C0-AMY-607

DISCARDED
UNIVERSITY OF WINNIPEG
PORTAGE & BALMORAL
WINNIPEG, MAN.   R3B 2E9
CANADA

REVIEW OF
Child Development Research

VOLUME FOUR

Advisory Committee

EDWARD DEVEREUX
   Cornell University

WALTER EMMERICH
   Educational Testing Service

MARTIN HOFFMAN
   University of Michigan

ROSS PARKE
   Fels Research Institute

ARTHUR PARMELEE
   University of California

WILLARD HARTUP, Ex Officio
   University of Minnesota

HQ
767
.8
.R47
v.4

REVIEW OF

Child Development

Research

VOLUME FOUR

Frances Degen Horowitz,
Editor

E. Mavis Hetherington
Sandra Scarr-Salapatek
Gerald M. Siegel
Associate Editors

Prepared under the auspices of the Society for Research in Child Development with a grant from the National Institute of Child Health and Human Development

THE UNIVERSITY OF CHICAGO PRESS

Chicago and London

FRANCES DEGEN HOROWITZ is chairman of
the Department of Psychology and a professor
in the Department of Human Development at
the University of Kansas.

E. MAVIS HETHERINGTON is a professor of
Psychology at the University of Virginia.

SANDRA SCARR-SALAPATEK is an associate
professor at the Institute of Child
Development, the University of Minnesota.

GERALD M. SIEGEL is professor of Communication Disorders at the University of
Minnesota.

The University of Chicago Press, Chicago 60637
The University of Chicago Press, Ltd., London

© 1975 by The University of Chicago
All rights reserved. Published 1975
Printed in the United States of America

Library of Congress Cataloging in Publication Data

Main entry under title:

Review of child development research.

"Prepared under the auspices of the Society for
Research in Child Development."
    Vol. 2 edited by L. W. Hoffman and M. L. Hoffman.
    Vol. 3 edited by B. M. Caldwell and H. N. Ricciuti.
has special title: Child development and social policy.
    Vol. 4: F. D. Horowitz, editor; E. M. Hetherington,
S. Scarr-Salapatek, G. M. Siegel, associate editors.
    Vol. 3– have imprint: Chicago, University of Chicago
Press.
    Includes bibliographies.
    1.   Children study—Addresses, essays, lectures.
    2.   Children—Research.   3.   Children in the United
States.   I.   Hoffman, Martin Leon, 1924–   ed.
    II.   Society for Research in Child Development.
    [DNLM: 1.   Child psychology—Yearbooks.   2.   Growth—
Yearbooks.   W1 RE252R]
    HQ768.8.R48   155.4   64–20472
    ISBN 0–226–35353–2 (v. 4)

Contents

Introduction

THE VISION with which this series was begun is still viable: to bring together a set of chapters that would each offer a review and integration of research so that practitioners in a diversity of fields could find and use a readable account of what is and is not known about important current topics and issues. With this volume we have begun to come full circle. Two of the chapters in this book update topics originally treated in volumes 1 and 2. Martin, on parent-child relations and Bloom, on language development, each reflects the growth and changes in knowledge since Becker wrote about the effects of parental discipline in volume 1 and Susan Ervin Tripp wrote about language development in volume 2.

The success of these volumes is attested to by the fact that students, active researchers, teachers, and lay people, in addition to practitioners, have found the chapters to be useful basic resources. As the literature on a particular topic becomes diverse, the need for an integrative review grows. But normal needs for summative discussions have intensified as child development has become more and more central to the issues of governmental policy and planning. Volume 3 of this series, under the editorship of Bettye Caldwell and Henry Ricciuti, was specially designed around the theme of relevance of developmental research to social policy. Volume 4 is less theme-oriented but reflects no less the pressures of our times. The topics in volume 4 include the controversies concerning genetic factors in development, the application of remedial and therapeutic techniques, and the increasing attention being given to the interplay of biological and environmental factors. The chapters also reflect the resurgence of interest in infant development, language development, the adolescent, and cross-cultural relativism. As with each of the previous volumes, the topics represent a part of the cosmos of the vast current enterprise that is concerned with discovering how development happens.

In light of these current issues, Sandra Scarr-Salapatek has provided a basic review of the data and controversies surrounding the topic of "Genetics and the Development of Intelligence." In this chapter the reader will find a definition of essential terms, a delineation of the issues, and a review of all available data. An attempt has been made to provide a balanced perspective with regard to how much is known and how much is speculation, in a manner that is relatively nontechnical but accurate. A related topic is treated by Elizabeth Reed in chapter 2. In "Genetic Anomalies in Development" there is a simple presentation of a selected set of the most common genetic syndromes that affect development. Again, a basic set of definitions, a glossary, and an annotated bibliography are provided in order to facilitate the understanding of individuals not highly sophisticated about patterns of genetic deviance.

In the last fifteen years there has been a major revival in the study of the human infant. In chapter 3, Appleton, Clifton, and Goldberg have surveyed a vast literature that tells an almost surprising story of the development of infant competencies; a much more competent young organism than had been supposed is pictured, while at the same time the impact of environmental factors on behavioral patterning is made clear. This point is made sharper in the fourth chapter, by Sameroff and Chandler, "Perinatal Risk and the Continuum of Caretaking Casualty," in which the review of the existing literature makes clear that the fate of an infant born at risk is partially determined by the total stimulus envelope of the environment in which the infant develops.

Lois Bloom has provided a succinct but complete review of language development in the fifth chapter. Taking up where the volume 2 chapter left off, this review offers the reader a clear perspective of where we stand with respect to our knowledge about the development of language in children. A less well-developed but growing area of interest is reviewed in chapter 6 by Glucksberg, Krauss, and Higgins. In "The Development of Referential Communication Skills" the authors provide a useful overview of the development of skills in children reflected against the kinds of competencies found in adults.

The control of deviance and behavior problems by the administration of drugs is a growing and, for some, alarming practice. In the seventh chapter Alan Sroufe offers an overview of the evidence of the effects of drugs and makes a helpful comparison to alternative procedures that both practitioners and lay people will find helpful and informative. Though the chapters were written independently, there is an amazing compatibility between Sroufe's conclusions and the evidence offered by Sherman and Bushell in chapter 8 on the utilization of behavior modification techniques in educational settings. These procedures are reviewed, the standards for their utilization are specified, and the ethical issues that they engender are discussed.

Chapter 9, by Barclay Martin, on parent-child relations, probably offers the most dramatic example of change in a field. Both in terms of differences and similarities in subtopic headings, as well as in the strength of the conclusions, there emerges a more self-confident picture about our understanding of the complexity of parent-child interactions than Wesley Becker was able to draw in 1964.

The influence of Piaget and the resurgence of interest in adolescent development is reflected in Edith Neimark's chapter on the development of formal operations during the adolescent period. This is perhaps the first review of the work in this area and in its detail and accuracy will be of enormous use to those interested in the intellectual development of adolescents and its implications. Finally, Joseph Glick has provided a review of our current level of understanding about cognitive development when cross-cultural factors are taken into account. The growing interest in this area reflects, in part, the concern for educational policy within the United States relative to ethnic and racial differences in cognitive style. While there are fewer firm conclusions that can be drawn for this topic, compared to the others reviewed in this volume, the chapter offers an opportunity for readers to become familiar with the issues and the current state of knowledge, with the possible result of increased sensitivity to the practical implications for current social policy decisions.

The appearance of this volume is a tribute to the commitment of many individuals to the field of child development. Everyone involved in the publication of this book met an incredible set of deadlines efficiently and with amazing good humor. In planning the volume we had some of the original guidelines proposed by Bettye Caldwell and Henry Ricciuti. The members of the Advisory Committee, who are listed at the front of the book, offered helpful counsel in the selection of topics, authors, and reviewers. The authors, ably represented by their own products herein, were prompt, efficient, and cheerful. Their responsiveness to the review process, their willingness to revise, and their adherence to the time schedule were in large part responsible for whatever timeliness this volume will have.

The willingness of Mavis Hetherington, Sandra Scarr-Salapatek, and Gerald Siegel to serve as associate editors of this volume was a significant factor in the quality of its contents. Their individual and collective competence ranged far beyond the capacity of any one editor. The pleasure of the working relationship that we were able to establish greatly enhanced the enjoyment of the editorial responsibility.

A cadre of reviewers helped us enormously in the process of improving first drafts to become final drafts. As in the case of everyone else associated with this volume, they responded fully and on time to their task. They included: Gordon Allen, Elving Anderson, Diana Baumrind, Courtney Cazden, Virginia Douglas, Lucy Rau Ferguson, John Flavell, Norman Garmezy, Jacqueline Goodenough, Lewis Lipsitt, Boyd McCandless, Gerald Patterson, Anne Pick, Howard Rosenfeld, Philip Salapatek,

Mark Stewart, Steven Vandenberg, Gerald Weiner, Ronald Wilson, and John Wright. The extent and care with which the basic reviews were done proved to be of enormous help both to the authors and the editors.

No volume comes to fruition without the dedication of a number of other professionals and nonprofessionals. Flora Thompson and Kay Hamm shared the final and awesome responsibility for typing the full manuscript of the book. Their concern with details and their intelligent attention to the task were responsible for some important improvements in the final product. Judith Castle was a helpful detective in proofreading and reference chasing. Jason Horowitz served ably and accurately in the initial bibliographical checks. The final proofreading and indexing of this volume required the united efforts of Patricia Linn, Jean Dempsey, Kathleen McCluskey, Howard Gallas, David Dempsey, Robert Grubbs, Jan Carpenter, Max Royle, and Jason Horowitz. It is gratifying to acknowledge their individual and excellent contributions to the production of this volume.

It has been a special pleasure for this editor to be associated with this volume. Not only are many of the specific topics covered of particular interest, but this volume and the tradition it represents are an expression of some of my strongest feelings. At a time when the cry for relevance and practical application threatens to smother the commitment to basic research, a volume such as this is an eloquent representation of the position that our success in the application of our knowledge to the solution of problems is in part determined by the extent of our basic understanding of the phenomena involved. Basic research without any contact with practical issues can become sterile and trivial. But attempts to solve practical problems are doomed to a relatively high percentage of failure unless the facts from basic research can be systematically utilized and our knowledge base about how development happens can be constantly increased. There is an important interaction between basic and applied work, and these volumes represent a significant recognition of that nexus. Thus, if there is any dedication to be made for this book, it is to the continuing efforts at communication between those involved in the endeavors of basic research and those involved in the practice of helping children and families.

Frances Degen Horowitz

1 Genetics and the Development of Intelligence

SANDRA SCARR-SALAPATEK
Institute of Child Development
University of Minnesota

IN THIS CHAPTER the three terms of the title, "genetics," "development," and "intelligence," will be defined and interrelated in several ways. The term "genetics" subsumes the two broad theoretical and methodological areas of Mendelian and biometrical genetics. Both are important to the study of intellectual development. "Development" is defined as a change over time in the direction of greater differentiation and integration of structure and function; developmental changes at biochemical, morphological, and behavioral levels are all important to the study of genetics and intelligence. "Intelligence" is a behavioral construct for which everyone can give many examples at all developmental stages but which often evades definition. A lack of consensus on the necessary and sufficient criteria for definition is the source of controversy. In this chapter psychometric, cognitive developmental, and cross-cultural approaches to intelligence will be related to genetic principles.

This chapter will explore the development of normal, human intelligence from a behavior-genetic point of view. The review is perforce largely theoretical because there is only a small (but growing) literature on the genetics of human intellectual development in the normal range. Two major goals of the chapter are to clarify behavior-genetic concepts of intellectual development and to frame questions about genetic aspects of intelligence that can be productively investigated.

There are several other goals which this chapter will *not* attempt to achieve. First, it will not describe in detail the basic principles of Mendelian and quantitative genetics, for which other sources are readily available (see Cavalli-Sforza and Bodmer 1972, for a particularly good

My deepest gratitude to Professors William Charlesworth, John Flavell, Irving I. Gottesman, Frances D. Horowitz, Anne D. Pick, Steven G. Vandenberg, and Ronald Wilson for their suggestions on the manuscript for this chapter. They are in no way responsible, however, for its content or conclusions. I received support during the period of research from the Grant Foundation and the National Institute of Child Health and Human Development (HD–06502, HD–08016).

1

treatment). Second, it will not review the endless controversy over the measurement of intelligence, for which recent sources are also available (see Cancro 1971; Butcher 1968). Third, it will not describe the growing literature on genetic anomalies in intellectual development, which are well reviewed by Reed in this volume (chapter 2). Fourth, this chapter will not recapitulate a half-century of the nature-nurture controversy, even as it pertains to intelligence; however, some of the research on foster children and related individuals will be discussed where relevant.

Lastly, this chapter will not offer a primary review of the excellent behavior-genetic literature on infrahuman species, which is well-represented in Manosevitz, Lindzey, and Thiessen (1969), Hirsch (1967), and Thiessen (1972*a*). Elegant experiments on strain and species differences in behavior development have value in demonstrating some of the mechanisms of development from genotype to phenotype, both theoretically and particularly for the populations studied. But the analogue to the mechanisms and course of development of human intelligence is tenuous indeed. Other surveys on behavior genetics and development have appeared that have reviewed the extensive animal literature (Lindzey, Loehlin, Manosevitz, and Thiessen 1971; McClearn 1964, 1970; Thiessen 1970).

Intelligence is a very complex phenotype with a very complex developmental sequence. For those reasons it is not an ideal phenotype for behavior-genetic analysis (Hirsch 1967, 1971). The importance of human intellect in human affairs is so great, however, that an abdication of the pursuit is not excusable either. The relative lack of information on human intelligence, compared to simpler genetic mechanisms in simpler organisms, is not surprising in light of the difficulty of analyzing phenotypes that arise from many genes and many pathways in varied environments.

Biases and Controversies

Theoretical and empirical controversies abound in the area of genetics and intelligence. Any chapter on the subject is necessarily biased by the author's interpretation of what we already know, what we need to discover, how research questions should be theoretically framed, and what inferences can be made from the findings. It is not possible to write a chapter on genetics and intelligence without these factors affecting the presentation of the topic. The following is a brief outline of the author's beliefs through which the material in this chapter has been filtered.

1. Our present knowledge of genetic factors in normal human intellectual development is primarily in the area of individual differences. The study of genetic and environmental contributions to individual differ-

ences is valuable, both in its own right and as an indication of where genetic research should be concentrated.

2. Generalizations from research on genetic and environmental differences are limited to the distributions of genotypes, environments, and measures actually sampled. The finding of substantial genetic variance in one population with one set of environments and one set of measures does not guarantee finding the same proportion in another.

3. At present we know that perhaps half of the variance of intellectual tests in the white population can be attributed to individual genetic differences. We know little or nothing about different populations reared under different sets of environments. Despite some assertions to the contrary, we know nothing about the sources of average intellectual differences between populations because appropriate methods have never been used to study these differences.

4. The application of genetic theory to normal intelligence has been limited to the analysis of variance and to biometrical models which assume that the phenotype is a static entity. Development is a dynamic concept that requires theoretical accounts of both stability and change in the organization of behavior and the plasticity of the developing phenotype.

5. Genetic theory has too often been applied to human behavioral development in a reductionist, linear manner. The necessary transactions between genotypes and environments have been paid lip service but have seldom been measured in research on developing phenotypes.

6. The methods of animal behavior-genetic research (e.g., selective breeding, uniform environments) have avoided many of the pitfalls cited above but are not themselves directly applicable to human studies. New models and methods are badly needed for the study of normal human development.

7. Knowledge gained from research on the abnormal development of abnormal genotypes is of limited use for the construction of models of normal development. Although it is very important to trace the effects of a single blocked pathway from gene action to mental retardation, knowing one source of error does not inform us of the other hundreds of pathways that must also function properly and together for normal intellectual development to occur.

8. The measurement of intelligent behavior at different developmental stages is fraught with so many conceptual and methodological problems that an open mind on IQ tests, operational measures, cross-cultural strategies, and possible psychophysical measures is absolutely required. Inferences from behaviors observed, under similar *or* different testing conditions, to the construct intelligence should be cautious and circumscribed.

What Shall We Call Intelligent?

Intelligence is a value-laden inference from behaviors that are generally considered to belong in the intellectual domain: problem-solving, concept formation, symbolic reasoning, hierarchical classification, and the like. Humphreys (1971, p. 36) defines intelligence as "the totality of responses available to the organism at any one period of time for the solution of intellectual problems." The domain of intellectual problems is defined by a consensus among psychologists.

It is possible to debunk operational definitions of intelligence as "what IQ tests measure," but in doing so one is surely ignoring the demonstrated value of the construct. There *is* some consensus among psychologists, and even people in general, as to what skills fall in the intellectual domain. There is substantial disagreement on how best to measure intelligent behavior: e.g., differential versus general ability (Butcher 1968), empirically-based normative versus theoretically-based operational tests (Almy, Chittenden, and Miller 1966; Cancro 1971; Pinard and Laurendreau 1964; Tuddenham 1970), culture-fair versus situation-specific behavior samples (Cattell 1971; Cole and Bruner 1971; Labov 1966).

A distinction between competence and performance in studies of intelligence, as in language, has assumed considerable importance for cognitive development. Competence is necessarily an inference from performance, and the crucial question concerns the basis of that inference. Shall intellectual competence be estimated from the best performance given by an individual in any situation (Cole, Gay, Glick and Sharp 1972; Labov 1970), by a specific performance under comparable conditions among individuals (IQ tests), or by an average of performances across many situations?

The distinction between cognitive competence and performance is like the distinction between intelligence and IQ scores. Both distinctions depend upon the latter being used as an estimate of the former. Although one can argue extensively for and against the various bases for estimation, the issue cannot be settled here.

Situational factors can influence the production of responses to intellectual problems, so that performances by the same individual may vary considerably from one situation to another. In cross-cultural research the best intellectual performance a person can give may not be sampled in unfamiliar testing or experimental situations posed by investigators (Cole, Gay, Glick and Sharp 1972; Ervin-Tripp 1972). Labov has argued that many U.S. black children who use cognitively and linguistically complex codes with their peers fail to perform well on IQ tests primarily because the testing situation elicits hostility and suspicion rather than motivation to perform well (Labov 1970). In contrast, Jensen (1973) has shown that the motivation to perform well on tests is equally high in black and white children.

A possible explanation for the conflicting results is that, apart from the motivation to behave appropriately and the competence to perform well, children learn to select and apply one of several alternative behaviors in any situation. Non-Western subjects and some U.S. black children may want to behave appropriately in the testing situation, may have the competence to do so, but may not have learned that categorization and complex problem-solving skills are appropriately applied to artificial testing situations. Their ability to perform at a higher intellectual level in other situations would suggest this conclusion. On the other hand, Jensen (1969, 1971b) has made a compelling argument for at least two factors in intelligence: one, conceptual ability, which we generally call IQ; the other, associative ability. High levels of the latter can account for the frequent finding of adequate social skills among people who perform poorly on tests of conceptual abilities. One must be careful, therefore, that the mental operations inferred from samples of social behaviors are actually the same conceptual skills sampled by IQ tests.

Interpretations of standard IQ tests and cognitive developmental measures should be restricted to statements about performance under given conditions. These performances have important implications and make quite good predictions of performance in school, job, and similar situations which call for conceptual skills. But they should not be used to infer "native ability" or ability to perform more or less adequately in situations that differ greatly from the testing conditions. *In this chapter, IQ tests and other operational measures will be used to infer intelligence, with the limitations noted above.*

The usefulness of IQ scores in behavior-genetic studies will be evident from the regular fit between polygenic theory and phenotypic IQ correlations among related individuals, from the fit between the theoretical and demonstrated effects of inbreeding, from the application of the reaction-range model to available IQ data, and from the prediction of parent-offspring regression. The usefulness of cognitive developmental measures and cross-cultural strategies in behavior-genetic research can be shown in a few recent studies. As in many other instances, seemingly competing and conflicting approaches turn out to provide complementary data.

GENETIC MECHANISMS IN DEVELOPMENT

Development is the process by which the genotype comes to be expressed as a phenotype. Development in any one case is the expression of only one of many alternative phenotypes in the genotype's range of reaction (Ginsburg and Laughlin 1971; Hirsch 1971). The degree to which an individual's genotype is expressed in his or her intellectual development depends upon many environmental factors that are critically present in adequate or inadequate amounts during the developmental process.

Genes are a primary part of the cellular system, being segments of chromosomes in the nucleus of every cell. Genes act, however, as constituents in all hierarchically organized systems from cellular to behavioral levels. Developmentally, gene action both initiates growth and is regulated by the growth of other constituents in the systems. To understand genetic factors in development is to know the ways in which gene action regulates and is regulated at every level and at every point in development, and to understand how individual variation develops.

The ultimate goal in behavior-genetic research is to understand the developmental pathways between genotypes and phenotypes. A complete knowledge of the biochemical-physiological-behavioral links from genotype to behavioral phenotype would encompass the understanding of both its Mendelian determinants and its individual variation.

This goal is far from being realized. At present, behavior-genetic studies of human intellectual development are primarily concerned with variation rather than with the role of genes in development. This section will outline what is known about genetic mechanisms in development. The third section will concentrate on genetic variation.

Mendelian and Biometrical Genetics

Mather (1971) has contrasted Mendelian and biometrical genetic analysis:

The Mendelian approach depends on the successful recognition of clearly distinguishable phenotypic classes from which the relevant genetical constitution can be inferred. It is at its most powerful when there is a one-to-one correspondence of phenotype and genotype, though some ambiguity of the relationship, as when complete dominance results in heterozygotic and one homozygote having the same phenotype, is acceptable (p. 351). The biometrical approach is from a different direction starting with the character rather than the individual determinant. It makes no requirement that the determinants be traceable individually in either transmission or action. It seeks to measure variation in a character and then, by comparing individuals and families of varying relationship, to partition the differences observed into fractions ascribable to the various genetical (or for that matter non-genetical) phenomena . . . (p. 352).

The two methods are entirely complementary (although they are often seen as competing) and, in fact, have somewhat different applications.

For polygenic traits like intelligence in the normal range of variation, the biometrical method has been applied almost exclusively because too many genes and pathways are involved to allow for Mendelian analysis. In the case of abnormalities, Mendelian analysis is used to establish the genotype-phenotype pathways. In some cases where major genes are involved in a polygenic system, Mendelian and biometrical analysis will give similar results (Mather 1971).

Both Mendelian and biometrical approaches depend ultimately upon a knowledge of environmental factors which regulate gene expression. The behavior-genetic analysis of intellectual development must proceed with knowledge of the many gene-action pathways, gene regulatory mechanisms, and environmental factors that affect the expression of the genotype in the phenotype for intelligence.

Gene Action and Behavioral Development

If gene-action pathways in human development were known, this chapter would be simple reporting rather than speculative construction. In fact, only bits and pieces of the genetics of developmental processes are known. The basic DNA-RNA, protein-synthesis code is well established. Knowledge of fetal development at a morphological level is fairly complete. But how does morphological development over the fetal period, and indeed the life span, relate to protein synthesis at a cellular level? What causes some cells to differentiate and develop into the cortex and others into hemoglobin? And how do gene action and morphological development relate to intellectual development from birth to senescense? How do cells, which all originate from the same fertilized ovum and all carry the same genetic information, come to program development into different organs and systems and in different behavioral stages of development?

The relation between gene action and behavioral development has been well summarized by Thiessen (1972a, p. 87).

The lengthy, often tortuous, path from DNA specificity to metabolic synchrony explains why behavior must be considered a pleiotropic reflection of physiological processes. Gene influence in behavior is always indirect. Hence the regulatory processes of a behavior can be assigned to structural and physiological consequences of gene action and developmental canalization. The blueprint for behavior may be a heritable characteristic of DNA, but its ultimate architecture is a problem for biochemistry and physiology. Explaining gene-behavior relations entails knowing every aspect of the developmental pattern: its inception, its relation to the environment, its biochemical individuality, and its adaptiveness. When these things are known, it is possible to enter an experimental wedge at any level and to adjust gene expression anywhere within the limits of modification.

It has been hypothesized (Jacob and Monod, 1961) that several kinds of genes exist: structural genes to specify the proteins to be synthesized, operator genes to turn protein synthesis on and off in adjacent structural genes, and regulator genes to repress or activate the operator and structural genes in a larger system (Jacob and Monod 1961; Lerner 1968; Martin and Ames 1964). The instructions that a cell receives must be under regulatory control that differentiates the activity of that cell at several points in development.

Genes and chromosome segments are "turned on" at some but not other points in development. Enlargements of a chromosome section (called "puffs") have been observed to coincide with RNA synthesis in the cell. Puffs occur on different portions of the chromosomes at different times in different cells, indicating the existence of regulatory mechanisms in development.

Regulatory genes are probably the ones responsible for species and individual differentiation through control of the expression of structural genes. Most of the structural genes, which are directly concerned with enzyme formation, are common to a wide array of species and function in approximately the same way. They provide the fundamental identity of life systems. The diversity of individuals and species is due in large part to the regulatory genes, which modify the expression of basic biochemical processes (Thiessen 1972*a*).

In other words, the greatest proportion of phenotypic variance, at least in mammalian species, is probably due to regulatory rather than structural genes—genes that activate, deactivate, or otherwise alter the expression of a finite number of structural genes (p. 124).

Several cellular regulatory mechanisms have been suggested (Lerner 1968). First, the cytoplasms of different cells contain different amounts of material and may contain different materials. As cell division proceeds, daughter cells receive unequal amounts of cytoplasm, and this may relate to their progressive differentiation. Second, the position of the developing cells may influence their course. Outer cells may have different potentialities for development than those surrounded by other cells.

Third, the cell nuclei become increasingly differentiated in the developmental process. Progressively older nuclei have a more limited range of available functions; they become more specialized in the cell activities they can direct. Specialization of nuclei is related to the differentiation of organs and functions in different portions of the developing organism.

The regulation of developmental processes over the life span is accomplished through the gene-encoded production of hundreds of thousands of enzymes and hormones. During embryogenesis there are precise correlations between changes in enzyme concentrations and development (Hsia, 1968).

For example, *cholinesterase* activity shows particularly close relationships with neural development. As early as the closure of the neural tube, high cholinesterase activity has been found in association with morphogenesis of the neuraxis. . . . Nachmansohn has shown that *cholinesterase* is synthesized in the developing nervous system of the chick embryo exactly at the time that synapses and nerve endings appear (pp. 96–97).

Any behavior represented phenotypically by the organism *must,* by definition, have a genetic and organismic representation. It does not appear without CNS regulation, and CNS regulation does not occur without brain myelenization, synaptic transmission, and previous experience encoded chemically in the brain.

Enzymatic differentiation is specific to the stage of development, the specific organ, specific regions within organs, and the type of enzyme. Development proceeds on a gene-regulated path by way of enzymatic activity. Generalizations are very risky from one point in time to another and from one organ part to another.

There are several enzyme systems that are active in the embryo but that disappear with the cessation of growth. Other enzymes that are absent or present in low activity in the embryo greatly increase in activity at the time an organ becomes functionally mature. These enzymes then remain active throughout life to regulate functional organ activity. A third class of enzymes is activated only with maturation and remains active the rest of adult life (Hsia 1968, pp. 96–107).

Interference with regulatory mechanisms at a cellular or organ-system level can result in a variety of phenotypic abnormalities. The result of interference is often related to the time it occurs during development. For example, male rabbit fetuses castrated on the nineteenth day of gestation resemble a female at birth. Castration on any day up to the twenty-fourth results in a gradation of femininity, but if castration is performed on the twenty-fifth day or later, there is no effect on the development of male genitalia. Figure 1 is a schematic presentation of the biochemical development of the embryo and the influence of environment at all levels of development.

Hormonal activity is critically important to the stimulation of protein synthesis and to the differentiation of male embryos from the basic female form. Minute quantities of fetal testosterone at critical periods in development affect genital differentiation as well as CNS differences that seem

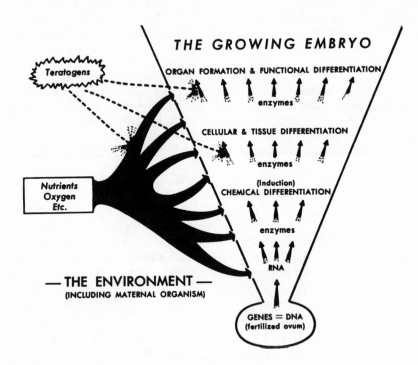

Fig. 1. Model of the biochemical development of the growing embryo and the influence of environment at all levels of development. (From Hsia 1968, after Wilson.)

to last a lifetime (Levine 1967). The variety of hormones that stimulate protein synthesis includes growth hormones as well as sex hormones, cortisone, insulin, and thyroxine (Thiessen 1972*a*, p. 95). A model of hormone-gene flow is presented by Thiessen, as shown in figure 2.

There are many known ways in which normal development can be

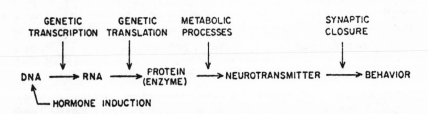

Fig. 2. Model of hormone-gene flow from cellular to behavioral levels. (From Thiessen 1972*b*.)

disrupted at a biochemical level. Defects in the biochemical pathways between gene action and normal cell metabolism number in the hundreds. In the glucose to glycogen pathway alone, there are seven independent genetic errors that result in different genetic anomalies (Hsia 1968).

Environmental pathogens can, of course, intervene in normal development. Radiation, infectious diseases, drugs, and other specific environmental factors are responsible for some congenital abnormalities in the developing fetus.

The effect of ionizing radiation on CNS development is detailed in figure 3. Rubella, mumps, toxoplasmosis, and viral infections produce

TIMETABLE OF RADIATION MALFORMATIONS IN MICE AND MAN

AGE (DAYS) Mouse	Man	EMBRYO (mm.)	NERVOUS SYSTEM	OTHER
0–9	0–25		No damage	
9	25½	2.4	Anencephaly (extreme defect of forebrain)	Severe head defects
10	28¼	4.2	Forebrain, brain stem, or cord defects	Skull, jaw, skeletal, visceral defects, anophthalmia
11	33½	7.0	Hydrocephalus, narrow aqueduct, encephalocele, cord, and brain stem defects	Retinal, skull, skeletal defects
12	36½	9.0	Decreasing encephalocele; microcephaly, porencephaly	Retinal, skull, skeletal defects
13	38	12.0	Microcephaly, bizarre defects of cortex, hippocarpus, callosum, basal ganglia, decreasing toward term	Decreasing skeletal defects

Fig. 3. Timetable of radiation malformations in mice and man. (From Hsia 1968, after Hicks.)

characteristic anomalies when contracted by the fetus in the first trimester of pregnancy. Mental retardation is a prominent feature of many genetic and environmental disturbances in the developmental process (see chapter 2 in this volume).

Another genetic pathway that has received considerable attention is that of phenylalanine. While many behavioral scientists recognize that a block in this pathway can produce PKU (phenylketonuria), most are not aware that four other identifiable genetic syndromes result from additional blocks in the same pathway, as shown in figure 4.

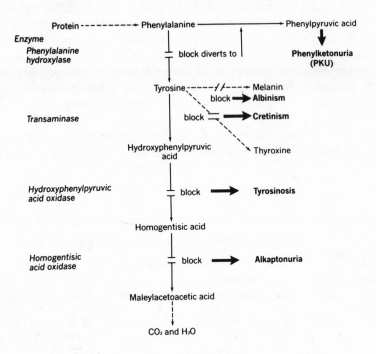

Fig. 4. Genetic blocks in the metabolism of phenylalanine. (From *Heredity, Evolution, and Society* by I. Michael Lerner [W. H. Freeman and Company. Copyright © 1968].)

Genetic Canalization

The concept of canalization in development accounts for many phenotypic phenomena. Canalization is the restriction of alternative phenotypes to one or a few outcomes. The developing phenotype is represented as more or less difficult to deflect from a growth path (creode), depending upon the degree of genotypic control, the force of the deflection, and the timing of the deflection. Waddington's epigenetic landscape, as shown in figure 5, is a model of the varying canalization in the development of different aspects of the organism (Waddington 1957, 1962).

The ball is the developing phenotype which rolls through valleys of varying widths and depths. At some points a minor deflection can send the phenotype into a different channel of development; at other points a major deflection would be required to change the course of development because genetic canalization (represented by a narrow, deep valley) is very strong.

Lesser canalization means greater modifiability. Greater canalization

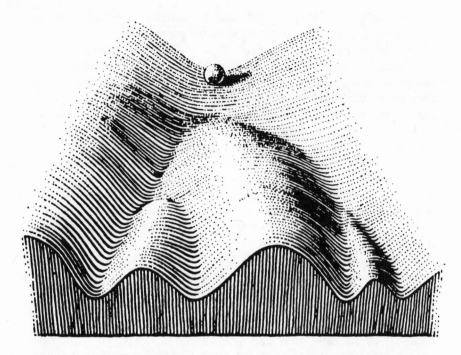

Fig. 5. Waddington's epigenetic landscape: a model of genetic canalization in development. (From Waddington 1957.)

means that a large array of environmental events may have little or no effect on the development of the phenotype. It has been suggested (Wilson 1972) that infant intellectual development has strong canalization, whereas later intelligence may be more easily modified. Similarly, infant babbling seems to be strongly canalized since even congenitally deaf infants babble (Lenneberg 1967).

The Concept of Expression

Phenotypic intelligence is an outcome of the developmental process by which genes were expressed in environments from the cellular to the fetal to the postnatal stages of growth.

The concept of *expression* is extremely important in developmental genetics. For example, the same genes that produce clinical diabetes in some people do not achieve clinical expression in others due to the modifying effects of environments and other genes during development. A common-sense example can be found in physical growth. The expression of height depends on a variety of growth hormones, protein and caloric intake, and many other regulatory mechanisms in growth. Final stature may be limited by many diseases, and by nutritional and biochemical deficiencies that affect the expression of the genotype.

Another polygenic characteristic, skin color, is not fully expressed when a single recessive locus for albinism blocks melanin production, even though normal genes for skin color are present. The expression of skin color is also affected by the amount of sunlight received shortly before the time of measurement. The same genotype will generally be expressed as a lighter phenotype as distance from the equator increases. It cannot be said, however, that skin color is any less genetically *determined* at greater, than at less, distances from the tropical sun. It is simply that many genotypes for skin color are less fully expressed in colder climates. Some genotypes, however, achieve pale phenotypes in most locations and, therefore, can be said to have a limited range of reaction.

The genotypic expression of intellectual development apparently works the same way, under better and worse environmental conditions. Intelligence can be said to be genetically determined, as is skin color, but the phenotypes achieved by the same genotype can vary, depending upon important features of the environment that affect the expression of the genotype.

One important feature of the child's environment is his or her mother. Maternal effects have been shown to affect the expression of familial mental retardation. Children reared by their retarded mothers but with normal IQ fathers have two and one-half times the rate of retardation found among children with equally retarded fathers and normal IQ mothers (Reed and Reed 1965). Whether the maternal effect is entirely postnatal can only be discovered through large studies of adopted children with a retarded natural parent.

Willerman's recent study of maternal effects (1972) shows that college students whose mothers are more highly educated than their fathers have higher aptitude scores than those whose fathers are more highly educated than their mothers, even though the socioeconomic status of the latter significantly exceeds the former. One is tempted to conclude that mothers have a greater effect on children's intellectual development in this society because they spend far greater amounts of time with children than do most fathers. Maternal effects on the development of IQ may influence the expression of genotypes by setting the intellectual level of the environment.

The Range of Reaction: A Developmental Model

The expression of the genotype in the phenotype can be shown in an adaptation of the *reaction range* model (fig. 6). The concept of reaction range refers to the quantitatively different phenotypes that can develop

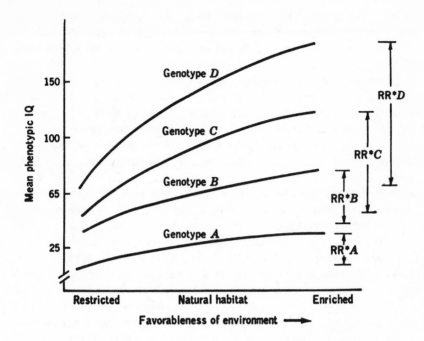

Fig. 6. The intellectual reaction ranges of several genotypes in more and less favorable environments. The phenotypic range of each genotype is indicated by RR. Genotype A, which achieves a very low phenotypic IQ under excellent conditions, is not part of the normal IQ range. The other curves represent genotypically unique responses to the changing favorableness of the environment. (From Gottesman 1963.)

from the same genotype under varying environmental conditions (Gottesman 1963).

The potential for development into any one of a number of phenotypes is called the *genomic repertoire* (Ginsburg and Laughlin 1971). A given genotype has only those degrees of freedom that are inherent in its genes. The actual phenotype that develops is achieved through genotypic expression in a set of environments over the entire span of development.

Every genotype has a unique range of reaction to a given set of environmental conditions, which accounts for the broad range of intellectual differences among children in the same family. It is not correct, however, to say that heredity sets the limits on development while environment determines the extent of development. Both are half-truths because they ignore the constant transaction between genotype and environment during development.

Under different environmental conditions the same genotype can become different phenotypes; under the same environmental conditions, different genotypes can become different phenotypes; and under uniform environmental conditions, different genotypes may result in the same phenotype.

Ginsburg and his colleagues (1966, 1968, 1971) have summarized evidence on the genomic repertoires of a number of inbred strains of mice. Since each strain is essentially made up of identical genotypes, strain differences can be treated as individual human differences. The important developmental findings are (1) genotype-environment interactions are frequent, (2) environmental circumstances that will alter the behavioral development of one strain will have no effect on another and an opposite effect on a third, (3) the period during development at which a given effect can be most readily induced by a given environmental circumstance is genotype-specific.

Just as there are many possible phenotypes for most genotypes, there are many genotypic routes to the same phenotype. A large number of genetic-environmental combinations will yield the same IQ score. Much of the genotypic variation within species is, in fact, masked by the strong canalization of development in a given range of environments. Phenotypes that apparently have little variation can, in fact, be shown in other environments to be based on different genotypes, whose differences were simply not expressed in the first set of environments (Thiessen 1972*b*).

There are no general laws of reaction range that can predict a priori the development of individuals. Only for certain abnormal genotypes can the reaction range be roughly specified under existing environments. As Hirsch (1971, p. 94) has said,

The more varied the conditions, the more diverse might be the phenotypes developed from any one genotype. Of course, different genotypes should not be expected to have the same norm of reaction; unfortunately, psycology's attention was diverted from appreciating this basic fact of biology by half a century of misguided environmentalism. Just as we see that, except for monozygotes, no two human faces are alike, so we must expect norms of reaction to show genotypic uniqueness. . . . Extreme environmentalists were wrong to hope that one law or set of laws described universal features of modifiability. Extreme hereditarians were wrong to ignore the norm of reaction.

Identical twins reared apart provide the best human data on reaction ranges in intelligence. Since monozygotic twins have the same genotype, all differences between co-twins must arise from environmental sources beginning at the first cell division and including pre- and postnatal events. If monozygotic twins are separated at birth into different families, how different can they become in intellectual level?

Jensen (1971*a*) combined the results of four published studies on a total of 122 MZ pairs separated in early childhood and reared apart.

TABLE 1. STATISTICS ON IQs OF MZ TWINS REARED APART

Study	N (Pairs)	Mean IQ	SD	$/\overline{d}/$	$SD_{/\overline{d}/}$	r_i	r_a
Burt	53	97.7	14.8	5.96	4.44	.88	.88
Shields	38	93.0	13.4	6.72	5.80	.78	.84
Newman et al.	19	95.7	13.0	8.21	6.65	.67	.76
Juel-Nielsen	12	106.8	9.0	6.46	3.22	.68	.86
Combined	122	96.8	14.2	6.60	5.20	.82	.85

SOURCE: Jensen 1971*a*.

The average absolute difference ($/\overline{d}/$) in IQ scores between MZ twins reared apart is about 6.5 points; between MZ twins reared together it is about 5 points; and between dizygotic twins reared together the difference is about 11 IQ points. Rearing in different families per se does not increase the average IQ differences between MZ twins by very much and certainly not to the level obtained from DZ twins reared together.

How different were the families in which co-twins were reared? This question has been answered anecdotally from the case histories of the separated twins. In general, between-family differences were within the average range of the population sampled, from working to upper-middle-class environments. The largest IQ differences between separated twins were associated with the largest life history differences, but there is no linear correlation between the phenotypic differences of co-twins and social class differences of the adoptive families.

Gottesman (1968) has estimated that the IQ reaction range under natural habitat conditions is about ± 12 points for average genotypes. Similarly, DeFries (1971) estimated that the IQ scores of children presently reared by parents with IQs of 80 could be raised by 25 points if they were reared under the best .01 percent of conditions. Thus, the reaction range of most genotypes probably falls in the ± 10 to 12 point range depending upon rearing conditions of low to high average values.

Very poor environments can radically lower IQ scores (Skeels 1966). Intellectually superior environments, such as those provided in intensive tutoring programs (Heber 1969) and kibbutzim (Smilansky, personal communication), may be able to radically raise IQ scores, at least for disadvantaged children. New interventions are conceivable. If the gene-action pathways to normal intellectual development were known, intervention would probably be possible at a biochemical level, especially for many forms of familial retardation, which do not now respond well to educational treatment.

Another line of evidence on reaction range comes from studies of adopted children (Burks 1928; Skodak and Skeels 1949). While a great deal of attention has been given to the greater *correlation* between adopted children's IQ and their natural parents' intellectual level, an equally important fact is the substantially higher mean of the adopted children's IQ scores compared to their natural mothers' average IQs. The children might well have had IQs in the low 90s (by regression toward the mean) instead of the average of 106 which was actually obtained (Skodak and Skeels 1949). Similarly, Burks' (1928) and Leahy's (1935) studies found the average IQs of adopted children well above the population mean. Burks' sample of 214 adopted children averaged IQ 107.4, and Leahy's 194 children averaged 110.5. Adopted children are unlikely to be retarded because they are a selected group, but it is also true that the greater environmental enrichment provided by the adoptive parents, in comparison to that given by the natural parents, acted on the reaction range of each genotype to produce higher than expected phenotypes for IQ. Further, the adopted children's IQ scores were correlated ($r \simeq .20$ to .30) with the adoptive families' socioeconomic characteristics, even though adoptive families constitute an attenuated sample of the SES range.

Based on the data from separated monozygotic twins and adopted children, a reasonable reaction range model for most genotypes (not severely retarded or extremely gifted) would include phenotypes in a 25-point IQ range. This figure is based only on currently existing environments, not on innovations that could shift the whole distribution of IQ scores to an unknown degree.

Intelligence as Species-Specific Development

The evolution of human intelligence is often presented in a phylogenetic frame with appropriate accounts of the increasing brain capacities of our progenitors. The crucial interplay of behavioral adaptation and morphological changes in the cortex have been well reviewed (Alland 1967; Washburn and Howells 1960): culture, language, and intelligence evolved together as genetic, species-specific characteristics.

The intellectual genotypes of man have changed through natural selection, i.e., the differential reproductive rate of better-adapted members of the species. Selection acts at a phenotypic level, but changes in the genotype are necessary for a continuation of the new adaptation.

It is not simply the final, adult phenotype that is the subject of selection. Selection can act at all points in a developmental sequence. In the human case, selection has acted to extend infancy and to increase the role of cultural learning in man's ontogeny (Dobzhansky 1962; La Barre 1965).

The ontogenesis of intelligence should be seen as an evolved pattern of development. The modal sequence of intellectual stages described extensively by Piaget and his colleagues (see Flavell 1963, 1970) can be understood as the development of normal human genotypes under a range of average to superior human environments. The modal progression from sensorimotor to preoperational, concrete, and perhaps formal operational stages is found in every normal member of the species who is exposed to a natural human environment. It is, of course, the *form* of the behavior, not the *content,* that is the evolved pattern of development.

Cross-cultural studies on conservation and related concepts find an invariant order for the major stages of intellectual development but not necessarily for their timing (Cole et al. 1972; deLacey 1970, 1971*a,* 1971*b;* DeLemos 1969; Hyde 1969; Price-Williams 1961; Prince (1968). The timing is doubtless influenced by the cultural milieux. The universality of cognitive developmental stages led Price-Williams (1961) to conclude, "As these children have had no formal instruction in abstract numbers, there is much to be said for the neuro-physiological interpretation for dealing with such concepts" (p. 303).

The normal human genotype is programmed for this sequence of development, having been adapted under rearing conditions of a family, peers, and a larger social group. The evolution of prolonged brain development in postnatal life and a prolonged learning period is as much a part of species history as is the evolution of the opposable thumb.

The gene-action pathways to the normal stages of intellectual development are not known. But one can reason backwards from observed development to genotype and be fairly sure that this regular species-specific progression in cognitive development has CNS representation and that CNS development is genetically programmed through enzymatic, hormonal, and other regulatory mechanisms.

"Much behavior that we see may be controlled by regulatory genes open to processes of canalization, early and later experiences, and natural selection" (Thiessen 1972*b,* p. 124). For intellectual development this means that, as the CNS matures, previously irrelevant aspects of the environment become relevant, learning occurs, and the CNS develops. The constant transaction between organismic development and environmental features produces intellectual, behavioral development.

Inbreeding Effects

One test for the effects of genes on intellectual development is the study of inbreeding. If some gene combinations are important for the development of high IQ, and others for low IQ, then IQ ought to be a sensitive measure of the generally depressing effects of inbreeding. It is.

When two related individuals mate, their offspring have an increased chance of receiving at many loci the same genes twice from the same ancestor. They are homozygous at these loci. Homozygocity at many loci increases the probability that some deleterious recessive characteristics will be expressed in the offspring. In some cases, however, particularly desirable combinations may result from homozygous genes at some loci, which explains the frequent use of brother-sister and parent-offspring matings by breeders of domestic animals. But the cost of inbreeding is increased fetal mortality, congenital defects, and depressed physical and intellectual growth for other offspring.

An extreme form of inbreeding in man is found in incestuous matings between brothers and sisters and between parents and their children. Carter (1967) reported the outcome of thirteen such unions: three of the children had died of rare recessive diseases, one was severely retarded, and four more had IQ scores between 59 and 76. The remaining five had IQs in the normal range. A second study turned up eighteen offspring of incestuous matings (Adams, Davidson, and Cornell 1967; Adams and Neel 1967). Three of the eighteen children had died in infancy, two were severely retarded, three had IQ scores between 60 and 70, and ten fell in the normal range of intelligence-test scores. Six of the ten children with normal IQs ranged from 110 to 119, which supports the notion that inbreeding does not always have bad to disastrous outcomes. The fact that eight of the eighteen children had serious mental impairments, however, demonstrates the dangers of severe inbreeding.

Less severe forms of inbreeding include the cousin marriages and uncle-niece unions that are common in some parts of the world. Three studies of cousin marriages have shown depression of IQ scores to be the most consistent outcome for offspring. Böök (1957) reported a mental retardation rate of 4.6 percent for offspring of cousin marriages, compared to 1.3 percent for the controls. Cohen and his colleagues (1963) found depression of all subtest scores on the WAIS for the offspring of cousin marriages, compared to matched controls.

In the largest study to date, Schull and Neel (1965) used the Japanese form of the WISC to evaluate 865 children of cousin marriages (first cousins, first cousins once removed, and second cousins) and 989 children of unrelated parents. The effects of socioeconomic class, age, and inbreeding were evaluated in a multivariate analysis. Inbreeding was found to depress IQ scores independent of socioeconomic status and the age of the child. Vandenberg (1971) has arranged the Japanese data to express inbreeding depression as a percentage of the mean of non-inbred children for each subtest in the WISC, as shown in table 2.

Since the IQ mean of the outbred group (children of unrelated parents) is about 100, the inbred children averaged only about IQ 93 on

TABLE 2.   EFFECT ON CONSANGUINITY ON
WISC IQ SCORES

| | Depression as percent of outbred mean | |
	Boys	Girls
Information	8.1	8.5
Comprehension	6.0	6.1
Arithmetic	5.0	5.1
Similarities	9.7	10.2
Vocabulary	11.2	11.7
Picture completion	5.6	6.2
Picture arrangement	9.3	9.5
Block design	5.3	5.4
Object assembly	5.8	6.3
Coding	4.3	4.6
Mazes	5.3	5.4
Verbal score	8.0	8.0
Performance score	5.1	5.1
Total IQ	7.0	7.1

SOURCE: Vandenberg 1971, based on Schull and Neel 1965.

the basis of inbreeding alone. Increased fetal mortality and congenital defects, as expected, have also been reported for the offspring of cousin marriages (Böök 1957).

A Polygenic Model of Intelligence

Intelligence, like many human characteristics that vary quantitatively among people, is probably determined by many genes acting together with the environment to produce the phenotype. Polygenic systems are assumed to be composed of many genes, each of which adds a little to the development of the trait. There may also be a few major genes, or ones with larger effects, that substantially reduce or increase intellectual levels beyond the additive effects of the polygenes (Bock and Kolakowski 1973; Jinks and Fulker 1970).

There are no genes specifically for behavior; all genes act at a more molecular level on the development and maintenance of structures that have consequences for behavior. Genes have pleiotropic (many) effects, and genes at one locus act on the expression of genes at other loci (epistasis). No one knows how many genes affect the development of intelligent behavior or how many pleiotropic and epistatic effects there are within the polygenic system.

The fact that at least twenty genes (Gottesman 1963) or as many as several hundred (Dewey et al. 1965; Wall 1967) are involved in intelligence, makes the inheritance of intelligence a quantitative matter. Li (1971) has presented a simple but comprehensive polygenic model for intelligence which explains parent-child regression, variability within families, and the other phenomena observed for phenotypic IQ. The most important single consequence of the genetic model is that, for any given class of parents, their offspring will be scattered in various classes; conversely, for any given class of offspring, their parents will have come from various classes. This effect is shown in figure 7.

Parents at the high and low *extremes* of the distribution contribute offspring primarily to the upper or the lower *halves* of the distributions, while

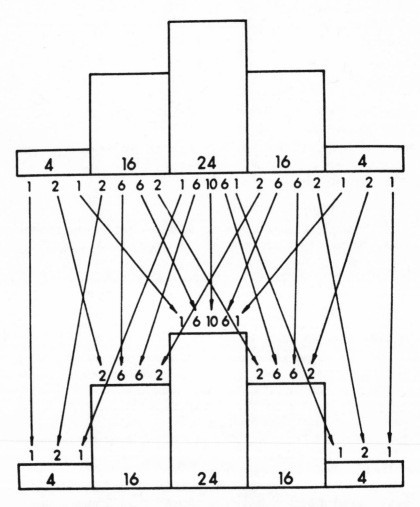

Fig. 7. The distributions of offspring and parents in five phenotypic classes in a random mating population. (From C. C. Li, in R. Cancro, ed., *Intelligence: Genetic and Environmental Influences* [Grune and Stratton 1971]. Used by permission.)

parents in the middle of the distribution contribute children to all classes in the distribution. On the average, the children will have less extreme scores than their parents, but the total distribution of phenotypic IQ will remain relatively constant from one generation to another (unless selective forces intervene).

To the redistribution of offspring from parental to offspring classes in each generation, Li adds the Markov property of populations: "The properties of an individual depend upon the state (in this case, genotype) in which he finds himself and not upon the state from which he is derived. A state is a state; it has no memory" (Li 1971, p. 173).

TABLE 3. TRANSITIONAL PROBABILITIES FROM ANCESTOR TO DESCENDANT

	State of ancestor	State of descendant				
		0	1	2	3	4
T	0	.2500	.5000	.2500	0	0
	1	.1250	.3750	.3750	.1250	0
	2	.0417	.2500	.4167	.2500	.0417
	3	0	.1250	.3750	.3750	.1250
	4	0	0	.2500	.5000	.2500
T^2	0	.1354	.3750	.3542	.1250	.0104
	1	.0937	.3125	.3750	.1875	.0312
	2	.0590	.2500	.3819	.2500	.0590
	3	.0312	.1875	.3750	.3125	.0937
	4	.0104	.1250	.3542	.3750	.1354
T^4	0	.0784	.2812	.3744	.2187	.0472
	1	.0703	.2656	.3750	.2344	.0547
	2	.0624	.2500	.3752	.2500	.0624
	3	.0547	.2344	.3750	.2656	.0703
	4	.0472	.2187	.3744	.2812	.0784
T^8	0	.0635	.2520	.3750	.2480	.0615
	1	.0603	.2510	.3750	.2490	.0620
	2	.0625	.2500	.3750	.2500	.0625
	3	.0620	.2490	.3750	.2510	.0630
	4	.0615	.2480	.3750	.2520	.0635

SOURCE: Li 1971.

Under conditions of random mating, successive generations form a Markov chain of probabilities (T, T^2, T^4, T^8) from parent state to offspring state. In table 3, the ancestors and descendants are divided into five classes (0–4). In the case of intelligence, the classes would correspond to IQ groups from retarded to very superior levels. Parents of class 0 (retarded) have children in the T generation, whose IQs are distributed in classes 0, 1, and 2 but not 3 or 4. Parents of class 4 have children distributed in classes 2, 3, and 4 but not 0 or 1. In the next generation (T^2), however, the grandchildren of class 0 ancestors are distributed in all classes, as are the grandchildren of class 4 ancestors, albeit in unequal proportions. By the eighth generation (T^8), the descendants of classes 0 and 4 are distributed about equally in all five classes.

Thus, the distant descendants of Jean Bernoulli are distributed into the various classes of mathematical ability in exactly the same way as the distant descendants of one whose mathematical ability belonged to class 0. Family members who are as much as six to eight generations apart are (genetically) practically unrelated even though they retain the same family name.

Environmentalists sometimes misunderstand the implications of population genetics, thinking that heredity would imply "like class begets like class." Probably the opposite is true. Only very strong social and environmental forces can perpetrate an artificial class; heredity does not (Li 1971, p. 172).

Whether present-day family groups and social classes are entirely artificial groups is debatable (Herrnstein 1971) because one assumption of Li's model is random mating, which is violated by an IQ correlation of about .40 between parents. The topic of assortative mating will be taken up in the next section.

Even under conditions of high assortative mating, however, there is considerable regression of offspring scores toward the population mean and considerable IQ variation among the offspring of the same parents. Burt's (1961) classic study of the IQ scores of some forty thousand adults and their children illustrates the polygenic system in IQ very nicely. Tables 4 and 5 give his results. When the fathers are grouped by occupational status, their mean IQs range from 140 in the highest professional groups to 85 in the unskilled occupations. Their children's IQ scores, however, varied from only 121 to 93 over the same social class range, thereby illustrating the regression effect predicted from a polygenic model of IQ.

The children had considerably more varied IQ scores within each occupational class than had their fathers ($\sigma = 14$ and 9.6 respectively), as Li (1971) has described. If one followed a single family line through several generations, one would find great variation in IQ scores and occupational achievements. It would be impossible to predict exactly a grandchild's score from the grandparents' scores, and vice versa.

The polygenic nature of familial retardation was explored by Roberts (1952) using sibling comparisons. Institutionalized retardates were divided into two groups of severely retarded and less severely retarded on the basis of IQ scores. In each group correlations were then calculated between the IQ scores of the retardates and their siblings. The IQ scores of severely retarded children (IQ < 50) showed no correlation at all with

TABLE 4.   DISTRIBUTION OF INTELLIGENCE ACCORDING TO
OCCUPATIONAL CLASS: ADULTS

IQ	Professional Higher I	Lower II	Clerical III	Skilled IV	Semi-skilled V	Un-skilled VI	Total
50–60						1	1
60–70					5	18	23
70–80				2	15	52	69
80–90			1	11	31	117	160
90–100			8	51	135	53	247
100–110			16	101	120	11	248
110–120		2	56	78	17	9	162
120–130		13	38	14	2		67
130–40	2	15	3	1			21
140+	1	1					2
Total	3	31	122	258	325	261	1000
Mean IQ	139.7	130.6	115.9	108.2	97.8	84.9	100

Source: Burt 1961.
N = 40,000, converted to a base of 1,000.

TABLE 5.   DISTRIBUTION OF INTELLIGENCE OF CHILDREN
ACCORDING TO FATHER'S OCCUPATIONAL CLASS

IQ	Professional Higher I	Lower II	Clerical III	Skilled IV	Semi-skilled V	Un-skilled VI	Total
50–60					1	1	2
60–70				1	6	15	22
70–80			3	12	23	32	70
80–90		1	8	33	55	62	159
90–100		2	21	53	99	75	250
100–110	1	6	31	70	85	54	247
110–120		12	35	59	38	16	160
120–130	1	8	18	22	13	6	68
130–140	1	2	6	7	5		21
140+				1			1
Total	3	31	122	258	325	261	1000
Mean IQ	120.8	114.7	107.8	104.6	98.9	92.6	100

Source: Burt 1961.
N = 40,000, converted to a base of 1,000.

those of their siblings, whose average IQ was 100. The IQ scores of the
less severe retardates, however, correlated about .50 with those of their
siblings, whose scores averaged only 85. The distribution of the siblings'
IQ scores is shown in figure 8.

These data support the important distinction between single-gene and
chromosomal anomalies, which produce severe retardation in a few children but which leave most sibs completely unaffected, and polygenic retardation, which may occur in various degrees of severity in other members of the same family.

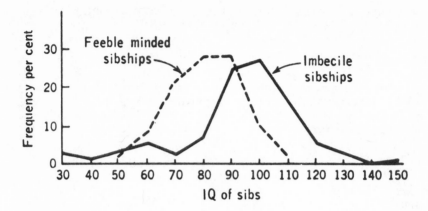

Fig. 8. Frequency distributions of the IQs of siblings of severe (imbecile) and less severe (feebleminded) retardates. (From Roberts 1952.)

Summary

In this section the basic genetic mechanisms have been reviewed. From the current state of knowledge in this field, it can be concluded that:

1. The role of genes in human behavioral development is poorly understood at present. A speculative construction of gene effects on development emphasized the mutual regulation of genes and environments acting in systems from cellular to behavioral levels.

2. The concepts of canalization, gene expression, and range of reaction are important in understanding the regulation of genotype-to-phenotype development. There is no one-to-one correspondence between genotypes and behavioral phenotypes; rather, there is a complex set of transactions between genotypic, physiological, and environmental factors that leads to the development of one of many possible phenotypes.

3. A polygenic model of intelligence accounts for the distribution of IQ values in a population, for the regression from parent to offspring IQ, and for the effects of inbreeding. Although there may be a few major genes that affect intellectual development, a multigene model fits the data very well.

4. Normal intellectual development can be seen as a species-specific, evolved pattern of development. The stage-sequence model described by Piaget and others may be modal for the species. All normal members of the human group with environments in the normal range show the same progressive development of intelligence.

VARIATION IN THE DEVELOPMENT OF INTELLIGENCE

The statement that variability in a given trait depends, in part, upon genetic variation implies necessarily that genetic variation contributed to differences *in the development of that trait.* McClearn (1970, p. 65) summarized the point:

In a very real sense it is the case that any demonstrated genetic control over an adult characteristic is, at the same time, an implication of genetic control over the developmental processes that culminated in that characteristic. Research aimed explicitly at studying the genetic control of behavioral development unfortunately has been rare, particularly with respect to man.

Since Mendelian models of genetics have not yet been fitted to the complex polygenic system of normal human intelligence, the only substantial literature to review concerns the determinants of *variation* of intelligence. Studies of environmental differences within and between families, social class, and ethnic groups try to account for portions of the variance in IQ scores, just as studies of genetic differences do. There is sometimes great confusion of meaning when authors of studies in *variation* call their variables *determinants* of intelligence. Certainly, some of the genotypic differences between people are also important determinants of intellectual development, but there must be many genes that produce little or no variation which are also important determinants of intelligence.

An example of a genetic characteristic that shows little genetic variation is human birth-weight (Morton 1955). Almost 90 percent of the variation in birth-weight does *not* depend on genotypic differences among fetuses. Most of the variation is environmental in origin even though the narrow range of normal birth-weight is clearly a species-specific, genetically determined characteristic.

It is a principle of genetic variation that characteristics particularly close to reproductive fitness and viability are allowed little variability within the species. Variants that are less fit or viable are selected out rapidly. Thus, birth-weight has a narrow range of largely nonheritable variation.

It is likely that many gene loci for normal intellectual development also have little polygenic variability within the species and that a minority of regulatory genes control most of the individual variation in the normal range (Thiessen 1972*b*).

Given some genetic and environmental variation, individual differences in phenotypic intelligence can be analyzed into genetic and environmental components of variance by appropriatic behavior-genetic methods. Most of the variation that has been studied has been individual variation *within* a population or breeding group. There is strong interest, however, in analyzing the phenotypic variations in IQ *between* populations (Jensen, 1973). The latter requires quite different assumptions: i.e., about distributions and values of genotypes and environments within and between different

populations. In the first part of this section, variation within a population
will be considered, followed by between-group comparisons.

Individual Variation within a Population

The relative contributions of genetic and environmental differences to
phenotypic diversity within a population depend upon six major parameters: (1) range of genotypes; (2) range of environments; (3) favorableness of genotypes; (4) favorableness of environments; (5) covariance of genotypes and environments; (6) interactions of genotypes and
environments.

The range of genotypes and environments can independently and together affect the total variance of a behavioral, polygenic trait in a population. The mean favorableness of genotypes and environments can independently and together affect the mean values of phenotypes.

Two separate problems are involved in understanding the effects of
mean favorableness and ranges of genotypes in a population: gene frequencies, and the distribution of genes among the genotypes. Gene frequencies are affected by two principal processes: differential reproduction, or
natural selection, and *sampling errors.* Genotype frequencies are affected
by *assortative mating.* Two populations (or two generations of the same
population) may have equal gene frequencies but different genotype frequencies if assortative mating for a behavioral trait is greater in one population than the other.

1. *Genotypic range and favorableness.* a. Natural selection. Changing
environmental conditions, such as the introduction of more complex technology, may affect the rate of reproduction in different segments of the
IQ distribution in a generation. We know, for example, that severely mentally retarded persons in the contemporary white populations of Europe
and the United States do not reproduce as frequently as those who can
hold jobs and maintain independent adult lives (Bajema 1968; Higgins,
Reed, and Reed 1962). Severe retardation renders one less likely to be
chosen as a mate and less likely to produce progeny for the next generation.

If one segment of the phenotypic IQ range has been strongly and consistently selected against, as severely mentally retarded persons are in
contemporary industrial populations, then the range and favorableness
of the total gene distribution will be slowly changed. If, in another population, high phenotypic IQ were disadvantageous for mate selection and
reproduction, then the genic distribution would be reduced at that end. It
is probably true that systematic selection against high phenotypic IQ does
not occur frequently. In any case, selection against polygenic characteristics is probably very slow (Stern 1960), especially when many gene loci
are involved.

b. Sampling. Gene frequencies can also be affected by genetic drift, a random sampling error. Not every allele at every gene locus is equally sampled in every generation through reproduction. Rare genes, especially, may disappear through random failure to be passed on to the next generation, and the frequencies of other alleles may be randomly increased or decreased from generation to generation.

A special case of restriction in genic range is nonrandom sampling from a larger gene pool in the formation of a smaller breeding group. If, for example, an above-median sample from the IQ group migrated to a distant locale and bred primarily among themselves, the gene frequencies within the migrant group might vary considerably from those of the nonmigrant group, all other things being equal.

c. Assortative mating. The distribution of genes in genotypic classes within a population can vary because of assortative mating. To the extent that "likes" marry "likes," genetic variability is decreased within families and increased between families. At the present time, within the U.S. white population, the assortative mating correlation for parental IQ is approximately .40, which increases the sibling correlation for phenotypic IQ to about .55 instead of the .50 expected, since they share, on the average, one-half of their genes in common (Jensen 1968, 1969). Assortative mating for IQ also increases the standard deviation of IQ scores within the total (white) population by increasing the frequency of extremely high and extremely low genotypes for phenotypic IQ. On a random mating basis, the probability of producing extreme genotypes is greatly reduced because extreme parental genotypes are unlikely to find each other by chance. The sheer frequency of middle-range genotypes makes an average mate the most likely random choice of an extreme genotype for both high or low IQ.

Since children's IQ values are distributed around the mean parental value (with some regression toward the population mean), the offspring of such matings will tend to be closer to the population mean than offspring of extreme parental combinations. The phenotypic distribution under conditions of random mating will tend to have a leptokurtic shape with a large modal class and low total variance.

2. Environmental range and favorableness. The range of environments within a population can also affect phenotypic variability. Uniform environments can restrict phenotypic diversity by eliminating a major source of variation. Since environments can be observed and manipulated, there are many studies on infrahuman populations to demonstrate the restriction of variability through uniform environments (Manosevitz, Lindzey, and Thiessen 1969).

Far more important, however, for the present discussion is the favorableness dimension of the environment. Environments which do not support the development of a trait can greatly alter the mean value of the trait. If environments in the unfavorable range are common to all or most members of a population, then the phenotypic variance of the population can be slightly reduced while the mean can be drastically lowered.

The most likely effects of very suppressive environments are that they lower the mean of the population, decrease phenotypic variability, and consequently reduce the correlation between genotype and phenotype (Henderson 1970; Scarr-Salapatek 1971*b*). A contrast can be made between uniform environments which support the development of a particular behavior and suppressive environments which may also be uniform but not supportive of optimal development (Nichols 1970). Uniform environments of good quality may reduce variability and raise the mean of the population.

The ranges of genotypes and environments and the favorableness of the environment control a large portion of the total phenotypic variance in IQ. The two additional factors—covariance and interaction—are probably less important (Jinks and Fulker 1970), at least within the white North American and European populations.

3. *Covariation.* Covariance between genotypes and environments is expressed as a correlation between certain genotypic characteristics and certain environmental features which affect phenotypic outcome: e.g., the covariance between the IQs of children of bright parents, which is likely to be higher than average, and the educationally advantaged environment offered by those same parents to their bright children. Retarded parents, on the other hand, may have less bright children under any environmental circumstances but also may supply those children with educationally deprived environments. Covariation between genotype and environment may also depend upon the genotype and the kind of response it evokes from the environment. If bright children receive continual reward for their educationally superior performance, while duller children receive fewer rewards, environmental rewards can be said to covary with IQ. The fact that the giving of rewards in this example depends upon the genotype of the child in a significant way does not remove covariance from the environmental side of the equation.

4. *Interaction.* Covariance is sometimes confused with interaction but they are quite different terms. When psychologists speak of genetic-environment interaction, they are usually referring to the reciprocal relationship that exists between an organism and its surroundings. The organism brings to the situation a set of characteristics that affects the environment, which in turn affects the further development of the organism, and vice versa. This is not what quantitative geneticists mean by interaction. A better term for the psychologists would be "transaction" between orga-

nism and environment because the statistical term "interaction" refers to the *differential* effects of various organism-environment transactions on development.

Behavioral geneticists, whose experimental work is primarily with mouse strains and drosophila, often find genotype-environmental interactions of considerable importance. The differential response of two or more genotypes or two or more environments is interaction. In general, m genotypes in n environments yield $\dfrac{(mn)!}{m!n!}$ types of interaction; for example, ten genotypes in ten environments can generate 10^{144} kinds of interaction (Hirsch 1971). In studies of animal learning, where both genotypes and environmental conditions can be manipulated, so-called maze-dull rats who were bred for poor performance in Tryon's mazes were shown to perform as well as so-called maze-bright rats when given enriched environments (Cooper and Zubec 1958) and when given distributed rather than massed practice (McGaugh, Jennings, and Thompson 1962). The interaction of learning conditions with genotypes is obvious in figure 9.

Studies of genotype-environment interaction in human populations are quite limited. Biometrical methods that include an analysis for interaction have failed to show any substantial variance attributable to nonlinear effects on human intelligence (Jinks and Fulker 1970; Jensen 1973). This is not to say that genotype-environment interaction may not account for some portion of the variance in IQ scores in other populations or in other segments of white populations (e.g., the disadvantaged).

5. *Total phenotypic variance.* Jensen (1969) has offered an array of variance terms that combine to produce total phenotypic variance in studies of human characteristics.

$$V_p = [(V_g + V_{AM}) + V_D + V_i] + [V_E + 2\,Cov_{HE} + V_I + V_e]$$

where:
V_p = phenotypic variance in the population
V_g = genic (or additive) variance
V_{AM} = variance due to assortative mating, $V_{AM} = 0$ under random mating
V_D = dominance deviation variance
V_i = epistatis (interaction among genes at two or more loci)
V_E = environmental variance
Cov_{HE} = covariance of heredity and environment
V_I = true statistical interaction of genetic and environmental factors
V_e = error of measurement (unreliability)

The first bracket contains the terms usually grouped under total genetic

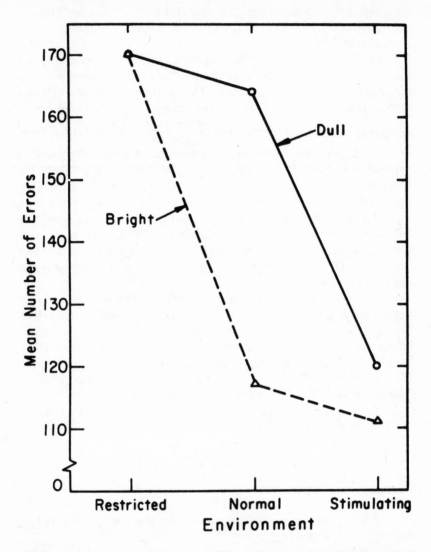

Fig. 9. Error scores in maze learning by Tryon "bright" and "dull" rats reared in restricted, average, and stimulating environments. (From Cooper and Zubek 1958.)

variance, the second those usually grouped as total environmental variance. The estimation of genetic variance leads to estimates of heritability.

6. Heritability is a summary statement of the proportion of the total phenotypic variance that is due to additive genetic variance (narrow heritability) or to total genetic variance (broad heritability). Heritability (h^2) is a *population statistic,* not a property of a trait (Fuller and Thompson 1960). Estimates of h^2 vary from population to population as genetic

variance varies as a proportion of the total variance. (For the calculation of various kinds of heritability estimates see Falconer 1960).

TABLE 6.   CORRELATIONS FOR INTELLECTUAL ABILITY:
OBTAINED AND THEORETICAL VALUES

Correlations Between	Number of Studies	Obtained Median r[a]	Theoretical Value[b]	Theoretical Value[c]
Unrelated Persons				
Children reared apart	4	−.01	.00	.00
Foster parent and child	3	+.20	.00	.00
Children reared together	5	+.24	.00	.00
Collaterals				
Second cousins	1	+.16	+ .14	+ .063
First cousins	3	+.26	+ .18	+ .125
Uncle (or aunt) and nephew (or niece)	1	+.34	+ .31	+ .25
Siblings, reared apart	3	+.47	+ .52	+ .50
Siblings, reared together	36	+.55	+ .52	+ .50
Dizygotic twins, different sex	9	+.49	+ .50	+ .50
Dizygotic twins, same sex	11	+.56	+ .54	+ .50
Monozygotic twins, reared apart	4	+.75	+1.00	+1.00
Monozygotic twins, reared together	14	+.87	+1.00	+1.00
Direct Line				
Grandparent and grandchild	3	+.27	+ .31	+ .25
Parent (as adult) and child	13	+.50	+ .49	+ .50
Parent (as child) and child	1	+.56	+ .49	+ .50

SOURCE: Jensen 1969, adapted from Burt 1961.
[a] Correlations not corrected for attenuation (unreliability).
[b] Assuming assortative mating and partial dominance.
[c] Assuming random mating and only additive genes, i.e., the simplest possible polygenic model.

The six parameters of individual variation within a population noted at the beginning of this section are the major contributors to the total phenotypic variance in any population. The proportions of genetic variance (additive, assortative mating, dominance, and epistasis) and environmental variance (biological-social, covariance, interaction) may well vary from one population to another depending upon the ranges and favorableness of the two sets of variables, their covariances and interactions. The variance terms and heritability statistics are frequently used in family studies to estimate the relative importance of genetic and environmental differences to account for phenotypic IQ differences.

7. *Family studies of IQ variation.* A number of excellent reviews of the behavior genetic literature on intelligence have appeared in the last five or six years.[1] The data shown in table 6 are representative of results from family studies.

[1] Readers who wish to pursue the methodological and substantive issue of IQ heritability should see Lindzey et al. 1971; Hirsch 1967; Huntley 1966; Jarvik and Erlenmeyer-Kimling 1967; Jensen 1969, 1973; Vandenberg 1966, 1967, 1968, 1971; Scarr-Salapatek 1971*a*, 1971*b*; Bouchard 1972.

There is increasing similarity in IQ scores as genetic relatedness increases. Rearing together has a relatively small effect on IQ correlations, as shown in figure 10.

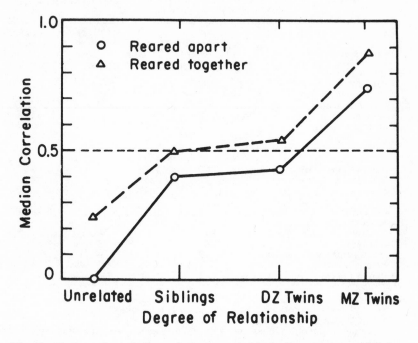

Fig. 10. Median values of all correlations reported in the literature up to 1963 for the indicated kinships. (From Jensen 1969, adapted from Erlenmeyer-Kimling and Jarvik, "Genetics and Intelligence: A Review," *Science* 142 [December 1963]: 1477–79, copyright © 1963 by the American Association for the Advancement of Science.)

When intellectual abilities are tested differentially, rather than as a summary IQ score, there emerge different heritabilities for different factors, over and above the heritability of general intelligence (Nichols 1965; Vandenberg 1965). Verbal and spatial abilities appear to be more highly heritable than other factors like numerical reasoning and memory. Multivariate analyses (see Vandenberg 1971) have shown that *separate* genetic variances are involved in spatial and verbal skills. Thus, besides general IQ, with which most research has been concerned, there are differential abilities that have still other degrees of heritability. Spatial abilities may, in fact, have a sex-related pattern of inheritance (Bock and Kolakowski, in press; Money 1968).

The research literature on genetic and environmental contributions to variation in IQ test scores is substantial. Within North American and European Caucasian populations, individual differences in IQ seem to be due more to genotypic differences than to measured environmental variation. (This may be due, in part, to failure to measure environmental differences as well as genetic differences.) Most biometrical and family studies suggest that half to three-quarters of the individual variation in the IQ arises from genotypic variation in those populations. The particular gene-action pathways and environmental determinants that create the developmental differences in IQ are unknown.

In less advantaged populations, particularly lower social-class groups, the full genotypic range may not be expressed in the distribution of their phenotypic IQ scores. Environments that limit the expression of genotypic differences can reduce phenotypic variability, lower the mean phenotypic value, and reduce the statistical contribution of the genotype to the phenotypic development (Scarr-Salapatek 1971a, 1971b).

There are many ways to produce a poor phenotype for intelligence. Neonatal starvation, prenatal rubella, extreme parental abuse, deprivation of learning opportunities are examples. Genotypic intelligence is not well expressed under these conditions. In the socially advantaged ranges of environmental variation, phenotypes may reflect more genotypic variability; in less advantaged ranges, genotypic expression may be reduced and environmental variation increased. New research on this issue will be forthcoming.

Between-group Differences

Mean differences in IQ scores between racial, ethnic, and social-class groups are too well known to be restated at any length (see Jensen 1969, 1973; Weyl 1969). Briefly, there is often found an average difference of 10 to 20 points on IQ tests between black and white samples, between lower- and upper-middle-class white samples, and between various ethnic groups, such as Irish and Jews. There is also a growing literature on population differences in cognitive developmental skills that reports similar results (Berry 1966; deLacey 1970, 1971a, 1971b; DeLemos 1969; Gaudia 1972; MacArthur 1968, 1969; Price-Williams 1961). In general, Caucasian, American Indian, Eskimo, and Oriental children are shown to have higher IQ scores and more rapid cognitive development than children of African or Australian aboriginal origin, particularly after the first two years of life (Bayley 1965; Geber 1958).

The finding of average differences between populations does not favor either a genetic or environmental explanation. Even if the heritabilities of intellectual performance *within* each of two populations have been shown to be high, there is practically no connection between within-group heritability and between-group heritability (DeFries 1971; Lewontin 1970; Scarr-Salapatek 1971a). Intelligence score differences within two populations can be related primarily to genetic differences among individuals while average differences between groups can be related primarily to environmental differences.

While most investigators prefer an environmental hypothesis to account for between-population differences (Jensen 1973), there is no a priori scientific basis for this stance (Scarr-Salapatek 1971*a*). Variation between populations on many characteristics like blood groups, skin color, height, physique, and so on are thought to be evolutionary adaptations to different environments. It is unlikely that any two relatively isolated populations have maintained exactly the same gene or genotype frequencies for any characteristic. This does not mean, however, that their reaction ranges for intellectual development need differ significantly, because important human qualities have tended to show convergent evolution among temporarily isolated groups (Gottesman 1968).

1. *Race and social class.* These are terms that refer to socially defined subgroups of the human population. Reproduction is more likely to occur between people in the same subgroup than between persons from different subgroups. There is no question that races are partially closed breeding groups with a great deal more mating within the group (endogamy) than mating outside of the group (exogamy). It is also true in modern times that social-class groups (groups whose members have attained a certain educational and occupational status) within races practice more endogamy than exogamy (Gottesman 1968; Kiser 1968).

Social mobility, based on IQ, from generation to generation actually helps to define social classes more sharply as rather distinct breeding groups with different average IQ levels. In older times, when social status was gratuitously ascribed because of family origin and when there was less social mobility, social-class groups were probably less distinct in their average IQ levels.

Because of social mobility in contemporary society, the IQ distribution within each social-class level tends to be reestablished in each generation of adults (Burt 1966; Herrnstein 1971). Brighter children in families at all but the top social levels tend to be upwardly mobile, whereas duller siblings at all but the bottom class level tend to be downwardly mobile (Waller 1971). Social-class groups may be thought of as endogamous primarily for IQ (as expressed in occupational and educational achievements).

The mean differences by social class in children's IQ reflect differences in both parental genotypes and rearing environments, which covary to a large extent in the development of IQ. Crucial evidence on the genetic and environmental components from adopted children is very limited, but, as mentioned before, Skodak and Skeels (1949) revealed a 20-point rise in the IQ of adopted children over that of their biological mothers.

The distribution of adopted children's IQs was even shifted beyond the values expected by regression to a mean above the average of the population, presumably by their better social environments.

Social-class groups, then, are subdivisions of the total population and represent different distributions of parental genotypes, as well as different rearing environments. There is no comparable statement that can be made about racial groups: whereas races represent different rearing environments, no statements can be made concerning different distributions of parental genotypes for IQ. Since there is no direct test possible for distributions of genotypic IQ (Thoday 1969), it is impossible to assert that such distributions for the two races are "equal" or "different."

The same six parameters of individual variation within a population describe the sources of variation between populations. The mechanisms that can produce population differences in gene and genotype frequencies are the same. The major difference, and the importance of this difference cannot be exaggerated, is that comparisons between racial populations require a set of assumptions different from comparisons between individuals and social-class groups within a population.

Only if one assumes that within the two populations the same environmental factors affect the development of intelligence in the same way, is it possible to make between-race comparisons. If one is unwilling to assume a complete identity in the distribution of environmental variables and in the ways they affect development, then between-race comparisons are not justifiable (Scarr-Salapatek 1971*b*). Jensen (in press) calls this reluctance to make quantitative comparisons between races "the factor X" hypothesis—one which proposes that some unknown environmental factor (like racial discrimination) affects one group and not the other or affects one group in a different way from the other (Chinese versus blacks). The reader must judge for himself which assumptions seem justified.

2. *Admixture studies.* To avoid direct comparisons between racial or ethnic groups, there is a better research strategy that uses hybrid populations: the study of admixture. Suppose that groups of children reared under comparable conditions but differing in racial admixture rates were also found to differ in mean IQ scores. Such evidence would suggest a genetic basis for at least part of the phenotypic differences between races.

Negro Americans and aboriginal Australians are examples of populations with varying degrees of Caucasian admixture that have accumulated over the several centuries. Since visible amounts of African and aboriginal ancestry cause the bearer to be classified as nonwhite, most of the persons of mixed ancestry have remained in these groups rather than in the populations of European ancestry (Reed 1969).

DeLemos (1969) presented Piagetian conservation tasks to full aboriginal and part-aboriginal children in the same mission. The part-aboriginal children had small percentages of Caucasian ancestry, most being classified from mission records as seven-eighths aboriginal. The European ancestry was, therefore, several generations removed from the present group:

there were no apparent differences in the present environment of part-Aboriginal and full-Aboriginal children in the Hermannsburg groups. Part-Aborigines and full-Aborigines formed a single integrated community, and the children were brought up under the same mission conditions and attended the same school (p. 257).

The results for several conservation tasks are presented in table 7. Children with some Caucasian ancestry performed significantly better than full-aboriginal children on four of the six tasks. DeLemos claims that an environmental hypothesis cannot account for these results.

TABLE 7. COMPARISON OF THE NUMBER OF PART-ABORIGINAL AND FULL-ABORIGINAL CHILDREN SHOWING CONSERVATION

Test	Full-Abor. $N = 38$	Part.-Abor. $N = 34$	X^2	p
Quantity	4	18	15.214	$< .001$
Weight	16	25	7.227	$< .01$
Volume	2	8	3.595	$.05 < p < .10$
Length	12	20	5.365	$< .05$
Area	3	10	4.225	$< .05$
Number	3	9	3.22	$.05 < p < .10$
Total	40	90	36.141	$< .001$

Source: DeLemos 1969.

DeLemos's results have not been replicated in several other studies. DeLacey (1970, 1971*a*, 1971*b*) has studied verbal intelligence, classificatory ability, and operational thinking in aboriginal, part-aboriginal, and white Australian children. Within each population, social-class differences have been shown to affect scores on all measures. Between the groups, smaller average differences were found on performance than on verbal tasks. From two separate reports it is possible to compare full- with part-aboriginal samples, both in schools with white children. On the Peabody Picture Vocabulary Test (PPVT), forty full-aboriginal children from six to twelve years of age scored an average of IQ 63.5 (S.D.=12.3). Thirteen part-aboriginal children scored an average of IQ 69.3 (S.D.=14.5). One hundred and five low SES white children scored an average of 94.1

THE
UNIVERSITY OF WINNIPEG
PORTAGE & BALMORAL
WINNIPEG, MANITOBA CANADA
DISCARDED

(S.D.=12.6). There is no question that white Australian children scored higher on verbal IQ tests in English than aboriginal children, but there was no clear difference between the part- and full-aboriginals.

For Piagetian operational tasks, deLacey (1971a) found no differences between aboriginal and white Australian children. Although the samples are small (three to ten at each age level) the data in table 8 show that increases in the percentage of children giving operational responses on classification tasks were similar in the two groups.

TABLE 8.   PERCENTAGE OF ITEMS ANSWERED OPERATIONALLY ON TWO CLASSIFICATION TESTS BY ABORIGINAL AND LOW SOCIOECONOMIC WHITE CHILDREN

	Age groupings						
Tests	6	7	8	9	10	11	12
Nixon Test[a]							
Aboriginals	26	52	67	64	89	88	95
Whites	35	48	72	77	90	90	
Matrices Test[b]							
Aboriginals	5	10	25	38	49	57	68
Whites	4	8	26	36	44	71	78

SOURCE: DeLacey 1971a.
[a] Chi square $= 3.24$, df 6, $p > .50$.
[b] Chi square $= 2.48$, df 6, $p > .50$.

DeLemos's samples also showed marked increases in cognitive skills with age. It is possible that age was confounded with full- and part-aboriginal background in DeLemos's study, thereby giving false positive results for the background variable. From his report (1969), it is impossible to find the age distributions in the full- and part-aboriginal groups. If more full-aboriginal children were in the younger age-groups, the results can be explained by age alone.

Unless more quantitative approaches are used in studies of racial admixture, it is difficult to form any firm conclusions about the effects of genotypic differences on intellectual differences between racial groups. A better method would use *degree* of white ancestry as a correlate of intellectual performance, where degree of ancestry would be measured from pedigree studies or from independent estimates of admixture obtained from blood group phenotypes. No studies of this sort have yet been done.

Studies of children from interracial marriages in the U.S. (Willerman, Naylor, and Myrianthropoulos 1970, 1971) have suggested substantial maternal effects on the development of intelligence. The children of white mothers and black fathers develop higher IQ scores over the first four years of life than the children of black mothers and white fathers. The

Scarr-Salapatek

educational levels of the parents in both types of interracial matings were quite comparable, but there was still a maternal effect on intellectual development.

3. *Cross-fostering studies.* The rearing of offspring from one group by mothers from another group is known as cross-fostering, a technique that is often used in animal behavior genetics to separate maternal environmental effects from genotypic effects. Cross-fostering periods can include the prenatal and postnatal environments, the former by means of ova transplants.

In human populations, cross-fostering is not arranged for experimental convenience, of course, but sometimes occurs naturally in adoptive families. To separate possible genetic racial differences from the effects of environments provided by the racial groups, one could compare the development of children reared by parents of their own race with those reared by parents of another race. A complete design would include children of both racial groups reared by same- and different-race parents, as follows:

Race of parents

		A	B
Race of child	A^1	A^1A	A^1B
	B^1	B^1A	B^1B

The reader can immediately see the pitfalls of a cross-fostering approach if average intellectual differences were found among the offspring groups. Racial classifications are primarily social—not genetic—categories and depend upon identifiably different phenotypes. Thus, the offspring of race A are identifiably different from the offspring of race B; and even though reared by parents from a different group, they may be treated by others as members of their own race. Any finding of average intellectual differences would not discriminate between a genetic-difference hypothesis and a social-discrimination hypothesis.

The finding of *no difference,* however, between the children of races A and B when reared by parents of a single race would be an interesting result, suggesting that the reaction range of the two racial groups included the same IQ values under similar rearing conditions. In other words, if combinations of child and parent $A^1A = B^1A > A^1B = B^1B$, then environmental differences between races A and B becomes the preferred hypothesis. The result $A^1A = A^1B > B^1A = B^1B$ does not discriminate between genetic differences and environmental differences. Several patterns of results would suggest interaction effects between race of child and race of parents: $A^1A > A^1B > B^1A > B^1B$, or $A^1A > B^1B > A^1B > B^1B$, and so forth.

Adoptive families may be seen as providing cross-fostering for many characteristics on which they differ from the natural parents. Children of retarded parents may be seen as cross-fostered when reared by adoptive families of normal IQ. Children of psychotic parents, when adopted, are reared in nonpsychotic environments. Children whose natural parents are alcoholic, drug addicted, psychopathic, and so forth are often adopted into families without those characteristics. Comparisons can then be made between the adopted children and others reared by similar natural parents. To complete the cross-fostering design one can also study the children of nonpsychotic, nonretarded, nonalcoholic natural parents reared by psychotic or retarded or alcoholic adoptive parents. (Since adoptive families are selected by social agencies for their virtues, however, pathological adoptive parents are probably a very small group.) The last group would be nonpathological families who rear their own offspring. For a review of the use of this design in studies of psychopathology, see Rosenthal (1970).

To my knowledge, there have been no studies of the effects of cross-fostering on the intellectual development of children from different racial or ethnic groups. Nor have there been any systematic studies on the postnatal effects of normal-IQ adoptive parents on the children of retarded natural parents. Only Skodak and Skeels (1949) considered the intellectual outcomes of adopted children with natural mothers of higher or lower IQs. The children of lower-IQ natural mothers did not achieve as high phenotypic levels of IQ as the children of higher-IQ mothers, regardless of adoptive family characteristics. Eleven adopted children whose natural mothers had IQs of less than 70 (mean = 63) had an average IQ of 104. Eight adopted children, whose mothers had IQs above 105 (mean = 111) had an average IQ of 129. Although the number of cases is very small, the results suggest (1) that there is a considerable reaction range shown by the children's IQ scores, and (2) that genotypic differences between groups of children with retarded natural mothers and those with above-average natural mothers were important in determining the rank order of the children's IQ scores. Note, however, that even the children with retarded natural mothers scored above the average IQ level of the population, a fact that demonstrates the importance of the adoptive home environments in raising the IQ level of the adopted children.

Developmental Differences in Intelligence

How malleable is the genotypic response to variations in the environment? How severe or prolonged must environmental effects be to deflect the developing phenotype from its genetically canalized, "normal" course of growth? How far above and below the average range of environments must treatments be to have substantial effects on raising or lowering IQ? Heritability tells us nothing about malleability (Crow 1969). For this we must look to the reaction ranges of genotypes under different environments, as in cross-fostering and intervention studies.

Tentative answers, or at least new questions, are provided by three current lines of developmental research: longitudinal studies on the intellectual development of related individuals (Honzik 1971; McCall 1970; Wilson 1972), life-span research on intellectual similarity in twins (Jarvik et al. 1971; Jarvik, Blum, and Varna 1972; Jarvik et al. 1957; Jarvik and Kato 1970; Kallman 1961), and new intervention studies on children of predictable intellectual level (Heber 1969; Rynders 1972; Smilansky and Smilansky, 1968).

With the exceptions noted above, nearly all studies of naturally occurring "environmental" variations have failed to separate genetic from environmental components of variance. Seemingly environmental measures such as socioeconomic status, parental education, number of books in the home, and the like reflect the parents' IQ level. The parents' IQs not only contribute to the child's environmental enrichment but are an indication of what the child received genetically from his parents. There is a confounding of genotypes and environments in sociological studies of the "environmental" variation among unselected families and unknown genotypes.

Similarly, psychological studies of maternal styles of child rearing fail to separate maternal contributions to the child's genotype from maternal behavior toward the child (Brophy 1970; Hess and Shipman 1965). If there is a substantial maternal-style effect in the development of IQ *differences,* then it must be demonstrated after eliminating genetic components of variance. When mothers taught their twins to sort blocks by one of several possible criteria, Fischer (1972) and Waterhouse (1972) failed to find any maternal-style effect on the magnitude of cognitive differences between MZ or DZ co-twins.

Better studies of maternal-style effects and the like can be accomplished by either controlling for genetic relatedness, as in twin and sibling studies, or by eliminating relatedness, as in studies of mothers with adopted children. Studies of larger social-class variation can be made more interpretable by equating parents for IQ while varying socioeconomic status, and vice versa, in order to compare the two components of variation. Behavior genetic methods can improve studies of true environmental variation by controlling for genetic variation.

Experimental treatment or training studies on intellectual or cognitive acceleration usually escape the covariance problem by randomly assigning genotypes to environments. Treatment effects are averaged across the varied genotypes, often lumping large with small, and even reverse, effects. What is to be learned from studies on just any group of fifty six-year olds, that show, for example, that a certain form of concrete manipulation accelerates the acquisition of a conservation concept? While one learns one way to increase average performance on that task in that sample, one learns nothing about the varied ways in which individual children learn conservation concepts (even under the artificial training conditions, and especially not in the real world). Behavior genetic methods of selecting children of known relatedness from stipulated populations would make experimental studies somewhat more meaningful.

   1. *Longitudinal family studies.* The Louisville Twin Study, organized by Vandenberg (1968*b*), has collected data on the development of intelligence in the first two years. Wilson (1972) separated environmental and genetic variation in infant mental development. The 261 pairs of monozygotic and dizygotic twins were measured repeatedly with the Bayley Mental Scales. Over the first two years of life, both absolute level of mental development and pattern of development were very similar for both MZ and DZ twins. Mental development was more similar for MZ than DZ twins, as shown in table 9.

   Socioeconomic variables in Wilson's average white sample correlated

TABLE 9.   ANALYSIS OF BAYLEY MENTAL SCALE SCORES
FOR TWINS IN FIRST AND SECOND YEARS

Source of variance	Within-pair correlations (R)	Test for MZ > DZ (P)	Range of 98 percent level of confidence	Mean square Between pairs	Within pairs	Degrees of freedom
Ages 3, 6, 9, and 12 months						
Overall level						
MZ pairs	.90	< .01	.80—.95	645.5	35.6	44/45
DZ pairs	.75		.57—.86	871.8	122.4	50/51
Profile contour						
MZ pairs	.75	< .01	.65—.83	280.0	39.1	132/135
DZ pairs	.50		.34—.63	228.5	76.0	150/153
Ages 12, 18, and 24 months						
Overall level						
MZ pairs	.89	< .05	.79—.94	677.8	40.7	50/51
DZ pairs	.79		.62—.89	614.5	71.0	45/46
Profile contour						
MZ pairs	.67	< .05	.53—.78	272.4	53.1	100/102
DZ pairs	.52		.33—.68	200.7	62.4	90/92

SOURCE: Wilson 1972.
NOTE: The within-pair correlation is given by $R = (MS_b - MS_w)/(MS_b + MS_w)$, where MS_b is the mean square between pairs and MS_w is the mean square within pairs.

only slightly (r ≃ .11 for the first year, r ≃ .20 for the second year) with intellectual status. Wilson concluded,

Therefore, the hypothesis is proposed that these socioeconomic and maternal care variables serve to modulate the primary determinant of developmental capability, namely the genetic blueprint supplied by the parents. . . .

Further, while there is a continuing interaction between the genetically determined gradient of development and the life circumstances under which each pair of twins is born and raised, it required unusual environmental conditions to impose a major deflection upon the gradient of infant development. . . . For the great majority of pairs, life circumstances fall within the broad limits of sufficiency that permit the genetic blueprint to control the course of infant mental development (p. 917).

These conclusions are very strong in light of the only moderate heritabilities that could be calculated from them both. The fact that DZ correlations are very high suggests a strong similarity of twins' gestation and early environment rather than genetic similarity. Note also that Wilson does *not* say that extraordinary environmental factors cannot have disastrous or extremely beneficial effects upon the course of intellectual development. But in a population of cooperative parents, who varied from welfare to upper-middle-class status, differences in their infants' mental development depended more upon genotypic differences than upon environmental differences.

At older ages, both genetic and social environmental differences between families may assume greater importance than in infancy. It is well known (Burks 1928; Honzik 1957; Jensen 1969) that children's IQ scores increasingly resemble their parents' scores over the preschool and early school years. The increasing similarity between parents and their children could be due to any of the following: (1) greater similarity of tasks on IQ tests at older ages, (2) increasing expression of genetic individual differences, and (3) longer and more effective exposure of the children to the parental environment. Studies of adopted children's increasing resemblance to their natural parents can only be interpreted as support for explanations 1 and 2. The extent to which their resemblance to natural, and not adoptive parents, increases with age, can only support 2, the increasing expression of genetic differences (Honzik 1957).

The *level* of IQ scores at any one age shows more genetic variation than does the *pattern* of IQ development over time. Wilson found correlations between .80 and .90 for level of IQ in MZ twins and around .70 for pattern of development. One MZ twin's IQ score was a better predictor of his co-twin's score at a single age than it was of his own score at another age. In other words, the patterning of development has two variable aspects: it is probably genotype-specific, so that MZ twins are fairly similar in their patterns of development in similar environments, but it is also environmentally variable depending upon prenatal effects, illnesses, preferential maternal care, and the like. The profiles of two MZ twins may be somewhat "offset" in time, so that their correlations are reduced. Absolute level of IQ score, however, takes into account the wide differences between families, which make MZ co-twins comparatively very similar.

McCall (1970) studied the levels and patterns of development in siblings and parents (as children) and their children. The IQs of one hundred pairs of siblings correlated around .55 consistently across ages from three and a half to eleven years. The thirty-five pairs of parents and children, who share half their genes in common, had lower correlation ($r \simeq .30$) than the expected .50, for unexplained reasons.[2] Differences in patterns of development for siblings and parents and children did not show substantial genetic variation. This again supports the reaction range model: that patterns of intellectual growth may be genotype-specific and environmentally variable. Since parent-child and sibling pairs receive only half of their genome by identical descent, and since their pre- and postnatal environments vary more than those of fraternal twins, they may have quite different patterns of growth. The resemblance of their phenotypic levels of IQ at any one age suggests some similarity in their reactions to similar environments, but they need not have achieved that intellectual status by the same profile of growth over the preceding years.

Wilson (1972) found significant correlations for patterns of intellectual growth between DZ co-twins ($r \simeq .51$). Although DZ co-twins share the same percentage of their genome in common as ordinary siblings, they are products of the same pregnancy and are reared at the same time. Environmental variation within families, therefore, seems to influence profiles of growth more than phenotypic levels of IQ within families.

Honzik (1971) reported WAIS correlations for three generations of family members (grandparents, parents, and children). Besides correlating the levels of IQ, as has been done in many studies (see table 6 from Burt), she used rank order correlations to ascertain their similarity in patterns of ability on the WAIS subtests, without regard to overall IQ level. To summarize the results of more than five hundred rhos, the percentage of positive and significantly positive rhos was computed (50 percent will be positive by chance if the expectation is zero correlation). These are shown in table 10.

---

[2] Correlations between parents and children are often found to be lower than those of siblings. Both parent-child pairs and siblings share about half of their genome in common, but only siblings can share dominance variance (see Mather and Jinks 1971). That can increase their similarities over those of the purely additive effects shared by parents and children. In addition, siblings share a common rearing environment which parents and their children cannot share.

TABLE 10.   THE PERCENT OF POSITIVE AND SIGNIFICANTLY
POSITIVE RANK ORDER CORRELATIONS FOR WAIS SUB-
TEST SCORES AMONG GRANDPARENTS, PARENTS,
AND THEIR CHILDREN

Relationship	N (Pairs)	% Positive	% Positive, p < .05
Father-son	12	92	
Father-daughter	20	85	21
Mother-daughter	27	89	
Mother-son	15	67	
Grandfather-grandson	26	54	
Grandfather-granddaughter	21	43	5
Grandmother-granddaughter	39	59	
Grandmother-grandson	36	58	
Mother-father	81	81	17
(assortative mating)			

SOURCE: Honzik 1971.

The finding of a positive rho is dependent upon variability in subtest scores. "In other words a significant rho tells us something (about similar patterns of abilities regardless of IQ level) but the large proportion of low positive and negative rhos are not informative" (p. 6). Significant parent-child similarity in WAIS pattern of ability is based on relatively higher vocabulary than block design scores, for example, not on level of performance in either. The study of pattern similarity suggests that children significantly reflect their parents' patterns of ability, probably on both genetic and environmental grounds. Parental correlations reflect assortative mating. Similar studies of siblings, adopted children, half-siblings, cousins, and so on would permit the analysis of the pattern differences into genetic and environmental components. In the Honzik study, however, the greater parent-child than grandparent-grandchild pattern similarity fits the polygenic model presented by Li (1971).

2. *Life-span genetic differences.* The control of the genotype over development throughout life is often ignored. Genetic influences on the acquisition *and maintenance* of intellectual level have now been shown to persist from infancy to the ninth decade of life. In their studies of 134 pairs of aging twins, first tested in their 60s (Kallman, 1961), Jarvik and her associates have shown that genotypic differences continue into late life to be highly related to phenotypic differences in intellectual skills. In the most recent publication (Jarvik et al. 1972) nineteen surviving intact pairs, with a mean age of 83.5 years, were evaluated. Among aging twins there is considerable concordance for survival in MZ pairs and much less similarity of life span in DZ pairs; hence, the 2:1 ratio of MZ:DZ intact pairs. Interestingly enough, the survivors had *not* deteriorated in intellectual level over the twenty-year period despite a decline in speeded motor performance. Test results for the survivors are given in tables 11 and 12.

TABLE 11. INTRACLASS CORRELATIONS[a] OF TEST SCORES FOR
13 MONOZYGOTIC (MZ) AND 6 DIZYGOTIC (DZ) PAIRS
TESTING INITIALLY IN 1947 AND RETESTED IN 1967

Tests	1947 MZ	1947 DZ	1967 MZ	1967 DZ	Tests	1967 MZ	1967 DZ
Vocabulary	0.89[b]	−0.31	0.87[b]	0.29	Stroop card 1	0.98[b]	0.24
Similarities	0.76[b]	−0.02	0.71[b]	0.38	Stroop card 2	0.70[b]	−0.29
Digits forward	0.23	0.09	0.42	0.24	Stroop card 3	−0.19	0.32
Digits backward	0.59[c]	−0.47	0.52[c]	0.19	Stroop card 3-card 2	−0.39	0.33
Tapping	0.77[b]	0.47	0.33	0.55	Graham-Kendall	0.08	0.10
Block design	0.77[b]	0.86[b]	0.56[c]	0.68[c]	Picture arrangement	0.35	0.32
Digit symbol substitution	0.87[b]	0.27	0.46	−0.38	Picture completion	−0.39	0.55

SOURCE: Jarvik et al. 1972.
[a] Fisher (1938)
[b] p < 0.01
[c] p < 0.05

TABLE 12. COMPARATIVE MEAN RAW SCORES OF AGING
MONOZYGOTIC (MZ) AND DIZYGOTIC (DZ) TWINS
TESTED IN 1947 AND 1967

	Original sample (N = 240) 1947 MZ	1947 DZ	Surviving subgroup (N = 38) 1947 MZ	1947 DZ	1967 MZ	1967 DZ
Tests						
Vocabulary	29.18	27.09	30.25	29.42	29.38	29.92
Similarities	9.24	8.21	11.38	11.08	9.81	9.92
Digits forward	5.94	5.69	6.29	6.00	5.71	6.08
Digits backward	4.15	4.10	4.32	4.58	3.82	4.00
Tapping	67.72	63.23	71.00[a]	74.00[a]	48.32[a]	54.92[a]
Block design	13.18	13.80	13.94[a, b]	18.80[b]	9.33[a, b]	15.30[b]
Digit symbol substitution	28.25	26.88	33.25[a]	33.50	21.66[a]	24.40
No. of subjects	150	90	26	12	26	12
Mean age	68.08	70.75	66.08	61.21	85.00	80.35

SOURCE: Jarvik et al. 1972.
[a] Difference within zygosity groups 1947–1967: significant (p < 0.01)
[b] Difference between zygosity groups: significant (p < 0.05)

Although the sample sizes are very small (hardly surprising at an average age of 83), at ages 60 and 80 the MZ pairs were clearly more similar in verbal intellectual skills than the DZ survivors. From the 60s to the 80s, however, there was a steep decline in the similarity of MZ twins in speeded motor tasks, "suggesting that there comes an age (possibly in the 70s) when nongenetic factors modify the genetic influences on motor performance to a significant extent" (Jarvik et al., 1972, p. 166). Verbal reasoning and vocabulary skills continued to show strong genetic variation near the end of life.

3. *Intervention studies.* Another strategy for behavior genetic research is the intervention study with children of known genetic relatedness or at

least predictable phenotypic outcome. A seldom-used strategy is the co-twin control study in which monozygotic twins are separated into different treatment conditions to evaluate the efficacy of various training procedures with the same genotypes. A few pairs of MZ twins have been used in this way to evaluate training in motor development (Dennis 1941). Provided the samples were large enough, excellent studies of educational treatments could be done by separating pairs of co-twins and exposing them to two curricula. Statistical tests for main and interaction effects can be done across treatment groups, controlling for genotypic differences. Reversals in the treatment effects for some pairs could lead to hypotheses about the limitations of the treatments on a much more economical basis than usually occurs in curriculum studies. This strategy is also more likely to show treatment × ability interactions than the usual one.

Another strategy is to provide treatments for children of predictable intellectual outcome. For those with poor prognoses the research strategy is to calculate the gain of actual over expected values. (One needn't expect a mean IQ of 100 in every group.)

Heber (1969) has tutored a group of infants whose mothers have tested IQs of less than 70. Their fathers IQ scores are unknown. One may generously assume the fathers' IQs to average 95 and the mothers' to average 65. The midparent IQ is, therefore, 80. By calculating the expected regression of offspring scores with a conservative heritability figure of .5, the expected average children's score is 90 if reared by their own mothers. The task of the experimental treatment, therefore, is to raise the average above 90 and not to beat the mothers' figure of 70 nor the population average of 100. The infants in Heber's group, whose intensive tutoring had extended from birth to three years by 1971, have average IQs in excess of 120, a very significant difference from the expected 90.

Rynders (1972) has successfully tutored a group of twenty-five Down's syndrome infants from birth. Their expected intellectual level was at severe retardation. The predicted IQ is less than 50, based on untreated samples of Down's children. The group now averages 85 at the age of three years. A control group of Down's infants in other treatment programs has an average IQ of 68. In the case of chromosomal anomalies, the midparent IQ is not important because the regressions expected for normal children may not occur predictably in case of abnormality.[3]

---

[3] In fact, I do not know of any study that has tried to regress mid-parent IQ scores on the scores of children with Down's Syndrome. It may be that some systematic depression of the children's IQ scores would be revealed by a sizeable parent-child correlation. A lack of parent-child correlation would suggest that the child's abnormal IQ level is not affected by the normal range of genotypic differences among parents.

An Israeli study (Smilansky, personal communication) reported on the IQ scores of children from Oriental and European Jewish families living on kibbutzim. Child-rearing on the 129 kibbutzim sampled was handled from shortly after birth to adolescence in communal nurseries and in small groups of children with their caretakers. Children visited with their parents daily for about two hours but resided in the children's groups. Their education was handled entirely within their communal setting.

Home-reared Oriental Jewish children are often found to have tested IQs of about 92 on the average, compared to about 108 for children of European Jewish parents. The populations from which the Oriental and European groups come have been separated for so many thousands of years that they constitute very different gene pools. In addition, they are culturally very different. Thus, the home-reared Oriental Jewish children probably differ both genetically and environmentally from home-reared European Jewish children.

Within each kibbutz the rearing conditions are uniform for all children, regardless of descent. The Smilanskys matched each of 670 Oriental children with a European child within the same kibbutz, controlling for parental educational level, length of residence in Israel, and several other factors. The children were tested with the Stanford-Binet (four- to five-year-olds) or the Wechsler Intelligence Scale for Children (six to fourteen).

At both kindergarten age and at elementary ages (six to fourteen), the two groups of children had equivalent, and high, average IQs ($\simeq$115). Since kibbutz residents are self-selected, one cannot conclude that all Israeli children would be as bright if they were similarly reared. But one can conclude that the reaction ranges of the present kibbutz children include the same IQ values whether they come from the Oriental or European Jewish populations.

Within each population, parental educational level correlated significantly ($r \simeq .25-.45$) with children's IQs. In part, the parent-child correlations may be due to parental environmental influence, although this is attenuated by the communal rearing. A probably more important fact is that parental education reflects parental IQ to a considerable extent (Jencks 1972) and that IQ has moderate heritability within Israeli, as well as other, populations.

Even if the heritability of IQ is substantial *within* each of two populations, and even if there are sizeable *average differences between* the populations, uniformly good rearing conditions can act on the reaction ranges of children in both populations and result in similar distributions of phenotypes.

Treatment studies of children whose phenotypic outcomes under environmental conditions are predictable can supply important data on the reaction ranges of various genotypes when other conditions are provided. (For a general review of the intervention-study literature, see Horowitz and Paden 1973.) Studies of twins and siblings, one of whom is provided with the treatment, can provide still better comparisons than ordinary control or comparison groups.

A sibling study on the effects of extremely low birth-weight (Dann, Levine, and New 1964) is an example of the use of related persons to evaluate the effects of a naturally occurring "treatment." The IQ scores of fifty low birth-weight children ($<$ 1,000 grams at birth) and their normal-weight sibs differed by 13 IQ points on the average (94 vs. 107). Since genotypes can be assumed to be randomly distributed between the two siblings and since they are reared in the same families, the decrement in IQ scores for the low birth-weight babies can be attributed to the sequelae of low birth-weight rather than to possible genetic and environmental differences between the families of prematures and normal birth-weight infants.

There is a great need for developmental studies that attend to genetic as well as environmental parameters of variation. The individual child, with his or her unique genotype and unique response to environmental contingencies, is the datum to be understood. Until we build theoretical models to better account for the individual child, our generalities based on average values will always dissolve into a mass of conflicting trends. Evolutionary theory, polygenic models of intelligence, and the reaction range concept suggest many approaches to the study of intellectual development. We should capitalize on the opportunities.

Summary

1. Individual variation in IQ has been extensively studied at the phenotypic level by variance analysis techniques. Studies of related and unrelated persons, living together and apart, suggest that the majority of the variance in IQ scores in white populations is due to genetic differences.

2. Little is known about the sources of variation in nonwhite populations.

3. Little is known about the sources of between-group average differences on IQ tests because appropriate methods have not been used.

4. The development of intellectual skills has been studied longitudinally in a few samples of twins, siblings, and parent-child pairs. The results suggest that the level of IQ is moderately heritable, and that the pattern of intellectual development is more variable than the level within families.

5. Behavior genetic methods can be profitably applied to developmental problems in intervention research, in longitudinal studies, and in

many other areas where it is important to separate genotypic from environmental effects.

CONCLUSIONS

Trends in Psychological Explanation

Psychology seems to be in the midst of an aperiodic swing between extreme forms of environmentalism and hereditarianism. More biological assumptions, variables, methods, and conclusions have crept into child development during the past ten years than in the preceding twenty-five. This trend must be critically evaluated. We must, first, be alert to the dangers of the reductionist thinking inherent in biological explanations of behavioral phenomena. Second, we must avoid an extreme form of hereditarianism that ignores the necessary transactions between genotypes and environments throughout the life-span development of human intelligence. A serious appraisal of the new genetics avoids both of these errors.

Much of the confusion in earlier hereditarian eras arose from the failure to distinguish between determinism and differences. Although genetic studies of intelligence were most often concerned with apportioning the sources of individual *differences,* some faulty conclusions were drawn concerning the importance of genes in *determining* intelligence. The conclusions from twin, family, and adoptive studies apply only to the sources of differences, not to the importance of genes in determining development. Even though environmental differences were found to be less important sources of IQ variation than genetic differences, there is no reason to conclude that the environment is less important than genes in determining intellectual development. It may simply be the case that all members in the population studied had functionally equivalent environments, but they all had environments!

A related, and equally faulty, conclusion is that, if genetic differences contribute more than environmental differences to the variance in IQ scores, then IQ is considered to be not very malleable. The myth of heritability limiting malleability seems to die hard. Until recently, the importance of the genotype's reaction range was underestimated; it provides alternative phenotypes for the same individual, depending upon crucial environmental factors in the development of that individual. There is no one-to-one correspondence between genotype and behavioral phenotype, regardless of the heritability of a characteristic. Even if the heritability for IQ in a population were one, meaning that present environmental differences contributed nothing to individual phenotypic differences, a change in the environments could dramatically shift the mean of the entire phenotypic distribution.

Studies of reaction ranges, canalization, genetic expression, and related issues have barely begun in human populations. From a developmental point of view, these are the critical concepts because they lead to research on the malleability of intellectual development and to questions about genetic mechanisms underlying that development.

An Overview

Studies of genetics and human intelligence have concentrated on the apportionment of statistical variation in IQ scores into environmental components. Although we still know virtually nothing about the sources of intellectual variation within nonwhite and disadvantaged populations, the methods are available to be applied. Further refinements of the variance theme will come from more careful studies of covariance and interaction effects, with samples of adoptive families and separated relatives. From the many twin and family studies of IQ variation, it is necessary to conclude that genotypic differences are a more important source of IQ differences than are environmental differences, within white U.S. and European populations. Most investigators estimate genetic sources of variation to account for half to three-quarters of the phenotypic differences in these populations. Covariance and interaction effects have not been well studied yet.

Although studies of variation are important, they are barely a prelude to the research that needs to be done before we will have any substantial knowledge of genetic differences in normal intellectual development and of genetic mechanisms in development. Some strategies for developmental genetic research have been suggested: Studies of interventions with groups of predictable phenotypic level, co-twin control strategies, longitudinal family studies, cross-fostering studies, admixture studies, and life-span genetic research. Many of the research studies now being done in child development can be improved by the inclusion of behavior-genetic strategies.

In this chapter there has been an attempt to review previous research on normal, human intellectual development, to construct a coherent account of the relation of genetics to human intellectual development, to evaluate the present state of our knowledge, and, primarily, to indicate our lack of knowledge. Perhaps a later volume in this series can include a more conclusive chapter on the subject.

REFERENCES

Adams, M. S., Davidson, R. T., & Cornell, P. Adoptive risks of the children of incest —a preliminary report. *Child Welfare,* 1967, *46,* 137–142.

Adams, M. S. & Neel, J. V. Children of incest. *Pediatrics,* 1967, *40,* 55–62.

Alland, A. *The Evolution of Human Behavior.* New York: American Museum of Natural History, 1967.

Almy, M., Chittenden, E., & Miller, P. *Young Children's Thinking: Studies of Some Aspects of Piaget's Thinking.* New York: Teacher's College Press, 1966.

Bajema, C. J. Relation of fertility to occupational status, IQ, educational attainments, and size of family of origin: a follow-up study of a male Kalamazoo public school population. *Eugenics Quarterly,* 1968, *15,* 198–203.

Bayley, N. Comparison of mental and motor test scores for ages 1–15 months by sex, birth order, race, geographical location, and education of parents. *Child Development,* 1965, *36,* 379–411.

Berry, J. W. Tenne and Eskimo perceptual skills. *International Journal of Psychology,* 1966, *1,* 207–222.

Bock, R. D. & Kolakowski, D. F. Further evidence of a major-gene influence on human spatial abilities. *American Journal of Behavior Genetics,* 1973, *25,* 1–14.

Book, J. A. Genetical investigation in a north Swedish population: The offspring of first-cousin marriages. *Annals of Human Genetics,* 1957, *21,* 191–221.

Bouchard, T. J. Genetic factors in intelligence. In A. R. Kaplan, ed., *Human Behavior Genetics.* Springfield: Thomas, 1972.

Brophy, J. E. Mothers as teachers of their own preschool children: the influence of socioeconomic status and task structure on teaching specificity. *Child Development,* 1970, *41,* 79–94.

Burks, B. S. The relative influence of nature and nurture upon mental development: a comparative study of foster parent–foster child and true parent–true child resemblance. *Twenty-seventh Yearbook of the National Society for the Study of Education,* 1928, 219–316.

Burt, C. Intelligence and social mobility. *British Journal of Statistical Psychology,* 1961, *14,* 3–24.

———. The genetic determination of differences in intelligence: a study of monozygotic twins reared together and apart. *British Journal of Psychology,* 1966, *57,* 137–153.

Butcher, H. J. *Human Intelligence.* London: Methuen, 1968.

Cancro, R., ed. *Intelligence: Genetic and Environmental Influences.* New York: Grune & Stratton, 1971.

Carter, C. O. Risk to offspring of incest. *Lancet,* 1967, *1,* 436.

Cattell, R. B. The structure of intelligence in relation to the nature-nurture controversy. In R. Cancro, ed., *Intelligence: Genetic and Environmental Influences.* New York: Grune & Stratton, 1971, 3–30.

Cavalli-Sforza, L. L. & Bodmer, W. F. *The Genetics of Human Populations.* San Francisco: W. H. Freeman, 1972.

Cohen, T., Block, N., Flum, Y., Kadar, M., & Goltschmidt, E. School attainments in an immigrant village. In F. Goldschmidt, ed., *The Genetics of Migrant and Isolate Populations.* Baltimore: Williams & Wilkens, 1963.

Cole, M. & Bruner, J. S. Cultural differences and inferences about psychological processes. *American Psychologist,* 1971, *26,* 867–876.

Cole, M., Gay, J., Glick, J. A., & Sharp, D. W. *The Cultural Context of Learning and Thinking.* New York: Basic Books, 1972.

Cooper, R. & Zubek, J. Effects of enriched and restricted early environments on the learning ability of bright and dull rats. *Canadian Journal of Psychology,* 1958, *12,* 159–164.

Crow, J. Genetic theories and influences: comments on the value of diversity. *Harvard Educational Review,* 1969, *39,* 153–170.

Dann, M., Levine, S. Z., & New, E. V. A long-term follow-up study of small, premature infants. *Pediatrics,* 1964, *33,* 945–955.

DeFries, J. C. Quantitative aspects of genetics and environment in the determination of behavior. Paper presented at the C.O.B.R.E. Research Workshop on Genetic

Endowment and Environment in the Determination of Behavior. Rye, New York, October 3–8, 1971.

deLacey, P. R. A cross-cultural study of classificatory skills in Australia. *Journal of Cross-Cultural Psychology*, 1970, *1*, 293–304.

————. Classificatory ability and verbal intelligence among high-contact aboriginal and low socio-economic white Australian children. *Journal of Cross-Cultural Psychology*, 1971a, *2*, 393–396.

————. Verbal intelligence, operational thinking and environment in part-aboriginal children. *Australian Journal of Psychology*, 1971b, *23*, 145–149.

DeLemos, M. M. The development of conservation in aboriginal children. *International Journal of Psychology*, 1969, *4*, 255–269.

Dennis, W. Infant development under conditions of restricted practice and minimum social stimulation. *Genetic Psychology Monographs*, 1941, *23*, 143–191.

Dewey, W. J., Barrai, I., Morton, N. E., & Mi, M. P. Recessive genes in severe mental defect. *Amercian Journal of Human Genetics*, 1965, *17*, 237–256.

Dobzhansky, T. *Mankind Evolving*. New Haven: Yale University Press, 1962.

Ervin-Tripp, S. Personal communication. February, 1972.

Falconer, D. S. *Introduction to Quantitative Genetics*. New York: Ronald, 1960.

Fischer, K. Genetic aspects of individual differences in language development. Ph.D. dissertation, University of Pennsylvania, 1972.

Flavell, J. H. *The Developmental Psychology of Jean Piaget*. Princeton: Van Nostrand, 1963.

————. Concept development. In P. H. Mussen, ed., *Carmichael's Manual of Child Psychology*. Vol. 1. New York: Wiley, 1970, 983–1059.

Fuller, J. L. & Thompson, W. R. *Behavior Genetics*. New York: John Wiley, 1960.

Gaudia, G. Race, social class, and age of achievement of conservation on Piaget's tasks. *Developmental Psychology*, 1972, *6*, 158–165.

Geber, M. The psycho-motor development of African children in the first year, and the influence of maternal behavior. *Journal of Social Psychology*, 1958, *47*, 185–195.

Ginsburg, B. E. & Laughlin, W. The multiple bases of human adaptability and achievement: A species point of view. *Eugenics Quarterly*, 1966, *13*, 240–257.

Ginsburg, B. E. Genotypic factors in the ontogeny of behavior. *Science and Psychoanalysis*, 1968, *12*, 12–17.

Ginsburg, B. E. & Laughlin, W. Race and intelligence, what do we really know? In R. Cancro, ed., *Intelligence: Genetic and Environmental Influences*. New York: Grune & Stratton, 1971, 77–87.

Gottesman, I. I. Biogenetics of race and class. In M. Deutsch, I. Katz, & A. R. Jensen, eds., *Social Class, Race, and Psychological Development*. New York: Holt, Rinehart & Winston, 1968.

————. Genetic aspects of intelligent behavior. In N. Ellis, ed., *Handbook of Mental Deficiency*. New York: McGraw-Hill, 1963, 253–296.

Heber, R. *Rehabilitation of Families at Risk for Mental Retardation*. Regional Rehabilitation Center, University of Wisconsin, 1969.

Henderson, N. D. Genetic influences on the behavior of mice as can be obscured by laboratory rearing. *Journal of Comparative and Physiological Psychology*, 1970, *3*, 505–511.

Herrnstein, R. IQ. *Atlantic Monthly*, 1971, *228* (September), 44–64.

Hess, R. D. & Shipman, V. Early experience and the socialization of cognitive modes in children. *Child Development*, 1965, *36*, 869–886.

Higgins, J., Reed, E. W., & Reed, S. Intelligence and family size: a paradox resolved. *Eugenics Quarterly*, 1962, *9*, 84–90.

Hirsch, J., ed. *Behavior-Genetic Analysis*. New York: McGraw-Hill, 1967.

Hirsch, J. Behavior-genetic analysis and its biosocial consequences. In R. Cancro, ed., *Intelligence: Genetic and Environmental Influences*. New York: Grune & Stratton, 1971.

Honzik, M. P. Developmental studies of parent-child resemblance in intelligence. *Child Development,* 1957, *28,* 215–228.

————. Resemblance in Wechsler Patterns in Three Generations. Paper presented at the Biennial Meetings of the Society for Research in Child Development, Minneapolis, April 2, 1971.

Horowitz, F. D. & Paden, L. Y. The effects of environmental intervention programs. In B. Caldwell & H. Riccuti, eds., *Review of Child Development Research.* Vol. 3. Chicago: University of Chicago Press, 1973.

Hsia, D. Y. Y. *Human Developmental Genetics.* Chicago: Yearbook Medical Publishers, 1968.

Humphreys, L. G. Theory of intelligence. In R. Cancro, ed., *Intelligence: Genetic and Environmental Influences.* New York: Grune & Stratton, 1971, 31–42.

Huntley, R. M. C. Heritability of intelligence: In J. E. Meade & A. S. Parkes, eds., *Genetic and Environmental Factors in Human Ability.* Edinburgh: Oliver & Boyd, 1966, 201–218.

Hyde, D. M. An investigation of Piaget's theories of the development of the concept of number as reported in DeLemos (1969).

Jacob, F. & Monod, J. Genetic regulatory mechanisms in the synthesis of proteins. *Journal of Molecular Biology,* 1961, *3,* 318–356.

Jarvik, L. F., Altschuler, K. Z., Kato, T., & Blummer, B. Organic brain syndrome and chromosome loss in aged twins. *Diseases of the Nervous System,* 1971, *32,* 159–170.

Jarvik, L. F., Blum, J. E., & Varna, A. O. Genetic components and intellectual functioning during senescence: A 20-year study of aging twins. *Behavior Genetics,* 1972, *2,* 159–171.

Jarvik, L. F. & Erlenmeyer-Kimling, L. Survey of family correlations in measured intellectual functions. In J. Zubin & G. Jervis, eds., *Psychopathology of Mental Development.* New York: Grune & Stratton, 1967, 447–459.

Jarvik, L. F., Kallman, F. J., Falek, A., & Klaber, M. M. Changing intellectual functions in senescent twins. *Acta Genetica Statistica Medica,* 1957, *7,* 421–430.

Jarvik, L. F. & Kato, T. Chromosome examinations in aged twins. *American Journal of Human Genetics,* 1970, *22,* 562–572.

Jencks, C. *Inequality: A Reassessment of the Effect of Family and Schooling in America.* New York: Basic Books, 1972.

Jensen, A. R. *Educability, and Group Differences.* New York: Harper & Row, 1973.

————. Social class and verbal learning. In M. Deutsch, I. Katz, & A. R. Jensen, eds., *Social Class, Race, and Psychological Development.* New York: Holt, Rinehart & Winston, 1968.

————. How much can we boost IQ and scholastic achievement? *Harvard Educational Review,* 1969, *39,* 1–123.

————. The IQs of MZ twins reared apart. *Behavior Genetics,* 1971*a, 2,* 1–10.

————. A Two-Factor Theory of Familial Mental Retardation. Paper presented at the Fourth International Congress of Human Genetics, Paris, 1971*b.*

Jinks, J. L. & Fulker, D. W. Comparison of the biometrical, genetical, MAVA, and classical approaches to the analysis of human behavior. *Psychological Bulletin,* 1970, *73,* 311–349.

Kallman, F. J. Genetic factors in aging: comparative and longitudinal observations on a senescent twin population. In P. H. Hoch & J. Zubin, eds., *Psychopathology of Aging.* New York: Grune & Stratton, 1961, 227–247.

Kiser, C. V. Assortative mating by educational attainment in relation to fertility. *Eugenics Quarterly,* 1968, *15,* 98–112.

LaBarre, W. *The Human Animal.* Chicago: University of Chicago Press, 1965.

Labov, W. *The Social Stratification of English in New York City.* Washington, D.C.: Center for Applied English, 1966.

————. The logic of nonstandard English. In F. Williams, ed., *Language and Poverty.* Chicago: Markham, 1970, 153–189.

Leahy, A. M. Nature-nurture and intelligence. *Genetic Psychology Monographs,* 1935, *17,* 235–307.

Lenneberg, E. H. *Biological Foundations of Language.* New York: John Wiley, 1967.

Lerner, I. M. *Heredity, Evolution, and Society.* San Francisco: Freeman, 1968.

Levine, S. Sex differences in the brain. In J. L. McGaugh, N. M. Weinberger, & R. E. Whalen, eds., *Psychobiology.* San Francisco: Freeman, 1967.

Lewontin, R. C. Race and intelligence. *Bulletin of the Atomic Scientists,* 1970, *26,* 2–8.

Li, C. C. A tale of two thermos bottles: properties of a genetic model for human intelligence. In R. Cancro, ed., *Intelligence: Genetic and Environmental Influences.* New York: Grune & Stratton, 1971.

Lindzey, G., Loehlin, J., Manosevitz, M., & Thiessen, D. Behavioral genetics. *Annual Review of Psychology.* Palo Alto: Annual Reviews, 1971.

MacArthur, R. S. Some differential abilities of northern Canadian native youth. *International Journal of Psychology,* 1968, *3,* 43–51.

———. Some cognitive abilities of Eskimo, White and Indian-Metis pupils age 9 to 12 years. *Canadian Journal of Behavior Sciences,* 1969, *1,* 50–59.

Manosevitz, M., Lindzey, G., & Thiessen, D., eds. *Behavioral Genetics.* New York: Appleton-Century-Crofts, 1969.

Martin, R. G. & Ames, B. N. Biochemical aspects of genetics. *Annual Review of Biochemistry,* 1964, *33,* 235–256.

Mather, K. On biometrical genetics. *Heredity,* 1971, *26,* 349–364.

Mather, K. & Jinks, J. L. *Biometrical Genetics.* Ithaca, New York: Cornell University, 1971.

McCall, R. Intelligence quotient patterns over age: Comparisons among sibling and parent-child pairs. *Science,* 1970, 644–648.

McClearn, G. E. Genetics and behavior development. In M. L. Hoffman & L. W. Hoffman, eds., *Review of Child Development Research.* Vol. 1. New York: Russell Sage, 1964.

———. Genetic influences on behavior and development. In P. H. Mussen, ed., *Carmichael's Manual of Child Psychology.* New York: John Wiley, 1970, 39–76.

McGaugh, J. L., Jennings, R. D., & Thompson, C. W. Effect of distribution of practice on the maze learning of descendants of Tryon maze bright and maze dull strains. *Psychological Reports,* 1962, *10,* 147–150.

Money, J. Cognitive deficits in Turner's syndrome. In S. G. Vandenberg, ed., *Progress in Human Behavior Genetics.* Baltimore: Johns Hopkins, 1968.

Morton, N. E. The inheritance of human birth weight. *Annals of Human Genetics,* 1955, *20,* 125–134.

Nichols, P. The effects of heredity and environment on intelligence test performance on 4- and 7-year-old white and Negro sibling pairs. Ph.D. dissertation, University of Minnesota, 1970.

Nichols, R. C. The National Merit twin study. In S. G. Vandenberg, ed., *Methods and Goals in Human Behavior Genetics.* New York: Academic Press, 1965, 231–243.

Pinard, A. & Laurendreau, M. A scale of mental development based on the theory of Piaget. *Journal of Research in Science Teaching,* 1964, *2,* 253–260.

Price-Williams, D. R. A study concerning concepts of conservation of quantities among premature children. *Acta Psychologica,* 1961, *18,* 297–305.

Prince, J. R. The effect of Western education on science conceptualization in New Guinea. *British Journal of Educational Psychology,* 1968, *38,* 64–74.

Reed, E. W. & Reed, S. C. *Mental Retardation: A Family Study.* Philadelphia: W. B. Saunders, 1965.

Reed, T. E. Caucasian genes in American Negroes. *Science,* 1969, 762–768.

Roberts, J. A. F. The genetics of mental deficiency. *Eugenics Review,* 1952, *44,* 71–83.

Rosenthal, D. *Genetic Theory and Abnormal Behavior.* New York: McGraw-Hill, 1970.

Rynders, J. Personal Communication, November, 1972, University of Minnesota.
Scarr-Salapatek, S. Unknowns in the IQ equation. *Science, 1971a, 174,* 1223–1228.
———. Race, social class, and IQ. *Science, 1971b, 174,* 1285–1295.
Schull, W. J. & Neel, J. V. *The Effects of Inbreeding on Japanese Children.* New York: Harper & Row, 1965.
Skeels, H. M. Adult status of children with contrasting early life experience. *Monographs of the Society for Research in Child Development,* 1966, *31,* (whole no. 105).
Skodak, M. & Skeels, H. M. A final follow-up of one hundred adopted children. *Journal of Genetic Psychology,* 1949, *75,* 85–125.
Smilansky, M. Personal communication, June 12, 1973.
Stern, C. *Principles of Human Genetics.* 2d ed. San Francisco: Freeman, 1960.
Thiessen, D. D. Philosophy and method in behavior genetics. In A. R. Gilgen, ed., *Scientific Psychology: Some Perspectives.* New York: Academic Press, 1970.
———. *Gene Organization and Behavior.* New York: Random House, 1972a.
———. A move toward a species-specific analysis in behavior genetics. *Behavior Genetics,* 1972b, *2,* 115–126.
Thoday, J. M. Limitations to genetic comparisons of populations. *Journal of Biosocial Science,* 1969, Supplement, 3–14.
Tuddenham, R. A "Piagetian" test of cognitive development. In B. Dockrell, ed., *On Intelligence.* Toronto: Ontario Institute for Studies in Education, 1970, 49–70.
Vandenberg, S. G. Contributions of twin research to psychology. *Psychological Bulletin,* 1966, *66,* 327–352.
Vandenberg, S. G., ed. *Methods and Goals in Human Behavior Genetics.* New York: Academic Press, 1965.
Waddington, C. H. *The Strategy of the Genes.* London: Allen & Unwin, 1957.
———. *New Patterns in Genetics and Development.* New York: Columbia University Press, 1962.
Wall, C. Paper presented at the Fourth International Congress of Human Genetics, Paris, September 6–10, 1967.
Waller, J. H. Achievement and social mobility: relationship among IQ score, education and occupation in two generations. *Social Biology,* 1971, *18,* 252–259.
Washburn, S. L., & Howells, F. C. Human evolution and culture. In S. Tax, ed., *Evolution after Darwin: The Evolution of Man.* Vol. 2. Chicago: University of Chicago Press, 1960, pp. 33–57.
Waterhouse, L. H. Genetic and sociocultural influence on language development. Ph.D. dissertation, University of Pennsylvania, 1972.
Weyl, N. Some comparative performance indexes of American ethnic minorities. *Mankind Quarterly,* 1969, *9,* 194–199.
Willerman, L. Personal communication. August, 1972.
Willerman, L., Naylor, A. F., & Myrianthropoulos, N. C. Intellectual development of children from interracial matings. *Science,* 1970, *170,* 1329–1331.
———. Children of interracial matings: evidence for environmental effects on intellectual performance. Paper presented at the Fourth International Congress of Human Genetics, Paris, September, 6–11, 1971.
Wilson, R. S. Twins: Early mental development. *Science, 1972, 175,* 914–917.

2 Genetic Anomalies in Development

ELIZABETH WAGNER REED
The Dight Institute for Human Genetics
University of Minnesota

INTRODUCTION

THE WAYS in which genetically controlled, biochemical processes can influence behavior raise fascinating and profound questions about how mental processes really function. As the answers are elucidated, much should be learned about the functioning of the brain. What is the physical basis of familiar, undifferentiated mental retardation? Why should an excess of some metabolites in phenylketonuria cause not only mental retardation but other behavioral disorders as well? What does abnormal purine metabolism have to do with self-mutilation in the Lesch-Nyhan syndrome? The questions do not end here, of course. They extend into the difficult area of the role of the individual and of society in the identification, treatment, and prevention of these genetic anomalies. Anderson and Siegel (1968) have pointed to the importance of the study of behavior in genetically defined syndromes. Mattsson (1972) has reviewed studies on long-term physical illness in childhood and the psychosocial problems connected with it.

Only recently have the questions about treatment and prevention of genetic anomalies become more serious, as new intervention techniques have become available. Now it is possible to identify the carriers of some genetic disorders, to screen infants for other genetic disorders which will develop later if not treated, and even to identify some genetic anomalies in fetuses long before birth. These procedures are being improved and expanded rapidly. How should such information be used? There are several sources available that discuss these issues: Lappe, Gustafson, and Roblin (1972) have written about screening for genetic diseases; the report from the Symposium on Intrauterine Diagnosis (Bergsma, ed. 1971) has papers on the various aspects of the prenatal detection of genetic disorders. As evidence of the widespread interest in these procedures, the World Health Organization (1972) has recently published a report covering the various aspects of the problem. Also see M. Harris (1971) for a symposium on the subject.

The field of human genetics is expanding so rapidly, and information is accumulating so fast that any review can cover only a small part of the material in any detail. Hence, the remainder of the chapter is divided into three parts. One will deal with patterns of inheritance, the calculation of genetic risk, and research procedures. A second will deal in some detail with certain genetic anomalies and their behavioral aspects. These disorders have been selected primarily because they can illuminate different facets of genetic and behavioral problems.

A third part of the chapter is an annotated reading list that provides information about books on genetic anomalies which cover the field much more extensively. These books contain current information about many disorders and provide large bibliographies for further reference. The 1971 edition of McKusick's comprehensive computer printout of references on human genetic disorders (exclusive of chromosomal abnormalities) lists 943 autosomal dominant traits, 783 autosomal recessive traits, and 150 X-linked traits, for a total of 1,876 currently known Mendelian traits in man. Many of these traits are rare and some are not expressed in children, but many affect behavioral development over the life span of affected individuals (McKusick 1971). Behavioral problems related to genetic disorders are not confined to the patient alone but affect all persons who interact with him or her. Their behavioral responses in turn, can influence the attitudes and behaviors of the patient.

Obviously the behavioral problems associated with a lethal disease will differ from those in which there is a good life expectancy requiring prolonged and restrictive medical treatment or where there is definite mental impairment without serious physical defects. In reality, the behavior of the child results from the interaction of two sets of factors. There is the direct effect of the genetic anomaly on his psychological functioning. There is also a second, perhaps equally important, set of factors: the attitudes of relatives, peers, and teachers toward the child's disorder, and the duration and kind of medical treatment needed. Talbot and Howell (1971) discussed these problems at some length in their paper on social and behavioral causes and consequences of disease among children.

One common disorder, obesity, illustrates the complexity of these interactions. The genetic components of obesity are not well understood, but there seems to be no doubt that there are some (Bruch 1958; Mayer 1966). Richardson (1963) reported a study in which normal and handicapped ten-year-old children were shown pictures of a normal child, a child in a wheelchair, one with crutches and braces, one with an amputated hand, one with a repaired cleft lip, and one who was fat. Both the normal and handicapped children selected as first preference for playmate the normal-appearing child, and as last choice the fat one. One can have little doubt that, while some behavioral traits in the obese child are related to the child's body chemistry (lethargy, clumsiness), others will develop in response to social rejection by his or her peers. Overt genetic traits can elicit a feedback from the reaction of other persons to the disorder that will in turn induce a compensatory behavior in the subject. (This can also hold true for obvious but normal differences, such as skin color, age, or sex.) Genetic traits which can be concealed, at least for a time (such as diabetes) cause other behavioral problems associated with fear of discovery and the reactions of others to the attempted concealment.

BASIC CONSIDERATIONS IN GENETIC RESEARCH

The Calculation of Genetic Risk

Information about genetic risk is very important to many individuals. Some fear they may develop a genetic disorder known to be present in their family, such as Huntington's chorea, and want to know what their chances are. Prospective parents may fear, or know, that they are carriers of a recessive or X-linked disorder, and need to understand the risk they take of having affected children so they can plan their families. Sometimes genetic counseling and the explanation of risk-figures alleviate the anxiety of troubled persons. If the persons seeking counseling have some idea of the common principles of inheritance, the counselor will find it easier to explain the basis of his calculations of risk for their particular cases.

1. *Inheritance.* A short review of how inheritance works and what a few terms mean may be helpful at this point. Only since 1956 has the correct number (46) of human chromosomes been known. As in all sexually reproducing organisms, these chromosomes come in pairs, one of each pair coming from the father via the sperm and the other one of the pair coming from the mother via the egg. The fertilized egg, then, unless something goes awry, has 46 chromosomes in its nucleus. These 46 packages of DNA contain the genetic code which will direct the development of the future person and will make him or her genetically different from everyone else except his or her identical twin. This DNA will provide the individual's *genotype,* the set of genes derived from his or her ancestors. This genotype may or may not be expressed in visible or measurable traits as the individual's *phenotype*. The phenotypic expression of the genotype depends on the genotype itself and on all the environmental influences that impinge upon the individual from the time of conception to death.

2. *Autosomes and sex chromosomes*. The genetic code that each individual carries is in the DNA in the chromosomes. There are two kinds of chromosomes. One kind comprises the 22 pairs of *autosomes*. These chro-

mosomes are in matched pairs and carry most of the genetic code for development. In addition, each person has one pair of *sex chromosomes*. This pair is alike in females, XX, and unlike in males, XY. The X chromosome is large and carries many genes, while the Y found in males is considerably smaller and appears to be primarily involved with initiating the development of the male sex glands, or gonads. Thus, males are vulnerable to any deleterious genes carried on their single large X. Unlike females, they have no second X to supply the corresponding genes for normal processes which can overrule or mask the unfortunate effects of the deleterious genes. Hence, there are a number of X-linked disorders like hemophilia that occur almost exclusively in males. The male needs only the one gene to exhibit symptoms of the disease, while the female needs two genes, one on each of her X chromosomes, to have this disease. This can only happen if her father has the disease and her mother is a carrier, so that 50 percent of the time she would get both X chromosomes carrying the gene. Affected males rarely reproduce, however, so the chances are remote of finding a hemophiliac woman.

The pattern of inheritance in X-linked disorders is that of unaffected carrier women having half of their sons affected. This happens because each son gets one or the other of his mother's X chromosomes. Half the time, on an average, the son will get the X chromosome which carries the gene for the disorder. Half the daughters of carrier women will be themselves carriers (since they, too, get one of their mother's X chromosomes) and will have a risk of having half their sons affected. The well-known historical example is that of Queen Victoria, who had hemophiliac sons and affected grandsons via her carrier daughters.

3. *Autosomal recessive and dominant inheritance.* There are two other simple patterns of genetic inheritance in addition to the X-linked type. These are related to the genes located on the 22 pairs of autosomes. Many disorders in which the presence of the abnormal gene affects the production of an enzyme needed for a biochemical process, appear only when the abnormal gene is present on both members of the chromosome pair. In the case of albinism, production of the pigment melanin is prevented, and albinism is the resulting phenotype. If, however, one defective gene is present but its mate on the other chromosome is not defective, then enough enzyme can be produced to supply sufficient melanin and the carrier appears to be normal.

Albinism is an example of *autosomal recessive* inheritance, where the gene for the defect must be present in the double dose in the *homozygous* individual before the phenotype of albinism is seen. If the genotype is heterozygous, one gene for the production of normal pigment being present, then the carrier, or *heterozygote,* is phenotypically normal. Such recessive genes can remain undetected for many generations until both members of the gene pair come together in the offspring of two carriers. The risk of this occurring is 25 percent, since one-fourth of the offspring will inherit both genes for normal pigment, one-half of the offspring will inherit one deleterious gene from one parent or the other (and be carriers), and one-fourth will get both deleterious genes, one from each parent. Phenotypically, the homozygous normals and the carriers will look essentially alike. Recently it has been shown that there are at least three different types of albinism involving mutations at different steps in the enzyme pathway. This is an illustration of the genetic heterogeneity which can emerge from a careful study of what appears to be a single trait. One of the important areas of research in genetics today is the detection of carriers of deleterious recessive genes before they have to suffer the disaster of having a homozygous child with a serious autosomal recessive genetic defect. Parents who are related to each other have a greater chance of being carriers of the same recessives, hence run a greater risk of having affected children.

On the other hand, when the presence of one deleterious gene is enough to cause the appearance of the anomaly, the inheritance is that of an *autosomal dominant,* and the trait appears in every generation, going from affected parent to affected child. The heterozygote almost always shows the trait phenotypically. The double dose of the gene in the homozygote may have such a severe effect that the affected fetus may be aborted spontaneously. The chance of an affected individual having an affected child is about 50 percent. One example is achondroplastic dwarfism.

Many human traits are affected by several genes, or have a *multigenic* inheritance. These traits show a continuous gradation in phenotype in contrast to those recessive or dominant ones in which there is an "all or none" discrete ratio. One example is height, which has a range in the population from very short to very tall, with most phenotypes clustering around an average or mean height. Genetic predictions in regard to multigenic traits have to be based on empiric data from population statistics. The only figures which can be given are derived from what has been known to have happened in similar cases reported in previous studies.

4. *Chromosomal anomalies.* Gross chromosomal abnormalities involve much more DNA than differences between single genes. They usually produce very serious disorders which are generally manifest at birth and which present an array of seemingly unrelated symptoms. When the normal balance of the chromosome complement is upset by the absence of a chromosome, the presence of an extra one, or the lack of some parts of chromosomes, the total development of the individual is disrupted. Down's syndrome, with its many congenital defects of the eye, heart,

skeleton, and brain, is one example. Many early spontaneous abortions are the result of such chromosomal abnormalities. Estimates go as high as 22 to 46 percent for the proportion of aborted fetuses that may have *monosomies* (one chromosome missing), *trisomies* (one extra chromosome present), or other chromosomal abnormalities (Witschi 1971).

About 1 in 200 live births shows some sort of gross chromosomal abnormality. These mishaps appear to be due either to a failure in the separation of the chromosomes in the last meiotic division of the oocyte which forms the egg or to a similar occurrence in the first or very early mitotic divisions of the egg itself. If the failure occurs in the first few divisions of the fertilized egg, *mosaicism* usually results, with some cell lines in the body showing one chromosome complement and some showing another. The risk of recurrence here depends upon the type of chromosomal anomaly involved. Often the risk is related to the age of the mother.

The above classification of autosomal recessives and dominants, X-linked, multigenic, and chromosomal aberrations may seem quite clear-cut. However, since each individual has many thousands of other genes acting upon his development, and each person, even an identical twin, has had a different environment from conception on, it follows that the phenotypic expression of a certain genotype will differ somewhat from person to person. In some cases the trait may not be expressed at all (reduced penetrance), while in other cases it may be made more severe by the action of other genes in the chromosome complement or by special environmental stresses. There are conditions resembling known genetic disorders that are the result of special environmental influences, for example, the blindness, deafness, and retardation in infants born to mothers who had rubella during early pregnancy. These are called *phenocopies*.

Methods of Research on Genetic Anomalies

Since the expression of a trait can vary greatly from person to person, it is apparent that it may be difficult to ascertain the incidence of a given disorder in the population with an acceptable degree of accuracy. The trait must be clear-cut enough and measurable enough that a diagnosis can be made. This presents a difficult problem in the assessment of mental retardation and psychosis.

The genetics of a particular trait cannot be understood fully until the incidence of the trait in a particular population, for example, a kinship, can be contrasted with its incidence in the population as a whole. Does a particular family show an unusual incidence of schizophrenia? Is mental retardation more frequent in certain socioeconomic levels? Does close proximity to nuclear power plants increase the incidence of genetic defects? It is difficult to obtain accurate data to study such problems, but it is important to try to do so.

The selection of appropriate populations to study presents many problems. Sometimes entire populations, such as those in institutions, are surveyed for the incidence of specific gene or chromosomal defects. These groups do not supply a representative distribution for sex or age, however. At other times an attempt is made to get representative samples from large, heterogeneous populations. The incidence of some genetic traits has been found to vary by geographic location, country of origin, socioeconomic status, age, and sex.

Control samples for comparison with index study groups may be derived from large populations or they may be especially tailored to match each individual in the study group as to age, sex, education, and the like. Control samples are necessary if valid differences in incidence are to be established.

Longitudinal studies of family pedigrees can reveal patterns of inheritance through several generations of persons within different degrees of relationship to each other. A strong case can be made for the high heritability of a trait that increases in frequency with closer degrees of relationship.

Because identical twins share the closest degree of genetic relationship, that of the same DNA, they have been favorite subjects for research, since the differences between them can be ascribed to environmental influences. Often such studies include fraternal twins who have only half their genes in common and are essentially siblings born at the same time. If the concordance of a trait in identical twins is greater than that in fraternal twins (that is, the trait in one identical twin appears also in the other identical twin more often than is the case in fraternal twins), an estimate of heritability can be made. Twin methods are used very frequently in studies of behavioral traits.

Rare recessive disorders are more often found in the offspring of first- or second-cousin marriages. The offspring of related parents have an increased risk of inheriting the same deleterious recessive gene from a common ancestor of the parents. Thus, a useful technique in defining the pattern of inheritance for a particularly rare trait is to look for an increased incidence of cousin marriages among the parents of affected children.

There is a great range in the heritability of traits because the phenotypes of some traits are more susceptible to environmental differences than others. As far as anyone knows, blood groups have 100 percent genetic variance. No environmental differences have been found that can affect the ABO blood groups. At the other end of the range one might put starvation, an environmental factor which is 100 percent effective in eliminating genetic differences! However, even with starvation, some persons will survive longer than others, perhaps by virtue of their particular genotype (better utilization of food, lower metabolic rate, and so on). Even epidemics of contagious disease usually spare some individuals who for some reason or other survive the infection.

The importance of genetic differences is most clear in the cases of ge-- netic anomalies where the phenotypes can be divided into discrete classes of those affected and those not affected. Even with discrete classes of phenotypes, however, there are genetic and environmental modifiers that affect the development of the trait. In cases of multigenic inheritance, both genetic and environmental differences are likely to be implicated in the observable phenotypic differences.

The methods used to measure the phenotypes and to investigate the mode of inheritance will vary widely with the trait. Phenotypes may be defined by biochemical analysis, by intelligence tests, by personality inventories, by neurological examination, and so forth. Suspected modes of inheritance can be investigated by chromosome counts, by pedigree analysis, by population studies, by the incidence of cousin marriages, by twin and family studies, and so forth. The sort of trait being investigated determines the techniques used to evaluate its inheritance.

Summary

1. A short review of the modes of inheritance described as autosomal are sex-linked, dominant and recessive patterns, multigenic inheritance, and gross chromosomal anomalies.

2. Methods for investigating genetic anomalies include population studies, pedigree analysis, twin studies, the incidence of cousin marriages, chromosome counts, and longitudinal studies of families.

3. The choices of phenotypes to study and methods for the investigation of modes of inheritance depend upon the trait.

SPECIFIC GENETIC ANOMALIES

The following portion of this chapter deals with some of the more common genetic anomalies found in children and with some which are rare but have unusual behavioral components. They have been selected chiefly to illustrate six different aspects of family and medical genetic problems: (1) severe genetic anomalies with early death; (2) chronic genetic anomalies with good life expectancy; (3) treatable genetic anomalies with recurrent severe episodes; (4) remediable genetic anomalies with amelioration of symptoms; (5) congenital sense deprivation; and (6) genetic anomalies primarily behavioral in nature.

Each disorder is defined medically, and described, as far as possible, as to symptoms, incidence, diagnosis, treatment, mode of inheritance, and the behavioral problems both of the child and of the other persons concerned with him or her. Genetic counseling appropriate to the situation is also included.

In genetic counseling for specific disorders, the counselor tells the client about the inheritance of the disorder and evaluates the probable risk of a repetition in future offspring. The counselor presents the possible courses of action but does not advise the clients what to do about the situation. Only the clients know what their personal situation is and how they can cope with it. They need a sympathetic hearing, a review of possible strategies, and an accurate and understandable explanation of the risks as far as they are known. With disorders for which affected persons can be treated and survive to reproductive age, two kinds of counseling are needed. One of these is for the parents to be informed about the risk of a repetition in any additional children they may have. The other concerns the reproductive future of their affected child and his or her siblings.

Severe Genetic Anomalies with Early Death

Many of these disorders are very rare, although the proportion of carriers in a population may be fairly high. No disease is rare, however, to the couple faced with such a family disaster. The behavior of the child is related to the nature and progress of the disease. The behavior of the parents is influenced by their own upbringing and their attitudes toward themselves and their children. The approach used by the physician who makes the diagnosis may be crucial to the couple's acceptance of the calamity.

Sibinga and Friedman (1971) reported a study of parental understanding of the facts told them about phenylketonuria. Tests showed that only 19 percent of the sample of seventy-nine parents appeared to have good comprehension of the facts. They found that capability of the parents to understand was not related to their educational level but to their emotional reaction to the situation.

Kanof, Kutner, and Gordon (1962) studied the impact of Tay-Sachs disease on the family. They found that, in the sample of forty-six parents interviewed, over half the individuals reported that they were told only that their child had an inherited lethal disease. They were given no explanation and no directions as to how to proceed. Most were advised to hospitalize the child immediately and to have no more children. Only in four cases did the parents feel they had received helpful support from physicians. The situation was naturally very devastating to the parents, who tended to blame the physician, to feel guilty about the genetic aspect, and to withhold the information from relatives. Tay-Sachs disease and Lesch-Nyhan syndrome will be discussed as examples of severe genetic anomalies with early death.

1. *Lesch-Nyhan syndrome.* This severe neurologic disorder is caused

by the lack of the enzyme hypoxanthine-guanine phosphoribosyl transfer-ase, which is essential for proper purine metabolism. It is an X-linked trait affecting males only. The overt biochemical sign is a great excess of uric acid in the urine, but carriers and affected fetuses as early as twenty weeks of age can be detected by tests for the level of the enzyme. It is a rare trait with an incidence of about 1 in 50,000 males but it is included here because of its unique behavioral aspects.

The symptoms develop at around age six months, when the neurologi-cal signs appear. The infant cannot sit unsupported or crawl. He has choreoathetoid movements and scissoring of the legs develops. The pa-tients appear to be severely retarded. Later, at about age three, the char-acteristic behavioral symptom develops: compulsive self-mutilation. The patients bite their fingers and lips, bang their heads, and hit or bite other objects and persons. They rarely live beyond their teens. No effective treatment has been developed. Physical restraints and tooth extraction reduce the self-mutilation.

Hoefnagel, Andrew, Mireault, and Berndt (1965) reported on three children in two families, describing the physical symptoms and the be-havior. They stated that the patients appeared to be more comfortable with restraints which prevented their self-mutilation. The same observa-tions have been made by Berman, Balis, and Dancis (1969) in their re-port on four cases. Their patients, when restrained and supported, ap-peared to be happy, placid, and anxious for attention; when the supports and restraints were removed, they screamed and cried. The authors stated that it was clear that the children were frightened by their compulsion to bite.

Michener (1967) found in a study of six patients that each had a unique personality and each gave the impression that he had a higher learning ability than that revealed by tests. The question of how mentally retarded these children may be has also been raised by Scherzer and Ilson (1969). They reported that in the thirty case reports reviewed by them, only fourteen gave a specific estimate of the patient's intelligence. Most patients were reported as having IQ scores below 50 but one had an IQ of 90 at age eight, and one had an IQ of 84 at age eight and a half. One case had an IQ in the normal range for his age (six years), although he exhibited all the severe symptoms of the disease and was in restraints and toothless. Scherzer and Ilson described the difficulties of testing a child who is aggressive and hostile, can barely speak, and cannot use his hands. The patient was tested by the Picture Vocabulary Sub-test of the Stanford Binet and by the Full Range Picture Vocabulary Test. His comprehen-sion of language was normal for his age but his expressive vocabulary was at the four-year level. This child was put in a preschool program for the handicapped.

If, indeed, these severely disabled children have a fairly average intelligence, the hostility and aggression they display might well be the reaction of acute frustration induced by their physical handicaps and their real fear of the compulsive self-mutilation. Careful investigation of the behavior problems of other children with severe disorders may reveal that mental retardation may not be a necessary concomitant of these anomalies. Very sophisticated techniques of testing need to be developed to reveal the real abilities of these patients.

Genetic counseling for parents with an affected son is straightforward. The chance that the next son will be affected is 50 percent. No daughters will be affected but half of them will be carriers and will face a risk of their own sons having the disease in half the cases, since the deleterious gene is on the X-chromosome. Carriers and affected fetuses can be detected and the pregnancies of women at high risk can be monitored by amniocentesis. The abortion of an affected fetus can enable the parents to avoid a disaster and try again for a happier outcome.

2. *Tay-Sach's disease.* Tay-Sach's disease results from a disorder in lipid metabolism. The affected individuals show a deficiency in hexosaminidase A. Lipids in the form of gangliosides accumulate in the cells of the brain and nervous system with concomitant degeneration of myelin. The disorder is much commoner in some populations than in others. Ashkenazi Jews have an incidence of about 1 in 5,000 births with as many as 1 in 30 being carriers. In the non-Jewish population in the United States it occurs at the rate of about 1 in 200,000 to 1 in 500,000 births (Hsia 1966).

The infant appears normal at birth but by age four to six months development slows, and there is irritability and hyperacusis. The infant shows progressive mental and motor deterioration, becomes blind and may develop convulsions, an enlarged head, and emaciation. Death usually comes by age three to four years. The only treatment is for the alleviation of the symptoms as they develop. The heredity is the autosomal recessive type with complete penetrance. Carrier parents can expect a 25 percent chance of a repetition in any one birth.

The behavioral aspects of the disease in the child are apparently related to the accumulation of fatty materials in the cells of the brain and nervous system. At the present time there is no known way to alter the course of the disease.

In situations like this, the chief behavior problems relate to the reactions of the physician, the affected child's parents, siblings and other relatives, the in-laws, and even the neighbors (Kanof et al. 1962). Naturally, parents fear a repetition of such a disaster. The 25 percent chance may seem too great to take. Now that carriers can be identified biochemically and the affected fetus can be diagnosed in utero, couples at high risk have organized to protect themselves. In several cities, groups of these parents arrange for the testing of spouses to detect any carriers. If two carriers are married to each other, arrangements are made to monitor each pregnancy by amniocentesis. The procedure of amniocentesis has been well described in an article by Friedmann (1971). If an affected fetus is found, the option of abortion may be exercised. Parents can then try again for the 75 percent chance of having an unaffected child. Since any subsequent normal offspring of these parents have a two out of three chance of being carriers, such procedures are somewhat disgenic (compared to the alternative of no further reproduction). However, the humane value of giving concerned parents an opportunity to have normal children outweighs the eugenic considerations, even though the number of carriers in the population will slowly increase over the course of many generations. (For estimates see Bergsma [1971, pp. 23–32].)

Chronic Genetic Anomalies with Good Life Expectancy: Down's Syndrome

Genetic disorders that are chronic with good life expectancy pose problems different from those which, however devastating at the time, are soon over. Here there are more behavioral problems with the growing child, and there is a need for future planning, perhaps for the lifetime of the parents. Quite a lot depends on the approach of the physician, who may present a very discouraging prognosis to the parents at the first interview or, conversely, may enable them to see possibilities for future adjustment.

Down's syndrome, formerly called mongolism, is the most common syndrome caused by the presence of an extra chromosome, number 21 in the 22 pairs of autosomes. This extra chromosome interferes with orderly fetal development, so that the child is born with multiple, seemingly unrelated, defects. These include mental retardation, retarded motor development, broad flat face with protruding tongue, lens opacities and other eye defects, heart defects and other developmental anomalies, including the epicanthal eye-fold that gave the disease its former name. The clinical diagnosis can be made in the newborn. The disorder appears in about 1 in 500–600 births. One-third of these children are born to women over the age of forty years. Ten percent of the retardates in institutions have Down's syndrome.

Since the disorder is the result of faulty fetal development and the cause is an extra chromosome in every body cell, there is no treatment except a palliative one of continuous special education and good medical supervision. However, research to find a treatment, perhaps chemical, which may alleviate the mental retardation in these patients is continuing. Formerly these children died young, often of pneumonia. Now, with the use of antibiotics, they may live to middle age or older. They seldom reproduce, although a few births to affected girls have been recorded. (As expected, the offspring were affected in half the cases.)

There are certain behavioral characteristics that are typical of Down's syndrome children. Bartalos and Baramki (1967) reported that most have IQs in the range of 25 to 45, although a few may have IQs as high as 70. About 4 percent can read. These patients are usually cheerful, although they may be stubborn. They have a sense of rhythm and a faculty for mimicry. They enjoy singing, dancing, and listening to music.

Formerly, at the time the diagnosis was made, parents were advised to have these infants institutionalized. However, it became apparent that Down's children varied considerably in their symptoms. Many developed better in the more stimulating atmosphere of a home, and many parents found they could cope with the problems if they were given the proper orientation when the diagnosis was first made.

The success of home-rearing depends on the severity of the case, the attitudes and financial status of the parents, and the willingness and ability of the mother to undertake the task. There is hope of improvement, but at present practically no hope of an independent existence for the child. Milunsky et al. (1970) reported that in Massachusetts about one-third of the children with Down's syndrome are institutionalized at birth, one-third by age ten, and the remainder by age thirty. This points up the problem faced by aging parents who can no longer look after a retardate who needs constant supervision.

One has only to look at letters written to the editor in publications for lay people like *Mental Retardation News* to discover the range of parental attitudes toward home care of retardates. The range is from the bearing of an almost intolerable burden to the feeling that the presence of an affected child has been a blessing. The effect on siblings is unpredictable. Grossman (1972) reported that often the oldest girl is required to assume too much care for the retarded sibling and comes to resent him or her greatly. Other less involved siblings may be neutral or accepting.

The genetic counseling for the parents differs according to the mechanism that caused the trisomy. If the extra chromosome 21 got into the egg because of failure to separate from its mate at meiosis (*nondisjunction type*), the chances of it happening as a first event or as a recurrence depends upon the age of the mother. The risk is small in young mothers, about 1 in 1,200. On the contrary, in women over forty-five the risk may be as great as 1 in 40. The risk of recurrence is slightly greater than that of the first happening.

If the Down's syndrome is the result of a *translocation* in which the extra chromosome 21 has become attached to another chromosome, the possibility of a recurrence is greatly increased. Cytological examination of dividing cells from the affected child can determine whether or not the extra chromosome is free (nondisjunction type) or attached (transloca- tion type). If the latter is the case, the cells of both parents can be exam- ined to discover whether or not one is a carrier of the translocation. Car- riers will have one free chromosome 21 and one attached one. If one of the parents is a carrier, the chance of the disorder in the offspring is about 15 percent. This is a risk parents may be unwilling to take.

At present, the chromosome complement of the early fetus can be de- tected by amniocentesis. Couples at high risk because one of them carries the translocation and women at high risk because of their age (late thir- ties or older) are candidates for an amniocentesis so that a prenatal diag- nosis can be made with the option of abortion.

Other autosomal trisomies in which the extra chromosome is larger usually cause early spontaneous abortion or multiple severe defects in infants, who die early.

Treatable Genetic Anomalies with Recurrent Severe Episodes

The problems faced by the patient and his family with a disorder in this category, in which treatment can alleviate symptoms and prolong life but where there are life-threatening episodes, are in many ways greater than those faced by the family in which the patient dies young or has a disorder which runs a fairly even course. Prolonged medical treatment is expensive, and recurrent crises are very traumatic for both the parents and the child. The issue of long-term care and the advisability of repro- duction for the patient both present problems not experienced by families in the first two categories.

The disorders described below have been selected because they pre- sent different kinds of behavioral problems. The genetics of three (hemo- philia, sickle cell disease, and cystic fibrosis) are well understood. The others (diabetes and epilepsy) show much variability in their degree of expression. The pattern of inheritance is not well understood nor are the underlying causes of the symptoms all known. All five are more or less "invisible"; that is, the patient usually appears to be normal physically.

1. *Hemophilia.* Hemophilia A (Factor VIII deficiency) is the classi- cal hemophilia, or bleeders' disease, of historical interest in the royal houses of Europe. A history of the Russian royal family gives a very interesting study of the disorder (Massie 1967).

Hemophilia A is the most common hereditary coagulation defect and occurs in about 1 in 10,000 male births (Abildgaard and Schulman 1968). One-third of these are presumed to be the result of new mutations. The defective gene is a recessive located on the X chromosome; hence, females are very seldom affected. The symptoms are the result of a deficiency in the antihemophilic Factor VIII. The deficiency may vary from severe to mild (from less than 1 percent of Factor VIII in the blood to 5–25 percent of Factor VIII present).

The disorder may become evident shortly after birth, especially at circumcision, or may not appear until the child walks and suffers trauma from falls. There may also be spontaneous bleeding into soft tissues or joints. Bleeding into the joints can result in great pain and crippling.

Treatment includes the prevention of trauma as much as possible. In the crises, transfusions of Factor VIII (via fresh plasma or plasma concentrates) are given, followed by therapy to prevent joint damage. The crises require hospitalization and the treatment is very expensive. Factor VIII disappears rapidly from the blood and must be administered again at the next crisis.

Agle (1964) made a study of thirteen patients with hemophilia A, with the object of finding out what effect the illness had on the personality and what effect psychological factors had on the illness. His subjects described their fears of bleeding, severe pain, crippling, and death. Nine patients thought their mothers were overprotective and their fathers inattentive. They reported that they felt inferior to siblings and peers. Psychiatric syndromes seen were anxiety and recurrent depression. These were severe enough in eight patients to interfere with normal activities. He also found that the child may be forced into one of two responses— fearful and passive or rebellious. The rebellious ones undertook risks such as riding motorcycles, indicating a denial of the disease. He reported many clinical data on psychophysiological bleeding following emotional stress and on the effects of emotions on capillaries. Tense, frightened hemophiliacs appeared to have more frequent and more severe bleeding episodes. Hypnotic suggestion aided hemostasis in oral surgery.

Browne, Mally, and Kane (1960) reported similar results in their comparison of twenty-eight hemophiliac children with twenty-seven matched controls. There appeared to be seasonal variations in the bleeding, with episodes at holidays, the beginning of school, and in association with other illnesses, although blood studies did not show a change in the amount of Factor VIII. Spontaneous episodes were more frequent, but those resulting from trauma were more severe.

They reported that the major problem of the affected children was conflict about activity. Not only the patients but the siblings were restricted in activity. Schooling was often interrupted, and career choices were limited. The patients were outwardly passive but rebellious in subtle ways. The mothers felt intensely guilty as carriers, the fathers tended to remain aloof, leaving the care of the patient to the mother. The fathers appeared to feel that the disorder was the mother's "fault."

Genetic counseling for the normal parents of a hemophiliac child gives a risk of 50 percent among sons. Fifty percent of the daughters will be carriers but none will be affected. Counseling for the hemophiliac himself is different. None of his sons will be affected (because they receive his Y chromosome), but all of his daughters will be carriers (because they receive his X), giving a risk of 50 percent hemophiliacs among the sons of the patients' daughters. This is a risk he might not want to take. On the outside chance that a hemophiliac might marry a carrier female, he then runs the risk of 50 percent affected daughters, 50 percent carrier daughters, and 50 percent affected sons. In hemophilia the genetic risk of propagating the gene is high. Other risks taken by an adult hemophiliac as husband and father involve his health, longevity, and earning capacity.

2. *Sickle cell anemia.* Sickle cell anemia is a severe chronic hemolytic anemia found chiefly in persons of African descent whose ancestors came from malarial regions. About 10 percent of American blacks are heterozygous and have sickle cell trait, a mild disorder that may go undetected unless the individual is subjected to oxygen deprivation, for example at high altitudes.

The homozygotes (about 0.2 percent in the black population) suffer from a chronic anemia and also from severe episodes when the sickle-shaped red cells occlude the small blood vessels, causing severe pain and swelling with possible tissue damage and the plugging of essential vessels in the lungs or brain. Many affected persons do not survive the first two decades of life but others may live much longer, depending upon the severity of manifestation of the disease and the kind of medical care they receive.

Sickle cell anemia is interesting biochemically in that the genetic defect which causes it has been traced to the exact locus on the DNA molecule where the deleterious mutation occurred. The sickling of the normally disc-shaped red cells is caused by the presence of hemoglobin molecules that assume an abnormal shape under low oxygen tension, thus changing the shape of the red cells that contain them to the sickle shape.

Treatment consists, first, of protecting the homozygous child from infections, strenuous exercise, and situations where oxygen may be scarce, such as high altitudes. Second, the life-threatening crises require expensive hospitalization, bed rest, analgesics for the severe pain, and often transfusions. Crises can be brought on by various factors such as infections, exercise, and oxygen lack, but in some instances no precipitating factor has been found. For a description of this disorder and its treatment, see Pearson and Diamond (1971).

Screening programs are being set up to discover the carriers. Carriers have about 35 percent abnormal hemoglobin and are usually symptom-free. A simple blood test will reveal the sickled cells, which appear under conditions of low oxygen tension.

Screening has raised questions about the propriety of locating carriers. There have been charges of racism in some quarters. Some blacks have suffered employment and insurance problems because of the ignorance of the public about the disease and the misleading information which has been disseminated by the news media. It is particularly important to find the homozygotes because the life-threatening crises present many kinds of symptoms so that the real cause may be overlooked. Blacks considering marriage may want to find out whether or not they are carriers. In a population where 10 percent are carriers, 1 marriage in 100 would involve two spouses who are carriers.

For genetic counseling there is no real problem since the heterozygotes can be identified. Two heterozygotes then have a 25 percent chance of having a severely affected child. Methods are being developed for the detection of the affected fetus by amniocentesis.

It is interesting to geneticists that this very deleterious gene has survived in a population where homozygotes die young (in Africa, as small children). Research has uncovered the fact that the carriers of the gene for sickle cell survived malarial attacks better than did their relatives with completely normal hemoglobin. Hence, the carriers reproduced more and kept the gene frequency stable in the population. Its presence among Afro-Americans reflects their past history but has no significance for their survival in malaria-free regions. Its frequency can be expected to decrease in our population, unless there is selective abortion of homozygotes and an increase in the number of carrier offspring of carrier parents. In this case, the gene frequency may slowly increase over many generations.

3. *Cystic fibrosis.* In the population of the United States, cystic fibrosis (mucoviscidosis) is the most frequent severe genetic disease of childhood. The incidence of affected individuals is in the range of about 1 in 1,200 with about 1 in 20 to 30 who are carriers. The disorder is a malfunctioning of the exocrine glands, and it is inherited as an autosomal recessive. The underlying cause is not yet known, and treatment is only palliative.

The symptoms are varied but all relate to the malfunctioning of the exocrine glands with the production of sticky mucus. There is chronic pulmonary disease which tends to get worse, digestive insufficiency from lack of digestive enzymes, especially from the pancreas (trypsin, lipase, and other enzymes may be deficient or lacking), and excessive salt loss from sweat with susceptibility to heat exhaustion. No really reliable tests have been developed yet for the detection of carriers.

Treatment must be on a daily basis with intermittent hospitalization for the crises. McCollum and Gibson (1970) provided a detailed and sympathetic description of what this disease means to family adaptation. Constant, expensive medical care is required. The child is difficult to care for on a day to day basis for he must have daily therapy for the respiratory problems (aerosols, mist tent, drainage posturing) and a regulated diet with oral antibiotics, supplementary doses of vitamins and pancreatic extracts at each meal. The child has a persistent cough and foul-smelling stools. In the crises of infections with pulmonary involvement, several weeks of hospitalization with antibiotic therapy may be required. Now that the children live longer (primarily because of antibiotics) they go to school, where some of the problems of daily medication, diet, and psychological support fall on the teacher.

Obviously the whole family has problems of adjustment. The child is subjected to continuous treatment with frightening episodes of crises in hospitals. As he grows older he realizes that his prospects for survival are uncertain, as are his chances for marriage and a career. Shwachman, Kulczycki, and Khaw (1965) reported on 1,700 patients they had seen in the past twenty-five years. Sixty-five were older than seventeen years. Four were college graduates, one was in medical school, seven were married but had no children. They estimated that only seven of the sixty-five were essentially normal in ability to work. In spite of excellent care, some patients become progressively worse. The significance of psychological factors in an expensive chronic disease with an uncertain future cannot be overlooked.

In another paper, Shwachman, Redmond, and Khaw (1970) reported on 130 patients diagnosed under three months of age and followed for twenty years. They stressed the need for early diagnosis and vigorous therapy. There were 101 survivors to age twenty (77 percent). The more severely affected died at younger ages. Of the 101 survivors, only 14 were considered in "excellent" condition.

Genetic counseling for the parents gives the usual risk for an autosomal recessive of 25 percent repetition in other offspring. Parents may not want to take this risk in a disorder where so much time, effort, and money must be expended in caring for one affected child.

The survival of the homozygotes to marriageable age poses the question of their reproduction. However, in studies of adult affected males, Denning et al. (1968), and Kaplan et al. (1968) reported aspermia in twenty-five patients. These men had normal sexual development and formed sperm, but defects in the vas deferens prevented the movement of the sperm into the ejaculate. Only one male has been reported as fathering a child. Such children would all be carriers unless the mother also was a carrier. Then half the children would be affected.

Female homozygotes appear to have abnormal cervical mucus (Oppenheimer and Esterly 1970), but there are records of ten women who had eleven children, all of whom were normal (but of necessity carriers). Pregnancy is a serious risk for these patients because of their continuing respiratory problems. Grand, Talamo, de Sant'Agnese, and Schwartz (1966) reported on the pregnancies of ten mothers. Two died postpartum, four had severe and persistent pulmonary difficulty, and four had no change in pulmonary status.

4. *Diabetes.* Diabetes is a chronic metabolic disorder resulting in elevated blood glucose levels. It occurs both in children and in adults. Before the discovery of insulin, the child diabetic had a life expectancy of about two years, with a rigid diet. Today the incidence of diabetes is increasing in the population, first because all diabetics live longer, and second because juvenile diabetics survive to reproduce. Some of their children may be affected, and all will be carriers.

Accurate statistics on the incidence of diabetes are difficult to obtain since many persons who do not have overt symptoms have been found to have abnormal blood sugar levels. Nelson (1969) reported that about 4 percent of the 3,000,000 diabetics in the United States were under the age of fifteen. Weil (1968) reported that, in affected children, the disease appears under age five in 20–25 percent of the cases; 35 percent of the cases appear between the ages of five to ten; and the remainder have an age of onset between ten and fifteen years. He found that rapid onset of diabetes in children was accompanied by polyuria, weight loss, fatigue, and lethargy.

The overt cause of diabetes is the failure of the body to metabolize carbohydrates properly. This may be accompanied by disorders in fat and protein metabolism as well, with the possibility of the later development of vascular problems including blindness. The diagnostic signs are excess sugar in the blood and urine.

The basic genetic mechanisms in diabetes are still unknown. There may be a deficiency of insulin production by the pancreas, a defect in the proinsulin molecule, the presence of an insulin inhibitor, some sort of transport barrier, or others not yet found. These different defects may even have different modes of inheritance.

Treatment includes prompt hospitalization, the regulation of diet, and the determination of the correct amount and kind of insulin needed for the daily injections. The parents and the child need good instruction so that they understand the disease and can cope with the complexity of dietary exchanges, urine tests, and the regulation of the insulin injections. In young children the mother must assume most of the responsibility. Older children can learn the techniques. All the requirements for care presuppose that family members are able to accept the restrictions and are sufficiently well educated and intelligent enough to follow the myriad directions.

Fischer and Dolger (1946) made a study of forty-three young diabetics who were followed from childhood through adolescence. All had been under treatment for ten to twenty years. They found that young children do not realize the implications of the disease, but that the parents are greatly shocked and may react by being either overly solicitous or rejecting. Some parents so feared their child's death by insulin shock that they slept with him or her. Normal siblings resented the extra care and attention that the diabetic child received.

These authors also reported that the diabetic child felt stigmatized. Some children tried to conceal their affliction from their classmates. Some refused to attend diabetic camps. Control of diet became more difficult among adolescents, and their management of their disease became more careless. Adolescents worried about the possible complications of circulatory problems and blindness. Girls were frequently rejected as future spouses. If married and pregnant, they faced obstetrical crises.

Despite improved management of the disorder today, diabetes is still a disease that the victim is aware of all the time and that presents an uncertain future. The older child must make his own urine tests, administer his own injections, watch his diet, and be aware of the premonitory symptoms of diabetic coma or insulin shock. Hypoglycemia, or low blood sugar, brings about behavioral symptoms of irritability, erratic behavior, violent outbursts, and, as it progresses, to insulin shock, dizziness, sweating, tremors, convulsions, and unconsciousness. Diabetic coma can result from insufficient insulin with the resulting increase in blood sugar. Teachers need to be watchful of diabetic children, alert to symptoms of shock and coma, and protective of their dietary needs.

When one considers the burden placed on children by such a disease, it is little wonder that they suffer behavioral disorders. Some behaviors are related to the level of blood sugar but others, anxiety and depression, are probably related to the restrictions imposed by the disease and are less remediable. The children's fears have a real basis in the possibilities of severe life-threatening crises, shortened life expectancy, and blindness.

The genetics of diabetes is far from known. Even the definition of an "affected" individual is not easy. Much depends on the kinds of tests used. Biochemically and genetically, diabetes is probably not a single defect. The disease with early onset in childhood may be different in nature from that which appears in elderly persons. Risk figures for offspring are difficult to provide because of the differences in risk related to different ages of onset. Reed (1963) quoted a risk of 10–15 percent for children of a diabetic parent, with a risk for siblings of a diabetic with a diabetic parent at about 18 percent if they live to the age of eighty. There are also cases of two diabetic parents having an unaffected child, probably because the parents have different genetic defects.

Rimoin and Schimke (1971) reviewed much of the research on the genetics of diabetes and described many of the difficulties encountered in the study of this complex disorder. They quoted risks for first-degree relatives corrected for age of onset in the proband. If the proband becomes diabetic before age nineteen, the siblings have a 10–14 percent risk over that of the general population and children of the proband have an 18–41 percent increased risk. If the original patient develops the disease after age nineteen but before age forty, then the siblings have an increased risk of 4–5 percent and children a risk of 6–13 percent. If the age of onset is beyond forty, the risk to first-degree relatives of developing the disease is again reduced, with the siblings having a risk of 2–4 percent and children of 1–3 percent over that of a general population. One figure given for the incidence of diabetes in a population of ten- to nineteen-year-old males is 3 percent. It is obvious that the disease itself is not well defined and often appears as a part of other genetic syndromes (Rimoin and Schimke 1971, list 32). The mode or modes of inheritance have not been clarified, and even the biochemistry of this common disorder is not well understood.

The indications are that diabetes has a multigenic basis so that only empirical risk figures can be given. Of more moment for reproductive planning by diabetics seems to be the future health of the prospective mother and the future earning power and life expectancy of the father.

5. *Epilepsy*. Epilepsy is a convulsive disorder which has carried with it a great social stigma. There are several kinds of seizures, from massive generalized convulsions with periods of unconsciousness (grand mal) to transient (perhaps less than thirty seconds) losses of consciousness with few outward signs (petit mal). Many genetic disorders are accompanied by convulsive seizures, as for example Lesch-Nyhan syndrome and Tay-Sach's disease. The epilepsy described here is an affliction of otherwise apparently normal individuals.

Reed (1963) in his chapter on convulsive seizures, quoted a frequency of 1 in 250 for all kinds of epilepsy, both idiopathic and organic. Electroencephalography is sometimes useful in diagnosis.

The symptoms result from recurring excessive neuronal discharges within the brain. Since the causes of these discharges vary, the treatment must be adapted to the particular case. All patients must be protected from bodily injury during the seizures. If brain lesions are found, surgery may be successful. Anticonvulsant drugs have been helpful, but the kind and amount given must be carefully adjusted to the child. Sometimes the

diet is adjusted also. The treatment requires long-term medical supervision and the cooperation of the parents and child.

The child may be fearful. He or she may resent the continuous medication and the restrictions on diet or activity, especially at school. Baird
(1969) suggested that the child may use the disease as a shield or weapon
(attacks can be mimicked) or the child may deny that he or she has the
disease and "forget" to take the required medication. Deutsch and Wiener
(1948) reported in a study of seventy affected children that there was a
wide variation in children's reactions to the disease depending on the personality of the particular child. Aggression was inhibited in these patients.
In some, the release of tension and anxiety reduced the frequency of the
attacks.

Deutsch and Wiener (1948) noted that some parents fostered dependency in the children. Parents need help to overcome their feelings of
guilt and anxiety. Teachers must be told of the child's condition so that
they will understand the medical problems and know how to manage an
emergency in the classroom.

A predisposition to seizures in phenotypically normal parents can be
detected by an electroencephalogram. Some believe that epilepsy is a
threshold effect—that the level of the threshold is lower in those who have
the seizures, but that perhaps nearly everyone might have a seizure under
the proper triggering conditions.

Reed (1963) estimated the chance of normal parents having a second
child with seizures at about 10 percent. The chances of two normal parents with dysrhythmia (apparent on their electroencephalograms) of having an affected child range from 1 in 20 to 1 in 40.

Bray and Wiser (1964) in a study of temporal-central abnormalities
in focal epilepsy, studied families of forty index cases and compared them
with families of forty controls. They made 750 electroencephalograms
of siblings, parents and children. They found focal temporal lobe spikes,
or sharp waves, in 30 percent of the relatives of epileptics but in only 5
percent of the relatives of controls. Siblings and children of affected pro-
bands showed abnormal waves in 19 of 53 cases (36 percent), compared
with only 3 of 151 first-degree control group relatives who showed abnormal brain waves (1.9 percent). Four of 21 parents of index cases (19
percent) but only 1 of 51 parents of controls (2 percent) showed the
abnormality. They found that nearly all the relatives with abnormal wave
forms had no overt symptoms. For a summary of the kinds of epilepsy,
the types of research done, and a bibliography, see Slater and Cowie
(1971).

The chief handicap in considering reproduction of an epileptic person
is not the genetic risk of having affected children, which is about 2 to 10

percent (Reed 1963), but the attitude of society toward them. Affected persons have trouble getting employment. If the disorder is known, such individuals may have problems of being accepted socially or of finding a spouse. Many children and adults try to conceal the fact that they are epileptics, and this information may even be withheld from potential mates. Until recently many states had laws against the marriage of epileptics, who were often classified with retardates. Fortunately, with better education of the public, these outmoded attitudes are changing.[1]

Remediable Genetic Anomalies with Amelioration of Symptoms

Two of the three disorders described below are caused by aberrant numbers of sex chromosomes (Turner's syndrome and Klinefelter's syndrome). Affected persons cannot reproduce, but they can be treated to ameliorate the overt symptoms. These disorders, therefore, have psychological aspects somewhat different from the others reported in this chapter. The third disorder is phenylketonuria.

1. *Turner's syndrome.* Turner's syndrome (gonadal dysgenesis) occurs in about 1 in 2,500 live-born females. In most cases these girls have only one X chromosome instead of the normal number of two. Sometimes they show mosaicism or have another partially deleted X. They are short, with a stocky build, webbed neck, low hairline, and shield-like chest. Bodily defects are more apparent in some cases than in others. Most patients have intelligence in the normal range. They have only streak-like gonads, which are nonfunctional, but they do have female internal and external genitalia. They fail to mature and develop secondary sex characteristics at puberty because of the lack of hormones. Diagnosis is made from a chromosome count.

Treatment consists of the continued administration of estrogens (at the time of puberty) which will bring about the development of the feminine form and regular menstrual periods. The patients remain sterile.

Money and Mittenthal (1970) reported a study of seventy-three patients. They showed a low incidence of disabling psychopathology. Only three patients had symptoms of hostility, paranoia, or suicidal interest. Most were accepting, phlegmatic, and tolerant of adversity. They had an unambiguous gender identity as feminine, and showed feminine attributes even before treatment with hormones. All were treated with hormones at the age requested by the girls. Nine of the adults in the sample had married, and two had adopted children. The authors reported that the atti-

1. Another childhood disorder similar in some ways to epilepsy is asthma. For information on behavioral problems associated with asthma and allergies in general, see Randolph (1947), Deamer (1971), and Creak and Stephen (1958) all of whom described allergic children as chronically tired, irritable, and depressed.

tude of the parents was more of a psychological hazard to the affected girls than the problems caused by the deficit itself. The small stature and immature appearance of the patients led parents and others to treat them in an overprotective manner.

The writers concluded that the differentiation of a feminine identity was not dependent on the presence of the normal XX karyotype. In regard to intellectual functioning, they cited studies which indicated that Turner's syndrome patients may have a specific cognitional defect in space-form relations which shows up in their scores on the nonverbal portions of intelligence tests. Their verbal ability is not affected. (Consult Money and Mittenthal [1970] for studies on space-form disability.)

Genetically, there is not much chance of a repetition in a family since this condition is the result of an accident in the division of the cells making the egg. Early abortions of fetuses with XO and other deficiencies are common. The chances of a repetition are higher among older mothers, as is the case with nondisjunction type of other chromosomal anomalies such as Down's syndrome.

2. *Klinefelter's syndrome.* Klinefelter's syndrome is a gonadal dysgenesis in which the phenotypical male has at least two X chromosomes and one Y chromosome (XXY, XXXY, and so on). It occurs as the result of meiotic nondisjunction of the X chromosomes in gametogenesis, and appears in about 2 out of 1,000 live-born males. It is often not diagnosed until puberty, when secondary male characteristics fail to develop and when there may be breast enlargement. The patients have small genitalia (phenotypically male), and the internal sex organs are male but reduced in size. Very seldom are viable sperm found. About 25 percent of the affected males are retarded (DiGeorge 1969).

Treatment consists of surgery to reduce the breast size and the administration of androgens to promote the development of male secondary sex characteristics. The patients remain sterile, however.

There appear to be more behavior problems among the males with Klinefelter's syndrome than among the females with Turner's syndrome. In addition to the rather high proportion of retardation, there seems to be an increase in antisocial behavior and delinquency. Forssman and Hambert (1963) investigated 760 males of subnormal intelligence who were described as hard to manage. Fifteen, or 1 in 50, were found to have an extra X chromosome. This was not as many as the 1 in 42 found among 336 boys in special classes for the retarded but more than the 1 percent found in heterogeneous populations of retardates. In three mental hospitals, 10 of 1,625 men were found to have two or more X chromosomes. Most of these males also had abnormal electroencephalograms. There seems to be an excess of Klinefelter males in populations of retarded males with behavioral disorders.

Genetically, the risk of a recurrence to parents is not very great but it increases somewhat with the increasing age of the mother. There are many other abnormal combinations of sex chromosomes, most of which are very rare. Defects including mental retardation and the impairment of male attributes become more severe as extra X chromosomes are added. The extra-Y-chromosome male (XYY) has aroused some interest with reports that he is unusually tall, often subnormal in intelligence, and likely to engage in violent, antisocial acts. There seems to be some evidence for this. For more information see Price and Whatmore (1967), Nielsen (1969), and Hook (1973). Hook (1973) provided an exhaustive review of the subject, with a large bibliography. The relationship of abnormal chromosome numbers to behavioral problems presents many possibilities for research.

3. *Phenylketonuria.* Phenylketonuria, or PKU, is a good example of how altering the environment, in this case the diet, can prevent the expression of the most serious consequences of an autosomal recessive genetic disorder. PKU is a disorder of amino acid metabolism in which the enzyme phenylalanine hydroxylase is missing. This enzyme has a crucial role in the utilization of phenylalanine, a very common component of the diet. In its absence, phenylalanine cannot be converted to tyrosine but instead accumulates in the tissues and is partly transformed into phenylpyruvic acid and other metabolites. In some way, as yet unknown but perhaps related to myelin formation, the accumulation of these abnormal metabolites prevents normal development of the brain, and mental retardation is the usual result. Other symptoms are irritability, athetoid movements, hyperactivity, and blond coloration. About one-third of the children have convulsive seizures. The incidence of homozygotes is about 1 in 10,000 births, with about 1 in 50 being heterozygous carriers.

The success of the treatment depends on very early restriction of intake of phenylalanine to prevent the brain damage which becomes apparent at the age of a few months. Nyhan (1968) reported that treatment after the age of three years had no effect on the retardation although it did ameliorate the other behavioral symptoms. Many states now require that all newborns be tested for PKU. The Guthrie test is made twenty-four to forty-eight hours after the infant has had dietary protein (age three to six days) to detect the level of phenylalanine in the blood. If this test is negative, a second test is made four to six weeks later on the urine. If the first test is positive and a definitive diagnosis of PKU has been made, excluding false positives, then the infant is put on a milk substitute composed of the essential amino acids (except phenylalanine) together with added carbohydrates and fats. The intake of natural foods must be limited. The child must be kept on the diet until the brain matures to the point where it will not be damaged by the abnormal metabolites. Physicians usually try to keep the children on the diet until middle childhood, although some clinics stop by age six. Dietary control becomes increasingly difficult with school-age children.

There are behavior problems associated with the disorder itself. In addition to the mental retardation associated with nearly all untreated cases, there is schizoid behavior, athetoid movements, hyperkinetic activity, uncontrollable temper, and seizures. Abnormal electroencephalograms have been found in about 80 percent (Nyhan 1968).

Siegel et al. (1968) reported school-behavior profile ratings of thirteen treated PKU children which were measured against thirteen matched controls. There were significant differences between the two groups on three items—clumsiness, talkativeness, and hypersensitivity, with the PKU subjects rated higher in all three categories.

The diet will prevent the mental retardation if it is begun early enough and may alleviate the behavioral problems even if it is started too late to prevent the retardation. However, the strictness and unpalatability of the diet brings new behavioral problems with it. While some children are faithful about the diet even when at school, others resent it and refuse to abide by it.

The diet requires constant monitoring because there is a danger of inducing a phenylalanine deficiency. The treatment and the diet necessitate acceptance of the problem and constant cooperation in the treatment. Keleske, Solomons, and Opitz (1967) reported on the reactions of thirty-two parents to PKU and the difficulties they had in coping with the disease. They found that parents were helped by group meetings where problems of guilt, fear, and anxiety could be aired. Many parents expressed their hostility in their attitudes toward the diet (which indeed is difficult to administer in a family setting of growing children).

Genetically, the inheritance pattern is that of an autosomal recessive with a 25 percent chance of a repetition. Early screening enables the detection of affected siblings and a phenylalanine loading test can detect the heterozygotes. So far no test useful for prenatal detection has been devised.

Now that PKU patients can be protected from mental retardation and grow up free to marry, the problem of genetic counseling arises for these individuals. A "cured" phenylketonuric still has the two genes for the disorder and all the offspring will be heterozygous. If the spouse happens to be a carrier, half the offspring would be affected. If by some chance both spouses have PKU, all their children would be affected.

The problem of reproduction is very serious for PKU women, where a fetus must grow in an abnormal uterine environment. Howell and Stevenson (1971) reviewed the data on the offspring of thirty-three PKU women, none of whom had been on the diet in their early years (because it has only been in use for about ten years). Most of these women, however, had escaped the severe retardation characteristic of the disease. These women had 121 live births and 25 spontaneous abortions. Of these 121 offspring, only *16* were apparently normal. Seven had PKU, 87 had subnormal IQs with other defects, the most common one being microcephaly, 10 died young, and 1 was not seen. Intrauterine growth retardation was the single most prominent characteristic of these children. A myelin deficiency may also be associated with the mental disorders of the offspring. One difficulty in treating PKU mothers by putting them on the diet to reduce their blood phenylalanine levels is that the damage to the fetus may have been done by the time the pregnancy has been diagnosed. The authors felt that the risk of congenital malformations in the children is very high and that it would be advisable for these women not to reproduce. Male phenylketonurics would simply pass on one gene to each of their offspring.

Congenital Sense Deprivation

It is obvious that sense deprivation can lead to severe learning difficulties and serious handicaps in later life. There are many genetic syndromes which number blindness or deafness among their components. McKusick (1971) reported about seventy forms of hereditary deafness, twelve with no associated abnormality and the rest associated with various other genetic defects. It is impossible to cover in this chapter all the genetic anomalies which have blindness or deafness, partial or complete, associated with other defects. Here congenital blindness and congenital deafness will be considered in those cases where they are the only defects in an otherwise normal child.

One has only to read Helen Keller's life story to realize that such defects, in her case the combined one of early blindness and deafness, can conceal the genetic potentialities of the individual (Keller 1954). A great teacher was needed to enable this child to learn about her world. Helen Keller described vividly her struggles to express herself and the outbursts of temper which occurred daily as she invariably failed to communicate. One wonders if the aggressive behavior of other children trapped by defects may not stem from the same frustrations.

Shirley (1963), in his book on pediatric psychiatry, reported that blind children need much stimulation, for otherwise they will lose interest in their environments. Deaf children, however, are more aware of their environments. Such disabilities necessarily impede activities that are usual in childhood and can cause frustrations which may lead the child to desperate efforts to compensate or can cause the victim to lose interest and feel inadequate. Handicaps interfere with family relationships, and the child may tyrannize, become resentful and hostile, or become self-deprecatory. Myklebust (1964) reviewed many aspects of sense deprivation and behavior.

1. *Congenital blindness*. A discussion of the professional techniques needed to aid children deprived of sight are beyond the scope of this chapter. It is essential that blindness be diagnosed as early as possible. The incidence of children blind from birth ranges from 1 in 2,000 to 1 in 5,000 (Shirley 1963). Children who have been able to see at one time are easier to teach, but it may be that their psychological problems are greater.

Sussman (1969) reported that the disability aggravates the child's struggle between dependence and independence. Such children score lower on internal controls, and they have a lowered self-concept. Society is ambivalent toward them, and their parents suffer anger, disappointment, and guilt.

Davis (1969) reported that blind children have the problem of knowing their own body image and also that of knowing the image of the body of the opposite sex (which they may be forbidden to explore). They need to be taught appropriate gestures and facial expressions. Adolescents cannot do the things their peers do, such as drive cars. These older children may tend to the one extreme of being self-deprecatory or to the other of being vigorously self-assertive. Cole and Tabaroff (1955) described the blind child's lot as "social separateness." Society tends to regard blind persons as permanently dependent.

It is obvious that blind children are restricted in many activities, in career choices, and in chances for marriage. Even with high intelligence, they can hardly expect to become physicians or research scientists who need to read great amounts of literature or manipulate laboratory equipment.[2] Those with high motor-drive are denied many avenues of physical expression in sports. It takes a great deal of courage to attempt to ski in the dark. Training is very helpful, but it needs to be done on an almost one-to-one basis, is expensive, and, of course, can never really remedy the basic defect.

Genetically, the situation varies from case to case. Retinoblastoma is inherited as an autosomal dominant with approximately a 50 percent chance of appearing in the offspring. Cases differ as to the involvement of one or both eyes, the amount of penetrance, and the possibility of mutation in the germ cells of normal parents. Other kinds of blindness can be recessive, and associated with genetic syndromes or caused by envi-

2. Recently, the first blind student was admitted to medical school at Temple University.

ronmental insult, from rubella in the pregnant woman to physical trauma
at any age. Families requesting counseling would have to be evaluated
individually. Probably, the difficulties of finding a spouse and becoming
self-supporting outweigh the question of reproduction in many cases. The
problem of the care and support of children, seeing or blind, may be
the deciding factor which restricts the family size. Persons interested in
the medical aspects of childhood blindness should consult Fraser and
Friedman (1967).

2. *Congenital deafness*. The report of a conference on deaf children
and adolescents (Smith, ed. 1963), stated that in Britain about 1 in 1,000
children is born deaf to speech and cannot learn to speak normally. Such
children have severe problems of communication. The small child is un-
aware of his defect because it is "covered up" with vision and touch. Such
children should be provided with hearing aids very early, and the parents
and child taught to use them if at all possible. The deaf child becomes
very frustrated when he or she cannot understand or be understood, and
is subject to tantrums. The segregation of such children is not advised.

A similar research project has been reported for New York State by
Rainer, Altshuler, and Kallmann, eds. (1963). The total New York State
population of literate deaf persons over twelve years of age was investigated with a view to collecting data on adjustment and behavior patterns
related to their life performances. Deafness was defined as a "stress-pro-
ducing hearing loss, from birth or early childhood, rendering a person
incapable of effecting meaningful and substantial auditory contact with
the environment."

The investigation included performance as adults in marriage, socialization, and social behavior. The chapter on the genetic aspects of early
total deafness by Diane Sank, and a summary by Franz Kallmann, are
of particular interest to persons concerned with deaf children. Sank
(1963) found that about one-half of all deafness was due to exogenous
causes or new genetic mutations or complicated modes of inheritance.
About 10 percent of the deafness was accounted for by autosomal dominant genes; the remainder, approximately 40 percent, seemed to be mainly
of autosomal recessive origin, with perhaps as many as forty-five different genes involved in different cases.

Psychologically, the deaf subjects were found to be socially isolated
(Kallmann 1963). Their marriage rate was lower (only 69 percent married) and was highly assortative (less than 10 percent of the deaf women
who ever married were married to hearing men.) Only 10 percent of the
children born to deaf parents, however, are themselves deaf. Hearing
children can introduce problems into a family of deaf parents, as children
and parents try to adjust to each other. Kallmann reported that in families

with both deaf and hearing children, the deaf parents had more problems
of control and obedience with their hearing children than with the deaf
ones. He pointed out the need for deaf children to receive more guidance,
especially in preparation for family living.

One problem is that deafness is not a visible handicap. Hearing people
often do not have much patience for the deaf, and both the deaf and their
respondents are under great strain. Opinions vary as to how to teach the
deaf. They really need to speak in order to communicate with hearing
persons. Hand signs are useful between deaf children but the vocabulary
is limited. Lipreading is sometimes used by the deaf but the communication is one-way. Deaf individuals are probably more comfortable in social groups with other deaf persons, as the high assortative marriage rate
indicates. The trend is to prevent segregation of deaf children in special
schools or classes, although they do need help from special techniques.

Since there are so many kinds of deafness, the mode of inheritance has
to be worked out for individual cases. In addition to Sank, cited above,
Brown (1967) reported similar results. Neither author gives risk figures
for particular kinds of inherited deafness. Each family requesting counseling would have to be evaluated individually.

Genetic Anomalies Which Are Primarily Behavioral in Nature

At the present time there are two great needs in the whole field of behavioral research. One is greatly improved methods of evaluating mental
ability and of measuring mental "normality." Intelligence tests have good
predictive value for academic and economic success but are not culture-
free or precise enough. Personality inventories and psychiatric diagnosis
are even less precise.

The second task, that of finding ways to evaluate the environmental
situations that contribute to mental disorders, is even more difficult. Obviously good nutrition is important, but even that is difficult to define
(some children cannot tolerate milk!). What are the physical and psychological situations most traumatic to children and how can they be rem-
edied? How do individual children differ in their requirements? What is
good mothering? Good teaching? How do you measure their results? Are
the same methods good for every child, every parent, and every teacher?
All these questions need a great deal of painstaking, well-designed research before valid answers can be found. (See chapters 7, 8, and 9 in
this volume for further discussion of these issues.)

1. *Mental retardation.* Mental retardation has been described as a
chronic handicapping condition that is responsive, within limits, to reha-
bilitative techniques. This definition covers a host of different etiologies,
from single-gene defects and chromosomal anomalies to multigenic dis-

orders with a considerable environmental component, and includes some that are completely environmental in nature. It is primarily characterized by an impairment in intelligence with inadequate mental development, slow and incomplete maturation, impaired learning ability, and poor social adjustment. It may be the most handicapping of all childhood disorders since peak recognition comes between the ages of six and sixteen (Bartram 1969). The cause of much retardation is unknown.

Retardates exhibit many kinds of behavior, from responses peculiar to some definite disorder to behavior which does not really set them apart from others, except as judged by their learning capacities. Most undifferentiated retardates of higher IQ levels live in the population, more or less under the supervision of relatives or social workers. Some may exhibit psychotic symptoms in addition to their retardation, others work regularly and adjust well in sheltered environments. Some have a chance of successful marriages if they are not burdened with children and do not have too many economic problems.

About 3 percent of the population is considered retarded, using a cutting score of about IQ 70. The retardates fall into two groups, the first of which includes those with well-defined, usually severe, genetic disorders related to gene or chromosomal abnormalities, and some who may be retarded as the result of severe injury or serious infection. These severely retarded children are in the minority. Anderson (1972) reported 159 genetic disorders associated with mental retardation in McKusick's 1968 catalogue of Mendelian disorders in man. Of the 159 disorders, 136 were autosomal recessives, 7 were autosomal dominants, and 16 were X-linked. (Chromosomal anomalies associated with retardation, such as Down's syndrome, were not included.)

The second, larger group includes those retardates whose IQ scores fall at the lower end of the normal distribution curve of IQ. They have no definite stigmata and apparently represent the interaction of many genes with the environment. The fact that chromosome deletions often result in lowered IQs suggests that many genes, perhaps hundreds, are involved in intelligence. However, some children may be retarded solely because of environmental insult, and some show pseudo-retardation. More males than females are retarded. Bartram (1969) classified the kinds of retardation as prenatal (genetic or due to infections or drugs), perinatal (birth-injured); and postnatal (infection, poisoning, and the like). All children thought to be retarded should be screened for peripheral sensory defects (at least by the age of 3 or 4), for language and speech disorders, and neurological disturbances. Any of these handicaps may be confused with mental retardation.

Prevention, in some cases, lies with the identification and treatment of biochemical disorders found in retardates with well-defined symptoms. Menkes and Migeon (1966) have summarized information about some biochemical disorders. Retardates with these disorders constitute a small proportion of the total population of retardates, but any successful treatment is helpful in reducing their numbers. The prevention of retardation in phenylketonurics is an encouraging example. Much research is being done on treatments that utilize enzyme replacement or biochemical activators designed to improve brain function.

Research papers in the field of behavior modification of the mentally retarded are reported by Thompson and Grabowski, eds. (1972). Their book includes papers on background and principles, illustrative programs, implementation, and special applications. Behaviors were modified by selecting a single goal (for example, establishing speech) and then proceeding towards this goal in very small programmed steps (a patient looked at the staff, then imitated mouth movements, then made sounds, and so on). Each appropriate response was reinforced, usually with food. Inappropriate behaviors were extinguished by nonreinforcement.

Genetic counseling will differ with the type of problem faced by particular parents. For those parents with a child retarded because of some specific genetic syndrome, the risk figures can be given according to the type of inheritance; if recessive, the risk of a repetition is 25 percent; if dominant, the risk of a repetition is 50 percent; if X-linked, the risk is 50 percent for males; if a chromosome anomaly, the risk usually increases with the increasing age of the mother (unless a translocated chromosome is involved).

When the child has an undifferentiated type of retardation, empiric risk figures are about 5.7 percent for a repetition. The risk of having a retarded child for normal couples with no retarded siblings of their own is about 0.5 percent. If one parent has a retarded sibling, the risk is increased to about 2.5 percent (Reed and Reed 1965).

The risk of having a retarded child is much greater if one or both parents are themselves retarded. If only one parent is retarded, the risk is about 12 percent. If both parents are retarded, the risk rises to about 40 percent. The IQs of the children of retardates regress toward the mean and hence tend to average somewhat higher than the IQ scores of the parents. Contrary to common opinion, retardates do not reproduce more than normals. Many retardates do not reproduce at all. However, when they do have large families, they are unable to cope with them and hence come to the attention of social agencies. See Reed and Reed (1965) for data on the reproductive rate and kinds of children produced by 2,156 retardates. Reproducing retardates (about 2 percent of the population) supply about 17 percent of the retardates for the next generation (E. W. Reed 1971).

Aside from the genetic risks, retardates function better if they do not have children. Some of the children born to these parents may have IQs above 70, but it is possible that these nonretarded children may suffer more damage from their parental environment than their retarded siblings. Retardates should not be denied the means to control their own reproduction.

2. *Childhood psychoses.* Only in recent years have mental disorders in children been recognized. The genetic aspects of some of these are only now coming to be known. The mental disorders considered here are not the more severe behavioral aspects of other anomalies but are unaccompanied by any overt physical defects.

Aug and Ables (1971) outlined a clinician's guide to the childhood psychoses which is very helpful in differentiating the behavioral signs at different ages. They defined childhood psychoses as a heterogeneous group of clinical syndromes, with onset any time from birth to eleven years, which present severe disturbances in the following key areas: relationship to the social environment; sense of personal identity, affect and its expression; use of speech for social communication; and total integration and organization of personality. The incidence is much less in children than in adults, 2.1 as against 9 per 10,000 reported, 4 as against 7.5 per 10,000 treated. For behavioral disturbances requiring psychiatric treatment, the psychoses of childhood comprise about 10 to 24 per 100 cases. Two to four times as many males as females are affected. For a detailed description of childhood psychoses and an extensive bibliography, see Hingtgen and Bryson (1972).

Aug and Ables (1971) classified these psychoses as, first, early infantile autism, a rare disorder which begins in the first six months of life and is characterized by a total absence of social contact or relatedness and an obsessive insistence on sameness. Second is the symbiotic psychosis, a disorder in which a good social rapport is broken at two, three, or four years, usually precipitated by separation from mother, birth of a sibling, or other trauma. The child then exhibits autistic symptoms. Third, childhood schizophrenia with unusual motor behaviors, thought disorders, disturbances in perception, lack of affect, poor contact even with the inanimate environment, impairment of speech (mute or singsong or private language), overreaction to stimuli, and a lack of genuine play. The authors regarded those symptoms as severe disturbances in ego development.

Szurek and Berlin (1956) reported on the results of treatment of one hundred cases of psychotic children. Of the one hundred, nine became well or were much improved. The rest had varying degrees of response with some being hospitalized. They reported that the greater the integration of the child and the younger and better adjusted the parents, the better the prognosis.

Bakwin and Bakwin (1958) described the symptoms of schizophrenic children and pointed out that such children are often mistaken for retardates. The primary symptom is withdrawal from the realities of everyday living. Many had physical complaints and quite a few were considered deaf. The child has extreme compulsions and anxieties. Some may be precocious, brilliant, and overactive. The parents are likely to feel guilt, rejection, and hostility. The results of the treatment depend on the severity of the disorder.

There is a continuous search for biochemical indications, which was prompted originally by the discovery that LSD could produce symptoms like schizophrenia in normal people. Until the psychoses can be separated into clear diagnostic categories, the genetic prognosis must rest on empiric risk data. Extensive studies on twins, siblings, parents and children, and adopted children of schizophrenic parents indicate that there is a genetic component in such disorders. Estimates of risks are dependent on the diagnosis. For schizophrenia, with an incidence of about 2 in 100, the risk of normal parents having a child who will become schizophrenic at some time in the future is somewhat less than 2 percent. However, a schizophrenic parent's risk of having a child affected at some future time is about 15 percent if the mother is the one affected and about 5 percent if the father is schizophrenic (S. C. Reed 1971). The risk of a child of two schizophrenics becoming schizophrenic is about 40 percent.

Heston (1966) followed a sample of forty-seven children who were removed from their mothers at age three days and reared in foster homes. They were matched with a control sample of similar children from nonschizophrenic mothers who were also adopted. The age range for both samples was twenty to fifty. None of the forty-seven controls became schizophrenic, but five of the children reared apart from their schizophrenic mothers developed the disorder. Current research indicates that many genes are involved in the development of mental disorders. For a comprehensive study of the genetics of mental disorders, see Reed et al. (1973).

Summary

1. This chapter describes several kinds of genetic anomalies in children in terms of diagnosis, treatment, genetic risk, and behavioral problems. A brief description of genetic ratios, calculations of risk, and meth-

ods of research is followed by a consideration of the different sorts of medical and social problems posed by different types of genetic disorders.

2. Severe genetic anomalies with early death pose more problems for parental adjustment in regard to genetic risk, guilt feelings, and planning for future children than they do for the patient. However, the patient will exhibit behavioral disorders peculiar to his particular disease. Lesch-Nyhan syndrome and Tay-Sach's disease are the examples discussed.

3. Down's syndrome presents a different picture, that of a disorder not greatly ameliorated by treatment but with fairly good life expectancy. The whole constellation of symptoms, physical and behavioral, are related to the presence of a single, extra autosomal chromosome. The mental retardation and good life expectancy combine to make severe problems for family members and for society, since eventually many patients are institutionalized.

4. Treatable genetic anomalies with recurrent severe episodes requiring expensive hospital care not only carry with them the behavioral disorders associated with their particular biochemistry but a host of others related to the adjustment of the patients and their relatives to their illness. Individuals with hemophilia, cystic fibrosis, sickle cell anemia, diabetes, and epilepsy have many personal problems in adjusting to their disease and in attempting to make plans for their future occupations and family lives.

5. Turner's and Klinefelter's syndromes are the results of unusual conditions in the sex chromosome complement. The Turner's patients, who are females, usually lack one X chromosome. The Klinefelter's patients, who are males, usually have an extra X chromosome. Some of the symptoms in these two disorders can be alleviated by hormone therapy, but some behavioral difficulties remain, both in the physical reaction to the abnormal chromosome setup and in the patients' reactions to their situations.

6. Another genetic anomaly, phenylketonuria, is not connected with the presence or absence of sex chromosomes but with an enzyme deficiency caused by a pair of recessive genes. In this case, the chief behavioral symptom, mental retardation, can be prevented by very early dietary restriction, although other abnormal behavior patterns may remain. Here the rigid dietary restrictions make many problems for the family, the school, and the child.

7. Congenital sense deprivation—blindness and deafness—are not yet treatable by chemical means. Here the procedures of correct management and teaching are of prime importance. Needless to say, affected children and their families will have difficulties in adjusting to their situation.

8. Genetic anomalies which are primarily behavioral in nature, some

forms of mental retardation and childhood psychoses, present many problems and challenges to teachers, psychologists, and biochemists. Their etiology and treatment are even less well defined than the other genetic anomalies discussed.

Conclusions

The diverse array of genetic anomalies described in this chapter is only a small sample of the varied conditions which have some genetic etiology. Genetics is a frontier with vast areas of needed research; many new genetic anomalies are discovered every year, and many of these have important behavioral aspects.

The behavioral problems associated with genetic disorders are one of the least explored areas but one of the most promising for future research. Not only are many genetic disorders expressed at a behavioral level, but, when one considers the physical and mental handicaps imposed by many genetic anomalies and the problems connected with the proper care and treatment of the children, it is no wonder that there are many behavioral problems associated with these disorders.

H. Harris (1971) in his book on biochemical genetics concluded that, to date, social and medical applications of genetic research lie chiefly in the modification and control of the environment. From a developmental point of view, amelioration and even prevention of the often disastrous outcomes of genetic disorders must be sought in the environmental modification at proper times in the developmental sequence. Very little human research has yet been directed toward these issues.

Annotated Reading List

Bartalos, Mihaly and Baramki, Theodore A. *Medical Cytogenetics.* Williams and Wilkins Company. Baltimore. 1967.
   This book will be of interest to those wanting more information about human chromosomes, chromosome anomalies in sexual development, and autosomal chromosome disorders such as Down's syndrome.
Barnett, Henry L., ed. *Pediatrics.* Appleton-Century-Crofts. New York. 1968.
   A standard medical school textbook covering childhood disorders.
Cornblath, Marvin and Schwartz, Robert. Disorders of carbohydrate metabolism in infancy. Vol. 3 in the series *Major Problems in Clinical Pediatrics.* W. B. Saunders Co. Philadelphia. 1966.
   This book includes material on hereditary metabolic disorders.
Hamerton, John L. *Human Cytogenetics.* Vol. 2. Academic Press, N. Y. 1971.
   A second reference with a great deal of information on chromosomal disorders.
Harris, Harry. *The Principles of Human Biochemical Genetics.* American Elsevier Publishing Company, Inc. N. Y. 1971.
   This book will be of interest to those interested in biochemistry and in the

author's observations on the environment and the expression of genetic anomalies.

Hsia, David Yi-Yung. *Inborn Errors of Metabolism*. Second Edition. Part 1. Year Book Medical Publishers, Inc. Chicago. 1966.

This book covers the clinical aspects of inborn errors, together with a chapter on biochemical variations in normal humans.

Lynch, Henry T. *Dynamic Genetic Counseling for Clinicians*. Charles C Thomas Publishers. Springfield. 1969.

This book covers many aspects of genetic counseling and includes many rare disorders.

McConnell, R. B. *The Genetics of Gastro-Intestinal Disorders*. Oxford University Press. Oxford. 1966.

The material is organized according to the structures involved, starting with the mouth and continuing to the intestinal tract. A large bibliography is provided.

McKusick, Victor A. *Mendelian Inheritance in Man*. Catalogues of autosomal dominant, autosomal recessive, and X-linked phenotypes. Third Edition. The Johns Hopkins Press. Baltimore. 1971.

A comprehensive computer printout of the most recent information in the literature.

Nelson, Waldo E., Vaughan, Victor C. III, and McKay, R. James, eds. *Textbook of Pediatrics*. W. B. Saunders Co. Philadelphia. 1969.

Both the Nelson and Barnett books offer a wealth of information and many bibliographical references on the physical and mental disorders of children.

Pratt, R. T. C. *The Genetics of Neurological Disorders*. Oxford University Press. Oxford. 1967.

Half of the book is a description of the disorders and half is a bibliography.

Reed, Sheldon C. *Counseling in Medical Genetics*. W. B. Saunders Company. Philadelphia. 1963.

A genetics counseling book which gives information on genetic risks in many common disorders.

Reisman, Leonard E. and Matheny, Adam P. *Genetics and Counseling in Medical Practice*. The C. V. Mosby Company. St. Louis. 1969.

This book includes some basic genetics in its counseling material.

Rimoin, David L. and Schimke, R. Neil. *Genetic Disorders of the Endocrine Glands*. C. V. Mosby Company. St. Louis. 1971.

Comprehensive reference book.

Slater, Eliot and Cowie, Valerie. *The Genetics of Mental Disorders*. Oxford University Press. London. 1971.

This book covers the psychoses, epilepsy, mental subnormality, and the mental disorders associated with chromosome anomalies and neurometabolic disorders.

Stanbury, John B., Wyngaarden, James B., and Frederickson, Donald S., eds. *The Metabolic Basis of Inherited Disease*. McGraw-Hill Book Company. N. Y. 1972.

A comprehensive summary of disorders classified as to kind of chemical disorder. There is an extensive bibliography and an appendix describing methods of coding and filing family records.

Steiner, Mathew M. *Clinical Approach to Endocrine Problems in Children*. C. V. Mosby Company. St. Louis. 1970.

Included here are disorders such as overweight and underweight, tallness and shortness, and anomalies in sexual development, together with a large bibliography.

Talbot, Nathan B., Kagan, Jerome, and Eisenberg, Leon, eds. *Behavioral Science in Pediatric Medicine*. W. B. Saunders. Philadelphia. 1971.

This book has some interesting data and case histories.

Wolman, B., ed. *Manual of Child Psychopathology*. McGraw-Hill. N. Y. 1972.

A comprehensive reference book on etiologic factors, organic, sociogenic and other disorders, and the diagnosis and treatment of children with behavioral disorders.

REFERENCES

Abildgaard, C. F. & Schulman, I. Disorders of hemeostasis. In H. L. Barnett, ed., *Pediatrics*. New York: Appleton-Century-Crofts, 1968.

Agle, D. P. Psychiatric studies of patients with hemophilia and related states. *Archives of Internal Medicine*. 1964, *114*, 76–82.

Anderson, V. E. Personal communication to the writer, 1972.

Anderson, V. E. & Siegel, F. Studies of behavior in genetically defined syndromes in man. In S. G. Vandenberg, ed., *Progress in Human Genetics, Recent Reports on Genetic Syndromes, Twin Studies, and Statistical Advances*. Baltimore: Johns Hopkins Press, 1968, 7–17.

Aug, R. G. & Ables, B. S. A clinician's guide to childhood psychoses. *Pediatrics*, 1971, *47*, 327–338.

Baird, H. W. Chronic or recurrent convulsions. In W. E. Nelson, V. C. Vaughan III, & R. J. McKay, eds. *Textbook of Pediatrics*. Philadelphia: W. B. Saunders, 1969, 1250–1259.

Bakwin, H. & Bakwin, R. M. Schizophrenia in childhood. In H. Bakwin, ed., Symposium on behavior disorders, *Pediatric Clinics of North America*, 1958, *5*, 699–708.

Bartalos, M. & Baramki, T. A. *Medical Cytogenetics*. Baltimore: Williams & Wilkins, 1967.

Bartram, J. B. Mental retardation. In W. E. Nelson, V. C. Vaughan III, & R. J. McKay, eds., *Textbook of Pediatrics*. Philadelphia: W. B. Saunders, 1969, 119–121.

Bergsma, D., ed. Symposium on intrauterine diagnosis. In *Birth Defects: Original Article Series*. National Foundation—March of Dimes. Vol. 7. No. 5. White Plains, New York, 1971.

Berman, P. H., Balis, M. E., & Dancis, J. Congenital hyperuricemia. *Archives of Neurology*, 1969, *20*, 44–53.

Bray, P. F. & Wiser, W. C. Evidence for a genetic etiology of temporal-central abnormalities in focal epilepsy. *The New England Journal of Medicine*, 1964, *271*, 926–933.

Brown, K. S. The genetics of childhood deafness. In F. McConnell and P. H. Ward, eds., *Deafness in Childhood*. Nashville: Vanderbilt University Press, 1967, 177–203.

Browne, W. J., Mally, M. A., & Kane, R. P. Psychosocial aspects of hemophilia: a study of twenty-eight hemophiliac children and their families. *American Journal of Orthopsychiatry*, 1960, *30*, 730–740.

Bruch, H. Obesity. In H. Bakwin, ed., Symposium on behavior disorders. *Pediatric Clinics of North America*, 1958, *5*, 613–627.

Cole, N. J. & Tabaroff, L. H. Psychological problems of the blind child. *American Journal of Orthopsychiatry*, 1955, *25*, 627.

Creak, M. & Stephen, J. M. The psychological aspects of asthma in children. In H. Bakwin, ed., Symposium on behavior disorders. *Pediatric Clinics of North America*. Philadelphia: W. B. Saunders, 1958, *5*, 731–747.

Davis, C. J. In M. H. Goldberg & J. R. Swinton, eds., *Blindness Research: The Expanding Frontiers*. University Park, Penn.: The Pennsylvania State University Press, 1969.

Deamer, W. C. Pediatric allergy: some impressions gained over a 37 year period. *Pediatrics,* 1971, *48,* 930–938.

Denning, C. R., Sommers, Sheldon, C., & Quigley, H. J. Infertility in male patients with cystic fibrosis. *Pediatrics,* 1968, *41,* 7–17.

Deutsch, L. & Wiener, L. L. Epileptic children, emotional problems and treatment. *American Journal of Orthopsychiatry,* 1948, *18,* 65–72.

DiGeorge, A. Disorders of the gonads. In W. E. Nelson, V. C. Vaughan III, & R. J. McKay, eds., *Textbook of Pediatrics,* Philadelphia: W. B. Saunders, 1969, 1127–1128.

Fischer, A. E. & Dolger, H. Behavior and psychologic problems of young diabetic patients. *Archives of Internal Medicine,* 1946, *78,* 711–732.

Forssman, H. & Hambert, G. Incidence of Klinefelter's syndrome among mental patients. *The Lancet,* no. 7284, vol I., 1963, 1327–1328.

Fraser, G. R. & Friedmann, A. I. *The Causes of Blindness in Childhood.* Baltimore: The Johns Hopkins Press, 1967.

Friedmann, T. Prenatal diagnosis of genetic disease. *Scientific American,* 1971, *225,* 34–42.

Grand, R. J., Talamo, R. C., de Sant'Agnese, P. A., & Schwartz, R. H. Pregnancy in cystic fibrosis of the pancreas. *The Journal of the American Medical Association,* 1966, *195,* 993–1000.

Grossman, F. K. Brothers and sisters of retarded children. *Psychology Today,* 1972, *5,* 82–84, 102–104.

Harris, H. *The Principles of Human Biochemical Genetics.* New York: American Elsevier Pub. Co., 1971.

Harris, M., ed. *Early Diagnosis of Human Genetic Defects: Scientific and Ethical Considerations.* HEW Pub. No. (NIH) 72–25, 1971.

Heston, L. L. Pediatric disorders in foster-home-reared children of schizophrenics. *British Journal of Psychiatry,* 1966, *112,* 819–825.

Hingtgen, J. N. & Bryson, C. Q. Recent developments in the study of early childhood psychoses: infantile autism, childhood schizophrenia, and related disorders. *Schizophrenia Bulletin.* National Institute of Mental Health. Rockville, Md., 1972, *5,* 8–54.

Hoefnagel, D. E., Andrew, D. E., Mireault, N. G., & Berndt, W. O. Hereditary choreoathetosis, self-mutilation and hyperuricemia in young males. *The New England Journal of Medicine,* 1965, *273,* 30–135.

Hook, E. B. Behavioral implications of the human XYY genotype. *Science,* 1973, *179,* 131–150.

Howell, R. R. & Stevenson, R. E. The offspring of phenylketonuric women. *Social Biology Supplement,* 1971, *18,* S19–S29.

Hsia, D. Y-Yung. *Inborn Errors of Metabolism.* Part I. Clinical aspects. 2d ed. Chicago: Year Book Medical Pub., 1966, 326.

Kallmann, F. J. Main findings and some projections. In J. D. Rainer, K. Z. Altshuler, & F. J. Kallmann, eds., *Family and Mental Health Problems in a Deaf Population.* Department of Medical Genetics, New York State Psychiatric Institute. New York: Columbia University, 1963, 234–248.

Kanof, A., Kutner, B., & Gordon, N. B. The impact of infantile amaurotic familial idiocy (Tay-Sach's disease) on the family. *Pediatrics,* 1962, *29,* 37–45.

Kaplan, E., Shwachman, H., Perlmutter, A. D., Rule, A., Khaw, Kon-Taik, & Holsclaw, D. S. Reproductive failure in males with cystic fibrosis. *The New England Journal of Medicine,* 1968, *279,* 65–69.

Keleske, L., Solomons, G., & Opitz, E. Parental reactions to phenylketonuria in the family. *The Journal of Pediatrics,* 1967, *70,* 793–798.

Keller, H. *The Story of My Life.* Garden City, New York: Doubleday, 1954.

Lappe, M., Gustafson, J. M., & Roblin, R. Ethical and social issues in screening for genetic disease. *The New England Journal of Medicine,* 1972, *286,* 1129–1132.

Massie, R. K. *Nicholas and Alexandra.* New York: Dell, 1967.

Mattsson, A. Long-term physical illness in childhood: a challenge to psychosocial adaptation. *Pediatrics,* 1972, *50,* 801–811.

Mayer, J. Some aspects of the problem of the regulation of food intake and obesity. *The New England Journal of Medicine,* 1966, *274,* 662–673.

McCollum, A. T. & Gibson, L. E. Family adaptation to the child with cystic fibrosis. *The Journal of Pediatrics,* 1970, *77,* 571–578.

McKusick, V. A. *Mendelian inheritance in man.* Catalogues of Autosomal Dominant, Autosomal Recessive and X-linked Phenotypes. Third Edition. Baltimore: The Johns Hopkins Press, 1971.

Menkes, J. H. & Migeon, B. R. Biochemical and genetic aspects of mental retardation. *Annual Review of Medicine,* 1966, *17,* 1–11.

Michener, W. M. Hyperuricemia and mental retardation. *American Journal of Diseases of Children,* 1967, *113,* 195–206.

Milunsky, A., Littlefield, J. W., Kanfer, J. N., Kolodny, E. H., Shih, V. E., & Atkins, L. Prenatal genetic diagnosis. *The New England Journal of Medicine,* 1970, *283,* 1502.

Money, J. & Mittenthal, S. Lack of personality pathology in Turner's syndrome: relation to cytogenetics, hormones and physique. *Behavior Genetics,* 1970, *1,* 43–56.

Myklebust, H. R. *The Psychology of Deafness.* New York: Grune & Stratton, 1964.

Nelson, W. E. Diabetes mellitus. In W. E. Nelson, V. C. Vaughan III & R. J. McKay, eds., *Textbook of Pediatrics.* Philadelphia: W. B. Saunders, 1969, 449–450.

Nielsen, J. Klinefelter's syndrome and the XYY syndrome. *Acta Psychiatrica Scandinavica.* Supp. 209. Munksgaard. Copenhagen, 1969.

Nyhan, W. L. Anomalies of amino acid, purine and pyrimidine metabolism. In H. L. Barnett, ed., *Pediatrics,* New York: Appleton-Century-Crofts, 1968, 411–424.

Oppenheimer, E. H. & Esterly, J. R. Observations on cystic fibrosis of the pancreas. VI. The uterine cervix. *The Journal of Pediatrics,* 1970, *77,* 991–995.

Pearson, H. A. & Diamond, L. K. The critically ill child: sickle cell disease crises and their management. *Pediatrics,* 1971, *48,* 629–635.

Price, W. H. & Whatmore, P. B. Criminal behavior and the XYY male. *Nature,* 1967, *213,* 815.

Randolph, T. G. Allergy as a causative factor of fatigue, irritability and behavior problems of children. *The Journal of Pediatrics,* 1947, *31,* 560–572.

Rainer, J. D., Altshuler, K. Z., & Kallmann, F. J., eds. *Family and Mental Health Problems in a Deaf Population.* Department of Medical Genetics, New York State Psychiatric Institute. New York: Columbia University, 1963.

Reed, E. W. Mental retardation and fertility. *Social Biology Supplement,* 1971, *18,* S42–S49.

Reed, E. W. & Reed, S. C. *Mental Retardation: A Family Study.* Philadelphia: W. B. Saunders, Co., 1965.

Reed, S. C. *Counseling in Medical Genetics.* Philadelphia: W. B. Saunders, 1963.

————. Mental illness and reproduction. *Social Biology,* Supplement 18, 1971, S95–S102.

Reed, S. C., Hartley, C., Anderson, V. E., Phillips, V. P., & Johnson, N. *The Psychoses: Family Studies.* Philadelphia: W. B. Saunders, 1973.

Richardson, S. A. Some social psychological consequences of handicapping. *Pediatrics,* 1963, *32,* 291–297.

Rimoin, D. L. & Schimke, R. N. *Genetic Disorders of the Endocrine Glands.* St. Louis: C. V. Mosby, 1971.

Sank, D. Genetic aspects of early total deafness. In J. D. Rainer, K. Z. Altshuler, & F. J. Kallmann, eds., *Family and Mental Health Problems in a Deaf Population.* Department of Medical Genetics. New York: New York State Psychiatric Institute, Columbia University, 1963, 28–81.

Scherzer, A. L. & Ilson, J. B. Normal intelligence in the Lesch-Nyhan syndrome. *Pediatrics,* 1969, *44,* 116–119.

Shirley, H. F. *Pediatric Psychiatry.* Cambridge, Mass.: Harvard University Press, 1963, 498–537.

Shwachman, H., Kulczycki, L. L., & Khaw, Kon-Taik. Studies in cystic fibrosis. *Pediatrics,* 1965, *36,* 689–699.

Shwachman, H., Redmond, A., & Khaw, Kon-Taik. Studies in cystic fibrosis. Report of 130 patients diagnosed under 3 months of age over a 20 year period. *Pediatrics,* 1970, *46,* 335–343.

Sibinga, M. S. & Friedman, C. J. Complexities of parental understanding of phenylketonuria. *Pediatrics,* 1971, *48,* 216–224.

Siegel, F. S., Balow, B., Fisch, R. O., & Anderson, V. E. School behavior profile ratings of phenylketonuric children. *American Journal of Mental Deficiency,* 1968, *72,* 937–943.

Slater, E. & Cowie, V. *The Genetics of Mental Disorders.* London: Oxford University Press, 1971, 160–184.

Smith, G. M. L., ed. *The Psychiatric Problem of Deaf Children and Adolescents.* The National Deaf Children's Society. Report of a conference at British Medical Association House. London, 1963.

Sussman, M. B. Family structure, parent-child relationships disability. In M. H. Goldberg & J. R. Swinton, eds., *Blindness Research: The Expanding Frontiers.* University Park, Penn.: The Pennsylvania State University Press, 1969, 36–53.

Szurek, S. A. & Berlin, I. N. Elements of psychotherapeutics with the schizophrenic child and his parents. *Psychiatry,* 1956, *19,* 1–19.

Talbot, N. B. & Howell, M. C. Social and behavioral consequences of disease among children. In N. B. Talbot, J. Kagan, & L. Eisenberg, eds., *Behavioral Science in Pediatric Medicine.* Philadelphia: W. B. Saunders, 1971, 1–89.

Thompson, T. & Grabowski, J., eds. *Behavior Modification of the Mentally Retarded.* New York: Oxford University Press, 1972.

Weil, W. B., Jr. Diabetes mellitus in children. In H. Barnett, ed., *Pediatrics.* New York: Appleton-Century-Crofts, 1968, 433–447.

Witschi, E. Overripeness of the egg as a possible cause in mental and physical disorders. In I. I. Gottesman & L. Erlenmeyer-Kimling, eds., Differential reproduction in individuals with mental and physical disorders. *Social Biology Supplement,* 1971, *18,* S9–S15.

World Health Organization Technical Report Series No. 497. Genetic disorders: prevention, treatment and rehabilitation. World Health Organization. Geneva, 1972.

3 The Development of Behavioral Competence in Infancy

TINA APPLETON
RACHEL CLIFTON
SUSAN GOLDBERG
University of Massachusetts

INTRODUCTION

THE PURPOSE of this chapter is to review the literature related to the development of infant abilities or skills in order to highlight recent research in this area. There have been several recent reviews devoted to specific infant skills such as perception (Spears and Hohle 1967) and learning (Sameroff, 1972). Such reviews have dealt with specific topics and were primarily addressed to research psychologists. In this review we have attempted to bring together research findings on behavioral competence within a developmental framework and to relate some of these findings in nontechnical terms to applied aspects of infant care. Most of the basic research on infant development has been conceived within the framework of "pure" research. For the most part, the investigators did not plan their research in order to answer practical, immediate questions. However, by making this basic information available to a broad audience, including persons who are responsible for constructing environments and caring for very young children, we hope that the knowledge of developing skills in infancy can be integrated into practical settings.

This review is selective rather than comprehensive; the abundance of research studies on human infants makes it impossible to include many important studies. With rare exceptions, research in progress, but as yet unpublished, is not included here, nor is research pertaining to the enormously important area of social and emotional development. (These aspects of development are discussed in chapter 1 in volume 3 of this series [Ainsworth 1973]). An annotated list of reviews of the literature on infant development will be found in the annotated reading list at the end of this chapter.

In the present chapter, the weight given to various periods of infancy reflects the amount of research available in a particular area rather than our judgment that one period is more important than another. For example, the newborn has received the lion's share of attention, probably because hospital newborns are more readily available for study than are older infants. In contrast, relatively little information is available on development in the second year of life, and this gap is reflected in this review.

There are many different ways to organize our current knowledge about infant development. In this chapter we have chosen to start with a description of specific abilities—auditory, language, visual, sensorimotor, and cognitive skills. Audition and vision are included as the most important perceptual skills and the basis for more complex skills which develop later. Since language is highly dependent upon auditory skills, the section on preverbal communication and language reception follows that on audition. The major developments in visual sensory abilities appear to occur in the first few months of life. Thereafter, the most important aspect of visual development is the coordination of vision with other senses and with motor skills, which leads to the consideration of sensorimotor development. The sections that follow, on sensorimotor and cognitive development, are closely connected. Inclusion of data into one of these sections rather than the other is at times somewhat arbitrary, because many early abilities have both sensorimotor and cognitive elements. In the discussion of sensorimotor development, we have chosen to emphasize the views of Piaget, including his cognitive framework, since this has been the orientation of many recent studies. The section concerned with learning and cognitive development includes both the more traditional learning approach and cognitive skills such as problem-solving and concept formation. Such skills provide an important foundation for later development. In the final section of this chapter, we have made an effort to coordinate some of the research knowledge reviewed and to formulate some general principles of caring for infants which are geared to the course of development. The need to advise parents and professionals working with infants, and the increasing interest in the development of day-care facilities for infants suggest the importance of applying basic knowledge to practical situations.

The fact that a chapter is being written about the "competence" of infants reflects a significant change in our view of the infant. During the first half of the twentieth century, the "infant" was generally considered to be a passive organism who was the object of forces which determined development: maturational forces (Gesell 1928; McGraw 1943); psychosexual drives (Freud 1953); or environmental shaping (Watson 1928). During this period, there was extensive research about what infants normally do in the course of development (Bayley 1933; Bühler and Hetzer 1935; Gesell 1928; Shirley 1931, 1933). These studies helped to chart the normal developmental sequence, but they did not experimentally analyze what infants *can* do when provided with appropriate opportunities. Aside from numerous studies of neonatal behavior (see Pratt 1954), experimental work with infants was limited. Although the importance of the opening years was recognized, many of the theoretical constructs about infant development were based upon clinical interviews with adults concerning their childhood and on parents' retrospective accounts of infant-care practices.

In the last fifteen years there has been an explosion of infant research of all kinds, and our knowledge continues to expand at a rapid rate. Recently developed methods and equipment have enabled us to test some of the limits of infant capacities, permitting a remarkably different view of the infant to emerge. In comparison with the "theoretically constructed" infant who was passive, helpless, and shaped primarily by experience (Kessen 1963), the "real world" infant has come to be viewed as skilled, active, and socially influential. In short, he or she is competent.

What is meant by "competence" in infants? According to the dictionary, competence is synonymous with "capability, capacity, efficiency, proficiency, skill." Several authors (Chomsky 1957; Flavell and Wohlwill 1969) have stressed the importance of distinguishing between competence and performance. This distinction is made to emphasize that competence in any domain is *inferred* from behavior. Failure to perform on any specific occasion does not necessarily imply lack of competence. An assessment of competence can be no better than the demands of the tasks on which the estimate is based (Fowler 1971).

The more recent intensive investigation of behavioral competence in infancy has focused on mapping out the limits of the infant's basic abilities as they develop. From the sometimes separate literatures of cognitive psychology and learning psychology, a compelling and fascinating picture of infant development is emerging. The full appreciation of developing infant competence should eventually have profound effects on the practical issues of infant care. This chapter is intended as a beginning contribution toward this long-term goal.

INFANT ABILITIES

The way the infant experiences the world is initially determined by the capabilities of his or her sense organs. Auditory and visual systems function at birth and mature rapidly. However, the environment does play an important role in early perceptual development. For example, studies of the effects of visual deprivation in animals have indicated that environmental sensory input is necessary for maintenance of existing systems and the development of new ones (Riesen 1961). Without light, the neural connections between the eye and the brain that are present at birth will not be maintained. We know that children who have little or no sound experience because of deafness will not learn to speak unless given special training.

In addition, the competence of the older child in manipulating and comprehending the environment is probably based on interactions with the environment which are dependent upon processing sensory information. Through development of perceptual and sensorimotor abilities the infant can learn about his or her surroundings and can develop a practical understanding of reality. Early learning of skills and expectations appears to contribute to further learning and development.

This section is organized so that the basic perceptual functions (audition and vision) are discussed first and lead into discussion of more complex abilities which are dependent upon them (language reception, sensorimotor and cognitive skills). Although in each section there is mention of the behavior of newborns and later development, this organization roughly parallels the course of infant development, in which basic perceptual abilities through experience come to serve more complex behavior systems.

Auditory Competence

1. *Maturation of the auditory system.* The anatomical development of the auditory receptor system is virtually complete before the end of gestation, enabling the infant to hear even while *in utero*. Fetuses as young as seven months gestational age show heart-rate acceleration in response to auditory stimuli (Bernard and Sontag 1947). Myelinization of the auditory nerve is well advanced at the time of birth in comparison to myelin deposition in other cranial nerves, indicating rapid conduction of acoustic information to the cortex (Peiper 1963). However, the immature state of the auditory cortex and lack of EEG synchronization between the two hemispheres suggests that integration of sound from the two ears may be limited during the early months (Conel 1952; Dreyfus-Brisac 1966).

Hearing acuity also improves during the first few months of life. At the time of birth, the middle ear is filled with fluid and remnant tissue, resulting in inefficient conduction of sound vibration. Much of this material disappears within a few days and is completely reabsorbed by the end of several months (Spears and Hohle 1967).

2. *Auditory abilities.* The earliest research on audition during infancy related to the question of whether the newborn could hear. Subsequent research has concentrated on questions about the aspects of sound stimulation that can be discriminated by the infant. The initial research did establish the fact that the newborn does respond to sound (see Pratt 1954 for a review of these studies). Table 1 contains selected recent references on

TABLE 1. AUDITORY COMPETENCE

Age	Auditory Skills	Effects of Sound
Fetal		Heart-rate acceleration to auditory stimuli at 7 months (Bernard & Sontag 1947)
Newborn	Responds differentially to stimuli varying in duration (Clifton, Graham, & Hatton 1968; Stubbs 1934)	Soothed by low frequency sounds (Birns et al. 1965; Bench 1969) and continuous or rhythmic sounds (Brackbill et al. 1966; Salk 1962; Weiss 1934)
	Can discriminate sounds varying in intensity; heart-rate change present to low intensity tones (40–55 db), suggesting that most speech is audible (Bartoshuk 1964; Eisenberg 1965; Steinschneider, Lipton, & Richmond 1966)	More sensitive to complex sounds than pure tones (Eisenberg 1965; Hutt et al. 1968; Hoversten & Moncur 1969)
	Can localize sound soon after birth (Hammond 1970; Leventhal & Lipsitt 1964; Wertheimer 1961)	Startle to sudden onset of sounds (Peiper 1963)
	Response thresholds measured at 62.8 db using respiration as the response (Suzuki, Kumiyo, & Kuichi 1964), and 105 db using eye-blink as the response (Wedenberg, 1956)	Gradual onset of moderately intense (75 db) tones eliminated heart-rate acceleration typically given to sudden onset sounds (Jackson, Kantowitz, & Graham 1971)
To 2 months		Can alert infant to visually attend (Culp 1971; Self 1971)
3–6 months	Sharp decrease in auditory threshold between 3 and 8 months (Hoversten & Moncur 1969)	Elicits head-turn in direction of sound when object making sound is out of sight (Bayley 1969; Cattell 1940)
6–9 months		
9–12 months	Can use sound to direct manual search for object (Freedman et al. 1969)	
12–18 months		

the newborn's differential response to sounds varying in intensity, duration, and localization. Newborn infants show reliable changes in heart-rate acceleration when presented with a loud tone (85 db) and a milder acceleration with softer tones (70 db) (Steinschneider, Lipton, and Richmond 1966). The effect of stimulus duration is dependent upon the intensity of the sound presented; the lower the stimulus intensity, the longer a stimulus must be presented in order to elicit an equivalent response from the infant (Clifton, Graham, and Hatton 1968; Stubbs 1934). Several studies have indicated that neonates can localize sound (see table 2). Although one study reported no localization until six months of age (Chun, Pawset, and Forster 1960), test norms suggest that infants four to five months old will turn toward the sound of a bell or rattle out of view (Cattell 1940; Bayley 1969). Present evidence indicates that not until late in the first year does the infant manually search for an object he has seen and heard, when only a sound indicates its presence (Freedman, Fox-Kolenda, Margileth, and Miller 1969).

As the infant develops, auditory threshold sharply decreases (see table 1). Fluid trapped in the middle ear during the first two weeks following birth may contribute to an initially high threshold. The particular threshold level reported by various investigators has varied greatly according to the response measured, the background-noise level, frequency of sound stimulus, and other variables. For example, neonatal heart rate and respiration changes have been elicited by low intensity tones in the 40–65 db range, while eyeblinks required high intensity stimuli (105 db). At three months the infant's threshold is 43 db above that of the adult, and by eight months this difference is reduced to 34 db (see table 1 for specific references). In making these comparisons, one should remember that whereas adults can be instructed to report the occurrence of a sound, we can never be sure that infants do not hear even when no response is observed.

3. *Effects of sound upon the infant.* Infants respond to sounds in at least three different ways. They are soothed by them, are alert to them, or are distressed by them. Low-frequency sounds and continuous or rhythmic stimulation have been found to be particularly soothing to infants (see table 1). Many kinds of continuous stimulation have been associated with a reduction in arousal level and inhibition of crying. Although Salk (1962) reported that mother's heartbeat was particularly effective in this respect, subsequent research has not substantiated this finding. Tape-recorded heartbeats, a metronome, and a lullaby have all been found to be more soothing than silence, but these stimuli did not differ from one another in effectiveness (Brackbill, Adams, Crowell, and Gray, 1966).

Various characteristics of auditory stimulation are especially successful in capturing the infant's attention. Frequency and band-width are important in this respect. The adult human ear can perceive frequencies from 20 to 20,000 Hz, but is most sensitive to sounds in the 1,000–3,000 Hz range (Keele and Neil 1965, p. 319). Frequencies between 1,000 Hz and 3,000 Hz are also the most important in speech perception (Keele and Neil 1965, p. 319). Infants are most responsive to sounds within this range and less sensitive to sounds greater than 4,000 Hz (Eisenberg 1965; Hoversten and Moncur 1969). Complex sounds of wide band-width (wide range of frequency), compared to pure sine waves, elicit greater responsivity in both newborns (Hutt, Hutt, Lenard, Von Bernuth, and Muntjewerff 1968) and older infants between three and eight months (Hoversten and Moncur 1969). There are almost no studies of older infants which observe responsiveness to more complex nonlanguage auditory stimuli. A single exception has demonstrated that the addition of music can re-recruit infant visual attending behavior at five and six weeks of age (Self 1971).

Some auditory stimuli are distressing to the newborn. High frequency pure tones (over 4000 Hz) and very low frequency square waves (70 Hz) appear to have this effect (Haller 1932; Hutt, Von Bernuth, Lenard, Hutt, and Prechtl 1968). It has been hypothesized that the immaturity of the basilar membrane in newborns may account for this finding (Hutt et al. 1968). In addition, particularly loud or sudden sounds produce a startle defensive reaction in the infant (Peiper 1963). Cardiac acceleration has been interpreted in terms of a startle or defense reflex to sound stimuli with sudden onsets (Graham and Jackson 1970). Even moderately loud sounds (75 db) elicit cardiac acceleration in newborns when the tone is produced with a sudden stimulus onset (Graham, Clifton, and Hatton 1968) while the same intensity tone with a gradual onset does not have this effect (Jackson, Kantowitz, and Graham 1971).

From the wealth of studies on newborns, a data base for the infant's initial auditory behavior has emerged. However, an apparent lack of interest in the older infant's auditory abilities has resulted in a paucity of information regarding subsequent auditory development. This lack of research on older subjects may be partly due to the common dichotomous characterization of auditory competence as "deaf" or "not deaf." Contrary to this view, auditory competence involves the ability to code and organize acoustic information, and goes far beyond the capacity simply to respond to sound (Eisenberg 1971). Communication disorders seen in school-age children might be detected earlier if normative data on complex auditory skills were available. We know very little about how normal hearing develops. Unexplored developmental competencies in auditory behavior include the ability to detect signals from a noisy background, the ability to integrate information coming into different ears, the ability to detect changes in complex acoustic patterns, and the ability to coordinate across different sensory modalities such as auditory and visual. Basic research is needed on how these abilities develop in normally hearing children and how the failure to develop such abilities may impair later competencies.

Summary. We can cite the following about auditory competence in infants.

1. The infant has fairly well-developed auditory skills at birth or soon after.

2. There is growing evidence that the infant can make a wide variety of discriminations of auditory signals (e.g., intensity, duration, location) in the first few weeks of life.

3. Certain types of auditory stimulation appear to be soothing (low frequency tones, continuous or rhythmic sounds), while other types are distressing (frequencies over 4,000 cps, loud or sudden sounds).

4. There is almost no information about the normal development of more complex auditory skills during infancy.

Preverbal Communication and Language Reception

The study of language acquisition has generally been concerned with speech production. Early theories were based on the assumption that language acquisition could be understood as a special case of learning. The infant's initial sounds were gradually shaped into speech sounds and acquired meaning by association. Within this framework normative studies attempted to determine the age at which specific sounds and words occurred (see McCarthy 1954; Palermo 1970; Rebelsky, Luria, and Starr 1967).

In the 1960s the focus of research shifted to the grammar of young children. Samples of early speech were collected for the purpose of inferring their grammatical structure (see McNeill 1970; also chapter 5 below). Since this approach was not suitable for the study of preverbal infants, the precursors of speech, the listening experience, and the language comprehension of young infants received little attention (Friedlander 1970).

Standardized infant tests are also oriented toward assessing language production rather than reception. Of 126 language items from infant tests included in a summary table by McCarthy (1954), only 42 were concerned with listening behavior or comprehension. Yet in the first two years infants must listen to speech far more often than they produce it. "Infancy" literally means (according to its Latin derivation) "the period without language" (McCarthy 1954). What are the preverbal developments that pave the way for speech? To what extent can infants discriminate speech sounds and voices? Are these capacities functional in the newborn and to what extent are they dependent upon maturation and specific experiences?

These are questions asked in current research. The following summary of evidence for special language capacities and structures provides the context for a review of infant language reception.

1. *Evidence for language-specific structures.* Analysis of the nature of language and language acquisition has suggested to some authors that some parts of the human brain must be specially adapted to language functions (Chomsky 1965; Lenneberg 1967; McNeill 1966, 1970). Accumulating neurophysiological data (e.g., Matsumiya, Tagliasco, Lombroso, and Goodglass 1972; Wood, Goff and Day 1971) and studies of aphasia suggest that there are indeed neural structures and mechanisms specialized for language. This review, however, is confined primarily to consideration of the nature of language and speech perception.

Language is species-specific. We are the only species that speaks. Exposure of other animals to human speech does not lead to language learning; but most infants learn to speak, and exposure to human speech does appear to lead to language learning.

Language is species-uniform. Although languages differ, they seem to share important characteristics. All languages use only a limited sample of vocal sounds. We can all make snorting and clapping sounds, but there is no language which makes use of these. All languages depend on word sequences which conform to some rules (grammar). There appears to be no language in which one can generate meaningful utterances by random ordering of words. Although grammars vary among languages, many of the underlying meanings expressed are similar (Lenneberg 1969).

Language acquisition has maturational characteristics. The age at which children engage in sound production and acquire speech is the same regardless of the language being learned (Lenneberg 1967; Slobin 1966). Some aspects of language development are correlated with motor and neurological development. Infants babble at the same age whether they hear or not (Lenneberg 1964). Babbling appears to depend on physiological maturation rather than experience. There may also be an optimal period for language learning. Until puberty, children can learn any language with sufficient exposure and can achieve the fluency of native speakers. After puberty, language learning seems to be more difficult, requires more deliberate training, and rarely approaches the fluency of native speakers (Lenneberg 1967).

Speech perception differs radically from sound perception in general. Experiments with adults, using input to one ear only, indicate that speech signals are comprehended more readily by the left hemisphere of the brain while nonspeech sounds are interpreted primarily by the right hemisphere. We understand speech at extremely rapid rates. If we define a phoneme as the shortest speech segment in which a change produces a change in meaning (e.g., the difference between *lip* and *lap* is accounted for by different middle phonemes), we can follow speech at rates up to thirty phonemes per second (normal speaking rate is about fifteen phonemes per second) but cannot discriminate thirty nonspeech sounds per second (Liberman 1970).

Categorical perception is another unique feature of speech perception. We hear a wide range of sounds as belonging to a single category but cannot discriminate among them. For example, there are pairs of consonants (e.g., *b* and *p*, *v* and *f*) for which the oral cavity is shaped in the same way; the main difference is the timing of sound production (vocal chord vibration). In one member of the pair (*p* or *f* in the above example) vocal chord vibration begins later than for the other pair member. It is possible in artificially produced speech to vary continuously the time when voicing or sound begins. Over a wide range of variation in onset of voicing, one hears *b*. Over another broad range of voice onset times, one hears *p*. We hear either *b* or *p* and nothing in between. This phenomenon, known as categorical perception, is uniquely present for speech sounds. Nonspeech sounds are discriminated on a continuous basis rather than within categorical boundaries (Liberman 1970).

The above evidence supports the notion that the capacity to learn language is part of our genetic endowment. Evidence with respect to the linguistic capacities of preverbal infants is an important addition to the evidence presented above.

2. *Preverbal communication.* Table 2 outlines some of the major developments in early language reception and communication. Long before the infant appears to intentionally influence or control others, the infant can exert control through the signaling quality of his or her behavior (Bell and Ainsworth 1972). At first, cries are the infant's most effective signals. Cries, however, are acoustically quite different from speech sounds (Lenneberg 1964; Tonkova-Yampolskaya 1962). The importance of cries for later speech probably lies in the opportunity to discover that making sounds brings caretaker attention. Four types of newborn cries can be differentiated spectrographically (Wolff 1969). Furthermore, caretakers can identify these types of cries and respond to them differentially. Thus, in the first few months the infant can also learn that different sound patterns bring different results. One study which supports this view followed the course of infant crying over the first year of life in relation to maternal responsiveness to crying (Bell and Ainsworth, 1972). If caretaker responses enable the infant to learn that the vocal mode is an effective way to communicate and that use of different sounds increases its effectiveness, then, the more responsive the caretaker, the more rapidly the infant should learn to use other vocal sounds. Indeed, in the above study, mothers who

were most responsive to cries in the first few months had infants who cried least and had the most effective noncrying communications at nine to twelve months. Mother-infant interaction can be viewed as a communication system that develops between caretaker and infant from birth (Richards 1972). Analysis of mother-infant communication patterns at twelve weeks indicated that these early patterns were predictive of later language competence (Lewis and Freedle 1972). The function of language is to communicate, and some aspects of communication, including the use of sound, probably develop long before an infant learns to speak. Possibly, effective preverbal communicative interaction is a necessary precursor of spoken language.

3. *Early vocalizations.* First vocalizations include a variety of sounds. The repetition of consonant-vowel syllables or babbling (which begins around three to six months), has been studied, although there is no consensus about its role in language development (McCarthy 1954; Lewis 1951; Rebelsky et al. 1967). Babbling is neither necessary nor sufficient for later language. Deaf infants babble but do not learn to speak normally, while children who cannot articulate and do not babble may comprehend complex language (Lenneberg 1967; Fry 1966). While the initial occurrence of babbling does not depend upon auditory experience, continued sound production does.

As the studies listed in table 2 indicate, babbling can be increased and shaped by appropriate reinforcement procedures. Social reinforcement will increase general vocal output of infants (Rheingold, Gewirtz, and Ross 1959) and is more effective in that respect than comparable nonsocial reinforcement (Weisberg 1963). More specifically, reinforcement can selectively increase production of consonant or vowel sounds made by infants (Routh 1969). These studies all used auditory reinforcement, usually the experimenter saying "tsk, tsk, tsk" along with smiling and patting the infant. Although the presence of the adult (visual reinforcement) increases its effectiveness, the human voice alone is an effective reinforcer of babbling (Todd and Palmer 1968). One study indicates, however, that auditory, visual, and tactile reinforcement alone or in combination are equally effective reinforcers of babbling (Schwartz, Rosenberg and Brackbill 1970).

Some of the effective parameters of auditory stimulation have also been explored. At six months it has been found that presentation of vowel sounds was accompanied by reduction of vowel sounds in babbling while presentation of consonant sounds led to reduction in babbled consonants (Webster 1969). In a related study (Dodd 1972) responses of nine- to twelve-month infants to consonant-vowel combinations were compared under three conditions: taped presentation, babbling by the experimenter

TABLE 2. PREVERBAL COMMUNICATION AND LANGUAGE RECEPTION

Age	Preverbal Communication	Early Vocalization	Response to Voices	Phoneme Perception	Word Comprehension
0–3 months	Cries may be interpreted by caretakers and responded to appropriately (Wolff 1969) Maternal responsiveness to cries predicts effectiveness of 9–12 month communication (Bell & Ainsworth 1972)		Upset if voice and appropriate face are not at same location (Aronson & Rosenbloom 1971)	Discrimination of voiced and unvoiced consonants (Trehub & Rabinovitch 1972), categorical perception of "ba-pa" (Eimas et al. 1971)	
3–6 months	Mother-infant communication patterns predict later language competence (Lewis & Freedle 1972)	Babbling (McCarthy 1954), babbling increased by social reinforcement (Rheingold et al. 1959; Schwartz et al. 1970; Todd & Palmer 1968; Weisberg 1963) Selective shaping of babbling (Routh 1969) Presented vowel or consonant sounds decrease production of same type sound (Webster 1969)	Differential smiling to mother and stranger (LaRoche & Tcheng 1963) More quieting to female than male voice (Kagan and Lewis 1965) Distress if sight of mother does not accompany voice (Turnure 1971) Responds differentially to voice of mother and its distortion (Turnure 1971)	Vowels & some initial consonants discriminated (Moffitt 1971; McCaffrey 1971), initial consonant discrimination requires following vowel (Morse 1972) Discrimination of rising and falling intonation (Kaplan 1969; Morse 1972)	

Age			
9–12 months	Social play and babbling increases number and length of utterances containing consonants (Dodd 1972) First words	Differential looking and smiling to voice of mother and stranger (Tulkin 1971)	Girls show increased vocalization to high-meaning passage and decreased vocalization to low-meaning passage (Kagan 1971) Conditioning to words faster than to other sounds (Fradkina 1971)
2d year	Two-word utterances	Differential attention to same voice different inflection (Friedlander 1968)	Differential attention to familiar and unfamiliar vocabulary (Friedlander 1968) Response to simple commands (Bayley 1969; Bühler & Hetzer 1935; Cattell 1940; Frankenberg & Dodd 1967; Gesell & Thompson 1938) Points to and names pictures (Bayley 1969; Cattell 1940; Gesell & Thompson 1938; Griffiths 1954) Recognition and comprehension of well-formed commands (Shipley, Smith & Gleitman 1969)

while playing with the infant, and play only. Only social stimulation plus babbling led to an increase in number and length of utterances containing consonants. No group showed actual change in the range of vowels or consonants produced. Adult vocalization may, therefore, play only a limited role in encouraging new articulation. The pitch of spoken sounds can influence the pitch of infant babbling (Webster, Steinhardt and Senter 1972). When seven-month-olds heard high-pitched vowels, the pitch of their babbling rose. A similar result with low-pitched vowels was noted but was not significant.

4. *Language reception.* Some linguists have argued that the linguistic environment of infants is too complex to allow language learning without special processors and strategies (Chomsky 1965; McNeill 1966, 1970). With the exception of one exploratory study (Friedlander, Jacobs, Davis, and Wetstone 1972), there has been little analysis of what infants hear in their natural environments. One study (Snow 1972) analyzed the speech of mothers to two- and ten-year-olds. Speech to the younger children was characterized by grammatical simplifications, short sentences and sentence fragments, and more repetitions than speech to the older children. Similar differences were found in the speech of mothers to eighteen- and twenty-eight-month-olds. However there were no differences between speech of mothers addressed to eight-month-olds and speech addressed to older infants (Phillips 1973). It has been suggested that speech to preverbal infants is different from that addressed to infants beginning to speak, in that, in the latter case mothers are guided by verbal feedback from the child (Phillips 1973). Although extensive analysis of speech to infants has not been done, this work suggests that infants beginning to speak are exposed to special samples of speech uniquely designed to facilitate comprehension and language learning.

Description of what is said to infants does not give us the whole picture. We must also ask whether selective attention mechanisms direct infants to detect particular features of speech, and we should seek to discover which features are discriminated.

Phoneme perception. Speech perception in adults is characterized by special decoding processes, unlike nonspeech processing. Evidence of phoneme perception and discrimination by young infants points to early ability to operate in this special speech mode.

We have already noted that adults have categorical perception of voiced and unvoiced consonants such as *b* and *p*. Infants four to fourteen weeks old can discriminate voiced and unvoiced consonants (Trehub and Rabinovitch 1972). When voice onset time is varied continuously, infants of one and four months respond with differential sucking behavior only when the adult boundary between *b* and *p* is crossed (Eimas, Siqueland, Jusczyk and Vigorito 1971).

At five months, differential heart-rate responses indicate that infants discriminate *bah* and *gah,* which differ only in initial phoneme (Moffitt 1971). Similar response measures have been used to demonstrate that at this age infants also discriminate vowels and the consonants *p, t, k, s,* and *n* (McCaffrey 1971). In these studies consonants were always followed by vowel sounds. When the vowel is stripped away, five-month-olds do not show clear-cut discriminations (Morse 1972). Adults presented with the latter stimuli hear chirps and glides unlike speech sounds. It seems that discrimination of initial consonants by infants follows the adult pattern in depending upon contextual cues.

These recent studies represent an area which promises to expand rapidly in the next few years. Although these first reports are limited, they begin to sketch in a picture of the infant's early competence in phoneme perception.

Response to voices. We have noted that infants are especially attentive to voices. As the studies listed in table 2 indicate, an early association between hearing speech and seeing persons is suggested by the finding that infants of one to two months are distressed when their mother's voice suddenly shifts 90 degrees as a result of changing speaker balance and seems to come from a place other than where they see her (Aronson and Rosenbloom 1971). Six-month-olds may be distressed upon hearing their mother's voice when they cannot see her (Turnure 1971). Differential smiling to voice of the mother and another female has been reported as early as four months (LaRoche and Tcheng 1963). Female voices produced more quieting during presentation and more subsequent vocalizing in six-month-olds than a male voice reading the same passage (Kagan and Lewis 1965). At ten months, female infants from middle-class homes looked at their mothers after hearing her taped voice and looked at the female experimenter after hearing a strange female voice. They also vocalized more after the mother's voice than after the stranger's voice (Tulkin 1971). Infants in the first year also seem to be capable of discriminating rising and falling voice intonation (Kaplan 1969; Morse 1972). At two months of age infants can discriminate different voices on tape (Boyd 1972), and the addition of a tape of the mother's voice can re-recruit visual attending behavior (Culp 1971).

Selective attention, discrimination of voices, and early phoneme perception show that preverbal infants are able to process speech sounds in their appropriate mode. This is further support for the view that the ability to discriminate language components may be an innate capacity and is operative in the first weeks of life.

Word comprehension. Conditioning studies in the Soviet Union (Fradkina 1971) find that until seven or eight months of age, conditioning to word stimuli is no different than conditioning to other auditory stimuli. By ten or eleven months, conditioning to words occurs four times faster than to other sounds. Most infant tests begin to include responses to simple commands (e.g., "come here," "give me the ball") between eleven and eighteen months (Bayley 1969; Bühler and Hetzer, 1935; Cattell 1940; Frankenburg and Dodd 1967; Gesell and Thompson 1938). The number of pictures the child can point to and name increases over the second year (Bayley 1969; Cattell 1940; Gesell and Thompson, 1938; Griffiths 1954). In these normative studies, language comprehension is tested in lifelike situations which include many supplementary cues. Controlled experiments are necessary to determine which cues are actually used by the child. When the tester says "Bring me the doll" and points, does the child respond to the sentence, part of it, the gesture, or some combination? A promising technique for answering such questions is illustrated by an experiment conducted by Shipley, Smith, and Gleitman (1969). After determining six familiar nouns for each child, a set of forty-eight commands was constructed, with eight variations for each noun generated by systematic variation of structure and meaning. Different responses to the eight variants made it possible to determine which cues were used. For example, children eighteen to thirty-three months old who spoke in two-word sentences (e.g., "throw ball") made more appropriate responses to the well-formed command "throw the ball" than to the imitation of their own speech. These children therefore recognized and understood grammatical structures which they were unable to produce.

When infants begin to learn spoken language, their thought is more developed than their language (Piaget 1951; Sinclair-de-Zwart 1969; Vygotsky 1962). Symbolic representation does not appear until after sensorimotor representation is achieved (Bruner 1964; Piaget 1951; Werner and Kaplan 1963). Macnamara (1972) recently proposed that infants learn language by application of previously acquired cognitive strategies. They first determine meaning from situational cues and then associate heard sounds with meaning. One such strategy may be to take the emphasized word as the name of the object involved. An infant thus decides that the name of the stove is "hot" when he has heard "Don't touch that, it's *hot!*" Anecdotal evidence suggests that infants' first words are names of objects or people that have special importance for them. Names of family members, food words, and "no" are usually among the first reported words. The importance of particular people or objects may depend upon emotional experiences, action involvement, and so on. Systematic exploration of the way in which infants learn words should provide important clues for understanding language development. An account of later language development may be found elsewhere in this volume (see chapter 5).

Summary. Our review of the literature on early language reception and preverbal communication leads us to conclude that:

1. Language is a uniquely human function and appears to depend upon specialized biological structures.

2. Communication begins between the infant and his or her caretaker from birth, and this preverbal communication may be important for later speech.

3. Although babbling can be increased and shaped by appropriate reinforcement procedures, it now seems doubtful that speech develops primarily through the gradual shaping of babbling.

4. Infants are particularly attentive to voices and by the middle of the first year listen selectively to different voices and different speech passages.

5. Recent studies of phoneme perception indicate that infants as young as one to five months can make some of the same discriminations as adults. The ability to process acoustic information in the speech mode is present very early in life.

6. There has been little research on the cues infants use in early word comprehension although it is clear that infants understand words and sentences which they cannot produce.

Visual Competence

Humans are visually oriented organisms. Adult human vision is more highly developed than other senses such as taste or smell and tends to dominate human interactions with the environment. Long before reaching, voluntary grasping, or crawling is possible, the infant explores the world visually. This early visual behavior appears to provide the basis for the gradual development of both sensorimotor and social competence. Increasingly more complex patterns of sensorimotor behavior seem to be achieved through the coordination of vision with other sensory systems. The infant learns to crawl toward, pick up, and manipulate interesting objects he sees. The infant learns to associate the visual perception of the object with the sound it makes and the way it feels. Recognition of familiar people and discrimination of strangers leads to new social competence. Thus, the infant's visual abilities affect many areas of competence in early development. Visual development has probably received more research attention than any other sensory system. The reader is referred to Bond (1972), Gibson (1969), Hershenson (1967), Kessen, Haith and Salapatek (1970), and Spears and Hohle (1967) for excellent reviews of this research area. Much of the data discussed in the following sections is presented in capsule form in table 3. The table should aid the reader in seeing the developmental progression of certain kinds of visual behavior, as well as the age relationships among these behaviors.

1. *Basic visual capacities.* The infant's visual system is immature at birth but develops significantly in the early postnatal months. An area of the retina called the fovea, which is the most highly developed part of the

TABLE 3. DEVELOPMENT OF VISUAL ABILITIES

Age	Basic Capacities	Brightness	Color	Movement
Newborn	Does not easily accommodate, average focal distance of 19 centimeters (Haynes, White & Held 1965) Acuity based on optickinetic nystagmus found to range from 20/440 to 20/150 (Dayton, Jones, Aiu, Rawson, Steele & Rose 1964; Gorman, Cogen & Gellis 1957) Some convergence of both eyes on nonmoving objects (Wickelgren 1967; Hershenson 1967) Acuity based on voluntary visual preferences found to be 20/800 (Fantz, Ordy & Udelf 1962) Scanning of the visual environment occurs 5–10% of awake time (White 1971) Scans tend to be larger in the horizontal than vertical plane (Salapatek & Kessen 1966); adjusts scanning according to the size of the stimulus (Salapatek 1968) but often scans only a portion of the stimulus (Salapatek & Kessen 1966)	Prefers lights of moderate brightness (Hershenson 1964) Shows sluggish pupillary constriction to moderate lights (Peiper 1963)	Photic system functioning at birth (Barnet, Lodge & Armington 1965) Numerous studies suggest that the infant can probably discriminate colors (Kessen, Haith & Salapatek 1970, for a review)	Can locate and track a moving stimulus (Dayton, Jones, Steele, Rose 1964; Wickelgren 1969); reduces rate of nonnutritive sucking when presented with moving lights (Haith 1966) Saccadic eye movements are poorly controlled (Dayton et al. 1964)

TABLE 3. *Continued*

Depth & Distance	Response to Face	Complexity
	Prefer to look at regular face over scrambled face (Fantz 1961); failure to replicate this result (Fantz & Nevis 1967; Koopman & Ames 1968)	Looks more at patterned than nonpatterned stimuli (Fantz 1965; Stirnimann cited by Kessen et al. 1970)
		Looks longer at 2×2 checkerboards than 12×12 checkerboards (Hershenson 1964); this result not replicated by Friedman, Nagy, & Carpenter 1970
		Prefers stimuli with 10 angles over 5 angles (Hershenson, Munsinger & Kessen 1965)

TABLE 3. *Continued*

Age	Basic Capacities	Brightness	Color	Movement
1–4 months	Ability to focus at varying distances approaches adult performance by 4 mo. (Haynes et al. 1965)	By 3–4 mo. responds to lights of much weaker intensities, indicating a lowering of brightness threshold (Doris and Cooper 1966)	Red and blue preferred over gray (Spears 1964)	By 2 mo. prefers moving over stationary stimuli (Ames & Silfen 1965)
	Acuity based on voluntary visual preference has improved to 20/200 (Fantz et al. 1962)			Can track objects as they move toward and away from him or her (Ling 1942; Gesell 1967)
	Tracking is more smooth and efficient (Ling 1942; Gesell, Ilg, & Bullis, 1949)			By 3 mo. anticipates a regular pattern of movement (Nelson 1968)
	Scans the environment 35% of the time awake (White 1971)			By 3–5 mo. shows greater suppression of nonnutritive sucking to moving light than to stationary light (Haith 1966)
	Scans stimulus more broadly, including internal elements when present (Salapatek 1972)			
	Capacity for binocular vision has improved (Brown 1961)			
6 months	Acuity measured at 20/100 (Fantz et al. 1962)			No difference in preference for single blinking light, light moving horizontally, and light moving in square helix (Kagan & Lewis 1965). But found to prefer lights blinking in 4 to 16 positions over stationary blinking light (Cohen 1969)
1 year			Color preferences more definite by 1 year, may indicate better color discrimination (Saples 1931, 1932)	13-mo.-old prefers single blinking light over light moving horizontally or in square helix (Kagan & Lewis 1965)

TABLE 3. *Continued*

Depth & Distance	Response to Face	Complexity
Shows defensive reactions to objects approaching on a collision course (Ball & Tronick 1971; White 1971)	Under 3–5 weeks of age fixates facial areas 21% of the time and then concentrates on areas of high contrast (Bergman, Haith, & Mann 1971); 7 weeks and older fixates facial areas over 90% of the time (Bergman et al. 1971)	With increasing age prefers more complex checkerboards (Brennan, Ames, & Moore 1966; Caron & Caron 1969; Karmel 1969*b*; Greenberg 1971); this result not found when the same infants were treated repeatedly over several weeks (Horowitz et al. 1972)
Shows HR deceleration visual cliff (Campos, Langer, & Krowitz 1970)		
Prefers 3-dimensional over 2-dimensional stimuli (Fantz 1961; Fantz & Nevis 1967)	Prefers to look at a regularly arranged face rather than a distortion of facial features (Haaf & Bell 1967; McCall & Kagan 1967b)	Between 13 and 20 weeks prefers stimuli with more contour at older ages; the complexity dimension did not fit these data (Karmel 1969*b*; McCall & Kagan 1967*a*)
Found to have size constancy and discriminate distance without relying on retinal image (Bower 1964, 1965*a*); distance from object determines length of fixation; no indication of size constancy (McKenzie & Day 1972)	Eyes elicit smiling at 2–3 months of age (Ahrens, 1954); visual fixation is longer to two dots in the eye position than to two dots in another position (Fantz 1967)	Physiological data support the fixation results on contour, indicating this as the stimulus variable responsible for the age shift in preference for smaller checkerboard patterns (Harter & Suitt 1970; Karmel, White, Cleaves, & Steinsick 1970)
Avoids visual cliff (Walk 1966)	At 7 mo. different facial expressions are distinguished (Ahrens 1954)	

human eye, undergoes extensive cellular changes from the eighth month of intrauterine life to the fourth month after birth (Mann 1964). Since the fovea is the retinal area where visual images are focused most sharply, its immaturity would indicate that objects might not be in sharp focus for the newborn. The newborn's eye has been described as having a relatively high refractive index of the cornea and a shorter eyeball that reduces the distance between the retina and lens, both of which produce a tendency toward farsightedness (Mann 1964; Spears and Hohle 1967). The optic nerve is incompletely myelinated; immaturity of the visual cortex has been indicated histologically and by rapid fatigue and long latency of evoked responses recorded from the occiput (Conel 1939; Ellingson 1967).

Accommodation and acuity. At birth, weak ciliary muscles that control the shape of the lens limit the infant's ability to adjust his focus to varying distances (Peiper 1963). The newborn tends to maintain a relatively short focal length of about 19 cm (Haynes, White, and Held 1965). Measures of reflexive eye movements have shown that most newborns tested had acuity around 20/440, with the best subjects scoring 20/150 (Dayton, Jones, Aiu, Rawson, Steele, and Rose 1964; Gorman, Cogen, and Gellis 1957). That is, the infant perceives objects that are 20 feet away about as clearly as the adult perceives objects that are 440 feet away. Nevertheless, infants are still able to distinguish light-dark contrasts. Estimates of acuity based upon the infant's voluntary visual preferences have found that infants under one month of age reliably prefer a striped stimulus at a distance of 10 inches as long as the stripes are at least one-eighth of an inch wide (Fantz, Ordy, and Udelf 1962). When this method was used, acuity was found to be about 20/800.

During the first three or four months the infant's visual system rapidly matures. The ability to focus on objects at varying distances improves greatly by two months and approaches adult performance by three to four months of age (Haynes et al. 1965; White 1971, p. 69). Acuity also becomes much sharper, enabling the infant to discriminate stripes at least as narrow as one-sixteenth inch at a distance of 10 inches, a Snellen equivalent of 20/200 (Fantz et al. 1962). By six months of age the infant's acuity permits discrimination of one-sixty-fourth inch stripes at 10 inches, about 20/100 (Fantz et al. 1962). All of the above considerations lead one to conclude that the newborn's visual system is functional at birth and that continued development during the first six months produces increasingly acute vision.

Eye movements. The newborn is able to follow a moving stimulus with conjugate eye movements; that is, both eyes move together in the same direction (Dayton, Jones, Steele, and Rose 1964; Wickelgren 1969). The optokinetic nystagmus reflex, which is elicited by moving a series of images such as dots or stripes across the visual field, has been demonstrated in newborns (Dayton et al. 1964; McGinnis 1930). The saccadic eye movements necessary to keep the visual image on the retina were large and poorly controlled. The newborn tended to fixate and refixate the moving stimulus many times. Pursuit movements, or the smooth tracking of a moving stimulus, have not been observed until around three to four months of age (Gesell, Ilg, and Bullis 1949). Since pursuit and saccadic systems are neurologically distinct, it would not be surprising if these two types of eye movements develop at different rates. The three-month-old infant can visually pursue objects in depth as they are brought nearer or moved farther away from him, and he can follow through a visual arc of 180 degrees (Gesell et al. 1949; Ling 1942). It should be noted that there are large individual differences in the ability to track moving stimuli; even some newborns can follow a moving stimulus through a wide arc, although the tonic neck reflex allows most newborns a visual arc of only 90 degrees, approximately.

There is disagreement about how much the newborn fixates a nonmoving stimulus with both eyes simultaneously. Such convergence has been reported as occurring frequently (Hershenson 1964) or rather infrequently (Wickelgren 1967, 1969). Difference in the relative attractiveness of stimuli may partially account for this result (Wickelgren 1969). When convergence was not present, the infant's eyes tended to flare, with the right eye looking right and the left eye looking left. The major problem in practical terms is that researchers working with newborns need to determine the relative frequency of convergence in their particular experimental setting and not assume convergence during an entire testing session (Hershenson 1967).

During the first month of life the infant spends only 5 to 10% of his or her awake time in scanning the visual environment (White 1971). Typically, scanning is rapid, with frequent changes of direction and larger horizontal than vertical sweeps (Salapatek and Kessen, 1966). Vertical contours attract more attention than horizontal contours, perhaps because the infant's scanning pattern produces more frequent boundary encounters, hence more retinal stimulation, when the contour is vertically oriented (Kessen, Salapatek, and Haith 1972). When a pattern is encountered, the scope of scanning is adjusted to a length appropriate to the size of the stimulus (Salapatek 1968). When scanning a stimulus, the newborn will often look at only one portion of it (Salapatek and Kessen 1966). By two and a half months of age the infant spends considerably more awake time (35 percent) in scanning the visual environment (White 1971). Scanning patterns are less confined, and the infant frequently scans the entire stimulus, devoting particular attention to internal stimulus elements when present, as well as outside contours (Salapatek 1972). As the child grows older, scanning patterns continue to play an important role in cognitive tasks. Preschool children often use poor scanning strategies which can limit their performance on visual comparison tasks (Vurpillot 1968).

In summary, the infant responds actively to the visual world from birth, scanning and seeking stimulation. Acuity, accommodation, and control over eye movements greatly improve by six months of age. With maturation of the visual system, the infant is increasingly more capable of processing information from the visual world.

2. *Stimulus qualities affecting the infant.* Although sensitivity increases greatly during the first months of life, the newborn infant is probably responsive to most of the stimulus dimensions that an adult perceives. While we don't know very much about some of the specific stimulus dimensions, brightness, color, movement, depth, and form are probably all important stimulus qualities affecting the attending behavior of infants.

Brightness. Historically, observers of infant behavior have noted the baby's attraction to bright objects such as lights (Blanton 1917; Hall 1891). More recent investigations have verified these early observations, concluding that different brightnesses are discriminated by the newborn (Hershenson 1964). Light of intermediate brightness elicits a sluggish, but functional, pupillary constriction (Peiper 1963) and is preferred by newborns to very bright or dim light (Hershenson 1964). During the first four months of life, brightness sensitivity continues to increase, enabling the infant to perceive and respond to stimuli of much weaker intensities than was previously possible (Doris and Cooper 1966).

Color. Color discrimination in infancy has been studied extensively (Chase 1937; Peiper 1963; Trincker and Trincker 1967). However, because of the difficulty of equating stimuli of different colors for brightness, the results of many studies are difficult to interpret. In other words, the baby may be responding to changes in brightness (which we know can be discriminated) rather than differences in color. Nevertheless, physiological evidence suggests that the photopic system, necessary for color discrimination, is functioning in the neonate (Barnet, Lodge, and Armington 1965). And, although brightness has not always been adequately controlled, numerous studies suggest that very young infants are able to discriminate colors (see Kessen et al. 1970, for a review of this research). There is little agreement, however, on which colors are preferred by infants, except that gray is least preferred. Up until the age of fourteen months the infant becomes progressively more consistent in his choice of colors over gray, providing some indication that color discrimination may improve during the first year of life (Staples 1931, 1932).

Movement. As previously noted, the newborn baby can track a moving stimulus (Dayton, Jones, Steele, and Rose 1964). When infants are presented with moving lights, they reduce their rates of nonnutritive sucking, which indicates attention to the stimuli (Haith 1966). By eight weeks the infant shows a definite preference for stimuli that move (Ames and Silfen 1965). By three months of age the infant is able to anticipate regular patterns of movement, such as sequentially moving lights (Nelson 1968). It is not clear, however, what types of movement are most preferred. Kagan and Lewis (1965) found no preference among three different light patterns (single blinking light, horizontal row, and square helix) in infants six months of age. These same infants, when retested at thirteen months, preferred the single blinking light. Cohen (1969) testing six-month-olds, found lights blinking in four positions and sixteen positions to be preferred over single blinking lights.

Depth. Another aspect of the visual environment that the young infant responds to is depth. Beginning at around two months of age infants start to prefer three-dimensional stimuli over two-dimensional stimuli and will look longer at a solid representation of a head than at a flat form (Fantz 1961; Fantz and Nevis 1967). Conflicting reports have appeared concerning the presence of size constancy in infants of this age. Two early reports claimed that two- to three-month-old infants used motion parallax (cues obtained by moving the head in this situation) to discriminate between a small cube at a near distance and a larger cube placed farther away which produced the same size retinal image as the small cube (Bower 1964, 1965a). A recent nonreplication of these findings reported that infants between six and twenty weeks of age showed little regard for objects placed more than 1 meter away regardless of the size of the retinal image (McKenzie and Day 1972). A marked increase in visual attention was shown to objects at 1 meter, leading the authors to conclude that object distance is a critical determinant of visual fixation at these ages. The earlier evidence for size constancy was not supported by this work, leaving the question open and in need of further study.

Babies can also use cues of spatial depth to react defensively to potentially dangerous situations. As early as one to two months of age, infants show defensive reactions to objects approaching on a collision course but not to objects approaching on a miss course (Ball and Tronick 1971; White 1971). Infants six months and older cannot be coaxed to crawl across a surface which appears to be a cliff but is actually covered with glass (Walk 1966). When the glass covers a solid surface (shallow side), however, they do not show avoidance. Younger infants, not yet able to crawl, show mild heart-rate acceleration when placed on the shallow side of the visual cliff and large heart-rate deceleration when placed on the deep side (Campos, Langer, and Krowitz 1970). Apparently infants at this age can distinguish the difference in depth between the two sides of the visual cliff but do not show marked fear responses to the deeper side.

Form. The vast literature on form perception can only be covered thoroughly in a chapter devoted to this topic. The reader is referred to Bond (1972), Gibson (1969), and Hutt (1970) for reviews of topics not covered here, such as response to novelty, stimulus change, and to Bower's work on gestalt characteristics of form perception (Bower 1965*b*, 1966*a*, 1966*b*). We have chosen somewhat arbitrarily to limit our review to two hypotheses that have received much attention: (1) certain forms such as the human face have an initial attraction for the infant; (2) preference for stimulus complexity varies with age such that with increasing age more complex stimuli will be preferred.

Response to faces. The impetus for recent work on early preference for certain forms grew out of animal work. Newly hatched chicks were observed to peck ten times more often at round objects that resembled food than at angular ones, without receiving any reinforcement or having had prior experience (Fantz 1957). Research with monkeys has provided further evidence of early visual recognition at a higher phylogenetic level. Three different species of infant monkeys, raised in isolation, were found to prefer and orient toward the adult monkey of their own species over adult monkeys from the other two species (Sackett 1970). In a second study, isolated monkeys exposed only to pictures of monkeys in numerous postures began to show avoidance, when they reached three to four months of age, of the pictures depicting monkeys exhibiting threat facial expressions. This avoidance behavior appeared suddenly and seemed due to postnatal maturation of fear responses to specific visual stimuli (Sackett 1970). These data remind us that initial preferences or avoidance for certain stimuli need not be observable at birth, but may appear much later, even when the releasing stimuli have been present from birth.

Research that extended this animal work to infants indicated that infants from four days to six months of age preferred to look at schematic features arranged as a "real" face, rather than at scrambled features (Fantz 1961). This finding raised the possibility that human infants might have very early recognition of the human face. However, later attempts to replicate this finding have failed (Fantz and Nevis 1967; Koopman and Ames 1968). A recent study using real faces as stimuli suggested a developmental shift in attention to certain features of the face. Mirror reflections of real faces were presented to four groups of infants, ranging in age from three to seventeen weeks (Bergman, Haith, and Mann 1971). Prior to seven weeks of age infants attended little to the faces; when they did attend, they primarily scanned the border areas such as the hairline, where high contrast was present. By seven weeks of age infants directed 90 percent of their visual fixations toward a facial stimulus as compared to only 21 percent at younger ages, with scanning concentrated in the eye region. Infants three to four months of age responded along a dimension of "faceness" rather than stimulus complexity (Haaf and Bell 1967). They preferred regular faces over distorted faces and over abstract stimuli of equal complexity (McCall and Kagan 1967a). Thus, by at least four months of age, the infant discriminates the face as a particular visual array, although it is unclear whether this discrimination is based on particular features or the entire arrangement. Infants probably discriminate the eyes as a separate feature around two to three months, while the mouth is not distinguished until around five months (Ahrens 1954; Fantz 1967; Spitz 1965). Facial expressions are distinguished even later, around 7 months (Ahrens 1954). The reader is referred to Gibson (1969) for a more detailed summary and interpretation of the data on the infant's reaction to the face.

Complexity and contour. The most frequently tested hypothesis about complexity is that, with increasing age, infants will prefer increasingly complex stimuli. Although the hypothesis can be stated simply, it has not proved to be easy to test. One of the major difficulties is that different authors have defined "complexity" in a variety of ways. Stimulus qualities such as amount of contour, number of parts, number of random turns in a figure, and redundancy of pattern have all been investigated under the rubric of complexity. Critics have also pointed out that the meaning of "preference" is unclear (Hutt 1970; Kessen et al. 1970). What does it mean to say that the infant prefers one stimulus over another? The question is not clarified by looking at the response side of the problem. Total fixation time, first fixation time, number of fixations, evoked potentials recorded from the visual cortex, heart-rate change, and smiling are some of the responses that have been used to index the infant's response to complexity. When multiple response measures are taken, results differ depending on which measure is being considered. Given these conceptual and methodological problems, it is not surprising that conflicting results abound.

At the simplest level the complexity hypothesis would predict that the infant should prefer a pattern over no pattern at all, and indeed this has been consistently found for both newborns (Fantz 1963) and older infants between three and fourteen weeks (Brennan, Ames, and Moore 1966). When more complicated visual distinctions are to be made, results are not as clear. A number of studies have used checkerboard stimuli, with the 2×2 checkerboard considered the least complex pattern, and more complex stimuli formed by increasing the number of squares. It should be noted that this procedure simultaneously increases the number of parts and amount of contour (perimeter of the figure), as well as increasing "complexity." In an early study, newborns were found to prefer (fixate longer) the least complex checkerboard offered, a 2 × 2, over the most complex, a 12 × 12 (Hershenson 1964). However, when complexity was varied by manipulating the number of angles in random shapes, newborns preferred a ten-turn figure over a five-turn figure (Hershenson, Munsinger, and Kessen 1965). Since a more recent study using reproductions of Hershenson's checkerboard stimuli has also failed to replicate the finding that newborns prefer less complex stimuli, this point is still in question (Friedman, Nagy, and Carpenter 1970).

When both age and complexity of stimuli were varied, three-week-olds preferred the least complex checkerboard (2 × 2), eight-week-olds preferred a medium complexity (8 × 8), while fourteen-week-olds preferred the most complex checkerboard (24 × 24) (Brennan, Ames, and Moore 1966). This finding was bolstered by subsequent studies testing infants within this same age range, which reported that increasingly complex stimuli were preferred by older infants (Caron and Caron 1969; Greenberg 1971; Karmel 1969b). However, when a longitudinal approach was applied to this problem so that the same infants were tested weekly between three and fourteen weeks, the preference for increasing complexity with age was not found (Horowitz, Paden, Bhana, Aitchison and Self 1972).

Not all authors have interpreted their results in terms of the complexity hypothesis (Karmel 1969a, 1969b; McCall and Kagan 1967a). Contour, obtained by summing the lengths of all black-white transitions in the stimulus pattern, has been suggested, rather than complexity, as the stimulus variable responsible for the preference-age shift. In tests of infants between thirteen and twenty weeks old, both random shapes (McCall and Kagan 1967a) and checkerboards (Karmel 1969b) were used in studies that controlled for contour and complexity. The contour dimension fitted the resulting preference data better than the complexity dimension. The results paralleled the complexity data in that twenty-week-olds preferred patterns with more contour than did thirteen-week-olds (Karmel 1969b).

Many investigators working with the complexity hypothesis have assumed that cognitive changes are responsible for the increasing preference for more complex stimuli with age. That is, the baby can handle more information as more complex cognitive structures are formed with age. However, with the use of contour as a more compelling way to describe or dimensionalize the data, a less cognitive and more physiological explanation has been proposed (Harter and Suitt 1970; Karmel 1969a). Changes in preference have been linked to the visual system itself; specifically, increasing acuity may in part account for the changes in response with age. As previously noted, the fovea is still undergoing development up through the fourth postnatal month. All of the above studies that reported increasing preference for complexity with age have tested infants four months or under. The only exception is Karmel's (1969) twenty-week-old group, which he compared to a thirteen-week-old group, but again this comparison encompasses a period of improvement in acuity. The data supporting an acuity interpretation come from both adults and infants (Harter and Suitt 1970; Harter and White 1968; Karmel, White, Cleaves, Steinsiek 1970). If the complexity hypothesis is to be retrieved, it would appear necessary to demonstrate the preference-age shift with infants beyond the age when rapid acuity changes are taking place. Critics have suggested that the term "complexity" be discarded entirely (Hutt 1970; Karmel 1969b). Obviously, this is one area of visual behavior that requires further research before firm conclusions can be drawn.

Summary. The following statements may be made about visual competence in infants:

1. The infant's visual system matures in a number of ways in the months immediately following birth; as a result, the infant experiences improved acuity, accommodation, and better control over eye movements. The period of most rapid maturation is probably between birth and six months.

2. The newborn can discriminate different levels of brightness, is attracted by movement, and prefers to look at a pattern rather than no pattern at all. By four months of age, the brightness threshold has lowered, regular patterns of movement can be anticipated, and patterns with more contour (or complexity) are fixated longer than patterns with less contour.

3. Numerous studies have indicated that infants can discriminate color, but methodological problems have prevented any clear conclusions, particularly regarding which colors are preferred.

4. Around two months of age, infants find the face an attractive visual stimulus, and the eyes alone are sufficient to elicit smiling. By four months, they prefer to look at a regularly arranged face rather than distorted face, although different facial expressions may not be differentially responded to until around seven months of age.

5. A number of investigators have presented checkerboard patterns to infants from birth to four months of age, and have reported an increasing preference with age for stimuli containing smaller checks. This finding has been variously interpreted as an increasing preference for greater complexity or contour; also, more physiological explanations dealing with the visual system itself have been offered.

Sensorimotor Development

1. *Definitions and overview.* The distinction between sensorimotor and motor acts is a difficult one to make. "Sensorimotor" implies coordination

of sensory and motor functions, but all motor acts require processing of sensory information. On standardized infant tests, large-muscle activities related to posture and locomotion are considered motor items while small-muscle activities, such as manipulation of objects, are classified as sensorimotor or adaptive behavior. Another, perhaps more important distinction, is that sensorimotor acts involve more complex cognitive processing than "pure" motor acts. Building a tower of cubes involves judgments of spatial relations in addition to manual skill. Pulling a string to obtain a toy requires understanding of the relationship between the string and the toy beyond ability to pull the string. Even with this criterion (complexity of cognitive processing), it is not easy to differentiate motor and sensorimotor behavior, for it is through motor responses to stimulation that the infant begins to know and cope with the environment. In this section we will not review postural and locomotor development, as detailed information on these topics is available from numerous sources (Crowell 1967; Gesell 1954; Kessen, Haith, and Salapatek 1970; Shirley 1931). We will, however, discuss the importance of locomotion in the development of infant competence. The major portion of this section is concerned with the development of manipulatory skills and correlated cognitive developments.

The entries in table 4 summarize some of the major milestones in sensorimotor development. Two important trends are illustrated. Development proceeds from head to foot (cephalocaudal gradient). Control of the head precedes control of arms which precedes control of the trunk. Development also progresses from central to peripheral segments (proximodistal gradient). Arm control precedes hand control which in turn precedes finger control.

A third feature of sensorimotor development is the continued combination and integration of simple acts into complex behaviors. Grasping, looking, and arm movement are temporally sequenced and coordinated to achieve successful reaching. Once accomplished, reaching becomes available as an element of more complex activities such as putting objects into containers. During the initial achievement of sensorimotor coordination, success requires focal attention. When coordination is perfected, the infant executes the same behavior with minimal attention. The infant who is building a tower of blocks concentrates upon the placement of blocks, with reaching being smooth and almost automatic in nature. The infant who is just beginning to reach must focus upon the act of reaching itself.

2. *Sources of information.* The normative studies upon which infant tests are based provide valuable information about sensorimotor development. Early workers in the development of infant tests made the assump-

TABLE 4.   SENSORIMOTOR DEVELOPMENT

Age	Motor Control	Prehension and Manipulation	Object Permanence
newborn	Little coordination, strong tonic neck reflex (Prechtl & Beintema 1964; Andre-Thomas et al. 1960)	Arm movements, reflex grasping, sucking-looking present but not co-ordinated Cries if object cannot be touched where image appears (Bower 1967)	
1–4 months	Tonic neck reflex diminishes (White, Castle & Held 1964) Control of eye muscles and movement (Gesell 1954)	Defensive reactions to looming (Ball & Tronick 1971; Bower 1967) *Chance coordinations* Spontaneous hand-mouth activity (Brazelton, et al. in press; Escalona & Corman 1966; Griffiths 1954)	Recognition of events—anticipation of feeding (Bühler 1930; Cattell 1940; Piaget 1954) Smooth tracking of moving objects (Ling 1942; McGinnis 1930)
	Tonic neck-reflex disappears (White et al. 1964)	Grasps object in hand (Griffiths 1954; McGraw 1943; Shirley 1933; White 1969); occasionally object in hand brought to mouth without looking (Escalona & Corman 1966; Piaget 1952) *First coordinations* Hand-watching (Bayley 1969; Bühler & Hetzer 1935; Cattell 1940; Escalona & Corman 1966; Piaget 1952; Uzgiris & Hunt 1966); object in hand brought immediately to mouth, hands brought to object in mouth (Bayley 1969; Griffiths 1954; Escalona & Corman 1966; Piaget 1952; Uzgiris & Hunt 1966) sucking and mouth-opening at sight of object (Bruner 1969; Escalona & Corman 1966; Piaget 1952)	Follows object behind screen (Bower et al. 1971; Gardner 1971); no surprise if object passes behind screen and a different one emerges on the same trajectory (Bower et al. 1971; Gardner 1971)

TABLE 4. *Continued*

Age	Motor Control	Prehension and Manipulation	Object Permanence
		Reaching for object that touches hand, reaching for object if hand and object seen at same time (Escalona & Corman 1966; Piaget 1952)	
		Increased activity while viewing object, swiping (Bayley 1969; Cattell 1940; Bruner 1969; Escalona & Corman 1966; Halverson 1931; Piaget 1952)	
		Hands to midline when viewing object (Gesell & Thompson 1938; White et al. 1964)	
		Successful reaching under enrichment conditions (White 1969)	
4–7 months	Control of head and arms (Gesell 1954)	Successful reaching, palmar grasp, object brought to mouth (Bruner 1969; Escalona & Corman 1966; Piaget 1952; Shirley 1933; Halverson 1931)	Anticipation of trajectories (Bower et al. 1971)
			Surprise if object changes when behind screen (Bower et al. 1971; Gardner 1971)
		Reaching for objects out of range (Cruikshank, 1941; Shirley, 1933)	Removes cloth from face (Escalona & Corman 1966; Piaget 1954)
			Anticipates trajectories, looks for fallen objects, no search for covered objects (Piaget 1954; Bühler & Hetzer 1935; Escalona & Corman 1966; Gesell & Thompson 1938; Griffiths 1954; Uzgiris & Hunt 1966)
		Successful reaching (Halverson 1931)	*Partial success with hidden objects*
		Reach with manipulation (Piaget 1952; Escalona & Corman 1966; Bruner 1969)	Toy covered with transparent cloth after grasp (Gratch 1972)

TABLE 4. *Continued*

Age	Motor Control	Prehension and Manipulation	Object Permanence
			Partially visible object (Bell 1968; Bühler & Hetzer 1935; Decarie 1965; Gratch & Landers 1971; Piaget 1954); object covered with opaque cloth after reach begins (Bell 1968; Decarie 1965; Uzgiris & Hunt 1966)
7–10 months	Control of trunk and hands (Gesell 1954)	Refines grasp-partial thumb opposition (Bayley 1969; Halverson 1931)	Searches for hidden objects if hiding is observed (Bayley 1969; Bell 1968; Bühler & Hetzer 1935; Cattell 1940; Charlesworth 1966; Decaries 1965; Corman & Escalona 1969; Piaget 1954; Uzgiris & Hunt 1966)
	Sitting	Fingers holes in pegboard (Bayley 1969; Cattell 1940)	Puzzled if different object is revealed—picks it up (LeCompte & Gratch 1972)
10–12 months	Control of legs	Places pegs in board (Bayley 1969; Cattell 1940)	Searches in place where object is first found (Bell 1968; Escalona & Corman 1966; Gratch & Landers 1971; Evans & Gratch 1972; Landers 1971; Piaget 1954)
		Opens and closes boxes (Cattell 1940; Bühler & Hetzer 1935; Shirley 1933)	Searches longer if handles as well as sees toy (Harris 1971)
2d year	Walking and running	Holds crayon—later imitates lines (Bayley 1969; Cattell 1940; Frankenberg & Dodd 1967)	Searches in second place if unsuccessful at first (Bell 1968; Piaget 1954; Uzgiris & Hunt 1966)
		Builds cube towers (Bayley 1969; Cattell 1940; Frankenberg & Dodd 1967; Gesell & Thompson 1938)	Returns to first location but is correct if allowed second attempt on delayed search (Webb et al. 1972)
		Success on form-	Successful in two or

TABLE 4. *Continued*

Age	Motor Control	Prehension and Manipulation	Object Permanence
		boards (Bayley 1969; Cattell 1940; Gesell & Thompson 1938)	more hiding places immediately (Bell 1968)
		Uses spoon (Frankenberg & Dodd 1967)	Follows one invisible displacement (Miller et al. 1970) Follows serial displacements (Bell 1968; Escalona & Corman 1966; Piaget 1954; Uzgiris & Hunt 1966)
			Representation of displacements One invisible displacement (Bell 1968; Escalona & Corman 1966; Piaget 1954; Uzgiris & Hunt 1966)
			Searches in place where object is first found
			Searches in two or more locations
			Serial displacement

tion that sensorimotor functions and simple adaptations were the intellectual components of infant behavior (Bayley 1933). Most tests of infant development in use today include many sensorimotor items (Stott and Ball 1965). These items are typically combined with apparently unrelated items on the basis of empirical observations. Items are selected because they are characteristic of a given age, and there is little attempt to follow the development of specific behaviors.

A second source of information, from a different point of view, is the work of Piaget and his followers. Piaget (1952) called the first major developmental period "the period of sensorimotor intelligence" to indicate that the major developmental task in this period is the achievement of a coherent organization of sensorimotor behavior. Like the test developers, Piaget considered sensorimotor behavior to be the beginning of intelligence. He further assumed that from careful observations of sensorimotor development we can make inferences about an infant's knowledge of the physical world, particularly concepts relevant to the basic categories of experience: space, time, causality, and the permanence of objects. In contrast to the test developers, Piaget's theoretical orientation leads him to follow the development of specific behaviors and to show cognitive relationships between apparently unrelated behaviors. There is little concern in this approach for the specific age at which achievement occurs. It is rather the sequence and pattern of development which are important. (Summaries of Piaget's theoretical views may be found in Elkind [1967], Flavell [1963], Hunt [1961], and Stott and Ball [1965]. A full discussion of Piaget's last developmental stage will be found in chapter 10 of this volume.) We will emphasize the Piagetian approach in early infant development, especially in regard to prehension and object permanence because this has been the orientation of many recent studies. Material from normative studies and published test norms will be incorporated where relevant. The development of causal and spatial relations will be concurrently indicated. Several of these topics might be appropriately discussed in the subsequent section on cognitive development. They are included here as a reflection of the Piagetian view, since these are the cognitive correlates of sensorimotor development as discussed by Piaget (1954). Object permanence has received such extensive attention in recent literature that it is one of the few concepts for which we can give a detailed account of development. The following section on cognitive development and learning is concerned with non-Piagetian concepts.

3. *Changing test norms.* In gathering information for this section, we studied published test norms which provide ages of achievement for many sensorimotor behaviors. The ages given in these norms vary widely (see, for example, table 2 in Kessen et al. 1970). Hence the interpretation of these norms was difficult. An important consideration was the current validity of the norms in question.

Underlying the construction of traditional infant tests is the notion that they measure a quantitative phenomenon that is incremented over time. An infant's competence is judged in relation to his age-mates by comparing the number of items he or she passes with the average number of items passed by other infants of the same age. Thus, good estimates of average performance of infants at various ages are required. In fact, with the exception of the recent standardization of the Bayley Scales (1969) and the Denver Developmental Screening Test (Frankenburg and Dodd 1967), most infant tests were standardized on small and poorly representative samples many years ago. Recent evidence indicates that norms vary not only over different populations but over time. Studies of African infants often report that they are developmentally advanced over American and European infants (Falade 1955; Geber 1958; Geber and Dean 1957; Goldberg 1972; Leiderman et al. 1972; Lusk and Lewis 1972). A few contradictory reports exist (Falmagne 1959; Parkin and Warren 1969), and these are for studies in which the authors did not use norms, but tested both African and European samples themselves. The use of norms rather than comparison samples has been severely criticized by Warren (1972), and at least one recent investigator has found that the use of different standardizations of the Bayley Scales led to different conclusions (Kilbride 1969). Comparison with 1936 norms led to the conclusion of greater precocity of the African sample. Bayley herself (1965) reported that the 1958–61 sample was more precocious than the previous standardization sample, and there are several reports that test norms underestimate the development of current American infants (Cobb, Goodwin, and Saelens, 1966; Honzik 1962; Klatskin 1952; Klatskin, Jackson, and Wilkin 1956). Although this change in normal performance may be attributable to inadequacy of earlier standardizations or changes in test procedures, better medical care and nutrition and changes in child-rearing practices may have led to actual changes in infant behavior (Cobb et al. 1966; Klatskin 1952). In support of this view are the results indicating that over the past hundred years there has been an increase in the rate of physical growth and maturation of children (Tanner 1970). Current infants in the United States may be more advanced developmentally than the infants who participated in early normative studies. Available test norms developed in the United States may be appropriate measurement guidelines only for American infants. Thus, in describing sensorimotor development, we will emphasize sequences of development with general (rather than specific) indication of ages of attainment.

4. *Prehension.* Prehension is the ability to reach for and grasp objects with the hands. As an exploratory pattern, it requires the coordination of vision, grasping, and arm movement. At the time infants begin to reach successfully, objects grasped are usually brought to the mouth. Most components of the look-reach-grasp-suck sequence are in the infant's repertoire before successful reaching occurs. Some infants can focus on and follow objects in the first few days of life. Grasping reflexes are present at birth (Andre-Thomas, Chesni, and Saint-Anne-Dargassies 1960; Prechtl and Beintema 1964; reviewed by Crowell 1967), and sucking is one of the first acts infants voluntarily control. Very young infants can learn to vary their sucking pattern according to different conditions of milk delivery (Kessen 1967; Sameroff 1968) and control the brightness of a picture (Siqueland and DeLucia 1969). Thus, in "designed" environments infants are competent in control of the environment through sucking. Arm movements, however, are relatively uncontrolled in the neonate. Successful reaching requires accurate depth perception, voluntary control of grasping from early reflexes (Twitchell 1965), arm control, and sequential and temporal organization of these behaviors (Bruner 1969).

Cognitive significance. According to the Piagetian view, the first conceptions of the physical world are inseparable from the actions by which the infant knows the world. Each type of sensorimotor act is a unique way of organizing experience which Piaget calls an "action schema." There is a sucking schema, a looking schema, and a grasping schema (among others), and objects are things to be sucked, grasped, or looked at. The infant does not conceive of a single object with specific features, only unrelated schema-experiences. Likewise, there is a visual space, an auditory space, a tactile space, and so on, but the infant does not understand these as being related. Nor does the infant conceive of events having causes, for events are not distinguished from activities (Piaget 1954). As the infant coordinates action schemas, he or she is also coordinating spatial, causal, temporal, and object concepts and is constructing the world as we know it, a unified space containing objects.

It has been argued that vision-touch connections are congenitally organized since infants as young as two weeks show defensive reactions to looming visual objects (Ball and Tronick 1971; Bower 1967) and are surprised or upset if they reach for an object and cannot touch it in the expected place (Bower 1967). However, many prereaching behaviors are characterized by failure to coordinate visual and tactual information. The infant learning to reach begins to combine pattern elements with increasing effectiveness in order to reach a goal—for example, grasping something he sees.

Initial behaviors. At birth, independent arm and head movement are restricted by the tonic neck reflex (Andre-Thomas et al. 1960; Prechtl and Beintema 1964). This reflex diminishes in strength, and head and arms can act independently by three and one-half to four months of age (White, Castle, and Held 1964). Hand-mouth activity may occur spontaneously in the fetus (Humphrey 1969) in the newborn (Brazelton 1971), and within the first month (Escalona and Corman 1966; Griffiths 1954). In tactile exploration, grasping occurs in chance encounters with objects (Bühler and Hetzer 1935; Escalona and Corman 1966; Griffiths 1954; McGraw 1943; Piaget 1952). An object placed in the hand is grasped (Griffiths 1954; McGraw 1943; Shirley 1933) and sometimes brought to the mouth without looking (Escalona and Corman 1966; Piaget 1952). The quality of coordination at this age is that of chance occurrences in which the movements are not smooth or coordinated. Coordinations of this type probably enable the infant to perceive momentary associations of visual, tactile, and buccal space and to experience contingencies.

First coordinations. The sequence described in table 4 goes from handwatching through rudimentary hand-mouth, mouth-eye, and hand-eye coordination. In these sequences two or more schemas are coordinated, yet reaching and grasping are unsuccessful. The hand may reach the object improperly oriented for grasping, with the fist closed (Bruner 1969) or with the hand opening at the wrong time (White, Castle, and Held 1964). Twitchell (1965) suggested that the delay between swiping and accurate reaching depends upon maturation of the orientation component of the grasp reaction. But these partial successes allow the infant to observe the effects of actions. Piaget (1954) has suggested that the feeling of efficacy derived from such observations may be the first notion of causality.

Successful reaching. When reaching is successful, the object is immediately brought to the mouth, but at a later stage it is looked at and manipulated (Bruner 1969; Escalona and Corman 1966; Piaget 1952; Shirley 1933). Successful reaching is reported as early as two and one-half to three months when babies are given special stimulation (White 1969), and as late as seven or eight months (Halverson 1931). This range is accounted for by different criteria for success as well as individual variation among infants. When infants were provided with increased visual and tactile experience, successful reaching occurred before some of what we have called "prereaching" behaviors (White 1969). This raises the question of which behaviors necessarily precede successful reaching and which are coincidental.

Later developments. Subsequent achievements in reaching include a smoother, more direct path to the object (Halverson 1931), reflecting better coordination and an increasing understanding of spatial relations (Piaget 1954). Grasping is refined to the thumb-forefinger grip, and the infant learns to anticipate the size of an object in the opening of the hand (Bayley 1969; Escalona and Corman 1966; Frankenburg and Dodd 1967; Gesell and Thompson 1938; Griffiths 1954; Halverson 1931; McGraw 1943). At first the infant reaches for objects that are out of range. These inappropriate attempts initially increase and then decline as the infant comprehends the relationship between arm length and the object's location (Cruikshank 1941; Shirley 1933). As reaching becomes smooth and coordinated, it is executed with minimal attention (Bruner 1969). Once the need for total involvement declines, reaching can become integrated into more complex patterns of behavior. According to the Piagetian view, it is through complex manipulation of the environment that causality and spatial relations come to be understood. After the infant becomes successful at reaching, behavior becomes increasingly systematic and intentional, and the infant can recognize himself or herself as a causal agent (Piaget 1954).

Complex manipulation. As the child grows older, manipulation of objects becomes more complex and precise. Infant tests include many situations in which this is demonstrated. The ability to place one cube on top of another leads to building increasingly higher cube towers (Bayley 1969; Cattell 1940; Frankenburg and Dodd 1967; Gesell and Thompson 1938). The child can use a stick to retrieve a toy out of reach and manipulate one toy with another toward the end of the first year, which indicates comprehension of the causal relation between objects in contact and their movements (Bayley 1969; Bühler and Hetzer 1935; Escalona and Corman 1966).

At nine or ten months, the infant only fingers the holes in the pegboard, but in the second year he or she puts in and removes pegs with increasing speed (Bayley 1969; Cattell 1940). Understanding of spatial relationships improves, and the infant can fit simple shapes into a formboard (Bayley 1969; Cattell 1940; Gesell and Thompson 1938) and can open and close boxes (Bühler and Hetzer 1935; Cattell 1940; Shirley 1933). Ability to grasp a pencil voluntarily is later part of the ability to make drawing movements and to imitate lines (Bayley 1969; Cattell 1940; Frankenburg and Dodd 1967). Accurate use of a spoon is another second-year accomplishment (Frankenburg and Dodd 1967). Many complex manipulative skills emerge rapidly in the second year, but we have little experimental documentation of these developments.

5. *Object permanence.* The assumption that objects continue to exist independently of our perceptual contact with them is an assumption of object permanence. Although ultimately this does not depend upon remembering a particular object, memory is involved, and the tasks used to test memory in young children are similar to tests of object permanence. However, in Piaget's system, recognition alone is not sufficient for object permanence, for the infant may recognize an event as an action or sensation previously encountered without attributing it to an external source (Piaget 1954). As noted in table 4, recognition memory has been identified in the first few months of life as evidenced by anticipatory behavior to the sight of the bottle (Bühler 1930). The achievement of object permanence and parallel and related achievements with respect to space, time, and causality result in a coherent organization of sensorimotor behavior and a stable conceptualization of the physical world. It is assumed that sensorimotor coordinations eventually become internalized as the infant's first representations. Such representation or action memory is considered a necessary precursor to true symbolization and language (Bruner 1969; Piaget 1951, 1952, 1954; Werner and Kaplan 1963).

Several tests of object permanence have been constructed that replicate Piaget's observations on the stages of development with respect to the major steps (Bell 1968; Decarie 1965; Escalona and Corman 1966;

Uzgiris and Hunt 1966). Additional information for the following description comes from infant tests, memory studies with infants, and studies of object permanence.

Initial coordinations. The first stage in development of object permanence corresponds in time to the achievement of successful reaching. The infant is able to restore interrupted vision by removing a cloth from his face, but when an object is removed from the visual field the infant acts as if it no longer exists (Escalona and Corman 1966; Piaget 1954). Later, the infant looks for it at the point of disappearance and may repeat actions previously associated with the object. Piaget (1954) interprets such actions as attempts to make the object reappear, reflecting a "magico-phenomenalistic" view of causality. Infants under sixteen weeks of age continue to track a moving object even when it stops in view (Bower, Broughton, and Moore 1971). When an object passes behind a screen, infants under twenty weeks are not disturbed by the appearance of a different object as long as it appears at the right time (Bower 1971). These observations support the notion that the action of tracking is more important than the specific features of the object.

Anticipating trajectories. The baby's next accomplishment is the anticipation of the trajectory of an object that has moved too quickly to be followed. If a toy is dropped while the infant is looking at it, he or she will look down for it. The path of an object moved horizontally is also anticipated. If a toy is covered by a screen while the infant watches, there is no search for it at this stage (Bühler and Hetzer 1935; Escalona and Corman 1966; Gesell and Thompson 1938; Griffiths 1954; Piaget 1954; Uzgiris and Hunt 1966). Nevertheless, these successful anticipations indicate some understanding of an object's movement in space.

Searching for hidden objects: partial successes. Before a completely hidden object can be found, the infant can retrieve partially hidden objects. Retrieval of an object covered with a transparent cloth after the object is grasped is the first partial success (Gratch 1972). The infant can next succeed at the same task with an opaque cloth (Gratch 1972; Gratch and Landers 1971), and later the infant can recover an object covered with an opaque cloth after reaching has begun (Bell 1968; Decarie 1965; Gratch and Landers 1971; Piaget 1954; Uzgiris and Hunt 1966). Recovery of a partially visible object (Bell, 1968; Bühler and Hetzer 1935; Decarie 1965; Gratch and Landers 1971; Piaget 1954; Uzgiris and Hunt 1966) is achieved before retrieval of the grasped and opaquely covered object (Gratch and Landers 1971). This has been interpreted to indicate that vision provides more convincing evidence of existence than touch. However, in these tasks the object was first presented visually so that infants were visually rather than tactually attentive (Gratch 1972).

When eight- and twelve-month-old infants saw, or both saw and handled a toy before it was hidden, younger infants searched longer when allowed to handle the toy as well as view it (no infant was actually allowed to find the toy), demonstrating that when engaged both tactually and visually, eight-month-olds can use tactile information effectively (Harris 1971).

Initial successes and limitations. The ability to find a completely hidden object, an ability which marks the initial achievement of object permanence, is generally reported to occur in the last third of the first year (Bayley 1969; Bell 1968; Bühler and Hetzer 1935; Cattell 1940; Charlesworth 1966; Decarie 1965; Corman and Escalona 1969; Piaget 1954; Uzgiris and Hunt 1966). When a hidden object apparently disappears (through a trapdoor beneath the screen), infants show surprise at about the same age that they begin to search for hidden objects (Charlesworth 1966). It has been argued (Bower 1967) that surprise at the disappearance of hidden objects can be detected at an earlier age through heart-rate responses. Lack of information about the specific criteria for a "surprise" heart-rate response makes it difficult to evaluate this report. In a study where nine-, twelve-, and eighteen-month-olds searched for hidden objects, the screen was removed to reveal a different object on two trials (LeCompte and Gratch 1972). Younger infants were mildly surprised but accepted the new toy. Older infants acted puzzled and continued to search for the first toy. Thus, when infants are first able to find hidden objects, the specific features of the object are not necessarily clearly conceptualized or remembered.

Another limitation of this first form of object permanence is that the infant is unable to dissociate the object from the place where it is first found. It is as if location were a characteristic of the object, and changes in place were equated with changes in state (Piaget 1954). After finding an object at place A, the infant searches for it again at A *even when he or she has just seen it hidden at B* (Bell 1968; Escalona and Corman 1966; Evans and Gratch 1972; Gratch and Landers 1971; Landers 1971; Piaget 1954). In one study (Gratch and Landers 1971) infants were tested biweekly beginning at six months until they were able to find an object at either of two places. Searching at A after hiding in B (hereafter abbreviated $A\overline{B}$) persisted from one to three months. In a second experiment (Landers 1971) the number of times the infant found the object at A was varied. The more A tests the infant experienced, the more $A\overline{B}$ behavior he or she showed. Observation of the experimenter finding the object at B did not affect $A\overline{B}$ behavior, indicating the importance of the infant's own action at this stage. In a three-choice hiding task with delayed search, sixteen-month-olds returned to the location where they had previously been successful (Webb, Massar, and Nadolny 1972). If allowed to make a second choice, however, they chose the correct location. The authors suggest that the infant has two conflicting memories: the visual memory of seeing the object hidden and the action memory of finding it. The strategy at this stage is to attend to the action memory first. Even in the third year, this behavior pattern has been observed in a hiding task when a delay of twenty-five seconds occurs (Loughlin and Daehler, in press).

Subsequent developments in object permanence involve ability to find the object after increasingly complex (but still visible) hiding procedures. Once he or she can follow direct displacement to two or more hiding places, the infant begins to cope with serial displacements in which the object is moved to one or more screens before it is hidden. A transition stage occurs in which the infant looks in one or more incorrect places before finding the object (Bell 1968; Piaget 1954; Uzgiris and Hunt 1966). Ability to follow visible displacements is consolidated when the infant can observe serial displacements and search directly in the correct location. At this stage the infant comprehends that different paths can lead to the same place and that different actions can have the same effect. Objects can be removed one by one from a container or the container may be inverted. The infant comprehends the nature of space in practical ways. Likewise the existence of causes unrelated to his or her activity and the relation between spatial contact and influence is recognized (Piaget 1954).

Representation of displacements. The final stage of object permanence, completed toward the end of the second year, involves representation of the object and its displacements in space (Piaget 1954). When the object is displaced in a closed container or the closed hand the infant is able to follow the displacements mentally. The sequence of developments with respect to invisible displacements is identical to that reported for visible displacements (Bell 1968; Decarie 1965; Escalona and Corman 1966; Piaget 1954; Uzgiris and Hunt 1966). At first there is difficulty in dissociating the object from its place, and then the development of ability to follow serial displacements. Only one study has found that infants could follow a single invisible displacement before serial visible displacements (Miller, Cohen, and Hill 1970). Causal representation is also achieved. The infant actively reconstructs causes from their effects. For example, if the child cannot push a chair that he or she has previously moved, the child looks for the impediment.

It is clear that object permanence, spatial relations, and causality are interdependent developments. However, temporal, causal, and spatial concepts have not been studied extensively except by Piaget (1954), Escalona and Corman (1966), and Uzgiris and Hunt (1966).

Although we have only described object permanence for inanimate objects, there is evidence that a similar progression occurs with respect to persons and that person permanence is generally more advanced (Bell 1970). Studies relating mother-infant interaction variables to the development of person permanence and object permanence provide an important link between conceptual and emotional development (Bell 1970; Decarie 1965; Serafica and Uzgiris 1971).

6. *The importance of locomotion.* Toward the end of the first year, the infant begins to crawl and then to walk. The sequence of postural and locomotive developments culminating in walking is well documented and is described and illustrated in all standard texts in child development. With each new accomplishment in locomotion, the infant succeeds in gaining voluntary control of his or her own body and of the environment in a new way. The baby who spends much of his or her time on the back or stomach experiences and therefore perceives the environment differently than the infant who sits alone for long periods. But the most dramatic change occurs when the infant first becomes mobile. He or she is no longer at the mercy of the immediate locale and what others have placed within reach. The infant's opportunities for independent exploration and manipulation suddenly increase with the achievement of mobility. New aspects of the environment become accessible as "he gets into everything." People and objects can be approached as a result of his or her own movements. Withdrawal from situations which are unpleasant or uninteresting is another new possibility. If a ball rolls away, the infant can follow it; if the toy within reach becomes boring, he or she can look for another one.

Whereas comprehension of space previously depended upon observation of movements of others, mobility allows the infant to observe the effects of his or her own locomotions and the resulting perspectives. The infant has moved into new dimensions of control of both the physical and social environment and awareness of this new power must enhance feelings of competence. Perhaps it is not coincidental that soon after learning to walk infants begin to assert themselves by saying "no." This is certainly the time when the infant hears "no" most often, for the infant's mobility makes new demands on caretakers. The relationship between mobility and self-assertion is one worth exploring, for it may be an important element in second-year development.

Sensorimotor coordination continues to be important as the child matures, and through refinement of these abilities the child becomes more sophisticated in interactions with the environment. With the acquisition of prehension the infant is able to manipulate objects actively and to integrate information from several sensory modalities. The mental representation of object permanences, spatial relations, and causality provides an organizational framework for further comprehension and elaboration of the real world. Increased mobility contributes to this organizational framework, to the infant's ability to control the environment, and to feelings of competence. Thus, early sensorimotor developments are important for infant competence and are intricately related to cognitive development.

Summary. Sensorimotor development has been studied more extensively than other aspects of infant development. We can see that:

1. Age norms reported in early studies of sensorimotor development must be considered in light of recent evidence which indicates that today's American infants are more precocious than those in early samples.

2. Though arm movements, grasping, and looking are present at birth, these behaviors must be gradually coordinated in the first few months before the infant can reach for and retrieve objects successfully.

3. Complex manipulative skills which develop in the second year have not been adequately studied.

4. The infant begins to search for hidden objects in the second half-year of life. At first infants may search in the wrong place when given two choices and may not conceptualize or remember the features of the object adequately.

5. The achievement of locomotion appears to mark a discontinuity in development, in that it dramatically increases the child's control of the environment and places new demands on caretakers.

Learning and Cognitive Development

Through learning and development, the infant's initial perceptual and sensorimotor skills are integrated into sophisticated and complex patterns of behavior. It is thought that learning that takes place later in life may be highly dependent on this early cognitive development, since it appears to build upon, rather than replace, skills already mastered. Indeed, it is likely that the rapidity and efficiency of later learning occurs, in part, through the association and transfer of knowledge previously acquired. Studies with animals further suggest that early learning may interact with rapid maturation in infancy to influence the structure of receptor and central processing systems. Differences in cortical and subcortical development have been found in rats following selective learning experiences during infancy (Altman 1970), while experiments with kittens have shown that the visual receptor system is modifiable through manipulation of the early environment (Hubel and Wiesel 1963). Although no concrete data exist for humans, the extremely rapid maturation of the central nervous system during the first two years (brain weight increases 350 percent) suggests that learning during this period may influence structural development. The observation that early learning is not easily reversed lends some support to this hypothesis. Certainly, early cognitive development is an important determinant of competence in infancy and is the foundation on which all subsequent learning is based.

In the following discussion we will consider some of the basic cognitive skills used by the infant to assimilate information from the environment, how the infant functions as an active problem-solver who attempts to organize his world coherently, and some of the concepts the infant acquires during the first two years of life.

1. *Basic processes.* Every infant, even when very young, produces a great deal of his or her own experience, namely the sensory feedback arising from each action. Eye and head movements produce changes in visual stimulation. As the infant's head turns on the mattress, there are accompanying tactile sensations and kinesthetic feedback from the active muscles. The infant's cries provide distinct auditory sensations. They also produce tactile sensations in the throat and pressure sensations in the chest. Simple behaviors are accompanied by complex sensory experiences involving several modalities. We assume that the infant does not continuously attend to all these sensations and events. One of the major tasks of infancy is the control of attention. At first, the attentional processes are directed toward simple tracking of sensory change, but eventually the infant is able to utilize these processes for problem-solving (Bruner 1968).

Orienting and habituation. The earliest example of attentional control by the infant is the orienting response (OR). This response consists of those behaviors elicited by change in the environment (Pavlov 1927). These include turning the appropriate receptors toward the source of the change, cessation of ongoing activity, and physiological changes which facilitate registration of the change (Lynn 1966). If the event that elicits orienting occurs repeatedly, these responses will ordinarily diminish even in the absence of organism or receptor fatigue. This process of response decrement is known as habituation. A popular theoretical account for the habituation of the OR states that repetition of a stimulus enables the organism to establish an internal representation or neuronal model of the stimulus event (Sokolov 1960). Each occurrence of the stimulus adds further information to the model. As long as the event and the model do not match (the stimulus is unfamiliar or the model does not incorporate all of its salient features), orienting continues. When a match occurs (the stimulus is familiar), the OR decreases. If a new stimulus is presented or the model fades (that is, the infant forgets), the OR reappears.

This explanation suggests that the ability of the infant to process and store the information in a stimulus event determines the course of habituation. The more efficiently the infant can use stimulus information to elaborate a neuronal model, the more rapidly attention to that stimulus declines. Studies in which visual stimuli are presented repeatedly, report that as infants grow older they habituate more rapidly to a given stimulus (Cohen 1969; Lewis Goldberg and Campbell 1969; Wetherford and Cohen 1971). Habituation of visual attention has been reported for ten-week olds (Wetherford and Cohen 1971) and for newborns (Friedman, Nagy and Carpenter 1970). However it is not clear how reliable or general habituation to visual or auditory stimuli is before three months of age (Graham and Jackson 1970; Jackson, Kantowitz, and Graham 1971; Kearsley 1971; Jeffrey and Cohen 1971; Lewis et al. 1969; Pomerleau-Malcuit, and Clifton, in press; Wetherford and Cohen 1971).

Another theoretical model to account for attention to relatively complex stimuli has been suggested in the notion of "serial habituation" (Jeffrey 1968). In "serial habituation" the infant is thought to orient first to the most salient cue in the stimulus configuration. As a model for this cue is established, the OR to it habituates and a different aspect of the stimulus commands attention. This process continues until a model for the complex stimulus is established. For example, a baby might first be attracted by the brightness of a television set. As an internal model is established for brightness, the infant may shift his or her attention to sound or movement. During this time, if the model for brightness fades, the baby may attend to brightness again. Attention to the television set continues until the infant has elaborated a model for it or until some other stimulus intrudes. The notion of serial habituation suggests that more complex stimuli elicit different patterns of attention than simple ones and that a constantly changing stimulus such as television can successfully maintain attention for long periods of time. This hypothesis also suggests that when an infant has been exposed repeatedly to a complex stimulus, some parts of it may be remembered more clearly than others. There is some recent evidence to support this notion (Horowitz 1972; Miller 1972).

Implications for early memory. Thus far we have been concerned with theories relative to internal representations or neuronal models thought to be established during short exposures in the laboratory. In natural settings, models are probably built up over longer time-periods and may be more permanent. Decreases in orienting responses over repeated exposures imply that the stimulus is recognized and therefore at least partially remembered in the time between exposures. It is not clear how early in life this process occurs, though, as noted previously, under limited conditions there is some indication it may be a process that, in rudimentary form, is present at birth.

Research with older infants suggests that familiarization taking place within one session is maintained for at least short periods of time. Infants three to six months old were exposed to a visual stimulus for two minutes.

Then the familiar stimulus was paired with each of two novel stimuli immediately after familiarization and again two hours later (Fagan 1970). On both immediate and delayed testing the novel stimuli received more attention than the familiar one. Thus, these infants remembered the familiar stimulus for two hours after a two-minute exposure. In a second experiment, (Fagan 1971) five-month-olds had three sequences of two-minute familiarization followed by pairing of familiar stimuli with novel ones. Delayed testing at one, four, and seven minutes showed preference for novel stimuli in all three problems, indicating that all three familiar patterns were recognized and that presentation of later material did not interfere with memory of the earlier stimuli over a span of seven minutes.

Formation of schemas. Repeated attending to stable stimulus configurations in the infant's environment is thought to result in the elaboration of a neuronal model. Piagetians use the term "schema" to refer to the experienced stimulus represented in a neuronal model. A schema is considered to be a remembered representation of an event in which essential elements and spatial and temporal configuration are preserved without necessarily being isomorphic with the event (Kagan 1971). It is thought that the formation of a schema is the event that enables the infant to recognize and assimilate information. The establishment of basic schemas appears to result in increased discrimination of novel versus familiar elements in stimulus configurations. It has been suggested that maximal attention is given to a stimulus which is moderately discrepant from the event(s) which generated a schema (Kagan 1971). Novel events are those for which schemas have not been established. For example, before three months of age, when the infant is thought not to have acquired a schema for the face, photos and line drawings of regular or irregular faces are equally novel and elicit equivalent attention. In the second half of the first year, when the face schema is thought to be well elaborated, infants look longer at scrambled faces than at regular faces (Kagan, Henker, Hen-tou, Levine, and Lewis 1966; Lewis 1969).

Numerous studies report that attentional preference for novelty changes with age. One method of investigating this phenomenon is to expose the infant to a stimulus daily over a period of weeks, testing at various intervals to see whether infants will attend more to the familiar stimulus or to a novel one. It is consistently reported that until around eight weeks of age, infants prefer the familiar stimulus and thereafter prefer the novel one (Weizman, Cohen, and Pratt 1971; Wetherford and Cohen 1971; Uzgiris and Hunt 1970). Older infants show a preference for novelty even when short familiarization periods are used in a single session (Fagan 1970, 1971; Saayman, Ames, and Moffett 1964).

Violation of an established schema also influences attending behavior

in older infants. After a stimulus has been presented repeatedly and become familiar, transformation of the stimulus (e.g., change in color, position, arrangement of elements) can result in renewed attentive responses.
The complexity of the stimulus, the age of the infant, and the familiarity
of the surroundings appear to be important determinants of this effect
(Fantz 1964; McCall and Kagan 1970; McGurk 1970; Schaffer and
Parry 1969; Weizman et al. 1971). After a number of familiarization
trials with a two-dimensional geometric figure, six-week-olds showed a
waning of attention. When the figure was changed so that it was presented
upside down, attention was renewed. However, when the same procedure
was followed with a three-dimensional head, the effect was present only
in infants twenty weeks of age or older (McGurk 1970). In a series of
auditory studies, five-month-olds heard a sequence of tones (such as an
ascending C major scale) repeated over a number of trials. On a subsequent test trial, a different arrangement of the same tones was played.
Attention to the transformation, as indicated by heart-rate responses, increased as a function of the amount of discrepancy from the familiar
pattern and the number of familiarization trials (McCall and Melson
1970; Melson and McCall 1970).

Presentation of contrived events which cannot occur in everyday life
(e.g., man with an upside-down head) is one way of testing infants' cognitive schemas. If the infant acts surprised, we can conclude that he or
she has developed expectations which the event violated (Charlesworth
1969). For example, this technique has been used to investigate the role
of object features in object permanence. By four or five months of age,
infants who visually track an object behind a screen do not continue to
track if a different object emerges from the other side of the screen. Instead, they look back, as if searching for the first object (Bower et al.
1971; Gardner 1971). Infants twelve months and older appear to attend
more to discrepant stimuli, and this effect increases with age (Finley,
Kagan, and Layne 1972; Kagan 1971; Lewis, Wilson, and Baumel 1971).
In a study with nine- to eighteen-month olds (LeCompte and Gratch
1972) a toy was hidden in a box, but on some trials a different toy was
there when the box was opened. At nine months, infants acted mildly
puzzled but played with the new toy; at eighteen months, infants refused
to accept the new toy and continued to search for the first one. During
the second year and beyond, determinants of attention to discrepant
events may become more complex. It has been suggested that by two
years and older the child may be attempting to form hypotheses to account for the discrepancy (Kagan 1971).

Thus, at first, attention is "captured" by any stimulus change. As the
environment becomes familiar, events which confirm expectations and

match past stimulus configurations receive minimal attention, and the infant focuses upon discrepant events. Possibly complex processes of habituation and dishabituation underlie these attending patterns.

2. *Early associations.* In addition to habituation, simple and complex schema-formation and attention probably also involve learned associations between elements representing event characteristics. In this section we consider some of the ways in which these associations are established. The process by which infants form these early connections has been studied extensively with the techniques of classical and operant conditioning. Our coverage of this literature will be brief, as excellent reviews are available elsewhere (Brackbill and Koltsova 1967; Fitzgerald and Porges 1971; Lipsitt 1963; Siqueland 1970).

In classical conditioning experiments a neutral stimulus (CS) is typically presented slightly before a second stimulus (UCS) that reliably elicits a response from the infant. For instance, a tone might be presented just prior to offering the infant a bottle of milk, which elicits sucking. After a number of presentations the infant comes to anticipate the sequence and responds to the tone with sucking motions. Newborns are capable of associating two stimuli in this manner. For example, infants can learn that certain signals such as sounds (Lipsitt and Kaye 1964; Marquis 1931) or lights (Mirzoiants 1954, cited by Brackbill and Koltsova 1967) or vestibular stimuli (Denisova and Figurin, cited by Brackbill and Koltsova 1967) are always followed by food. Elapsed time can also serve as a stimulus. If fed on a regular schedule, the infant learns to anticipate his next feeding. As feeding time approaches, he becomes more active and shows physiological changes in preparation for the ingestion of food (Irwin 1930; Krachkovskaia 1959; Marquis 1941). Infants as young as ten days have been conditioned to blink when a tone signaled a puff of air to the eye (Little 1971). In addition, premature infants were conditioned to anticipate the presentation of noxious odors (Polikanina 1961), but a subsequent study with full-term infants was unsuccessful in replicating this result (Lipsitt 1963).

Operant conditioning is another technique that has been used to investigate infant learning. It involves positive or negative reinforcement of spontaneous behavior. For example, if the baby's smiling is followed by the caretaker's talking and playing with him or her, the baby is likely to associate smiling with pleasant consequences and increase the rate of smiling. Thus, operant conditioning is based on the infant's ability to modify an ongoing response in order to gain reinforcement or avoid punishment. Since the newborn lacks adequate control over most response systems, the demonstration of successful conditioning has been limited to sucking and head-turning. Infants can learn to modify their styles of sucking (Sameroff 1968) and can differentiate between two types of nipples when one is associated with reinforcement and the other is not (Lipsitt and Kaye 1965; Lipsitt, Kaye, and Bosack 1966). Most head-turning studies have used a combination of operant and classical conditioning techniques. In the earliest work, an auditory stimulus was presented and if the infant turned his or her head milk was offered (Papousek 1959). If the infant did not respond, the experimenter attempted to elicit a head-turn by stroking the infant's cheek. Failure to respond to the tactile stimulation resulted in the experimenter manually turning the infant's head, then delivering reinforcement. Using a modification of this procedure, Siqueland and Lipsitt (1966) found that newborn infants quickly increased head-turning when reinforced. Subsequent work has indicated that arousal level influences both acquisition and maintenance of conditioned head-turning (Clifton, Meyers, and Solomons 1972; Clifton, Siqueland, and Lipsitt 1972).

Although newborns can be conditioned, most of the associations formed at this time are weak and unstable (Janos 1959; Kasatkin 1969; Papousek 1967). For example, neonates required an average of 177 trials to establish reliable head-turning whereas three-month-old infants took only 42 trials and five-month-olds 28 trials (Papousek 1967). It is not clear whether such differential acquisition rates are a function of increased learning capacity in older infants due to maturation or if other factors such as experience, state, motivation, or the degree of coordinated response capabilities are responsible. Difficulty in establishing stable classical conditioning in particular may be due to the fact that many of the signal stimuli used in this kind of research are completely new to the infant (Sameroff 1971). If the infant has not had sufficient experience with a particular signal stimulus, he or she may not be able to associate the signal stimulus with the later event. If this interpretation is correct, previous experience with the stimulus modality of the neutral stimulus should facilitate the ease with which conditioning is established (Sameroff 1971). While there is some evidence that repeated exposure to relevant stimulation facilitates learning (Papousek 1967), some investigators report that more exposure had either no effect or a negative influence (Janos 1959; Papousek and Bernstein 1969).

A second possibility is that the newborn infant learns the connection between the CS and UCS but does not possess the necessary coordination of behavior to reliably perform the conditioned response (CR). Can learning be shown in this situation in any way other than by the appearance of a CR? If two stimuli have been presented in a close temporal sequence, and the second stimulus is then omitted, an OR will be elicited to the absence of the stimulus (Sokolov 1963). Unlike the CR, which is an anticipatory response, a "getting ready" for the UCS, the OR in this situation is characterized more as a "what happened?" response, when the expected event does not occur. After tone and glucose presentation were paired a number of times, newborns showed large heart-rate deceleration to the absence of the UCS during extinction (Clifton, in press). This deceleration was interpreted as an OR to the absence of an expected stimulus. It may be that the newborn forms expectancies about event sequences, and by disrupting these temporal sequences we can determine whether the relationship has been learned, regardless of the CR's appearance.

Learning situations in which the infant controls the reinforcement seem to produce rapid and effective learning in young infants. Conjugate reinforcement refers to the situation in which the amount of reinforcement is dependent upon the amount of effort expended. For example, infants may be allowed to operate a mobile by kicking (Rovee and Rovee 1969; Smith 1969). A light string was tied to the infant's right leg so that the harder he or she kicked, the more the mobile moved. Infants from two to five months of age rapidly learned the response, and their rate of kicking increased from a base rate of less than 10 kicks per minute to 25 or 30 kicks per minute during conditioning (Rovee and Rovee 1969). Infants also learned to suck harder when sucking controlled the intensity of a visual display (Siqueland and DeLucia 1969).

3. *Problem-solving strategies.* Quite early, the infant seems to begin to develop strategies for responding to the environment. One of the earliest strategies is that of maximizing reinforcement. For example, infants between one and five months of age who were learning to discriminate direction of head turn to receive milk, on the basis of a buzzer and a bell, responded in consistent patterns (Papousek 1967). Some infants always turned to the side where milk had been presented on the previous trial. Others alternated, turning first to one side and then to the other. A third solution was turning to one side and then, if the milk did not quickly appear, turning to the other side.

However, in the first few months, the infant has difficulty changing responses so as to inhibit behavior which is no longer appropriate. When the reinforcement contingencies learned in a head-turning discrimination were reversed, infants were slow to change their response (Papousek 1967). In this study, infants had received milk in response to a bell, and quinine solution in response to a buzz. When the contingencies were changed, so that the bell signaled quinine and the buzz signaled milk, infants continued to respond positively to the bell, sucking the previously rejected quinine, while responding negatively to the buzz and refusing the milk. Eventually appropriate responses were acquired. Similarly, infants continued to make head-turns even when satiated, although they refused the milk.

Apparently, infants in the first year lack the ability to inhibit well-established behaviors. Even at one and a half to two years, children were observed to experience more difficulty inhibiting an incorrect response than initiating a correct one (Luria 1961) and at two to three years this difficulty persists. In a two-choice task where the correct response is rewarded, two- to three-year-olds repeat a response whether or not it has been rewarded, while older children shift their choice after nonreward (Berman and Graham 1964; Daehler and Myers 1972). In the same situation, when children are rewarded for whatever choice they make, one-and-a-half- to two-and-a-half-year-olds repeat the same choices over long trial sequences while older children generate alternating or random patterns (Daehler and Myers 1972). As noted in a previous section, infants in the second year return to the place where they remember finding an object rather than to where they saw it hidden, when search is delayed.

During the second and third years, children use task information selectively, attending to some cues and not to others. Several studies report that position errors account for a significant proportion of errors in choice tasks for children under three (Babska 1965; Hicks and Stewart 1930; Hill 1965). For example, in one study (Miller 1934) children eleven-and-a-half to thirteen-and-a-half months were trained to find a reward under one of two boxes; the boxes were different colors and remained in the same positions during training. Then the child was given three test trials in which the positions of the boxes were changed so that he or she could respond to the color of the box, the absolute position of the box, or its relative left-right position. Up to age three, left-right position of the box was the cue chosen. In a series of similar tasks it was demonstrated that, developmentally, position was the earliest cue used, followed by configuration and then color. The addition of pictorial cues on boxes in a choice task has not been helpful to children under three (Babska 1965; Loughlin and Daehler, 1973).

However, strategies become more sophisticated with age. Infants from twelve to twenty-four months of age had to rotate a lever to bring a toy within reach (Koslowski and Bruner 1972). Only the oldest children succeeded. In the earlier strategies, the child either tried to obtain the toy by direct reach (although it was too far away) or manipulated the lever but failed to reach for the toy when it was in the appropriate position.

Although the data on use of strategies is sparse, it appears that infants as young as one month exhibit consistent behavior patterns in solving problems. Initial strategies are modifiable only with difficulty. Position and spatial information are the first cues used effectively, and young children continue to use them in situations where they are not appropriate.

4. *Early concepts*. The ability to categorize stimuli according to common attributes enables an individual to respond to many stimuli in the same way on the basis of a common characteristic and without detailed consideration of each instance. It is possible that the changing ability to categorize may underlie the development of schema formation discussed earlier. Successful categorization requires attention to and discrimination of the attributes on which stimuli vary. Early in life, infants learn to discriminate on the basis of a single attribute. For example, infants learn to respond to the positive stimulus when two different colors (Lipsitt 1963; Simmons 1964) or sounds are varied in position.

The ability to respond selectively to stimuli varied in position and differing in two dimensions appears to be acquired much later. Infants from six to twelve months learned to respond on the basis of form, while position and one other attribute (e.g., orientation, size) were irrelevant cues. Many trials over an extended period of time were required. At twelve to fifteen months infants solved a two-choice discrimination problem where all trials were given in one session, only if three redundant cues were provided (e.g., small red cylinder versus large blue square) while position was an irrelevant cue (Hill 1965; White 1972). By twenty-one months this discrimination was learned with only two redundant cues (size and shape), and by two years the task could be learned on the basis of color alone (White 1972).

Several studies have investigated infants' ability to categorize spontaneously. In one study, infants played with a collection of objects which could be sorted into two groups on the basis of one or more attributes (Ricciuti 1965). Fifty percent of the year-old infants handled first the objects of one group and then the objects of the other when the two object-groups differed in color, form, and texture (hard yellow beads and gray clay balls). When objects differed in size alone, only 25 percent of the year-olds showed ordering, but 50 percent of the eighteen-month-olds and 63 percent of the two-year-olds did so. Few infants at any age ordered stimuli differing only in shape. In two other studies, two-year-olds were asked to group forms differing in size, shape, and color. The infants either did not group objects on the basis of similarity or did so only partially (Denney 1972a, 1972b). Partial groupings reflected attention to size and shape (Denney 1972b).

Although two-year olds have obviously learned to make discriminations requiring attention to multiple dimensions (e.g., recognizing a person), reports of simultaneous categorization on two dimensions are sparse. When two-year-olds were trained to drop blocks into separate holes according to form or color, only four of twenty-four infants were able to sort successfully when attention to both form and color was required (Watson and Danielson 1969). However, color is apparently not a very salient cue for infants (Denney 1972*b;* Miller 1934; Collard and Rydberg 1972). Perhaps more successful sorting would be obtained on the basis of form and size in the same task.

The infant's ability to relate objects to each other along a common dimension such as size is relatively undeveloped. When playing with nesting cups, infants under sixteen months were described as demonstrating a binary concept of size (Greenfield, Nelson, and Saltzman 1972). One cup was treated as the large one, and the others were placed in it without regard for the size relationships of the inner cups. Although two-year-olds can learn to select the smaller of two boxes to obtain candy, they cannot pick "the middle-sized stimulus" and do not understand the meaning of "biggest" (Hicks and Stewart 1930; Thrum 1935; Welch 1939).

There is some evidence in an early study that two-year-olds can learn to choose the "box of a different color" and the "box outside the square" (Miller 1934), but studies of such complex relational concepts have not often been attempted with infants.

With increasing experience, details become more important in the identification of exemplars of a concept. For example, "mommy" may be applied to all females at an early period, but later this concept refers to one specific female. Fifteen eighteen- to twenty-four-month-olds were shown black and white photos, outline and detailed drawings of familiar and unfamiliar objects. Familiar objects were recognized most easily in pictures with detail, but unfamiliar objects required less detail for identification (Nelson 1972). This suggests that as a concept becomes familiar, its definition incorporates more information about relevant details which must be discriminated before an exemplar can be identified. This kind of research and these results fit very well with the data used to infer schema formations discussed earlier. The literature on categorization is not often discussed conjointly with the literature on schema formation because the research in each area tends to be undertaken by different sets of investigators whose work is related to different theoretical backgrounds. However, the eventual integration of the two research areas may lead to a greater understanding of the development of complex cognitive behavior and the processes that control this development.

5. *Emergence of symbolic representation.* The ability to act with reference to objects and events in their absence probably requires some internal representation. When an infant in the first few months of life has learned to turn his or her head to receive milk at the sound of a bell, we can say that he or she expects the milk to follow the sound of the bell. Although this expectation is probably engaged only when the bell sounds

and may endure only in the brief interval between the sound and the delivery of milk, it involves a representation of the event sequence. In the example above, the infant "represents" the sequence "bell—milk delivery" by turning appropriately and perhaps beginning to suck before the time when the milk is delivered. Objects are first represented by the actions in which the child contacts them (Piaget 1951; 1952). A rattle may be represented, for example, by the continuation of hand-shaking after the infant has dropped the rattle. Early imitation involves immediate repetition of observed behaviors and reflects an attempt to understand the event through its continuation and reproduction (Piaget 1951). Longitudinal study of vocal and gestural imitation in the first two years suggests a consistent sequence (Piaget 1951; Uzgiris 1971). At first the infant only imitates familiar sounds and gestures (that is, those that have previously been produced spontaneously). The earliest imitations are not morphologically exact reproductions, but later the infant reproduces unfamiliar behaviors with attempts at accuracy and begins to use imitation as a way of learning new behaviors. The reproduction of observed behaviors can be viewed as an external reproduction, but later this external representation is internalized (Piaget 1951). Toward the end of the sensorimotor period, the infant begins to deliberately imitate behaviors seen hours or even days earlier. This delayed imitation, according to Piaget (1951), is a necessary precursor of words and more abstract symbolic representation. Language is undoubtedly the most important symbolic system acquired by the child. It opens a new domain of cognition and changes the relationship between the child and other persons.

6. *Implications for later development.* Although later learning and cognition appear to be based upon these early developments, in over thirty years of longitudinal research, it has been consistently reported that infant developmental tests are not good predictors of later scores on intelligence tests (Bayley 1955; Elkind 1967; Knobloch and Pasamanick 1962; Stott and Ball 1965). A number of explanations have been offered to account for this predictive failure.

First, intelligence is not a unitary function which grows through steady accretions. It may be more like a dynamic succession of developing functions which proceed on separate time-schedules such that the organization of these functions is different at different times. Thus the behaviors assessed on tests at different ages are distinctly different (Bayley 1955). Furthermore, standardized-test scores are based on comparison of a child with his or her age peers. In order to obtain the same score at different ages, the rate of growth must remain constant. But, in fact, the rate of growth can vary over different periods of childhood and for different individuals. The infant, even at age two, is a relatively plastic organism. We can expect behavior to be modified through continuing experience. For any selected group of infants at a given level of development, we can expect wide variations in subsequent experience. Thus we can expect that they will differ more at school-age than they did as infants, in part as a reflection of divergent experiences. Intelligence tests sample only a limited group of behaviors. A child's acquisition of these behaviors depends on their adaptive value in his environment.

In spite of failure to predict future developmental status accurately, infant tests do evaluate progress in infancy and may alert parents and caretakers to possible problems. Although early abilities are necessary for later development, they alone are not sufficient. Advanced functions depend upon the maturation of early skills plus others (Bayley 1955). For example, form recognition must develop before a child can learn to read. But, since reading involves many other skills, we cannot predict success in reading on the basis of skill at form recognition. However, we *can* predict that if a child is *not* able to recognize forms, reading will not be learned. For this reason, infant tests are successful in predicting within broad ranges those individuals who are likely to be retarded, average, or superior, and prediction is most successful for identifying developmental failures (Elkind 1967; Frankenburg, Camp, and Van Natta 1971; Knobloch and Pasamanick 1962). For a full discussion of intelligence and the genetic-environmental issues, the reader should refer to chapter 1 in this volume.

Summary. From the above review of learning and cognitive development in infancy, we can conclude that:

1. The ability to control attention is one that develops during infancy. At first infants attend to sensory change. Later they attend to discrepant events.

2. We know very little about infant memory. The ability to habituate to a stimulus involves memory since the stimulus must be recognized when it is repeated. Habituation to visual stimuli is difficult to demonstrate in infants under three months of age although older infants do habituate reliably to visual stimuli.

3. Classical and operant conditioning have been demonstrated in the newborn, but stable conditioned responses have been difficult to obtain until later ages.

4. Infants as young as one to five months show consistent patterns of behavior in learning situations, which suggests that simple strategies are operative at this age.

5. In the second and third years children frequently use position of test materials in relation to their own bodies as a salient cue, even when it is inappropriate. The ability to use pictorial information, configuration,

and color as salient information appears to develop later, although few studies have been conducted.

6. In the first year infants can be trained to respond regularly to one of two stimuli differing on a given attribute. Attention to more than one attribute (e.g., color and form; size and form) develops later, and two-year-olds still experience difficulty in sorting or grouping with respect to two attributes.

7. Infants' earliest representations are actions including imitation. Delayed imitation may be evidence of the first internal representation and is believed to be necessary for development of linguistic symbols, although there are few studies of infant imitation.

8. Although later learning depends upon early skills, infant tests do not predict later ability because other variables are also involved. These include integration of skills, individual differences in rate of development, and individual differences in subsequent opportunities and experience.

EARLY ENVIRONMENT AND THE DEVELOPMENT OF COMPETENCE

The Competent Infant

The research findings reviewed in this chapter indicate the current state of knowledge about what the infant can and cannot do. From the data gathered thus far, there emerges a view of the neonate as active and skilled with the potential for developing competence in many areas. On an absolute scale the competence level during infancy is low, since the infant's repertoire of cognitive, motor, and social skills is limited when compared to that of an older child or adult. Yet these same skills are very effective when the type of environment in which the infant functions is taken into account. When hungry, the newborn can cry loudly to signal the caretaker to provide nutriment and can suck effectively when it is provided. Later, the infant can control much of his or her own experience and can affect environmental events. For example, during the first two years the infant develops the ability to influence the caretaker, maintain attention, manipulate objects, and control position in the environment through motor activity and locomotion. Thus, in terms of controlling the environment the infant can be considered quite competent.

Investigators who are impressed with infant competence note that infant behavior shows direction, selectivity, and persistence (Wenar 1964; B. White 1972; R. White 1959). These motivational attributes do not appear to result from a physiological drive such as hunger or thirst, nor can they be explained through association with such drives. The infant cannot directly satisfy primary needs through manipulation of the environment until the particular skill involved is highly practiced (White

1959). For example, an infant spends many months perfecting his or her grasp before self-feeding is possible. Likewise, when the infant first learns to walk, there is frequently a transition period when crawling is the preferred mode of travel if the baby wants to get somewhere (or something) fast. At this stage, walking is tedious and slow, with frequent falls, whereas crawling has usually been perfected as a fairly rapid means of locomotion. Yet, with a persistence few adults can muster when mastering a new motor skill, every normal infant eventually walks.

A number of authors have pointed out the apparent pleasure infants derive from mastering a new skill. Papousek and Bernstein (1969) commented about infants learning a head-turning discrimination: "Sometimes we even had the impression that successful solving of the problem elicited more pleasure in the subject than did the reward" (p. 246). Others have observed smiling and cooing in infants who have learned to operate a mobile or recognize a slightly discrepant stimulus (Watson 1972; Zelazo 1972), while laughter has been related to mastery in cognitive tasks (Sroufe and Wunsch 1972).

Thus, it is likely that the infant is a self-motivated organism who learns at least partly through self-rewarding experience. If the learning of motor control were not self-rewarding, the many failures and falls would quickly condition the infant to cease his efforts. In a responsive environment this motivation is maintained as the infant learns new and better ways to affect the objects and surrounding events.

Experience is probably extremely important in this respect. The infant learns to learn by finding that attention and activity result in new and interesting experiences. Stimulus change observed or produced by the infant probably functions as a reinforcing event which maintains the infant's attention and causes repetition of the behavior (Horowitz 1969). But if these activities produce no results, the infant may learn not to respond. In an experiment that illustrates this point infants were given the opportunity to learn to move a mobile (Watson and Ramey 1972). Each infant in one group was given a mobile that could be controlled by head-turning. A second group had the same amount of experience with a stabile, while a third group had a mobile that moved but could not be controlled. When presented with the opportunity to control a mobile in the laboratory, the infants in the third group performed poorly, unable to learn the task, while infants in both of the other two groups were successful. Six weeks later, when the infants were retested at this task, the results remained the same (Watson 1971). Thus, previous experience with the noncontingent mobile had taught the infants that their behavior had no effect and prevented further efforts toward mastery in this situation.

We have seen that infants begin life with an initial readiness to learn and are already competent in many respects. However, the acquisition of almost every ability described is contingent upon appropriate environmental experience. In the following sections we discuss why the early environment is important, skills that caretakers may consider valuable, and activities that are likely to facilitate acquisition of these skills.

Facilitating Infant Development

Both animal and human studies have demonstrated that early experience can affect structural development, intersensory coordination, and behavioral maturation. Chimps reared in darkness early in life developed permanent structural damage to the eye (Reisen 1961). Kittens reared without sight of their forepaws failed to show visual-motor coordination in a task requiring correct placement of paws on wooden slats (Hein and Held 1967). Even motor behaviors whose onset is primarily determined by maturation (e.g., sitting, standing, and walking) were retarded in institutionalized infants experiencing severe physical restriction (Dennis 1960). Also, retarded performance on cognitive tasks has been found to be related to severe malnutrition during infancy (Brockman and Ricciuti 1971; Cravioto, DeLicardie, and Birch 1966; Cravioto and Robles 1965).

Although it is known that early deprivation may retard development in some areas, it is not clear what effect environmental variations have beyond a certain level of adequacy. Most homes probably provide an environment sufficient for normal development to take place during infancy, but no clear evidence exists regarding long-term effects produced by adding further special stimulation (see Horowitz and Paden 1973). Nevertheless, use of the available knowledge to structure the infant's environment may increase the infant's developmental opportunities and is our best chance of bringing infants at least above the threshold environment for normal development. Thus, caretakers of all kinds might wish to take into consideration the available knowledge about infant development in order to organize the environment for maximal developmental opportunities for infants.

As a result of the increasing number of women wishing to enter the work force, an urgent need for quality day-care has arisen. Because large numbers of children will be affected by the programs created at day-care centers, guidelines based on our current knowledge are needed to assure the child of a beneficial environment. An unresolved issue is whether the emphasis of day-care centers will be educational or custodial. Unfortunately, federal and state legislators involved in establishing and regulating day-care facilities are rarely experts on the needs of young children. As research on institutional deprivation has repeatedly indicated, poorly run custodial facilities not only fail to develop the child's full potential but can be highly detrimental (Provence and Lipton 1962).

Papousek (1970) has enumerated some advantages and some risks involved in infant group-care. On the positive side there is the opportunity to provide a higher-quality, more stimulating environment than infants might otherwise receive. A number of well-run experimental day-care centers have already demonstrated that infants can make substantial developmental progress under these conditions and may even surpass home-reared infants in some respects (Caldwell and Richmond 1968; Fowler 1971; Haith 1972; Keister 1970). A day-care center can furnish "Adequate space for play and outdoor activities, outdoor naps, selection and production of toys in agreement with pedagogic and hygenic principles, adequate nutrition, physical exercise, and inoculation and other preventative medical measures" (Papousek 1970, p. 54). In addition, contact with other children is likely to stimulate positive social behavior and facilitate language acquisition. Finally, interactions between parents and day-care personnel may enhance the environment at home. There are also risks involved. Poorly trained staff or overcrowded conditions can lead to impersonal, routine care and lack of attention to individual needs. Also, too much group contact may tire or overstimulate young children. Care must be taken to provide children with adequate opportunity to work or play alone. Even in the best day-care centers the child may miss everyday situations common to our society (e.g., visiting, shopping) and human interactions he or she might encounter by remaining with a parent. Lastly, while some parents may profit from their contact with the day-care center, others may abdicate their child-rearing responsibilities to the center and belittle the parental role. Clearly, the day-care center cannot be a substitute for the role of the parents. Thus, while these centers have great potential for developing competence, this result can only be achieved in a well-staffed and well-equipped setting, in conjunction with responsible parenthood.

An environment which offers children a variety of experiences might be achieved through a combination of day-care and home (Caldwell 1967). At least two intervention programs have used this strategy (Dunham 1969; Fowler 1971). Although only preliminary results are available, it appears that infants are progressing very well under these programs. There is evidence that a stimulating home environment "primes" the child to take advantage of the day-care experience (Caldwell and Richmond 1968), which may in turn relieve stress at home by providing some time when the caretaker is free of child-rearing activities.

What Skills Should the Child Develop?

Those designing child-rearing programs must first decide on the relative value of different skills before determining what kind of experience to provide for the child. While the underlying goal in the development of competence involves insuring adequate growth through interaction with the environment, growth can proceed in many directions and emphasis in one area often narrows the opportunity for full development in other areas. Which skills will be the most valuable for any particular child is determined by the environment the child is preparing to enter. For example, a child competent by middle-class standards will not necessarily be prepared to cope with the ghetto environment and vice versa. Different subcultural groups have values of their own, and the worth of specific skills is relative to these values. In current American society, a standard of living adequate for physical and mental health usually requires success in the educational system, a middle-class institution. Though one can be critical of some middle-class values, they are the predominant standards in our society. Most of the skills discussed below are therefore consistent with middle-class standards, although they may also be consistent with other value orientations. The applicability of any skills should be judged in accordance with the needs of children in a specific setting.

A number of specific abilities have been suggested by various authors as child-rearing goals and as indications of competence, (Fowler 1972; Rohwer 1970; Wenar 1964; White 1972). These abilities can be categorized as cognitive, behavioral, and social skills. Cognitive skills include: (1) attentional skills such as persistence, curiosity, and exploration; (2) perceptual skills, including the ability to notice discrepancies and learn from observation; and (3) conceptual skills such as the anticipation of consequences, taking the perspective of another person, planning and carrying out activities, developing strategies for problem-solving, and the acquisition of basic knowledge. Behavioral abilities consist of: (1) motor skills such as manipulation of objects and control of body position; (2) control skills, including the ability to carry out instructions and to inhibit impulsive behavior; and (3) self-care skills such as toileting, eating in a regular manner, and so on. Finally, social skills include: (1) the understanding and use of language; (2) the ability to use adults as resources by getting their attention and help at appropriate times; and (3) the development of such personal attributes as feelings of self-worth, independence, ability to express feelings, warmth, flexibility, and cooperation. These skills prepare the child for successful learning in school, independent behavior, and effective communication with people.

Toward the Acquisition of Skills During Infancy

1. *General principles.* There are a number of general principles helpful in constructing an environment designed to facilitate acquisition of the
skills outlined above (see also chapter 9, this volume). First, let us consider the physical environment. According to one current view (Hunt
1961), cognitive development is determined by the match between the
child's existing cognitive level and the environmental stimulation present.
The child is interested in and enjoys discrepancy within his or her capacity
for integration (that is, mild variations of stimuli with which he or she is
already familiar). Stimulation beyond the infant's integrative level results
in distress and avoidance, while stimuli already well mastered by the infant produce "stultifying boredom."

The infant's level of cognitive development is not simply a function of
age. Individuals vary considerably according to previous experience and
natural ability. Each infant is continually evolving new cognitive structures so that the match between cognition and environment is in constant
flux. In order to assure the infant of challenging stimulation, an environment providing a wide range of stimuli is desirable.

A research study designed to isolate the environmental variables associated with competence found that the early environments in families
which produced competent children were varied and highly conducive to
exploration (White 1972). Interesting manipulatable objects (both common household articles and toys) were available within the child's reach.
The child was allowed access to furniture and stairs for climbing. Larger
toys such as tricycles or scooters provided the child with the opportunity
to develop other motor skills. People, television, and the physical surroundings offered interesting visual stimulation. The parents of these children did not inhibit the children's exploratory activities. For example,
they tended not to use confining playpens and gates and allowed the
children considerable freedom. Other studies have also emphasized the
importance of freedom to explore. For example, floor freedom has been
found to correlate with infants' ability to internalize controls (Stayton,
Hogan, and Ainsworth 1971). In addition, engagement in exploratory
activities has been suggested as a source of schema development (Kagan
1971; Piaget 1952) and a limitation of the opportunity for exploration
has been related to use of fewer schemas and lower scores on infancy tests
(Collard 1971).

Opportunity to explore a varied environment allows the child to develop both cognitive and motor skills at his own pace. Novel or discrepant
stimuli are likely to be encountered and to maintain the infant's attention
while he takes in the new information. Stimulation which is not excessive

or chaotic, and proceeds in a predictable manner, is thought to be conducive to the development of basic concepts of object permanence and causality. On the other hand, an overstimulating environment may cause infants to ignore important stimuli in order to reduce incoming information to a manageable level (Klaus and Gray 1968; Wachs, Uzgiris, and Hunt 1971).

In addition to the physical environment, the primary caretaker is probably a major influence on the level of competence attained by the infant. The caretaker structures the infant's interaction with the physical environment, gives emotional support and encouragement, and provides interesting stimulation by playing with the infant and talking to him or her. Infants differ greatly in their responsiveness to both the physical characteristics and the pacing of stimulation (Horowitz 1969). Where environmental events may elicit attention from one infant, these same events may go unnoticed by another. A responsive caretaker can structure the environment so as to facilitate a good match between the events and the infant's ability to comprehend and respond to them. When a good match occurs, the infant learns that his or her actions are effective in getting attention or food and in reducing discomfort (Lewis and Goldberg 1969). Although most mothers automatically adjust environmental stimulation (cuddling, feeding, and so on) to accommodate the characteristics of their infants, institutionalized infants may not be so fortunate. When a few caretakers are responsible for the care of many infants, individual differences are more difficult to take into account. Thus, the retardation found in infants raised in institutions may be partially due to a poor match between the environment and their individual needs, while the institutionally raised infants who show normal development may have experienced a good match with the environment (Horowitz 1969).

It is probably the case that the caretaker need not spend inordinate amounts of time in structuring the infant's experience. It has been noted that the mothers of competent infants rarely spent concentrated amounts of time instructing the child (Wenar 1972; White 1972). Instead, these mothers tended to stop briefly, attend to, and encourage their children's ongoing behavior. White (1972) writes:

These mothers very rarely spend five, ten or twenty minutes teaching their one or two-year-olds, but they get an enormous amount (in terms of frequency) of teaching in "on the fly," and usually at the *child's* instigation. Though they do volunteer comments opportunistically, they mostly react to overtures by the child (p. 33).

An important characteristic of this teaching style is that the caretaker shows interest in what the child is doing and is sensitive and responsive to the child's needs. One evaluation of three preschool curricula found that the child's cognitive development was more closely related to the social atmosphere and enthusiasm of the teacher than to the material being taught (Weikart 1969). An alert and enthusiastic caretaker or teacher, who is genuinely interested in what a child is doing, is likely to interact with him or her in a way that facilitates a good match between the child's abilities and environmental stimulation. Genuine interest must be distinguished from applying pressure to achieve. When an optimal match is maintained, the infant is not being "pushed" or overstimulated and enjoys learning. High levels of motivation or anxiety interfere with solving complex problems and acquiring a wide breadth of information. Instead, high motivation tends to result in learning that is rapid but narrow in scope (Bruner, Matter, and Papanek 1955). Allowing the infant or young child to interact with the environment at a leisurely pace, with an anxiety level lowered by adult acceptance and interest, probably results in broader and more enjoyable learning.

A second characteristic of the caretaker-infant interactions described as leading to competence was that most interactions occurred at the child's request (White 1972). Consequently, a connection was established between the child's behavior and the caretaker's response. Numerous studies have pointed out the importance of the child's learning that a response from the environment is contingent upon something he or she does. Infants whose mothers were responsive to crying during early infancy showed less distress and more effective communication later in infancy (Bell and Ainsworth 1972). Infants of responsive mothers also showed better internal control and obedience (Stayton et al. 1971). Mother vocalization in response to infant vocalization has been found to be significantly related to infants' vocalization, while noncontingent remarks from mothers were unrelated to infant vocalization (Yarrow, Rubenstein, and Pedersen 1971).

Thus, control over stimulation is important to the development of competence. To acquire such control the infant must perceive the connection between the action and its effect and must repeat the behavior while this contingency awareness is still in memory. For example, young infants may perform a response such as kicking the side of the crib and produce an interesting noise, but, lacking the ability to reproduce this event before contingency awareness has faded, they are unable to learn the sequence (Watson 1966). At a later age, increase in memory span and maturation of motor abilities make it possible for the infant to master a contingency previously beyond his capability.

In addition to helping the child interact with the environment, the caretaker is also a source of interesting and important stimulation. As noted earlier, babies are particularly attentive to sensory stimulation coming from people. One of the most important forms of such stimulation is language. Only in the last few years have we become aware of the receptive language abilities of infants. While normal home environments probably provide a lot of receptive language experience, unless group-care centers are planned carefully they may not provide adequate speech samples for infants, to the detriment of development. Many studies have noted the relationship between language competence and overall competence (Beckwith 1971; Golden, Birns, Bridger, and Moss 1971; White 1972). Language probably needs to occur in a clear, meaningful context and needs to be related to what the child is doing at the time. This is likely to be the most effective set of conditions for facilitating the development of language skills. Exposure to live language rather than language coming from the television or radio, and the use of language directed toward the child's level of understanding, have been found to be related to the development of competence (White 1972).

2. *Application of principles and knowledge.* A varied environment, freedom for exploration, an interested and responsive caretaker, and contingent stimulation all appear to be conducive to the development of competence. There are a growing number of sources that contain suggestions for infant-care activities and environments. They are based upon much of the research reviewed in this chapter and contain examples of activities appropriate to various ages (Evans and Saia 1972; Fowler 1972; Provence 1967). However, the basic responsibility for providing the infant with activities appropriate to his or her developmental level must lie with an observant and responsive caretaker. Described below are some general recommendations for caretaking of infants that reflect the current state of our knowledge as reviewed in this chapter. These recommendations are intended to serve as examples of the way practical applications can be drawn from the existing literature.

Birth to two months. The feeding situation offers important opportunities for interaction with the infant, since much of the infant's awake time is spent feeding. When held and fed by the caretaker, the infant is likely to be receptive to various types of stimulation. The human face provides an interesting visual stimulus. Eyes and hair provide areas of high contrast, the mouth and eyes provide movement, and the distance between the face and the infant is usually seven or eight inches, a distance considered within the focal range at this age. In addition, speech provides an effective auditory stimulus, and the infant receives tactile and vestibular stimulation while being held. The feeding situation also enables the child to begin forming simple associations (that is, being held in a certain way is connected with being fed). Leaving the infant to feed alone prevents all of this important stimulation from occurring during feeding.

Any of the infant's spontaneously emitted behaviors such as smiling, vocalizing, or looking can be reinforced by the caretaker's talking, singing, smiling, or touching the infant immediately following his or her behavior. In this way the infant learns to attend to the caretaker and can exert some control over the environment. The adult must select the most appropriate moments for such play by taking the cue from the infant, when he or she is alert, rested, and not hungry. Immediately after feeding is often a playful period for infants (Wolff 1965), but great individual variation exists.

During the first weeks of life much of an infant's crying is probably the result of discomfort. Thus, responding to the crying of a very young infant and alleviating the discomfort probably establishes an association between comfort and caretaker. As we have seen, the infant's cry represents the first attempt at communication and is one of the few means by which he or she is able to exert some control over the environment. The infant probably learns rather quickly whether or not crying brings attention from someone. As pointed out earlier, infants seem to cry less at an older age if the caretaker responds quickly to crying during early infancy (Bell and Ainsworth 1972). (Crying in older infants probably takes on different characteristics, and undiscriminated attention to crying can lead to high levels of such behavior.)

Picking up and carrying the infant often quiets crying and provides sensory stimulation. When picked up, infants become alert and begin visual scanning of the environment (Korner and Thoman 1970). One cross-cultural study has indicated that Zambian infants carried frequently on their mothers' backs exhibited more precocious motor behavior than did infants who remained in a crib (Goldberg 1972). Comfortable cloth back-carriers are now commercially available which allow the caretaker to continue work while providing the baby with visual, tactile, and vestibular stimulation.

Two to six months. A variety of small manipulatable objects, safe for the infant to put in his mouth but not small enough to swallow, can be made available. The infant's visual ability has now improved, and the coordination of eye-hand-mouth is a major task at this age. Objects hanging across the crib give the infant something to swipe at and will move contingently when the infant shakes the crib.

Talking to the infant about activities taking place probably facilitates language acquisition. Simple direct phrases, labeling objects and describing activities in a warm friendly tone, allow the infant to become acquainted with speech sounds. Although the infant does not necessarily know the meaning of words at this age, important receptive language is probably being acquired. Talk is not "wasted" on babies at any age.

Six to twelve months. During the second half of the first year fine motor coordination is developing which enables the child to perform more complex manipulations with objects. The infant can now make use of more complex toys and enjoys objects that make noise or move (e.g., toy car). Objects with parts that fit together or containers with contained objects help the child to form spatial relations. Allowing the infant freedom to crawl and explore the environment provides the opportunity to discover other interesting objects and their relations to each other. To insure safety, some confinement may be necessary, depending upon the specific situation.

With increased motor coordination the infant is capable of more independent behavior. Allowing the infant to take a more active role in routine caretaking activities helps him or her to develop new skills and acquire a sense of autonomy. For example, providing the infant with his or her own spoon and encouraging any attempts made at self-feeding facilitate the learning of skills necessary for this behavior.

During this period the infant is becoming aware of the existence of objects in space as separate from his or her body. Several games such as peek-a-boo can increase opportunities to use this concept. Such activities are interesting to the infant and capitalize upon learning of object permanence or spatial relations.

Towards the end of the first year and throughout the rest of early childhood, reading to the infant is an enjoyable activity. Even before babies can produce words they begin to understand the meanings of words. At this age, pointing out and labeling the objects on the page for the child, is an activity he or she will find interesting. Use of action words and dramatic expressions maintains interest.

One to two years. As the infant begins to walk, toys that require large motor skills are appropriate. Large toys such as a rocking horse or kiddie car help the child coordinate different kinds of movements. Toys that can be manipulated to make something happen (wind-up jack-in-the-box or music toys), toys that can be banged or pounded, and toys that can be cuddled and loved are enjoyed at this age. The availability of such objects or toys probably enables the infant to improve motor skills and actively manipulate the environment. The infant can learn about causal relations and how to make things happen.

Allowing the child to feed himself or herself and help with other caretaking activities (e.g., toilet, dressing) is likely to encourage an independent attitude. Encouragement and praise of his or her efforts gives the infant a feeling of accomplishment. Freedom to initiate activities and explore the environment continues to facilitate learning and independence. At the same time definite and consistent limits necessary for safety teach the infant that there is regularity in the effects of his or her actions. The infant can learn to inhibit inappropriate behaviors. Because the ability to inhibit is not well developed during the second year of life, it may be best to concentrate on a few important behaviors rather than to make many demands for inhibition at once. Diverting attention from forbidden objects by offering an attractive toy is often more effective than verbal warnings. Physical and gestural intervention are more effective than talking.

Language development occurs rapidly between the first and second year (see chapter 5 of this volume), and exposure to language in many contexts facilitates the infant's understanding and use of speech. Talking to the infant, describing current activities, and explaining what will take place next are important sources of linguistic stimulation. Short trips and various experiences accompanied by explanations about where you are going, what you are doing, and attempting to relate these experiences to other things that have happened or will happen, probably help the child to learn to use language to organize experience in a meaningful way. Appropriate word and movement games such as labeling objects and parts of the body ("Where is baby's nose?") can provide important tuition in a fun context. Instructions can be geared to the infant's level of understanding. Giving instructions that stress the names and relations of objects ("put the *blocks under* the *chair*"), not only help the child to master new words, but provide the child with opportunities to bring behavior under verbal control and to connect language with spatial relations.

There are probably innumerable ways in which the caretaker facilitates the infant's development. Unfortunately, almost no research is available concerning the long-term effects of either specific experiences or groups of experiences. Consequently, the structuring of activities must proceed to some extent on a trial-and-error basis. A recent article suggests that child-care workers must constantly be aware of possible adverse effects of specific programs (Watson 1971). Programs designed to stimulate development may fail either by having the opposite effect of that anticipated or by producing the desired result in one area but causing negative effects in other areas of behavior. An example used to illustrate this point is that of increasing a child's attention to speech by providing meaningful speech through a record system. Although the intention is to increase the infant's perception of speech, the infant might instead learn to ignore speech since it is not presented in contingent or relevant contexts. This example demonstrates the advisability of careful monitoring of planned environments such as day-care centers and emphasizes the great need for further research in this area.

Summary

In this section the discussion of early environmental influences suggests that:

1. Knowledge gained from basic research with infants can be used in planning early environments for children, which will help provide for adequate development in both home and group settings.

2. Day-care settings can be beneficial if well planned, but should not be considered a substitute for parental involvement.

3. In facilitating the acquisition of skills for a particular child, his or her individual needs and cultural background should be taken into consideration. It is important that early experiences are appropriate to an infant's level of development and are responsive to the child's behavior and interests.

4. The opportunity to explore a varied environment, including exposure to language, and a responsive but not intrusive caretaker appear to facilitate the infant's development.

Conclusion

Our knowledge about the infant is rapidly expanding, and it seems the more carefully we look the more capable we find the infant to be. Where we once wondered whether newborns could see, we now know that some patterns are discriminated in the first months of life and that even very young infants can make some fairly complex discriminations. The possible importance of early auditory experience for later language learning is a recent area of exploration. While sensorimotor development in the first year is well documented, the development of complex skills in the second year has been neglected. In the area of learning and cognitive development there is a great deal of current activity, yet our information about infants in the second year is still sparse. Although we know a great deal more about infant development than we knew twenty or even ten years ago, we are still at the threshold of understanding infant development. There have been only a few studies specifically designed to study the course of development. Many of the studies discussed above demonstrate a particular ability within a relatively narrow age-span. Our picture of development must currently be patched together from many disparate studies. While longitudinal studies are time-consuming and costly, the tracing of individual development over an extended period of time provides information that cannot be obtained otherwise, and this approach is particularly needed for second-year development. Although our current data base enables us to draw some implications for practical situations, we may benefit in this respect from future studies in applied settings designed to answer practical questions. With the increasing need for child-care services, adequate evaluation of experimental attempts is essential if long-term programs are to be instituted. There is, therefore, a continuing need for communication between the community of basic and applied researchers and the community of professionals and practitioners involved with children in natural settings.

ANNOTATED READING LIST

Advances in Child Behavior and Development. Vols. 1–6. New York: Academic Press, 1963, 1965, 1969, 1970, 1972.

A series edited by Spiker, Lipsitt, and Reese in which authors contribute reviews of their own research on a specific topic. Most volumes include one or more chapters on infancy, some of which are outstanding.

Bond, E. Perception of form by the human infant. *Psychological Bulletin,* 1972, *77,* 225–246.

A thorough review of recent research on infant visual perception.

Brackbill, Y., ed. *Infancy and Early Childhood.* New York, Free Press, 1967.

An edited collection of topical reviews of research on infants' sensory and perceptual processes, motor development, conditioning and learning, language development and cognition.

Brackbill, Y. & Thompson, G. G. *Behavior in Infancy and Early Childhood.* New York: Free Press, 1967.

An edited collection of significant articles on various topics such as perceptual, motor, and cognitive growth, learning and language development.

Dennenberg, V. H., ed. *Education of the Infant and Young Child.* New York: Academic Press, 1970.

A collection of contributed chapters on the effects of early educational experiences.

Eisenberg, R. The organization of auditory behavior. *Journal of Speech and Hearing Research,* 1970, *13,* 453–471.

A description of auditory development and a model for the organization of auditory behavior.

Flavell, J. H. Concept development. In P. H. Mussen, ed., *Carmichael's Manual of Child Psychology.* New York: John Wiley, 1970, 983–1060.

A comprehensive review of research in concept development from infancy to adolescence.

Friedlander, B. Z. Receptive language development in infancy: issues and problems. *Merrill-Palmer Quarterly,* 1970, *16,* 9–52.

A recent review which emphasizes the importance of listening experience for language development and provides a theoretical framework for studying early language reception.

Gesell, A. The ontogenesis of infant behavior. In L. Carmichael, ed., *Manual of Child Psychology.* New York: John Wiley, 1954, 295–331.

An excellent overview of infant development which reflects maturational principles of development based on early normative studies.

Gibson, E. J. *Principles of Perceptual Learning and Development.* New York: Appleton-Century-Crofts, 1967.

A review of research in perceptual learning and development within a coherent theoretical framework.

Hess, R. D. & Bear, R. M., eds., *Early Education,* Chicago: Aldine, 1968.

A collection of readings about preschool education and cognitive development.

Kessen, W., Haith, M. M., & Salapatek, P. H. Human infancy: a bibliography and a guide. In P. H. Mussen, ed., *Carmichael's Manual of Child Psychology*. 3d. ed. New York: John Wiley, 1970, 287–445.

A recent and comprehensive review of studies of infants from the nineteenth century up to 1968.

McCarthy, D. Language development in children. In L. Carmichael, ed., *Manual of Child Psychology*. 2d ed. New York: John Wiley, 1954, 476–681.

A review of early normative studies of language development with a good discussion of early babbling and imitation.

Peiper, A. *Cerebral Function in Infancy and Early Childhood*. New York: Consultants Bureau, 1963.

An excellent and detailed discussion of early behavior in relation to neurological and physiological development.

Pratt, K. C. The neonate. In L. Carmichael, ed., *Manual of Child Psychology,* 2d ed. New York: John Wiley, 1954, 190–254.

An excellent review of early studies (pre-1950) of neonatal behavior and capacities.

Provence, S. *Guide for the Care of Infants in Groups*. New York: Child Welfare League of America, 1967.

An informative but nontechnical manual which explains important principles of infant development and suggests techniques for appropriate interacting with infants.

Siqueland, E. Basic learning processes: I. Classical conditioning. Basic learning processes: II. Instrumental conditioning (Instrumental conditioning in infants); Discrimination learning (Discrimination learning in infancy). In H. W. Reese and L. P. Lipsitt, eds., *Experimental Child Psychology*. New York: Academic Press, 1970, 65–102, 157–183.

A textbook discussion of studies of learning and conditioning in infants.

Stone, J. L., Murphy, L. B., & Smith, H. T., eds., *The Competent Infant*. New York: Basic Books, 1973.

A comprehensive handbook of infant development which includes more than two hundred selections of original research studies.

Stott, L. H. & Ball, R. S. Infant and preschool tests: review and evaluation. *Monographs of the Society for Research in Child Development,* 1965, 30 (serial no. 101).

A review of theories of intelligence, measurements of intelligence, and current uses of infant tests with analysis of the behaviors sampled by infant tests.

References

Ainsworth, M. D. S. The development of infant-mother attachment. In B. Caldwell and H. Ricciuti, eds., *Review of Child Development Research*. Vol. 3. Chicago, University of Chicago Press, 1973.

Ahrens, R. Beiträge zur Entwicklung des Physiogriomie-und Mimikerkennes. Zeitschrift für experimentelle und angewandte Psychologie, 1954, 2, 412–454.

Altman, J. Postnatal neurogenesis and the problem of neural plasticity. In W. Himwich, ed., *Developmental Neurobiology*. Springfield, Illinois: Charles Thomas, 1970.

Ames, E. & Silfen, C. Methodological issues in the study of age differences in infant's attention to stimuli varying in movement and complexity. Paper presented at meeting of Society for Research in Child Development, Minneapolis, 1965.

Andre-Thomas, Chesni, Y., & Saint-Anne-Dargassies, S. *The Neurological Examination of the Infant*. London: Medical Advisory Committee of the National Spastics Society, 1960.

Aronson, E. & Rosenbloom, S. Space perception in early infancy: perception within a common auditory-visual space. *Science,* 1971, *172,* 1161–1163.

Babska, Z. The formation of the conception of identity of visual characteristics of objects seen successively. *Monographs of the Society for Research in Child Development,* 1965, *30* (2), 113–124.

Ball, W. & Tronick, E. Infant responses to impending collision: optical and real. *Science,* 1971, *171,* 818–820.

Barnet, A. B., Lodge, A., & Armington, J. C. Electroretinogram in newborn human infants. *Science,* 1965, *148,* 651–654.

Bartoshuk, A. K. Human neonatal cardiac responses to sound: a power function. *Psychonomic Science,* 1964, *1,* 151–152.

Bayley, N. Mental growth during the first three years: An experimental study of sixty-one children by repeated tests. *Genetic Psychology Monographs,* 1933, *14,* 1–92.

————. On the growth of intelligence. *American Psychologist,* 1955, *10,* 805–818.

————. Comparisons of mental and motor tests scores for ages 1–15 months by sex, birth order, race, geographical location and education of parents. *Child Development,* 1965, *36,* 379–411.

————. *Bayley Scales of Infant Development.* New York: Psychological Corporation, 1969.

Beckwith, L. Relationships between attributes of mothers and their infants' IQ scores. *Child Development,* 1971, *42,* 1083–1097.

Bell, S. M. The relationship of infant-mother attachment to the development of the concept of object permanence. Doctoral dissertation. Johns Hopkins University, 1968.

————. The development of the concept of object as related to infant-mother attachment. *Child Development,* 1970, *41,* 291–312.

Bell, S. M. & Ainsworth, M. D. S. Infant crying and maternal responsiveness. *Child Development,* 1972, *43,* 1171–1190.

Bench, J. Some effects of audio-frequency stimulation on the crying baby, *Journal of Auditory Research,* 1969, *9,* 122–128.

Bergman, T., Haith, M., & Mann, L. Development of eye contact and facial scanning in infants. Paper presented at meeting of Society for Research in Child Development, Minneapolis, 1971.

Berman, P. W. & Graham, F. K. Children's responses to relative, absolute, and position cues in a 2-trial size discrimination. *Journal of Comparative and Physiological Psychology,* 1964, *57,* 393–397.

Bernard, S. & Sontag, L. W. Fetal reactivity to tonal stimulation: a preliminary report. *Journal of Genetic Psychology,* 1947, *70,* 205–210.

Birns, B., Blank, M., Bridger, W. H., and Escalona, S. K. Behavioral inhibition in neonates produced by auditory stimuli. *Child Development,* 1965, *36,* 639–645.

Blanton, M. G. The behavior of the human infant during the first thirty days of life. *Psychological Review,* 1917, *24,* 456–483.

Bond, E. Perception of form by the human infant. *Psychological Bulletin,* 1972, *77,* 225–246.

Boyd, E. Voice responsibility and discrimination in two-month-old infants. Doctoral dissertation. University of Kansas, 1972.

Bower, T. G. R. Discrimination of depth in premotor infants. *Psychonomic Science,* 1964, *1,* 368.

————. Stimulus variables determining space perception in infants. *Science,* 1965a, *149,* 88–89.

————. The determinants of perceptual unity in infancy. *Psychonomic Science,* 1965b, *3,* 323–324.

————. Heterogeneous summation in human infants. *Animal Behavior,* 1966a, *14,* 395–398.

————. The visual world of infants. *Scientific American,* 1966b, *215,* 80–92.

————. The development of object permanence: some studies of existence constancy. *Perception and Psychophysics*, 1967, *2*, 311–318.

————. The object in the world of the infant. *Scientific American*, 1971, *225*, 30–38.

Bower, T. G. R., Broughton, J., & Moore, M. K. Development of the object concept as manifested in changes in the tracking behavior of infants between 7 and 20 weeks of age. *Journal of Experimental Child Psychology*, 1971, *11*, 182–193.

Brackbill, Y., Adams, G., Crowell, D. H., & Gray, M. L. Arousal level in neonates and preschool children under continuous auditory stimulation. *Journal of Experimental Child Psychology*, 1966, *4*, 178–188.

Brackbill, Y., & Koltsova, M. Conditioning and learning. In Y. Brackbill, ed., *Infancy and Early Childhood*. New York: Free Press, 1967, 207–289.

Brazelton, T. Berry, Young, Grace C., & Bullova, M. Inception and resolution of early developmental pathology: a case history. *Journal of the American Academy of Child Psychiatry*, 1971, *10*, 124–135.

Brazelton, T. B., Freedman, D. A., Horowitz, F. D., Koslowski, B., Robey, M., Ricciuti, H. N., & Sameroff, A. *Neonatal Behavioral Assessment Scale*. In press.

Brennan, W. M., Ames, E. W., & Moore, R. W. Age differences in infants' attention to patterns of different complexities. *Science*, 1966, *151*, 1354–1356.

Brockman, L. M. & Ricciuti, H. N. Severe protein-calorie malnutrition and cognitive development in infancy and early childhood. *Developmental Psychology*, 1971, *4*, 312–319.

Brown, C. A. The development of visual capacity in the infant and young child. *Cerebral Palsy Bulletin*, 1961, *3*, 364–372.

Bruner, J. S. The course of cognitive growth. *American Psychologist*, 1964, *19*, 1–15.

————. *Processes of Cognitive Growth: Infancy*. Worcester: Clark University Press, 1968.

————. Eye, hand, and mind. In D. Elkind & J. H. Flavell, eds., *Studies in Cognitive Development: Essays in Honor of Jean Piaget*. New York: Oxford University Press, 1969, 223–236.

Bruner, J. S., Matter, J., & Papanek, M. K. Breadth of learning as a function of drive level and mechanization. *Psychological Review*, 1955, *62*, 1–10.

Bühler, C. *The First Year of Life*. New York: John Day, 1930.

Bühler, C. & Hetzer, H. *Testing Children's Development From Birth to School Age*. New York: Farrar Rinehart, 1935.

Caldwell, B. M. What is the optimal learning environment for the young child? *American Journal of Orthopsychiatry*, 1967, *37*, 8–21.

Caldwell, B. M. & Richmond, J. B. The children's center in Syracuse, New York. In C. P. Chandler, R. S. Lourie, & A. P. Peters, eds., *Early Child Care*. New York: Atherton Press, 1968.

Campos, J. J., Langer, A., & Krowitz, A. Cardiac responses on the visual cliff in prelocomotor human infants. *Science*, 1970, *170*, 196–197.

Caron, R. F. & Caron, A. J. Degree of stimulus complexity and habituation of visual fixation in infants. *Psychonomic Science*, 1969, *14*, 78–79.

Cattell, P. *The Measurement of Intelligence of Infants and Young Children*. New York: Psychological Corporation, 1940.

Charlesworth, W. R. Development of the object concept: a methodological study. Paper presented at American Psychological Association, New York, 1966.

————. The role of surprise in cognitive development. In D. Elkind & J. H. Flavell, eds., *Studies in Cognitive Development: Essays in Honor of Jean Piaget*. New York: Oxford University Press, 1969.

Chase, W. P. Color vision in infants. *Journal of Experimental Psychology*, 1937, *20*, 203–222.

Chomsky, N. *Syntactic Structures*. The Hague: Mouton, 1957.

————. *Aspects of the Theory of Syntax*. Cambridge, Massachusetts: MIT Press, 1965.

Chun, R. W. M., Pawset, R., & Forster, F. M. Sound localization in infancy. *Journal of Nervous and Mental Disorders,* 1960, *130,* 472–476.

Clifton, R. K. Cardiac conditioning and orienting in the infant. In P. A. Obrist, J. Brener, A. H. Black, & L. DiCara, eds., *Cardiovascular Psychophysiology— Current Issues in Response Mechanisms, Biofeedback, and Methodology.* Chicago: Aldine Press, in press.

Clifton, R. K., Graham, F. K., & Hatton, H. M. Newborn heart rate response and response habituation as a function of stimulus duration. *Journal of Experimental Child Psychology,* 1968, *6,* 265–278.

Clifton, R. K., Meyers, W. J., & Solomons, G. Methodological problems in conditioning the headturning response of newborn infants. *Journal of Experimental Child Psychology,* 1972, *13,* 29–42.

Clifton, R. K., Siqueland, E. R., & Lipsitt, L. P. Conditioned headturning in human newborns as a function of conditioned response requirements and states of wakefulness. *Journal of Experimental Child Psychology,* 1972, *13,* 43–57.

Cobb, K., Goodwin, R., & Saelens, E. Spontaneous hand positions of newborn infants. *Journal of Genetic Psychology,* 1966, *108,* 225–237.

Cohen, L. B. Observing responses, visual preferences and habituation to visual stimuli. *Journal of Experimental Child Psychology,* 1969, *7,* 419–433.

Collard, R. R. Exploratory and play behaviors of infants reared in an institution and in lower- and middle-class homes. *Child Development,* 1971, *42,* 1003–1015.

Collard, R. R., & Rydberg, J. Generalization of habituation to objects in human infants. *Proceedings, 80th Annual Convention, APA,* 1972.

Conel, J. L. *The Postnatal Development of the Human Cerebral Cortex,* Vol. I: *Cortex of the Newborn.* Cambridge, Mass.: Harvard University Press, 1939.

———. Histologic development of the cerebral cortex. In *The Biology of Mental Health and Disease.* New York: P. B. Hoeber, 1952, 1–8.

Corman, H. H. & Escalona, S. K. Stages of sensori-motor development: A replication study. *Merrill-Palmer Quarterly,* 1969, *15,* 352–361.

Craviato, J., DeLicardie, E. R., & Birch, H. G. Nutrition, growth and neurointegrative development: an experimental and ecologic study. *Pediatrics,* 1966, *38,* 319–372.

Craviato, J., & Robles, B. Evolution of adaptive and motor behavior during rehabilitation from Kwashiorkor. *American Journal of Orthopsychiatry,* 1965, *35,* 449–464.

Crowell, D. H. Infant motor development. In Y. Brackbill, ed., *Infancy and Early Childhood.* New York: Free Press, 1967, 125–203.

Cruikshank, R. M. The development of visual size constancy in early infancy. *Journal of Genetic Psychology,* 1941, *58,* 327–351.

Culp, R. Looking response, decrement and recovery, of eight- to fourteen-week-old infants in relation to presentation of the infant's mother's voice. Master's thesis, University of Kansas, 1971.

Daehler, M. W. & Myers, N. A. Cognitive development in one- to three-year-old children. Progress report to the Spencer Foundation, 1972.

Dayton, G. O., Jones, M. H., Aiu, P., Rawson, R. A., Steele, B., & Rose, M. Developmental study of coordinated eye movement in the human infant. I. Visual acuity in the newborn human: a study based on induced optokinetic nystagmus recorded by electrooculography. *Archives of Opthalmology,* 1964, *71,* 865–870.

Dayton, G. O., Jones, M. H., Steele, B., & Rose, M. Developmental study of conditioned eye movements in the human infant. II. An electrooculographic study of the fixation reflex in the newborn. *Archives of Opthalmology,* 1964, *71,* 871–875.

Decarie, T. G. *Intelligence and Affectivity in Early Childhood.* New York: International Universities Press, 1965.

Dennis, W. Causes of retardation among institutional children: Iran. *Journal of Genetic Psychology,* 1960, *96,* 47–59.

Denisova, M. D. & Figurin, N. C. An investigation of the first combination feeding reflexes in young infants. Cited by Brackbill, Y. & Koltsova, M. Conditioning and learning. In Y. Brackbill, ed., *Infancy and Early Childhood*. New York: Free Press, 1967.

Denney, N. W. A developmental study of free classification in children. *Child Development*, 1972a, *43*, 221–232.

———. Free classification in preschool children. *Child Development*, 1972b, *43*, 1161–1170.

Dodd, B. J. Effects of social and vocal stimulation on infant babbling. *Developmental Psychology*, 1972, *7*, 80–83.

Doris, J. & Cooper, L. Brightness discrimination in infancy. *Journal of Experimental Child Psychology*, 1966, *3*, 31–39.

Dreyfus-Brisac, C. The bioelectric development of the central nervous system during early life. In F. Faulkner, ed., *Human Development*. Philadelphia: W. B. Saunders, 1966, 286–305.

Dunham, R. M. Project know-how: a comprehensive and innovative attack on individual familial poverty. Institute of Human Development, Florida State University Progress Report, April, 1969.

Eimas, P. D., Siqueland, E. R., Juczzyk, P., & Vigorito, J. Speech perception in early infants. *Science*, 1971, *171*, 303–306.

Eisenberg, R. B. Auditory behavior in the human neonate. I. Methodological problems and the logical design of research procedures. *Journal of Auditory Research*, 1965, *5*, 159–177.

———. Pediatric audiology: shadow or substance? *Journal of Auditory Research*, 1971, *11*, 148–153.

Elkind, D. Cognition in infancy and early childhood. In Y. Brackbill, ed., *Infancy and Early Childhood*. New York: Free Press, 1967, 361–394.

Ellingson, R. J. The study of brain electrical activity in infants. In L. P. Lipsitt & C. C. Spiker, eds., *Advances in Child Development and Behavior*, 1963, 81–91.

Escalona, S. K., & Corman, H. H. Albert Einstein scales of sensorimotor development. Unpublished test manual. Albert Einstein School of Medicine, 1966.

Evans, W. F., & Gratch, G. The stage IV error in Piaget's theory of object concept development: difficulties in object conceptualization or spatial localization. *Child Development*, 1972, *43*, 682–688.

Evans, B. & Saia, G. *Day Care of Infants*. Boston: Beacon Press, 1972.

Fagan, J. F. Memory in the infant. *Journal of Experimental Child Psychology*, 1970, *9*, 217–226.

———. Infants' recognition memory for a series of visual stimuli. *Journal of Experimental Child Psychology*, 1971, *11*, 244–250.

Falade, S. *Contribution à une Étude sur le Développement de l'Enfant d'Afrique Noire*. Paris: Foulon, 1955.

Falmagne, J. Étude comparative du développement psychomoteur. *Académie Royale des Sciences d'Outre-Mer, Mémoires*, 1959, *13* (5).

Fantz, R. L. Form preference in newly hatched chicks. *Journal of Comparative Physiological Psychology*, 1957, *50*, 422–430.

———. A method for studying depth perception in infants under 6 months of age. *Psychological Record*, 1961, *11*, 27–32.

———. Pattern vision in newborn infants. *Science*, 1963, *140*, 296–297.

———. Visual experience in infants: decreased attention to familiar patterns relative to novel ones. *Science*, 1964, *146*.

———. Visual perception from birth as shown by pattern selectivity. *Annals of the New York Academy of Science*, 1965, *118*, 793–814.

———. Visual perception and experience in early infancy: a look at the hidden side of behavior development. In H. W. Stevenson, E. H. Hess, & H. L. Rheingold, eds., *Early Behavior: Comparative and Developmental Approaches*. New York: John Wiley, 1967.

Fantz, R. L. & Nevis, S. The predictive value of changes in visual preferences in early infancy. In J. Hellmuth, ed., *Exceptional Infant*. Vol. I. Seattle: Special Child Publications, 1967.

Fantz, R. L., Ordy, J. M., & Udelf, M. S. Maturation of pattern vision in infants during the first six months. *Journal of Comparative and Physiological Psychology*, 1962, *55*, 907–917.

Finley, G. E., Kagan, J., & Layne, O., Jr. Development of young children's attention to normal and distorted stimuli: A cross-cultural study. *Developmental Psychology*, 1972, *6*, 288–292.

Fitzgerald, H. E. & Porges, S. W. A decade of infant conditioning and learning research. *Merrill-Palmer Quarterly*, 1971, *17*, 80–117.

Flavell, J. H. *The Developmental Psychology of Jean Piaget*. Princeton: D. Van Nostrand, 1963.

Flavell, J. H. & Wohlwill, J. F. Formal and functional aspects of cognitive development. In D. Elkind & J. H. Flavell, eds., *Studies in Cognitive Development: Essays in Honor of Jean Piaget*. New York: Oxford University Press, 1969, 67–120.

Fowler, W. Cognitive baselines in early childhood: Developmental learning and differentiation of competence rule systems. In J. Hellmuth, ed., *Cognitive Studies*. Vol. 2. New York: Brunner/Mazel, 1971, 231–280.

————. A developmental learning approach to infant care in a group setting. *Merrill-Palmer Quarterly*, 1972, *18*, 145–177.

Fradkina, F. T., Vozniknovenie rechi u nebeuka [The beginning of speech in the child]. Cited in A. V. Zaporozhets & D. B. El'Konin, eds., *The Psychology of Preschool Children*. Trans. by J. Shybut & S. Simon. Cambridge, Massachusetts: MIT Press, 1971.

Frankenburg, W. K., Camp, B. W., & Van Natta, P. A. Validity of the Denver Developmental Screening Test. *Child Development*, 1971, *42*, 475–485.

Frankenburg, W. K. & Dodd, J. B. The Denver Developmental Screening Test. *Journal of Pediatrics*, 1967, *71*, 181–191.

Freedman, D. A., Fox-Kolenda, B. J., Margileth, D. A., & Miller, D. H. The development of the use of sound as a guide to affective and cognitive behavior. *Child Development*, 1969, *40*, 1099–1105.

Freud, S. Three essays on the theory of sexuality. *Standard Edition of the Complete Psychological Works of Sigmund Freud*. Vol. 7. London: Hogarth, 1953, 73–102.

Friedlander, B. Z. The effect of speaker identity, voice inflection, and message redundancy on infants' selection of vocal reinforcement. *Journal of Experimental Child Psychology*, 1968, *6*, 443–459.

————. Receptive language development in infancy: issues and problems. *Merrill-Palmer Quarterly*, 1970, *16*, 7–52.

Friedlander, B. Z., Jacobs, A. C., Davis, B. B., & Wetstone, H. S. Time sampling analysis of infants' natural language environments in the home. *Child Development*, 1972, *43*, 730–740.

Friedman, S., Nagy, A. N., & Carpenter, G. C. Newborn attention: differential response decrement to visual stimuli. *Journal of Experimental Child Psychology*, 1970, *10*, 44–51.

Fry, D. B. The development of the phonological system in the normal and the deaf child. In F. Smith & G. Miller, eds., *The Genesis of Language*. Cambridge, Mass.: MIT Press, 1966, 187–206.

Gardner, J. K. The development of object identity in the first six months of human infancy. Paper presented at meeting of the Society for Research in Child Development, Minneapolis, Minnesota, 1971.

Geber, M. The psychomotor development of African children in the first year and the influence of maternal behavior. *Journal of Social Psychology*, 1958, *47*, 185–195.

Geber, M. & Dean R. F. A. The state of development of newborn African children. *The Lancet*, 1957, *1*, 1216–1219.

Gesell, A. L. *Infancy and Human Growth*. New York: Macmillan, 1928.

———. The ontogenesis of infant behavior. In L. Carmichael, ed., *Manual of Child Psychology*. 2d ed. New York: John Wiley, 1954, 335–373.

Gesell, A., & Amaturda, C. Developmental diagnosis: normal and abnormal child development, clinical methods and practical applications, 3d ed. New York: Harper, 1962.

Gesell, A. L., Ilg, F. L., & Bullis, G. O. *Vision: Its Development in Infant and Child*. New York: Paul Hoeber, 1949.

Gesell, A., & Thompson, H. *The Psychology of Early Growth*. New York: Macmillan, 1938.

Gibson, E. J. *Principles of Perceptual Learning and Development*. New York: Appleton-Century-Crofts, 1969.

Goldberg, S. Infant care and growth in urban Zambia. *Human Development*, 1972, *15*, 77–89.

Golden, M., Birns, B., Bridger, W., & Moss, A. Social-class differentiation in cognitive development among black preschool children. *Child Development*, 1971, *42*, 37–45.

Gorman, J. J., Cogen, D. G., Gellis, S. S. Testing the visual acuity of infants. *Pediatrics*, 1957, *19*, 1088–1092.

Graham, F. K., Clifton, R. K. & Hatton, H. Habituation of heart rate responses to repeated auditory stimulation during the first five days of life. *Child Development*, 1968, *39*, 35–52.

Graham, F. K. & Jackson, J. C. Arousal systems and infant heart rate responses. In H. W. Reese & L. P. Lipsitt, eds., *Advances in Child Development and Behavior*. Vol. 5. New York: Academic Press, 1970.

Gratch, G. A study of the relative dominance of vision and touch in six-month-old infants. *Child Development*, 1972, *43*, 615–623.

Gratch, G. & Landers, W. F. Stage IV of Piaget's theory of infant object concepts: A longitudinal study. *Child Development*, 1971, *42*, 359–372.

Greenberg, D. Accelerating visual complexity levels in the human infant. *Child Development*, 1971, *42*, 905–918.

Greenfield, P. M., Nelson, K., & Saltzman, E. The development of rulebound strategies for manipulating seriated cups: a parallel between action and grammar. *Cognitive Psychology*, 1972, *3*, 291–310.

Griffiths, R. *The Abilities of Babies: A Study in Mental Measurement*. New York: McGraw-Hill, 1954.

Haaf, R. A & Bell, R. Q. A facial dimension in visual discrimination by human infants. *Child Development*, 1967, *38*, 895–899.

Haith, M. The response of the human newborn to visual movement. *Journal of Experimental Child Psychology*, 1966, *3*, 235–243.

———. Day care and intervention programs for infants under two years of age. Preprint, University of Denver, 1972.

Hall, G. S. Notes on the study of infants. *Pedagological Seminary*, 1891, *1*, 127–138.

Haller, M. W. The reactions of infants to changes in the intensity of pitch of pure tone. *Journal of Genetic Psychology*, 1932, *40*, 162–180.

Halverson, H. M. An experimental study of prehension in infants by means of systematic cinema records. *Genetic Psychology Monographs*, 1931, *101*, 107–284.

Hammond, J. Hearing and response in the newborn. *Developmental Medicine and Child Neurology*, 1970, *12*, 3–5.

Harris, P. L. Examination and search in infants. *British Journal of Psychology*, 1971, *62*, 469–473.

Harter, M. R. & Suitt, C. D. Visually-evoked cortical responses and pattern vision in the infant: a longitudinal study. *Psychonomic Science*, 1970, *18*, 235–237.

Harter, M. R. & White, C. T. Effects of contour sharpness and check size on visually evoked cortical potentials. *Vision Research,* 1968, *8,* 701–711.

Haynes, H., White, B. L., & Held, R. Visual accommodation in human infants. *Science,* 1965, *148,* 528–530.

Hein, A. & Held, R. Dissociation of the visual placing response into elicited and guided components. *Science,* 1967, *158,* 390–392.

Hershenson, M. Visual discrimination in the human newborn. *Journal of Comparative Physiological Psychology,* 1964, *58,* 270–276.

———. Development of the perception of form. *Psychological Bulletin,* 1967, *67,* 326–336.

Hershenson, M., Munsinger, H., & Kessen, W. Preference for shapes of intermediate variability in the human newborn. *Science,* 1965, *147,* 630–631.

Hicks, J. A. & Stewart, P. P. The learning of abstract concepts of size. *Child Development,* 1930, *1,* 195–203.

Hill, S. D. The performance of young children on three discrimination-learning tasks. *Child Development,* 1965, *36,* 425–435.

Honzik, M. The mental and motor test performance diagnosed or suspected of brain injury. Final report Contract SA43 PH 2426. Washington, D. C.: National Institute of Health, National Institute of Neurological Diseases and Blindness, Collaborative Research, 1962.

Horowitz, A. B. Habituation and memory: Infant cardiac responses to familiar and discrepant auditory stimuli. *Child Development,* 1972, *43,* 43–53.

Horowitz, F. D. Learning, developmental research and individual differences. In L. P. Lipsitt & H. W. Reese, eds., *Advances in Child Development and Behavior.* Vol. 4. New York: Academic Press, 1969.

Horowitz, F. D. & Paden, L. Y. The effects of environmental intervention programs. In B. Caldwell & H. N. Ricciuti, eds., *Review of Child Development Research.* Vol. 3. Chicago: University of Chicago Press, 1973.

Horowitz, F. D., Paden, L. Y., Bhana, K., Aitchison, R. & Self, P. Developmental changes in infant visual fixation to differing complexity levels among cross sectionally and longitudinally studied infants. *Developmental Psychology,* 1972, *7,* 88–89.

Hoversten, G. H. & Moncur, J. P. Stimuli and intensity factors in testing infants. *Journal of Speech and Hearing Research,* 1969, *12,* 687–702.

Hubel, D. H. & Wiesel, T. N. Receptive fields of cells in striate cortex of very young, visually inexperienced kittens. *Journal of Neurophysiology,* 1963, *26,* 994–1002.

Humphrey, T. Postnatal repetition of human prenatal activity sequences with some suggestions of their neuroanatomical basis. In R. J. Robinson, ed., *Brain and Early Behavior.* New York: Academic Press, 1969, 43–84.

Hunt, J. McV. *Intelligence and Experience.* New York: Ronald Press, 1961.

Hutt, C. Specific and diversive exploration. In H. W. Reese & L. P. Lipsitt, eds., *Advances in Child Development and Behavior.* Vol. V. New York: Academic Press, 1970, 120–180.

Hutt, C., Von Bernuth, H., Lenard, H. G., Hutt, S. S., & Prechtl, H. F. Habituation in relation to state in the human neonate. *Nature,* 1968, *220,* 618–620.

Hutt, S., Hutt, C., Lenard, H., Von Bernuth, H., & Muntjewerff, W. Auditory responsivity in the human neonate. *Nature,* 1968, *218,* 888–890.

Irwin, O. C. The amount and nature of activities of newborn infants under constant external stimulating conditions during the first ten days of life. *Genetic Psychology Monographs,* 1930, *8,* 1–92.

Jackson, J. C., Kantowitz, S. R., & Graham, F. K. Can newborns show cardiac orienting? *Child Development,* 1971, *42,* 107–121.

Janos, O. Development of higher nervous activity in premature infants. *Pavlov Journal of Higher Nervous Activity,* 1959, *9,* 760–767.

Jeffrey, W. E. The orienting reflex and attention in cognitive development. *Psychological Review,* 1968, *75,* 323–334.

Jeffrey, W. E. & Cohen, L. B. Habituation in the human infant. In H. W. Reese, ed., *Advances in Child Development and Behavior*. Vol. 6. New York: Academic Press, 1971.

Kagan, J. *Change and Continuity in the First Two Years: An Inquiry into Early Cognitive Development*. New York: John Wiley, 1971.

Kagan, J., Henker, B., Hen-Tou, A., Levine, J., & Lewis, M. Infants' differential reactions to familiar and distorted faces. *Child Development*, 1966, *37*, 519–532.

Kagan, J. & Lewis, M. Studies of attention in the human infant. *Merrill-Palmer Quarterly*, 1965, *11*, 95–127.

Kaplan, E. L. The role of intonation in the acquisition of language. Doctoral dissertation, Cornell University, 1969.

Karmel, B. Z. Complexity, amounts of contour, and visually dependent behavior in hooded rats, domestic chicks, and human infants. *Journal of Comparative and Physiological Psychology*, 1969a, *69*, 649–657.

———. The effect of age, complexity and amount of contour on pattern preferences in human infants. *Journal of Experimental Child Psychology*, 1969b, *7*, 339–354.

Karmel, B. Z., White, C. T., Cleaves, W. T., & Steinsick, K. J. A technique to investigate evoked potential correlates of pattern perception in infants. Paper presented at Eastern Psychological Association, April, 1970.

Kasatkin, N. I. The origin and development of conditioned reflexes in early childhood. In M. Cole & I. Maltzmen, eds., *Handbook of Contemporary Soviet Psychology*. New York: Basic Books, 1969.

Kearsley, R. B. Neonatal response to auditory stimulation: a demonstration of orienting behavior. Paper presented at meeting of the Society for Research in Child Development, Minneapolis, 1971.

Keele, C., & Neil, E., eds. *Samson Wright's Applied Physiology*. London: Oxford University Press, 1965.

Keister, M. E. A demonstration project: group care of infants and toddlers. Final report submitted to the Children's Bureau, Office of Child Development, U. S. Department of Health, Education, and Welfare, 1970.

Kessen, W. Research in the psychological development of infants: an overview. *Merrill-Palmer Quarterly*, 1963, *9*, 83–94.

———. Sucking and looking: two organized congenital patterns of behavior in the human newborn. In E. H. Hess, H. W. Stevenson, & H. L. Rheingold, eds., *Early Behavior: Comparative and Developmental Approaches*. New York: Wiley, 1967.

Kessen, W., Haith, M., & Salapatek, P. H. Human infancy: a bibliography and guide. In P. Mussen, ed., *Carmichael's Manual of Child Psychology*. Vol. I. 3d ed. New York: John Wiley, 1970, 287–447.

Kessen, W., Salapatek, P. H., & Haith, M. The visual response of the human newborn to linear contour. *Journal of Experimental Child Psychology*, 1972, *13*, 9–20.

Kilbride, J. E. The motor development of rural Baganda infants. Master's thesis, Pennsylvania State University, 1969.

Klatskin, E. H. Intelligence test performance at one year among infants raised with flexible methodology. *Journal of Clinical Psychology*, 1952, *8*, 230–237.

Klatskin, E. H., Jackson, E. B., & Wilkin, L. C. The influence of degree of flexibility in maternal child care practices on early child behavior. *American Journal of Orthopsychiatry*, 1956, *26*, 79–93.

Klaus, R. A. & Gray, S. W. The early training project for disadvantaged children: a report after five years. *Monographs of the Society for Research in Child Development*, 1968, *33*, no. 4 (whole no. 120).

Knobloch, H. & Pasamanick, B. The developmental behavioral approach to the neurologic examination in infancy. *Child Development*, 1962, *33*, 181–198.

Koopman, P. R. & Ames, E. W. Infants' preferences for facial arrangements: a failure to replicate. *Child Development,* 1968, *39,* 481–488.

Korner, A. T. & Thoman, E. B. Visual alertness in neonates as evoked by maternal care. *Journal of Experimental Child Psychology,* 1970, *10,* 67–78.

Koslowski, B. & Bruner, J. S. Learning to use a lever. *Child Development,* 1972, *43,* 790–799.

Krachkovskaia, M. V. Reflex changes in the leukocyte count of newborn infants in relation to food intake. *Pavlov Journal of Higher Nervous Activity,* 1959, *9,* 193–199.

Landers, W. Effects of differential experience on infant's performance in a Piagetian Stage IV object task. *Developmental Psychology,* 1971, *5,* 48–54.

LaRoche, J. L. & Tcheng, F. C. Y. *Le Sourire du Nourrison.* Louvain: Publications Universitaires, 1963.

LeCompte, G. K. & Gratch, G. Violation of a rule as a method of diagnosing infant's level of object concept. *Child Development,* 1972, *43,* 385–396.

Leiderman, P. H., Babu, B., Kagia, J., Kraemer, H. C., & Leiderman, G. F. African infant precocity and some special influences during the first year. *Nature,* 1973, *242, 247.*

Lenneberg, E. H. Speech as a motor skill with special references to nonaphasic disorders. In U. Bellugi & R. Brown, eds., The acquisition of language. *Monographs of the Society for Research in Child Development,* 1964, *29,* no. 1 (whole no. 92), 115–127.

————. *Biological Foundations of Language.* New York: John Wiley, 1967.

————. On explaining language, *Science,* 1969, *164,* 635–643.

Leventhal, A. S. & Lipsitt, L. P. Adaptation, pitch discrimination, and sound localization in the neonate. *Child Development,* 1964, *35,* 759–767.

Lewis, M. Infants' responses to facial stimuli in the first year of life. *Developmental Psychology,* 1969, *1,* 75–86.

Lewis, M. & Freedle, R. Mother-infant dyad: the cradle of meaning. Paper presented at Symposium on Language and Thought: Communication and Affect, University of Toronto, March, 1972.

Lewis, M., & Goldberg, S. Perceptual cognitive development in infancy: a generalized expectancy model as a function of the mother-infant interaction. *Merrill-Palmer Quarterly,* 1969, *15,* 81–100.

Lewis, M., Goldberg, S., & Campbell, H. A developmental study of information processing within the first 3 years of life. *Monographs of the Society for Research in Child Development,* 1969, *34* (whole no. 133).

Lewis, M., Wilson, C., & Baumel, M. Attention distribution in the 24-month-old child: variations in complexity and incongruity of the human form. *Child Development,* 1971, *42,* 429–438.

Lewis, M. M. *Infant Speech.* New York: The Humanities Press, 1951.

Liberman, A. M. The grammars of speech and language. *Cognitive Psychology,* 1970, *1,* 301–323.

Ling, B. C. Form discrimination as a learning cue in infants. *Comparative Psychology Monographs,* 1941, *2,* 17, 1–66.

————. A genetic study of sustained visual fixation and associated behavior in the human infant from birth to six months. *Journal of Genetic Psychology,* 1942, *6,* 227–277.

Lipsitt, L. P. Learning in the first year of life. In L. P. Lipsitt & C. C. Spiker, eds., *Advances in Child Development and Behavior.* Vol. 1. New York: Academic Press, 1963, 147–194.

Lipsitt, L. P. & Kaye, H. Conditioned sucking in the human newborn. *Psychonomic Science,* 1964, *1,* 29–30.

————. Change in neonatal response to optimizing and nonoptimizing sucking stimulation. *Psychonomic Science,* 1965, *2,* 221–222.

Lipsitt, L. P., Kaye, H., & Bosack, T. N. Enchancement of neonatal sucking through reinforcement. *Journal of Experimental Child Psychology,* 1966, *4,* 163–168.

Little, A. Eyelid conditioning in the human infant as a function of the ISI. Paper presented at meeting of the Society for Research in Child Development, Minneapolis, 1971.

Loughlin, K. A. & Daehler, M. W. The effects of distraction and added perceptual cues on the delayed reaction of very young children. *Child Development,* 1973, *44,* 384–388.

Luria, A. R. *The Role of Speech in the Regulation of Normal and Abnormal Behavior.* New York: Liveright, 1961.

Lusk, D., & Lewis, M. Mother-infant interaction and infant development among the Wolof of Senegal. *Human Development,* 1972, *15,* 58–69.

Lynn, R. *Attention, Arousal and the Orientation Reaction.* Oxford: Pergamon Press, 1966.

Macnamara, J. Cognitive basis of language learning in infants. *Psychological Review,* 1972, *79,* 1–13.

Mann, I. *The Development of the Human Eye.* New York: Grune & Stratton, 1964.

Marquis, D. P. Can conditioned responses be established in the newborn infant? *Journal of Genetic Psychology,* 1931, *39,* 479–492.

————. Learning in the neonate: the modification of behavior under three feeding schedules. *Journal of Experimental Psychology,* 1941, *29,* 263–282.

Matsumiya, Y., Tagliosco, V., Lombroso, C. T., & Goodglass, H. Auditory evoked response: meaningfulness of stimuli and interhemispheric asymmetry. *Science,* 1972, *175,* 790–792.

McCaffrey, A. Speech perception in infancy. Doctoral dissertation, Cornell University, 1972.

McCall, R. B. & Kagan, J. Attention in the infant: effects of complexity, contour, perimeter, and familiarity. *Child Development,* 1967a, *38,* 939–952.

————. Stimulus-schema discrepancy and attention in the infant. *Journal of Experimental Child Psychology,* 1967b, *5,* 381–390.

————. Individual differences in the distribution of attention to stimulus discrepancy. *Developmental Psychology,* 1970, *2,* 90–98.

McCall, R. B. & Melson, W. H. Amount of short term familiarization and the response to auditory discrepancies. *Child Development,* 1970, *41,* 861–869.

McCarthy, D. A. Language development in children. In L. Carmichael, ed., *Manual of Child Psychology.* 2d ed. New York: John Wiley, 1954, 492–630.

McGinnis, J. M. Eye movements and optic nystagmus in early infancy. *Genetic Psychology Monographs,* 1930, *8,* 321–430.

McGraw, M. *The Neuromuscular Maturation of the Human Infant.* New York: Columbia University Press, 1943.

McGurk, H. The role of object orientation in infant perception. *Journal of Experimental Child Psychology,* 1970, *9,* 363–373.

McKenzie, B. E. & Day, R. H. Object distance as a determinant of visual fixation in early infancy. *Science,* 1972, *178,* 1108–1110.

McNeill, D. Developmental psycholinguistics. In F. Smith & G. Miller, eds., *The Genesis of Language.* Cambridge, Mass.: MIT Press, 1966, 15–24.

————. The development of language. In P. Mussen, ed., *Carmichael's Manual of Child Psychology.* 3d ed. New York: John Wiley, 1970, 1061–1161.

Melson, W. H. & McCall, R. B. Attentional responses of five-month-old girls to discrepant auditory stimuli. *Child Development,* 1970, *41,* 1159–1172.

Miller, D. J. Visual habituation in the human infant. *Child Development,* 1972, *43,* 481–494.

Miller, D. J., Cohen, L., & Hill, K. T. Methodological investigation of Piaget's theory of object concept development in the sensory motor period. *Journal of Experimental Child Psychology,* 1970, *9,* 59–85.

Miller, N. E. The perception of children: a genetic study employing the critical choice delayed reaction. *Journal of Genetic Psychology,* 1934, *44,* 321–339.

Mirzoiants, N. S. The conditioned orienting reflex and its differentiation in the child. Cited by Brackbill, Y. & Koltsova, M., Conditioning and Learning. In

Y. Brackbill, ed., *Infancy and Early Childhood.* New York: Free Press, 1967.

Moffitt, A. R. Consonant cue perception by twenty- to twenty-four-week-old infants. *Child Development,* 1971, *42,* 717–731.

Morse, P. A. Speech perception in six-week-old infants. *Journal of Experimental Child Psychology,* 1972, *14,* 477–492.

Nelson, K. Organization of visual tracking responses in human infants. *Journal of Experimental Child Psychology,* 1968, *6,* 194–201.

————. The relation of form recognition to concept development. *Child Development,* 1972, *43,* 67–74.

Palermo, D. Language acquisition. In H. W. Reese & L. P. Lipsitt, eds., *Experimental Child Psychology.* New York: Academic Press, 1970, 425–478.

Papousek, H. A method of studying conditioned food reflexes in young children up to the age of six months. *Pavlov Journal of Higher Nervous Activity,* 1959, *9,* 136–140.

————. Experimental studies of appetitional behavior in human newborns and infants. In H. W. Stevenson, E. H. Hess, & H. L. Rheingold, eds., *Early Behavior: Comparative and Developmental Approaches.* New York: John Wiley, 1967.

————. Effects of group rearing conditions during the preschool years of life. In V. H. Denenberg, ed., *Education of the Infant and Young Child.* New York: Academic Press, 1970, 51–61.

Papousek, H. & Bernstein, P. The functions of conditioning stimulation in human neonates and infants. In A. Ambrose, ed., *Stimulation in Early Infancy.* London: Academic Press, 1969, 229–248.

Parkin, J. M. & Warren, N. A. Comparative study of neonatal behavior and development. Proceedings, University Social Science Conference, University of East Africa, Nairobi, 1969.

Pavlov, I. P. *Conditioned Reflexes.* Oxford: Clarendon Press, 1927.

Peiper, A. *Cerebral Function in Infancy and Childhood.* New York: Consultants Bureau, 1963.

Phillips, J. R. Syntax and vocabulary of mother's speech to young children: age and sex comparisons. *Child Development,* 1973, *44,* 182–185.

Piaget, J. *Play, Dreams and Imitation.* New York: Norton, 1951.

————. *The Origins of Intelligence in Children.* New York: International Universities Press, 1952.

————. *The Construction of Reality in the Child.* New York: Basic Books, 1954.

Polikanina, R. I. The relation between autonomic and somatic components in the development of the conditioned defense reflex in premature infants. *Pavlov Journal of Higher Nervous Activity,* 1961, *11,* 51–58.

Pomerleau-Malcuit, A. & Clifton, R. K. Neonatal heart rate response to tactile, auditory, and vestibular stimulation in different states. *Child Development,* in press.

Pratt, K. C. The neonate. In L. Carmichael, ed., *Manual of Child Psychology.* 2d ed. New York: John Wiley, 1954, 215–291.

Prechtl, H. F. R. & Beintema, D. J. *The Neurological Examination of the Full-term Newborn Infant.* London: Heinemann, 1964.

Provence, S. *Guide for the Care of Infants in Groups.* New York: Child Welfare League of America, 1967.

Provence, S. & Lipton, R. C. *Infants in Institutions.* New York: International Universities Press, 1962.

Rebelsky, F. G., Starr, R. H., Jr., & Luria, Z. Language development: the first four years. In Y. Brackbill, ed., *Infancy and Early Childhood.* New York: Free Press, 1967, 289–360.

Reese, H. W. & Lipsitt, L. P. *Experimental Child Psychology.* New York: Academic Press, 1970.

Rheingold, H. L., Gewirtz, J. L., & Ross, H. W. Social conditioning of vocalizations in the infant. *Journal of Comparative and Physiological Psychology,* 1959, *52,* 68–72.

Ricciuti, H. N. Object grouping and selective ordering behavior in infants 12–24 months old. *Merrill-Palmer Quarterly*, 1965, *11*, 129–148.

Richards, M. P. M. The development of communication in the first year of life. In K. Connelly & J. S. Bruner, eds., *Infant Competence, CIBA Foundation Conference*, 1972.

Riesen, A. H. Stimulation as a requirement for growth and function in behavioral development. In D. W. Fiske & S. R. Maddi, eds., *Functions of Varied Experience*. Homewood, Illinois: Dorsey Press, 1961.

Rohwer, W. D. Implications of cognitive development for education. In P. Mussen, ed., *Carmichael's Manual of Child Psychology*. 3d ed. New York: John Wiley, 1970, 1379–1455.

Routh, D. K. Conditioning of vocal response differentiation in infants, *Developmental Psychology*, 1969, *1*, 219–226.

Rovee, C. K. & Rovee, D. T. Conjugate reinforcement of infant exploratory behavior. *Journal of Experimental Child Psychology*, 1969, *8*, 33–39.

Saayman, G., Ames, G. W., & Moffett, A. Response to novelty as an indicator of visual discrimination in the human infant. *Journal of Experimental Child Psychology*, 1964, *1*, 189–198.

Sackett, G. P. Innate mechanisms, rearing conditions, and a theory of early experience effects in primates. In M. R. Jones, ed., *Effects of Early Experience: Miami symposium on the prediction of behavior*. Coral Gables, Florida: University of Miami Press, 1970, 11–55.

Salapatek, P. Visual scanning of geometric figures by the human newborn. *Journal of Comparative Physiological Psychology*, 1968, *66*, 247–258.

————. The visual investigation of geometric patterns by the one- and two-month-old infant. In C. S. Lavatelli & F. Stendler, eds., *Readings in Child Behavior and Development*. New York: Harcourt Brace, 1972, 147–152.

Salapatek, P. & Kessen, W. Visual scanning of triangles by the human newborn. *Journal of Experimental Child Psychology*, 1966, *3*, 155–167.

Salk, L. Mother's heart beat as an imprinting stimulus. *Transactions of the New York Academy of Science*, 1962, *24*, 753–763.

Sameroff, A. J. The components of sucking in the human newborn. *Journal of Experimental Child Psychology*, 1968, *6*, 607–623.

————. Can conditioned responses be established in the newborn infant? *Developmental Psychology*, 1971, *5*, 1–12.

Sameroff, A. J. Learning and adaptation in infants. In H. Reese, ed., *Advances in Child Development and Behavior*. Vol. 6. New York: Academic Press, 1972.

Schaffer, H. R. & Parry, M. A. Perceptual motor behavior in infancy as a function of age and stimulus familiarity. *British Journal of Psychology*, 1969, *60*, 1–9.

Schwartz, A., Rosenberg, D., & Brackbill, Y. Analysis of the components of social reinforcement of infant vocalization. *Psychonomic Science*, 1970, *20*, 323–325.

Self, P. A. Individual differences in auditory and visual responsiveness in infants from three days to six weeks of age. Doctoral dissertation, University of Kansas, 1971.

Serafica, F. C. & Uzgiris, I. C. Infant-mother relationship and object concept. Paper presented at American Psychological Association, Washington, D. C., 1971.

Shipley, C. F., Smith, C. S., & Gleitman, L. R. A study in the acquisition of language: free responses to commands. *Language*, 1969, *45*, 322–342.

Shirley, M. M. *The First Two Years: A Study of Twenty-five Babies*. Vol. I. *Postural and Locomotor Development*. Minneapolis: University of Minnesota Press, 1931.

————. *The First Two Years: A Study of Twenty-five Babies*. Vol. II. *Intellectual Development*. Minneapolis: University of Minnesota Press, 1933.

Simmons, M. W. Operant discrimination learning in human infants. *Child Development*, 1964, *35*, 737–748.

Sinclair-de-Zwart, H. Developmental psycholinguistics. In D. Elkind & J. H. Flavell, eds., *Studies in Cognitive Development: Essays in Honor of Jean Piaget*. New York: Oxford University Press, 1969, 315–336.

Siqueland, E. R. Basic learning Processes: I. Classical conditioning. Basic learning processes: II. Instrumental conditioning (Instrumental conditioning in infants); Discrimination learning (Discrimination learning in infancy). In H. W. Reese & L. P. Lipsitt, eds., *Experimental Child Psychology.* New York: Academic Press, 1970, 65–102, 157–183.

Siqueland, E. R. & DeLucia, C. A. Visual reinforcement of non-nutritive sucking in human infants. *Science,* 1969, *165,* 1144–1146.

Siqueland, E. R. & Lipsitt, L. P. Conditioned head-turning in human newborns. *Journal of Experimental Child Psychology,* 1966, *3,* 356–376.

Slobin, D. I. The acquisition of Russian as a native language. In F. Smith & G. A. Miller, eds., *The Genesis of Language.* Cambridge, Mass.: MIT Press, 1966, 129–148.

Smith, L. Unpublished study cited by L. P. Lipsitt. Learning capacities of the human infant. In R. J. Robinson, ed., *Brain and Early Behavior.* London: Academic Press, 1969, 227–249.

Snow, C. E. Mother speech to children learning language. *Child Development,* 1972, *43,* 549–565.

Sokolov, E. N. Neuronal models and the orienting reflex. In M. A. Brazier, ed., *The Central Nervous System and Behavior.* New York: J. Macy, 1960.

————. *Perception and the Conditioned Reflex.* New York: Macmillan, 1963.

Spears, W. C. Assessment of visual preference and discrimination in the four-month-old infant. *Journal of Comparative and Physiological Psychology,* 1964, *57,* 381–386.

Spears, W. C. & Hohle, R. H. Sensory and perceptual processes in infants. In Y. Brackbill, ed., *Infancy and Early Childhood.* New York: Free Press, 1967, 51–125.

Spitz, R. A. *The First Year of Life.* New York: International Universities Press, 1965.

Sroufe, L. A. & Wunsch, J. A. The development of laughter in the first year of life. *Child Development,* 1972, *43,* 1326–1344.

Staples, R. Color vision and color preference in infancy and childhood. *Psychological Bulletin,* 1931, *28,* 297–308.

————. The responses of infants to color. *Journal of Experimental Psychology,* 1932, *15,* 119–141.

Stayton, D. J., Hogan, R., & Ainsworth, M. D. S. Infant obedience and maternal behavior: the origin of socialization reconsidered. *Child Development,* 1971, *42,* 1057–1069.

Steinschneider, A., Lipton, E. L., & Richmond, J. B. Auditory sensitivity in the infant: effect of intensity on cardiac and motor responsivity. *Child Development,* 1966, *37,* 233–252.

Stirnimann, F. Über das farbempfinden neugeborener. *Annalen der Paediatrie,* 1944, *163,* 1–25. Cited by Kessen, W., Haith, M., & Salapatek, P. Human infancy: A bibliography and guide. In P. Mussen, ed., *Carmichael's Manual of Child Psychology.* New York: John Wiley, 1970, 287–445.

Stott, L. H. & Ball, R. S. Infant and preschool mental tests: review and evaluation. *Monographs of the Society for Research in Child Development,* 1965, *30* (whole no. 101).

Stubbs, G. M. The effect of the factors of duration intensity, and pitch of sound stimuli on the responses of newborn infants. *University of Iowa Studies of Child Welfare,* 1934, *9,* 75–135.

Suzuki, T., Kumiyo, Y., & Kiuchi, S. Auditory tests of newborn infants. *Annals of Otology,* 1964, *73,* 914–923.

Tanner, J. M. Physical growth. In P. Mussen, ed., *Carmichael's Manual of Child Psychology.* 3d ed. New York: John Wiley, 1970.

Thrum, M. E. The development of concepts of magnitude. *Child Development,* 1935, *6,* 120–140.

Todd, G. A. & Palmer, B. Social reinforcement of infant babbling. *Child Development*, 1968, *39*, 591–597.

Tonkova-Yampolskaya, R. V. On the question of studying physiological mechanisms of speech. *Pavlov Journal of Higher Nervous Activity*, 1962, *12*, 82–87.

Trehub, S. E. & Rabinovitch, M. S. Auditory-linguistic sensitivity. *Developmental Psychology*, 1972, *6*, 74–77.

Trincker, D. & Trincker, I. Development of brightness in infants. In Y. Brackbill & G. G. Thompson, eds., *Behavior in Infancy and Early Childhood: a Book of Readings*. New York: Free Press, 1967.

Tulkin, S. Infants' reaction to mother's voice and stranger's voice: social class differences in the first year of life. Paper presented at meeting of the Society for Research in Child Development, Minneapolis, 1971.

Turnure, C. Response to voice of mother and stranger by babies in the first year. *Developmental Psychology*, 1971, *4*, 182–190.

Twitchell, T. E. The automatic grasping responses of infants. *Neuropsychologia*, 1965, *3*, 247–259.

Uzgiris, I. C. Patterns of vocal and gestural imitation in infants. Paper presented at the first symposium of the International Society for the Study of Behavioral Development, University of Nijmegen, Netherlands, July, 1971.

Uzgiris, I. C. & Hunt, J. McV. An instrument for assessing infant psychological development. Unpublished test manual. Psychological Development Laboratory, University of Illinois, 1966.

———. Attentional preference and experience: II. An exploratory longitudinal study of the effect of visual familiarity and responsiveness. *Journal of Genetic Psychology*, 1970, *117*, 109–121.

Vurpillot, E. The development of scanning strategies and their relationship to visual differentiation. *Journal of Experimental Child Psychology*, 1968, *6*, 632–650.

Vygotsky, L. S. *Thought and Language*. E. Hanfmann & G. Valear, eds. and trans. New York: John Wiley, 1962.

Wachs, T., Uzgiris, I., & Hunt, J. McV. Cognitive development in infants of different age levels and from different environmental backgrounds. *Merrill-Palmer Quarterly*, 1971, *17*, 283–313.

Walk, R. D. The development of depth perception in animals and human infants. *Monographs of the Society for Research in Child Development*, 1966, *31*, 82–108.

Warren, N. African infant precocity. *Psychological Bulletin*, 1972, *78*, 353–367.

Watson, J. B. *Psychological Care of the Infant and Child*. New York: Norton, 1928.

Watson, J. S. The development and generalization of contingency awareness in early infancy: some hypotheses. *Merrill-Palmer Quarterly*, 1966, *12*, 123–135.

———. Cognitive perceptual development in infancy: setting for the seventies. *Merrill-Palmer Quarterly*, 1971, *17*, 139–152.

———. Smiling, cooing and "The Game." *Merrill-Palmer Quarterly*, 1972, *18*, 323–340.

Watson, J. S. & Danielson, G. An attempt to shape bidimensional attention in 24-month-old infants. *Journal of Experimental Child Psychology*, 1969, *7*, 467–478.

Watson, J. S. & Ramey, C. I. Reactions to response-contingent stimulation in early infancy. *Merrill-Palmer Quarterly*, 1972, *18*, 219–229.

Webb, R. A., Massar, B., & Nadolny, T. Information and strategy in the young child's search for hidden objects. *Child Development*, 1972, *43*, 91–104.

Webster, R. L. Selective suppression of infants' vocal responses by classes of phonemic stimulation. *Developmental Psychology*, 1969, *1*, 410–414.

Webster, R. L., Steinhardt, M. H., & Senter, M. G. Changes in infants' vocalizations as a function of differential acoustic stimulation. *Developmental Psychology*, 1972, *7*, 39–43.

Wedenberg, E. Determinants of the hearing acuity in the newborn. *Nordisk Medicine,* 1956, *50,* 1022–1024.
Weikart, D. A comparative study of three preschool curricula. Paper presented at meeting of Society for Research in Child Development, Santa Monica, California, 1969.
Weisberg, P. Social and nonsocial conditioning of infant vocalizations. *Child Development,* 1963, *34,* 377–388.
Weiss, L. P. Differential variations in the amount of activity in newborn infants under continuous light and sound stimulation. *University of Iowa Studies of Child Welfare,* 1934, *9,* 9–74.
Weizman, F., Cohen, L. B., & Pratt, R. Novelty, familiarity and the development of infant attention. *Developmental Psychology,* 1971, *4,* 149–154.
Welch, L. The development of size discrimination between the ages of 12 and 40 months. *Journal of Genetic Psychology,* 1939, *55,* 243–268.
Wenar, C. Competence at one. *Merrill-Palmer Quarterly,* 1964, *10,* 329–342.
———. Executive competence and spontaneous social behavior in one-year-olds. *Child Development,* 1972, *43,* 256–260.
Werner, H. & Kaplan, B. *Symbol Formation.* New York: John Wiley, 1963.
Wertheimer, M. Psychomotor coordination of auditory and visual space at birth. *Science,* 1961, *134,* 1692.
Wetherford, M. J. & Cohen, L. Developmental changes in infant visual preferences. Paper presented at meeting of the Society for Research in Child Development, Minneapolis, 1971.
White, B. L. The initial coordination of sensorimotor schemas in human infants. Piaget's ideas and the role of experience. In D. Elkind & J. H. Flavell, eds., *Studies of Cognitive Development: Essays in Honor of Jean Piaget.* New York: Oxford University Press, 1969, 237–256.
———. *Human Infants: Experience and Psychological Development.* Englewood Cliffs: Prentice-Hall, 1971.
———. Fundamental early environmental influences on the development of competencies. In M. E. Meyer, ed., *Third Symposium on Learning: Cognitive Learning.* Bellingham, Washington: Western Washington State College Press, 1972.
White, B. L., Castle, P., & Held, R. Observations on the development of visually directed reaching. *Child Development,* 1964, *35,* 349–364.
White, R. W. Motivation reconsidered: the concept of competence. *Psychological Review,* 1959, *66,* 297–333.
Wickelgren, L. Convergence in the human newborn. *Journal of Experimental Child Psychology,* 1967, *5,* 74–85.
———. The ocular response of human newborns to intermittent visual movement. *Journal of Experimental Child Psychology,* 1969, *8,* 469–482.
Wolff, P. H. The development of attention in young infants. *Annals of New York Academy of Science,* 1965, *118,* 783–866.
———. The natural history of crying and other vocalizations in early infancy. In B. Foss, ed., *Determinants of Infant Behavior.* 4. London: Methuen, 1969.
Wood, C. C., Goff, W. R., & Day, R. S. Auditory evoked potential during speech perception. *Science,* 1971, *173,* 1248–1251.
Yarrow, L. J., Rubenstein, J. L., & Pedersen, F. A. Dimensions of early stimulation: differential effects on infant development. Paper presented at meeting of the Society for Research in Child Development, Minneapolis, 1971.
Zelazo, P. R. Smiling and vocalizing: a cognitive emphasis. *Merrill-Palmer Quarterly,* 1972, *18,* 349–367.

4 Reproductive Risk and the Continuum of Caretaking Casualty

ARNOLD J. SAMEROFF
MICHAEL J. CHANDLER
University of Rochester

INTRODUCTION

DURING THIS CENTURY great strides have been made in reducing the risks once associated with early growth and development. Children born in this decade are more likely to survive and grow to healthy maturity than were children born only a generation ago. Despite these accomplishments children continue to face a gamut of natural and man-made hazards to healthy development. Almost every family in the nation is directly touched by some such miscarriage in development, and no one fully escapes their consequences. Without the knowledge necessary to develop effective prevention programs, developmental casualties continue to occur, resulting in enormous human and physical costs.

In recent years increasing attention has been directed toward the study and early identification of various factors which place children at a greater than average risk to later disease or disorder. The impetus behind this shifting research emphasis is, according to Garmezy (in press), traceable to a variety of features of the contemporary social and scientific climate. A principal factor which has contributed to the escalation of interest in risk research has been a growing disenchantment with retrospective or "followback" studies as a means of increasing our understanding of the etiology of various disorders. As Robins, Bates, and O'Neal (1962) have pointed out, efforts to reconstruct events that may have led to the occurrence of a disease by studying persons who currently suffer from it often create the impression of an inevitability of outcome which is not justified. These efforts also risk confounding causes and effects. As a result of such concerns there has been a shift in emphasis toward prospective, follow-up studies, the conduct of which typically involves the early identification and longitudinal study of high-risk populations (Garmezy 1971).

A second contributing factor in the growth of risk research has been the recent increase in public and professional attention to the health needs of socially and economically disenfranchised groups. As Riegel (1972) has pointed out, shifting political ideologies and preoccupations often inspire parallel shifts in the focus of research attention. As marginal groups in our society have achieved some weight in influencing the balance of power, they have also become the focus of more serious and concerted research efforts. Because many of the same factors of substandard living that define these marginal groups are also known to constitute serious growth and health hazards, the study of developmental risk and family poverty have become intertwined. An additional factor in the growth of risk research is the recent accomplishment in the treatment and control of once common childhood illnesses that has made possible a reallocation of professional resources to problems of early detection and prevention.

The topography of the recent literature on risk research reflects the imprint of these various changes in the professional climate. Many of the studies to be considered in this review are principally concerned with unraveling the etiology of specific disorders. The remainder of the studies reviewed are of a somewhat more practical cast and have had as their explicit goal the identification of specific hazards which threten the developmental integrity of the child. These studies are principally concerned with documenting the potentially deleterious effects of substandard physical and psychological environments on pre- and postnatal growth and development. When taken in combination, the studies that fall into one or another of these classes constitute an extremely large and scattered literature. The present survey focuses on only a portion of this literature and, with a few exceptions, concentrates on risk factors operative during the prenatal and early postnatal periods.

Linear Models of Development

Although persons of all ages are menaced by a range of life hazards, most of the available research literature has focused on a variety of trauma that are suffered early in infancy and that are expected to play a principal role in the developmental outcome of the affected individual. The seriousness of such early hazards is underscored by the fact that the death rates during the perinatal period are four times greater than those for other ages (Niswander and Gordon 1972). Of perhaps even greater significance is the broad continuum of reproductive casualty, including congenital malformations, cerebral palsy, mental retardation, deafness, blindness, and other neurosensory defects, some forms of which are thought to result from early hazards and traumas (Lilienfeld and Parkhurst 1951; Pasamanick and Knobloch 1966). It has been estimated that approximately 10 percent of the population in the United States has handicaps or defects that are present at or soon after birth (Niswander and Gordon 1972; see chapter 2 in this volume for more detailed discussion of congenital defects).

Although the studies reviewed have been conducted under various auspices and for various purposes, almost all have proceeded on the general assumption that it is possible to specify particular characteristics of either the child or his parents that will permit long-range predictions regarding the ultimate course of growth and development. Despite the popularity and the apparent reasonableness of this position, the present review has found little evidence that such predictions are possible. On the contrary, studies that have followed the developmental course of supposedly vulnerable infants have typically found that the initial difficulties were attenuated with the passage of time and that the earlier expectations of negative outcomes were not realized. Instead, many of the children studied appear to overcome their initial handicaps and liabilities and to adapt successfully to their environment.

One's interpretation of the frequent failure to predict later pathology is primarily dependent upon the model of development that one espouses. Much of the research reviewed in this chapter assumes a generally mechanistic (Reese and Overton 1970) orientation toward the processes of human growth and, consequently, interprets development as a linear chain of efficient causes and invariant effects. With a mechanistic model one may attempt to bridge large segments of this causal chain and to directly link early traumas to subsequent symptomatology. Predictive inefficiency is viewed as a result of some failure to locate the critical links in the chain of causation and as a mandate to initiate a new search for the elusive cause.

Organismic Models of Development

Alternative developmental models are available that regard the process of human growth as a more circuitous course, in which linear chains of efficient causality are rare. An organismic interpretation would view children and their environments as undergoing regular restructuring in ways that relegate past events and characteristics to the status of ancient history. Discontinuity, rather than continuity, is expected between development stages. Early factors that have enduring consequences are assumed to do so because of persistent influences acting throughout the life span, rather than at discrete points in development. Self-righting influences are powerful forces toward normal human development, so that protracted developmental disorders are typically found only in the presence of equally protracted distorting influences.

From an organismic perspective predictive failures in the study of developmental disorders are not attributable to missing links or other "simple and sovereign solutions." They are assumed instead to be the result of a lack of adequate knowledge regarding the complex of mutual influences that operate between the child and his environment and that together serve to dissipate or amplify the effects of earlier developmental insults. According to this transactional view, successful predictions regarding long-range developmental outcomes cannot be made on the basis of a continuum of reproductive casualty alone. An equally important continuum of caretaking casualty exists to moderate or perpetuate earlier developmental difficulties. The continuum of caretaking casualty will be seen to run from lethal conditions in which the child dies from abuse or neglect, through sublethal variations such as battered children and infants who fail to thrive, to more subtle manifestations of mental retardation and psychiatric disturbance. Transactions between the child and his caretaking environment serve to break or maintain the linkage between earlier trauma and later disorder and must, according to this view, be taken into account if successful predictions are to be made. To gain predictive validity from the continuum of reproductive casualty one must take into account the maintaining environment. Similarly, to gain predictive validity from the continuum of caretaking casualty one must take into account the characteristics of the victimized child.

With few exceptions the available studies on high-risk infants have selectively focused attention on *either* reproductive *or* caretaking aspects of these casualties. Long-range predictions based on these unilateral assessments have been uniformly disappointing, and many investigators have been led to question whether it will ever be possible to anticipate deviant developmental outcomes. As the following review will attempt to show, however, a number of suggestive findings indicate that, if one couples information regarding *both* the reproductive and caretaking histories of the child, many more successful predictions are possible. In what follows special emphasis will be placed on the need for studies that attempt such transactional analyses and explore the interface of caretaking and temperament.

PERINATAL RISK FACTORS

Continuum of Reproductive Casualty

The high death rates found in the perinatal period combined with the later disorders presumed to originate in the perinatal period led Lilienfeld and Parkhurst (1951) to adopt the term "continuum of reproductive wastage" to describe the range of deviant pregnancy outcomes. The continuum was conceived of as extending from extreme conditions such as perinatal death and abortion, through sublethal conditions including cerebral palsy and epilepsy, to subtle forms of retardation, cerebral dysfunction, and learning disability.

Babson and Benson (1971) reported that of the 5–10 million conceptions occurring annually in the United States, 2–3 million result in spontaneous abortions due to genetic or chromosomal defects and pathogens, and another one million are terminated legally or illegally. Of the approximately 3.5 million fetuses that reach twenty weeks of gestational age, 50,000 die before delivery, 50,000 die in the first postnatal month, 50,000 have severe congenital malformations, while another 300,000 have learning disorders that range from mild to severe retardation.

The large number of general learning disorders and specific deficits in behaviors such as reading are of great concern to clinicians. The lack of either a clear genetic basis or anatomical damage in many children with sensory and behavioral disorders, was puzzling to investigators who adhere closely to a traditional "medical model." If, according to this point of view, a disorder existed, there should be some clear etiological factor, preferably biological, somewhere in the patient's history. If such a factor could not be located, it was presumably because diagnostic techniques were not yet sufficiently sophisticated to detect it. Gesell and Amatruda (1941), strong advocates of such a straightforward cause-effect model, proposed the concept of "minimal cerebral injury" as an explanation. The supposed reasons for not being able to document the existence of such injury is because it is, by definition, minimal—that is, undetectable. Current usage of terms like "minimal brain damage" or "special learning disabilities" are expressions of the continuing need for clinicians to be able to explain disorder on the basis of simple cause-effect relationships, rather than on the basis of complex developmental processes which, from the data to be reported here, seem not only to be more appropriate but necessary. (See chapter 7 in this volume for further discussion of some of these issues.)

The research of Pasamanick and Knobloch (1961) further expanded the range of deviant developmental outcomes considered to result from minor central nervous system dysfunction caused by damage to the fetus or newborn child. On the basis of their findings these authors suggested replacing the expression "continuum of reproductive wastage" with the somewhat more general expression "continuum of reproductive casualty." The term "casualty" includes a range of minor motor, perceptual, intellectual, learning, and behavioral disabilities that were not included in Lilienfeld and Parkhurst's (1951) original "wastage" continuum. The latter referred primarily to gross neurological disorders such as cerebral palsy and epilepsy.

Pasamanick and Knobloch (1966) reviewed a series of their own earlier retrospective studies, in which they examined the delivery and birth complications of children with a variety of subsequent disorders. They found five such later disorders to be significantly associated with greater numbers of complications of pregnancy and prematurity. These were cerebral palsy, epilepsy, mental deficiency, behavior disorders, and reading disabilities. Another condition, tics, was found to be related to pregnancy complications but not to prematurity. These same disorders were, however, less strongly related to the various complications of labor or instrumental procedures, such as Ceasarean sections and forceps extractions. The correlations were much higher with pregnancy complications like toxemia and maternal bleeding (Pasamanick and Knobloch 1966). In the comparisons between the disordered groups and controls, those evidencing more severe conditions, e.g., cerebral palsy, were more sharply differentiated from controls in the number of obstetrical complications than were subjects who expressed milder disorders, e.g., tics. An ancillary finding, to be discussed more fully later, was that the absolute number of such abnormalities of pregnancy was found to be higher among nonwhite than white groups.

Retrospective studies implicated four factors in early development as related to later disorder: (1) anoxia, (2) prematurity, (3) delivery complications, and (4) social conditions. They will be reviewed in the next four sections. An inescapable conclusion that will emerge from this review is that, even if one continues to believe that a "continuum of reproductive casualty" exists, its importance pales in comparison to the massive influences of socioeconomic factors on both prenatal and postnatal development.

Anoxia

Little (1861) is generally credited with being the first to focus on asphyxia as a cause of brain damage in the child. It seemed logical to assume that a generalized deficit in brain functioning could be related to cerebral oxygen deprivation early in development. Studies in which animals were deprived of oxygen seemed to indicate that asphyxia at birth led to learning deficits and brain damage (Windle 1944).

Human research on asphyxia was stimulated by a report by Schreiber (1939) that 70 percent of a group of mental retardates had histories of anoxia at birth. Although suggestive, Schreiber's study was far from definitive in that it was retrospective, had no control groups, and did not differentiate anoxia from a variety of other complications of birth and development that his subjects had suffered.

Moreover, retrospective approaches have serious problems of selection bias since only those subjects who have the later disorder are ever studied. Prospective research, by contrast, permits the selection of subjects with early characteristics thought to be implicated in the etiology of later disorders. The early characteristics assume the status of independent variables and later outcomes the status of dependent variables. In the current example anoxia would be an experimental variable and mental retardation the outcome studied.

Despite the methodological advantages offered by prospective over retrospective designs, several problems still remain (Graham, Ernhart, Thurston, and Craft 1962). These include the technical problem of maintaining the sample and making certain that sample loss is not related to the independent variable, e.g., death due to prematurity. A more basic problem in the prospective design, as applied to perinatal complications, is the lack of random assignment into the complicated versus noncomplicated comparison groups. As a consequence, even if a relationship is found between the independent and dependent variable, e.g., between anoxia and mental retardation, a causal connection is still not certain since both of these conditions might be determined by a third variable not included in the study. The seriousness of this issue will become evident when the effects of maternal emotional factors are examined in a later section.

To overcome some of the selection biases in retrospective studies, early hospital records have often been reviewed to identify a study population on the basis of risk factors rather than outcome measures. In the case of anoxia, groups of children with known histories of anoxia can be selected and evaluated for their current functioning.

1. *School age intelligence.* Two early studies (Darke 1944; Preston 1945) that used the "prospective" methodology of earlier records were able to find effects of anoxia on later intelligence, but both of these studies had serious design flaws. Preston (1945) used no control groups. Although Darke (1944) did have controls, some of his subjects were matched with siblings, while others were matched with parents. Of his nineteen anoxic subjects, nine were identified by inference rather than the recording of anoxia in birth records. In addition to the limitations of a small subject population, the age of the subjects at testing ranged from two to eleven years, raising questions about the homogeneity of the sample.

Two other studies found IQ differences between anoxics and normal controls at school age. From the birth records of 40,000 babies, Benaron, Tucker, Andrews, Boshes, Cohen, Fromm, and Yacorzynski (1960) selected a sample of forty-three seriously apneic infants who had from twelve minutes to over an hour of the delayed onset of respiration. These subjects, all of whom were of low social status, were matched with controls ranging in age from three to nineteen years. The authors concluded that severe anoxia may have deleterious effects; however, the expectation that these subjects would be uniformly poor in intellectual performance was not met, since they had both higher and lower IQs than their controls. Schachter and Apgar (1959) succeeded in testing their subjects when they were all eight years of age. They found a mean 5-point IQ deficit in a small sample of anoxic infants but no differences on special neurological tests designed to detect brain damage. They noted that the small IQ differences observed were of questionable clinical significance.

A larger number of "prospective" studies have found no later effects on intelligence in children who had reached school age. Campbell, Cheseman, and Kilpatrick (1950) examined children born in a three-year period at a Belfast hospital when they reached eight to eleven years of age and found no differences in physique, hemoglobin levels, or intelligence between sixty-one children who had suffered anoxia of two minutes or more and a control group with normal births. Usdin and Weil (1952) studied forty-one children with an anoxic period of longer than three minutes when they reached thirteen years of age and again found no IQ differences between these subjects and a group of matched controls. McPhail and Hall (1941) divided their anoxic subjects into those who had suffered severe apnea and those who had suffered mild apnea. Neither group was different from controls in intelligence quotient. Fraser and Wilks (1959) also divided their anoxic subjects into a moderate and severe group. The severe group included subjects who took longer than three minutes before their first breath and at least five minutes before the onset of regular respiration. At seven-and-a-half to eleven-and-a-half years of age sixty moderately apneic and forty severely apneic subjects were compared with controls, and no intellectual differences were found. Benaron, Brown, Tucker, Wentz, and Yacorzynski (1953) also found no IQ differences between children who had been apneic and controls when they were tested at five to fifteen years of age.

The evidence indicates that there are only small (if any) differences in school-age intelligence quotients between infants who have suffered anoxia and those who have not. It is surprising that such a massive perinatal trauma as thirty minutes without respiration should not affect later behavior. Yet, even the animal research is not unambiguous. Windle (1944) reported that the effects of anoxia on animal learning might be transient. Himwich (1951) reported that young animals seemed to be especially resistant to the effects of oxygen deprivation. Bailey (1958), reviewing studies of the effects of oxygen deficiency at birth, indicated that if one were to arrive at any conclusions from these studies it would first be necessary to overlook "defects such as improper selection of subjects or inaccuracies of case histories in the clinical reports and inadequate techniques or unreliable trends in the animal experiments."

Although predictions from early high-risk to the eventual intellectual status of anoxic infants is the major consideration, it is also of interest to determine if any transient effects appeared early but disappeared by school age. Longitudinal studies of anoxic infants will be discussed in the next section.

2. *Longitudinal studies*. Graham and her associates (Graham, Caldwell, Ernhart, Pennoyer, and Hartman 1957) criticized most previous studies because the possible presence of subtle brain damage was poorly determined by gross, undifferentiated IQ measures. If a variety of measures including neurological, personality adjustment, and perceptual-motor tasks had been included, more differences might have been found. In many prior studies control groups had not been adequately matched and the criteria of anoxia had not been carefully defined. They proposed a longitudinal study beginning at birth with multiple contemporary assessments of anoxia and its effects on newborn behavior, followed by assessments during later years.

Several hundred infants in St. Louis were seen in the newborn period (Graham, Matarazzo, and Caldwell 1956) followed-up at three years (Graham, Ernhart, Thurston, and Craft 1962), and again at seven years (Corah, Anthony, Painter, Stern, and Thurston 1965). As expected, when examined during the first days of life, anoxic infants were found to be "impaired" on a series of five measures which included maturation level, visual responsiveness, irritability, muscle tension, and pain threshold (Graham, Pennoyer, Caldwell, Greenman, and Hartman 1957). When the performance on these measures was compared with a prognostic score based on the degree of prenatal anoxia, postnatal anoxia, and the clinical assessment of central nervous system disturbance, those infants with the poorest prognostic scores performed the poorest on the newborn assessments.

These same infants were seen again at three years of age and tested with a battery of cognitive, perceptual-motor, personality, and neurologic tests (Graham et al. 1962). The group of anoxic infants scored lower than controls on all tests of cognitive function, had more positive neurological findings, and showed some personality differences. There were, however, no differences on tests of perceptual-motor functioning. The anoxic effect seemed to be strongest in the children with postnatal anoxia, that is, delayed onset of respiration. Those with prenatal anoxia, inferred from disturbances of pregnancy, performed as well as control subjects. There were small but statistically significant correlations between the degree of anoxia and the three-year intelligence test scores. (The highest of these correlations was −.15.) Thus, about 98 percent of the variance in the three-year intellectual functioning of previously anoxic infants is left unexplained by the anoxia.

At seven years of age these children were again tested (Corah et al. 1965). Significant IQ differences had disappeared between the anoxic group and the control population. Of the twenty-one cognitive and perceptual measures, only vocabulary and one perceptual task seemed still to be deficient in these children. Corah et al. concluded that anoxics showed minimal impairment of functioning at seven years and that efforts to predict current functioning on the basis of severity of anoxia were highly unreliable.

To summarize, the St. Louis study showed that anoxic infants did poorly on newborn measures, still showed effects at three years of age, but by seven performed almost as well as nonanoxic controls. Other studies have found similar developmental patterns among anoxics. Stechler (1964) followed seven apneic infants for three years. In the newborn period they showed some statistically unreliable deficits in behavior which became more pronounced during the first year and a half of development. By two these deficits had disappeared and the anoxics were performing as well as the controls. MacKinney (1958) followed twenty-four infants who had been rated in poor clinical status as newborns. At three years they had a 5-point IQ deficit compared with controls, but this difference disappeared by five years of age.

Although the size and quality of the St. Louis study would tend to make its results definitive, it must be noted that there are other studies that have assessed anoxic infants in the preschool period and that did not find them to be different from normals. Ucko (1965) tested anoxic infants repeatedly from six months to five years and found no differences in IQ at any age. Using umbilical cord blood oxygenation as their measure of anoxia, Apgar, Girdany, McIntosh, and Taylor (1955) found no relation to IQ at two or four years of age. Keith, Norval, and Hunt (1953) found no effects in children one to five years of age who had prenatal or postnatal anoxia. In addition, these investigators found no relationship between IQ and birth condition in fifty-seven children who had shown evidence of having brain lesions. In a further follow-up of these children at eight to fourteen years of age, Keith and Gage (1960) noted that prolonged labor, asphyxia, or delayed respiration did not cause abnormalities in children who survived the early months of life.

Graham et al. (1957) showed that the apparent contradiction between prospective and retrospective studies of the effects of perinatal complications could be explained by base rate differences in the variables assessed. If one accepts Pasamanick and Lilienfeld's (1955) finding that 15 percent of a mentally retarded group had suffered delivery complications, and that 2 percent of the general population is mentally retarded, then, by multiplying the two rates together, only 0.3 percent of the general population should be expected to have suffered both delivery complications and mental retardation. About 5 percent of births have some anoxia associated with them (Keith et al. 1953). The percentage of anoxic births that result in mental deficiency should then be the ratio of children with both complications and mental deficiency to children with complicated births. The result of this computation $(0.3\%/5\%)$ would suggest that approximately 6 percent of children with anoxia should become mentally retarded. At best, then, delivery complications constitute an extremely inefficient predictor of subsequent mental retardation. Prospectively, very few infants who suffer delivery complications will show mental retardation in later years.

3. *Effects of anoxia on personality.* Graham et al., (1957a) have criticized studies of anoxia for their excessive concentration on intelligence. They suggested that other behavioral effects might be found. Although the data on neurological and perceptual-motor functioning seem to be as ambiguous as those for intelligence, some reliable effects have been noted on personality variables. Stevenson (1948) found that a group of infants judged to be in poor physical condition at birth showed twice the maladjustment at ages five to eight that was shown by a group of infants judged to be in good physical condition. Bolin (1959), in a psychoanalytically oriented study searching for the effects of birth trauma, found that infants with longer durations of labor showed more fears, anxiety, and negativism than those who had shorter durations of labor when tested in a follow-up at seven to twelve years of age.

In the St. Louis study, psychologists rated their subjects on variables associated with a "brain injury syndrome." Only a composite score based on all the personality measures was reliably different for the anoxic subjects. Of the individual scales only distractability reached statistical significance. The authors found that in three-year follow-up there was little evidence for any personality constellation that could be related to brain injury. By the seven-year follow-up, Corah et al. (1965) again found no data to support a hyperkinetic personality syndrome in their anoxic group but did find significant impairments in social competence. The anoxic subgroup with the better newborn prognostic score was rated as more impulsive and distractible than were the controls, but, paradoxically, the subgroup having the poorer prognosis was found to be significantly less distractible than were the normal controls. The anoxics had lower scores on the Vineland social maturity scales and were judged to be more maladjusted.

4. *Summary.* How is one to explain the developmental disappearance of the effects of a severe trauma to the early physiological functioning of the brain? The preceding review has focused mainly on intellectual functioning. The fact that impairment in the preschool period tends to disappear by school age might be explained by changes in the quality of cognitive functioning between these ages (Piaget 1950; White 1965). McCall, Hogarty, and Hurlbut (1972), in a review of longitudinal studies of intelligence, examined the common finding of low correlations be-

tween assessments of "intelligence" during infancy and later "intelligence." These investigators concluded that low correlations were not a consequence of unreliabilities in the test instruments but were rather consequences of qualitative shifts in what is defined as "intelligence" at different ages. They argued against the belief in a "pervasive and developmentally constant intelligence" on which most longitudinal comparisons have been based. From the available data it would appear that there is no basis for assuming a simple continuity in intellectual competence.

Although long-term continuities in development are not found, short-term stabilities could occur. Even this compromise appears unjustified because of the rapid transitions in early behavior. Lewis and McGurk (1972) tested infants six times at three- to six-month intervals during the first two years of life. Of the fifteen intercorrelations between testings with the Bayley scales, only two were statistically significant. They found the same result in successive testings using a Piaget object-conservation task. Scores on infant tests seem to bring little prognostic power to bear on later functioning. Kagan (1972), in a study of Guatemalan infants, reported that what would be regarded as severe retardation by Western standards did not prevent these children from growing up to be competently functioning adults.(See chapter 1 in this volume for a discussion of patterns of intellectual development.)

These qualitative shifts in development are not restricted to intellectual functioning. Bell, Weller, and Waldrop (1971) noted a complete reversal in some behaviors between the newborn and preschool periods. Newborns who had been easy to arouse, with low thresholds to stimulation, tended to be passive and quiet in the preschool period, while newborns who had been difficult to arouse and had high thresholds to stimulation tended to be active and outgoing later. McGrade (1968) found a similar transition between the newborn period and eight months of age. Since qualitative shifts in development do occur during childhood, it would be surprising if children did show continuity in their intellectual performance. If continuity in intelligence is found, especially intellectual deficit, it can probably be explained by one of two reasons: either the child has suffered sufficient brain damage that he is incapable of moving from a sensorimotor to a conceptual mode of thinking or there are environmental conditions that promote deficient functioning in the child both early and late.

Prematurity

Prematurity is another of the classic perinatal hazards that has been related to later deviance in behavior. Since prematurity is an outcome of many complications in pregnancy and represents the most prevalent abnormality of birth, Birch and Gussow (1970) suggested that it was the modal problem for assessing the effects of the continuum of reproductive casualty.

As in studies of anoxia, the data on long-term effects of prematurity do not lead to any clear-cut conclusions. Wiener (1962), in a review of eighteen studies of prematurity, found only one that did not report an IQ deficit in the premature group. Parmelee and Haber (in press) have, however, argued that it is by no means clear whether the later adverse consequences associated with prematurity are a function of the prematurity itself, the accompanying low birth-weight, an extended period of living in an incubator, accompanying perinatal trauma, or the social climate in which the child is raised. A gestationally premature infant who suffers no prenatal, perinatal, or postnatal traumas other than prematurity itself, and is raised in an optimal home environment may, according to these investigators, be no different from a full-term infant raised under the same circumstances. Parmelee and Haber's views are consistent with those studies of prematurity undertaken by Hess, Mohr, and Bartelme (1939), who found generally good childhood outcomes for their subjects. Those premature children who did perform less well than normals were typically those who had evidenced additional neonatal complications as well.

Several large studies that have followed premature infants from infancy through school age did find small intellectual deficits associated with low birth-weights. Douglas (1960) reported that when compared with controls the prematures did less well at eight and eleven years of age. Drillien (1964), in an extensive study of the effects of prematurity, found that the lighter the infant had been at birth, the greater the deficit in developmental quotient at four years. The mean IQ scores ranged from 107 for the full-term control group to 80 for a group of infants under three and a half pounds at birth.

A sample of premature infants initially studied by Knobloch, Rider, Harper, and Pasamanick (1956) was followed up with intelligence testing when they were six to seven years old (Wiener, Rider, Oppel, Fischer, and Harper 1965) and again when they were eight to ten years old (Wiener, Rider, Oppel, and Harper 1968). The prematures, who at birth had weighed between 1,500 and 2,000 grams scored 5 points lower at ages six to seven, and 6 points lower at ages eight to ten. In another study the effects of physical defects were separated from the intellectual deficits in prematures. McDonald (1964) eliminated from her sample infants who were twins or had cerebral palsy, blindness, deafness, or IQs below 50. The resulting sample had an average IQ of 102 when tested at ages six to eight, no different from the national mean in Britain. Still, within her sample those infants with birth weights under three pounds had an average IQ 5 points less than those with birth weights between three and four pounds.

It seems clear that low birth-weight infants are disadvantaged in physical development. Harper and Wiener (1965) found that they were persistently shorter and lighter than full-term controls, tended to be hospitalized more often for illness, and suffered from a number of sensory defects. The amount of impairment increased as birth weight declined. Drillien (1965) reported that 75 percent of school-age children who had weighed under three pounds at birth had some congenital defect; while Dann, Levine, and New (1964) found 59 percent of their prematures to have visual defects. It is not clear, as Parmelee and Haber (in press) point out, whether the reported deficits in the intelligence functioning of prematures is due to some minimal cerebral damage or the disabling effects of other physical impairments.

It is interesting that the studies of the effects of prematurity have shown consistent, albeit small, IQ deficits, while studies of the effects of anoxia have not. A possible explanation, to be more fully explored in a later section, is that the premature infant is more easily recognized and labeled by his parent than the anoxic infant. The parents may not even know if their infant had some form of asphyxia, while the premature, and especially the lower birth-weight premature, is quite easily identified not only by its physical appearance but also by the initial separation from the parents and by the subsequently intense caretaking demands. It will be seen that the parent's perception of the child can play a major role in its deviant development exclusive of any actual deficit that may be present in the child.

Newborn Status as Outcome and Predictor

1. *The Collaborative Study.* The largest of the prospective studies of risk factors in infancy is the Collaborative Perinatal Study of the National Institute of Neurological Disease and Stroke. Fourteen hospitals collaborated in this study of over fifty thousand pregnancies. The study focused on the relation between perinatal factors and the later development of infants. These factors included abnormal conditions of pregnancy, environmental variables, and biological characteristics of the parents. The intake of pregnant subjects into the study ended in 1965. Follow-ups have been planned until the youngest subjects reach eight years of age.

Although a number of preliminary articles have appeared, the first major report was published in 1972 (Niswander and Gordon 1972). The report focused on the character of the pregnancies and their immediate effects on perinatal death or survival, birth weight, and the surviving infant's neurological status at twelve months of age. The report was based on forty thousand infants, half of them Caucasian and half Negro. Reports on the infants' psychological functioning are to be published in a second volume.

Niswander and Gordon (1972) reported that the incidence of low birth-weight infants among Negroes is twice as high as among Caucasian infants of the same gestational age (13 percent vs. 7 percent). In addition, Negroes were typically found to deliver a week earlier than Caucasians. Despite the difference in birth-weights between those groups and the assumed relationship between low birth-weights and neurologic abnormality, there was no difference in the percentage of infants found to be neurologically abnormal at twelve months of age.

A shortcoming of the Niswander and Gordon (1972) report is that there was no breakdown of the pregnancy outcomes by socioeconomic status. The variable that comes closest to reflecting some measure of economic circumstance was the education of the mother. A slight increase of perinatal deaths was found among mothers characterized by less education and presumably lower socioeconomic status. In particular there was a large increase in the frequency of abnormal twelve-month neurological examinations among infants of women of lower educational levels. There is little one can conclude about the long-range implications of risk factors from the first report of the Collaborative Study, since it encompassed only the first year of the infant's life and since within that period only death or neurological status were considered.

Educational background of the mother seemed to be unrelated to the rate of perinatal complications. However, when the infants of the Collaborative Study were assessed at one year, those with teenage mothers of lower educational background were shown to have a greater than average chance of evidencing neurologic abnormalities. This result could, however, be the consequence of the poor developmental environment these mothers provide for their infants.

The Collaborative Study also investigated the effects of a variety of pregnancy and delivery variables on outcome. Various maternal illnesses during pregnancy were found, for example, to increase the risk to the child of low birth-weight and perinatal death. These included cardiovascular conditions, thyroid dysfunction, and urinary tract and gastrointestinal infections. Among them, however, only frank diabetes mellitus seemed to produce neurological abnormalities measurable at the time of the twelve-month follow-up. Single maternal complications of pregnancy, while producing increased perinatal deaths and low birth-weight, were not shown to be related to the outcome of the twelve-month neurological examination.

Complications during labor were shown to constitute a risk for later neurological abnormalities. This increased risk was primarily confined to breech presentation and duration of labor variables. For multiparous mothers, labors which were either too short or too long were also related to more deaths and neurological abnormalities. For primiparous mothers, the longer the duration of labor the better. The increased risk associated with the shorter labor for primiparous mothers might, however, be a function of the increased incidence of low birth-weight infants which also characterizes this group.

In a separate publication, Niswander et al. (1966) reported the relation of pregnancy complications to Bayley Infant Assessment Scales at eight months of age. As with the twelve-month neurological examination, there seemed to be no effect of the potentially anoxic pregnancy variables on later psychological test performance. In light of these findings and the earlier reviews, it would appear that, in general, pregnancy variables taken alone do little to predict deviant outcomes during the first year of life and in a strict sense, do not, by themsleves, constitute risk factors.

2. *Multiple predictors.* Parmelee and Haber (in press) have argued that studies that make use of single events or scores based on neonatal health or adjustment often sample acute variables, the effects of which may be highly transitory. They concluded that while there is some limited basis for the widely held belief that many prenatal and perinatal factors do place an infant at risk, there is little agreement about the degree of such risk or what pathological outcomes are associated with the hazards. While large-scale investigations such as the Collaborative Study have documented the relationship between certain perinatal factors and perinatal mortality, the risk of later sequelae for infants who survive the neonatal period is still unclear. Surviving infants often become very ill, but, after recovery, they typically show little residual damage. By contrast, other more chronic, but less dramatic events, may lead to permanent damage which manifests itself only later in life. Combinations of pregnancy and delivery complications also appear to increase the likelihood of both immediate damage and the risk for subsequent disorder. The most successful prediction of later deviance would then appear to result from a combined criterion of prenatal, postnatal, and perinatal events.

The research literature summarized above offered little evidence to suggest a relationship between specific pregnancy and delivery complications and later abnormal behavior. Another source for specific predictions of later deviance has been aberrations in newborn behavior. Parmelee and Michaelis (1971) have provided an excellent review of the relationship between newborn neurological status and later deviance. Although the diagnostic search for neurological signs was a successful means of identifying infants with contemporary neurological problems, there was little evidence to suggest that such signs were of any utility as predictors of later adaptational problems.

In those prognostic studies in which a variety of different items from newborn examinations have been combined, predictive validity has been shown to increase. On the basis of such multivariate predictors, Prechtl and Beintema (1964) have, for example, successfully defined four different syndromes of disorder: apathy, hyperexcitability, hemisyndrome, and coma. Schulte and his colleagues (Joppich and Schulte 1968; Schulte, Michaelis, and Filipp 1965), using a similar set of multiple predictors, succeeded in identifying three additional syndromes: hypertonia, hypotonia, and seizures.

Prechtl (1965), for example, found early signs of hemisyndrome—defined as an asymmetry in motility, posturing, or response to stimulation —to be predictive of more pronounced forms of the same syndrome in later childhood. Such comparability across time should, however, probably be understood as an instance of successful early diagnosis rather than as identification of a set of risk factors which heighten a child's vulnerability to later disorder. Apathy, defined by Prechtl as low frequency and intensity of responses and high threshold for responses, was shown to carry the most serious prognosis for later development. This was especially the case when combined with hypotonia—a syndrome characterized by weak resistance to passive limb movements. The abnormal sequelae associated with this syndrome pattern were, however, shown to be quite diverse, and this clustering of symptoms seems to predict more than it explains. The last of the syndromes identified by Prechtl, hyperexcitability, proved to be the poorest predictor of later developmental problems. Significant correlations were, however, reported between twitching of the arms and fingers and hyperkinetic problems at two to four years of age. As was the case with the other predictive measures described earlier, none of the syndromes defined by Prechtl were particularly powerful when considered singly but proved to be reasonably prognostic of later neurological problems when taken in combination.

In summarizing the literature on newborn neurological examinations, Parmelee and Michaelis (1971) pointed out that those diagnostic signs that have demonstrated the most predictive validity have typically depended less on specific neurological signs than on general indices of behavioral state, activity level, and threshold considerations. According to these authors, it is not the disturbance of some specific reflex which appears to produce later problems but rather the occurrence of some distorting influence which disrupts the more general reprogramming capabilities of the nervous system. Parmelee and Michaelis concluded that much more needs to be known about how the nervous system compensates for brain injury before early neurological signs can be effectively employed as predictors of later pathology.

The general conclusion suggested by these various research findings would appear to be that the long-range effects of chronic or multiple traumas is to block the neural equilibratory processes that typically occur after some single insult or trauma. A more complete understanding of such complex regulations in the development of the nervous system would probably require a change in orientation from focusing upon single events or even combinations of events, to focusing upon an understanding of the integrative and organizing capacities of the whole organism.

The prediction of pathological outcome based on scores combining both prenatal and neonatal variables has been used with some success in a number of studies. When, for example, Niswander et al. (1966) used combined criteria of pregnancy complications, an Apgar score of 6 or less, and an abnormal newborn neurological examination, a strong relationship was found between these predictors and deviant scores on the eight-month Bayley and the twelve-month neurological examination. Using a similar set of multiple predictions, Drage and Berendes (1966) also found a relation between infants with both low birth-weight and low Apgar scores, and later evidence of disorder on the Bayley and neurological examination.

Despite these encouraging beginnings and short-range successes achieved by the use of these multiple criterion, their predictive power appears to be relatively short-lived and rarely goes beyond a few years. When, for example, Drage, Berendes, and Fisher (1969) retested their subjects at four years, the relationship between low birth-weight and low Apgar scores which had been demonstrated previously had all but disappeared. The mother's education level and socioeconomic status were, at this point, much more powerful predictors than were any combination of measures collected in infancy.

The St. Louis study reviewed earlier attempts to use multiple criteria based on newborn behavior to predict later deviance (Graham et al. 1962). However, the investigators were forced to conclude that none of the later effects could be predicted from newborn behavior or neurological status, even if these scores were part of a compound predictive criterion (Corah et al. 1965).

Other results (Smith, Flick, Ferriss, and Sellmann 1972) have run counter to this trend of poor predictability from neonatal events. With data collected at one of the participating hospitals in the Collaborative Study, seven-year-olds were divided into normal and abnormal groups based on a linear combination of intelligence and achievement tests. The normal group consisted of children a standard deviation or more above the mean, and the abnormal group consisted of children a standard deviation or more below the mean.

The two criterion groups were used to perform a discriminant function analysis of selected predictor variables from the prenatal and perinatal periods. The result of the analysis produced an equation capable of correctly classifying 77 percent of the abnormals and 84 percent of the normals. Adding variables from the eight-month Bayley and twelve-month neurological examination, improved the equation's discriminating ability so that 94 percent of the seven-year-olds were correctly assigned to their normal or abnormal criterion groups. When variables from a four-year follow-up were included, the hit rate rose to 98 percent.

On the surface, Smith et al. (1972) seem to demonstrate the strength of sophisticated statistical techniques in predicting later outcome from prenatal and perinatal variables. When, however, one examines the loadings of the variables used in the discriminant function, the education and IQ of the mother had by far the greatest weights. Although Smith et al. (1972) defined mother's IQ and education as (genetic) prenatal variables, they are also one-year-, four-year-, and seven-year-old variables, since the mother continues to make a contribution to the child's environment during the entire period of development.

A recurrent theme that has run through much of the preceding review is that social status variables seem to play an important role in modulating the effects of perinatal factors. In the next section it will be seen that the environment may have a much greater impact in producing deviance than any of the biological factors examined so far.

Socioeconomic Influences

Birch and Gussow (1970), in an extensive review of the effects of disadvantaged environments on development, concluded that high risk to infants is associated with both depressed social status and ethnicity. The highest rates of infant loss were found among populations which are both poor and black. Pasamanick, Knobloch, and Lilienfeld (1956) found in their sample that the proportion of infants having some complication increased from 5 percent in the white upper-social-class strata, to 15 percent in the lowest white socioeconomic group, to 51 percent among all nonwhites. These data imply that the biological outcomes of pregnancy are worse for those in poorer environments. Birch and Gussow (1970) summarized their review by noting that there were also many data to indicate that the developmental outcomes for these children were also far worse.

Drillien's (1964) data on Scottish premature infants show that for the highest social "grades" the deficit in developmental quotient (DQ) for children under 3.9 pounds is reduced from 26 to 13 points between the ages of six months and four years. For the lowest social grade, the DQ deficit increased from 26 to 32 points. When the same children were tested in school between the ages of five and seven, Drillien found that few children from middle-class homes were retarded except when birth weight had been below 3.5 pounds, while in poor homes there was a "marked excess of retarded and very dull children" in all weight categories studied.

McDonald (1964), in contrast, found that while prematurity affected intelligence in lower social groups, there were no deficits evident in the upper social class group in her sample. Similarly, Illsley (1966), who used a large sample of wide social background in Aberdeen, Scotland, found that while in lowest social class IQ scores were seriously depressed in low birth-weight groups, little effect was noted on IQ scores in the upper social class.

One of the most ambitious and revealing of the longitudinal studies of the effects of early complications has recently been completed in Hawaii. Werner, Bierman, and French (1971), reported on all 670 children born on the island of Kauai in 1955. Because of the multiracial nature of Hawaii and the variety of social classes sampled when the whole population was used, Werner et al. were able to provide ample controls for both variables.

Each infant was initially scored on a four-point scale for severity of perinatal complications. Twenty months later these perinatal scores were related to assessments of physical health, psychological status (as expressed in Cattell infant intelligence scores and Vineland social maturity scores), and the environmental variables of socioeconomic status, family stability, and mother's intelligence.

At the time of the initial perinatal assessment it was found that 56 percent of the children studied had no complications, 31 percent mild complications, 13 percent moderate complications, and only 3 percent showed severe complications. The distribution of complication scores was not found to be related to ethnic origin, socioeconomic class, age of mother, family stability, or mother's intelligence. This unusual lack of correlation between socioeconomic status and complications was probably a result of the prepaid health plan that provided good prenatal care to all women on the island. Evidence of the mothers' good health was that 80 percent showed no chronic illness during pregnancy.

At the twenty-month examination 14 percent of the children were found to be below average in health status, 16 percent in intellectual development, and 12 percent in social development. These findings closely approximate those of other comparable studies. Increasing severity of perinatal stress was related to lower scores in the three assessment areas. There was, however, a clear interaction between the impairing effect of perinatal complications and environmental variables, especially socioeconomic status. For infants living in a high socioeconomic environment, with a stable family, or with a mother of high intelligence, the IQ differences between children with and without complication scores was only 5–7 points. For infants living in a low socioeconomic environment, with low family stability, or with a mother of low intelligence, the difference in mean Cattell IQs between the high and low perinatal complications groups and between infants without perinatal complications ranged from 19 to 37 points.

The results of the Kauai study seem to indicate that perinatal complications were consistently related to later physical and psychological development only when combined with and supported by persistently poor environmental circumstances. In addition, when good prenatal care is available, socioeconomic differences in the initial distribution of perinatal complications are found to disappear.

The infants of the Kauai sample were again examined when they reached ten years of age (Werner, Honzik, and Smith 1968). Data from the perinatal and twenty-month examinations were correlated with intelligence and school performance at ten years of age. There was no correlation between the perinatal-stress score and the ten-year measures. Some correlation was, however, found between the twenty-month and ten-year data, especially when socioeconomic status and parents' educational level were taken into consideration. Stability of intellectual functioning was much higher for those children who had IQs below 80 at the ten-year testing. All of these children had twenty-month Cattell scores of 100 or less, with almost half below 80. The majority of these children had parents with little education and low socioeconomic status. In general, the correlation of the child's IQ with the parents' increased across the eight-year period. The Kauai study seemed to suggest that risk factors operative during the perinatal period disappear during childhood as more potent familial and social factors exert their influence.

Werner and her associates (1971) noted that of 1,000 live births in Kauai, by age ten only 660 were adequately functioning in school with no recognized physical, intellectual, or behavior problem. In the 34 percent of children who had problems at the age of ten, only a minor proportion of the problems could be attributed to the effects of serious perinatal stress. The major impact of biological defects associated with reproductive casualty occurs in the first weeks of pregnancy, when 90 percent of fetal losses occur in the form of spontaneous abortions. After this initial period, environment increasingly becomes the dominant influence. The biologically vulnerable child makes up only a small proportion of those children who will not function adequately. The authors concluded that, in their study, "ten times more children had problems related to the effects of poor early environment than to the effects of perinatal stress."

The data from these various longitudinal studies of prenatal and perinatal complications have yet to produce a single predictive variable more potent than the familial and socioeconomic characteristics of the caretaking environment. The predictive efficiency of the variable of socioeconomic class is especially pronounced for the low end of the IQ scale (Werner, Simonian, Bierman, and French 1967). Willerman, Broman, and Fiedler (1970), using another sample from the Collaborative Study, compared Bayley developmental scores obtained at eight months with Stanford-Binet IQs at age four. For children with a high socioeconomic status there was little relationship between their eight-month Bayley scores and their four-year scores. For children with a low socioeconomic status, however, those who did poorly at eight months continued to do so at four years of age. In addition, there was a crossover effect by which the high socioeconomic status children who were in the lowest quartile at the eight-month examination were performing better at four years than were the low socioeconomic status children who scored in the highest quartile at eight months. Willerman et al. see poverty as amplifying IQ deficits in poorly developed infants.

Ireton, Thwing, and Gravem (1970) also separated socioeconomic status variables from early developmental scores in their efforts to predict intelligence test scores at four years. In their Minnesota sample from the Collaborative Study, socioeconomic status was closely related to Stanford-Binet scores at four years but not to eight-month Bayley scores in the same subjects. A low eight-month mental score was a better prediction of low four-year IQ than was social class, but, conversely, high socioeconomic status was a better predictor of high scores than the eight-month mental test. Because of the small proportion of subjects who scored in the abnormal range on the twelve-month neurological examination, the relationships between this examination and four-month IQs were small and inconclusive.

Ireton et al. concluded that prediction of later intellectual functioning would require a model including early mental scores, the infant's biological and neurological status, and environmental opportunities. Their model would necessitate an evaluation of factors leading to deviancies in the prenatal environment and the subsequent characteristics of the newborn, followed by an analysis of how the infant interacts with his environment to increase or reduce the probability of later problems. A later section will make such an analysis by examining factors that play an early role in influencing the course and outcome of pregnancy.

Summary

1. In the preceding sections we have reviewed the long-term effects of a variety of complications of reproduction which had been thought to be associated with later subnormal behavior in the child. A continuum of reproductive casualty had been hypothesized which was thought to be positively related to the degree of abnormality present in the course of development; that is, the greater the reproductive complication, the greater the later deviance. This hypothesis has not been generally supported by the data reviewed. There is a serious question as to whether a child who has suffered perinatal trauma but shows no obvious brain damage is at any greater risk for later deviance than a child who has not suffered perinatal trauma.

2. Abnormalities have been found in populations with specific reproductive complications, but these tend to disappear with age. Postnatal anoxia may affect newborn behavior and intellectual functioning through the preschool periods, but, by school age, IQ differences between affected and control populations have all but disappeared. When infants born prematurely were followed through school age, the deficits in their intelligence at earlier ages were greatly reduced in later years. The lowest intelligence test scores were found in groups of infants with the lowest birth-weights.

3. In the studies reviewed, the effects of social status tended to reduce or amplify intellectual deficits. In advantaged families, infants who had suffered perinatal complications generally showed no significant or small residual effects at follow-up. Many infants from lower social class homes with identical histories of complications showed significant retardations in later functioning. Social and economic status appear to have much stronger influences on the course of development than perinatal history.

4. Three hypotheses emerge from the above review and will be examined in the following sections.

a) A major flaw in prospective studies of traumatic variables is that such traumas cannot be randomly assigned to subjects. Behavioral deviation found in children who have had complicated births may not be caused by the complications themselves but rather by a third factor which influenced both the behavioral deviation and the birth complication. Low socioeconomic status appears to be such a variable. A more specific factor that is correlated with social level is emotional health. Emotional stress and its influence on the birth process will be discussed in the next section.

b) The effects of birth complications on later development can be mediated by the attitudes of the child's caretakers. To the extent the child is seen as being different, troublesome, sick, or retarded, the par-

ents' attitudes may be altered and lead to their treating the child as difficult, troublesome, sick, or retarded. The study of the child's effect on his
parents has become a topic of increasing importance in developmental
research.

c) The organization of intelligence in the child appears to change with
age. As the child moves from a sensorimotor mode of functioning to a conceptual mode, early deficits tend to disappear in the child's restructured
cognitive functioning. When continuities in development are found (in
contrast to the normal discontinuities), their source must be sought in the
maintaining environment. Parental attitudes in particular, and social status
in general, seem to be strong candidates for such a maintaining role.

REPRODUCTION AND STRESS

The attitudes of the general public regarding potential risks and hazards
to unborn children have, according to Stott (1971), passed through a full
pendulum swing during the last half-century. Two generations ago, expectant mothers were routinely cautioned by their elders about the dangers
of fetal marking as a result of certain presumably hazardous experiences.
Expectant mothers were cautioned, for example, against eating strawber-
ries, lest their child develop a strawberry birthmark. In subsequent decades
gynecologists and pediatricians succeeded in relegating these concerns to
the status of old wives' tales. This shift in views appears, however, to have
carried beyond the mark, and the general public has come to assume that
the intrauterine environment is a sanctuary against potential hazards. This
countermyth has all but removed from public awareness the possibility
that a fetus could suffer intrauterine trauma.

Physical Anomalies

The public and sometimes professional notion, that nature completely
protected the fetus, began to be dispelled with discoveries of the harmful
effects of prenatal rubella (Gregg 1942). This and related discoveries have
precipitated a second pendulum shift leading to the development of a large
contemporary literature on the hazards of pregnancy and delivery. Although there is a sizeable cultural lag, the general public is again being sen-
sitized to such prenatal risks.

This history of fads and fickle beliefs should alert one to the possibility
that the pendulum may again swing too far too quickly and again overstress
or oversimplify the potential hazards to unborn children. Despite the relatively high proportion (16 percent) of physical malformations resulting
from maternal rubella, for example, mental defects during infancy which
could be attributed to such an illness history have been found in only 2 percent of the case studies (Manson, Logan, and Loy 1960). Such negative

outcomes were also not found to be associated with the severity of the rubella symptoms in the mother. Sheridan (1964) examined approximately two hundred school-age children whose mothers had had rubella during the first sixteen weeks of pregnancy. At ages eight to eleven their IQ distribution was no different than that of the normal population. Of the thirty-seven children with IQs less than 85, thirteen had significant hearing losses that could account for their poor performance. Stott (1971) concluded that infection may have a triggering effect on potential deviation, but that the long-range outcome for the child is the result of many other important factors.

Even such gross malformations as anencephaly seem to be strongly influenced by environmental factors. Pleydell (1960) found that anencephaly was four times more common in industrial areas than in rural areas. In some situations multiple cases were found to occur on the same street within a period of a day. Klebanov (1948) found that among children born to Jewish women released from concentration camps, the incidence of malformation was four to five times the normal rate. The incidence of Down's syndrome, for example, was 1 in 35 compared to 1 in 650 found in other European populations. The majority of these defective infants were born to women under thirty, which argues against the possibility that advanced maternal age was a cause of these high incidence figures in this population.

Stott (1971) also argues that emotional stress during pregnancy is related to the incidence of congenital malformations. He reviewed the literature on birth defects in Great Britain and Germany during World War II and found an increase in anomaly rates that could not be adequately explained by changes in nutrition during the war years. Stott goes on to argue that the increased incidence of birth malformations in teenage women is not the result of any biological immaturity of the mother but rather of the emotional stresses created by pregnancy at such a young age with a child often conceived out of wedlock. In fact, a number of studies have shown that teenage girls who are not subject to such stresses probably have more uneventful pregnancies than do older women (Niswander and Gordon 1972).

A number of infant anomalies have been found to be associated with genetic or chromosomal malformations. (See chapter 2 in this volume.) Despite these findings Stott (1971) argues that such genetic deviances do not, in themselves, account for all anomalies in infancy. Typically, malformed fetuses are aborted spontaneously during early pregnancy. Why are some infants born with Down's syndrome or other congenital malformation rather than being spontaneously aborted? In a study of severe mental retardation, Stott compared 739 children with Down's syndrome with 400 other retarded children. He found a higher incidence of prolonged prenatal stress among the mothers of the mongoloid children than among mothers of the other children studied. He argued that such prolonged stress during the second and third month of pregnancy changed the mothers' biochemical balance in a way that blocked the spontaneous abortion of malformed fetuses.[1] A similar argument linking prenatal stress and the inhibition of the natural aborting function can be applied to the cases of nonfamilial cleft lip and palate studied by Drillien, Ingram, and Wilkinson (1966). Drillien and Wilkinson (1964) also found a relationship between factors of emotional stress during pregnancy and an increased incidence of Down's syndrome.

Although major physical anomalies like cleft palate and mongolism claim attention because of their dramatic quality, there is a more common series of minor physical anomalies which have also been related to stress factors. Such anomalies include misshapen ears and toes, head circumference beyond the normal range, epicanthal folds, widely spaced eyes, curved fifth finger, and wide gaps between first and second toe. The occurrence of such anomalies has been repeatedly associated with factors operating in the first few weeks of pregnancy. Along with Down's syndrome, these anomalies are genetic in determination but generally are not hereditary in that they are not passed from generation to generation. They involve, instead, breakage and damage to the normal chromosomal material (McClearn 1964).

These minor physical anomalies have been thought, by a number of investigators, to be related to a variety of adaptational problems. Goldfarb (1967) reported a higher incidence of these anomalies among schizophrenic children than among normal children. Waldrop and Halverson (1971) reported on studies of more subtle behavior deviation than explicit mental illness. They found that in a sample of two-and-a-half year-old children, the more minor anomalies a child demonstrated, the more likely he was to be aggressive, hyperkinetic, and intractable. In a follow-up study, when the children were seven-and-a-half-years old, a persistently high correlation between the number of such anomalies and hyperactivity was again found.

Waldrop and Halverson (1971) emphasize that it is the total number of such anomalies which is related to hyperactivity and not the presence or absence of any particular anomaly. As in the case of perinatal and neonatal complications, no linear relationships have been found between

1. The tragic circumstances surrounding the use of thalidomide can be viewed as a demonstration of the biochemical mechanism which Stott has proposed. The usual outcome of the malformations produced by thalidomide would have been the spontaneous abortion of the fetus. However, thalidomide appears to have had a second property of suppressing this spontaneous abortion mechanism.

single characteristics of the child and later problems. Even when combined scores have shown predictive efficiency, the particular constellation of risk factors has proven to be secondary to the total number of risk factors.

Emotional Factors in Perinatal Complications

In the previous section connections between psychological stress during pregnancy and physical malformations were discussed. Emotional factors have also been shown to be related to an increase in the incidence of delivery complications. Several reviews of the effects of emotional factors on pregnancy have described relationships between a variety of labor complications and aspects of maternal personality (Ferreira 1969; Joffe 1969). Ferreira (1965) has pointed out the reluctance of many investigators to assume that the mother's emotional state represents a part of the fetus's environment. A number of studies report associations between maternal emotional state and prolonged pregnancy, nausea and vomiting during pregnancy, toxemia, prematurity, and abortion.

The clearest manifestation of the operation of an emotional complication is the psychologically triggered death of the infant through miscarriage or abortion. Javert (1962) summarized his experience with 427 women who had a history of habitual abortion. He remarked that most of the women had clear psychic conflicts and little desire for additional children. Grimm (1962) compared a group of habitual aborters with a control group, using a standard psychological battery. Although no differences were found in age, education, or intelligence, the habitual aborters demonstrated poorer emotional controls and stronger dependency needs. While the emotional difficulties which characterize these women could well have been the consequence rather than the cause of their previous spontaneous abortions, the stress associated with subsequent pregnancies, whatever its source, probably contributed to their continuing difficulties.

Prematurity has also been found to be associated with psychosomatic factors. Blau, Slaff, Easton, Welkowitz, and Cohen (1963), in a retrospective study, found mothers of prematures to be more emotionally immature and to have more negative attitudes towards their pregnancies than did controls. Gunter (1963) found that the mothers of premature infants had more feelings of inadequacy and greater anxiety than controls. Although a prospective study demonstrating that these emotional difficulties predated the occurrence of these premature births would be necessary to firmly establish the causative role of such emotional factors, these data do implicate such variables and suggest the need for additional research.

Labor difficulties have been related to high anxiety in a number of studies. McDonald, Gynther, and Christakos (1963) found a positive relation between anxiety and duration of labor. Scott and Thomson (1956) evaluated over two hundred primigravidas and found that uterine dysfunction tended to be associated with higher covert anxiety levels.

McDonald (1968), in reviewing the effects of emotional factors on obstetrical complications, found that the best results were obtained in studies which considered such complications to be derivatives of a single underlying process. The mothers' emotional status showed stronger relationships to a combined criteria of prenatal and perinatal complications than to any single complication. When women who had normal pregnancies and deliveries were contrasted with those who had delivery irregularities, disorders of the gestational period, or developmental abnormalities of the infant at birth, the abnormal group was consistently found to have been more anxious (McDonald and Christakos 1963). McDonald and Parham (1964) repeated these findings with a group of unwed mothers assessed in the last trimester of pregnancy. Davids and DeVault (1962) also tested a sample of women during their pregnancies and found that those who had been more anxious tended to have longer labor times and more delivery-room difficulties.

McDonald (1968) concluded that most studies in the area suffer from shortcomings of random clinical observation, lack of controls, and retrospective collection of data. When only the better studies are examined, they point to the same consistent psychological differences between samples of women who have had complications, and samples who have not. The groups with abnormal consequences were characterized by higher anxiety and less use of repressive-type defenses. In addition, these high-anxiety levels were found to be associated with high levels of dependency, particularly in women who were sexually immature and who had ambivalent feelings toward their pregnancies.

Ferreira (1965) argued that any interference with the process of pregnancy is an interference with the product of pregnancy. He suggested a number of pathways by which the mother's emotions can affect the fetus. Maternal hostility may be expressed in accident-proneness, improper diet, obesity, excessive smoking, or drug use. The mother's emotions may also have an impact on the fetus through her endocrine system. Emotional factors have been shown to effect adrenocortical function and peripheral vascular tone. Ferreira concluded that emotionally unwelcome pregnancies may have inevitable effects on the prenatal and postnatal life of the infant.

McDonald (1968) also focused on the endocrine system as the mediator between the psychological aspects of the mother's emotional disturbances and the somatic aspects of the subsequent prenatal and perinatal complication. He points out that many anxious women do have normal pregnancies and deliveries, and raises the question as to what conditions are necessary for obstetric complications to occur. He sees anxiety as the "necessary" condition, with an adaptive failure occurring when the anxiety reaches the "sufficient" condition of overwhelming intensity or duration.

Stott (1971) has argued that the breakdown will take the form of physical malformations if the stress occurs early in the pregnancy when gross biological differentiations are occurring. If the fetus survives these early developmental stages, continued stress is less likely to result in additional malformations and is more likely to produce deviations in the course of the pregnancy.

Smoking and Pregnancy Outcome

A study that has underscored, more than almost any other, the complex role played by perinatal variables has been Yerushalmy's investigation (1971, 1972) of the relation between smoking and pregnancy outcomes. Smoking during pregnancy has been generally associated with lower birth-weights. Although low birth-weight infants (less than 2,500 grams) typically have twenty times the neonatal mortality rate of infants with higher birth-weights (Shapiro, Schlesinger, and Nesbitt 1968), the neonatal mortality rate for the low birth-weight infants born to smoking mothers is no greater than for high birth-weight infants in general.

Yerushalmy (1971) reported that in addition to the neonatal mortality rate of low birth-weight infants being related to the mother's smoking, it was also related to the father's smoking. The lowest mortality rate among the low birth-weight group was found for those infants with a smoking mother and a nonsmoking father. The highest mortality rates were among infants with a nonsmoking mother and a smoking father. If one assumes that the connection between low birth-weight and mother's smoking is a physiological one, it would be quite difficult to understand how the husband's smoking is able to effect it. The only available interpretation of such a complex interaction is that smoking is somehow related to other personality variables and that the psychological characteristics that accompany smoking in the husband can affect the variables in the mother that produce low birth-weight infants.

Yerushalmy (1972) directed himself to answering the question of whether it was the smoking or the smoker that produced low birth-weight infants. He found that women who did not smoke when their child was born but began afterwards had the same rate of low birth-weight infants as those that had smoked all along. Women who had smoked during their pregnancies but had stopped afterwards did not have the increased rate of low birth-weight babies. Yerushalmy concluded that it was the smoker and not the smoking that affected the rate of low birth-weight babies. Women who smoked continually or who began smoking later had the low birth-weight babies. Women who never smoked or were able to give up smoking did not have more low birth-weight babies.

Yerushalmy's data demonstrate how, upon closer scrutiny, an apparently straightforward physiological phenomenon may prove to have a strong psychological component. In both this and related studies there is, then, strong evidence for the role of psychosomatic factors in pregnancy outcome.

Psychiatric Conditions

One area in which the relationship of biological and social variables has been most explicitly detailed has been the study of the etiology of schizophrenia. Because of the great body of data pointing to genetic factors in schizophrenia (Rosenthal 1970), researchers in this area have searched for the constitutional precursors of schizophrenia breakdown. Risk research has become one of the major areas in the study of schizophrenia, and the designs used in such investigations have provided sophisticated models for the study of risk factors in other areas (Garmezy 1971).

When the pregnancies of diagnosed schizophrenics were examined in a series of studies, there appeared to be a disproportionately large number of prenatal and perinatal complications. Pasamanick and Knobloch (1966) reported a study in which fifty children with infantile autism were found to have had high rates of prematurity, pregnancy complication, as well as neurologic signs of brain damage. Pollack and Woerner (1966), in an analysis of five studies of childhood schizophrenia, found a higher incidence of prenatal complications, in particular bleeding, toxemia, and severe maternal illness, in the birth records of schizophrenic as compared to normal control groups. Higher levels of prematurity were not, however, reported. Similarly, Taft and Goldfarb (1964) also found prenatal and perinatal complications to be a factor in childhood schizophrenia, especially for boys.

Other investigators have focused on the offspring of specific psychiatric groups in the hope of identifying differential risk factors in these various illness groups. Pollin and Stabenau (1968), for example, reported that, in a retrospective study of identical twins discordant for schizophrenia, the twin who became schizophrenic had a greater incidence of perinatal complications including anoxia, low birth-weight, and soft neurological signs.

The finding of more perinatal complications in the history of diagnosed schizophrenics led some investigators to consider obstetrical complications as predisposing factors in the etiology of schizophrenia. The higher incidence of schizophrenia in the offspring of schizophrenic women might then be attributable in part to their having had a higher proportion of pregnancy and delivery complications than nonschizophrenic women. Mednick (1970) proposed that reproductive complications affected the infant's brain through anoxia, producing autonomic reactivity patterns that would predispose the child to mental disorder. In order to further explore this potential relationship, Mednick and Schulsinger (1968) studied a sample of adolescent children of schizophrenic women. Twenty of their subjects required mental-health care during the first decade of their study. Mednick (1970) compared the pregnancy and delivery records of these "sick" subjects with a second group who had shown improvement in their mental-health status during the study, and found a greater number of pregnancy and delivery complications in the "sick" group. Mednick and his associates (Mednick, Mura, Schulsinger, and Mednick 1971) further examined the birth records of the offspring of schizophrenic, personality-disordered, and normal women. A greater number of birth complications was found in the offspring of the schizophrenic women. Lower birth-weight was the most frequent of these complications. They (Mednick 1970; Mednick et al. 1971) attributed the increased perinatal complications directly to the schizophrenic condition of the mothers.

Sameroff and Zax (1973) examined perinatal complications of women with a variety of psychiatric diagnoses. The severity of mental illness was separated from the effects of specific syndrome clusters such as schizophrenia. In a study comparing three groups of women—schizophrenics, neurotic depressives, and normals—Sameroff and Zax found that both the schizophrenic and neurotic depressive groups had more complications than the normal group. No differences were found between the two psychiatric groups. When the two psychiatric groups were divided on a dimension of chronicity, however, those who had the greatest number of psychiatric contacts and hospitalizations had infants with the most perinatal complications. This was true irrespective of the particular diagnostic group into which these women fell. Thus, the degree of severity rather than the specific type of mental illness proved to be the better predictor of infant perinatal complications. Sameroff and Zax (1973) also compared the deliveries of four groups of women—schizophrenics, neurotic depressives, personality disorders, and normals. When the four groups were divided into categories of severity of mental illness, infants of the women who had had the most previous psychiatric contacts again had the most perinatal complications. Before one can be sure of the relationship between a particular mental illness and increased delivery complications, one has to be sure that other possible causative factors have been controlled. The presence of a severe mental disturbance does seem to indicate an increased probability of obstetrical complications. Although the exact nature of the causal linkage underlying this empirical correlation is not known with certainty, the deleterious effects of anxiety and stress, described in the previous section, may provide a partial explanation for the observed covariation between severity of emotional illness and obstetrical complications.

Summary

1. Little evidence has been found to support the assumption of a direct causal relation between reproductive complications and later intellectual deficit. The evidence suggests that other factors might be present that are responsible for both of these outcomes.

2. Emotional stress has been identified as such a potential factor. Studies of women with high levels of anxiety, stress, or psychiatric disorder have been found to have a greater proportion of pregnancy complications and a greater proportion of physical anomalies in their offspring.

3. It would appear that emotional problems of the mother can create a disturbed physical climate for the child before and during birth.

CONTINUUM OF CARETAKING CASUALTY

The preceding sections of this chapter have reviewed research efforts to establish determinant connections between prenatal or perinatal complications and subsequent long-term developmental consequences. As a general rule, only when information regarding the nature of the subsequent caretaking environment has also been taken into account have such long-range predictions about the later consequences of pregnancy and birth complications been successful. These results argue strongly against any "simple and sovereign" approach to the definition of risk and emphasize the necessity of assuming a much more transactional attitude toward the study of childhood vulnerability. Unfortunately, those investigators who have directed their attention to the study of the caretaking environment have, in turn, largely ignored the contributions of the child, and of his or her cumulative prenatal and perinatal complications, to his or her own social environment. As a consequence this literature has tended to be as one-sided and unilateral as the research on prenatal complications already reviewed, and rarely reflects the transactional emphasis which seems to be required. Despite these limitations, research into the developmental implications of early caretaking practices does characterize many circumstances that contribute to risk.

Because the list of parental and other environmental hazards to a child's normal development is almost endless, our attempt to review the research literature on these topics must be selective and incomplete. Since anything from nutritional standards to disciplinary techniques might be legitimately included, some arbitrary delimiting of this domain was required. The present review will focus on only the most flagrant form of deviant caretaking, where the hazards to the child are immediate and unqualified. Specifically, attention will be focused on research concerned with child abuse and neglect. Even this "tip of the iceberg" is represented by a large and unwieldy literature. Selective emphasis will be given to those more transactional studies that have stressed or implied the possible contributions of children to the quality of their own care.

Postnatal Risk Factors

Risk factors which threaten to jeopardize the healthy growth and development of the child are in no sense exclusive to the prenatal and perinatal periods. Once delivered into the "booming, buzzing" world outside the womb, the infant is suddenly subject to a whole new constellation of influences and hazards from which he or she was insulated in utero. Although, as the previous pages have documented, the prenatal environment contains many more hazards than is commonly believed, the intrauterine environment is something of an evolutionary masterpiece as a sanctuary against many classes of threat. Once born, however, the child is rendered into the hands of parents whose qualifications for their new roles are often questionable. The growth context created by the parents of newborn infants must, like the intrauterine environment occupied earlier, provide ways of protecting the child and permitting him or her to grow and flourish. Parenting behaviors which do not meet minimal standards constitute a risk to the child's normal development. Breakdowns in the parent-child relationship may take a great variety of forms. The most heavily researched and carefully documented of these transactional failures, however, relate to the inability of parents and their children to work out an interactional style which both guarantees the child a reasonable margin of safety and satisfies the child's basic biological and social needs. These minimal requirements for adequate growth and development, while probably closely linked, have traditionally been discussed independently in the research literature under the separate rubrics of *abuse* and *neglect*.

The Battered Child

Although the infliction of serious physical injury on a child by a parent or parent substitute is only one of the many ways in which caretakers can and do abuse their children, physical abuse is dramatic evidence of a disorder in the parent-child relationship. In cases of physical injury, evidence of maltreatment is documented in a way not usually possible in other serious but less overt cases of psychological neglect. Consequently, an extensive literature has emerged on the medical and legal aspects of the problem of child abuse.

The degree of risk posed to infants by the threat of physical assault from their caretakers is difficult to estimate. It is obviously in the self-interest of abusive parents to prevent their assaultive behavior from coming to public attention. Although all fifty states have recently enacted laws regarding the reporting of suspected cases of battering, physicians are understandably reluctant to enter the legal entanglements that may follow from publicly accusing a parent of abuse (Gil 1970). Minimal estimate of the incidence of such maltreatment is provided by a nation-wide review of officially reported abuse cases (Gil 1970). This survey found approximately 1,200 cases of suspected physical abuse and 6,500 cases of confirmed child abuse reported during 1967. The true incidence is undoubtedly much greater. Holter and Friedman (1968) reported that as many as 20 percent of all children brought to hospitals for emergency room care may have sustained injuries resulting from parental neglect or abuse. DeFrancis (1972), reporting at a recent national symposium on child abuse, estimated that as many as a half million children a year may be victims of one or another forms of abuse or neglect. The most recent report of the Joint Commission on Mental Health of Children (1970) estimated that two to three thousand children are injured each month and one or two killed each day by abusive parents. Kempe and Helfer (1970) have suggested that the number of children under five years of age killed by parents each year is higher than the number of those who die from diseases.

Although the short-range consequences of serious abuse are obvious, its status as a risk factor for infants is also partially dependent on its long-range implication for growth and development. Very few studies have traced the subsequent development of abused children or assessed the long-range consequences of such maltreatment. Elmer and Gregg (1967), in an extensive physical and psychological evaluation of twenty children treated for abuse over a thirteen-year period, documented a broad range of developmental difficulties and continuing disorders. At the time of follow-up, 90 percent of the study population evidenced some form of residual damage. More than half of the children studied were judged to be mentally retarded, and more than half were thought to be emotionally disturbed. Growth failures, speech disturbances, and a variety of other signs of developmental delay and arrest were present to such an extent that only two of the study children were judged to be completely normal at the time of the follow-up. Only children who had sustained bone injuries as a result of suspected abuse were included in this study, however, and the authors concluded that this inclusion criterion led to the selection of cases whose prognosis was particularly unfavorable.

A three-year follow-up study of twenty-five suspected abuse cases was conducted by Morse, Sahler, and Friedman (1970). The selection criterion employed in this study was somewhat broader than that of Elmer and Gregg (1967), and, consequently, the cases of abuse were less extreme and possibly more representative. At the time of the three-year follow-up more than 70 percent of the children were judged to be below the normal range in either intellectual, emotional, social, or motor development. As in Elmer and Gregg's study, approximately half (43 percent) were found to have displayed symptoms of mental retardation or motor hyperactivity preceding the incident of abuse or neglect that led to their inclusion in the study.

The findings of these two studies, while not answering the question of cause and effect, do suggest that caretaking settings in which battering and abuse are believed to occur do constitute unusually hazardous environments that seriously jeopardize the healthy development of children who live in them. It is not at all clear from these studies whether the negative outcomes observed are the result of the abusive incidents which brought the study population to public attention, the generally poor quality of caretaking in these homes, or the attributes of the children on whom those abusive acts were perpetrated. Much of the research on child abuse has focused on characteristics of the abusive parents and their home environments that may have distorted the caretaking process. The literature on abusive parents and the few studies on possible child factors in abuse are summarized below.

Parental Factors in Child Abuse

Studies on the etiology of child abuse have typically concentrated on unearthing characteristics that differentiate abusive from nonabusive parents. Spinetta and Rigler (1972) have recently summarized research on the personality characteristics of abusive parents: they have been shown to be less intelligent, more aggressive, impulsive, immature, self-centered, tense, and self-critical than nonabusive parents. A number of investigators (Delsordo 1963; Merrill 1962; Zalba 1966) have gone beyond a mere listing of separate personality attributes and have attempted to identify clusters of descriptive terms which characterize different types of abusive parents.

The personal histories of abusive parents tend to include evidence that they were themselves abused or neglected as children (Fontana 1968; Steele and Pollack 1968) and, as a consequence, lack parenting skills and an adequate understanding of appropriate child-rearing practices (Galdston 1965). Spinetta and Rigler (1972) concluded their review of the literature on the child-rearing attitudes of abusive parents by stressing that they have typically been found to lack appropriate knowledge of child-rearing. Oliver and Taylor (1971) studied forty of the closest relatives of a seriously battered child and found evidence of battering, reported physical cruelty, abandonment, and serious neglect in all but thirteen of the cases studied. These data on three generations of family members led the authors to conclude that ill-treatment and neglect of a child seriously undermined later parenting skills and sustained maltreatment across generations. Parents who were abused as children may have unrealistic expectations which they enforce with inconsistent and poorly chosen parenting techniques. Of particular relevance is the finding of Gregg and Elmer (1969) that abusive mothers were particularly ineffective in their efforts to provide adequate care when their children were ill.

Despite the apparent convergence of these data, the attributes of the abusive parent have been pieced together without appropriate comparisons to families with other social problems. It is not at all clear that the defining features of the abusive group uniquely identify them as abusive or merely characterize them as belonging to the same multiproblem families that are routinely overrepresented in any study of social disorganization. Abusive parents may be all that they are claimed to be, but any attempt to predict abuse on the basis of these characteristics would almost certainly result in a large group of false positives (Gil 1970).

Socioeconomic Factors in Child Abuse

Because data on actual parental behaviors are not often available, investigators have turned to more indirect measures to assess the psychological climate of abusive families. These investigations have focused primarily on demographic variables such as socioeconomic and health status that may influence the amount of disorganization within the family unit. With minor exceptions these studies have been ex post facto in character, and contemporary information concerning the children who were the targets of abuse has not been available.

Abusing families have, according to these studies, been shown to be overrepresented in the lower socioeconomic classes; to be characterized by higher than average rates of divorce, separation, and unstable marriages (Kempe et al. 1962); and to be socially isolated, highly mobile, frequently unemployed, and isolated from the support of extended family members (Elmer 1967; Young 1964). All of these extrinsic economic and social factors have been assumed to be stressors for the family groups, to exhaust their physical and psychological resources, and to precipitate the uncontrolled expression of assaultive impulses.

One possible explanation of the observed relationship between socio-economic level and battering is offered by Galdston (1971), who suggested that the lower incidence of battering among the more affluent may simply reflect their ability to avoid attacking their children by relegating their care to others. The poor, because they cannot hire others to care for their children, are locked into a relationship from which they cannot escape.

Taken in combination, these studies portray the abusive parent as a member of a multiproblem family whose list of deficits and liabilities covers the whole spectrum of personal and social pathology. It is not at all clear how the various difficulties and disorders are translated into patterns of child abuse, why many families who can be similarly characterized do not abuse their children, and why the same families abuse some of their children and not others.

Children's Contributions to Their Own Abuse

A number of recent studies (Gil 1970) have provided evidence which suggests that, in addition to the more carefully explored relationship between child abuse and parental and family pathology, various abnormalities in the child may also predispose the parents to battering or neglect. Elmer and Gregg (1967) and Klein and Stern (1971), for example, have pointed to an apparent association between low birth-weight and the battered-child syndrome. One explanation for such an association is that both factors are related to low socioeconomic status. Mothers of low socioeconomic status more frequently have children of low birth-weight (Niswander and Gordon 1972) and are also disproportionately represented among groups of abusive parents (Spinetta and Rigler 1972). Klein and Stern (1971), however, found a significant association between battering and low birth-weight even after appropriate controls for socioeconomic level had been applied. More disturbed mothers not only tend to have more low birth-weight infants, but they are also more likely to abuse them. Klaus and Kennell (1970) suggested that the birth of a premature child may function to overtax the limited resources of certain mothers and precipitate an acute emotional crisis. This interpretation is lent credence by an additional finding of the Klein and Stern study (1971) which suggested that many of the battered children in their sample whose birth weights were within normal limits did have other significant medical illnesses which might also have served to deplete their mothers' emotional resources.

In summarizing the findings on child battering and child neglect, Klaus and Kennell (1970) hypothesized that these problems may be partly the result of separation in the newborn period. Because of prematurity or serious illness, a high proportion (44 percent) of battered children had been separated from their parents for prolonged periods. Early, prolonged separation may permanently impair the affectional ties between parents and children and leave the children vulnerable to parental abuse and neglect. Here again, one can see the potential consequences of emotional disorder in the mother. The anxious mother whose pregnancy ends prematurely might be the same disturbed mother who avoids visiting her infant in the premature nursery and does not form close ties with her child at home afterwards.

Although it is not always possible to separate truth from self-justifying rationalization, the parents of abused children frequently describe their offspring as difficult and unmanageable. In a follow-up study (Morse et al. 1970), for example, fifteen of the twenty-five children studied were considered "different" by their parents. Follow-up data collected by these investigators also tended to support the impressions of the parents that many of those children studied were problem children preceding the reported abuse or neglect.

Several lines of evidence suggest that abused children frequently present special caretaking problems. As previously indicated, high incidences of mental retardation are reported by both Elmer and Gregg (1967) and Morse et al. (1970). Holter and Friedman (1968) reported that 25 percent of their subjects were physically ill and required special attention at the time they were abused. Milowe (cited in Gil 1970) reported that many abused children are unusually difficult, irritating, and have particularly grating cries. The results of Gil's (1970) nationwide survey suggested that almost a third of the abused children studied revealed deviations in social interaction and general functioning during the year preceding the abusive incident. Another quarter of the sample suffered from deviation in physical functioning or revealed deviation in intellectual functioning. In addition, nearly a quarter of the sample was described as showing persistently atypical behavior, which is in accord with parental reports that abusive acts were often perpetrated in direct response to "provoking" behaviors by the child. Child-originated abuse can be seen as one of the principal factors implicated in legally reported, physical child abuse (Gil 1970).

Somewhat anecdotal evidence supports the hypothesis that infants may act in ways that precipitate the abuse which they experience. McKay (cited in Milowe and Lourie 1964) reported that the same children were occasionally battered by different and unrelated caretakers. McDovy (cited in Milowe and Lourie 1964) reported similar findings indicating that already abused children are sometimes battered a second time by foster parents who had assumed responsibility for their care.

In summary, the preliminary data on abused children would suggest that there are relatively high rates of bio-psycho-social deviance in the victims, as well as in the perpetrators, of child abuse and that any singular emphasis on one of these factors to the exclusion of the others fails to come to terms with the true interactional character of child abuse.

Failure-to-Thrive Syndrome

Gross parental inattention to the needs of their children, abandonment, starvation, and unusual isolation of the child from the family and the community is, according to the 1970 Report of the Joint Commission on Mental Health of Children (1970), an extremely widespread and largely unresearched problem of national importance. As suggested earlier, there is no clear demarcation between neglected and abused children; in fact, many children initially identified as victims of battering are later discovered to be seriously neglected as well (Gil 1970). Koel (1969) reported three cases of infants hospitalized because of failure to thrive who were later readmitted as the result of subsequent violence or assault.

These findings are consistent with other reports in the literature (Bullard, Glaser, Heagarty, and Pivchik 1968; Gil 1970; Helfer and Kempe 1968; Simons, Downs, Hurster, and Archer 1966) which document cases of coexisting failure to thrive and trauma. These studies suggest a number of interrelated maltreatment patterns, including rejection, neglect, "accidental" injury, and abuse, that are included in our continuum of caretaking casualty.

In contrast to battering, where the evidence for assault is relatively objective, the events surrounding periods of protracted neglect are much more difficult to specify. As Bullard et al. (1968) indicated, many distortions in parent-child interaction that result in failures to thrive may be themselves the result of excessive and ill-timed handling (rather than the absence of care) and cannot properly be referred to as "neglect."

As with battered children, infants who fail to thrive have long-range pathological sequelae. In a follow-up study of forty-one children re-examined eight months to nine years after initial hospitalization, Bullard et al. (1968) found a high frequency of pathologic sequelae. More than half of their follow-up group evidenced continued growth failure, emotional disorder, mental retardation, or some combination of these.

Like the literature on battering, the majority of research reports and case studies on failure to thrive have sought to link growth failures to a variety of social and psychological characteristics of neglectful parents. Bullard et al. (1968) reported that neglectful parents often showed signs of serious personal instability as evidenced by severe marital strife, erratic living habits, alcoholism, and an inability to maintain employment or provide financial support for the care of their children. Growth failures have also been shown to be associated with parental poverty, lack of a stimulating environment, harsh and dominating child-rearing approaches, and malnutrition (Joint Commission on Mental Health of Children 1970).

The quality as well as the quantity of mothering is of obvious importance in determining the course of a child's development. Prugh and Harlow (1962) have coined the term "masked deprivation" to characterize the failure of children to thrive in environments where parents are physically present but psychologically unavailable to their children. Many examples of psychologically deprived children were found by Leonard, Rhymes, and Solnit (1966) to be children who had been unwanted and unexpected.

As in the case of the battered child, the neglected child also may make a contribution to his own neglect. The extent to which the physical health or temperamental characteristics of infants are implicated in their own failure to thrive is partially obscured by the fact that the failure-to-thrive syndrome is typically diagnosed only when past medical histories are free of evidence of obvious gestational, birth, and disease complications. It is still difficult, however, to distinguish cause and effect in subsequent behavioral disorders since the presumed behavioral consequences of inadequate caretaking and the disruptive behaviors of the child which might cause breakdowns in mothering are essentially indistinguishable. When cause and effect cannot be distinguished, arguments about etiology become circular and nonproductive (Leonard et al. 1966).

Despite the confusion between cause and effect, a number of studies have reported consistent features in many children who fail to thrive. Galdston (1971) reported that the neglected child is often described by parents as having fussy eating habits, poor food intake, and frequent regurgitations. Histories of chronic diarrhea, coeliac disease, and intestinal allergies are also described. These symptoms have been traditionally interpreted as the results of parental neglect. Only recently have a number of investigators considered the possibility that these characteristics may be part of the etiology rather than the sequelae of parenting failures (Gil 1970).

Children who fail to thrive are often reported to be irritable, difficult to manage, to have unusually irritating cries, and to be "unappealing" to the hospital staff. The children who were later neglected by their parents were almost invariably placed in a nursery bed as far away from the nursing station as could be arranged. Thus, Milowe and Lourie (1964) suggested that defects in the child often serve to precipitate neglectful behavior by his or her parents.

Both the children and the mothers in a study of "failure-to-thrive" could be classified into one of two general personality or temperamental types (Leonard et al. 1966). More than half of the infants studied were

active, vigorous, irritable, hypertonic, and difficult to comfort. The mothers of these children were seen as tense, high-strung, and aggressive. The
remainder of the children and their mothers both tended to be passive,
quiet, and placid. In addition, these mothers were depressed and often
failed to initiate many contacts with their undemanding children.

Bidirectionality of Child-Caretaker Effects

In all of the risk categories of this survey (including prenatal and perinatal pathology, parental characteristics, and other inter- or extrafamilial
environmental factors) it is possible to identify significant numbers of
children who, although subjected to these influences, nevertheless develop
normally (Chess 1971). Only some of the children subjected to these
presumed pathological influences do in fact develop disturbances, and
only small quantitative relationships have been demonstrated to exist between pathology in either the parents or the environment and pathology
in the child (Beiser 1964).

The failure of prospective studies to predict adequately the causes of
child neglect and abuse appears to have been the result of a research
strategy which has been almost exclusively concerned with differentially
characterizing the psychosocial environments of normal and deviant children. Detailed studies of the characteristics of the children subjected to
these presumptive hazards are practically nonexistent.

Retrospective attempts to recapture the defining characteristics of such
high-risk children have been infrequent, and, when they have been undertaken, are themselves so vulnerable to distortions and selective recall as
to be of questionable value (Yarrow, Campbell, Burton 1970).

Children labeled "at risk" have often been regarded as passive victims
of external forces and as a consequence are thought to be incapable of
having in any way provoked or participated in the difficulties in which they
have found themselves (Galdston 1971). As a consequence the victims
have often been purposefully excluded from study because their roles have
been presumed to be irrelevant. Because much of the research on child
neglect and abuse has been prompted by concerns with prevention and
remediation, attention has been focused on those aspects of the problem
which have been thought to be more easily changed. The parents and their
child-rearing practices, rather than the children themselves, have been
most frequently nominated for this role. Thus, the research literature on
postnatal risk factors has generally adopted what Chess (1971) has labeled the "mal de mère" (bad mother) approach to the study of developmental failures.

Bell (1968) has reinterpreted the literature on direction of effects in
the caretaking interaction. He pointed out that viewing the infants as help-

less victims does fit a one-sided model of parental determination of behavior. Many studies have, however, shown that the infant is more involved in determining the nature of the interpersonal relationship than
was once supposed. Many parent behaviors are not spontaneously emitted in the service of educating the child but rather are elicited by many
of the child's own characteristics and behaviors.

The infant's appearance of helplessness and dependence appears to be
a strong contributor to the parent's desire to provide care (Rheingold
1966). However, the response of all caretakers is not necessarily the
same. The helplessness of a child can arouse negative as well as positive
parental response. To the extent that the helplessness and dependence are
accompanied by aggravating factors (such as restlessness, colic, and digestive difficulties), the chance of eliciting negative caretaking responses
is increased (Bell 1968).

The frequent assumption that the newborn is too ineffectual to carry
any legitimate burden of responsibility for the quality of his or her relationship with various caretakers is contradicted by much current research.
Wolff (1971), for example, reported that congenital differences in muscle
tonus, motility, duration of alertness, vigor of sucking, frequency of smiling, and stability of the sleep-waking cycle all contribute as much to the
mother-infant relationship as does the mother's individuality. Prechtl and
Stemmer (1962) reported that hyper- and hypotonicity resulting from
complicated births also markedly influence the quality of the mother-child
relationship. These studies tend to dispel the illusion that infants are simply the hapless victims of relational disturbances imposed by their parents.

Constitutional variability in children strongly affects the parents' attitudes and caretaking styles. The systematic investigation of such idiosyn-
crasies in the child's behavioral organization is, however, of fairly recent
origin. The studies of Escalona and Heider (1959), Escalona (1968) and
Thomas et al. (1963), have described some parameters of individual
variation in both the temperament of the child and the quality of the
parent-child interaction. These reported individual differences are not
characteristics of the child that will remain unmodified throughout development, because they are subject to alteration as a function of environmental transactions. Escalona and Heider present an explicit statement of
this issue:

These and similar observations suggest the hypothesis that infantile
patterns or schemata of behavior are most likely to continue into later
childhood (in overtly identical or very similar forms) among children who
experience significant developmental irregularity and maladaptation. In
optimal circumstances, early forms of behavior tend to be dissolved during transition stages of development so that reintegration and the forma-

tion of new schemata can take place at each new level of maturity. When earlier schemata are not dissolved it will be more difficult for the child to move from one developmental level to the next, and this in and of itself may constitute a kind of maladaptation. If, in this fashion, patterns from early infancy were carried along from one stage to the next, this would account for the fact that maturational unevenness has been found to be characteristic of many emotionally disturbed children (1959, p. 243).

Thomas, Chess, and Birch (1968) discussed the changes that occur in the child's temperament as a function of the transactions with his family environment. These investigators have described a temperamental constellation which they have labeled "the difficult child." Difficult infants were found to have low thresholds for arousal, intense reactions when aroused, and irregularity in biological functioning. Although only 10 percent of their sample was categorized as difficult, 25 percent of the children who later had behavioral disturbances fell in this group. Without the benefit of longitudinal studies, one could easily misinterpret these difficulties of temperament as constitutional weaknesses that predisposed the child to later emotional difficulties. Such static predictions would not, however, prove to be very accurate. In fact, when Thomas et al. examined the relationship between behavior in the first and fifth year of life, significant correlations were found for only one of their nine temperamental categories, threshold to stimulation. What made the difference in outcome for these children appeared to be the behavior of their parents. If the parents were able to adjust to the child's difficult temperament, a good behavioral outcome was likely. If not, the difficulties were exacerbated and behavioral disturbance often resulted.

The transaction was not simply the unidirectional influence of the parents on the child, but also the reciprocal influence of the child on his parents. The impact of these difficult children was such as to disrupt the normal caretaking abilities of their parents. Thomas et al. (1968) reported that before the children of their study were born there were no marked differences in child-rearing attitudes expressed among the various parents in the sample. Whatever differences eventually characterized the parental attitudes of the deviant children apparently arose as a consequence of experience in the parent-child interaction.

Changes in a mother's view of her child as a factor in vulnerability were also demonstrated by Broussard and Hartner (1971). They administered a questionnaire to primiparous mothers two to three days after delivery and again a month later. The questionnaire assessed how the mother saw her child in relation to her view of the average infant. The infants were divided into a high- and low-risk sample on the basis of whether their mothers saw them as worse or better than the average child. When the children reached four years of age, they were given a clinical assessment and divided into categories according to the apparent need for therapeutic intervention. The infants identified as high-risk on the basis of the mothers' attitudes after one month, were significantly more likely to require clinical intervention at four years of age. The risk identification based on the mothers' attitudes at two to three days did *not* relate to later need for intervention, which suggests that later behavioral problems were not the result of mothers' prejudicial attitudes but rather their early experiences with their infants. Broussard and Hartner concluded that the process of a successful or unsuccessful mother-child relationship was already well established at one month of age and that mothers were instrumental in, as well as predictive of, their children's later mental health.

The range of findings cited in the preceding section tends to support the hypothesis that knowing only the temperament of the child or knowing only the child-rearing attitudes and practices of the parents would not allow one to predict the developmental outcome for the child. It would appear, rather, that it is the character of the *specific* transactions that occurred between a given child and his parents which determined the course of his subsequent development.

Summary

1. Two broad spectra of disorder have been identified by investigators of deviant development and are described here as the continuum of reproductive casualty and the continuum of caretaking casualty. The notion of such continua possessed important advantages over earlier models that tried to deal with each of these classes of disorder as a unique entity with a unique etiology.

2. There has not been an equal advance in our understanding of the causal mechanisms underlying these deviant outcomes. Following a "medical model" of disease, most investigators have attempted to trace a linear chain of efficient cause and effect assumed to underlie the connection between earlier trauma and later deviant outcome. These attempts have not met with a great deal of success.

3. Retrospectively, the range of later developmental difficulties does appear to be related to pregnancy and perinatal complications, but, prospectively, the majority of infants who experience such complications have not been found to have later difficulties.

4. While abused children do appear to have parents with particular personality constellations, other parents with apparently identical personalities do not abuse their children.

5. Although seemingly unrelated, reproductive complications and caretaking aberrations appear on closer inspection to be interdependent. The

characteristics of both parents and children must be considered to predict accurately the children's developmental outcome. When infants with reproductive complications were followed longitudinally, their developmental outcomes could be anticipated only if environmental factors such as family constellation or socioeconomic status were taken into account. Those children who were raised in affluent socioeconomic environments, with an intact family and a mother with a good education, showed few if any negative effects from their earlier complications. Children with identical complications, but raised in a socioeconomically depressed environment, with an unstable family situation and a mother with little education, were often found to be mentally retarded or to evidence a variety of personality problems.

6. Similarly, the deviancies in caretaking behavior which characterize the parents of abused children can only be understood if the nature of the child's contributions to this disordered relationship are also taken into consideration. The syndrome of personality disturbance which often characterizes abusive parents may appear to explain their assaultive and neglectful behavior but cannot account for the fact that such parents do not abuse and neglect all of the children in their family. The child chosen for abuse appears to be selected because of unique characteristics such as irritability and demandingness or because of the added attentional needs caused by illness, restlessness, or a difficult temperament.

Conclusions

Models of Development

Escalona (1968) has pointed out that although developmental research had been able to successfully define patterns of normalcy throughout the age span, it has been unable to explain the processes by which a child reached, maintained, or diverged from such patterns. Explanations as to why children experiencing what appears to be the same quality of care have different developmental outcomes, or how children can emerge from both the most supportive and the most brutalizing environments as equally able and competent, have not been forthcoming.

Escalona attributes our lack of knowledge of these developmental processes to the use of an inappropriate level of analysis. Methodologies derived from physics and chemistry are, according to Escalona, used to study biological phenomena which operate at a different order of complexity. Boulding (1956) has made a similar point and has argued further that it is not the methodologies of physics and chemistry which are deficient for understanding psychological phenomena but the level of analysis they apply to the phenomenon of concern. While it is true that biological organisms do function in accordance with the laws of the natural sciences, their more complex operation requires additional principles of organization, especially in regard to the developmental process.

Reese and Overton (1970) have elaborated the historical roots of two models that underlie most current theories of development, the mechanistic and the organismic, which use as metaphors the machine and the biological organism, respectively. While Reese and Overton offer these models as examples of different points of view which can be alternately applied to any developmental process, it will be argued here that these alternate explanatory models have grown out of and are best suited to explanations of phenomena at differing levels of complexity.

The lack of explanatory power found in analyses of psychological behavior can be understood as deriving from two sources. One source is our general lack of empirical knowledge that only more research could overcome (Escalona 1968). The second is our attempt to guide and interpret such research in terms of levels of analysis more appropriate to lower levels of organization (Boulding 1956). To ultimately understand how the organization of information found in biological processes influences behavior on a more psychological level will probably require that we come to appreciate additional principles of functioning which are only now being approached by such theorists as Piaget (1971).

For many, a discussion of the choice of developmental models may seem superfluous in the study of the concrete factors leading to behavioral disorder. It is possible, however, that a change in such a level of analysis will reveal important relationships in existing data on the etiology of disorder which were not previously evident, in addition to pointing out fruitful directions for seeking new data. To illustrate the significance of such issues in interpreting data, three different models will be applied to the data previously summarized regarding the relative roles of constitution and environment in developmental outcomes.

1. *Main-effect model.* The central premise of what is referred to here as the main-effect model is that constitution and environment exert influences on development which are independent of each other. A defect in the constitution of an individual will, according to this model, produce a defective adult irrespective of environmental circumstance, and a pathogenic environment will produce a defective adult independent of his constitution. Such a model is attractive to many investigators because of its parsimony and has been given strong currency in etiological research. Constitutional defects caused by pregnancy and delivery complications have often been assumed to exert such unilateral influences on development. We have seen how retrospective investigations showed that individuals suffering a wide range of disorders, from cerebral palsy to mental

retardation and schizophrenia, were more likely to have experienced complicated births than individuals without the disorders. The general findings of prospective studies have not, however, supported the inference drawn from these retrospective studies that such birth complications provide direct, causal explanations for later disorder. Although some of the effects of early trauma can still be detected at three years of age, by seven these effects have become almost completely attenuated. The typical 3- to 5-point IQ difference found at school age between children who had suffered reproductive complications and those who had not is small, indeed, when compared with the 15-point difference typically found between blacks and whites and the 50-point difference found between adults at the top and bottom of the socioeconomic scale.

The conclusion to which one is led by these studies is that while many persons with later developmental difficulties can be shown, retrospectively, to have had pregnancy and perinatal complications, the majority of infants experiencing such complications are not found to have later difficulties when studied prospectively. Interactions have, however, been noted between obstetrical complications and the child's environment. For infants raised in a middle-class home, with a stable family structure and with educated parents, there was, for example, no relationship between obstetric complications and later intelligence or personality. When children with similar complications were raised in a lower SES home, or in an unstable family situation, or with uneducated parents, they were more likely to suffer mental retardation and behavioral problems. In other words, unless the environmental context is also specified, few predictions can be made about developmental outcome based on perinatal difficulties. A similar conclusion can be drawn for the vast literature concerning the effects of pregnancy and delivery complications based on early intellectual functioning or the child's temperamental characteristics. It would appear then that the influence of constitutional characteristics of the child on his development do not seem to fit a main-effect model.

Similar conclusions about the inadequacy of predictions based exclusively on environmental effects also seem warranted. The general finding of studies of aberrant caretaking (Spinetta and Rigler 1972) has been that parents who neglect or abuse their children have different personalities from those who do not. The ability to identify personality characteristics of abusing parents after-the-fact might lead one to presume that predictions can be made before-the-fact that parents having such characteristics would abuse their children. Unfortunately, however, those attributes found to characterize such parents are sufficiently broad and commonplace that they are of little value in attempting to predict which parents actually will abuse their children. Also, as we have noted earlier, abusing parents are themselves selective in the choice of the child they abuse, and the same static personality variables cannot account for the abuse of some but not all of their offspring. A missing element in the predictive equation for child abuse would seem to be characteristics specific to the child. As was the case with obstetrical complications taken alone, parental characteristics taken alone are not effective predictors of developmental outcome.

Clearly, there are extremes of constitutional disorders, such as severe brain damage, the developmental consequences of which would be deviant in any environment. Similarly, there are obvious extremes of environmental disorder which may well produce deviance in a child of any constitution. These extreme examples are not, however, representative of the vast majority of children who evidence poor developmental outcomes. A main-effects model seems to apply neither to constitutional nor environmental components in development.

2. *Interactional model.* The preceding discussion would suggest that, at a minimum, any prognostic equation for predicting long-range developmental outcomes must include information concerning both the child's constitutional makeup and his caretaking environment. Horowitz (1969) has presented an articulate description of such an interactional model. From this point of view one should be able to create a two-dimensional array of constitutions and environments, with an entry describing the child's developmental outcome for any combination of these two factors. Children with constitutional problems raised in a deviant environment would have poor outcomes. Children with constitutional problems raised in supportive environments and children without problems raised in deviant environments would have better outcomes. The best outcomes of all would be expected for children without constitutional problems raised in a supportive environment.

While this interactive model substantially increases the general efficiency of predictions regarding risk factors leading to poor developmental outcome, it may, nevertheless, be insufficient to facilitate our understanding of the etiological mechanism leading to later disorder. The major reason behind the inadequacy of this model would appear to be that neither constitution nor environment is necessarily constant over time. At each moment, month, or year the characteristics of both the child and his environment change in important ways. Moreover, these differences are interdependent and change as a function of their mutual influence on one another. The child alters his environment and in turn is altered by the changed world he has created. In order to incorporate these progressive interactions, one must move from a static interactional model to a more dynamic theory of developmental *transaction* where there is a continual and progressive interplay between the organism and its environment.

3. *Transactional model.* Any truly transactional model must stress the plastic character of the environment and of the organism as an active participant in its own growth. From this position the child's response is thought to be more than a simple reaction to his environment. Instead, he is thought to be actively engaged in attempts to organize and structure his world. The child is, in this view, in a perpetual state of active reorganization and cannot properly be regarded as maintaining an inborn deficit as a static characteristic. In this view, the *constants* in development are not some set of traits but rather the processes by which these traits are maintained in the transactions between organism and environment.

Breakdown from this organismic or transactional point of view is not seen simply as the function of an inborn inability to respond appropriately but rather as a function of some *continuous* malfunction in the organism-environment transaction across time which prevents the child from organizing his world adaptively. Within this view, forces preventing the child's normal integration with his environment act not just at one traumatic point but must operate throughout his development.

A second shortcoming of a static interactional model is that there is not only change but directionality in development. In light of the great variety and range of influences on development, there are a surprisingly small number of developmental outcomes. The human organism appears to have been programmed by the course of evolution to produce normal developmental outcomes under all but the most adverse of circumstances (Waddington 1966). Any understanding of deviancies in outcome must be seen in the light of this self-righting and self-organizing tendency which appears to move children toward normality in the face of pressure toward deviation. (For further discussion of this see chapter 1 in this volume.)

Deviant Development

Given the "self-righting" tendencies of the organism, two possibilities are available to produce deviant development. The first possibility is an insult to the organism's integrative mechanisms which prevents the functioning of its self-righting ability, while the second possibility is that environmental forces present throughout development prevent the normal integrations that would occur in a more modal environment. The former possibility can be seen in the pregnancy and delivery complications related to the "continuum of reproductive casualty" (Pasamanick and Knobloch 1966). The latter possibility can be seen in the familial and social abnormalities related to our "continuum of caretaking casualty."

Rather than being considered separately, these two sources of risk appear to be closely interrelated in the production of positive or negative developmental outcomes. Where the child's vulnerability is heightened through massive or recurrent trauma, only an extremely supportive environment can help to restore the normal integrative growth process. A seriously brain-damaged child requiring institutional care would be an instance of such an extreme case of reproductive casualty. On the other extreme, a highly disordered caretaking setting might convert the most sturdy and integrated of children into a caretaking casualty.

Summary

An attempt has been made to review the research on the identification of variables that increase the "risk" that a child will have a poor developmental outcome.

1. From this review we can conclude most research in the area, whether retrospective or prospective in character, has been based on a mechanistic level of analysis which has focused on discovering missing links in a chain of efficient causality leading from early traumas to later abnormality.

2. Retrospective studies have often given the impression of having established clear relationships between pregnancy and delivery complications and later deviance. Prospective studies of the same variables have, however, not succeeded in demonstrating the predictive efficiency of these supposed risk factors. Most infants who suffer perinatal problems have proven to have normal developmental outcomes.

3. By contrast, the literature on perinatal complications has shown a strong connection between the course of the pregnancy and the emotional state of the mother. Psychosomatic factors do appear to increase sharply the risk of complications and of physical anomalies in the fetus. An unanswered question, however, is whether these pregnancy and delivery complications are a part of a causal chain leading to later disorder or whether both are parallel disorders resulting from the poor psychological state of the mother.

4. The large role given to socioeconomic and familial factors in producing emotional difficulties and intellectual retardation tends to overshadow the effects of early perinatal difficulties. The environment appears to have the potential of minimizing or maximizing such early developmental difficulties. High socioeconomic status dissipates the effects of such perinatal complications as anoxia or low birth-weight. Poor social environmental conditions tend to amplify the effects of such early complications. Since the caretaking environment plays such a major role in determining developmental outcomes, a "continuum of caretaking casualty" was hypothesized to describe the range of deviant outcomes which would be attributed to poor parenting.

5. Abused children clearly suffer from an extreme of deviant caretaking behavior. However, the temperament of the child appears to contrib-

ute in important ways to the abusing tendencies of his parents. Children with difficult temperaments or physical disorders may increase their own chances of being abused, whereas siblings of a less bothersome nature are likely to receive only minimal abuse.

6. A transactional model was felt to be necessary to understand the range of developmental outcomes described in the literature. The child and his caretaking environment tend to mutually alter each other. To the extent that the child elicited or was provided with nurturance from the environment, positive outcomes were a consequence. To the extent that the child elicited negative responses from the environment, he was found to be at a "high risk" for later difficulties.

REFERENCES

Apgar, V., Girdany, B. R., McIntosh, R., & Taylor, H. C., Jr. Neonatal anoxia. I. A study of the relation of oxygenation at birth to intellectual development. *Pediatrics*, 1955, *15*, 653–662.

Babson, S. G. & Benson, R. C. *Management of High-risk Pregnancy and Intensive Care of the Neonate*. St. Louis: Mosby, 1971.

Bailey, C. J. Interrelationship of asphyxia neonatorum, cerebral palsy and mental retardation: present status of the problem. In W. F. Windle, ed., *Neurological and Psychological Deficits of Asphyxia Neonatorum*. Springfield, Ill.: Thomas, 1968.

Beiser, H. R. Discrepancies in the symptomology of parents and children. *Journal of American Academy of Child Psychiatry*, 1964, *3*, 457–468.

Bell, R. Q. A reinterpretation of the direction of effects in studies of socialization. *Psychological Review*, 1968, *75*, 81–95.

Bell, R. Q., Weller, G. M., & Waldrop, M. F. Newborn and preschooler: Organization of behavior and relations between periods. *Monographs of the Society for Research in Child Development*, 1971, *36*, 2 (whole no. 142).

Benaron, H., Brown, M., Tucker, B. E., Wentz, V., & Yacorzynski, G. K. The remote effect of prolonged labor with forceps delivery, precipitate labor with spontaneous delivery, and natural labor with spontaneous delivery on the child. *American Journal of Obstetrics and Gynecology*, 1953, *66*, 551–568.

Benaron, H., Tucker, B. E., Andrews, J. P., Boshes, B., Cohen, Fromm, F., & Yacorzynski, G. K. Effects of anoxia during labor and immediately after birth on the subsequent development of the child. *American Journal of Obstetrics and Gynecology*, 1960, *80*, 1129–1142.

Birch, H. & Gussow, G. D. *Disadvantaged Children*. New York: Grune & Stratton, 1970.

Blau, A., Slaff, B., Easton, D., Welkowitz, J., & Cohen, J. The psychogenic etiology of premature births: a preliminary report. *Psychosomatic Medicine*, 1963, *25*, 201–211.

Bolin, B. J. An investigation of the relationship between birth duration and childhood anxiety. *Journal of Mental Science*, 1959, *105*, 1045–1052.

Boulding, K. General systems theory—the skeleton of science. *Management Science*, 1956, *2*, 197–208.

Broussard, E. R. & Hartner, M. S. S. Further consideration regarding maternal perception of the first born. In J. Hellmuth, ed., *Exceptional Infant: Studies in Abnormalities*. Vol. 2. New York: Brunner/Mazel, 1971.

Bullard, D., Glaser, H., Heagarty, M., & Pivchik, E. Failure to thrive in the "ne-glected" child. In S. Chess & A. Thomas, eds., *Annual Progress in Child Psychiatry and Child Development,* New York: Brunner/Mazel, 1968.

Campbell, W., Cheseman, E., & Kilpatrick, A. The effect of neonatal asphyxia on physical and mental development. *Archives of Diseases in Childhood,* 1950, *25,* 351–359.

Chess, S. Genesis of behavior disorder. In J. G. Howells, ed., *Modern Perspectives in International Child Psychiatry,* New York: Brunner/Mazel, 1971.

Corah, N. L., Anthony, E. J., Painter, P., Stern, J. A., & Thurston, D. L. Effects of perinatal anoxia after seven years. *Psychological Monographs,* 1965, *79,* 3 (whole no. 596).

Dann, M., Levine, S. Z., & New, E. V. A long term follow-up study of small pre-mature infants. *Pediatrics,* 1964, *33,* 945–955.

Darke, R. A. Late effect of severe asphyxia neonatorum. *Journal of Pediatrics,* 1944, *24,* 148–158.

Davids, A. & DeVault, S. Maternal anxiety during pregnacy and childbirth ab-normalities. *Psychosomatic Medicine,* 1962, *24,* 464–470.

DeFrancis, V. Protecting the abused child—a coordinated approach. In *A National Symposium on Child Abuse.* Denver: American Humane Society, Children's Division, 1972.

Delsordo, J. D. Protective case work for abused children. *Children,* 1963, *10,* 213–218.

Douglas, J. W. B. "Premature" children at primary schools. *British Medical Journal,* 1960, *1,* 1008–1013.

Drage, J. S. & Berendes, H. W. Apgar scores and outcome of the newborn. *Pediatric Clinics of North America,* 1966, *13,* 635–643.

Drage, J. S., Berendes, H. W., & Fisher, P. D. The Apgar score and four-year psychological examination performance. In *Perinatal Factors Affecting Human Development.* Pan American Health Organization WHO. Scientific Publication no. 185 (1969), 222–226.

Drillien, C. M. *The Growth and Development of the Prematurely Born Infant.* Baltimore: Williams & Wilkins, 1964.

———. Prematures in school. *Pediatrics Digest,* September, 1965, 75–77.

Drillien, C. M., Ingram, T. T. S., & Wilkinson, E. M. *The Causes and Natural History of Cleft Lip and Palate.* Edinburgh: Livingstone, 1966.

Drillien, C. M. & Wilkinson, E. M. Emotional stress and mongoloid birth. *Developmental Medicine and Child Neurology,* 1964, *6,* 140–143.

Elmer, E. *Children in Jeopardy: A Study of Abused Minors and Their Families.* Pittsburgh: University of Pittsburgh, 1967.

Elmer, E., & Gregg, C. D. Developmental characteristics of the abused child. *Pediatrics,* 1967, *40,* 596–602.

Escalona, S. K. *The Roots of Individuality.* Chicago: Aldine, 1968.

Escalona, S. K. & Heider, G. M. *Prediction and Outcome: A Study in Child Development.* New York: Basic Books, 1959.

Ferreira, A. J. Emotional factors in prenatal environment: a review. *Journal of Nervous and Mental Disease,* 1965, *141,* 108–118.

———. *Prenatal Environment.* Springfield, Ill.: Thomas, 1969.

Fontana, V. J. Further reflections on maltreatment of children. *New York State Journal of Medicine,* 1968, *68,* 2214–2215.

Fraser, M. S. & Wilks, J. The residual effects of neonatal asphyxia. *Journal of Obstetrics and Gynecology of the British Commonwealth,* 1959, *66,* 748–752.

Galdston, R. Dysfunction of parenting: the battered child, the neglected child, the emotional child. In J. G. Howells, ed., *Modern Perspectives in International Child Psychiatry.* New York: Brunner/Mazel, 1971.

———. Observation on children who have been physically abused and their parents. *American Journal of Psychiatry,* 1965, *122,* 440–443.

Garmezy, N. Vulnerability research and the issue of primary prevention. *American Journal of Orthopsychiatry,* 1971, *41,* 101–116.

————. Research strategies for the study of children who are at risk for schizophrenia. In M. Katz, R. Littlestone, L. Mosher, M. Roath, & A. Hussaini, eds., *Schizophrenia: Implications of Research Findings for Treatment and Teaching.* In press.

Gesell, A. & Amatruda, C. *Developmental Diagnosis.* New York: Hoeber, 1941.

Gil, D. *Violence Against Children.* Cambridge, Mass.: Harvard University, 1970.

Goldfarb, W. Factors in the development of schizophrenic children: an approach to subclassification. In J. Romano, ed., *The Origins of Schizophrenia.* Amsterdam: Excerpta Medica Foundation, 1967.

Graham, F. K., Caldwell, B. M., Ernhart, C. B., Pennoyer, M. M. & Hartman, A. F. Anoxia as a significant perinatal experience: a critique. *Journal of Pediatrics,* 1957, *50,* 556–569.

Graham, F. K., Ernhart, C. B., Thurston, D. L. & Craft, M. Development three years after perinatal anoxia and other potentially damaging newborn experiences. *Psychological Monographs,* 1962, *76,* 3 (whole no. 522).

Graham, F. K., Matarazzo, R. G., & Caldwell, B. M. Behavioral differences between normal and traumatized newborns: II. Standardization, reliability, and validity. *Psychological Monographs,* 1956, *70,* 21 (whole no. 428).

Graham, F. K., Pennoyer, M. M., Caldwell, B. M., Greenman, M., & Hartman, A. F. Relationship between clinical status and behavior test performance in a newborn group with histories suggesting anoxia. *Journal of Pediatrics,* 1957, *50,* 177–189.

Gregg, N. M. Congenital cataract following German measles in the mother. *Transactions of the Opthalmological Society of Australia,* 1942, *3,* 35–46.

Gregg, G. S., & Elmer, E. Infant injuries: accident or abuse? *Pediatrics,* 1969, *44,* 434–439.

Grimm, E. R. Psychological investigation of habitual abortion. *Psychosomatic Medicine,* 1962, *24,* 369–378.

Gunter, L. Psychopathology and stress in the life experience of mothers of premature infants. *American Journal of Obstetrics & Gynecology,* 1963, *86,* 333–340.

Harper, P. A. & Wiener, G. Sequelae of low birth weight. *Annual Review of Medicine,* 1965, *16,* 405–420.

Helfer, R. E. & Kempe, C. H., eds. *The Battered Child.* Chicago: University of Chicago Press, 1968.

Hess, J., Mohr, G., & Bartelme, P. F. *The Physical and Mental Growth of Prematurely Born Children.* Chicago: University of Chicago Press, 1939.

Himwich, H. E. *Brain Metabolism and Cerebral Disorders.* Baltimore: Williams & Wilkins, 1951.

Holter, J. C. & Friedman, S. Child Abuse: early case findings in the emergency department. *Pediatrics,* 1968, *42,* 128–138.

Horowitz, F. D. Learning, developmental research, and individual differences. In L. P. Lipsitt & H. W. Reese, eds., *Advances in Child Development and Behavior.* Vol. 4. New York: Academic Press, 1969.

Illsley, R. Early prediction of perinatal risk. *Proceedings of the Royal Society of Medicine,* 1966, *59,* 181–184.

Ireton, H., Thwing, E., & Gravem, H. Infant mental development and neurological status, family socio-economic status, and intelligence at age 4. *Child Development,* 1970, *41,* 937–945.

Javert, C. T. Further follow-up on habitual abortion patients. *American Journal of Obstetrics and Gynecology,* 1962, *84,* 1149–1159.

Joffe, J. M. *Prenatal Determinants of Behavior.* Oxford: Pergamon, 1969.

Joint Commission on Mental Health of Children. *Crisis of Child Mental Health: Challenge for the 1970's.* New York: Harper & Row, 1970.

Joppich, G. & Schulte, F. J. *Neurologie des Neugeborenen.* Berlin: Springer-Verlag, 1968.

Kagan, J. Cross-Cultural perspectives on early development. Paper presented at meeting of the American Association for the Advancement of Science, Washington, December 1972.

Keith, H. M. & Gage, R. P. Neurologic lesions in relation to asphyxia of the newborn and factors of pregnancy: long-term follow-up. *Pediatrics,* 1960, *26,* 616–622.

Keith, H. M., Norval, M. A., & Hunt, A. B. Neurologic lesions in relation to the sequelae of birth injury. *Neurology,* 1953, *3,* 139–147.

Kempe, C. H. & Helfer, R. E. In *Crisis in Child Mental Health: Challenge for the 1970's.* New York: Harper & Row, 1970.

Kempe, C. H., Silerman, F. N., Steele, B. F., Droegemueller, W., & Silver, H. K. The battered-child syndrome. *Journal of the American Medical Association,* 1962, *181,* 17–24.

Klaus, M. H. & Kennell, J. H. Mothers separated from their newborn infants. *Pediatric Clinics of North America,* 1970, *17,* 1015–1037.

Klebanov, D. Hunger and psychische Erregungen als Ovar und Keimschadigungen. *Geburtshiffe und Frauenheilkunde,* 1948, *8,* 812–820.

Klein, M. & Stern, L. Low birthweight and the battered child syndrome. *American Journal of Diseases of Children,* 1971, *122,* 15–18.

Knobloch, H., Rider, R., Harper, P. & Pasamanick, B. Neuropsychiatric sequelae of prematurity: a longitudinal study. *Journal of the American Medical Association,* 1956, *161,* 581–585.

Koel, B. S. Failure to thrive and fetal injury as a continuum. *American Journal of Diseases of Children,* 1969, *118,* 565–567.

Leonard, M. F., Rhymes, J. P., & Solnit, A. J. Failure to thrive in infants. *American Journal of Diseases of Children,* 1966, *111*(6), 600–612.

Lewis, M. & McGurk, H. Evaluation of infant intelligence. *Science,* 1972, *170,* 1174–1177.

Lilienfeld, A. M. & Parkhurst, E. A study of the association of factors of pregnancy and parturition with the development of cerebral palsy: a preliminary report. *American Journal of Hygiene,* 1951, *53,* 262–282.

Little, W. J. On the influence of abnormal parturition, difficult labor, premature birth, and asphyxia neonatorum on the mental and physical condition of the child especially in relation to deformities. *Lancet,* 1961, *2,* 378–380.

MacKinney, L. G. Asphyxia neonatorum in relation to mental retardation: current studies in man. In W. F. Windle, ed., *Neurological and Psychological Deficits of Asphyxia Neonatorum.* Springfield, Ill.: Thomas, 1958.

Manson, M. M., Logan, W. P. D., & Loy, R. M. *Rubella and Other Viral Infections During Pregnancy.* London: Her Majesty's Society of Obstetrics, 1960.

McCall, R. B., Hogarty, P. S., & Hurlbut, N. Transitions in infant sensorimotor development and the prediction of childhood IQ. *American Psychologist,* 1972, *27,* 728–748.

McClearn, G. E. Genetics and behavior development. In M. L. Hoffman and L. W. Hoffman, eds., *Review of Child Development Research.* Vol. 1. New York: Russell Sage Foundation, 1964.

McDonald, A. D. Intelligence in children of very low birth weight. *British Journal of Preventive and Social Medicine,* 1964, *18,* 59–74.

McDonald, R. L. The role of emotional factors in obstetric complications: a review. *Psychosomatic Medicine,* 1968, *30,* 222–237.

McDonald, R. L. & Christakos, A. C. Relationship of emotional factors during pregnancy to obstetric complications. *American Journal of Obstetrics and Gynecology,* 1963, *86,* 341–348.

McDonald, R. L., Gynther, M. D., & Christakos, A. C. Relations between maternal anxiety and obstetric complications. *Psychosomatic Medicine,* 1963, *25,* 357–363.

McDonald, R. L. & Parham, K. J. Relation of emotional changes during pregnancy to obstetric complications in unmarried primigravidae. *American Journal of Obstetrics and Gynecology,* 1964, *90,* 195–201.

McGrade, B. J. Newborn activity and emotional response at eight months. *Child Development,* 1968, *39,* 1247–1252.

McPhail, F. L. & Hall, E. L. Consideration of cause and possible late effect of anoxia in newborn infants. *American Journal of Obstetrics and Gynecology.* 1941, *42,* 686–701.

Mednick, S. A. Breakdown in individuals at high risk for schizophrenia. Possible predispositional perinatal factors. *Mental Hygience,* 1970, *54,* 50–63.

Mednick, S. A., Mura, E., Schulsinger, F., & Mednick, B. Perinatal conditions and infant development in children with schizophrenic parents. *Social Biology,* 1971, *18,* Supplement, 103–113.

Mednick, S. A. & Schulsinger, F. Some premorbid characteristics related to breakdown in children with schizophrenic mothers. In D. Rosenthal & S. S. Kety, eds., *The Transmission of Schizophrenia.* Oxford: Pergamon, 1968.

Merrill, E. J. *Protecting the Battered Child.* Denver, Colorado: American Humane Association, 1962.

Milowe, F. D., & Lourie, R. S. The child's role in the battered child syndrome. *Journal of Pediatrics,* 1964, *65,* 1079–1081.

Morse, C., Sahler, O. & Friedman, S. A three-year follow-up study of abused and neglected children. *American Journal of Diseases of Children,* 1970, *120,* 439–446.

Niswander, K. R., Friedman, E. A., Hoover, D. B., Pietrowski, R., & Westphal, M. Fetal morbidity following potentially anoxigenic obstetric conditions. I. Abrupto placentae. II. Placenta previa. III. Prolapse of the umbilical cord. *American Journal of Obstetrics and Gynecology,* 1966, *95,* 838–846.

Niswander, K. R. & Gordon, M., eds. *The Collaborative Perinatal Study of the National Institute of Neurological Diseases and Stroke: The Women and Their Pregnancies.* Philadelphia: W. B. Saunders, 1972.

Oliver, J. E. & Taylor, A. Five generations of ill-treated children in one family pedigree. *British Journal of Psychology,* 1971, vol. 1, 19 [issue 552], pp. 473–480.

Parmelee, A. H. & Haber, A. Who is the "risk infant"? In H. J. Osofsky, ed., *Clinical Obstetrics and Gynecology.* In press.

Parmelee, A. H. & Michaelis, R. Neurological examination of the newborn. In J. Hellmuth, ed., *Exceptional Infants: Studies in Abnormalities.* Vol. 2. New York: Brunner/Mazel, 1971.

Pasamanick, B. & Knobloch, H. Epidemiologic studies on the complications of pregnancy and the birth process. In G. Caplan, ed., *Prevention of Mental Disorders in Children.* New York: Basic Books, 1961.

———. Retrospective studies on the epidemiology of reproductive causality: old and new. *Merrill-Palmer Quarterly,* 1966, *12,* 7–26.

Pasamanick, B., Knobloch, H., & Lilienfeld, A. M. Socio-economic status and some precursors of neuropsychiatric disorders. *American Journal of Orthopsychiatry,* 1956, *26,* 594–601.

Pasamanick, B. & Lilienfeld, A. M. Association of maternal and fetal factors with development of mental deficiency. I. Abnormalities in the prenatal and paranatal periods. *Journal of the American Medical Association,* 1955, *159,* 155–160.

Piaget, J. *Psychology of Intelligence.* New York: Harcourt, Brace & World, 1950.

———. *Biology and Knowledge.* Chicago: University of Chicago, 1971.

Pleydell, M. J. Anencephaly and other congenital malformations. *British Medical Journal,* 1960, *1,* 309–314.

Pollack, M. & Woerner, M. Pre- and perinatal complications and "Childhood Schizophrenia": a comparison of five controlled studies. *Journal of Child Psychology and Psychiatry,* 1966, *7,* 235–242.

Pollin, W. & Stabenau, J. R. Biological, psychological, and historical differences in

a series of monozygotic twins discordant for schizophrenia. In D. Rosenthal &
S. S. Kety, eds., *The Transmission of Schizophrenia*. Oxford: Pergamon Press,
1968, 317–332.

Prechtl, H. F. R. Prognostic value of neurological signs in the newborn infant.
Proceedings of the Royal Society of Medicine, 1965, *58*, 1.

Prechtl, H. F. R. & Beintema, D. J. The neurological examination of the full term
newborn infant. *Little Club Clinics in Developmental Medicine*. No. 12. London:
National Spastics Society, 1964.

Prechtl, H. F. R. & Stemmer, C. J. The choreiform syndrome in children. *Developmental Medicine and Child Neurology*, 1962, *4*, 119–127.

Preston, M. I. Late behavioral aspects found in cases of prenatal, natal, and postnatal anoxia. *Journal of Pediatrics*, 1945, *26*, 353–366.

Prugh, D. & Harlow, R. "Masked deprivation" in infants and young children. In
Deprivation of Medical Care: A Reassessment of its Effects. Public Health
Papers, no. 14. Geneva: World Health Organization, 1962.

Reese, H. W. & Overton, W. F. Models of development and theories of development.
In L. R. Goulet & P. B. Baltes, eds., *Life Span Developmental Psychology:
Research and Theory*. New York: Academic Press, 1970.

Rheingold, H. L. The development of social behavior in the human infant. In H.
W. Stevenson, ed., Concept of development. *Monographs of the Society for
Research in Child Development*, 1966, 31, 5 (whole no. 107).

Riegel, K. Influence of economic and political ideologies on the development of
developmental psychology. *Psychological Bulletin*, 1972, *78*, no. 2, 129–141.

Robins, L. N., Bates, W. M., & O'Neal, P. Adult drinking patterns of former
problem children. In D. Pittman & C. Snider, eds., *Society, Culture, and Drinking Patterns*. New York: John Wiley, 1962.

Rosenthal, D. *Genetic Theory and Abnormal Behavior*. New York: McGraw-Hill,
1970.

Sameroff, A. J. & Zax, M. Perinatal characteristics of the offspring of schizophrenic
women. *Journal of Nervous and Mental Diseases*, 1973, in press.

Schachter, F. F. & Apgar, V. Perinatal asphyxis and psychologic signs of brain damage in childhood. *Pediatrics*, 1959, *24*, 1016–1025.

Schreiber, F. Mental deficiency from paranatal asphyxia. *Proceedings of the American Association of Mental Deficiency*, 1939, *63*, 95–106.

Schulte, F. J., Michaelis, R., & Filipp, E. Neurologie des Neugeborenen: I. Mitteilung
Uraschen und Klinische Symptomatologie von Funktionsstorungen des Neurensystems bei Neugeborenen. *Zeitschrift für Kinderheilkunde*, 1965, *93*, 242–263.

Scott, E. M. & Thomson, A. M. A psychological investigation of primigravidae: IV.
Psychological factors and the clinical phenomenon of labor. *Journal of Obstetrics and Gynecology of the British Empire*, 1956, *63*, 502–508.

Shapiro, S., Schlesinger, E., & Nesbitt, R. E. C. *Infant Perinatal, Maternal, and
Childhood Mortality in the United States*. Cambridge, Mass.: Harvard University, 1968.

Sheridan, M. D. Final report of a prospective study of children whose mothers had
rubella in early pregnancy. *British Medical Journal*, 1964, *2*, 536–539.

Simons, B., Downs, E. F., Hurster, M. M., & Archer, M. Child Abuse: epidemiologic
study of medically reported cases. *New York State Journal of Medicine*, 1966,
66, 2783–2788.

Smith, A. C., Flick, G. L., Ferriss, G. S., & Sellmann, A. H. Prediction of developmental outcome at seven years from prenatal, perinatal and postnatal events.
Child Development, 1972, *43*, 495–507.

Spinetta, J. J. & Rigler, D. The child-abusing parent: a psychological review.
Psychological Bulletin, 1972, *77*, 296–304.

Stechler, G. A longitudinal follow-up of neonatal apnea. *Child Development*, 1964,
35, 333–348.

Steele, B. F. & Pollack, C. B. A psychiatric study of parents who abuse infants and small children. In R. E. Helfer & C. H. Kempe, eds., *The Battered Child.* Chicago: University of Chicago Press, 1968.

Stevenson, S. S. Parental factors affecting adjustment in childhood. *Pediatrics,* 1948, *2,* 154–162.

Stott, D. H. The child's hazards in utero. In J. G. Howells, ed., *Modern Perspectives in International Child Psychiatry.* New York: Brunner/Mazel, 1971.

Taft, L. & Goldfarb, W. Prenatal and perinatal factors in childhood schizophrenia. *Developmental Medicine and Child Neurology,* 1964, *6,* 32–43.

Thomas, A., Chess, S., & Birch, H. *Temperament and Behavior Disorders in Children.* New York: New York University, 1968.

Thomas, A., Chess, S., Birch, H. G., Hertzig, M., & Korn, S. *Behavioral Individuality in Early Childhood.* London: University of London, 1963.

Ucko, L. E. A comparative study of asphyxiated and non-asphyxiated boys from birth to five years. *Developmental Medicine and Child Neurology,* 1965, *7,* 643–657.

Usdin, G. L. & Weil, M. L. Effect of apnea neonatorum on intellectual development. *Pediatrics,* 1952, *9,* 387–394.

Waddington, C .H. *Principles of Development and Differentiation.* New York: Macmillan, 1966.

Waldrop, M. F. & Halverson, C. F. Minor physical anomalies and hyperactive behavior in young children. In J. Hellmuth, ed., *Exceptional Infant: Studies in Abnormalities.* Vol. 2. New York: Brunner/Mazel, 1971.

Werner, E. E., Bierman, J. M., & French, F. E. *The Children of Kauai.* Honolulu: University of Hawaii Press, 1971.

Werner, E. E., Honzik, M., & Smith, R. Prediction of intelligence and achievement at ten years from twenty months pediatric and psychologic examinations. *Child Development,* 1968, *39,* 1036–1075.

Werner, E. E., Simonian, K., Bierman, J. M., French, F. E. Cumulative effect of perinatal complications and deprived environment on physical, intellectual, and social development of preschool children. *Pediatrics,* 1967, *39,* 480–505.

Wiener, C. Psychologic correlates of premature birth: a review. *Journal of Nervous and Mental Diseases,* 1962, *134,* 129–144.

Wiener, G., Rider, R. V., Oppel, W. C., Fischer, L. K., & Harper, P. A. Correlates of low birth weight: psychological status at 6–7 years of age. *Pediatrics,* 1965, *35,* 434–444.

Wiener, G., Rider, R. V., Oppel, W. C., & Harper, P. A. Correlates of low birth weight: psychological status at eight to ten years of age. *Pediatric Research,* 1968, *2,* 110–118.

Willerman, L., Broman, S. H., & Fiedler, M. Infant development, preschool IQ, and social class. *Child Development,* 1970, *41,* 69–77.

Windle, W. F. Structural and functional changes in the brain following neonatal asphyxia. *Psychosomatic Medicine,* 1944, *6,* 155–156.

White, S. H. Evidence for a hierarchical arrangement of learning processes. In L. P. Lipsitt & C. C. Spiker, eds., *Advances in Child Development and Behavior.* Vol. 2. New York: Academic Press, 1965.

Wolff, P. H. Mother-infant relations at birth. In J. C. Howells, ed., *Modern Perspectives in International Psychiatry.* New York: Brunner/Mazel, 1971.

Yerushalmy, J. The relationship of parents' smoking to outcome of pregnancy implications as to the problem of inferring causation from observed effects. *American Journal of Epidemiology,* 1971, *93,* 443–456.

———. Infants with low birth weight born before their mothers started to smoke cigarettes. *American Journal of Obstetrics and Gynecology,* 1972, *112,* 277–284.

Yarrow, M. R., Campbell, J. D., & Burton, R. V. Recollection of childhood: a study of the retrospective method. *Monographs of the Society for Research in Child Development,* 1970, *35,* 5 (whole no. 138).

Young, L. *Wednesday's Children*: *A Study of Child Neglect and Abuse*. New York: McGraw-Hill, 1964.

Zalba, S. R. The abused child: I. A survey of the problem. *Social Work*, 1966, *11*, 3–16.

5 Language Development Review

LOIS BLOOM
Teachers College, Columbia University

THE DATA for studying language development are abundant; virtually all small children are learning to talk. Moreover, it is possible to see in the study of language development a host of relevant issues and ideas that bear on the nature of language in general and, indeed, on the nature of mind and mental development. However, different investigators have observed and described the data differently and have asked different questions of the data. In reviewing recent research it will first be helpful to place the last decade within the larger perspective of the study of language development in the last half century. The themes that will be seen to emerge from this brief perspective are the primary issues that have concerned researchers in the 1960s and into the 1970s. These are: *the nature of the code—* what it is that is learned; *the process of language development—*how learning and maturation come together in the acquisition of the code; and *sociological and cultural differences—*as influences on differences among individuals.

PERSPECTIVE

Until the 1950s, there were two major thrusts in research in language development—the diary studies of individual children and the large-scale studies of large numbers of children across age and social class. The diary studies reflected the fascination of a linguist or psychologist parent with a young child's progress in learning to talk. They varied greatly in scope and duration and several have become landmarks in the literature: for example, Ronjat's study of his son's bilingual (French-German) development (1913); the four-volume study by Leopold of his daughter's bilingual (English-German) development (1939–49); the Sterns' study in German (1907); the studies of French-speaking children by Bloch (1921, 1924), Guillaume (1927), and Grégoire (1937); and the study by Chao of his

The preparation of this review was supported in part by Research Grant HD 03828 from the National Institutes of Health.

245

granddaughter's Chinese development (1951). Renewed interest in these studies is apparent in Bloom (1973), Slobin (1971a), Brown (1973), and Clark (1973).

By far, however, the greatest effort, in this same period of time, was devoted to normative studies of large numbers of children, who varied in age, social class, sex, birth position, and so on. These studies were comprehensively reviewed in McCarthy (1954). The study by Templin (1957) was, perhaps, the last and the most important of what have come to be called count, or normative, studies. It is interesting that the count studies came about in reaction to the diary studies, which had begun to appear in the literature at the turn of the century. The swing towards behaviorism and the striving for scientific rigor in psychology in the 1930s and 1940s resulted in a disparagement of information, however detailed and minutely recorded, gathered by a parent-investigator, who, it was presumed, was necessarily biased in what he chose to record in his notes and in what was overlooked as well. Only objective data that could be counted and described statistically were considered admissible. And, indeed, the major indexes of growth and development have made abundant use of precisely this kind of information.

The studies described certain properties of the *form* of children's speech; for example, the average length, parts of speech, numbers of different words, and so on, in a representative number (usually 50 to 100) of a child's utterances. The principal result was the specification of linguistic developmental milestones that allowed comparison among individual children or groups of children. For example, children produce a variety of babbled sounds in the first year, and some time around age twelve months, plus or minus several months, firstborn children generally utter their first words. In the last half of the second year, children begin to produce combinations of two and three words; between ages two and three years, children speak in sentences. Developmental milestones such as these have had widespread use in medicine, psychology, speech pathology, and education (see, for example, Lenneberg 1967).

These milestones provide only a very general and gross index of development, and, more seriously, they ignore the notion of development as continuous *change* over time. Within the single-word utterance period, to take one example, the fourteen-month-old child who is speaking single words but is not about to use syntax, is very different from the child of eighteen or nineteen months who is about to use syntax and is still saying only one word at a time. The specific vocabulary and the ways in which the words are used vary markedly within this particular "milestone" (Bloom 1973). As another example, children's two-word utterances are reductions of their subsequent three- and four-word sentences (Bloom 1970; Brown

1973). Thus, important differences in behavior that occur within a particular developmental milestone and the ways in which the different milestones are actually interrelated and interdependent were easily overlooked in the developmental studies of the 1930s and 1940s.

The reaction to the objective studies of children's utterances began in the 1950s. People began to seek different kinds of information about children and began asking different kinds of questions in language development research. Most important, there was a turn away from descriptions of the form of speech in an effort to discover what children *know* about language at any point in time. Research in the 1950s, for example, Brown (1957) and Berko (1958), began to inquire into the knowledge that underlies the ability to speak and understand—the "productive system . . . that [the child] employs in the creation of new forms" (Berko and Brown 1960).

The new questions required the development of new research techniques for observing children's response to the manipulation of certain kinds of language and situation variables. Such research generally involved fewer children than was typical of the earlier behaviorist-oriented research but aimed towards obtaining more basic kinds of information. This era in psycholinguistic research has been very amply summarized and described in a number of reviews (for example, Berko and Brown 1960; Ervin and Miller 1963; and Ervin-Tripp 1966). These studies convincingly demonstrated that children do not learn all of the sounds, words, and possible sentences in a language. Rather, what the child learns is an underlying linguistic system that is, itself, never directly available to the child or the adult. The studies of Brown (1957) and Berko (1958) made this point most explicitly and most elegantly. For example, when children in the Berko study were presented with a nonsense word like "wug" that named a small bird-like animal, they had no difficulty calling two of them "wugs." Rather than learning singular and plural nouns as separate lexical items, these children had learned one rule (with phonological variants) for marking the plural distinction.

The fact that children learned phonological and morphological rule systems had long been suspected by the earlier diarists and other linguists (see, for example, Jakobson 1968, and Jesperson 1922). Linguistic field research had generally emphasized discovery procedures in the phonology and morphology of languages. The study of syntax or grammar was quite another matter. It was not at all clear how one could discover the grammar of a language and it was even less clear how much of a grammar existed in early child language. However, with the advent of the theory of generative transformational grammar (Chomsky 1957), the search for grammar became the goal of language development research in the 1960s, evolving in a very natural way from the interest in underlying knowledge that began in the 1950s. In short, attempts to discover what a child knows were pursued in the 1960s as a search for grammar or the description of the rule systems that could account for the use of sentences.

The investigation of child grammar began with the procedures of structural linguistic analysis (Bloomfield 1933; Gleason 1961; Hockett 1958), but the goals of the research derived from developments in linguistic theory (most notably, Chomsky 1957, 1965; Harris 1957) with the assumption that underlying knowledge of language is equal to a transformational grammar (Braine 1963a; Brown and Fraser 1963; McNeill 1966a; Miller and Ervin 1964). It is at this point that the story of this particular review of the literature will begin, taking up, essentially, where the review for volume 2 of this series by Ervin-Tripp (1966) left off. All of these studies will be considered in detail in the next section. The children in these studies were a relatively homogeneous sample of firstborn children from middle-class university environments. The results of the studies were impressive in that they concurred in their essential findings, even though three different and geographically separate populations of children were involved. The children from whom these data were obtained were again fewer than in earlier research: Braine reported on the speech of three children; Brown and his associates described the speech of two children; and Miller and Ervin used a population of five children. However, each child was seen over a long period of time and was visited at home at periodic intervals (for up to several years by Brown and his associates). The important finding of these studies was that syntax was indeed systematic and the words were not juxtaposed at random even in the earliest sentences.

The finding that early sentences were constructed in an orderly and predictable way, and that all of these children, as well as others studied later (for example, Bloom 1970 and Bowerman 1973), used many of the same kinds of words (person names, object names, and relational terms like "more," "all gone," "this," "on," and the like), led to another important shift in child language research at the close of the 1960s. Attention was turned from *description* to an attempt at *explanation* of early sentences. Once the attempt was made to explain why some words occurred more than others and in orderly juxtaposition in early sentences, it became clear that the child's underlying knowledge did not equal a grammar in any simple way. The search began for the cognitive correlates of meaning in language and the cognitive processes involved in language learning (Bever 1970a; Bloom 1970 and 1973; Sinclair-de-Zwart 1969, Sinclair 1970; Slobin 1971a). The emphasis of the 1960s on linguistics and linguistic theory for *describing* language development, gave way in the

1970s to an emphasis on cognitive development and cognitive psychology for *explaining* language development.

THE NATURE OF THE CODE
DESCRIBING LANGUAGE DEVELOPMENT

What children learn in the course of their language development is the *substance* of language development and will be considered here apart from the *process* of development, to the extent that the two have been considered separately in the literature. The question of how language is acquired will be taken up in the next section. What is learned is a linguistic code—a system of signs and the possible relations among them which, together, allow for the representation of an individual's experience of the world of objects, events, and relations. There is, as yet, no adequate description of the nature of any linguistic code, and linguists have generally not been enthusiastic about the study of language development for just this reason. Nonetheless, linguistic theory and changes in linguistic theory have been major influences on research in language development. The descriptions of child grammar that have appeared in the last decade were derived from methods and theory in linguistics, beginning with the influence of structural linguistics, then generative transformational grammar, and then the relation between form and meaning.

Structuralism and Emphasis on Form

The structural analysis of language that followed from the work in this country of Bloomfield (1933), Sapir (1921), and much later, Harris (1955) was "distributional." It was concerned with discovering the inventory of linguistic items in a language and describing the ways in which these items were distributed or combined in relation with one another. For example, in English the plural morpheme has three different phonological shapes or allomorphs /-s, -z, -əz/. The distribution of each of those allomorphs is systematic and predictable according to phonological context: words ending in /s, z, š, ž, č, j/ add plural /-əz/, otherwise words ending in voiceless sounds add plural /-s/, and words ending in voiced sounds add plural /-z/. This distributional rule holds with only relatively minor exceptions (for example, "children" and "mice" and the fact that in certain words final /f/ is changed to /v/ and adds plural /-z/, as in "leaves" and "knives").

Since the goal of research was to describe the distribution of linguistic elements in speech, the evidence for analysis was obtained from actual utterances. Thus, given a sample of speech from a child, one could proceed to (1) isolate the different linguistic items in the sample, (2) list all of the phonemes, words, morphological markers, and phrase or sentence types, and (3) describe the linguistic contexts in which each linguistic item can occur. One would then have a taxonomy of linguistic units that occurred in the sample. Gleason (1961) and Hockett (1958) have outlined such procedures in considerable detail. The application of such procedures to child speech data has been described by Brown (1965), Berko and Brown (1960), Ervin-Tripp (1966), and Braine (1971*a*).

The structure of child speech during the single-word utterance period was largely described in terms of adult parts of speech. As the child's speech matured, it was compared to phrase- and sentence-types of the adult model. Structural grammars of adult speech consisted of lists of different sentence-types, and such a catalog of adult sentence-types was frequently used to chart children's progress in development toward the adult model (see, for example, Loban 1963, and Strickland 1963).

Generative Grammar and New Goals of Description

The introduction of generative transformational grammar (Chomsky 1957) in linguistic theory had a profound effect on the study of child language. Essentially, Chomsky proposed that a grammar of a language is something more than a taxonomy of structures or sentence-types such as declarative statements, imperatives, questions, and so on. Following Harris (1957), transformational theory pointed out that there was a closer relationship among such sentences as:

1. The man threw the ball.
2. The ball was thrown by the man.
3. Did the man throw the ball?
4. Who threw the ball?
5. What did the man throw?
6. It was the ball that the man threw.

than among sentences that were all of the same "type," such as declaratives, interrogatives, passives, and so on. That is, the sentences 1 to 6 above (and others) were more closely related to each other, as transforms of one another, even though each is a different sentence type, than were a group of simple active declarative sentences such as:

7. The man hit the ball.
8. The rat ate the cheese.
9. The girl swept the floor.

The theory of generative grammar (Chomsky 1957) attempted to account for this relatedness among sentences in terms of an underlying system of rules. Certain rules in a generative grammar are considered basic, phrase-structure rules that underlie all of the indefinitely many utterances that are possible in a language. The phrase-structure rules produce a single abstract structure that is considered the underlying basis for all of the sentences 1 to 6 above. Other rules, grammatical transformations, operate after the base rules and are optionally applied in generating such different sentences as 1 to 6 above. Thus, there is a set of optional rules which transform the underlying basis of the sentence into its related passive, interrogative, or other forms. The derivation of an interrogative sentence, for example, would involve the base rules plus an interrogative transformation.

The theory of generative transformational grammar evolved in a dynamic way in the 1960s, and there have been a large number of important theoretical advances (e.g., Chomsky 1965; Katz and Fodor 1963; Postal 1964). For a detailed description of the theory and an extensive list of related references in the early and mid-1960s, one ought to consult Jacobs and Rosenbaum (1968) or Stockwell, Schachter, and Partee (1968).

One way in which the new theory of generative grammar influenced the study of child language was to provide a new and more explicit account of the adult model with which to compare child utterances. Menyuk (1963b) was one of the first to use the phrase-structure rules and transformations proposed for the adult model by Chomsky (1957) to describe children's utterances. The children in Menyuk's study were divided into two groups of forty-eight children each, in nursery school (mean age: three years, eight months) and first grade (mean age: six years, five months). Menyuk found that a large proportion of the children's utterances fit the transformational rules of the adult model, although there were occurrences of redundancy, omission, and permutation that altered the adult rules. These latter operations resulted in structures that differed from the adult and appeared to be restricted to the speech of children.

There are at least two important shortcomings in descriptions of child speech in terms of the structure-types of the adult model, regardless of which adult model one assumes as a criterion (structural or generative). First, when researchers have explained child utterances in terms of an adult rule system, they have been willing to accept a single instance or example of a structure as evidence that the child has knowledge of the structure. A single instance may suffice to identify a structure in adult speech because one can ask the adult for related and supporting information. For example, one could ask the adult speaker, quite simply, if the utterance is or is not acceptable, that is, grammatical. One can also ask the adult for paraphrase and equivalence judgments. The linguist who attempts to write a grammar for an adult language depends upon such intuitive judgments from a native speaker.

There is an important distinction between implicit and explicit knowledge of grammar, and it is not clear how much children are aware of what they know (explicit knowledge). In the last decade, investigators have generally presumed that children know rules of grammar (implicit knowledge) that make it possible for them to speak and understand sentences (for example, Bloom 1970; Brown, Cazden, and Bellugi 1969). It has been notoriously difficult to get children to talk about what they know. On the other hand, some researchers (Bever 1970*a*; Bowerman 1973) have proposed that children do not know a grammar, per se, and so could not be expected to talk about it. It has been recently reported (Gleitman, Gleitman, and Shipley 1973) that it was possible to tap explicit knowledge with children as young as two years of age. But such research is only in its preliminary stages.

A single occurrence of an utterance type in the speech of a child is simply not enough evidence that he or she knows the rules for generating the structure. A single occurrence may be a well-learned steretoype or an echo of a previous adult utterance. It is necessary to have evidence of the productivity of structures—that is, the use of the structure v ith different forms in different situations. For example, Brown and Hanlon attempted "to treat the child's production of a construction, in quantity and over a good part of its proper range, together with evidence that he understands the construction when others use it, as *signs* that he has the grammatical knowledge represented formally by the derivation of that construction in the adult grammar" (1970).

However, there are a number of important arguments against assuming that utterances (or structures) that are identical in both child and adult speech can be attributed to the same underlying rule system. Watt (1970) made a very detailed and explicit case against what he called the "strong-inclusion hypothesis" which states, quite simply, that an utterance in child speech has the same underlying structure and derivational history as the same utterance if uttered by an adult. Watt's examples (in addition to references to stereotype and echo, or "parroting" utterances) are adult-based. He points out, for instance, that a syntactically ambiguous utterance with a single surface form can have two or more different underlying structures and, therefore, would differ derivationally as well (for example, "They are flying planes").

A much stronger argument can be made based on the available child-language data. It has been observed repeatedly (Bloom 1970; Brown and Bellugi 1964; Leopold 1939) that children characteristically talk about events that are immediately, perceptually available in the nonlinguistic context. Adults, in marked contrast, do not ordinarily talk about what they see and what they are doing when a listener is there to see for himself.

It appears that child utterances depend directly on the support of non-linguistic context whereas adult utterances do not. In adult discourse, an utterance that bears no relation to the perceivable situation can elicit an appropriate response that also does not relate to what the speakers see or hear or do at the same time. But an adult who asks a child a question "out of the blue," will usually draw a blank, unless it is part of a well-learned routine. Although adult and child utterances may be identical in their surface form, there are almost certainly important differences between their underlying cognitive and linguistic representations. The derivation or origin of the child and adult utterances would necessarily differ, probably in proportion to the extent to which the child utterance was dependent on the "here and now" in which it occurred.

Thus, one result of generative transformational grammar was to change the *means* of describing child utterances in terms of the adult model. But, more important, the theory of generative transformational grammar also changed the *goals* of child-language description. In asking, What does the child learn? it became apparent that an explanation of language development would need to involve an explanation of how the child achieves *linguistic creativity*.

Chomsky (1966) emphasized that one who knows a language has the ability to understand and speak an infinite number of grammatical and meaningful sentences that he has never heard or said before. In learning language, the child's linguistic input is necessarily limited to only those sentences (and nonsentences) presented to him in his environment, and this sample is an incredibly small proportion of the indefinitely many sentences that are possible. Since the child obviously cannot hear all possible sentences, he or she needs to learn the system of rules for semantic-syntactic combinations of words that underlies all the sentences that are possible in the language. That is, the child needs to learn a generative grammar, and that grammar, although manifest in the speech that he or she hears, is not directly accessible to him or her. The major goal of research in the first half of the 1960s was the search for grammar in child speech, and the major focus was on the emerging grammar of early two- and three-word sentences.

Before describing the syntax of early child sentences, it is worthwhile to consider three alternative views of early multiword utterances. If language develops as a trial-and-error process, there should be an early stage of chaotic nonlanguage when the child misses the mark more often than not. Early sentences would be incoherent, unpredictable, and non-systematic, and one could hope for little more than a catalog of the child's most frequent words and word combinations in whatever order. Although this is often the layman's view of what goes on in the years from ages two to four, it was, fortunately, not the original operating assumption of most research in the 1960s.

Most investigators, influenced by insights in the early diary studies and results of experimental research in the 1950s, assumed that early syntax was indeed systematic but potentially idiosyncratic in either of two possible ways. On the one hand, early syntax could be the result of an idiosyncratic child language in which some system, while different from the adult model, was nonetheless the same for all children. That is, one could speak of child language in much the same way as one spoke of the English language or the French language. This seems to have been the operating assumption in much of the work of Brown and his colleagues at Harvard, Miller and Ervin (1964), and McNeill (1966a), and data from different children were sometimes pooled as child-language data. On the other hand, child language was seen as potentially systematic but idiosyncratic for individual children. That is, each child could, conceivably, discover and evolve his or her own particular grammar in the course of his or her development. Although there would no doubt be a core of important similarities among all children, there might also be substantive differences as well. Thus, in the studies of Braine (1963a), Miller and Ervin (1964), Cazden (1968), Brown, Cazden, and Bellugi (1969), and Bloom (1970), the speech of individual children was described separately.

The third view is that child speech is a systematic reduction of the adult sentence-types, rather than idiosyncratic. It turns out that much of the research begun with the operating assumption that child language is idiosyncratic eventually yielded results that supported this third view. That is, although there were important individual differences, children were also alike in many ways. Moreover, child language was more like the adult model than it was different, and the deviations from the model were motivated and coherent rather than errors or mistakes. For example, Brown and Fraser (1963) aptly characterized child speech as "telegraphic"—the words that were left out of two- and three-word utterances were the small, minimally stressed prepositions, conjunctions, and morphological markers. The words that occurred were the content words—mostly nouns and verbs which were most salient and meaningful—and the order in which they occurred corresponded to adult word order, for example, "read book" and "Daddy coat." "Telegraphic" describes only the product of speaking and does not refer to the underlying process by which such utterances are produced.

1. *Neoformalism and descriptive child grammars.* The goals of research, derived from generative transformational theory, were to propose generative grammars for samples of child utterances at different times.

Such a grammar would specify a system or process to account for the generation of sentences. Given a large sample of child speech, the goal was to write rules that would account for as many as possible of the utterances that actually occurred or could occur, while not allowing utterances that were presumably ungrammatical. The focus was on the earliest syntax, with children who were about two years old. Brown (1970, 1973) has since labeled this period in which children begin to use two-word utterances as "Stage 1 speech." Mean length of utterance begins to increase from the single-word stage (1.0) to the time when the larger percentage of utterances consists of two words, and single-word and longer three- and four-word utterances may occur in about equal proportion. The end of Stage 1 speech occurs with mean length of utterance 2.0.

In retrospect, it no longer appears that all of these studies were indeed tapping early Stage 1 speech. Braine (1963a) apparently reported the earliest data. He instructed the mothers of three children to record all word combinations as they began to appear among the children's single-word utterances. The children, Adam and Eve, described by Brown and Fraser (1963) and Brown and Bellugi (1964), had mean length of utterance between 1.4 and 2.0. Miller and Ervin (1964) did not report mean length of utterance, but, from the examples that were given, mean length of utterance appears to have been greater than 2.0.

Although the goals of such grammar writing were derived from generative transformational theory, there was, unfortunately, no prescribed methodology or discovery procedures for obtaining generative grammars. Moreover, as was pointed out by Chomsky (1964) and Lees (1964), there was no generative grammar of adult syntax, except for the fragment of a grammar of adult English offered as examples of phrase-structure rules and transformations in Chomsky (1957). Consequently, the search for rules to account for the underlying productivity of child sentences began with methods of distributional analysis. Lists of child utterances were arranged according to frequently occurring words, and the pattern in which these words occurred with other less frequently occurring words was determined. For example, Brown and Fraser (1963) reported utterances with "Mom" and "Dad," "here" and "there"; Miller and Ervin (1964) reported all utterances with "off" and "on" and variants of "this" and "that."

The major result in which these studies concurred was that the words that occurred most frequently in the children's speech occurred in ordered relation to other words in sentences. That is, such words as "more" or "it" occurred in either first or second position in two-word utterances, but rarely in both positions ("more juice," "more read," "more cookie"; and, "fix it," "have it," "do it."). Braine (1963a) called this small group of frequently occurring words "pivots"; the remaining words in the child's lexicon, for example, "juice," "read," "cookie," "airplane," were grouped together as "x-words." These two classes of words appeared to correspond roughly to the two broad classes of function and content words in the adult model, and, indeed, Brown and his colleagues described them as "functors" and "contentives," and Miller and Ervin called them "operators" and "non-operators."

Transformed sentence types such as Wh-questions, and passives, were not present among these early sentences, and so the grammars that were proposed consisted of rules which defined a few basic sentence types. Braine's rules provided for three possible syntactic arrangements: pivot + x-word, x-word + Pivot', and x-word + x-word where Pivot and Pivot' were two classes of different words. Brown and Bellugi (1964) proposed a series of rules for the development of the early noun phrase. An initial, single, unified modifier class (essentially a pivot-like class) was gradually differentiated as length of utterances increased, with the eventual ordered arrangement of three different classes: articles, determiners, and adjectives in front of noun forms.

The notion of "pivot grammar" as the child's "first" grammar dominated language development research through the mid-1960s. The distributional evidence—the fact that a small group of words occurred with great frequency in fixed order relative to other words in child speech—was indeed impressive. Children were apparently learning different kinds of words and something about word order. However, the difficulties in the "pivot grammar" account were soon apparent. One problem was that the two classes of words did not really have counterparts in the adult grammar. Adult syntax, particularly in a generative grammar account, is considerably more than the juxtaposition of classes of words. There is a hierarchy of structure in rules of generative grammar, and rules are mutually dependent on one another. Such rules do not just label sentence-types. Moreover, the essence of sentence structure is the relationship among constituents, and the function of phrase-structure rules is to specify the grammatical relations among subject-verb-object. Pivot grammar rules said nothing about the meaning relations between words and gave little insight into how basic grammatical relations would ultimately evolve in child sentences.

McNeill (1966*a*) attempted to reconcile these difficulties and expanded the pivot grammar notion in an effort (1) to show that the two original classes were generic to the grammatical classes of the adult model, and (2) to account for the basic grammatical relations of adult sentences. He proposed more complex pivot grammar structures that were hierarchical in that the original "pivot + x-word" phrase was embedded in a still larger pivotal phrase. Such structures, he suggested, functioned as either subject noun-phrases or predicate phrases. McNeill proposed that the limitation to two-word utterances was due to the fact that children were unable to combine both subject and predicate phrases in a single utterance. However, the rationale for deciding whether the underlying function of a phrase was either a subject or predicate noun-phrase was not specified. The result was still tied to the distributional method.

All of the accounts of early child syntax that used generative transformational grammar as a heuristic resulted in a new kind of formalism. Child utterances were obviously systematic, but the nature of the system was described in terms of the form of linguistic elements and the way in which such elements were arranged relative to one another. The categorization of words as "pivots" or "x-words" was the result of the linguistic description. It had not been demonstrated that the two classes were, in fact, used categorically by the child.

Slobin (1966) found evidence of the same distributional phenomenon. In Russian diary studies, a small group of words occurred with great frequency and in fixed order relative to a larger group of relatively infrequent words. He found that, indeed, there was evidence of the same kind of early syntax in Russian, even though Russian, an inflectional language, depends far less on word order to signal semantic relationships than does English. This raised the issue of the extent to which linguistic development was language-independent, and inquiry was begun into the possibility of developmental universals as either a corollary, consequence, or cause of the linguistic universals that had long been sought by, for example, Sapir (1921), Greenberg (1963), and Chomsky (1965). Cross-cultural research in language development moved ahead rapidly at Berkeley with the development of a manual (Slobin 1967) that compiled research methods and provided further details of procedures used in the previous decade. A number of field studies began at Berkeley and elsewhere (for example, by Bowerman 1973, at Harvard, and Solberg 1971, at Cornell).

But while the cross-cultural work was begun as a search for pivot grammar, both the goals and the methodology were quickly changed. Parallel developments occurring in the study of language development and in linguistic theory made it apparent that underlying syntax was inextricably bound to the semantics of sentences and that the essence of language had to do at least as much with underlying meaning as with the surface form of linguistic representation.

The Relation between Form and Meaning

There were ample grounds for criticizing the pivot grammar account of child language, and many of these arguments have been presented extensively (Bloom 1968, 1970, 1971; Bowerman 1973; Brown 1973;

Schlesinger 1971). To begin with, the pivot grammar account ignored meaning entirely, and, as pointed out most explicitly by Schlesinger, it was the underlying semantic intention that was coded in the surface form of children's utterances. Further, there was no structure corresponding to pivot grammar in the grammar of the adult language, and the analogy with the function and content words of the adult lexicon simply did not fit. For example, the word "Mommy" could not be anything but a content word in referential function, but its distribution was pivotal in the data reported in Bloom (1970): for example, "Mommy pigtail," "Mommy kiss," "Mommy diaper." Moreover, it was not immediately apparent how one could account for the child's arriving at the basic grammatical relations represented in adult phrase-structure knowing only something about the permitted occurrences of individual words.

Both Bowerman (1973) and Brown (1973) advanced the case against pivot grammar by refuting the distributional phenomenon itself in the published, as well as unpublished, data. They pointed out that there were exceptions and that pivot words did occur in both positions, so that pivot grammar was not even accurate as a surface description. However, the exceptions that occurred were far less impressive than the overwhelming evidence of the distributional phenomenon that was available not only in the recent literature and the earlier diaries but in real-life situations— on any playground, in any preschool playgroup, or day-care center. It appears to be fact that children use a few words far more than other words, in relatively fixed position, and that the large majority of words that they use occur relatively infrequently in their speech.

The most compelling arguments against pivot grammar as an account of what children know when they first begin to use sentences are, first, that the distribution, which does indeed occur, has to do with what it is that children are learning to talk about. Second, the order in which words occur in multiword utterances is only superficially similar. The same order can occur with two very different underlying semantic relations between the words, indicating that children are learning different underlying structures rather than superficial word order. For example, in twenty-nine instances in which "Mommy" occurred in first position in the two-word utterances spoken by a single child described in Bloom (1970), it was possible to identify the following underlying relations being coded by the superficial form "*Mommy* plus x-word": agent-action, agent-object, and possessor-possessed.

Children use certain words far more than others because of what these words mean for them. Certain words happen to code important cognitive distinctions for children between the ages of one and three years. These distinctions have been represented in the speech of just about all of the children whose speech has been studied so intensively in the last decade, although we must keep in mind that the number of children involved in these longitudinal psycholinguistic investigations is still not many more than twenty. Brown (1973) has looked at both the available contemporary data and the older diary studies and has identified virtually a closed set of such distinctions.

Bloom (1970) and Schlesinger (1971) each reported independent studies in 1968 that attempted to account for the underlying semantics of early sentences. The basic grammatical relationships between *subject-verb-object* were represented in early two-word utterances, with *subject* apparently functioning as agent of an action most often. But whereas McNeill (1966a) had earlier proposed that the child's first phrases functioned as *either* subject *or* predicate, it became apparent that, in the speech of one of the children studied by Brown, such disjunction was not, in fact, the case. Although verb-object phrases (or predicates) occurred abundantly, subject-verb and subject-object phrases occurred as well. Thus, all of the basic grammatical relations occurred among the utterances in a corpus but could not be represented entirely within the bounds of a single utterance due, apparently, to some constraint on linguistic and psychological processing.

Bloom (1970) reported other semantic relations between two words that were identified on the basis of how certain of the words were used. The word "more" or "another" signaled another instance or *recurrence* of an object or an event after its previous existence; negative words like "no," "no more," or "all gone" signaled the *disappearance* or *nonexistence* of an object or action in situations where existence was somehow expected; and words like "this," "that," "Hi," or simply "ə" served to point out the *existence* of an object or action (this last function was referred to as "ostension" by Schlesinger and "nomination" by Brown). In two-word utterances of this type, the meaning of the relation between the words was derived from the meaning of one of the words, such as "more," "all gone," or "this."

The semantic relations *possession* and *location* were of a kind that were less adequately defined on the basis of the meaning of one of the component words. Bloom, Lightbown, and Hood (1974) found that, in the earliest data from three children (Kathryn, Gia, and Allison), possession was represented by two substantive words, for example, "daddy coat." Possession was subsequently signaled by a possessive marker such as "my" or "your." Location was first represented by two substantives in juxtaposition (for example, "sweater chair," which was said when Kathryn carried her sweater to the chair) and subsequently by a locative word such as "there," "up," "right here," or "on." Similarly, agent and object were most often nouns and pronouns when these functions appeared subsequently. However, in the speech of two other children (Eric and Peter), agent, object, possessor, and location were first signaled by a function form ("I," "it," "my," and "there") that determined the relational meaning between the two words in an utterance. This difference among these children represents the two alternative strategies for learning grammar that were suggested in Bloom (1973). One strategy depends upon the child learning to use certain words with constant form and constant meaning (such as the inherently relational terms "more," "this," "no," "my") in two-word utterances, where such words determine the semantic-syntactic relationship. The second strategy involves a linguistic categorization, where different words (such as "Mommy," "Daddy," "baby") form a class for the child because they can have the same meaning (for example, agent) relative to other words. In this case, the semantic-syntactic relationship between the words is independent of the lexical meaning of either of the words. Other relations between words occurred less often; the *attributive,* with forms other than those already reported, was apparently a later development, as was the *dative,* which was rare in all of the data.

The semantic-syntactic relations between words appeared to develop in two-word utterances as follows. Children used certain words that referred to the existence, nonexistence, disappearance, and recurrence of objects. These words (such as "this," "more," "no," or "all gone") operated as function forms in relation to other words such as "cookie," "book," "read," and "fit." At the same time, there were other relations between words that were not specified by the words themselves, such as the relation between object located and place of location, possessor and possessed, and agent and object of an action. After the appearance of these relations in two-word utterances, later development consisted of (1) specifying more than one such relation within a longer utterance, for example, "Mommy more juice," or "drink Mommy juice," and (2) specifying other relations, such as the dative, and attributes of relative size, color, or state. Thus, in the developmental sequence of syntactic structures, the noun phrase (with "adjectives" other than "more," etc.) and the morphological markers of plural and possessive /-s, -z, -z/, or verb tense, and so on, were relatively later developments. The explanation for this sequence appears to be largely a psychological one: the order in which children learn syntactic structures apparently reflects the order in which they learn to distinguish and organize aspects of their environment. Thus, plurality and relative size and color were not coded in the earliest utterances because they were apparently not among the earliest discriminations the children made.

There were two important conclusions to be drawn from these results. The first had to do with the fact that the distinction of certain words in children's early sentences could be *explained* as well as *described,* and the explanation had to do with underlying cognitive function. Specifically, the children were using the semantic-syntactic relations between words which coded certain of their mental representations of the world of objects and events. The second conclusion was that the children had learned something about grammatical structure for representing (and distinguishing among) these underlying conceptual representations, which said more about their linguistic knowledge than that they knew which word forms could follow one another in speech. Both conclusions influenced subsequent theorizing about language development, and two major questions in language development research after the 1960s had to do with (1) the cognitive prerequisites for language learning and (2) the best linguistic theory and formulation for representing children's linguistic knowledge.

1. *Cognitive prerequisites.* Cognitive development in relation to language learning became the dominant issue in theory and research in the beginning of the 1970s. The relations between language and thought, and their development in children, have been interesting to philosophers and psychologists for centuries. In its contemporary form, the issue has revolved around whether children acquire or somehow know the grammar of a language in the abstract sense proposed by Chomsky (1965) and McNeill (1966a, 1970), or whether they learn language as a representation of their logically prior conceptual learning as proposed by Piaget (1967).

One of the earliest attempts to deal with this question directly, both experimentally and theoretically, was reported by Sinclair-de-Zwart (1969), a close associate of Piaget. She distinguished between language as an object of knowing and a means for learning. Her intent in the series of experiments she reported was to determine (1) the linguistic forms used by children who had achieved certain stages in cognitive development, such as the notions of conservation and seriation, and (2) whether one might hasten the development of such notions in children who did not yet have them by teaching them the relevant speech forms. That is, would preoperational children who could not conserve or seriate be able to do so if they knew the right words and linguistic structures used by operational (conserving) children?

Sinclair reported, first, that the language used by the two extreme groups of conservers and nonconservers (there was also an intermediate, transitional group in her study) was different. Preoperational children who did not conserve described the materials presented to them in absolute terms, for example, "this one is big, this one is little." The children who were able to conserve used coordinate structures, such as "this one is fatter but shorter" or "this one is bigger than the other one." The two kinds of language were not actually confined to use by only one or the other kind of child. Apparently, some children from both groups used both kinds of language (Kowalski 1972). The major point made by Sinclair-de-Zwart was that while it was possible to teach the preoperational children the language used by the operational children (with different materials, of course), they still failed to demonstrate conservation or seriation when retested. Sinclair-de-Zwart concluded that knowing the words and structures was not enough and would not lead to the induction of the relevant cognitive operation.

Piaget's contention that language depends upon, as a logical consequence of, the prior development of relevant cognitive structures, is strongly supported by the results of research in early language development (Bloom 1970, 1973). Children learned precisely those words and structures which encoded their conceptual notions about the world of objects, events, and relations. Children learned that things exist, cease to exist, and then can recur; that people do things to objects; that objects can be owned and located in space. In retrospect, it seems quite obvious that these would be the things that children talk about at the end of their second year. The child's awareness of such phenomena has been described by Piaget (1954) as the essence of sensorimotor intelligence as it develops in the course of the child's first two years of life.

The counterargument, that children learn words and structures and then attempt to use these in order to make sense of their environment, can be refuted by several kinds of evidence. It is apparent that children know and can even talk about such phenomena as agency, possession, location, recurrence, disappearance, and the like, without knowing the corresponding linguistic forms for their representation. First, as reported in Bloom (1970), the basic grammatical relations were developmentally progressive, that is, children did not characteristically begin talking in sentences with subject-verb-object strings. Although they may have known these grammatical relationships among words, and have been limited to only one relation per utterance, they may also first have learned to use one or the other. For example, verb-object predominated in the speech of the three children studied by Bloom (1970); subject-verb predominated in the speech of the three children studied by Bowerman (1973). Moreover, younger children who used only single-word utterances also presented considerable evidence of an awareness of such relationships in experience, although they did not have the structural knowledge for linguistic representation (Bloom 1973; Greenfield, Smith, and Laufer, in press; Ingram 1971). Further, in the development of negation reported by Bloom (1970), the children learned to express different semantic categories of negation before they learned different contrasting linguistic structures. When the children began to use syntax to talk about a different concept (*rejection* and then *denial* as categories of negation), they used the primitive structure that they had used earlier to encode syntactically the notions of nonexistence and disappearance.

The search for linguistic universals in child-language data in the 1960s was largely motivated by the distributional evidence of word order in the early utterances of English-speaking children. Slobin (1966) had looked for the distribution of pivot and open class words in the Russian language development literature. Bowerman (1973) studied development in Finnish, a language that, like Russian, depends on inflectional processes rather than on word order, to determine how universal, that is, independent of specific languages, the systematic word order in early two- and three-word sentences would be. The early results of the search for universals in linguistic development, and the emphasis given to innatist views of the origin of language by Chomsky (1965), McNeill (1966a), and Lenneberg (1967), raised a number of questions concerning the child's cognitive development and the extent of universality of underlying cognitive function as it relates to language development. Slobin (1971a) compared the reports of research in about thirty languages and attempted to specify a set of linguistic-cognitive principles that could account for the cross-linguistic data.

Thus, the beginning of the 1970s marked a major shift in research in language development, away from the description of child language in terms of linguistic theory and towards the explanation of language development in terms of cognitive theory. There was an important change from the early research reports that described such utterances as "Mommy pigtail" and "bear raisin" as "noun + noun" or "x-word + x-word" (Braine 1963a; Brown and Bellugi 1964; McNeill, 1966a), to the description of the same utterances as "possessor-possessed" or "agent-object" by Bloom (1970) and Brown (1973). It is of considerable interest that there was a corresponding shift in the study of linguistics and linguistic theory in the same period of time. The role of semantics in grammar became the major issue in linguistics in the late 1960s as it became increasingly clear that semantics and syntax could not be separated and analyzed apart from one another. Several new semantically based models of linguistic theory began to appear (see Bach and Harms 1968; Lakoff 1968). Because of the new interest in meaning and function in child language occurring at the same time, different investigators began looking among these new linguistic models for the "best theory" for representing what children know about language.

2. *The best theory for describing child language.* The grammars proposed in Bloom (1970), following Chomsky (1965), were offered as an account of what children know about syntactic structure. It was explicitly assumed that the syntactic structure of utterances could be described only

in terms of the underlying meaning that is encoded in or represented by what the children said. An implicit assumption was that such grammars represent linguistic hypotheses about children's knowledge of sentence structure. Bloom (1970) did not attempt to specify the semantic component of a generative transformational grammar, which in Chomsky (1965) functioned somehow to interpret syntactic structure. It was assumed that syntax and semantics were mutually dependent and that one could not be described or accounted for without the other. The inferred meanings of the children's utterances were the primary data for arriving at the rules of grammar which accounted for the structure of their sentences.

Schlesinger (1971) suggested that children's sentences derived from an underlying semantic basis—specifically, the child's semantic intention— rather than the syntactic basis specified by the phrase structure of generative transformational grammar. The form of utterance would be determined by what the speaker intended to talk about, and the syntax of the utterance would depend directly upon its underlying meaning.

The issue of semantics in linguistic theory became a dominant concern in generative grammar after the emphasis on syntax in the original theory revealed that syntax was inseparable from underlying meaning. Innovations in semantic theory proposed that an underlying semantic basis derivationally precedes the operation of rules of syntax (see, for example, Bach and Harms 1968; Bierwisch 1970; Chafe 1971; Lakoff 1971; Leech 1970). Because semantics is an account of meaning, and meaning derives from mental representation of experience, the new descriptions of the semantic structure of language began to be used in accounts of early language development.

The one semantic theory that seemed most attractive and most immediately relevant to child-language data was case grammar as proposed by Fillmore (1968). Noun forms characteristically predominate in the speech of children, and many two-word utterances include at least one noun as a constituent. Case grammar accounts for the semantic structure of sentences in terms of the meanings of noun forms, as specified by certain prepositions, in relation to verb forms. The semantics of early child-language became the focus of research, and case grammar appeared to be most readily applicable to child-language data (Bowerman 1973; Greenfield, Smith, and Laufer, in press; Ingram 1971; Kernan 1970).

Bowerman (1973) recorded the speech of one English-speaking child, Kendall, and two Finnish-speaking children, Rina and Seppo, in order to compare development in two languages that code meaning differently. English is a language that depends primarily on word order, while Finnish is an inflectional language where word order is essentially variable. Bowerman described semantic structure in terms of case grammar for utterances with mean length less than 2.0 morphemes and compared these case grammars with transformational grammars in order to test the adequacy of the different linguistic theories. The children were found to code essentially the same set of conceptual notions in their speech as had been reported in Bloom (1970) for English-speaking children. Bowerman concluded that case grammars could account for more of the semantic information that was obtained for the utterances than could transformational grammar. For example, in Seppo's speech when mean length of utterance was 1.42, "father clock" was specified as dative (person-affected) + objective, and "chick shoe," where the chick was on the shoe, was specified as locative + objective. The case symbols were unordered in these specifications and did not necessarily correspond to the order in which the corresponding elements appeared in the children's utterances.

Bowerman proposed that children do not have knowledge of such grammatical structure as subject-of-sentence, or predicate, or object-of-verb. Rather, their knowledge is semantic, and they learn such semantic relationships as agent-object, possessor-possessed, person affected-location, and so on. However, she found that these relationships were, indeed, marked initially by consistent syntactic word order in both languages. In the Finnish children's speech, there was a preferred word order initially (which matched the preferred word order that she also found in the mother's speech), although word order became more variable, as in the adult model of Finnish, as mean length of utterance approached 2.0.

Bowerman's conclusions were similar to those offered by Schlesinger (1971): children first learn semantic relations between words, and these determine the subsequent development of such grammatical notions as subject and predicate. According to Schlesinger and Bowerman, early two- and three-word utterances represent semantic rather than syntactic relationships. However, syntax clearly exists if children discover, as they do virtually from the beginning, that the semantic relations between words can be marked by word order. Moreover, the facts that different words express the same semantic relation, and different semantic relations occur with the same words, such as (in Kathryn's speech) possessor-possessed in "baby (s) shoe" and "Mommy (s) sock"; agent-object in "bear raisin" and "Mommy pigtail"; and person-affected-state in "baby tire (d)" and "Mommy busy," appear to be evidence of the superordinate categorization of words as, for example, *sentence-subject*. Bloom, Lightbown, and Hood (1974) reported that Kathryn, Gia, and Allison expressed the same semantic relation with different words (for example, action-object— "eat *meat*," "comb *hair*," "read *book*"; and locative-action—"sweater *chair*," "sit *floor*"). However, Eric and Peter used a system in which the *same* semantic relation was marked by a constant relational term (for example, action-object—"fix *it*," "find *it*," "turn *it*"; and locative-action —"put *there*," "screw *there*," "sit *there*"). The fact that the same semantic relations can have two alternative and consistent representations in the speech of different children is evidence that children are learning semantic-syntactic structure, or *grammar*.

Brown (1973) has reviewed the arguments of Bowerman and Schlesinger and compared each with the analysis reported in Bloom (1970) in an effort to propose the "best theory" for representing children's linguistic knowledge. He concluded that the semantics of children's first sentences could not be as fully represented within the framework of the original theory of generative transformational grammar as they could be in case grammar terms. However, generative grammars of child language do account for the syntax of utterances. Generative grammars also represent the semantics of utterances to the extent that the order of elements is semantically determined; the underlying structure of the sentence is the meaning of the sentence. Finally, generative grammar appears to be more powerful than case grammar in accounting for a wider range of structure in the child's continuing and subsequent development and in the adult model.

Unfortunately, as promising as the developments of linguistic theory were for describing the language-acquisition data in the beginning of the 1960s, linguistic theory at the start of the 1970s appeared to be of little help. As linguists have begun to look to philosophy 'and cognitive psychology for the answers to many of their questions about the nature of language, there is no longer a unified theory of generative grammar. Writing grammars for later child-speech appears to offer more frustration than ever and no longer seems to be a promising endeavor. There is no available model of what such a grammar might look like nor a consensus of the kinds of information it might account for. Theories of linguistic meaning have come to be thought of as accounting for cognitive meaning and the result has been a blurring of the distinctions between *semantics* (meaning as it is coded by natural languages), and *cognition* (the mental structures and processes of thought).

However, one result of the interest in semantics and underlying cognitive function has been attention to the origins of early grammar in the study of children's use of single-word utterances before syntax.

Origins of Grammar in Single-Word Utterances

Research with one-year-old children has attempted to determine whether or not complex structures underlie the single-word utterances that the child actually says. McNeill (1970) argued extensively that such utterances are syntactically structured and that children already know about sentences and grammatical relations. Something like this view of single-word utterances as "one-word sentences" or "holophrases" has recurred throughout the history of research in language development.

However, children's knowledge about sentence structure thus far has not been testable when they say only one word at a time, even in comprehension tasks. One can only make inferences based on their relevant linguistic and nonlinguistic behaviors.

An alternative argument is that the structure that underlies single-word utterances is semantic rather than syntactic (Greenfield et al., in press; Ingram 1971). McNeill (personal communication) has also recently arrived at this conclusion. Ingram, from the data reported by Leopold (1939), observed that the same word, for example, "up," was used by Hildegard Leopold in a variety of situations, with different people and objects interacting in a variety of ways relative to the state of *upness*. Ingram concluded that such different occurrences of "up" could be explained only in terms of different underlying semantic structures; for example, the child as both reflexive object and agent when she has gotten up, in contrast with the child as nonreflexive object and the hearer as agent when she wants to be picked up.

Greenfield et al. (in press) used case grammar to describe the underlying semantic structure of the single-word and early two-word utterances in the speech of two children. They concluded that there was developmental progression in the children's use of different cases in the single-word utterance period, and that this sequence of development paralleled the subsequent development of cases in syntactic representation.

The argument against linguistic structure—semantic or syntactic—underlying single-word utterances has been presented at length in Bloom (1973). Using video taped data obtained over the six-month period before the use of syntax from one child (Allison, the author's daughter), it was possible to demonstrate that she used different kinds of words and used them differently at different points in time. However, the different words that Allison used, and the way in which she used them, appeared to be functions of her underlying cognitive development. There was convincing evidence that she did not know anything about syntax. She produced series of single words in succession which were obviously related by virtue of the state of affairs being referred to, but which appeared in variable order relative to one another and were not produced in combination as phrases:[1]

1. In examples of speech events, utterances on the right were spoken by the child. Utterances on the left were spoken by the mother or investigator. Material in parentheses on the left is description of behavior and situational context, and the convention used for the correspondence between linguistic and nonlinguistic data was as follows. Utterances follow one another on successive lines. Ongoing behavior or action is coded in the present progressive form and occurs on the same line as the utterance. Immediately previous (or immediately subsequent) behavior or action is coded in the simple present and occurs on the line preceding (or following) the utterance. Slashes indicate utterance boundary as determined by intervening pause and intonation contour.

At nineteen months, two weeks:

(Allison putting horse on chair)	there/
(Allison having trouble getting horse on chair; Mommy reaching out to help)	Mommy/

I'll help. Okay, Mommy'll help you.

(Allison trying to put horse on chair)	help/
(no room for horse, Allison giving it to Mommy)	horse/ help/

Help?

(Allison pointing to space on chair)	over there/

Although she evidently knew something about the lexical meanings of words, there was no evidence that she knew about grammatical meaning. She was evidently aware of certain recurrent relationships among people and objects in her experience, but this conceptual development was apparently not related to linguistic structure—either syntactic or semantic.

In an effort to trace the development of word meaning, Clark (1973) has searched the diary literature and has brought together many observations of how different single words have been used by children in a number of different languages. She concluded that a child learns the meaning of a word by acquiring certain semantic features that are based on perceptions of his world, features based on aspects of objects that can be seen, heard, felt, and so on. The child initially shares with the adult only a small portion of common semantic features, and his or her task, in the course of development, is to learn more and more of the features of a word. At a later time, according to Clark, the child will learn the linguistic function of such perceptually based features, that is, the rules for the combination of different lexical items. Clark illustrated the acquisition of perceptually based features by citing examples of overextension in the literature, where children were reported to have extended the use of a word to things which shared a perceptual likeness, such as size, shape, and the like.

However, children also use certain words that do not share such perceptually based features in each instance of use. For example, words like "more" and "there" or "this" also occur with great frequency among the early words. And yet, a child can call a second cookie "more" after he or she has eaten the first cookie and also call a second horse "more" after seeing the first horse go by. The meaning of "more" in the sense of the recurrence of an object depends upon conceptions or organizations of behavior which do not appear to lend themselves to the kind of feature analysis that is based on perceptual attributes of objects. Also, it is not always the case that children learn the linguistic rules for combination of lexical items after they learn the perceptually based semantic features of such words. Certain words, verbs, for instance, appear to be learned only in the sense of their meaning in combination with other words, so that it is difficult to know which kind of meaning, lexical or grammatical, came first.

There is, at present, considerable interest and research in progress having to do with the period of single-word utterances, and the reports of such research should be appearing within the next several years. People are looking more closely at what children say in relation to the semantic intent or meaning of their utterances, as has already been described, but also in relation to the speech of the mothers of their children (Nelson 1973), the function of such utterances in relation to context (Greenfield et al., in press), and in relation to the child's cognitive development. Both Sinclair (1970) and Bloom (1973) have concluded that the words that are used in the second year directly reflect the organizing activity of the child as he or she passes through the stages of sensorimotor development that have been described by Piaget (1954). The use of relational terms, such as "more" and "there" predominate in the first half of the second year, and noun forms, or references to classes of objects, do not come to predominate in child lexicons until the achievement of object constancy in the second half of the second year.

But there are a host of questions that remain to be answered in further explorations of children's use of single words before they use syntax. For example, it is not at all clear what the child's comprehension is in this same period of time, or what the function of different behaviors, such as imitation, might be for the process of language development. But it is already abundantly clear that the period in development between first words (at about twelve months, plus or minus a few months) and the use of two- and three-word utterances at the end of the second year is not a single "developmental milestone." Rather, it is a period of considerable growth and change. The child is learning more than a dictionary of word forms and word meanings. The child at thirteen to fourteen months is not about to use syntax, whereas the child of eighteen to nineteen months is about to use syntax—primarily because of the complex changes in cognitive development in that period of time—even though both are saying only one word at a time.

An almost inevitable consequence of, or correlate to, the upsurge in interest in language development in the second year has been a renewed interest in infancy which, for many people in the past, has been considered a "prelinguistic" stage in language development (see, for example, the review by Kaplan and Kaplan 1971, and chapter 3 in this volume). On the semantic, intonational, and phonetic levels, there appears to be at least some preliminary evidence that young infants do pay attention to what they hear. It can be expected that more studies of infants and children in the first two years of life will emerge and that the emphasis will be on the empirical observation of behavior, rather than on ad-hoc theorizing and speculation.

Semantics and Referential Function

In addition to the interest in underlying semantic intention in single-word utterances and early syntax, the recent focus on semantics in the study of child language has stimulated studies of the development of specific lexical items and domains of meaning. In particular, attention has been given to how children learn comparative terms (Clark 1972; Donaldson and Wales 1970; Klatzky, Clark, and Macken, in press; Milligan 1972; Weiner, in press); linguistic references to notions of time (Clark 1970, 1971; Cromer 1968, 1971; Harner 1973); and definite and indefinite reference (Maratsos 1971).

The acquisition of the comparative terms "more" and "less," and "same" and "different," are of considerable interest for several reasons. For psychologists these terms are central to the evaluation of cognitive functioning and the measurement of intelligence. For example, Piagetian tasks of conservation depend on the child's use of such terms to describe the outcome of certain transformations of the shape of objects or other matter. Judgments of relative amount (more or less) and identity and equivalence (same or different) are central in tests of intellectual achievement, such as the Stanford-Binet. For linguists and psycholinguists, the acquisition of these relational terms provides the opportunity to study how the two terms of an antonymous pair are related to one another.

Experiments by Donaldson and Wales (1970) appeared to confirm the notion that each pair—"more" and "less" and "same" and "different"—were, indeed, coding a particular dimension of meaning. Three- and four-year-old children were presented with (1) a figure of a tree with hooks on it, some of which had apples hanging from them and some of which were empty, and (2) extra apples. The children responded the same way in response to the two directions, "Make it so that there are *more* apples on the tree" and "Make it so that there are *less* apples on the tree." In both instances, they put *more* apples on the tree. Further, when presented with an array of objects and an exemplar of one of the objects, they responded the same way to the directions "Show me one that is the *same* in some way" and "Show me one that is *different* in some way." In both instances they picked an equivalent object. Donaldson and Wales interpreted these findings to mean that children first learn only one meaning for both members of a polar pair of adjectives; "less" means the same as "more" and "different" means the same as "same."

Subsequent research, however, has failed to replicate these findings. Weiner (in press) pointed out that there were certain problems in the design of the Donaldson and Wales experiments. For example, in the original experiment, items with "more" were presented to all subjects on one day and items with "less" on a subsequent day. The response to "less" may well have been influenced by this order of the presentation of the items. In Weiner's experiments, two- and three-year-old children were asked to judge the relative quantity of horizontal arrays of discrete objects arranged in one-to-one correspondence on a vertical board, when initially equal or unequal rows were added to, subtracted from, or left static. Addition and subtraction had little effect on the children's comprehension. Rather, they understood "more" first when number-characteristics of the arrays were relatively large, suggesting that "many" was an intermediate stage of meaning for "more"—between early understanding of the sense of "existence" and ultimate understanding in the sense of greater quantity. She found comprehension of the quantity "more" developed earlier than comprehension of the quantity "less," apparently because of the restricted sense of "less" as smaller in quantity. However, these children did not respond to items with "less" as though "less" meant "more."

Studies that have measured young children's comprehension of antonymous pairs of adjectives have reported that positive adjectives are understood earlier than negative adjectives: "more," "big," "tall," "high" were better understood than "less," "wee" (small), "short," "low" in the studies by Donaldson and Wales (1970); "more" was understood earlier than "less" in the study by Weiner (in press); "big," "long," and "fat" were easier to understand than "small," "short," and "thin" in a study by Milligan (1972). However, there have been conflicting results in studies reporting comprehension tasks with the temporal terms "before" and "after."

The semantic domain of *temporal* references has intrigued philosophers and linguists for centuries. Psychologists have long been aware that the conceptual notion of nonpresent time and linguistic reference to past and future events are relatively late developments in the preschool years. For example, among the Wh- questions that children learn to ask, questions beginning with "when" are usually among the last to occur. It is not clear whether children first learn time-language dealing with past or future. On the one hand, two-year-old children typically comment on their intentions, that is, on what they are about to do, more often than on what they have just done (Bloom and Hood, in preparation). However, it is also true that one can have a conception of future events only in relation to events already experienced. The ability to plan for and anticipate events that are yet to be depends in a fairly obvious way on the memory or mental organization of what one has already seen or done.

Studies of how children learn both the concepts and the language of time have not been conclusive. Cromer (1968) reported that the children studied by Roger Brown made reference to future time more often than to past time in the age range from two to five years. Other studies of temporal reference have offered conflicting evidence. In a study of temporal decentering by Cromer (1971), subjects did better in comprehending past-tense sentences than future-tense sentences, which is in essential agreement with the findings of Clark's (1971) study of comprehension of "before" and "after."

The terms "before" and "after" are of particular interest because they encode sequential time and are also linguistically polar opposites. In Clark's experiments, three- and four-year-old children were more often correct in responding to items with "before" than to items with "after." Her interpretation of this finding was not very different from the interpretation offered by Donaldson and Wales of the results of their study of "more" and "less." Clark concluded that children learn the semantic dimension of time, and that the first binary division in the dimension has to do with plus prior and minus prior events. As with the studies of "more" and "less," and "same" and "different," children apparently first learn the semantically positive term, that is, "more," "same," and "before," and then learn the semantically negative terms, "less," "different," and "after." Thus far, none of the explanations of this phenomenon appear to be satisfactory. Clark (1971) concluded that children learn semantic features of words in hierarchical order and that the first feature learned in the "before" and "after" domain is the feature [+ prior]. However, the statement that children learn the feature [+ prior] first and then [− prior] seems to be a restatement of the conclusion that they learn to understand "before" and then "after," and is more of a paraphrase than it is an explanation.

Bever (1970b) also found that subjects were better able to understand sentences with "before" rather than "after" when the terms preceded a subordinate clause. Bever concluded that the task was easiest for four-year-old children when order of mention corresponded to order of occurrence, and that the first event in a series was psychologically more salient: both (a) "we sang songs, before we went to bed" and (b) "after we sang songs, we went to bed" were easier than (c) "before we went to bed, we sang songs" or (d) "we went to bed after we sang songs." Amidon and Carey (1972) did not find a difference in comprehension of sentences with "before" and "after" by five-year-old children. They suggested that difficulty in comprehension was due to syntactic rather than semantic complexity, depending on the location of the subordinate clause: (a) and (d) were easier than (b) and (c) because the subordinate clause followed the main clause.

Most recently, Harner (1973) studied two- to four-year-old children's understanding of the notions of time in relation to the understanding of time language: verb tense and the terms "before," "after," "yesterday," and "tomorrow." She found that (1) in linguistic reference to immediate past or future action, verb tense was better understood than "before" (future reference, e.g., "The girl before she jumps") and "after" (past reference, e.g., "The girl after she has jumped"). (2) In linguistic reference to more *remote* times, both past verb tense and "after" having future reference (e.g., "toys for after this day") were understood better than future verb tense and "before" having past reference (e.g., "toys from before this day"). (3) Two-year-old children understood reference to immediate future best; and (4) three-year-old children understood "yesterday" better than "tomorrow." Interestingly, there was considerable variability in understanding of linguistic reference to past and future events, depending on the particular linguistic form and the situation in which it was used. The terms "before" and "after" were used to refer to both past and future time, and each was better understood when used to refer to the next event or action following the present. Harner suggested that "before" and "after" are each better understood in the context of future time and action rather than past time or action, and are not initially understood as relationally ordering two events with respect to each other.

Certain relational terms, such as before-after, more-less, same-different, inside-outside, and others, have constant meanings, but their referential meanings shift with respect to the contexts in which they are used. Thus, for example, "before" means prior and "after" means subsequent in the ordering of two events or the aspects of a particular event; "more" means larger in amount and "less" means smaller in amount; "inside" means contained within a space and "outside" means excluded from a space. However, the same event A can occur both "before" an event B and "after" an event C; the same quantity X can be described (or referred to) as both "more" than another quantity Y and "less" than a third quantity Z; the same object can be referred to as both "inside" a building but "outside" a particular room; and so on. Such shifting reference no doubt presents a problem for the child in learning the meaning of such words, and no less a problem for a theoretical account of the acquisition of such meanings.

Studies of semantic development have only just begun. In addition to the empirical studies that have appeared, there have also been several attempts to specify a theory of semantic development. One such theory, already discussed, is that children learn a set of hierarchical features of meaning.

For example, Clark (1971) proposed that children learn the following set of temporal semantic markers, *time, simultaneous,* and *prior* in the following order: plus or minus *time*; if plus time, then plus or minus *simultaneous;* if minus simultaneous, then plus or minus *prior.*

Anglin (1970) proposed a "generalization hypothesis" to account for the development of word meanings, with progress from concrete to abstract representation. He presented a series of verbal tasks that involved a total of twenty words to subjects ranging in age from seven to twenty-six years. The tasks involved free recall, free association, clustering, and so on. The youngest children were described as being "idosyncratic" in the ways in which they organized words, meaning that they did not treat the twenty words the same way as adults did in the same experiments. The essential difference between the youngest and the oldest subjects appeared to be in the extent to which they recognized the abstract semantic boundaries of form class membership. The syntagmatic-paradigmatic shift in word association responses of children in the age range of roughly five to seven years has been described by Ervin (1961); Entwisle, Forsyth, and Muuss (1964); McNeill (1966*b*); and, most recently, by Francis (1972). According to these studies, children before the age of six or seven years operate on the principle that words "go together" in a phrasal (that is, syntagmatic) unit. For example, "eat" and "apple" are more alike, that is, more closely related to one another, than words of the same form class such as "apple" and "cup." Anglin proposed that the semantically abstract nature of form class membership continues to be learned through adulthood, by a process of "generalization."

The syntagmatic-paradigmatic shift in word association data remains to be adequately explained. It may be related to Huttenlocher's (1964) finding that four-year-old children were unable to repeat a syntactic phrase in reverse order as well as they were able to repeat a series of unrelated words in reverse order. Most puzzling is the fact that even though five- and six-year-old children do not appear to use form class membership (the part of speech) as a criterion in word association, children as young as two and three years were apparently able to use information about part of speech membership to speak and understand sentences, and to learn something about the meanings of words (Brown 1957).

Another theory of semantic development, proposed by McNeill (1970), suggests that semantic features enter the child's dictionary of word-meanings at large in two possible ways and are not restricted to the meanings of individual lexical items. McNeill distinguished between two hypotheses to explain the development of dictionaries and when and how "a semantic feature spreads through the dictionary." Both hypotheses may be true for the dictionary as a whole. The first hypothesis specifies a *horizontal* development; when a word enters the child's dictionary, it may have different semantic features or properties than the same word in the adult dictionary. Semantic development would consist of completing the dictionary entry, that is, adding new features of meaning to those words already acquired, as well as adding new words.

The alternative hypothesis is described by McNeill as a vertical development in which most or all of the semantic features of a word enter the dictionary at the same time, but such features are unrelated to the features of other words already in the dictionary and are separate from them. Vertical development, then, would consist of collecting such features that are common to separate words "into unified semantic features" that transcend the whole dictionary. The horizontal and vertical development alternatives suggested by McNeill imply that the features of meaning in lexical entries are context-free, and it is not at all clear that this is the case.

Higgins and Huttenlocher (in preparation) have proposed that one critical aspect of the dictionary entry for certain words, especially concrete nouns like "dog" or "apple," consists of a prototypical or schematic representation of their perceptual properties. It is this stored perceptual information which makes possible the recognition of class members and the recollection of their perceptual properties. These authors have proposed that the schematic representation of an object class is linked to the schematic representation of the class of word-sounds for that object class.

Bierwisch (1970) specified a theory of semantics whereby components of linguistic meaning were related to the mental representation of physical objects and events. Semantic features do not represent

external physical properties, but rather the psychological conditions according to which human beings process the physical and social environment. Thus, they are not symbols for physical properties and relations outside the human organism, but rather for the internal mechanisms by means of which such phenomena are perceived and conceptualized (p. 181).

It is fairly clear that learning the lexical meanings of words, and the grammatical meaning-relationships between words, depends in a rather direct way on (1) how the child perceives and mentally represents objects and events around him, and (2) the ability to process linguistic messages relative to the contexts in which they occur.

It would appear, then, that there is not so much a rigid hierarchy of features of meaning for particular linguistic forms, as proposed by Katz and Fodor (1963) and applied to children's development by Clark (1971), as there is a network of features with sensitivity to situational context. Although the grammar of a language may have a fixed number of dictionary items and a finite rule system, its meaning components are probably neither fixed nor finite. A theory of semantic development needs to specify how the child takes into account situational and intrapersonal variability in arriving at the meaning components of linguistic items. The research by Johnson, Bransford, and Solomon (in press) and Bransford and Johnson (1972) with adults has demonstrated how the availability of context and prior knowledge can influence comprehension and recall of linguistic messages. We know that one-, two-, and three-year-old children understand and speak in the "here and now," with the necessary support of overt behavior and perceptual context, whereas adults do not. The facts that adults attempt mentally to create situational context when they hear prose passages, and understand more when provided with an overt context, as reported by Bransford and Johnson, indicate that the mental representation of linguistic features of meaning continues to be influenced through adulthood by the interaction of informational, contextual, and pragmatic constraints. The operation of such constraints in the acquisition of features of meaning needs to be specified in a theory of semantic development.

There is much in the child's cognition that is not linguistic; while he does talk about what he knows, he knows about things that he cannot talk about. To be sure, the child necessarily comes to the point where his linguistic capacities can structure his learning—the developmental shift from learning to talk and talking to learn. But the relation between the two and how this transition occurs are not at all clear at the present time.

The Later System

The study of the development of grammar, after the emergence of syntax, has been more fragmentary than the study of early sentences and single-word utterances. That is, there have been few attempts to describe the child's later linguistic system as a whole by proposing a grammar. Brown, Cazden, and Bellugi (1969) proposed a tentative grammar to account for the speech of one of their subjects, Adam, after the early stage of syntax in his speech. Gruber (1967) described the utterances of a somewhat older child in terms of topicalization, suggesting that utterances consisted largely of topic plus comment constructions. By and large, however, most accounts of the speech of older preschool children have focused on one or another particular grammatical subsystem.

1. *Emergence of subsystems of grammar.* Studies of questions (Brown 1968; Brown and Hanlon 1970; Ervin-Tripp 1970; Holzman 1972), negation (Bellugi 1967; Bloom 1970; Klima and Bellugi 1966; McNeill and McNeill 1968), noun and verb inflections (Brown 1973; Cazden 1968), pronouns (Huxley 1970) have provided data on the language

development of two- and three-year-old children. The information contained in these studies has not been brought together in a unified account of the development of particular subsystems, but all of the evidence does not appear to be in as yet. The studies of negation, for example, while complementary in several important aspects also present different conclusions about the sequence and stages of development. Other studies have offered only tentative conclusions and hypotheses that remain to be tested.

Brown's account (1973) of the development of morphological changes for the "modulation of meaning" expanded on the earlier study by Cazden (1968) that had described the noun and verb inflections in the speech of Brown's original three subjects, Adam, Eve, and Sarah. Brown compared these findings with other reports in the literature on the morphological development of children in the same age-range, and the result appears to be a fairly definitive account. He reported that the emergence of grammatical morphemes added to and intervening between the nouns and verbs in child speech begins when mean length of utterance is between 2.0 and 2.5 morphemes. He pointed out that the "modulations" and "tunings" of meaning by grammatical morphemes cannot exist apart from the things and processes that are tuned. But it is possible to talk about the things and processes without modulations, which is probably one reason why the nouns and verbs occur first in child utterances. Brown concluded that the various grammatical morphemes developed in a particular order over a period of two to three years. Although rate of development was widely variant, this order appeared to be relatively constant among different children, as follows: present progressive, *in, on,* plural, irregular past, possessive, uncontracted copula, articles, regular past, regular third person, irregular third person, uncontracted auxiliary, contracted copula, and contracted auxiliary.

The study of negation by Bellugi (Bellugi 1967; Klima and Bellugi 1966) described three stages in the speech of the three children in Brown's study in terms of the syntactic form of their negative utterances. In the first stage, Bellugi proposed that negation consisted of attaching a negative marker (such as "no" or "not") outside of a simple sentence, for example, "no drop mitten," "no the sun shining." In the second stage, the negative marker appeared inside of the sentence, for example, "you can't dance." In the third stage, the negative sentences approximated the transformationally derived negative sentences in the adult model.

In Bloom (1970), there was an alternative account of the development of negation that considered the syntactic form of negative utterances in relation to their meaning. The addition of semantic information complemented the Bellugi account but also revealed a critical difference in the specification of the form of children's first negative sentences in the first phase of development of syntactic negation.

In the speech of the three children reported in Bloom (1970), there was a clear progression in the development of different semantic categories of negation in the period from nineteen to about twenty-six months of age. All of the children used "no" as a single word to express *rejection* of something that they did not want to have or to do. At the same time, however, multiword utterances with a negative marker such as "no," or "no more" were comments on the *disappearance, nonexistence,* or *nonoccurrence* of an object or event in a context where the object or event was somehow expected; for example, Kathryn said "no pocket" when there was no pocket in her mother's skirt (nonexistence), and Eric said "no more noise" when the vacuum cleaner was turned off (disappearance). Subsequently, after the productive syntactic expression of nonexistence, the children began to use multiword utterances with "no" to express *rejection*; for example, "no dirty soap" as Kathryn pushed away a sliver of worn soap, wanting to be washed with a new bar of pink soap. The third semantic category that developed after nonexistence and rejection was *denial,* for example "no truck" (meaning "that's not a truck"):

> Kathryn, at twenty-two months, three weeks:
> (Kathryn, Mommy, and Lois looking for a truck)
> Where's the truck?
> (Mommy picking up the car, giving it to Kathryn)
> Here it is. There's the truck.   no truck/
> (Kathryn continued to look for the truck)

The three semantic categories appeared in the children's sentences in the order nonexistence, rejection, denial, and there was a corresponding development in the form of their syntactic representation. Expression of *nonexistence* was elaborated in complexity, with variation in the form of the negative marker, including "can't," "doesn't," "not," and so on, before elaboration of the expression of rejection. The form of utterances that signaled rejection increased in complexity before utterances expressing denial. McNeill and McNeill (1968) studied the semantic development of negation in a Japanese child, Izanami, and found a similar sequence of development. Izanami acquired the categories "existence-truth," "lack" of "internal desire," and "entailment-nonentailment" in that order.

When the meaning relation between the negative marker and the rest of the utterance was taken into account, it turned out that sentences in which the "no" appeared before the sentence-subject, were not negative sentences at all (Bloom 1970). Rather, "no" before a sentence was anaphoric in relating back to something else either said or implied, and the sentence itself was actually an affirmative statement. Although anaphoric "no" would be marked by a comma in adult speech, there was not a corresponding pause in the child utterances. For example, "no doll sleep" occurred without pause between "no" and "doll" and asserted that the doll was indeed going to sleep. The "no" negated an alternative action (in the following, *Gia* sleeping):

> Gia, at twenty-five months, two weeks:
> (Gia had pretended to sleep; getting up and
> taking her doll)   no doll sleep/
> (Gia put the doll to sleep)

It was not the case then that the first negative sentences in the children's speech consisted of a negative marker attached to a whole sentence. Rather, when the negative marker occurred in a sentence, the sentence did not include a subject. Such truly negative sentences were generally among the most primitive sentences to occur in the children's speech, usually consisting of either an object-noun, or a verb. There appeared to be a complexity limit on the children's sentences, so that the operation of negation within a sentence caused a reduction of complexity and, for example, sentence subjects did not occur. Subsequently, in the further development of syntactic negation, when sentence subjects did occur in negative sentences, they preceded the negative marker, which appeared within the sentence, before the verb. Thus, contrary to Bellugi's (1967) account, negative sentences in the speech of the children described in Bloom (1970), although primitive, were more like the adult model than they were different. Similar results have recently been reported in descriptions of the developmental syntax and semantics of negation in Italian (Volterra 1971) and French (de Boysson-Bardies 1972).

Brown (1968) described the development of the form of Wh- questions, from approximately two to four years of age. Brown was concerned primarily with tracing the child's acquisition of the transformational rules that relate question forms to the corresponding affirmative statements which appear earlier in child speech. He reported a developmental sequence in which an intervening syntactic structure occurred in the transition from a statement such as "John will read the book" to a question such as "What will John do?" or "What will John read?" The last two questions are acceptable in the adult model; that is, they are derived from the set of transformational rules that account for such forms in adult speech. However, before the children in Brown's study produced such questions as these, in which the subject "John" and the auxiliary verb "will," are transposed, and the Wh- word is preposed, they produced such questions as "What John will do?" "What John will read?" "Why he play little tune?" and "Why not you see any?"

In this intervening stage in the development of question forms, the children were only preposing the Wh- word, "what," "why," "why not," and so on; they were not transposing the subject and the verbal auxiliary. Thus, in the course of development, the children seemed to learn and apply a preposing operation before a transposing operation. Both operations are basic in the adult system so that the evidence indicated that the children were learning the grammatical structures that underlie adult Wh- questions, as described in the then current accounts of transformational grammar. However, there was evidently a systematic constraint on learning the operations that Wh- questions involve; the children preposed before they transposed. Brown offered several explanations of the sequence in learning how to ask Wh- questions which depended, primarily, on recurrent discourse patterns between mother and child.

Brown and Hanlon (1970) traced the development of tag and truncated questions in the speech of the same three children. They reported that such forms occurred in the children's speech in a particular order. Truncated forms ("he did" and "he didn't) occurred first and were frequent, before truncated affirmative questions ("did he?"). Tag questions, for example, "We didn't have a ball, *did we?*" and "We had a ball, *didn't we?*" appeared later. In the order of emergence of syntactic forms in the children's speech, truncate and tag forms appeared after declarative, question, and negative sentences. The order of progression in Brown and Hanlon's terms, according to the adult grammar, is from derivationally simple constructions to those that are derivationally complex—indicating that, at least for some developmental sequences, complexity in adult grammar can predict order of emergence of structures or the relative difficulty with which they are learned.

Ervin-Tripp (1970) reported the sequence in which five children responded to different question forms addressed to them after the age of about twenty-five months; "where," "what," "whose," and "who" were responded to in apparently that sequence and before "why," "how," and "when."

In summary, after the emergence of syntax in children's two- and three-word utterances, accounts of language development have focused on the acquisition of the linguistic form of particular subsystems of adult grammar. All such studies have reported that individual children were different in more or less important respects in the course of development. Most often, there were substantial differences among children in their relative rates of development. But, even if some children reach the target language sooner and trace the course of development more quickly and, perhaps, more smoothly, all of the children for whom data have been reported appear to have converged on the adult model from the beginning.

However, language development in the age range from three to five years has by no means been adequately described, much less explained. These were the neglected years in the last decade of research, just as they have often been the neglected years in studies of cognitive development. Children produce increasingly complex sentences and use increasing numbers of different words. But, as the studies of semantic development in this age range have shown, the words used and understood by children do not have precisely the same meanings as the same words in adult speech. Also, at about age three, or shortly before, children begin to use certain aspects of language that appear to be more mature than the underlying cognitive understanding of the children (Bloom 1970; Bruner 1966; Inhelder and Piaget 1964). On the one hand, children learn language in the first two years for coding what they know of the world of objects, events, and relations, and they apparently know a great deal more than they are able to talk about. However, there appears to be some sort of linguistic crossover between ages two and three. The syntax of speech, in particular, goes ahead of underlying thought, as in the following example:

Kathryn, at thirty months, three weeks:
(During the last sessions, six weeks previously, Mommy had been ironing in the kitchen while Lois and Kathryn played in the living room)

    you came here last night, when my mother was ironing/

I came here last night?

    yes/
    my mother, my mother ironed/

Oh, your mother ironed last night?
What did she iron?

    yes/
    oh, she ironed some clothes/

Hm. And what did Kathryn do?
Hm. Did you play with me tomorrow?
Yes? Will you play with me yesterday

    oh, I played with you/
    yes/
    yes/ last yesterday/ last night/

(Mommy had not been ironing the previous night)

Verb inflection was appropriate in Kathryn's speech in referring to past and future times. However, although temporal adverbs such as "today," "last night," and "next Monday" were syntactically correct in sentences, the reference of these forms was inaccurate or superfluous. Bever (1970*a*) has described a characteristic temporary drop between three and four years in the comprehension performance of two- to five-year-old children who were asked to act out different kinds of sentences. He attributed this apparently developmental dip in performance to a change that takes place, at this age, in the strategies that children use in perceptually processing sentences, as a result, apparently, of their learning more about language. The study of the changing relation between child language and child thought in the preschool years has only just begun, but it should become increasingly important.

2. *Language development in the school years.* There has been a general tendency to view child language after the age of five as being perilously close to the adult model, so that describing the speech of school children has entailed many (if not more) of the problems of describing the target language. There have been a number of such studies, however, and these have differed in methods and in scope. In a recent review, Palermo and Molfese (1971) pointed out that all such studies have reported developmental changes throughout the period from age five to about ten or twelve years. Some studies described the changes in this period in some detail.

Menyuk (1963*b*, 1964) described the spontaneous speech of nursery school and kindergarten children in terms of rules of grammar (that is, transformations) in adult grammar and syntactic forms that are apparently restricted to child speech. Loban (1963, 1966) collected yearly speech samples from 220 children from kindergarten through the ninth grade and described changes with age in syntactic structure and vocabulary. O'Donnell, Griffin, and Norris (1967) analyzed the oral and written language of children from five to fourteen years. They reported substantive changes in length of output as well as in complexity and variability of structural units.

Other studies have probed the nature of changes in language in seeking explanations of later language development. C. Chomsky (1969) devised a series of experiments in which she explored comprehension of certain linguistic forms which present a particular problem in their acquisition: "easy to see," which is ambiguous with respect to the subject of "see"; the verb "promise," which violates a fairly general rule with respect to the subject and object of certain kinds of verbs; the distinction between "ask" and "tell"; and pronominalization. Chomsky pointed out that there are two aspects of "knowing a word": "on the one hand, the speaker knows the concept attached to the word, and secondly, he knows the constructions into which the word can enter" (p. 5). Her studies were based on the assumption that evidence of the distinction between the two aspects of knowledge can be obtained from children who know the concept but who do not, as yet, know the constructions which can represent the concept.

The first three constructions tested by Chomsky were relatively specialized and dependent on particular lexical items, whereas the fourth, pronominalization, was more basic. She found that the basic principles governing pronominalization were acquired more uniformly with respect to age across children, and more quickly, at age five to six months. The more specialized constructions varied more among individual children and were acquired later: "easy to see" and "promise" were acquired by age nine; "ask/tell" was still imperfectly learned at age ten. In attempting to replicate these findings with different tasks, Kessel (1970) found that certain of the same distinctions were learned earlier: "ask/tell" at age eight, and "easy/eager" apparently before age nine.

Although these studies on language development in the school years have been only touched on here, it has become clear that children do not "know the language" by age three, or five, or even by age ten. On levels of syntax, semantics, and phonology, they go on learning the language throughout the school years. It is surprising that there have not, as yet, been attempts to tap the intuitions which school-age children have about their language except for the very recent, preliminary study by Gleitman, Gleitman, and Shipley (1973). As children's knowledge becomes less "implicit," it would seem that one could gain considerable insight into what older children know about their language—by such indirect means as paraphrase and equivalence judgment tasks, and by directly asking them to explain certain things that they can or cannot do with words and sentences.

Clearly, the most important development in language in the school years is the child's increasing ability to use the linguistic code, both to speak and understand messages, independently of eliciting states or conditions or of the circumstances in which speech occurs. Linguistic interaction among adults is relatively free from the context in which it occurs; adults do not talk about what is immediately apparent to their listener. Language becomes a means of knowing at about age twelve, when the child becomes capable of the logical operations of thought described by Piaget (1960). Language emerges as truly creative, in the sense described by Chomsky (1966), only through a very gradual process that has really not been touched on in any of the studies of language development in the school years.

The critical question about development that was stimulated by the theory of generative transformational grammar remains: how does the child achieve linguistic creativity—the ability to speak and understand indefinitely many sentences, never spoken or heard before, that are, moreover, free from eliciting conditions and internal states? There has been, thus far, only a partial answer in terms of the nature of the underlying rule system which the child induces from the samples of speech he hears. This induction of the underlying structure of language occurs, to a large extent, in the preschool years. What may be the more important aspect of the question—how the child subsequently comes to use the linguistic code to talk about events and to process messages about events that are not readily perceivable or imaginable—remains to be explained. This transition from maximum dependence on contextual support to speech which is independent of the states of affairs in which it occurs is the major accomplishment in language development in the early school years. It is not at all clear how empirical or theoretical inquiry can arrive at an adequate account of this transition. But it is clear that until such an account appears or is at least attempted, any theory of language development will be incomplete.

Summary

1. The first descriptions of language development that attempted to represent the syntax of child utterances reported that there was a distribution of different kinds of words in early sentences. A small number of words such as "more," "gone," "this," and "Mommy" occurred frequently in juxtaposition with a large number of other words, each of which occurred relatively infrequently. This result was formalized by rules of generative grammar.

2. It was soon apparent that such distributional rules of syntax could not be explained apart from the underlying meaning or semantics of early sentences. Subsequent inquiry into semantic development revealed that the antecedents of early language development could be found in early cognitive development.

3. Investigation of child language after the first three years centered on the development of such subsystems of grammar as Wh- questions and negation.

4. Language development in the school years has begun to receive attention but remains an unchartered course towards achieving competence with the model language at about age ten to twelve.

THEORIES, PROCESSES, AND STRATEGIES FOR EXPLAINING LANGUAGE DEVELOPMENT

An important theoretical conflict dominated attempts at explanation of language development in the early 1960s. On the one hand, the child was seen as the ever-changing product of his own *maturation*. On biological grounds (for example, Lenneberg 1967) and on linguistic grounds

(Chomsky 1965; Fodor 1966; McNeill 1966*a*, 1970) the child could not escape his fate—barring physical or mental complications, he could not help but learn to talk. Such a view placed heavy emphasis on the child— he learned to talk because he was biologically prepared for it or linguistically preprogrammed to do so. In contrast, other theorists (most notably, Braine, 1963*b*, 1971*a*; Jenkins and Palermo 1964; Staats 1971) placed heavy emphasis on the influence of the environment in shaping and controlling the child's *learning*. The child's role in this view was, again, essentially a passive one; his learning was largely determined by the ways in which individuals in his environment responded and reacted to what he said and did. Most recently, attempts at explaining language development have emphasized the active participation of the child, in terms of the *processes* (for example, Brown and Bellugi 1964; Cazden 1965; Shipley, Smith, and Gleitman 1969) or strategies (for example, Bever 1970*a*; Bloom 1973; Slobin 1971*a*; Watt 1970) that appear to influence his interactions with linguistic and nonlinguistic aspects of his environment as he learns to talk.

The argument between those who held that language is innate and that acquisition is the product of maturation, and those who believed that language is learned and is shaped by forces in the child's environment began, essentially, with the Chomsky (1959) critique of Skinner (1957). Since that time, a great deal has been written, and the argument can be followed in Bellugi and Brown (1964), Smith and Miller (1966), Lyons and Wales (1966), Jakobovits and Miron (1967), Dixon and Horton (1968), Reed (1971), and Slobin (1971*b*). As the dust has settled, it has become clear that neither explanation could be entirely correct, and there has been a shifting of positions in several directions.

Jenkins and Palermo (1964) had put forth one of the most explicit accounts of language learning in terms of mediation and reinforcement theory. Since that time, however, there has been modification of these views, and Palermo (1970) pointed out that explanations of language development in behaviorist terms had been too heavily influenced by learning theory and too little influenced by language theory. Attempts to explain language behavior, after all, must necessarily depend on the nature of language, on what it is that is being learned. Verbal learning studies, in general, had used language to investigate learning; emphasis on learning in order to explain language seemed to have been less fruitful.

There was also reconsideration and shifting of opinion among those to whom the nature of language and linguistic theory were primary. Bever, Fodor, and Weksel (1965) criticized the theory of contextual generalization proposed by Braine (1963*b*) as being too closely tied to the surface features of speech. Braine had suggested that language learning depended upon the child perceiving the positions of words in sentences. Bever, Fodor, and Weksel (1965) emphasized that most of what was important about language was beneath the surface—that the underlying rule system was not directly perceivable and thus not obtainable from actual utterances. However, in Hayes (1970) there were several papers, for example, Bever (1970a), that pointed out that actual speech was, after all, primary evidence for the child. The child necessarily must process utterances that he hears, and an adequate explanation for language development must include a specification of the strategies he uses in processing speech.

The function of imitation for language development has emerged as an important issue. Throughout the century, the tendency for children to imitate the speech they hear has been repeatedly acknowledged and has, at least tacitly, been considered as somehow important for learning language. Recently, views of the importance of imitation have been divided. Behaviorists, on the one hand, saw imitation as a necessary precondition for reinforcement and learning (Staats 1971) or a combination of imitation and reinforcement as relevant to language learning (Sherman 1971). The transformationalists, on the other hand, have argued that the most important information about a sentence is in its deep structure, so that repeating the surface structure would not be helpful (McNeill 1966a; Slobin 1968). In support of the transformationalist claim that imitation cannot be important, Lenneberg (1967) pointed out that it was possible to learn language without being able to speak at all, as in the case of individuals with paralysis of the speech musculature who, nevertheless, understand speech. Ervin-Tripp (1964) compared the spontaneous and imitative utterances in the speech of five children and reported that the same rules of surface word-order described both kinds of utterances.

However, in the study of the spontaneous and imitative speech of six children (Bloom, Hood, and Lightbown 1974), there were marked differences in the extent to which the different children imitated, and there were developmental differences between the spontaneous and imitative speech of the individual children. In the speech of two children, Peter and Jane, almost one-third of their utterances repeated something just said to them by someone else. In contrast, in the speech of two other children, Allison and Gia, fewer than 10 percent of the utterances that occurred were repetitions of a preceding model. The other two children, Eric and Kathryn, were somewhere between these two extremes. When the imitative and spontaneous utterances were compared for each child, there were differences between imitative and spontaneous speech. The individual lexical items and the semantic-syntactic structure in multiword utterances that were imitated did not occur spontaneously; the words and structures that were productive in spontaneous speech were not imitated. For example, in an eight-hour sample of speech from Jane, mean length of utterance was 1.29, and 42 percent of her utterances were imitative. Of six *agent-action* phrases, five were spontaneous and only one was imitative, whereas fifteen *action-affected-object* phrases occurred and only four were spontaneous. In the two instances, there was marked difference from the expected proportion of imitation (.42), in two directions. In six five-hour speech samples, three weeks apart, from Peter, with mean length of utterance increasing from 1.0 to 1.69, there was a statistically significant difference between imitative and spontaneous lexical items that occurred three times or more. Lexical items were either imitative or spontaneous, but not both. Moreover, there was a statistically significant change across the six samples as imitative words became spontaneous, but not vice versa. From the results of this study, it appears that imitation is not necessary for language development, but when imitation does occur it is developmentally progressive and provides evidence of an active processing of utterances relative to the contexts in which they occur.

These results of the analysis of imitative utterances that occur in naturalistic speech are in contrast with the underlying rationale for the use of elicited imitation as a task for evaluating children's knowledge of grammar (for example, Menyuk 1963a; Rodd and Braine 1971; Slobin and Welsh 1973). In elicited imitation, it is presumed that the child processes the presented stimulus sentence through his or her own rule system, and the resulting imitation reflects what the child knows about a particular structure. In the study of spontaneous imitation by Bloom, Hood, and Lightbown, imitative utterances reflected what the children did not yet know but were in the process of learning. The processes involved in elicited imitation tasks versus spontaneous production are discussed at length in Bloom (1974a).

Linguistic Determinism

A number of studies have emphasized the nature of language and the linguistic code for explaining the course of language development. The linguistic theory of generative transformational grammar (Chomsky 1965) provided a scheme for representing important information about the origin of sentences. A system of integrated rules was proposed for representing how an actual sentence in speech (the form of a spoken sentence) was related to its abstract underlying structure (the specification of the meaning of the sentence). The system of rules in a generative transformational grammar attempted to specify not only the origin of particular sentences but also the interrelatedness of all sentences that are possible in the language. Such a system of rules is a linguistic grammar proposed by a linguist to represent what a speaker-hearer knows about sentences. A *linguistic grammar,* then, attempts to explain sentences in terms of source or derivational history and represents an hypothesis about *mental grammar.* The mental grammar is what speakers know about language that makes it possible for them to speak and understand sentences.

The distinction between linguistic grammar and mental grammar has not always been clear, and the two have often been confused (see Watt 1970, for an elaborate discussion of such confusion, and Bloom 1974*b*). However, for many people, linguistic grammars and, in particular, generative transformational grammar have provided important hypotheses for describing and explaining the data of language development. Brown and Hanlon (1970) provided an account of children's development of truncated and tag-question forms that was strongly tied to the system of rules that linguists have proposed for such forms in adult speech.

Several studies of speech perception by transformational linguists (for example, Garrett, Bever, and Fodor 1966) attempted to determine the psychological reality of linguistic segments by studying how adult listeners process the linguistic units of sentences. Bever (1970*a*) extended this research to different kinds of studies with small children in an effort to determine the mutual interaction between the child's strategies for speech perception and the actual structure of language itself. Bever proposed a set of processing strategies whereby children were able to retrieve such basic information about sentences as the actor-action-object relations and the interaction between clausal segments. Watt (1970) proposed a somewhat similar processing strategy whereby children analyzed the structure of a sentence by temporally attributing structure to a string of words from left to right. In experiments by Huttenlocher and Strauss (1968), and Huttenlocher, Eisenberg, and Strauss (1968), the easiest sentences to understand were those in which the sentence-subject was the actor of an action. In each of these proposals and in research reported by Lahey (1972), the primary cue used by children for analyzing sentences to obtain their meaning was word order.

Certain basic capacities and information are already attributed to the child who would be using such processing strategies. For example, in order for the child to know that the string of words he hears contains an agent-action-object sequence, he must already know about such relations, that is, about sentences. Such basic linguistic capacities have been largely taken for granted in studies of speech perception and in the linguistically determined theories of language acquisition proposed by McNeill (1970). According to McNeill, the facts of sentences must be available to the child at a very early age, inasmuch as virtually all of his linguistic behavior depends upon it. McNeill's views were strongly influenced by generative transformational grammar, and he has used Chomsky's (1965) notion of "language acquisition device" to explain child language. Essentially, such a device would include the formal and substantive features which are common to all languages (linguistic universals) and would provide the child with the set of hypotheses which he would presumably need for determining those aspects of language which are specific to the language in his community. Thus, what the child already knows about language determines what he learns about language. The origin of such prior knowledge about language is not at all clear. Chomsky, McNeill, and others have proposed a strong innate component in acquisition—that children are necessarily born with certain linguistic competencies. Bever, Watt, and others have left the question open but have allowed the important possibility that the capacities that are "basic" to the processing strategies of two- and three-year-old children are the product of the child's earlier learning in his first two years.

Linguistically determined explanations of language development have attempted to account for children's behavior in terms of what is known or hypothesized about the target language or about language in general. Thus, the linguistic code itself is seen to be the major (if not the only) determining influence on the sequence of development (as, for example, in the Brown and Hanlon 1970 study), or the mechanism of development (as explained, for example, by McNeill 1970). Other descriptions of language behavior have implicated more than the linguistic code and have offered explanations or described strategies that are cognitively determined.

Cognitive Determinism

Piaget has described development as the result of the child's interaction with his environment. The child comes to know about objects and events through his actions on them. Learning language, in this view, depends upon this kind of interaction. The environment in which the child acts includes speech, and his or her interactions must include the speech that is heard in relation to what the child does and the objects and events that he or she sees. Thus, there is complementary interaction among the child's developing perceptual-cognitive capacities and his or her linguistic and nonlinguistic experience. Rather than language being the determining influence on what and how the child learns, what the child learns about language is determined by what the child already knows of the world (see Bloom 1973; Macnamara 1972; Sinclair 1970; Slobin 1971a). This is the point of view that has been emphasized throughout this review chapter.

Slobin (1971a) attempted to bring together the data from developmental studies in a number of languages. He proposed a set of operating principles that would appear to be the child's basis for learning any language. He proposed that, in all languages, semantic learning would depend upon cognitive development and that children will begin to talk about what they know, even though they do not as yet know the adult structure. Thus, sequence of development would be determined at least initially by semantic complexity rather than by structural or formal complexity. In a bilingual situation where the child may have the option to use one or the other language, he will presumably choose the language that uses the less complex linguistic form to express a particular notion if the two languages differ in their means of formal representation of the notion.

Bloom (1973) proposed two alternative strategies for explaining the transition from single words to the use of two- and three-word sentences in child speech. The strategies represent the inductions which children make about grammar, and so they are linguistic strategies for learning about language. As such, they seem to reflect the basic distinction between synthetic and analytic features of languages in general (see Bloom, Lightbown, and Hood 1974). However, which of the strategies a child uses is presumably determined by his or her cognitive development.

Certain conceptions that the child has, for example, notions of the existence, disappearance, recurrence, and so on, of objects, can be conveniently coded by words that are inherently relational ("there," "away," "more") and that combine in direct and linear relation with other words. The meaning of the relations between such words as these and the words with which they are combined is dependent upon the meaning of one of the relational words. For example, "more cookie" as an expression of recurrence depends upon the meaning of "more."

Other conceptual categories such as the relationship between object and location, or agent and object, or possessor and possessed, can be coded by two words in combination, where the meaning relation between the words is independent of the meaning of either of the words, and it is the structural relation between the words that determines meaning. For example, in the utterance "Mommy pigtail," meaning is independent of either "Mommy" or "pigtail." The combination of such words is hierarchical in that there are intervening linguistic categories that specify relationships between individual words. The kinds of distinctions the child has made in his or her organization of experience would appear to influence which of these inductions prevails in his or her early attempts at syntax.

Several experimental studies have demonstrated that what a child knows about an event will influence how he or she interprets a message about the event. Given the same linguistic message, the child will have greater or lesser difficulty interpreting it depending upon what the child already knows about the state of affairs encoded in the message. In a series of experiments, Huttenlocher and Strauss (1968), Huttenlocher et al. (1968) and Huttenlocher and Weiner (1971) have demonstrated that messages such as "The red truck pushes the green truck" will be responded to with varying delay depending on whether one or the other or neither of the objects is already placed in a three-space track or ladder. Thus, the child's ability to determine the relationship between two nouns in a sentence is determined in part by how the corresponding objects appear to him or her in the situation in which the sentence occurs.

A theory of language development must be able to account for different kinds of data that have emerged in child-language studies. Most important, as emphasized throughout this chapter, an explanation of language development depends upon an explanation of the cognitive underpinnings of language: what children know will determine what they learn about the code for both speaking and understanding sentences. Even though there has been a strong motivation to discover the universal aspects of language and language development, important individual differences among children have emerged (as exemplified above and earlier in descriptions of two alternative strategies for emerging syntax). Other differences among children have appeared in relation to certain group variables that have been sociologically defined. Both individual and group differences need to be accounted for in explanations of language development.

Summary

1. There have been two main thrusts in attempts to explain how children learn to talk. On the one hand, it was proposed that the course of language development depends directly on the nature of the linguistic system and, more specifically, on the nature of those aspects of language that might be universal and represented in an innate, predetermined program for language learning.

2. On the other hand, evidence began to accrue to support a different hypothesis that emphasized the interaction of the child's perceptual and cognitive development with linguistic and nonlinguistic events in his environment.

3. The issue remains to be resolved, and neither linguistic determinism nor cognitive determinism has yet received unequivocal empirical or theoretical support. However, research in semantic development has led to an increasing awareness of the correlates of language acquisition in the development of perception and cognition.

Sociological and Cultural Differences

Research in language development that has described children's behavior in relation to cultural and social variables has not been concerned with development in the preschool years, in contrast to most of the research that has been described so far. Thus, educators and psychologists have described the speech of black children in school systems and preschool programs in order to explain underachievement and to plan programs of intervention or remediation. Linguists who have studied the speech of black children were motivated initially by other considerations, primarily their interest in language differences and diachronic language change. The confrontation between educators and psychologists who described the speech of poor black children as deviant, and the linguists who explained that the speech of black children was different rather than deviant, was inevitable (see Williams 1970). Their motivations and their approaches to studying the speech of black children were distinctly different. One group saw the issue as a problem to be solved; the other saw the speech of black children as a linguistic fact to be described.

Studies of the speech of black children that have used standardized tests of one or another aspect of development such as vocabulary or reading readiness have invariably demonstrated performance below the expected "norm." This literature was extensively reviewed by Cazden (1966) and Raph (1967). The tests of language performance that were based upon the language skills of middle-class white children (the "standard" population in the "normative" or "count" studies referred to earlier) produced altogether different results with black children who, quite simply, did not speak the language. The performance of these children on such tests or development profiles was substandard, resulting in the use of such terms as "impoverished," "deficient," or "disordered" to describe their language. Such linguistic deficits were taken to be the cause of learning or reading difficulties and became the focus of remediation (see, for example, Bereiter and Engelmann 1966; Deutsch, Katz, and Jensen 1968; Horowitz and Paden 1973).

The speech of black children has been viewed altogether differently in a number of other studies that have been most recently reviewed by Baratz (1973):

Linguists have also learned that within a large complex society where individuals from different social classes and different ethnicities live in close proximity, they often speak many varieties (dialects) of the same language. One of these dialects may be considered socially more prestigious than the others. It, thus, may be used as the standard for the nation. Although one dialect may be chosen as the standard language, it is important to realize that this is an arbitrary, or at most, social decision which has nothing to do with that particular dialect's linguistic merits. That is to say, the dialect chosen as standard is no more highly structured, well formed, or grammatical than any of the other dialects. The evolution of a particular dialect as the standard is due to sociopolitical considerations rather than to intrinsic linguistic superiority. Some psychologists, however, have failed to consider the existence of these language variations and have thus mistakenly equated a single surface manifestation of the universal behavior, that is the development of the standard dialect, with the universal itself, that is the development of language.

And Labov (1970) has pointed out:

When linguists say that [nonstandard Negro English] is a system, we mean that it differs from other dialects in regular and rule-governed ways, so that it has equivalent ways of expressing the same logical content. When we say that it is a separate subsystem, we mean that there are compensating sets of rules which combine in different ways to preserve the distinctions found in other dialects (p. 185).

The dilemma in education has had to do with establishing the appropriate goals and determining the best procedures for teaching children whose language cannot be adequately assessed in what may be, essentially, a foreign culture for them. However, the situation has been considerably complicated by social and political issues, so that it is not at all clear at the present time what the relevant variables are for making program decisions for education.

It seems fair to say that the language development of black and disadvantaged children has not really been the object of study. Rather, the speech proficiency of these children at particular points in time has been described and compared with that of other children of comparable age while varying such factors as socioeconomic level, race, geographical origin, sex, etc. There are virtually no published studies that have described the speech of preschool black children, and no studies have looked at developmental changes in the speech of preschool black children. It is somewhat startling that the considerable attention given, in the last decade, to the structure and use of language by school-age and adult black people, on the one hand, and to the cross-cultural study of the development of language, on the other hand, has not stimulated the kind of psycholinguistic study of language development that has been reviewed at length in this chapter.

The presumption on the part of those who have described the speech of black children as substandard or retarded is that their development has been slow. In this view, one might expect, then, that these children follow the same developmental sequence but simply more slowly than children from middle-class homes. In contrast, the different-but-equal description of black speech by such researchers as Labov (1970); Baratz (1969); Wolfram (1969); and Stewart (1969) would lead to an altogether different set of hypotheses which seem to cry out for investigation. What are the language correlates of sensorimotor development in black children? What are the conceptual distinctions encoded in their use of single-word utterances and in their early two- and three-word sentences? And, most important, is it possible to identify the origins of the distinguishing features of adult black English in the early language of very young black children?

The questions just posed relate to the structure of children's speech in relation both to the children's underlying cognitive functioning and to their adult model. Another, no less important, question has to do with the functions of speech that have been identified in the speech of adult and school-age black speakers. According to Abrahams (1970, quoted in Baratz 1973):

The emphasis on effective talking found throughout Afro-America, the demand for copiousness and verbal adaptability on the part of the speaker, the expectation that he will elicit a high degree of verbal and kinesthetic feedback from his audience (feedback that will not only permit him but urge him to continue), the license to repeat and to utilize the entire range of vocal effects, all of these traits and many more are the features of the black English speaking system which must be considered in any discussion of the structure and maintenance of black English.

The particular manifestations of how older black speakers use language have been reported and described by Labov, Cohen, Robbins, and Lewis (1968); Kochman (1972); Hannerz (1969); and Baratz (1973). Studies of how very young children use their speech as they are learning language in the preschool years are rare. Horner (1968) used wireless microphones to record the speech of two three-year-old boys, in their home environments, for two days each. She analyzed the function of their speech according to the Skinnerian verbal behavior categories; she found a high proportion of mands and tacts, and very few instances of echoic and intraverbal behavior. We do not have similar kinds of information from either adult black speakers or middle-class white children.

There is a curious disjunction, then, between the language-development literature and the literature of black English. The language-development literature in the last decade has emphasized the emergence of grammar—the evolution of semantic-syntactic structure in the speech of children less than three years old. However, the beginnings of speech of children from lower-class black homes have not been reported on. Similarly, studies of the structure and function of black English have looked at the speech of adults and school children primarily, in order to identify and describe black English. None of these studies has been developmental.

One prevailing theme has come out of the controversy between educator-psychologists who want to teach standard English or the relevant "concepts" or whatever they deem to be missing in black children's speech, and linguists who want to preserve black English as a viable, fully developed linguistic system. The difference between the performance of black and white speakers on one or another task is as much cultural as it is linguistic. In order to evaluate the relevance of any particular research statistic, it is necessary to place it within the larger perspective of the child and the milieu from which both he and his speech originated. Thus, for language "difficulty" one can read language "difference"; for "cognitive deficit" one can read "cultural difference." Future research should be less influenced by linguistic, educational, and political considerations and more influenced by sociological and developmental considerations.

LANGUAGE DEVELOPMENT
SUMMARY AND PROSPECT

Reviews of the literature are necessarily selective; a great deal has been only touched on here and much has been unfortunately omitted, for example, developmental phonology and bilingualism. The last ten years has easily been the most exciting decade in research in language development. For one reason, there has been an unprecedented coming together of psychology and linguistics on both theoretical and empirical grounds. And there has also been an unprecedented sharing of information—this has been the decade of conferences and underground "publication." Preliminary reports of research have had wide circulation among others involved in similar kinds of research. As a result, research in progress has had the benefit of relevant findings and issues before publication. There has been extended and occasionally heated disagreement, but, far more important, there have also been shifts in position and orientation.

It is tempting to speculate on the evalution that will be given to the last decade of research in language development at the close of the 1970s or of the 1980s. After all of the many studies have been sorted out and the evidence sifted, what will remain as the contribution of the 1960s to the study of child language and language development? The speech of a few children was studied in considerable detail; aspects of the speech of a larger number of children were described in somewhat less detail. This was the decade of the search for the underlying system—fired initially by Chomsky's *Syntactic Structures* (1957) and coming around to Piaget's descriptions of the *Psychology of Intelligence* (1960) and *The Construc-*

tion of Reality in the Child (1954). This was also the decade of the search for the universals of language development. Important similarities were found in language development in different cultures, but there were also important differences—in the language development of different cultures and among children learning to speak the same language, as well.

This was the decade in which new demands were placed on the accountability of evidence. The former practice of describing a sample of fifty or a hundred utterances was discarded, and the data for analysis often included over a thousand utterances from a particular child during one particular period of time. The data of language development began to include more than just what children said; behavior and context became critically important variables. The audio tape recorder began to give way to the video recorder with the continually increasing demand for more information about the substance and process of language development than could possibly be obtained from just the spoken word.

New questions have been asked; new techniques have been developed; and new evidence has been brought to light. There have been a number of important insights, and a number of blind leads and illusions as well. There has yet to be a final period at the end of any account of one or another aspect of language development. Very aptly, in the beginning, there were Adam and Eve, and Andrew and Gregory, Christie and Hollie, Rina, Seppo, Izanami, Kathryn, Allison. . . .

REFERENCES

Abrahams, R. Black uses of black English. Conference on Continuities and Discontinuities in Afro-American Societies and Cultures, Social Science Research Council, 1970.

Amidon, A. & Carey, P. Why five-year-olds cannot understand *before* and *after*. *Journal of Verbal Learning and Verbal Behavior,* 1972, *11,* 417–423.

Anglin, J. *The Growth of Word Meaning.* Cambridge, Mass.: MIT Press, 1970.

Bach, E. & Harms, R., eds., *Universals in Linguistic Theory.* New York: Holt, Rinehart & Winston, 1968.

Baratz, J. A bidialectal task for determining language proficiency in economically disadvantaged Negro children. *Child Development,* 1969, *40,* 889–901.

———. Language abilities of black Americans, review of research. In Miller, K. & Dreger, R., eds., *Comparative Studies of Blacks and Whites in the United States.* New York: Seminar Press, 1973.

Bellugi, U. The acquisition of negation. Doctoral dissertation, Harvard University, 1967.

Bellugi, U. & Brown, R., eds. The acquisition of language. *Monographs of the Society for Research in Child Development,* 1964, no. 29.

Bereiter, C. & Engelmann, S. *Teaching Disadvantaged Children in Preschool.* Englewood Cliffs, N. J.: Prentice-Hall, 1966.

Berko, J. The child's learning of English morphology. *Word,* 1958, *14,* 50–177.

Berko, J. & Brown, R. Psycholinguistic research methods. In P. Mussen, ed., *Handbook of Research Methods in Child Development*. New York: John Wiley, 1960.

Bever, T. The cognitive basis of linguistic structure. In J. Hayes, ed., *Cognition and the Development of Language*. New York: John Wiley, 1970a.

———. The comprehension and memory of sentences with temporal relations. In G. B. Flores d'Arcais & W. J. M. Levelt, eds., *Advances in Psycholinguistics*. New York: American Elsevier, 1970b.

Bever, T., Fodor, J., & Weksel, W. On the acquisition of syntax: a critique of "Contextual Generalization." *Psychological Review*, 1965, *72*, 467–482.

Bierwisch, M. Semantics. In J. Lyons, ed., *New Horizons in Linguistics*. Harmondsworth, Middlesex.: Penguin, 1970.

Bloch, O. Premiers stades du langage de l'enfant. *Journal de Psychologie*, 1921, *18*, 693–712.

———. Le phrase dans le langage de l'enfant. *Journal de Psychologie*, 1924, *21*, 18–43.

Bloom, L. Language Development: Form and Function in Emerging Grammars. Doctoral Dissertation, Columbia University, 1968.

———. *Language Development: Form and Function in Emerging Grammars*. Cambridge, Mass.: MIT Press, 1970.

———. Why not pivot grammar? *Journal of Speech and Hearing Disorders*, 1971, *36*, 40–50.

———. *One Word at a Time: The Use of Single-word Utterances Before Syntax*. The Hague: Mouton, 1973.

———. Talking, understanding and thinking. In R. Schiefelbusch and L. Lloyd, eds., *Language Perspectives: Acquisition, Retardation and Intervention*. Baltimore, Md.: University Park Press, 1974a.

———. Review of J. Hayes, ed., *Cognition and the Development of Language*. 1974b, *50*, No. 2, 398–412.

Bloom, L., Hood, L., & Lightbown, P. Imitation in language development: If, when and why. *Cognitive Psychology*, 1974, *6*.

Bloom, L., Lightbown, P., & Hood, L. Structure and variation in child language. Monographs of the Society for Research in Child Development, 1975, no. 2.

Bloomfield, L. *Language*. New York: Holt, Rinehart & Winston, 1933.

Bowerman, M. *Learning to Talk: A Cross-Linguistic Study of Early Syntactic Development, with Special Reference to Finnish*. Cambridge: Cambridge University Press, 1973.

Braine, M. The ontogeny of English phrase structure: the first phase. *Language*, 1963a, *39*, 1–13.

———. On learning the grammatical order of words. *Psychological Review*, 1963b, *70*, 323–348.

———. On two types of models of the internalization of grammars. In D. Slobin, ed., *The Ontogenesis of Grammar*. New York: Academic Press, 1971a.

———. The acquisition of language in infant and child. In C. Reed, ed., *The Learning of Language*. New York: Appleton-Century-Crofts, 1971b.

Bransford, J. & Johnson, M. Contextual prerequisites for understanding: some investigations of comprehension and recall. *Journal of Verbal Learning and Verbal Behavior*, 1972, *11*, 717–726.

Brown, R. Linguistic determinism and the part of speech. *Journal of Abnormal Social Psychology*, 1957, *55*, 1–5.

———. *Social Psychology*. New York: Free Press, 1965.

———. The development of Wh questions in child speech. *Journal of Verbal Learning and Verbal Behavior*, 1968, *7*, 279–290.

———. The first sentences of child and chimpanzee. In R. Brown, *Psycholinguistics*. New York: Free Press, 1970.

————. *A First Language*. Cambridge, Mass.: Harvard University Press, 1973.

Brown, R. & Bellugi, U. Three processes in the child's acquisition of syntax. *Harvard Educational Review*, 1964, *34*, 133–151.

Brown, R., Cazden, C., & Bellugi, U. The child's grammar from I to III. In J. P. Hill, ed., *1967 Minnesota Symposia on Child Psychology*. Minneapolis, Minn.: University of Minnesota Press, 1969.

Brown, R. & Fraser, C. The acquisition of syntax. In C. Cofer & B. Musgrave, eds., *Verbal Behavior and Learning: Problems and Processes*. New York: McGraw-Hill, 1963.

Brown, R. & Hanlon, C. Derivational complexity and order of acquisition in child speech. In J. Hayes, ed., *Cognition and the Development of Language*. New York: John Wiley, 1970.

Bruner, J. On cognitive growth: II. In J. Bruner, R. Oliver, & P. Greenfield, eds., *Studies in Cognitive Growth*. New York: John Wiley, 1966.

Cazden, C. Environmental assistance to the child's acquisition of grammar. Doctoral dissertation, Harvard University, 1965.

————. Subcultural differences in child language: an inter-disciplinary review. *Merril-Palmer Quarterly*, 1966, *12*, 185–219.

————. The acquisition of noun and verb inflections. *Child Development*. 1968, *39*, 433–438.

Chafe, W. *Meaning and the Structure of Language*. Chicago: University of Chicago Press, 1971.

Chao, Y. R. The cantian idiolect: an analysis of the Chinese spoken by a twenty-eight-months-old child. *Semitic Philology*, University of California Publications, 1951, *11*, 27–44.

Chomsky, C. *The Acquisition of Syntax in Children from Five to Ten*. Cambridge, Mass.: MIT Press, 1969.

Chomsky, N. *Syntactic Structures*. The Hague: Mouton, 1957.

————. Review of "Verbal Behavior," by B. F. Skinner. *Language*, 1959, *35*, 26.

————. Formal discussion. In U. Bellugi & R. Brown, eds., The acquisition of language. *Monographs of the Society for Research in Child Development*, 1964, no. 29.

————. *Aspects of the Theory of Syntax*. Cambridge, Mass.: MIT Press, 1965.

————. *Cartesian Linguistics: A Chapter in the History of Rationalist Thought*. New York: Harper & Row, 1966.

Clark, E. How young children describe events in time. In G. B. Flores d'Arcais & W. J. M. Levelt, eds., *Advances in Psycholinguistics*. New York: American Elsevier, 1970.

————. On the acquisition of the meaning of *before* and *after*. *Journal of Verbal Learning and Verbal Behavior*, 1971, *10*, 266–275.

————. What's in a word? On the child's acquisition of semantics in his first language. In T. Moore, ed., *Cognitive Development and the Acquisition of Language*. New York: Academic Press, 1973.

————. On the child's acquisition of antonym pairs in two semantic fields. *Journal of Verbal Learning and Verbal Behavior*, 1972, *11*, 750–758.

Cromer, R. The development of temporal reference during the acquisition of language. Doctoral dissertation, Harvard University, 1968.

————. The development of the ability to decenter in time. *British Journal of Psychology*, 1971, *62*, 353–365.

de Boysson–Bardies, B. L'étude de la négation: aspects syntaxiques et lexicaux. Doctoral dissertation, L'Université de Paris, Paris, 1972.

Deutsch, M., Katz, I., & Jensen, A., eds., *Social Class, Race, and Psychological Development*. New York: Holt, Rinehart & Winston, 1968.

Dixon, T. & Horton, D. *Verbal Behavior and General Behavior Theory*. Englewood Cliffs, N. J.: Prentice-Hall, 1968.

Donaldson, M. & Wales, R. On the acquisition of some relational terms. In J. Hayes, ed., *Cognition and the Development of Language*. New York: John Wiley, 1970.

Entwisle, D., Forsyth, D. F., & Muuss, R. The syntagmatic-paradigmatic shift in children's word associations. *Journal of Verbal Learning and Verbal Behavior,* 1964, *3,* 19–29.

Ervin, S. Changes with age in the verbal determinants of word association. *American Journal of Psychology,* 1961, *74,* 361–372.

Ervin, S. & Miller, W. Language development. In H. Stevenson, ed., *Child Psychology*. 62nd yearbook of the National Society for the Study of Education, Part I. Chicago: University of Chicago Press, 1963.

Ervin-Tripp, S. Imitation and structural change in children's language. In E. Lenneberg, ed., *New Directions in the Study of Language*. Cambridge, Mass.: MIT Press, 1964.

Ervin-Tripp, S. Language development. In L. Hoffman and M. Hoffman, eds., *Review of Child Development Research*. New York: Russell Sage Foundation, 1966.

———. Discourse agreement: how children answer questions. In J. Hayes ed., *Cognition and the Development of Language*. New York: John Wiley, 1970.

Fillmore, C. The case for case. In E. Bach & R. Harms, eds., *Universals in Linguistic Theory*. New York: Holt, Rinehart & Winston, 1968.

Fodor, J. How to learn to talk, some simple ways. In F. Smith & G. Miller, eds., *The Genesis of Language*. Cambridge, Mass.: MIT Press, 1966.

Francis, H. Toward an explanation of the paradigmatic-syntagmatic shift. *Child Development,* 1972, *43,* 949–959.

Garrett, M., Bever, T., & Fodor, J. The active use of grammar in speech perception. *Perception and Psychophysics,* 1966, *1,* 30–32.

Gleason, H. *An Introduction to Descriptive Linguistics*. New York: Holt, Rinehart & Winston, 1961.

Gleitman, L., Gleitman, H., & Shipley, E. The child as grammarian. *International Journal of Cognition,* 1973.

Greenberg, J. Some universals of grammar with particular reference to meaningful elements. In J. Greenberg, ed., *Universals of Language*. Cambridge, Mass.: MIT Press, 1963.

Greenfield, P., Smith, J., & Laufer, B. *Communication and the Beginnings of Language*. New York: Academic Press, in press.

Grégoire, A. *L'apprentissage du langage*. Vol. 1, *Les Deux Premières Années*. Paris: Droz, 1937.

Gruber, J. Topicalization in child language. *Foundations of Language,* 1967, *3,* 37–65.

Guillaume, P. Les débuts de la phrase dans le langage de l'enfant. *Journal de Psychologie,* 1972, *24,* 1–25.

Hannerz, U. *Soulside: Inquiries into Ghetto Culture and Community*. Stockholm, Sweden: Almquist and Wiksele, 1969.

Harner, L. Children's understanding of linguistic reference to past and future. Doctoral dissertation, Columbia University, 1973.

Harris, Z. *Structural Linguistics*. Chicago: University of Chicago Press, 1955.

———. Cooccurrence and transformations in linguistic structure. *Language,* 1957, *33,* 283–340.

Hayes, J., ed., *Cognition and the Development of Language*. New York: John Wiley, 1970.

Higgins, T. & Huttenlocher, J. Symbols and other signs. In prep.

Hockett, C. *A Course in Modern Linguistics*. New York: Macmillan, 1958.

Holzman, M. The use of interrogative forms in the verbal interaction of three mothers and their children. *Journal of Psycholinguistic Research,* 1972, *1,* 311–336.

Horner, V. The verbal world of the lower class three-year-old: a pilot study in linguistic ecology. Doctoral dissertation, University of Rochester, 1968.

Horowitz, F. D. & Paden, L. Y. The effectiveness of environmental intervention programs. In B. Caldwell, & H. Riccuiti, eds., *Review of Child Development Research*, Vol. 3. Chicago: University of Chicago Press, 1973.

Huttenlocher, J. Children's language: word-phrase relationship, *Science*, 1964, *143*, 264–265.

Huttenlocher, J. & Strauss, S. Comprehension and a statement's relation to the situation it describes. *Journal of Verbal Learning and Verbal Behavior*, 1968, *7*, 300–304.

Huttenlocher, J., Eisenberg, K., & Strauss, S. Comprehension: relation between perceived actor and logical subject. *Journal of Verbal Learning and Verbal Behavior*, 1968, *7*, 527–530.

Huttenlocher, J. & Weiner, S. Comprehension of instruction in varying contexts. *Cognitive Psychology*, 1971, *2*, 369–385.

Huxley, R. The development of the correct use of subject personal pronouns in two children. In G. B. Flores d'Arcais & W. J. M. Levelt, eds., *Advances in Psycholinguistics*. New York: American Elsevier, 1970.

Ingram, D. Transitivity in child language. *Language*, 1971, *47*, 888–910.

Inhelder, B. & Piaget, J. *The Early Growth of Logic in the Child*. New York: Harper & Row, 1964.

Jacobs, R. & Rosenbaum, P. *English Transformational Grammar*. Waltham, Mass.: Blaisdell, 1968.

Jakobovits, L. & Miron, M., eds., *Readings in the Psychology of Language*. Englewood Cliffs, N. J.: Prentice-Hall, 1967.

Jakobson, R. *Child Language, Aphasia and Phonological Universals*. The Hague: Mouton, 1968 (originally in German, 1941).

Jenkins, J. & Palermo, D. Mediation processes and the acquisition of linguistic structure. In U. Bellugi & R. Brown, eds., The acquisition of language. *Monographs of the Society for Research in Child Development*, 1964, no. 29.

Jespersen, O. *Language: Its Nature, Development, and Origin*. London: Allen and Unwin, 1922.

Johnson, M., Bransford, J., and Solomon, S. Memory for tacit implications of sentences. *Journal of Experimental Psychology*, in press.

Kaplan, E. & Kaplan, G. The prelinguistic child. In J. Eliot, ed., *Human Development and Cognitive Processes*. New York: Holt, Rinehart & Winston, 1971.

Katz, J. & Fodor, J. The structure of semantic theory. *Language*, 1963, *39*, 170–210.

Kernan, K. Semantic relationships and the child's acquisition of language. *Anthropological Linguistics*, 1970, *12*, 171–187.

Kessel, F. The role of syntax in children's comprehension from age six to twelve. *Monographs of the Society for Research in Child Development*, 1970, no. 139.

Klatzky, R., Clark, E., & Macken, M. Asymmetries in the acquisition of polar adjectives: linguistic or conceptual? *Journal of Experimental Child Psychology*, in press.

Klima, E. & Bellugi, U. Syntactic regularities in the speech of children. In J. Lyons & R. Wales, eds., *Psycholinguistics Papers*. Edinburgh: Edinburgh University Press, 1966.

Kochman, T. Black English in the classroom. In C. Cazden, D. Hymes & V. John, eds., *The Functions of Language in the Classroom*. New York: Teachers College Press, 1972.

Kowalski, R. The development of the concept of speed and its associated language. Doctoral dissertation, Columbia University, 1972.

Labov, W. The logic of nonstandard English. In F. Williams, ed., *Language and Poverty: Perspectives on a Theme*. Chicago: Markham, 1970.

Labov, W., Cohen, P., Robbins, D., & Lewis, J. A study of nonstandard English of Negro and Puerto Rican speakers in New York City. Vols. I and II. Final Report, Cooperative Research Project, Office of Education, 1968.

Lahey, M. The role of prosody and syntactic markers in children's comprehension of spoken sentences. Doctoral dissertation, Teachers College, Columbia University, 1974.

Lakoff, G. Instrumental adverbs and the concept of deep structure. *Foundations of Language*, 1968, *4*, 4–29.

——. On generative semantics. In D. Steinberg & L. Jakobovits, eds., *Semantics: An Interdisciplinary Reader in Philosophy, Linguistics and Psychology*. New York: Cambridge University Press, 1971.

Leech, G. *Towards a Semantic Description of English*. Bloomington, Indiana: Indiana University Press, 1970.

Lees, R. Formal discussion. In U. Bellugi & R. Brown, eds., The acquisition of language. *Monographs of the Society for Research in Child Development*, 1964, no. 29.

Lenneberg, E. *Biological Foundations of Language*. New York: John Wiley, 1967.

Leopold, W. *Speech Development of a Bilingual Child*. 4 vols. Evanston, Ill.: Northwestern University Press, 1939–49.

Loban, W. *The Language of Elementary School Children*. Champaign, Ill.: National Council of Teachers of English, Research Report No. 1, 1963.

——. *Problems in Oral English*. Champaign, Ill.: National Council of Teachers of English, Research Report No. 5, 1966.

Lyons, J. & Wales, R. *Psycholinguistic Papers*. Edinburgh: Edinburgh University, 1966.

Macnamara, J. Cognitive basis for language learning in infants. *Psychological Review*, 1972, *79*, 1–13.

Maratsos, M. The use of definite and indefinite reference in young children. Doctoral dissertation, Harvard University, 1971.

McCarthy, D. Language development. In L. Carmichael, ed., *Manual of Child Psychology*. New York: John Wiley, 1954.

McNeill, D. Developmental psycholinguistics. In F. Smith & G. Miller, eds., *The Genesis of Language*. Cambridge, Mass.: MIT Press, 1966*a*.

——. A study of word association. *Journal of Verbal Learning and Verbal Behavior*, 1966*b*, *10*, 392–399.

——. *The Acquisition of Language*: *The Study of Developmental Psycholinguistics*. New York: Harper & Row, 1970.

McNeill, D. Personal communication, 1972.

McNeill, D. & McNeill, N. What does a child mean when he says "no"? In E. Zale, ed., *Language and Language Behavior*. New York: Appleton-Century-Crofts, 1968.

Menyuk, P. A preliminary evaluation of grammatical capacity in children. *Journal of Verbal Learning and Verbal Behavior*, 1963*a*, *2*, 429–439.

——. Syntactic structures in the language of children. *Child Development*, 1963*b*, *34*, 407–422.

——. Alternation of rules in children's grammar. *Journal of Verbal Learning and Verbal Behavior*, 1964, *3*, 480–488.

Miller, W. & Ervin, S. The development of grammar in child language. In U. Bellugi & R. Brown, eds., The acquisition of language. *Monographs of the Society for Research in Child Development*, 1964, no. 29.

Milligan, C. Children's understanding of regular and comparative adjectival forms. Paper presented to the Eastern Psychological Association, 1972.

Nelson, K. Structure and strategy in learning to talk. *Monograph of the Society for Research in Child Development*, no. 149, 1973.

O'Donnell, R., Griffin, W., & Norris, R. *Syntax of Kindergarten and Elementary School Children*: *A Transformational Analysis*. Champaign, Ill.: National Council of Teachers of English, Research Report No. 8, 1967.

Palermo, D. Research in language development: do we know where we are going? In L. Goulet & P. Baltes, eds., *Lifespan Developmental Psychology*. New York: Academic Press, 1970.

Palermo, D. & Molfese, D. Language acquisition from age five onward. Pennsylvania State University: Laboratory for the Study of the Symbolic Processes, 1971.

Piaget, J. *The Construction of Reality in the Child*. New York: Basic Books, 1954.

———. *The Psychology of Intelligence*. Patterson, N. J.: Littlefield, Adams, 1960.

———. *Six Psychological Studies*. New York: Random House, 1967.

Postal, R. Underlying and superficial linguistic structure. *Harvard Educational Review*, 1964, *34*, 246–266.

Raph, J. Language and speech deficits in culturally disadvantaged children: implications for the speech clinician. *Journal of Speech and Hearing Disorders*, 1967, *32*, 203–214.

Reed, C., ed., *Language Learning*. Champaign, Ill.: National Council of Teachers of English, 1971.

Rodd, L. & Braine, M. Children's imitations of syntactic constructions as a measure of linguistic competence. *Journal of Verbal Learning and Verbal Behavior*, 1971, *10*, 430–443.

Ronjat, J. *Le développement du langage observé chez un enfant bilingue*. Paris: Librairie Ancienne H Champion, 1913.

Sapir, E. *Language*. New York: Harcourt, Brace & World, 1921.

Schlesinger, I. M. Production of utterances and language acquisition. In D. I. Slobin, ed., *The Ontogenesis of Language*. New York: Academic Press, 1971.

Sherman, J. A. Imitation and language development. In H. W. Reese, ed., *Advances in Child Development and Behavior*. Vol. 6. New York: Academic Press, 1971.

Shipley, E., Smith, C., & Gleitman, L. A study in the acquisition of language: free responses to commands. *Language*, 1969, *45*, 322–342.

Sinclair-de-Zwart, H. Developmental psycholinguistics. In D. Elkind & J. Flavell, eds., *Studies in Cognitive Development*. New York: Oxford University Press, 1969.

Sinclair, H. The transition from sensory-motor behavior to symbolic activity. *Interchange*, 1970, *1*, 119–126.

Skinner, B. F. *Verbal Behavior*. New York: Appleton-Century-Crofts, 1957.

Slobin, D. I. The acquisition of Russian as a native language. In F. Smith & G. Miller, eds., *The Genesis of Language*. Cambridge, Mass.: MIT Press, 1966.

———. Imitation and grammatical development in children. In N. Endler, L. Boulter, & H. Osser, eds., *Contemporary Issues in Developmental Psychology*. New York: Holt, Rinehart & Winston, 1968.

———. Developmental psycholinguistics. In W. D. Dingwall, ed., *A Survey of Linguistic Science*. College Park, Md.: University of Maryland Press, 1971*a*.

Slobin, D. I., ed., *A Field Manual for Cross-cultural Study of the Acquisition of Communicative Competence*. Berkeley: University of California Press, 1967.

———. *The Ontogenesis of Grammar*. New York: Academic Press, 1971*b*.

Slobin, D. I. & Welsh, C. A. Elicited imitation as a research tool in developmental psycholinguistics. In C. A. Ferguson & D. I. Slobin, eds., *Studies of Child Language Development*. New York: Holt, Rinehart & Winston, 1973.

Smith, F. & Miller, G., eds., *The Genesis of Language*. Cambridge, Mass.: MIT Press, 1966.

Staats, A. Linguistic-mentalistic theory versus an explanatory S-R learning theory of language development. In D. I. Slobin, ed., *The Ontogenesis of Grammar*. New York: Academic Press, 1971.

Stern, C. & Stern, W. *Die Kindersprache*. Leipzig: Barth, 1907.

Stewart, W. Historical and structural bases for the recognition of Negro dialect. In J. Alatis, ed., *School of Languages and Linguistics Monograph Series*, no. 22, Washington, D. C.: Georgetown University Press, 1969.

Stockwell, R., Schachter, P., & Partee, B. *Integration of Transformational Theories of English Syntax*. Vols. I & II. Los Angeles, Calif.: University of California Press, 1968.

Strickland, R. How children learn their language. *Childhood Education,* 1963, *39,* 316–319.

Templin, M. *Certain Language Skills in Children.* Minneapolis, Minn.: University of Minnesota Press, 1957.

Volterra, V. Il "no." Prime fasi di sviluppo della negazione nel linguaggio infantile, *Istituto Psicologico,* Italy, Sept. 1971.

Watt, W. On two hypotheses concerning developmental psycholinguistics. In J. Hayes, ed., *Cognition and the Development of Language.* New York: John Wiley, 1970.

Weiner, S. On the development of *more* and *less, Journal of Experimental Child Psychology.* In press.

Williams, F., ed., *Language and Poverty.* Chicago: Markham, 1970.

Wolfram, W. *Sociolinguistic Description of Detroit Negro Speech.* Washington, D. C.: Center for Applied Linguistics, 1969.

6 The Development of Referential Communication Skills

SAM GLUCKSBERG
Princeton University

ROBERT KRAUSS
Columbia University

E. TORY HIGGINS
Princeton University

INTRODUCTION

Overview

DURING THE PAST TWO DECADES there has been a sharp increase of interest in the psychology of language and, among developmental psychologists especially, in the processes of language acquisition (see chapter 5 in this volume). Surprisingly, this interest in language and language acquisition has not been paralleled by much concern for the processes by which children learn to use language for one of its primary functions, communication.

The chapter reviews the major contemporary approaches to the problem of referential communicative competence and the developmental research that has been generated by these approaches. For the most part, studies and analyses of language acquisition per se will not be considered except where there is direct relevance to the communicative functions of language. The focus is on referential communication, that is, on situations in which the participant's task is to construct a message that enables someone else to know what that message refers to. In general, knowing what a message refers to can be characterized as being able to select or identify a target stimulus (the referent) from among a set of implicit or explicit alternatives (nonreferents). There are, of course, other important functions of interpersonal communication (such as expression of affect or emotion), but reference has been the most frequent concern of empirical developmental work. Reference is also the simplest of communicative functions to conceptualize and one of the most basic of communicative

Preparation of this paper was facilitated by USPHS Grant HD 01910 to Princeton University. The review of the literature includes materials published up until January 1973. We thank J. Flavell, F. Horowitz and G. Siegel for their perceptive comments and critiques of an earlier draft.

functions, particularly if requests and questions are subsumed under this topic.

One more explicit limitation of the chapter should be made clear at the outset. We will be concerned almost exclusively with verbal communication. No attempt will be made to review the literature on nonverbal or paralinguistic communicative modes such as gesture, facial expression, and so on. Although nonverbal communication is intrinsically interesting and necessary for a complete picture of the multifaceted ability of humans to communicate, there has been relatively little work done on its developmental aspects, and in our judgment the topic is in too early a stage of development to permit much in the way of sensible conclusions (see Wiener, Devoe, Rubinow, and Geller 1972). Nor will we attempt to review the voluminous social psychological literature on mass media and social influence. The findings of such studies frequently bear upon the use of language for communication purposes, but their focus is rather different from the sorts of interpersonal and referential processes we want to consider.

The organization of this chapter is as follows. First we make some distinctions of terminology. Then, we outline the developmental goal (what children apparently must and do acquire) by sketching an abstract and idealized version of speaker-listener interactions in a referential communicative situation, with some indications of the component processes involved. Next, we will discuss the specific theoretical approaches and models that investigators have used as a framework for their research. In the later sections we will review the data that bear on the theoretical issues raised previously, first in terms of the overall performance of communicating dyads, second in terms of the correlates of and component processes underlying communicative performance, and third in terms of the evidence from attempts to train communication skills. The final sections consider the implications of research and theory on referential communication for the study of language behavior in general.

1. *Linguistic skills and communication skills.* The emphasis on acquisition rather than usage stems from at least two sources. First, the availability of formal models describing the system of rules presumed to underlie linguistic competence has led directly to investigations of the processes by which such rules might be learned. On the other hand, the available models describing the nature of the specific skills or processes underlying communicative competence are relatively primitive, and consequently there has been far less impetus to pursue such models empirically.

A second factor that seems to have contributed to the relative paucity of interest in referential communication skills is the assumption, implicit in much of the linguistic and psycholinguistic literature, that linguistic competence is in some sense equivalent to or sufficient for communicative competence. A number of authors have taken issue with this point of view (e.g., Cazden 1970; Hymes 1964; Krauss and Glucksberg 1970; Olson 1970; Rommetveit 1968). In general these authors, among others, have argued that effective communication requires the development of a set of skills, many of them extralinguistic, and that these skills are not incorporated in models of linguistic competence per se.

2. *The process of reference. Referential versus denotative meaning.* One way to characterize the distinction between linguistic and communicative processes is to consider the distinction between referential and denotative meaning. The referential meaning of a word or phrase is the *particular* event, object, or relationship which the word represents in a specific context. For example, the referential meaning of the word "table" is a particular piece of furniture or a particular class of furniture. This meaning is highly specific and is context-bound.

In contrast, denotative meaning refers to that class of items which are exemplars of the generic idea or concept represented by a word. Consider the sentences: *Look at Mars* and *Look at that planet.* In the context of these sentences *Mars* refers to a particular object in the sky and *planet* refers to that same object. Hence, in this communicative context, the referential meanings of *Mars* and *planet* are identical. However, the denotative meanings of *Mars* and *planet* are quite different.

One aspect of the development of linguistic competence is the acquisition of at least some of the lexicon, and a central aspect of that is the acquisition of the denotative meanings of words. Learning how to use those words for referential purposes is, we shall argue, a central aspect of acquiring communicative competence.

The developmental task. The distinction between reference and denotation would be unnecessary if language could be characterized as a code, where one-to-one relationships were to hold between words and the things they represented. However, as Brown (1958) and others have pointed out, any given word can be used to refer to a large number of different things, and any given thing can be referred to by any one of a large number of words. In learning to use a language, children must not only acquire a vocabulary, they must also learn to select words from that vocabulary in order to communicate effectively. For example, in talking about a dime, one can conceivably use any of the following words: "dime," "coin," "ten-cent piece," "money," "change," "metal object," "cash." The word "dime" is most often used since it best specifies the referent among a set of potential alternatives (Brown 1958). The words "coin" or "money" are not usually as useful in talking about dimes because these words also refer to other objects and so do not uniquely specify the referent, "dime." These words are usually too general. Similarly, the phrase "1952 Roosevelt dime" would normally be too specific. The choice of the word "dime," in most circumstances, conforms to what Brown (1958) referred to as the level of usual utility: the most frequent name for a thing is that name which most usually discriminates the referent from potentially confusable nonreferents.

However, there are circumstances when the most usual name for something fails to specify the referent. The most usual name for a particular kind of vehicle may be "car," but that word would have little discriminating value to the attendant at a parking ramp. Similarly, an adequate reference for one person may not be adequate for another. One might use the word "reinforcement" to refer to a food pellet when talking with an experimental psychologist, but one would use the word "reward" when talking with a young child. These few examples suggest that the task of selecting the particular words to suit particular social and physical contexts may not be a trivial one and that learning how to do so may pose formidable developmental problems to be solved as children learn how to use their language effectively.

This analysis is strongly supported by recent findings on the course of the development of referential communication skills. In those circumstances where the most usual or most common name for something is either not available or not adequate for communication, young children perform well below adult levels, and adult levels of performance are not attained until the early teens (Flavell, Botkin, Fry, Wright, and Jarvis 1968; Glucksberg and Krauss 1967). The relative difficulty of such tasks for young children and the slow, protracted growth of the overall skill to communicate in referentially ambiguous contexts poses the central question for this chapter: what is involved in referential communicative performance, and how do children acquire referential communicative competence?

The Developmental Goal: An Idealized Speaker-Listener Interaction

In our view, communicative interaction can most usefully be viewed as the resultant of a set of component processes, only some of which are linguistic in nature. In this section we will outline in a general way the component processes involved and the manner in which they might fit together to permit effective communication. Details of the specific mechanisms involved will be left to the section that follows on theoretical models.

In the simplest referential communication situation, there are two people whom we arbitrarily label speaker and listener.[1] (Although these labels designate somewhat different functions in our idealized situation, it should be clear that each person will function as both speaker and listener over the course of an interaction.) In this situation there is a stimulus (or class of stimuli) which we will designate as the referent stimulus (or referent) and one or more additional stimuli designated the nonreferent(s). These nonreferents are at least potentially discriminable from the referent. It is the speaker's task to transmit a verbal message that will enable the listener to select the referent from among the nonreferents, and it is the listener's task to select the referent on the basis of the speaker's message. For convenience, we will assume that both speaker and listener have intentions that are consistent with the task requirements—that is, the speaker does not intend to confuse or mislead his or her listener and the listener does not intend deliberately to misunderstand his or her speaker. We will also assume, for purposes of analysis, that the verbal communication channel (oral or written) is the only mode available to speaker and listener for the transfer of information. Finally, we assume that both speaker and listener are competent speakers of a common language, at least insofar as syntax, semantics, and phonology are concerned. It is not, however, assumed that the lexicon of each is adequate to describe any particular set of referents.

The speaker's initial task is to determine the nonreferents from which the referent stimulus must be distinguished. Ordinarily, especially in experimental situations, this is not problematic, since both referent and nonreferents are explicitly defined for the speaker and are perceptually available to both participants. In many real-life situations, however, the nonreferents are not explicitly defined and must be inferred on the basis of the speaker's experience, as, for example, when one must describe oneself to a stranger to be met at an airport. In such cases, the speaker must infer, on the basis of his or her experience, the set of potential nonreferent persons with whom the other person might possibly confuse him. For example, if you are an adult male, it would be reasonable to infer that the set of potentially confusable nonreferents includes adult males between the ages of twenty and fifty who are not wearing working clothes or uniforms. On the basis of this inference it would not be particularly useful to tell someone meeting you at the airport to look for an adult male wearing trousers; most males at the airport will be wearing trousers, just as you will be.

Having defined the nonreferent set, the speaker must then determine

---

[1] For purposes of clarity the terms *speaker* and *listener* are used instead of the more precise terms *encoder* and *decoder*. The communication channel, unless specified, may be either oral or written.

which attributes are criterial—that is, which attributes potentially can be used to distinguish the referent from the nonreferents. In doing this he or she is, in effect, performing an information analysis on the set of stimuli. The task here is to define those stimulus elements or dimensions that are discriminating and those that are nondiscriminating (redundant). In doing so, a number of considerations must be kept in mind. First, depending upon the nature of the task, it may be necessary to distinguish stimulus dimensions that are permanent from those that are temporary. For example, a woman may be identifiable on a particular occasion by the clothes she is wearing, but such information may not be very helpful in identifying her on another occasion. The speaker must also make some judgment regarding the perceptual saliency of the various available dimensions. A particular dimension may be criterial in that it distinguishes referent from nonreferent, but may also involve so difficult a perceptual discrimination for the listener that it cannot be dependably used for communicative purposes. This is likely to be especially important when reliable discrimination requires special knowledge or skill, as with, say, fine wines.

Following this, the speaker must formulate a tentative message or encoding which denotes verbally those elements the speaker believes will aid the listener in distinguishing referent from nonreferents. It should be borne in mind that such encodings will virtually always consist of a less-than-complete representation of the referent. It is seldom possible or desirable to refer to every attribute (or even every criterial attribute) of the referent.

Having formulated a potential message, the speaker must subject it to some sort of test or evaluation regarding its communicative adequacy. For a competent speaker of a language, any particular encoding is one of a large number of potential encodings. In the test or evaluation phase, the speaker must decide whether to transmit the tentative encoding he or she has formulated or to formulate another (presumably more effective) encoding. In making this evaluation of his or her potential message, the speaker must bear a number of considerations in mind—and it must be stressed that these considerations are viewed by the speaker *from the point of view of the listener*. First, the speaker must determine whether the encoding incorporates those stimulus dimensions that adequately characterize the distinction between referent and nonreferent in terms of the perspective and capacities of the listener. For example, although in a particular situation color might be a criterial attribute, it would be ineffective for a speaker to encode the distinction between referent and nonreferent in terms of this attribute if he knew his listener was totally color blind. (Although this may appear to be a trivial point, the research by Flavell et al. [1968] and Higgins [1973] to be discussed below demonstrates it is not uniformly and automatically observed by children.) The speaker must also take into account the linguistic competence of his or her listener vis-à-vis the particular encoding he or she is evaluating. It may be the case that an encoding is adequate from a speaker's point of view but contains unfamiliar lexical items or complicated syntactic constructions that would render it ineffective insofar as a particular listener is concerned. For example, an automobile may be describable as a "phaeton," and such a characterization may, in principal, adequately distinguish it from among a set of other automobiles. But it would communicate effectively only if the listener was aware of the attributes subsumed under the term "phaeton" that define it as a subset of the larger category "automobile."

Presumably the speaker will decide whether or not a particular encoding is an adequate characterization of the referent. If it does not meet his or her subjective criterion of adequacy, he or she will reject it and formulate a new one, again subjecting it to the same sort of evaluation. This process will continue until the speaker generates an encoding that is adequate (or that is the most adequate of those available in his repertoire) given his view of the perceptual, conceptual, and linguistic resources of the listener. It is this encoding that will be transmitted to the listener.

At this point it is the listener's task to receive and decode the message that has been transmitted. Presumably he examines each stimulus and calculates the match between its perceptual features and the features encoded verbally in the speaker's message. He may decide that the match between stimulus and message is sufficient to permit a decision at a reasonable level of confidence, in which case he will perform whatever response the situation requires of him, or he may decide that the information contained in the message is inadequate to permit a choice. In the latter case, he may be forced to make a choice on the basis of insufficient information if no alternative is available or occurs to him. Alternatively, if the situation permits, he may himself assume the role of speaker and transmit a message designed to elicit additional information. This message may take the form of a simple request for more information (e.g., "You'll have to tell me more about it.") or it may itself refer to potentially criterial attributes not incorporated in the speaker's message (e.g., "Do you mean the tall one with the red stripes?"). In the latter case, of course, the listener has engaged in the same sorts of analytic and encoding processes that have been described above for the speaker. (Actually, the situation from the listener's point of view can be somewhat more complicated because the listener, too, may take into account the cognitive, perceptual, and linguistic capacities of the speaker, as when a parent makes allowances for the fact that a child calls all four-legged animals "Doggie.")

The feedback from the listener will ordinarily elicit a response from the speaker. This may consist of an entirely new message, a modification of the original message, or a repetition of the original message. In the case of a listener message that encodes information about the stimulus set, it may consist of a simple affirmation or negation (e.g., L: "Do you mean the tall one with red stripes?" S: "Yes, that's the one."). In most cases new speaker messages will require the same sorts of analyses and encodings as did the original.

It should be remembered that the above description is of an idealized speaker-listener interaction, and we are not contending that every communicative interaction incorporates all of these components. Rather, we have tried to describe the component processes that would optimize the effectiveness of communication. Also, we have been deliberately vague on the precise mechanisms that underly each component process. The theoretical models that are discussed in the next section, though consistent with the general description we have presented, provide alternative conceptualizations of some of these mechanisms, and these will be noted where they occur.

Although our description of the communicative process is an idealized one, can it serve as a developmental goal? There is some evidence from the research literature that this idealized description does reflect the communicative behavior of adults. We will refer briefly to some relevant findings here. There is clear evidence that adult speakers do take the characteristics of their listener into account in formulating messages. Ratner and Rice (1963) found differences in encoding depending upon whether a fictitious listener (a mechanic who needed directions) was characterized as knowledgeable or not about the area he had to travel through. Kingsbury (1968), in an analogous field experiment, found both qualitative and quantitative differences in the directions to a destination given to a questioner depending on whether or not the questioner implicitly or explicitly characterized himself as being "from out of town." Krauss, Vivekananthan, and Weinheimer (1968) found that speakers encoded information about the same stimulus array differently, depending on whether the message was to be used by themselves or by another person. They also found that the communicative effectiveness of such messages varied according to the user (self or other) at which they were aimed. Similar findings have been reported by Danks (1970). Both Rosenberg and Cohen (1966) and Krauss and Weinheimer (1967) have shown (for adults at least) that the nature of an encoded message varies as a function of the relation among the referent and nonreferent stimuli (Rosenberg and Cohen's stimuli were word pairs of varying associative overlap while Krauss and Weinheimer used color chips that varied in perceptual similarity). There is also reasonably clear evidence from the adult literature that feedback (listener-initiated messages) has a strong effect on speaker encoding. Maclay and Newman (1960), Krauss and Bricker (1967), and Krauss and Weinheimer (1966) found that accessibility to feedback (a two-way versus a one-way communication channel) affected both the quality and adequacy of speaker encodings.

The available evidence thus suggests very strongly that the major elements of our idealized speaker-listener interaction are represented in adult speaker and listener behaviors. Can this schematic outline be translated into a theoretical framework which can serve as an explicit guideline for research on and analysis of the development of these skills?

Theoretical Approaches to Speaker-Listener Interactions

Much of the research on referential communication with adults and with children seems to have been implicitly guided by conceptualizations of the competent speaker and listener that are similar to the schematic descriptions offered above. However, relatively few investigators have been explicit about the details of listener-speaker interactions, and few have based their work on formal models of that interaction. This section describes two approaches to the formalization of at least some of the mechanisms underlying communicative interactions and some of the research generated by these attempts.

1. *Two-stage stochastic models.* Rosenberg and Cohen (1966) have described both speaker encoding and listener decoding in terms of a two-stage stochastic choice process. Their typical experimental situation is one in which both speaker and listener are presented with a word pair (e.g., *woman* and *lady*). One of the words (e.g., *lady*) is designated as the target word (the referent) and the speaker is required to provide a one-word clue (like *Godiva*) that will enable the listener to select the target word *lady*. The listener's task is to select the target word, *lady,* on the basis of this clue, say, *Godiva*. According to the Rosenberg-Cohen model, the encoding process operates in two stages. In the first stage, the speaker samples from his repertoire of associative responses to the referent. The probability of a word's being sampled is a function of the strength of its association with the referent word. In the second stage (which Rosenberg and Cohen term the comparison stage) the speaker compares the associative strength of the tentatively selected clue word (message) to the referent word with its strength of association to the nonreferent word. The likelihood that a speaker will actually transmit a sampled word is a function of the magnitude of the difference between these two associative strengths: the greater the difference in favor of the target word (that is, the greater the associative strength of the clue word to the referent, relative

to its associative strength to the nonreferent), the greater the probability that the speaker will emit it. In the case where a sampled clue word is rejected in the comparison stage, the speaker resamples from his or her repertoire, the initial word being replaced in the pool of potential responses. The speaker repeats this two-stage process until a clue word is both sampled and emitted. The listener's choice process is equivalent to the speaker's comparison process. The listener compares the associative strength of the clue word both with the referent and with the nonreferents and chooses as a probabilistic function of the difference.

The Rosenberg-Cohen model identifies three distinct aspects of the encoding process which can contribute to communicative performance. First, because the content of the repertoire varies among speakers, a given speaker may simply not have available for sampling a clue word with sufficient associative strength to the referent to afford his or her listener the basis for a reliable selection. This seems likely to be a problem for young children whose vocabularies may be small relative to those of adult speakers. It also may be a problem as regards languages that do not provide lexicons that differentiate precisely within particular classes of referents. For example, Heider and Olivier (1972) found that Dani (the native language of an indigenous and relatively isolated people in West New Guinea) has only two lexical entries to encode the attribute of color—roughly translatable as "light" and "dark." Not surprisingly, speakers of this language are relatively ineffectual at encoding referents when color is the criterial attribute. Second, inadequate messages may derive from failures in the comparison stage. Clue words with strong association to the nonreferent (e.g., *female* for *woman-lady*) may be emitted because the speaker has inadequately compared the two associative strengths. Third, the model predicts that even competent speakers will occasionally emit inadequate messages. This is so because the comparison stage (like the sampling stage) is probabilistic. As a consequence, even clue words that are more strongly associated with the nonreferent than with the referent have a greater than zero (albeit small) probability of being emitted.

According to this model, when a speaker evaluates a particular clue word, he or she does so from the point of view of the listener—that is to say, the speaker necessarily takes into account the listener's perceptual and linguistic resources. This aspect of the model, however, has not been formally developed, and little of the work by Rosenberg, Cohen and their associates has been directed at it. Rather, most of their research has been aimed at testing the stochastic nature of the two processes, either assuming commonality of repertoire based upon word association norms or ensuring commonality of repertoire through training procedures. For the most part, these studies have found a close quantitative fit between the distributions of responses predicted by the model and those obtained from adult subjects (Rosenberg and Cohen 1966; Rosenberg and Donner 1968). The data from children shed further light on the operation of the model and are discussed below.

Glucksberg and Cohen (1968) have proposed a revision of the Rosenberg-Cohen model with respect to the nature of the comparison (or, as they term it, "editing") stage. They agree on the details of the sampling stage, but Glucksberg and Cohen have postulated a two-step comparison stage that differs from that of Rosenberg and Cohen. Reasoning that a speaker is unlikely to emit a clue word that will enable the listener to choose with less accuracy than he or she would achieve by simply guessing (that is, with a probability of .5 when only two stimuli are involved), Glucksberg and Cohen have posited that at least initially no clue words that are judged by the speaker to have an informative value less than .5 are emitted. In this context, the informative value of a clue word refers to the probability that a listener would make a correct choice from two alternatives if he or she were given that clue word. Poor clues are those with informative values of .5 or less. These should be categorically rejected. Good clues are those with informative values greater than .5 and, as in the Rosenberg and Cohen model, should be emitted with a probability that is a monotonic function of their informative value.

Furthermore, sampled words that are not used (those that are rejected) are not replaced in the repertoire to serve as candidates for future, repetitive sampling but instead are stored in a buffer of finite capacity while sampling continues from the remainder of the repertoire. If, due to time pressure, exhaustion of the repertoire, or other reasons, the speaker stops sampling without having used any of the messages he or she has thought of, he or she searches the buffer to determine the best available clue word of the ones he or she has already rejected. Here, as before, the likelihood of a clue word being used is a function of its informative value relative to that of the other words in the buffer.

In the vast majority of cases the two versions of the model do not make differential predictions, and each can serve as a formal model of a developmental target. One could use either model to assess whether children engage in the same kinds of social editing processes as do adults. However, there is one aspect of the differences between the two versions which has potentially important developmental significance. The Glucksberg and Cohen model states that an ideal speaker categorically rejects poor clues; the Rosenberg and Cohen model simply states that clues are used as a monotonic function of their informative value. What does an adult speaker actually do? In a test of this aspect of the models, Glucksberg and Cohen

(1968) found that adults (college students) do categorically reject poor clues. They evaluate and use good clues in accord with the Rosenberg and Cohen model. This means that children must learn not only to evaluate the quality of messages and to base message choice upon some evaluation of message adequacy, but they must also learn actively to inhibit messages below a certain level of adequacy if they are to achieve full adult competence. This particular issue will be addressed later in this chapter.

2. *Role-playing.* The message-evaluation component of the models outlined above is but one kind or instance of role-playing behavior, and a rather specialized and limited one at that. Flavell and his associates (1968) have proposed an approach which is less explicit but far more general than the approach represented by Rosenberg and Cohen. Great stress is placed on the necessity of the speaker's taking the role of a listener in evaluating the adequacy of a message. According to Flavell, a speaker first encodes a referent for himself or herself. Then a speaker attempts to discern those role attributes of his or her listener that are relevant to the referent, the set of nonreferents, and the potential message(s). On this basis, the speaker attempts to recode the message to suit his or her listener. The recoding may be identical to the speaker's initial self-encoding, or it may involve either a modification of the self-encoding or an entirely new message. Flavell does not detail the mechanisms that underlie the initial self-encoding or the recoding. This approach has generated a good deal of research by Flavell and his students. Since virtually all employ children as subjects, it will be described below in the relevant sections of the chapter. Suffice it to say that there are findings in the adult literature which demonstrate that encoding for self and encoding for others do differ markedly (see Krauss et al. 1968; Slepian 1959; Werner and Kaplan 1963). These findings, among others, are certainly consistent with Flavell's characterization of referential communication processes.

It is clear that the two general approaches discussed above are consistent with one another and with the generalized outline of communication processes sketched earlier. It is also clear that linguistic competence in the sense of syntactic, semantic, and phonological competence may be necessary but is still not sufficient for communicative competence. The developmental task of acquiring a language is not identical with the developmental task of acquiring verbal referential communication skills. We turn now to some direct evidence on this assertion in terms of the growth of communication skills.

Summary

1. A distinction must be made between linguistic competence and communicative competence.

2. In the perspective of this chapter communicative competence involves several component skills on the part of a speaker. These skills, in an idealized model, occur in a series of phases, the culmination of which is the receipt of a message by a listener.

3. Two approaches were described that have attempted to formalize some of the mechanisms underlying communicative interactions: two-stage stochastic models, and role-playing.

PERFORMANCE OF COMMUNICATION SKILLS

Communicative Performance of Dyads as a Function of Age

The earliest modern observations of the communicative behavior of children are contained in the now classic studies of egocentric and socialized speech by Piaget (1926). Piaget's observations and the inferences he drew from them are quite germane to the research to be discussed here. In general terms, Piaget observed that the utterances of children below the ages of seven or eight were communicatively inadequate, even when the intent to communicate was evident. He termed such utterances "egocentric speech" and speculated that it derived from the young child's inability to appreciate the differing points of view of others. This he contrasted with the "socialized speech" that is characteristic of older children and adults, in which the listener's point of view is taken into account in the formulation of the message.

Similar findings in a more structured experimental setting have been reported by Glucksberg, Krauss, and Weisberg (1966). These investigators employed a communication task in which visually separated speaker-listener pairs in the four to five year age-range had to communicate about novel graphic forms. Glucksberg et al. found that dyads were incapable of adequate communicative performance with these stimuli, although when pictures of familiar objects were used their performance was quite satisfactory. The young subjects' inadequate performance was attributed to their inability to take their listener into account in encoding the novel stimuli. In Flavell's terms, the children's messages were self-encodings, and familiar stimuli presented no problems since all had consensually agreed upon names. Glucksberg et al. (1966) found that the children's performance was virtually perfect when they responded to their own encodings, although these same messages communicated relatively little to others. Glucksberg et al. (1966) viewed their results as supporting Flavell's self-coding interpretation.

Cohen and Klein (1968) contended that the Glucksberg et al. findings could have been the result of paired-associate learning. The Cohen and Klein study employed a variation of the Rosenberg and Cohen referential word game. Using subjects in third, fifth, and seventh grades (mean ages 8.8, 10.8, and 12.8, respectively) they found that communication accuracy increased as grade level increased. The authors considered two alternative explanations of their findings: (1) that the deficient performance of their younger subjects was attributable to limitations in their associative repertoires (their vocabularies), or (2) that it was due to defects at the comparison stage. The latter explanation is compatible with the Glucksberg et al. (1966) conclusion, and the former is not. On the basis of internal analyses of their data, Cohen and Klein concluded that the former explanation appeared the more tenable. However, results of studies by Asher (1972), Saunders (1969), and Pietrinferno (1973) have cast considerable doubt on Cohen and Klein's conclusion.

The growing capacity of children to communicate as a function of age was also demonstrated in an experiment by Krauss and Glucksberg (1969). The procedure followed the Glucksberg et al. (1966) experiment described above. Matched-age pairs in kindergarten, first, third, and fifth grades differed little in their communicative adequacy on the first few trials but varied in the rate at which they decreased errors as a function of grade level. Kindergarteners showed no improvement over eight repetitive trials. Since both members of the dyads in this experiment were of the same age, it is conceivable that defective performance of dyads was due to the inability of young listeners to decode the messages rather than to age-related differences in speaker encoding. This possibility may be discounted on the basis of two kinds of evidence. First, as part of the experiment, Krauss and Glucksberg (1969) submitted the encodings used by children in their experiment to a sample of adults and asked them to identify the referents that had elicited each. Clear differences as a function of grade were found for the likelihood that an encoding would permit identification of the correct referent. Second, in an unpublished experiment by the same authors (discussed in Krauss and Glucksberg 1970), the ages of speaker and listener were varied orthogonally, making it possible to assess the relative contributions of the two roles to overall performance. Although the ages of speaker and listener were both significantly associated with overall dyad performance, the proportion of variance attributable to the speaker role was by far the greater of the two. However, there was no interaction between the two factors. This result, of course, need not hold for any and all situations. Tasks could be designed in which listener skills far outweigh speaker skills, or at least where variability in listener skills could be an important source of the variability of dyad or group performances.

Most recently, Higgins (1973) tested pairs of children where the referents and nonreferents were pictures of scenes from a story that takes place in a small model town. For dyads where the speaker (encoder) and listener (decoder) had no information in common ("stranger" dyads), significant age-related differences in performance were found for both oral and written channels. However, when the members of each dyad had important information in common ("neighbor" dyads), age-related differences were found only for the oral channel. These data point up the care that should be taken in generalizing age- or grade-related performance differences.

A study by Fishbein and Osborne (1971) demonstrated this point in the context of another task-specific variable. First-grade speakers played a communication game using novel graphic forms (as in Glucksberg et al. 1966) with either first- or fifth-grade listeners. The relative performances of first- and fifth-grade pairs varied as a function of knowledge of results. For example, when feedback conditions are held constant, fifth graders perform better than do first graders. However, first graders under "optimal" feedback conditions do as well as fifth graders under less optimal conditions, indicating that the relatively poor performance of young children may be, at least in part, situation-bound. Hence task-specific variables must always be considered quite carefully.

The developmental picture obtained from studies of dyad performance in communication tasks as a function of age or grade is relatively straightforward and clear. Both speaking and listening skills contribute to communicative performances, and both sets of skills develop with age, with children in their early teens demonstrating normal adult competence levels. Because of their nature, however, studies of overall dyadic performance can only provide this kind of general information about the shape of the development of communication skills. These studies cannot, in themselves, provide much insight into the development of the component elements and processes that contribute to and underlie the overall performance. They also cannot provide much information about those factors that may be correlated with communicative behaviors. For that it is necessary to consider studies that are specifically directed to the specific correlates of and component processes underlying the development of speaker and listener skills.

Correlates of Communication Performance

1. *Intelligence measures.* It would seem that the relation between measured intelligence and communicative performance would have been explored rather thoroughly and that generally positive results would have been found. This has not been the case. There have not been many studies of the relation between intelligence measures and measures of communicative performance, and the few studies that have explored this

relation do not provide sufficient evidence for any definite conclusions.

Finfgeld (1966) found no relationship between a measure of the ability to select words to convey an intended meaning and measures of intelligence, verbal-reasoning ability, or vocabulary. The subjects in this study were young adults, and neither sex nor choice of college major were related to a measure of commuication ability. These data suggest that communication abilities are relatively independent of standard reasoning and verbal abilities, but this interpretation cannot be strongly defended. To begin with, the subject sample was highly restricted, consisting entirely of college freshmen. Second, it is not at all clear what Finfgeld's communication test measured because no external validity criteria other than the ratings of "expert" judges were provided.

Rackstraw and Robinson (1967), using three different communication tasks, found no relations among IQ and their measures of communicative performance. Similarly, Ruth (1966) found no reliable correlations between IQ scores and communicative accuracy (except for cross social-class pairs in one of two schools). Krauss and Glucksberg (1969) also found no relation between IQ and either dyad's accuracy or the effectiveness of an encoder's message. However, relations between IQ scores and communication accuracy scores were found in two other studies (Baldwin, McFarlane, and Garvey 1971; Higgins 1973). Both of these studies involved larger samples than the studies mentioned above. Unfortunately, there are so many other differences among these various studies that no firm conclusions can be drawn at this time.

2. *Role-taking and measures of egocentrism.* To the extent that adequate referential communication requires a speaker to assume the perspective of others, role-taking abilities should be related to the ability to communicate accurately and efficiently. The empirical support for this assumption is sparse. Virtually all cognitive abilities will improve or increase with age. Therefore, to find that both role-taking and communicative performances improve with age, or that egocentrism (however measured) declines with age while communicative performance improves, says very little about the functional relations among these variables. The nature of most of the available evidence, unfortunately, hardly goes beyond this. Piaget is clear about the relations. Egocentric thought is partly responsible for the communication behavior of young children, a view shared by Flavell et al.: "Thus, intellectual egocentrism is fundamentally an inability to take roles; it is an inability . . . to search out the role attributes of others, compare them with one's own, and make effective use of the comparison in any of a variety of adaptations" (1968, p. 17). One of these adaptations is communication, and Flavell et al., while expressing caution and awareness of the difficulties in drawing causal in-

ferences from correlational data, have taken the position that cognitive egocentrism is a major contributing factor to the communication inadequacies of children.

What are the data relating role-taking, cognitive egocentrism, and communication behaviors? Anecdotal observations of egocentric-like behavior in the context of poor communication performance are abundant. For example, Glucksberg, Krauss, and Weisberg (1966) reported that a nursery-school child described two different referents (geometric forms) in the same way: one referent was *daddy's shirt*; the other was *another daddy's shirt*. In a similar context, where four-year-old children attempted to communicate with one another without visual contact, the following conversation clearly qualifies as egocentric:

> Speaker: It's a bird.
> Listener: Is this it?
> Speaker: No.

Neither speaker or listener in this case seemed to display any awareness of an important characteristic of their mutual situation—they could neither see one another nor see what they were each talking about. The difficulty with an interpretation or explanation in terms of egocentrism is that the same behaviors are, at one and the same time, judged as poor in communication terms and as egocentric. Lacking an independent criterion or clear definition for egocentrism, virtually any poor message (that is, a message conveying no useful information) could be characterized as egocentric. Similarly, poor messages are used to infer inadequate role-taking abilities.

This problem permeates the studies that examine the relations among these concepts. Role-taking abilities do increase with age and so does communication performance. Milgram and Goodglass (1961) had children from grades two through eight judge which of two word-association responses would be given by adults and by children, using a 48-item stimulus list. Their measure of role-taking was the difference between the two instructional sets (adults vs. children). Children in grades four through eight made differential choices under these two instructions; children in the lower grades did not. The differences among the four higher grades were minimal. To the extent that this task measures role-taking ability, fourth- through eighth-graders displayed more of that ability than did second- and third-graders. Similarly, Dymond, Hughes, and Raabe (1952) reported differences between second- and sixth-graders on projective measures of empathy and on social insight scores. However, the relations among the scores are not striking. Feffer and Gourevitch (1960) also reported increases in both role-taking scores and scores on a battery of

Piagetian tasks (including conservation of mass, conservation of number, class inclusion tasks) as a function of age. Here, too, the data were not as striking as one would like, given the growth of communication skills beyond the age of thirteen (cf. Glucksberg and Krauss 1967). Indeed, Feffer and Gourevitch's (1960) measure of role-taking ability suggested that twelve-year-olds are better than thirteen-year-olds, if they differ at all. If role-taking ability is a major contributor to the variance in communicative performance, then currently available measures have too low a ceiling to discriminate among children aged twelve and older.

The most thorough and ambitious study of role-taking in the context of communicative behavior was conducted by Flavell in collaboration with Botkin, Fry, Wright, and Jarvis (1968). Using a variety of role-taking tasks and communication tasks involving role-taking, these investigators found, in general, that role-taking performance increased with age and that communicative performance also increased with age. The communication performances differed from role-taking performances only in the sense that role-taking was assessed in the context of a communication task. An example of a role-taking task is the well-known Mountains task devised by Piaget, in which a child is asked to indicate which of several alternative views of a scene some specified observer sees. An example of a role-taking task in a communication context was provided by Cooper and Flavell (in press). They required the child to judge, either implicitly or explicitly, what someone else's view or information was, and to provide someone else with information. In this latter study, Cooper and Flavell applied distinctions that have been proposed by Flavell et al. (1968) among five components of role-taking behavior. These are: "*existence,* the awareness of . . . perspectives in general; *need,* knowing that analyzing perspectives is useful . . . ; *prediction,* the ability to infer the task-relevant role attributes of another . . . ; *maintenance,* the ability to maintain these inferences over time . . . ; and *application,* the ability to apply (that) awareness . . . to particular situations" (Cooper and Flavell, in press). Using two tasks in which second- and sixth-graders communicated information about a game and about visual displays, respectively, Cooper and Flavell found that the variance in second-graders' performance was primarily accounted for by variance in *general role-taking abilities* (the first three components listed above), while the variance in sixth-graders' performance was related to variance in *task-specific role-taking abilities* (the last two components listed above). However, the relation between role-taking abilities and communicative behaviors is still obscure in this study because both role-taking and communication abilities were inferred from the same set of behaviors. For example, one measure of task-specific role-playing was the extent to which two versions of a story differed; one version intended to be told to a child, the other to an adult. Operationally, role-taking ability here is primarily communication ability.

Bailey (1971) developed a graded series of tasks in which adequate message selection required subjects to assume increasingly complex perspectives from their listener's point of view. Using school children in grades one, three, five, and seven, he found that his tasks formed a highly reliable Guttman Scale. In Bailey's experiment, grade level was positively related to Guttman Scale score—that is, to the ability to select adequate messages over the range of tasks. However in this study, as in most of those discussed above, no separate assessment of role-taking ability apart from the communication tasks was made.

In the few studies where role-taking, egocentrism, and communication ability were assessed independently, the data are merely suggestive. Cowan (1967) found a fairly strong relation between a spatial perspective test of egocentrism and measures of communication style (egocentric vs. non-egocentric) and a weak relation between the former measure and the communicative accuracy of nine to ten-year-old pairs, with no relation at all for eight-year-old pairs. Kingsley (1971) independently measured communicative performance and egocentrism in kindergarten and third-grade children. He took three measures of communication and an additional measure of communication-related egocentrism. He also took two measures of communication-task-specific abilities (one perceptual, the other verbal) and three measures of egocentrism (spatial, pictorial, and verbal). He then intercorrelated these nine measures. For kindergarten children virtually none of the variance in communicative performance was accounted for by the variance in the egocentrism measures. Indeed, the three egocentrism task scores did not even correlate with one another. About 25 percent of the variance in these children's communication scores could be accounted for by their scores in *communication-task-specific* perceptual and labeling tasks. For the third-graders the pictorial and spatial egocentrism scores did correlate reliably with one another and these scores did, in general, correlate with communication scores. Overall, in contrast to the kindergarten children, about 25 percent of the variance in the third-graders' communicative performance could be accounted for by their performance in the spatial and pictorial egocentrism tasks.

These findings, which were limited to third-graders, seem, in any case, to lack generality. When Kingsley used a different communication task (Glucksberg and Krauss's [1967] stack-the-blocks task) none of the noncommunication tasks was related to kindergarteners' communicative performance.

Feffer and Gourevitch (1960) developed a test of role-taking abilities (the RTT) and reported that scores on this test were related to scores on a variety of Piagetian tests of cognitive development. A moderate relation between these two sets of scores remained after both age and Wechsler Intelligence scores had been partialled out. With this as the only index of the validity of the RTT, Feffer and Suchotliff (1966) examined the relationship between adults' RTT scores and performance in a communication task, the game of password (similar to Rosenberg & Cohen's [1966] test). In this game the speaker must give a listener a series of single clue words so that the listener can guess a target word. The measures of performance were the number of clue words needed and the time taken to guess the target word. When the listener could speak freely and provide feedback to the speaker, a reliable but moderate relation between communication performance and RTT scores was found. When the listener was silent, then RTT scores were not related to communication performance.

Higgins (1973) also compared role-taking and communication ability, using a modified version of Sarbin and Jones's (1956) "As-If" test of role-taking ability. In general, the findings were inconclusive. In only one of four grades tested was the speaker's communicative performance related to the measure of role-taking ability, and in only one of the four grades (not the same one) was the listener's performance related to role-taking performance.

The available evidence leads to the conclusion that egocentrism and role-taking are too general as concepts to be very useful for an analysis of the development of referential communicative competence. The most promising approach at the moment would seem to be Flavell's (1968) attempt to develop a taxonomy of role-taking behavior within the general context of the development of children's abilities to make inferences about others.

3. *Social-class correlates of communication skills.* The interest in intellectual and cognitive correlates of communication abilities stems primarily from a concern for an analytic understanding of communicative processes and their development. The interest in difference in communication skills as a function of group membership does not seem to be motivated in quite the same way. This latter interest seems to be derived from three sources. First, to the extent that there are distinctive subcultural languages (dialects, jargons, and so on) associated with group membership, the possibility exists that members of certain groups will be better or worse equipped to encode particular classes of referents by virtue of the properties of their natural language. For example, in Heider and Olivier's (1972) study, speakers of Dani (a West New Guinea language with a very meager color lexicon) were found to communicate poorly about referents that had color as criterial attributes although they were apparently able to communicate adequately about other classes of referents. Although it is true

that there are identifiable differences among class-related dialects in the same language, it should be borne in mind that such differences are generally minor in nature and do not approach in magnitude the differences one finds between historically unrelated languages. As Labov (1970) has argued, the differences between Standard American English and Northern Black English (perhaps the most divergent of American standard dialects) are relatively superficial, the most striking being the differences in the transformational rules that relate deep structure to surface structure in the system of negation. Even if one takes the opposing view that the differences are major, it is difficult to see how class-related differences in communicative abilities might be attributed to formal differences among subcultural languages per se.

Another source of interest derives from the speculation that class-related experience (especially in socialization) gives rise to different communicative orientations which in turn lead to different uses in communication of the same language. Bernstein's (1965, 1970) theory of "elaborated" and "restricted" codes makes such an assumption and attempts to detail differences in "communicative style" deriving from differences in socialization. Bernstein's work, because it has been directed primarily at properties of the two dialects (or "codes" as he terms them) rather than at their function in communication situations, will not be reviewed in this chapter. On the basis of the presently available evidence, it is our judgment that the theory still lacks empirical support. A number of criticisms of Bernstein's approach are presented in Labov (1970). To the best of our knowledge, there have been no direct measures of the communicative effectiveness of "elaborated" and "restricted" codes, where effectiveness is objectively defined.

A final source of interest in group-related differences in communication abilities derives from an interest in group differences. Although there is certainly adequate scientific justification for such interests, it does seem to us that there is an unfortunate tendency, in English and American psychology particularly, to apply indiscriminately to groups measures that appear to differentiate reliably among individuals, and vice versa. It must be stressed here that observed differences in communication skills associated with group membership can derive from a variety of factors that are irrelevant to the intrinsic abilities of speakers. Among them are differential familiarity with the stimulus materials employed, the reactive nature of experimental settings, and so on. Given the rudimentary state of our knowledge of the components of communication abilities, it should be clear that observed differences must be interpreted with great caution.

Assuming for the moment that such differences do exist, what might their nature be?

Two kinds of differences might exist. First, we may be able to detect differences in overall performance on any one or another type of communication task. These differences would be analogous to the differences in communicative performance among children of varying ages discussed above. Second, we may also be able to detect differences in one or more of those component skills and abilities that contribute to communication performance, such as the knowledge of the listener, the ability to use that knowledge, and so forth.

Rather than review the literature on these matters in detail, we will summarize the relevant findings and offer some interpretations and conclusions that may be drawn, given the available evidence. In this summary we will restrict the discussion to the literature on referential communication. The literature on class-related differences in language and linguistic abilities has been extensively reviewed and discussed elsewhere (see chapter 5 in this volume).

Overall, we have a rather confusing and contradictory picture. Some investigators have found clear social-class differences in communicative performance (Baldwin and Garvey 1970; Heider 1971; Krauss and Rotter 1968; Schatzman and Strauss 1955). Others have not (Higgins 1973; Rackstraw and Robinson 1967; Ruth 1966). Still other results have been unclear on this issue (Brent and Katz 1967; Cowan 1967). Three factors seem important in this context. First, are social-class differences found when the social-class groups are matched for intelligence test scores? Second, are social-class differences found when the social-class groups are matched for educational background and experience? Finally, how different are the social-class groups being compared?

With respect to social-class differences in communicative performance when intelligence differences have been controlled for, the picture is still unclear. In two studies where social-class groups did not differ on intelligence test scores, no communicative performance differences were found (Higgins 1973; Ruth 1966). In two studies where communicative performance of social classes differed, no intelligence measures were reported (Heider 1971; Krauss and Rotter 1968), and in a third study (Baldwin, McFarlane, and Garvey 1971) social-class differences in communicative performance were found even when the effect of IQ differences was partialed out through a covariate analysis. In any case, as we have seen above, it is not clear that intelligence test performance is related to communicative performance, or, if it is, under what circumstances. More evidence is clearly needed on this point.

With respect to educational background and communicative performance, the general pattern seems to be that one is more likely to find social-class differences when the subject populations come from different schools than when they come from the same schools. In the two studies where the social-class groups were drawn from the same schools, no social-class differences were found (Higgins 1973; Ruth 1966). However, there is an alternative explanation for these findings. When two social-class groups are in the same school it is quite unlikely that they would differ as markedly from one another in terms of socioeconomic status (SES) measures as they would if they were from two different schools. Similarly, it is more likely that groups from different schools would include an extremely low SES group, and it may be that only extremely low SES groups differ from all other SES groups. The Krauss and Rotter (1968) study, the Heider (1971) study, and a study by Baldwin and Garvey (Thelma Baldwin, personal communication) included children from different schools and extremely low SES groups. The Higgins and the Ruth studies drew their samples from the same schools and did not include extremely low SES groups. One plausible hypothesis concerning social-class differences is that SES groups do not, in general, differ from one another. If one compares a middle-class group with a working-class group, no differences would be expected. However, both of these groups would differ from unskilled and/ or unemployed groups. This hypothesis does fit the available data, but obviously requires a direct test and careful diagnostic research to explain or account for any differences that might be obtained.

Finally, how should we interpret whatever differences we may find? In our discussion so far we have tended to imply that age-related differences in communicative performances are similar in kind to social-class differences. Both kinds of differences have been implicitly treated as reflecting the same kinds of differences in underlying processes. This may be grossly misleading. When one compares social-class groups, one compares people of the same chronological age. If there are cognitive differences among such groups, they need not be of the same kind as cognitive differences among children of different ages. For example, differences among age groups may reflect differences in general cognitive development, while differences among social-class groups may reflect differences in task-specific abilities. If this is the case, then one would expect that practice effects would be more marked for social-class group differences than for age group differences. In other words, the sources of the differences among different age groups might very well be quite different than the sources for any differences among different social-class groups. Unfortunately, all we have at the moment are gross measures of overall performance and confusing ones at that. If there are differences among SES groups in communication skills, they have not been clearly demonstrated. If such differences were to be found, we would not know what they meant.

In our view, meaningful assessment of social-class differences needs to proceed from a fuller and deeper understanding of the particular behaviors involved. When we understand both the tasks we use and the behaviors required for those tasks, we can then assess diagnostically and perhaps do something about whatever specific differences we may find. In short, our failures with training studies, described below, are paralleled by our failures in coming to any firm conclusions regarding group differences, and the reasons underlying these two failures overlap considerably.

Component Processes Underlying Communicative Performance

We have yet to address directly the question, "What do children learn or acquire when they develop referential communicative competence?" One approach to this question is represented by the literature on cognitive and other correlates of communication ability. A second approach is represented in this section, where the focus is on the development of those component processes which, taken together, comprise referential communicative behavior.

1. *Sensitivity to the referent-nonreferent array.* From the studies described previously it seems clear that adults vary their description of a referent as a function of the context in which it appears. That is, adults generally provide information to a listener that discriminates between the referent and potentially confusable nonreferents. This ability to tailor one's descriptions to fit the referent-nonreferent array does vary with age. Typically, younger children provide more unnecessary or nondiscriminating information than do older children (Flavell et al. 1968; Higgins 1973). For example, if two faces in an array are smiling, then reference to a smile is useless in discriminating between those faces. In an unpublished study by Glucksberg and Kim (1969) nursery-school children had to tell a listener how to stack a set of colored blocks on a peg. If the children were set to use one-word descriptions and two blocks differed with respect to one color but shared a second color, then the children were just as likely to name the redundant color as the informative color— that is, if one block was red and blue and the other red and green, then "red" was just as probable a description as blue or green. At least some of the variance between children of different ages can be attributed to this component of the editing process, namely, discriminating between criterial and noncriterial attributes of referents and nonreferents. The specific proportion of variance attributable to this component should, of course, vary from task to task as well as with the age or stage of development.

2. *Sensitivity to characteristics of the listener and the listener's situa-*

tion. Just as a message about a referent should vary as a function of the context of that referent, messages should also vary as a function of the particular listener or set of listeners. The messages should, ideally, take into account who the listener is (one wouldn't speak in French to someone who knows no French), what the listener already knows, and what the listener needs to know. In order to adapt messages to the particular needs of a listener a speaker must (a) know what those needs are and (b) be able to make the appropriate decisions on the basis of that knowledge. Knowledge of other people obviously increases with age (Milgram and Goodglass 1961), and the apparent ability to adapt messages to particular listeners as a function of their situation and the information they have also increases with age (Flavell et al. 1968; Higgins 1973). For example, younger children's messages to a blindfolded person versus their messages to a person who can see what is being talked about did not differ as much as did older children's messages (Flavell et al. 1968). The same was true of children's messages to a "stranger" versus those to a "neighbor" who has information in common with them (Higgins 1973). Flavell et al. and Higgins found that older children were more likely to take into account what other people already knew or did not know and modified their messages accordingly.

Even very young children, however, display this kind of sensitivity to the needs of others. Gelman and Shatz (1972) found that four-year-olds spoke differently to adults as compared to two-year-old children. Speech directed to two-year-olds was shorter, simpler, and contained more attention-maintaining utterances (like "look") than was speech directed to adults.

Whether one classifies these behaviors as role-taking or as communication skills (or both), they generally do covary with age and with overall communicative performance.

3. *Sensitivity to listeners' behavior (feedback).* Skilled adult speakers do not only tailor their messages to fit the referent arrays and the perceived characteristics of their listeners; they also respond appropriately to feedback from their listeners. If a listener indicates that he or she doesn't understand a message, then an adult will usually provide a longer message (Maclay and Newman 1960). If the listener indicates understanding, then subsequent messages become shorter and more code-like (Krauss and Weinheimer 1964, 1966; Loewenthal 1968; Maclay and Newman 1960). This particular effect of listener feedback is usually absent in younger children, partly because their messages are brief to begin with. In one study of communication between pairs of children, third-, fifth-, seventh-, and ninth-graders were tested in the Glucksberg et al. (1966) stack-the-blocks game. Grade three through five children did not differ

among themselves in communicative accuracy, while ninth-graders approached adult performance (Glucksberg and Krauss 1967). Covarying with communicative accuracy was mean length of message. Ninth-graders' initial messages were relatively long and decreased systematically over trials. The younger children's messages were initially short and did not vary in length over trials. If length of an initial message can be taken as an indication of that message's adequacy, then only the ninth-graders in this study could be said to be tailoring their messages to their listeners' needs.

The effects of a listener's behavior upon communicative behavior was examined more directly by Glucksberg and Krauss (1967) by examining children's and adult's responses to feedback from a listener. Again employing the stack-the-blocks task, children in kindergarten, first, third, and fifth grades, as well as adults, were told, in three conditions respectively, "I don't understand which one you mean"; "Tell me more about it"; or "I don't understand which one you mean, tell me more about it." Taking adult behavior as the standard, no adult simply repeated the apparently inadequate message or responded with silence. All adults, as well as all third- and fifth-graders, either modified their initial description or provided a new description. Kindergarten children, however, tended to respond with a repetition or silence, and first-graders fell between the younger and older children. Similar effects of negative feedback as a function of age were reported by Jarvis (Flavell et al. 1968).

One source of difficulty for the younger children may be the rather inexplicit feedback provided. In a later study, Peterson, Danner, and Flavell (1972) compared the responses of four- and seven-year-old children to implicit and to explicit feedback. Implicit feedback was provided in two ways: either by a facial expression that was intended to indicate lack of understanding or by the statement "I don't understand. I don't think I can guess that." The explicit feedback consisted of the statements, "Look at it again. What else does it look like? Can you tell me anything else about it?" The results for the implicit feedback conditions were comparable to those of Glucksberg and Krauss. Only four four-year-olds and seven seven-year-olds (each out of twenty-four) gave at least one message reformulation in response to the facial expression. Seven four-year-olds and twenty seven-year-olds (each out of twenty-four) responded appropriately to the implicit verbal feedback by producing a different message, but all subjects responded appropriately to the explicit instruction by producing a different message. Apparently, explicit feedback must be quite specific, since Glucksberg and Krauss's (1968) instruction, "Tell me more about it" did not have the effect of the explicit instruction used by Peterson et al. (1972).

Young speakers, then, do worse than older speakers in virtually every aspect of communicative behavior that has been assessed so far. Do younger listeners also display deficiencies?

4. *The role of the listener.* In general, young listeners paired with adult speakers do quite well in communication tasks. Higgins (1973) found that for speakers (encoders) the developmental differences obtained were large and significant in both the oral and written channels, whereas for listeners (decoders) only the oral channel yielded any significant developmental effects. Still, the performance of a speaker-listener pair generally improves both when the speaker is older and when the listener is older. What sorts of things can a listener do to improve communicative performance?

Listeners can do at least three things within a communicative interaction. First, they can judge or estimate their confidence or certainty of understanding. That is, they can recognize ambiguous or noninformative messages as such. Second, if they recognize that a message or communication is inadequate, they can make this known to the speaker. Finally, they can specify the additional information that is needed in order to clarify the message.

A number of studies of adult listening behavior have illustrated these listener processes. Rosenberg and his associates (Rosenberg and Donner 1968; Rosenberg and Gordon 1968; Rosenberg and Markham 1971) have demonstrated that adult listeners, when faced with referentially ambiguous choices, recognized the ambiguity and made appropriate choices on a probabilistic basis. Adult listeners in the Krauss and Weinheimer paradigm also behaved appropriately; when messages were ambiguous, these listeners provided appropriate feedback to the speaker and postponed making a choice until they were fairly certain that their choice would be correct. The pattern of listener utterances during the task reflected this behavior. Initially, listeners did a lot of talking. After several repetitions of referents and messages, listeners said very little. This decrease in listener utterances paralleled the decrease in the length of reference phrases used by speakers. Children, on the other hand, said very little as listeners, and no pattern of change as a function of repetition was evident until about the ninth grade (Glucksberg and Krauss 1967). Ninth-grade listener behavior paralleled that of adults. Initially, there were many listener utterances, and these decreased over trials.

The only other study we found in this context was reported by Flavell et al. (1968). These investigators tested the ability of third-, seventh- and eleventh-graders to detect inadequacies in a message having to do with following directions using a map. The performance of the third-graders was poorer than that of the older children. Either they could not interpret maps adequately, or they could not detect the inadequacies in the message, or both.

*Why Do Children Perform Poorly in Referential
Communication Tasks?*

1. *Response repertoires and editing strategies.* Given the array of developmental differences in the components of communication skills, it is
not surprising that young children communicate poorly. Poorer performance of younger children in any given communication task could result
from deficiencies in any one or any combination of the component skills
involved, including, of course, limited vocabularies. Attempts to specify
the source of young children's difficulties in communication tasks can be
classified into two categories. The first involves studies that have employed a specific experimental paradigm and a specific communication
model, with the sole exemplars to date done in the context of Rosenberg
and Cohen's two-stage communication model. The second involves demonstrations of changes in abilities that are presumed to underlie communicative performance; a number of these studies have been reviewed above
(cf. Flavel et al. 1968).

Three studies have been addressed to the question of whether differential performance in the Rosenberg and Cohen communication task is
attributable solely to deficiencies in the sampling stage of the speaker
process. That is, is it simply a vocabulary deficit that produced differential
performance as a function of age? The first study to demonstrate age differences within this paradigm was reported by Cohen and Klein (1968),
discussed above. Cohen and Klein concluded that their results "can be
interpreted most parsimoniously in terms of limitations in the . . . repertoires of the third-grade Ss compared with the older groups" (p. 608).
The data, however, are equivocal: either limitations in repertoires or
deficiences in the comparison (editing) stage or both could account for
the poorer performance of their third-grade subjects.

Asher (1972) dealt with this problem in three related experiments. In
the first experiment, second-, fourth- and sixth-graders were given a word-
communication task under two conditions: referent and nonreferent unrelated, or referent and nonreferent related. Asher argued that only sampling need be performed in order to communicate information about a
referent in the context of an unrelated nonreferent, while both sampling and
comparison processes must be performed in the related condition. That
is, in the former condition the first clue word to come to mind (the most
probable associative response to the referent) would be an adequate
response, while in the latter it would not be. The clue words provided by
the children under each of these conditions were then given to adult
listeners who tried to choose the intended referent in each pair of words.
The performance of adult listeners was used as the measure of child-

speaker performance. On unrelated pairs, speaker performance was uniformly high across all three grade levels. On related pairs, second- and sixth-grade speakers differed reliably, with second-graders worse. In a second experiment, Asher asked children to select the better of two clue words for each referent-nonreferent pair. Providing alternative clues, and thus circumventing the sampling stage, did not improve younger children's performance over a production condition which included the sampling stage, even though, in a third experiment, Asher found that the younger children could identify, *if asked,* which of several clue words were "good" or "bad." The problem was, they did not spontaneously ask *themselves* this question when left to their own devices. These data, of course, do not rule out the sampling or vocabulary deficiency hypothesis for all tasks, but they do clearly suggest deficiencies in the comparison process among young children. Either hypothesis provides a parsimonious explanation of developmental differences in communicative performance in general, while the comparison deficiency hypothesis is the most tenable one within the context of Asher's study.

Further data relevant to this issue have come from an experiment by Saunders (1969). Working with a paradigm developed by Rosenberg and Donner (1968), Saunders first trained her subjects to associate names with drawings of animal-like figures. For each pair of figures, there was one name that was associated equally with both figures and an additional name for each figure that was associated exclusively with it. By regulating the number of pairings of each type of name during the training phase of the experiment, Saunders presumably could control their associative strengths. Subjects then performed the standard Rosenberg and Cohen referential communication task, with pairs of figures rather than word pairs as the referents. Clearly, in such a situation the most effective encoding for a figure is the name that was associated with it exclusively, regardless of the frequency of its association. Saunders found some evidence that message choice of young children seems to have been determined more by sheer associative frequency than by informative value. Such a result is consistent with the "defect in comparison stage" hypothesis. It seems unlikely the Saunders's subjects lacked an appropriate associative repertoire, since the training procedure was explicitly designed to guarantee this. Unfortunately, the effects in Saunders's study were too weak to permit unequivocal conclusions, a fact that Rosenberg (1970) attributed to a sample size too small to permit stable estimates of the various probabilities. Certainly this is an experiment that warrants replication.

What, specifically, is the deficiency in the comparison process? Asher's younger subjects apparently could appropriately label a clue as "good" or "bad" when asked to do so. Does this mean that younger children are capable of adequate editing but do not deploy their abilities or skills when asked to communicate information to others? Pietrinferno (1973) tested an alternative hypothesis: younger children can and do select clue words on the basis of their informative values but (a) do not do as well as older children or adults in fitting choice behavior to informative value and (b) fail to categorically reject poor clue words. Third- and fifth-grade children were asked to pick one of three clue words that had previously been scaled for their informative value in discriminating between related referent-nonreferent word pairs. The informative value of the clue words ranged from 0.0 (listeners picked the referent with probability $= 0.0$ when given that clue word) to 1.0 (listeners picked the referent with probability $= 1.0$ when given that clue word). In an earlier study, Glucksberg and Cohen (1968) had found that adults categorically rejected poor clue words: all those within the range 0.0 to 0.5. Furthermore, their choice of clue words was reliably correlated with informative value within the range 0.5 to 1.0: the higher the informative value of a clue within this range, the more likely would an adult elect to use that clue as a message. In a forced-choice task employing such clue words, fifth-grade girls were indistinguishable from adults in the 0.5 to 1.0 range; however, their rejection rate for poor clue words was reliably lower. That is, they still elected to use clue words which were worse, as messages, than no message at all. Younger subjects' (third-graders) choice behavior was even less efficient. While their choices were related to informative values, they did not reject poor clues as systematically as did older children nor as categorically as did adults. These data on choice behavior correspond directly to overall communicative performance in the Cohen and Klein (1968) version of the Rosenberg and Cohen (1966) task. Adults did better than fifth-graders, and fifth-graders in turn did better than third-graders.

These differences in selecting from alternative responses are sufficient to account for the observed differences in communicative performance. It seems clear that deficiencies in comparison or editing processes as well as deficiencies in response repertoires could account for failures in any given communicative performance. Which of these two kinds of deficiencies is most important to any given situation or context should depend almost entirely on the demands of the task. In any case, sampling or vocabulary adequacy alone is not sufficient for adequate communicative performance.

Other questions are applicable to the analysis of the comparison or editing process. First, do young speakers engage in the comparison process at all? Second, if they do, how well is it done? How many factors do they take into account or are able to handle at once? Are they able to inhibit inadequate but prepotent responses? Are they able or willing to produce revised or altered messages? How well do they interpret in-explicit feedback from listeners? On the listeners' side, do they judge the adequacy of the messages they get in terms of the confidence of their judgments? Do they provide either general or specific requests for more information when to do so would be appropriate? Each of these skills is acquired by normal adults. What are the learning or acquisition conditions for these skills?

2. *Training referential communication skills.* Somewhat surprising is the small number of studies directed towards modifying or improving communicative behaviors in normal children and the lack of success encountered by those few studies that have been attempted. Fry (1966, 1967) reported two experiments in which he tried to provide facilitative experiences, with generally meager results. In the first, twelve-year-olds were given practice in a communication task as either speakers, listeners, or both. In a very similar transfer task some effect of training was found in that messages tended to be briefer and more to the point, as compared with messages produced by untrained speakers. Unfortunately, on a dissimilar transfer task, trained speakers' messages were also briefer but inappropriately so. The children had obviously learned that brief messages were desirable in the experimental context but had learned very little else. Fry tried again with more extended practice on three different tasks and essentially found the same negative results. Transfer to a similar communication task was marginal, and there was no transfer to dissimilar tasks at all.

We found only one other reported training study involving normal children, that of Shantz and Wilson (1972). Twelve second-grade children were given training in providing descriptions and instructions to one another. The children alternately played the roles of speaker, listener, and observer in groups of three. A control group of twelve children had no training. Small but reliable practice effects were obtained, and a moderate degree of transfer to dissimilar tasks was also obtained, although not on every measure in each of the three transfer tasks used. While these results were somewhat mixed, at least some effects of practice and training were obtained. What accounts for the differential success of the Fry and the Shantz and Wilson studies? The two studies differed in so many ways that it is impossible to say. Fry used twelve-year-olds; Shantz and Wilson used seven-and-a-half-year-olds. Fry's subjects practiced with minimal intervention from the experimenter; Shantz and Wilson were actively engaged in practice and training and conducted discussions with the children over six sessions. The effective variable or variables within the Shantz and Wilson study remain obscure. Systematic analysis of their procedures should be a worthwhile enterprise.

Summary

In reviewing the evidence on communicative performance the following summary statements can be made.

1. Both speaking and listening skills appear to improve with age, with nearly adult competence attained by early teens. Younger children do as well as older children in some aspects of the communicative performance. However, the development of the component processes that contribute to communicative performance is still not understood.

2. Neither intelligence measures nor social-class membership appear to have much correlation with communicative performance as currently measured, with the possible exception that extremely low SES may go with poor communicative performance.

3. While egocentrism and role-taking are probably too general as concepts for the analysis of the development of referential communicative competence, the attempt to develop a taxonomy of role-taking behavior may contribute to an understanding of the development of children's abilities to make inferences about others.

4. Research on several of the component processes identified as part of communicative performance have been investigated. These include: sensitivity to the domain of referents and nonreferents; sensitivity to the listener; feedback; and listener behavior. While each component appears to show increased competence with age, the factors controlling improved performance as well as the relative importance of specific deficiencies in communication remain unknown.

5. There have been few studies that have attempted to train or improve communicative behaviors in normal children. Those that have made an attempt have not had outstanding success.

Conclusions and Implications

Development of Referential Communication Skills

1. *What is acquired?* The research to date has concentrated heavily upon demonstrations of differential performance in a variety of communication and apparently communication-relevant tasks. Our lack of detailed knowledge of both the necessary and sufficient component processes and response repertoires and their interrelations, as well as of the differential demands of various experimental tasks is dramatically highlighted by the strikingly few attempts to train communicative behavior and the notable lack of success of such attempts when made. Among the promising approaches to these problems are Flavell's program directed at analyzing how children learn to make inferences about others (Flavell 1971), and

the efforts of Rosenberg and Cohen and their associates to tease out the variables underlying communicative performance in terms of their model of communicative performance. The former represents an effort to trace, in detail, the development of a communication-relevant set of processes; the latter the articulation and extension of a model to characterize the important aspects of communication tasks. In neither does the emphasis on sheer age-differences cloud the central issues: what must people do in order to communicate effectively, and how do children learn to do those things? We know virtually nothing about the latter question—how children learn those skills involved in referential communication. However, the research reviewed here does provide some conclusions about the skills, knowledge, and processes that must be acquired (or at least are displayed by adults) if children are to attain adult levels of referential competence. Acquisition of the language itself may be a necessary condition but is clearly insufficient. To language competence must be added all the component skills and processes discussed above, including knowledge of other persons, the ability to predict the potential effectiveness of messages, and the ability to provide alternative encodings when appropriate and necessary. In short, children must learn how to use their language effectively for communicative purposes, and referential communication is one of the more important functions of language usage. When we consider that other functions of verbal communication must also be served, such as persuasion, the developmental tasks faced by a child loom large indeed.

2. *What does it mean when a child fails?* Given that any particular communication task requires the existence and deployment of a variety of linguistic as well as nonlinguistic skills, how shall any instance of a failure in performance be interpreted? We have suggested that both age-related and group-related (social, ethnic, racial, national) differences in any particular performance cannot be interpreted unambiguously in terms of a specific deficit or a difference in particular abilities. Instead, as Cole and his colleagues have argued (Cole, Gay, Glick, and Sharp 1971), we need a coherent pattern of performances if we are to make meaningful interpretations of differences between any two groups, whether as a function of age or other criteria. (See chapter 11 for full discussion of this issue.) With respect to age-related differences in communicative performance, a pattern is beginning to emerge. Younger children do as well as older children in some aspects of various communication tasks (e.g., understanding adequate messages from adults, as reported by Glucksberg et al. 1966); they display specific deficiencies in vocabulary, in a variety of role-playing skills as both speakers and listeners (cf. Flavell et al. 1968; Krauss and Glucksberg 1970), and in knowledge of

other persons (cf. Milgram and Goodglass 1961). In addition, some general behavioral and cognitive skills probably also contribute to differences among age groups.

Because poor performance can be attributed to any one or more of these components, behaviors, or processes, differences in performance within any given task are ambiguous. For example, consider the results obtained and conclusions drawn by Pascual-Leone and Smith (1969). Five-, seven-, and nine-year-old children were tested on symbol decoding and encoding in each of two modes, gestural and verbal. Within both modes the children did not differ among themselves in decoding performance. They did differ in encoding, and furthermore the gestural mode was superior to the verbal mode among the two younger age-groups. This result had been predicted by Pascual-Leone on the basis of an elegant extension and formalization of Piaget's model of cognitive development. His interpretation is consistent both with the general pattern of results obtained by others in communication tasks and with the theory. However, the gestural and verbal modes differed in more than just formal ways. In the verbal mode, the children were not permitted to use the name of an object as an encoding response. Hence, in this mode the child's dominant or most probable response had to be inhibited and another response provided instead. This is precisely what younger children have difficulty in doing (cf. Glucksberg and Krauss 1967). In contrast, in the gestural condition the initial, dominant response is acceptable. In addition, there was no control for the ease of pair discrimination across conditions. Hence, the differential performances as a function of age and mode of encoding may be attributable to the formal logical demands of the two tasks, to the response availability demands, to particular object pairs chosen, to none of these, or to all of these.

Similar arguments apply to interpretations of any age-related differences, and to socioeconomic class differences as well. Until coherent patterns of performance can be obtained, and until the demands of the experimental tasks and measurement instruments are well understood, interpretation of group differences remains ambiguous and uninformative.

Implications for psycholinguistics

1. *Language development and acquisition.* Until very recently, our sophistication and understanding of the mechanisms involved in children's acquisition of language had been aptly summarized by George Miller: "We have but two theories of language acquisition at the moment. . . . the miracle theory or the impossible theory" (personal communication). The first, of course, refers to the nativistic views expressed by Chomsky (1968) and McNeill (1966). The second refers to the inadequacy of traditional

mechanisms of learning to deal with anything but the simplest aspects of language behavior and learning. It is our view that so long as meaning, communication, and intentions to communicate are excluded from consideration as central to the interactive acquisition process, efforts to deal with acquisition of syntax per se or lexicons per se are doomed to failure. At least one reason is sufficient: it may very well be that children do not acquire just those kinds of knowledge that early transformational generative grammars dictated that they must acquire (cf. Hymes 1964). Macnamara (1972), for example, proposed that children first learn "meanings" and "intentions" and then learn to represent those "meanings" in linguistic forms. Schlesinger (1971), Bloom (1970), Roger Brown and his associates (1970), and Slobin (1971) among others have argued that formal syntactic models, such as pivot grammars, are inadequate characterizations of children's language. Instead of relying solely upon syntactic models of children's language, these investigators have suggested a form of propositional model, wherein a variety of "meanings" or sentence types are represented by a single surface form. The utterance "Mommy lunch" represents just one type of sentence in a pivot grammar. In Bloom's view, this utterance can represent a variety of meanings or "deep structures"; *Mommy's lunch, I want lunch, Mommy is eating lunch, look Mommy lunch,* to list but a few. It is not unreasonable to suppose that one source of pressure upon a child to differentiate his surface utterances in order to differentiate explicitly his propositions (meanings) is the need to be understood. The demands of interpersonal communication, not some idealized rule system, would seem to be a more likely source of motivation and information for language acquisition. In the same vein, Rommetveit (1968) has argued that analyses of message structure would be more promising as an organizing rubric than analyses of syntactic or other formal linguistic structures for an understanding of language behavior, including language development.

Whatever the ultimate utility of such an approach, we will (at the very least) learn something about communicative processes even if we do reach another dead end in our attempts to understand language acquisition. At the moment, in the absence of strong arguments or evidence to the contrary, we would tend essentially to agree with Rommetveit: in learning and using language, one's real concern is to learn how most effectively to engage in communication with those with whom one comes into contact. The name of the game is messages, not words, sentences, or paragraphs.

2. *Communicative bases for linguistic structures.* Bever (1970), in his seminal paper, "The Cognitive Basis for Linguistic Structures," argued that syntactic features of natural languages develop and are maintained

as a function of strategies used by people to produce and understand utterances. For example, a phonological system, if it is to survive, must be designed so that confusions are minimized and utterances can be pronounced. Similarly, syntactic structures are also "designed" to serve the perceptual and cognitive needs of speakers and listeners of a language. Among these needs are those specifically relevant to communication, and these would affect characteristics of natural language at the level of messages rather than at the level of phonology or syntax.

Two conceptually separable aspects of language and language usage can be considered in this context: lexical and syntactic. At the lexical level some progress has been made toward describing and accounting for natural language phenomena in terms of their communicative utility. As a case in point, consider the word-frequency, word-length relationship described by Zipf (1935). In a variety of languages, a word's length is inversely related to its frequency of usage. This relationship has been demonstrated in the laboratory by Krauss and his associates (Krauss and Weinheimer 1964, 1966), who showed that people performing in communication tasks systematically shortened the descriptive phrases they used as a direct function of their frequency of usage. The relation between word frequency and word length can also be treated stochastically (Mandelbrot 1953), with no necessary reference to functional utility or meaning (Cherry 1966). However, since the length of a "name" decreases monotonically with its frequency of usage in interpersonal communication tasks, it seems reasonable to infer that the word frequency/length relation found in natural languages does (or at least could) reflect the outcomes of social-interactive processes.

Roger Brown, in his paper, "How Shall a Thing Be Called?" (1958), deals with another aspect of the lexicon. He points out that natural languages do not provide one-to-one correspondences between names and the things they refer to (referents). A single "name" like *table* can be used to refer to any one of a number of referents: a piece of furniture, an arrangement of numbers, a level of water in the ground, a kind of terrain, or an action at a committee meeting. Conversely, a particular referent can have many "names." The family pet may be called *dog, Prince, pooch, mammal, hound,* or *pet.* What determines an adult's choice of a name for a child in regard to a particular referent or class of referents? Brown considered a number of alternatives and finally proposed a principle of level of usual utility. An adult will choose a name that "categorizes things in maximally useful ways: For most purposes Referent A is a spoon rather than a piece of silverware, and Referent B a dime rather than a metal object" (p. 17). This principle supersedes a frequency principle in that it is one way to account for relative word-frequencies. It also presents an alternative to the proposition that children acquire concrete words before they acquire abstract words (or vice versa). The words first learned by children are not determined by the words' locations on a dimension of concrete-abstractness but instead are determined by the naming practices of the adults around them. These naming practices presumably conform to the level of usual utility principle.

Can a similar approach be taken for analyses of syntactic phenomena? One syntactic phenomenon which has been approached from this point of view is the ordering of adjectives modifying a head noun. For example, in English, German, and many other languages the ordering of adjectives with respect to a modified noun seems to be constrained in a particular way. We would say "large red Turkish truck," not "Turkish red large truck." These order preferences are highly consistent in adults (Martin 1969), and appear early in children (Martin and Molfese 1971; Freedle and Hall 1972). One basis for this linguistic regularity (as well as various other syntactic conventions) might be its utility for referring to various states in the phenomenal world. Among linguists this point of view is expressed in a general way by Jesperson (1933) and specifically by Oller and Sayles (1969). Oller and Sayles proposed that, relative to a particular context, the adjective which appears first in a series within a noun phrase provides the most discriminative information to a listener. In the absence of an explicit restricting context, the ordering appropriate to the most frequent or usual context occurs. A related hypothesis has been proposed by Danks and Glucksberg (1971), who took the general requirements of a typical communication task as their point of departure (see, for example, Glucksberg and Krauss 1967; Olson 1970; Rosenberg and Cohen 1966). Communication can be likened to a problem-solving task where the speaker's goal is to provide a message to his or her listener which enables that listener to select a designated referent from a set of implicit or explicit alternatives (nonreferents) (see David Olson, 1970 for a theoretical approach to semantics based on this notion). When a speaker uses the adjective *red* as in *red table,* we may infer not only that the table is red. We may also infer that the table is *not* some other color and/or that there are tables which are not red and that these nonred tables are implicitly excluded by the message.

Other syntactic phenomena, such as the active-passive distinction, have been fruitfully approached from this point of view (cf. Carswell and Rommetveit, 1971; Glucksberg, Trabasso and Wald, 1973; Olson and Filby 1972). Huttenlocher and Higgins (1971) have pointed out how the choice of a comparative (e.g., "more than," "less than," "not as . . . as") may be determined jointly by the relative positions of the items being compared along some dimension, plus which item is to be the topic of the message. Not only psychology but linguistics as well seem to be moving in the direction of considering language within the context of social interaction and discourse (e.g., Chafe 1970; Fillmore 1968; Hymes 1964). The prospects for the future depend very heavily on our success in integrating our conceptions of the communication process with our conceptions of language. Only then will we be able to gain some insight into the refractory problem of language acquisition.

References

Asher, R. A. The influence of sampling and comparison processes on the development of communication effectiveness. Paper given at meeting of American Psychological Association, September, 1972.

Bailey, S. An analysis of the trend toward objective thought and speech in children's communication. Master's thesis, Rutgers University, 1971.

Baldwin, T. & Garvey, C. Studies in convergent communication: II. A measure of communication accuracy. Center for Social Organization of Schools, Report No. 91, November, 1970.

Baldwin, T. Personal communication, 1972.

Baldwin, T., McFarlane, P. T., & Garvey, C. Children's communication accuracy related to race and socioeconomic status. *Child Development,* 1971, *42,* 345–358.

Bernstein, B. A sociolinguistic approach to social learning. In J. Gould, ed., *Penguin Survey of the Social Sciences,* Baltimore: Penguin, 1965.

————. A sociolinguistic approach to socialization: with some reference to educability. In F. Williams, ed., *Language and Poverty: Perspectives on a Theme.* Chicago: Markham, 1970.

Bever, T. G. The cognitive basis for linguistic structures. In J. R. Hayes, ed., *Cognition and the Development of Language.* New York: John Wiley, 1970.

Bloom, L. M. *Language Development: Form and Function in Emerging Grammars.* Cambridge, Mass.: MIT Press, 1970.

Brent, S. B. & Katz, E. A study of language deviations and cognitive processes. Office of Economic Opportunity, Job Corps Research Contract 1209, Progress Report No. 3, March, 1967.

Brown, R. How shall a thing be called? *Psychological Review,* 1958, *65,* 14–21.

————. The first sentences of child and chimpanzee. In R. Brown, *Psycholinguistics: Selected Papers.* New York: Free Press, 1970.

Carswell, E. A. & Rommetveit, R., eds. *Social Contexts of Messages.* New York: Academic Press, 1971.

Cazden, C. B. The situation: a neglected source of social class differences in language use. *Journal of Social Issues,* 1970, *26,* 35–60.

Chafe, W. *Meaning and the Structure of Language.* Chicago: University of Chicago Press, 1970.

Cherry, C. *On Human Communication.* Cambridge: MIT Press, 1966.

Chomsky, N. *Language and Mind.* New York: Harcourt Brace, 1968.

Cohen, B. D. & Klein, J. D. Referent communication in school age children. *Child Development,* 1968, *39,* 597–609.

Cole, M., Gay, J., Glick, J. A., & Sharp, D. W. *The Cultural Context of Learning and Thinking.* New York: Basic Books, 1971.

Cooper, R. J. & Flavell, J. H. Cognitive correlates of children's role-taking behavior, University of Minnesota, mimeo (1972).

Cowan, P. A. The link between cognitive structure and social structure in two-child verbal interaction. Paper presented at meeting of the Society for Research in Child Development, 1967.

Danks, J. H. Encoding novel figures for communication and memory. *Cognitive Psychology*, 1970, *1*, 179–191.

Danks, J. H. & Glucksberg, S. Psychological scaling of adjective order. *Journal of Verbal Learning and Verbal Behavior*, 1971, *10*, 63–67.

Dymond, R. F., Hughes, A. S., & Raabe, V. L. Measurable changes in empathy with age. *Journal of Consulting Psychology*, 1952, *16*, 202–206.

Feffer, M. H. & Gourevitch, S. Cognitive aspects of role-taking in children. *Journal of Personality*, 1960, *28*, 383–396.

Feffer, M. H. & Suchotliff, L. Decentering implications of social interaction. *Journal of Personality and Social Psychology*, 1966, *4*, 415–422.

Fillmore, C. J. The case for case. In E. Bach & R. T. Harms, eds., *Universals in Linguistic Theory*. New York: Holt, Rinehart & Winston, 1968.

Finfgeld, T. E. The ability to select words to convey intended meaning. *The Quarterly Journal of Speech*, 1966, *52*, 255–258.

Fishbein, H. D. & Osborne, M. The effects of feedback variations on referential communication of children. *Merrill-Palmer Quarterly*, 1971, *17*, 243–250.

Flavell, J. H. The development of inferences about others. Paper presented at interdisciplinary conference on our knowledge of others: person perception and interpersonal behavior. SUNY-Binghamton, New York, 1971.

Flavell, J. H., with Botkin, P. T., Fry, C. L., Wright, J. C., and Jarvis, P. E. *The Development of Role-taking and Communication Skills in Children*. New York: John Wiley, 1968.

Freedle, R. & Hall, W. S. Effects of prenominal adjective ordering on children's latencies in an immediate sentence recall task. Paper presented at meetings of the American Psychological Association, September, 1972.

Fry, C. L. Training children to communicate to listeners. *Child Development*, 1966, *37*, 674–685.

————. A developmental examination of performance in a tacit coordination game situation. *Journal of Personality and Social Psychology*, 1967, *5*, 277–281.

Gelman, R. & Shatz, M. Listener-dependent adjustments in the speech of 4-year-olds. Paper given at meeting of the Psychonomic Society, 1972.

Glucksberg, S. & Cohen, J. A. Speaker processes in referential communication: message choice as a function of message adequacy. Proceedings of the seventy-sixth annual convention, American Psychological Association, 1968.

Glucksberg, S. & Kim, N. Unpublished study, 1969.

Glucksberg, S., Krauss, R. M., & Weisberg, R. Referential communication in nursery school children: method and some preliminary findings. *Journal of Experimental Child Psychology*, 1966, *3*, 333–342.

Glucksberg, S. & Krauss, R. M. What do people say after they have learned how to talk? Studies of the development of referential communication. *Merrill-Palmer Quarterly*, 1967, *13*, 309–316.

Glucksberg, S., Trabasso, T., & Wald, J. Linguistic structures and mental operations: an information-processing analysis of sentence comprehension. *Cognitive Psychology*, 1973, *5*, 338–370.

Heider, E. R. Style and accuracy of verbal communications within and between social classes. *Journal of Personality and Social Psychology*, 1971, *18*, 33–47.

Heider, E. R. & Olivier, D. C. The structure of the color space in naming and memory for two languages. *Cognitive Psychology*, 1972, *3*, 337–354.

Higgins, E. T. A social and developmental comparison of oral and written communication skills. Doctoral dissertation, Columbia University, 1973.

Huttenlocher, J. & Higgins, E. T. Adjectives, comparatives, and syllogisms. *Psychological Review*, 1971, *78*, 487–504.

Hymes, D. Introduction: toward ethnographies of communication. In J. J. Gumperz and D. Hymes, eds., The Ethnography of Communication. Special issue of *American Anthropologist*, 1964, *66*, 1–34.

Jespersen, O. *Language: Its Nature, Development, and Origin.* London & New York: Holt, 1933.

Kingsbury, D. Manipulating the amount of information obtained by a person giving directions. Senior Honors Thesis, Harvard University, 1968.

Kingsley, P. The relationship between egocentrism and children's communication. Paper read at meeting of the Society for Research in Child Development, 1971.

Krauss, R. M. & Bricker, P. D. Effects of transmission delay and access delay on the efficiency of verbal communication. *Journal of the Acoustical Society of America*, 1967, *41*, 286–292.

Krauss, R. M. & Glucksberg, S. The development of communication: competence as a function of age. *Child Development*, 1969, *40*, 255–256.

———. Socialization of communication skills: the development of competence as a communicator. In R. Hoppe, E. Simmel, and G. Z. Milton, eds., *Early Experience and the Process of Socialization.* New York: Academic Press, 1970.

Krauss, R. M. & Rotter, G. C. Communication abilities of children as a function of status and age. *Merrill-Palmer Quarterly*, 1968, *14*, 161–173.

Krauss, R. M. & Weinheimer, S. Changes in the length of reference phrases as a function of social interaction: a preliminary study. *Psychonomic Science*, 1964, *1*, 113–114.

———. Concurrent feedback, confirmation, and the encoding of referents in verbal communication. *Journal of Personality and Social Psychology*, 1966, *4*, 343–346.

———. Effect of referent similarity and communication mode on verbal encoding. *Journal of Verbal Learning and Verbal Behavior*, 1967, *6*, 359–363.

Krauss, R. M., Vivekananthan, P. S., & Weinheimer, S. "Inner speech" and "external speech": characteristics and communication effectiveness of socially and non-socially encoded messages. *Journal of Personality and Social Psychology*, 1968, *9*, 295–300.

Labov, W. The logic of nonstandard English. In F. Williams, ed., *Language and Poverty: Perspectives on a Theme.* Chicago: Markham, 1970.

Loewenthal, K. The effects of "understanding" from the audience on language behavior. *British Journal of Clinical and Social Psychology*, 1968, *7*, 247–252.

Maclay, H. & Newman, S. Two variables affecting the message in communication. In D. K. Wilner, ed., *Decisions, Values and Groups.* New York: Pergamon Press, 1960.

Macnamara, J. Cognitive bases of language learning in infants. *Psychological Review*, 1972, *79*, 1–13.

Mandelbrot, B. An informational theory of the structure of language based upon the theory of the statistical matching of messages and coding. In J. Willis, ed., *Proceedings of a Symposium on Application of Communication Theory.* London: Butterworth, 1953.

Martin, J. E. Semantic determinants of preferred adjective order. *Journal of Verbal Learning and Verbal Behavior*, 1969, *8*, 697–704.

Martin, J. E. & Molfese, D. Some developmental aspects of preferred adjective ordering. *Psychonomic Science*, 1971, *22*, 219–220.

McNeill, D. Developmental psycholinguistics. In F. Smith & G. A. Miller, eds., *The Genesis of Language: A Psycholinguistic Approach.* Cambridge, Mass.: MIT Press, 1966.

Milgram, N. & Goodglass, H. Role style versus cognitive maturation in word associations of adults and children. *Journal of Personality*, 1961, *29*, 81–93.

Miller, G. A. Personal communication, 1970.

Oller, J. W., Jr. & Sayles, B. B. Conceptual restrictions on English: a psycholinguistic study. *Lingua*, 1969, *23*, 209–232.

Olson, D. R. Language and thought: aspects of a cognitive theory of semantics. *Psychological Review,* 1970, *77,* 257–273.

Olson, D. R. & Filby, N. On the comprehension of active and passive sentences. *Cognitive Psychology,* 1972, *3,* 361–381.

Pascual-Leone, J. & Smith, J. The encoding and decoding of symbols by children: a new experimental paradigm and a neo-Piagetian model. *Journal of Experimental Child Psychology,* 1969, *8,* 328–355.

Peterson, C. L., Danner, F. W., & Flavell, J. H. Developmental changes in children's response to three indications of communicative failure. *Child Development,* 1972, *43,* 1463–1468.

Piaget, J. *The Language and Thought of the Child.* New York: Harcourt, Brace, 1926.

Pietrinferno, G. The development of comparison processes in children's communication. Doctoral dissertation, Princeton University, 1973.

Rackstraw, S. J. & Robinson, W. P. Social and psychological factors related to variability of answering behavior in five-year-old children. *Language and Speech,* 1967, *10,* 88–106.

Ratner, S. C. & Rice, F. E. The effect of the listener on the speaking interaction. *Psychological Record,* 1963, *13,* 265–268.

Rommetveit, R. *Words, Meanings, and Messages.* New York: Academic Press, 1968.

Rosenberg, S. The development of referential skills in children. In R. L. Schiefelbusch, ed., *Language of the Mentally Retarded.* Baltimore: University Park Press, 1972, 53–71.

Rosenberg, S. & Cohen, B. D. Referential processes of speakers and listeners. *Psychological Review,* 1966, *73,* 208–231.

Rosenberg, S. & Donner, L. Choice behavior in a verbal recognition task as a function of induced associative strength. *Journal of Experimental Psychology,* 1968, *76,* 341–347.

Rosenberg, S. & Gordon, A. Identification of facial expressions from affective descriptions: a probabilistic choice analysis of referential ambiguity. *Journal of Personality and Social Psychology,* 1968, *10,* 157–166.

Rosenberg, S. & Markham, B. Choice behavior in a referentially ambiguous task. *Journal of Personality and Social Psychology,* 1971, *17,* 99–105.

Ruth, D. Language, intelligence and social class: A study of communicative effectiveness within same-class and cross-class pairs. Senior Honors Thesis, Harvard University, 1966.

Sarbin, T. R. & Jones, D. S. An experimental analysis of role behavior. *Journal of Abnormal and Social Psychology,* 1956, *51,* 236–241.

Saunders, P. S. An experimental analysis of egocentrism in children's communication. Doctoral dissertation, Rutgers University, 1969.

Schatzman, L. & Strauss, A. Social class and modes of communication. *American Journal of Sociology,* 1955, *60,* 329–338.

Schlesinger, I. M. Production of utterances and language acquisition. In D. I. Slobin, ed., *The Ontogenesis of Grammar.* New York: Academic Press, 1971.

Shantz, C. U. & Wilson, K. E. Training communication skills in young children. *Child Development,* 1972, *43,* 693–698.

Slepian, H. A developmental study of inner vs. external speech in normals and schizophrenics. Doctoral dissertation, Clark University, 1959.

Slobin, D. I. *Psycholinguistics.* Glenview, Illinois: Scott Foresman, 1971.

Werner, H. & Kaplan, B. *Symbol Formation.* New York: John Wiley, 1963.

Wiener, M., Devoe, S., Rubinow, S., & Geller, J. Nonverbal behavior and nonverbal communication. *Psychological Review,* 1972, *79,* 185–214.

Williams, F., ed., *Language and Poverty: Perspectives on a Theme.* Chicago: Markham, 1970.

Zipf, G. K. *The Psychobiology of Language.* New York: Houghton-Mifflin, 1935.

7 Drug Treatment of Children with Behavior Problems

L. ALAN SROUFE
University of Minnesota

INTRODUCTION

AT LEAST 150,000 American children are currently being given stimulant drug medication for learning and behavior problems (NIMH testimony in the House of Representatives, Gallagher 1970, p. 16). Local estimates of the extent of this practice vary from less than 1 percent to 10 percent, but there is general agreement that the frequency of drug treatment is increasing rapidly (Maynard 1970; Richard 1972; Safer 1971; Stephen, Sprague, and Werry, unpublished; Witter 1971). In his recent book, which is certain to be influential, Wender (1971) has explicitly argued for a dramatic expansion of stimulant drug treatment and suggested that not offering drug treatment to some behavior problem ("minimal brain dysfunction") children may constitute medical malpractice. Also, discussions of screening procedures for the total school population are beginning to appear (Richard 1972; Steinberg, Troshinsky, and Steinberg 1971; Zedler 1968). Steinberg et al. (1971), for example, while not advocating large-scale, long-term drug treatment, did propose that entire schools be screened, based initially on teacher selection for "behavior disorder and/or difficulty concentrating on school work in the classroom," so that parents of children who might show a positive stimulant drug response would have the option of placing their children on medication. Clearly, proposals for large-scale screening and for an expanded use of medication suggest an urgent need for a critical review of the literature on drug treatment of children.

Clinical reports consistently have maintained that stimulant drugs produce positive and sometimes dramatic effects with variously labeled problem children (Eisenberg 1966; Sainz 1966; Solomons 1965; Wender 1971). And there are now scores of research studies in the literature concerning the effects of stimulant drugs on children with behavior problems. While many studies are methodologically poor or rely on global ratings of improvement, there are a number of well-controlled, well-described experiments that utilize objective and reliable measures. This substantial literature is conclusive concerning the potency of stimulant drugs for producing experimental effects in short-term evaluations (see Conners 1972*a,* and Eisenberg and Conners 1971, for reviews). Teachers and parents rate behavior as improved, certain classes of unwanted behavior are diminished, and performance scores are increased on a variety of tests and experimental tasks.

However, the meaning of this array of effects is far from clear. There are a number of empirical, conceptual, and ethical issues that must be examined in order to reach conclusions about the effects of stimulant drugs and the medical practice of prescribing these drugs to large numbers of children (Sroufe 1972). For example, given the variety of behavior and test-score changes following drug administration, can the underlying physiological mechanisms or the psychological locus of the effects be specified? Are there models that integrate existing findings and predict both positive and negative drug effects? What predictor variables, neurological and otherwise, are useful for isolating the subset of children who will show a positive drug response, objectively defined? Can a syndrome be defined, based on the intercorrelations among variables, and does it relate to underlying neuropathology and/or stimulant drug effects? Finally, do the children selected for treatment exhibit a response to stimulant drugs which is unique and therefore suggestive of central nervous system deviation?

Other questions concern the long-term effects of stimulant drugs and alternatives to drug treatment. There is a need to examine the evidence concerning the persistence of drug effects on behavior and performance, as well as the effects of drugs on learning and actual school achievement. Questions must also be raised about the physical, psychological, and social side effects of extensive and prolonged treatment of children with stimulant medications. To fully evaluate drug treatment of children, alternatives to pharmacological intervention and the possible interaction of drugs with these alternative techniques must also be examined.

Some introductory comments concerning terminology are required. Clements (1966) has catalogued thirty-eight terms which have been used to describe the type of children frequently given stimulant drugs. The government panel he chaired agreed on the term "minimal brain dysfunction," but other labels commonly used to describe the same set of children are "hyperkinetic-impulse disorder," "hyperactive child syndrome," and "special learning disability." The children are said to manifest a constellation of behaviors, usually including hyperactivity, distractibility, impulsiveness, short attention-span, coordination and/or "perceptual" problems, and poor schoolwork relative to tested IQ. While some investigators (e.g., Wender 1971) maintain that children having such a "syndrome" may sometimes be *hypo*active, the terms "hyperactive," or "hyperkinetic," and "minimal brain dysfunction" are frequently used interchangeably. In the following review, the terms "hyperactive" or "behavior problem" will be used predominantly, since these labels accurately reflect the referral basis for the majority of these children.

OVERVIEW OF STUDIES ON DRUG EFFECTS WITH CHILDREN

Methodological Considerations

Methodological problems in drug evaluation studies are numerous, and this is especially true for drug experiments with children conducted over a period of time. For example, one must insure that the child receives the medication consistently over the duration of the study, and one must be concerned about uncontrolled variables which might alter the child's behavior over the course of the drug trial. The various methodological problems in drug experiments with children have been the subject of several reviews (Baker 1968; Conners 1972a; Eisenberg 1968; Eisenberg and Conners 1971; Freeman 1966; Minde and Weiss 1970; Sprague and Werry 1971; Sprague, Werry, and Davis 1969), and the discussion here will be limited to a few key issues running through the literature.

The review of drug treatment studies that follows is restricted largely to double-blind, placebo-control experiments. "Double-blind" implies that neither the child nor the evaluators (parent, teacher, experimenter) know whether the child is in the placebo or active drug group (Chassan 1967). However, numerous studies suggest that blindness of evaluators is difficult to maintain due to side effects of the active drug (Cole 1968; Conners and Eisenberg 1963; Rickels, Lipman, Fisher, Park, and Uhlenhuth 1970; Sprague et al. 1969). For this reason the review will emphasize results based on standard psychological tests and laboratory tasks rather than ratings. Even objective measures of activity and task performance may, of course, be influenced by knowledge of the child, or significant persons in his environment, that he is on the active drug (Eisenberg 1968). Placebo effects and the role of set and expectations in mediating drug effects will be discussed in detail in a later section.

The studies reviewed in this chapter often employed crossover designs and used variable (optimal) rather than standard drug dosages. Both of these procedures have advantages and disadvantages. In the crossover design, where the same children are first in one condition (drug or placebo), then the other, main effects for condition are confounded with sequence effects (Sprague and Werry 1971). Sequence effects most often involve carryover from drug to placebo; that is, placebo scores obtained following a drug trial are higher than placebo scores prior to a drug trial (Cohen, Douglas, and Morgenstern 1971; Steinberg et al. 1971). There may also be a suppression of drug performance in subjects initially experiencing the placebo or rebound effects due to withdrawal from the drug (Eisenberg 1968). While such sequence effects may illuminate placebo reactions, they increase the difficulty of interpreting main effects for drug condition. Another disadvantage is that the crossover design requires multiple testing, which sometimes creates problems in terms of practice effects and subject attrition. On the other hand, the crossover design greatly reduces subject variance, allowing smaller sample sizes, and yields information concerning each participant's response to the active drug. (Such information is rightfully sought by parents who volunteer their children for study.) Subject heterogeneity has been stressed constantly as a problem in evaluating the effects of drugs (Conners 1972*a;* Fish 1969). In the absence of crossover designs, random assignment to group does sometimes lead to troublesome pretreatment differences (Conners, Kramer, Rothschild, Schwartz, and Stone 1971). Blocking or matching subjects in terms of pretests or variables known to be important can minimize the problem of initial differences but requires a large number of subjects.

A number of investigators have argued for the use of optimal dosages in drug experiments; that is, the dosage is gradually increased until an optimal clinical effect (usually in terms of parents' report) is reached or side effects occur. This dosage varies considerably from child to child. While such a procedure might be considered an alternative to administering large dosages to the entire sample (thus increasing side effects), there are a number of drawbacks to this common practice. These problems include confounding dosage variation with subject variance and increasing the likelihood that the double-blind will be broken. The argument for this procedure is that the individual sensitivity of children is highly variable (Minde and Weiss 1970), but, as Sprague and Werry (1971) have pointed out, this remains an empirical question.

Studies varying dosage from child to child and those employing a constant dosage across all children fail to provide needed information concerning the effects of dosage. It is axiomatic in psychopharmacology that drug effect and dosage are inseparable (Thompson and Schuster 1968). Millichap and Boldrey (1967), for example, reported that in both animals and children barbiturates will increase or decrease activity level depending on dosage. Therefore, it is perplexing that only two experiments are reported in the literature on drug treatment of children in which dosage level of a stimulant drug was parametrically manipulated. In the first (discussed in Sprague and Werry 1971), *linear* dosage effects were found for latency in a delayed recognition task, while a *curvilinear* effect was found for accuracy, with accuracy dropping off at high dosages. In the second study (Werry and Sprague, in press), there was no increase in drug effectiveness beyond a dosage of .3 mg/kg of body weight, though some investigators have used dosages higher than 1.0 mg/kg, the highest dosage used here. These studies have led Werry and Sprague (in press) to conclude that dosage levels commonly employed in stimulant drug studies with children are too high.

In conclusion, drug studies with children are extremely difficult to conduct, being given to the whole range of problems found in both laboratory and clinical research. A number of the studies to be reviewed below are commendable for their methodological rigor. There are studies, for example, in which drug administration was ensured with the aid of the school nurse, and raters were blind even to the fact that a crossover design was being used (Conners, Eisenberg, and Barcai 1967; Steinberg et al. 1971). Other investigators have used multiple dosage levels, carefully pretested; reliable indices; and/or converging measures (Cohen et al. 1971; Sprague, Barnes, and Werry 1970; Sykes, Douglas, Weiss, and Minde 1971).

Sedatives and Tranquilizers

It seems reasonable to attempt treatment of hyperactive and distractible children with sedatives (barbiturates) and tranquilizers; yet the research literature is completely uniform in contraindicating the use of these drugs to treat such children. While barbiturates (phenobarbital, seconal) are useful for preventing convulsions in young children, not a single controlled experiment can be found which indicates beneficial effects of these sedative drugs for children labeled as hyperactive, minimally brain-damaged, or behavior-disordered. In fact, clinical observation and controlled studies suggest that symptoms worsen and performance deteriorates following barbiturate administration with both children and adults (Blum, Stern, and Melville 1964; Eisenberg 1968; Kornetsky 1970; Laufer and Denhoff 1957; Millichap 1968).

The case with tranquilizers is only slightly more complicated. Phenothiazines such as chlorpromazine (Thorazine) and thioridazine (Mellaril) have been reported to improve some of the symptoms of active, behavior-problem children (Rapoport, Abramson, Alexander, and Lott 1971; Solomons 1965; Werry, Weiss, Douglas, and Martin 1966). However, such symptomatic improvement seems to be at the expense of a deterioration in performance. For example, in adults and children chlorpromazine and thioridazine have been found to impair both learning and performance, including accuracy of discrimination and reaction time (Cohen 1966; Conners 1971a; Garfield, Helper, Wilcott, and Muffly 1962; Hartlage 1965; Helper, Wilcott, and Garfield 1963; Werry 1970). Certainly, a medication for children should not reduce unwanted symptoms at the expense of the child's ability to learn or perform competently. As in the case with sedatives (Eisenberg 1966), studies making direct comparisons consistently show the major tranquilizers to be inferior to the stimulant drugs in the treatment of children (Rapoport et al. 1971; Sprague et al. 1969; Sprague et al. 1970; Werry 1970).

Stimulants

Over the past fifteen years stimulant drugs (methylphenidate, or Ritalin, and the amphetamines) have emerged clearly as the "drugs of choice" for behavior-problem or hyperactive children. This medical practice springs from the large number of positive clinical reports and the now substantial literature documenting the short-term potency of stimulant drugs for producing certain experimental effects.

1. *Early clinical studies.* Conners (1972a) has pointed out that greater control over relevant variables can sometimes be achieved in clinically oriented drug studies than in experiments with placebo control groups. It is probably for this reason that Bradley's (1937) early clinical report on amphetamine (here, Benzedrine) treatment of a heterogeneous group of institutionalized problem children has been supported by later controlled experiments. Bradley was able to control drug dosage and situational variables, as well as study the same children over a long time-period. He reported that amphetamine improved both interest in and ability to do schoolwork, increased feelings of well-being, and seemingly calmed overactive children without having a subduing effect. Though not employing placebo controls, this report gains credibility from the fact that neither Bradley nor his subjects were expecting such behavioral effects. As Stewart and Olds (in press) point out, Bradley was seeking a drug which would raise blood pressure in certain children, and it was the children themselves who first brought the behavioral effects to his attention. Later clinical studies, while sometimes informative (Burks 1964; Knobel, Wolman, and Mason 1959), are biased to an unknown extent by the investigator's preconceptions concerning stimulant drug effects.

2. *Controlled studies using ratings.* Since Bradley's (1937) report, there have been numerous double-blind, placebo-control studies supporting his finding that the behavior of problem children is rated as improved following administration of stimulant drugs, both the amphetamines and Ritalin (methylphenidate). A number of rating scales with established reliability have been developed. For example, the teacher rating-scale carefully developed by Conners (1969) was factor-analyzed using a large sample of hyperactive children. The scale had high test-retest reliability over one month, and five factors were derived. The four unambiguous

factors were labeled as follows: (1) defiance-aggressive conduct, (2) daydreaming-inattentive, (3) anxious-fearful, and (4) hyperactivity. Factors 1 and 4 were modestly correlated. Scales for parents are similar but place more emphasis on sleeping, health, and social problems (Conners 1970b). Other scales are described by Werry (1968b) and Werry and Sprague (1970).

Though based on variously defined and recruited samples and employing a variety of research designs, rating studies are consistent in showing greater improvement with active drug than with placebo. This is the case when a formal rating instrument is used by parents or teachers (Conners 1969, 1970b, 1971a; Conners, Eisenberg, and Barcai 1967; Conners and Rothschild 1968; Eisenberg 1966; Eisenberg, Conners, and Sharpe 1965; Finnerty, Greaney, Soltys, and Cole 1971; Knights and Hinton 1969; Rapoport et al. 1971; Steinberg et al. 1971) or when global ratings are made by professionals (Conners and Eisenberg 1963; Zrull, Westman, Arthur, and Rice 1964). The findings by Conners et al. (1967) are typical. Behavior-problem children given stimulant drugs for one month were rated as more improved on subscales relating to classroom behaviors (fiddling, inattentive, destructive, and so on), group participation (e.g., isolation, teasing other children), and attitudes toward authority (e.g., defiant, fearful, stubborn) than were control subjects.

In addition to a possible breakdown in the blindness of the raters due to side effects, the most serious difficulty with rating data concerns the likelihood of "halo" effects. This applies even to standardized instruments. A parent or teacher may note some changed behavior or attitude in the child, then rate the child as improved on items across the scale. This is particularly troublesome since all items are rated for a child at one time, and the dependent measure is often the sum across items. Also, it is not clear to which specific behaviors teachers are responding; these rating data have not been related to independent assessments of behavior based on time-sampled observations or other techniques, either before or after drug treatment. On the other hand, rating data are often relevant to the referral problem. Generally, children are referred to pediatricians because teachers or parents judge that they have a problem, not because of objective task performance. In addition, it may be that ratings are sensitive because their global, multivariate nature is responsive to complex drug effects (Werry 1970).

3. *Standardized tests and laboratory tasks.* While standard psychological tests and laboratory tasks are often only indirectly related to the referral problems of children treated with drugs, the objectivity and specificity of such measures is essential in the assessment of drug effects. Studies here have varied not only in the measures utilized but also in the types of

research design, dosage levels employed, and duration of the drug trial
from days to several weeks. The heterogeneity of the subject populations
studied merits special emphasis. A number of the studies reviewed involved children referred by teachers for learning and behavior disorders,
without any neurological evaluation (e.g., Conners et al. 1967, 1969). This
makes heterogeneity of subjects both within and across studies extremely
likely; yet the results to be reported are strikingly consistent in attesting
to the short-term potency of both methylphenidate (Ritalin) and the
amphetamines.

Standard Psychological Tests. Intelligence tests, achievement tests, tests
of "perceptual" development, maze performance, and figure drawings
have been employed in numerous studies, no doubt because of the availability of norms and standardized procedures for such instruments. The
Wechsler Intelligence Test for Children (WISC) has been used frequently
and results have been generally positive though not entirely consistent.
One study reported a significant drug-placebo difference in improvement
on full-scale IQ (Conners 1971*a*), another found a significant effect for
verbal IQ alone (Conners 1971*d*), and several studies reported either
clear trends or significant results for performance IQ (Conners 1971*d;*
Conners and Rothschild 1968; Epstein, Lasagna, Conners, and Rodriguez
1968; Knights and Hinton 1969). Other studies have failed to find drug-
placebo differences on either verbal or performance IQ (Conners et al.
1969; Finnerty et al. 1971). One explanation for this lack of total uni-
formity has been given by Conners (1972*a*). It seems unlikely, even given
a brain dysfunction hypothesis, that a trial of stimulant drugs over two to
eight weeks would actually affect general intellectual *ability.* Rather, one
would expect that aspects of the WISC dependent on motivation, concentration, or other *performance* factors would be more likely to yield
experimental results. This notion is supported by the apparently more
consistent results with performance subscales. The coding (digit symbol
substitution) subscale, for example, showed a drug advantage in every
study cited above.

Improvement on achievement tests in math (Conners, Rothschild, Eisenberg, Swartz, and Robinson 1969) and reading and spelling (Conners
1971*a*) has also been reported. Since these studies were only a few weeks
in duration, a performance rather than an ability interpretation is again
most plausible. One four-to-six-month study found no drug-placebo difference on spelling or reading achievement test scores over this period
(Conrad, Dworkin, Shai, and Tobiessen 1971).

Conners (1971*c,* 1972*a*) has also interpreted the consistent stimulant
drug effects with figure drawings (Conners 1970*a,* 1971*c;* Millichap,
Aymot, Sturgis, Larsen, and Egan 1968) and Porteus mazes in terms of

constructs such as attention span and test-taking attitude. In a series of well-controlled studies Conners and his colleagues consistently found both Dexedrine (an amphetamine) and Ritalin to be superior to placebo in improving Porteus maze performance (Conners 1971a; Conners and Eisenberg 1963; Conners et al. 1969; Epstein et al. 1968). Routinely, the Porteus IQ score, which presumably is affected by planning, judgment, and attention, yields positive results, while the "qualitative" score (motor coordination and other qualitative aspects of the performance) does not. Knights and Hinton (1969) also obtained a significant Ritalin effect using a mechanically scored stylus maze test. Specifically, Knights and Hinton found that *duration* of contacts with the sides of the maze, rather than number of contacts with the edges or speed of completion, was affected. This supports the contention that improvement on maze performance reflects motivation or attention variables (careful monitoring of performance) rather than intellectual or motor abilities.

Two standard developmental tests of "organicity" or "maturational lag," the Frostig Developmental Test of Visual Perception and the Bender Visual-Motor Gestalt Test (Koppitz scoring system), have been employed in several drug evaluation experiments. While results with the Bender have not been impressive, positive results have been obtained with the Frostig, especially for the figure-ground and spatial relations subtests (Conners 1971a; Conners et al. 1969; Conrad et al. 1971; Millichap et al. 1968). The figure-ground subtest involves locating designs within a complex background figure and may reflect the ability to concentrate and avoid being distracted.

Vigilance, learning, and other laboratory tasks. An impressive body of literature concerns the beneficial effects of stimulant drugs on perceptual judgments and stimulus detection. In some instances sustained performance is required, and here children on the active drug have shown a significantly greater reduction in errors of omission than have placebo subjects (Campbell, Douglas, and Morgenstern 1971; Conners and Rothschild 1968; Sykes 1969). Also, increased accuracy has been found in vigilance tasks and in other immediate and delayed (recognition) perceptual judgment tasks (Campbell et al. 1971; Conners and Rothschild 1968; Sprague et al. 1970; Sykes 1969). A typical vigilance procedure is the letter detection task of Conners and Rothschild (1968). The child views a continuous series of letters, each presented for .8 seconds. The task is merely to press a switch whenever the child sees the letter A. In an example recognition task the subject is required to rapidly press the "same" ("different") indicator if the test stimulus was present (not present) in a matrix shown seconds before. Where rapid responses are required, stimulant drugs reduce response latency (Sprague et al. 1970; Sykes 1969), and where deliberateness is an advantage, as in the matching-familiar-figures test, children in the drug group have responded more slowly than placebo subjects (Campbell et al. 1971). The work of Conners and Rothschild (1968), Spring, Greenberg, Scott, and Hopwood (unpublished), and Sykes (1969) suggests that these drug effects are due partially to deterioration in placebo group performance over time. Sykes, for example, reported both a main effect and a drug groups X period interaction in a vigilance task, indicating that the drug group was better able to maintain performance over the duration of the task. Spring, et al. reported similar findings for latency of same-different judgments. Improved concentration and ability to maintain concentration has also been cited by Conners et al. (1969) to account for the finding of improved auditory synthesis (assembling orally presented phonemes into words) on stimulant medication.

In light of the findings just discussed, it is not surprising that both simple and choice reaction-time (RT) and variability of RT have been found to be reduced by stimulant drugs (Cohen et al. 1971; Sroufe, Sonies, West, and Wright, 1973; Sykes 1969; Sykes, Douglas, and Morgenstern 1972). Both Sroufe et al. and Sykes found that Ritalin shortened response-time more than placebo, even though hyperactive and control samples were not initially different on this measure. Douglas, Cohen, Sykes, and their colleagues (e.g., Douglas 1972a) routinely pretest measures with hyperactive children and control subjects, and they can therefore determine when drug effects go beyond overcoming a deficit in the hyperactive children.

Children participating in these studies are often referred for "learning disorders," and the effect of stimulant drugs on learning tasks has been examined in a few studies. While the results have been positive, the tasks have been restricted to rote (paired associate) learning (Conners and Eisenberg 1963; Conners and Rothschild 1968; Conners, Eisenberg, and Sharpe 1964). The experiment by Conners and Rothschild is instructive, since they varied association strength of the lists and found no drug group X association strength interaction. This result, together with Conners and Eisenberg's (1963) finding of an effect only on the last block of trials, suggests that the drug effect is due to attention or motivation rather than association ability itself.

Activity level and motor skill. At first glance stimulant drugs seem to produce inconsistent effects on activity level in children with behavior problems, sometimes increasing and sometimes decreasing motor activity. The data are brought into harmony, however, when the studies are divided into those assessing activity level in free-field situations and those monitoring activity during task performance. Stimulant drugs *increase* activity level in free-field situations (Millichap and Boldrey 1967; Witt et al., in

Conners 1971*d*) but consistently *decrease* activity level and irrelevant behavior during task performance (Cohen et al. 1971; Millichap et al. 1968; Sprague et al. 1970; Sroufe et al., 1973). Likewise, time sampling studies in the classroom attest to the effectiveness of stimulant drugs in suppressing task-irrelevant behavior (Sprague et al. 1969, 1970). Conners (1972*a*) has concluded that such reduction in extraneous activity is secondary to improved concentration and the acquisition of a directed quality to activity. This contention is supported by Rapoport et al. (1971), who found a significant reduction in the number of location changes made by hyperactive children during structured play following Dexedrine administration.

Despite frequent clinical reports of increased jitteriness on stimulant drugs, several studies have reported increased visual-motor coordination and motor steadiness following drug administration (Knights and Hinton 1969; Epstein et al. 1968; Millichap et al. 1968). While these data are not completely unambiguous, they are consistent with the findings of increased deliberateness as reflected in results with the Frostig test, maze tests, figure drawings, and choice-discrimination tasks discussed above.

Physiological measures. Physiological measures are important in the evaluation of drugs, especially as they affect children with presumed CNS dysfunction. Unfortunately, both in predrug comparisons of normal and behavior-problem children and in assessments of drug effects, the data based on physiological measures are quite inconsistent. Absence of replication studies, failure to replicate, and frankly contradictory results are the rule.

One consistent finding is that stimulant drugs increase resting autonomic arousal (Cohen et al. 1971; Knights and Hinton 1969; Satterfield and Dawson 1971). However, it is not clear that hyperactive children are different from control children on arousal level prior to drug treatment. Only Satterfield (Satterfield and Dawson 1971) has found lower skin conductance and lower skin conductance lability (spontaneous GSRs), indicators of lower arousal. Others, including the present author, either have found no predrug difference in resting heart-rate, skin conductance and autonomic lability, or have found hyperactivity or impulsivity associated with greater autonomic lability (Boydstun, Ackerman, Stevens, Clements, Peters, and Dykman 1968; Boyle, Dykman, and Ackerman 1965; Cohen et al. 1971; Stevens, Boydstun, Ackerman, and Dykman 1968).

Results on the effects of stimulant drugs on autonomic responses to stimulation, or in anticipation of a stimulus, are also inconsistent. For example, Conners and Rothschild (1969) deduced that hyperactive children, being unable to inhibit responses to irrelevant stimuli, would be slower to habituate (stop responding) to a series of tones, and that Dexedrine would speed such habituation. They did not test the first part of this hypothesis, and others who have (Cohen and Douglas 1972) failed to find differences between hyperactive and control children. Concerning the second part of the hypothesis, Conners and Rothschild did find faster habituation of the finger blood-volume response on Dexedrine than on placebo. However, others have failed to find such differences with different autonomic measures (Cohen et al. 1971). Similarly, Sroufe et al. (1973) report that Ritalin increased the magnitude of heart-rate deceleration in anticipation of a stimulus (assumed to be an index of attentiveness), but Cohen (1970) failed to obtain such results using a similarly described group of hyperactive ("minimal brain dysfunction") children. Cohen used very short intertrial intervals, however, which may not have been sufficient for response recovery.

Not surprisingly, several investigators have reported results with clinical EEGs and other measures of brain function. Early studies reported negative results. Lindsley and Henry (1941), for example, demonstrated improved behavior on amphetamine but failed to find changes in the EEG pattern. More recent studies have used sophisticated measures such as photic driving thresholds (Laufer, Denhoff, and Solomons 1957; Shetty 1971), cortical evoked potentials, or power spectrum analyses of the EEG (Satterfield, Cantwell, Lesser, and Podosin 1972). These studies have produced suggestive results but raise a number of questions for interpretation. They will be discussed below in the section on physiological predictors of drug response.

In sum, both face valid ratings data, and data based on more objective and specific psychological tests and laboratory tasks consistently have shown that short-term treatment with stimulant drugs leads to greater change than does placebo. Task-irrelevant activity is reduced, performance on numerous psychological tests is improved, response latency is shortened, rote learning is better, and performance in vigilance and discrimination tasks is enhanced. In general, the types of tasks yielding positive results are repetitious, mechanical, and/or of long duration, and seem to require concentration, care, and sustained performance. On such tasks there is a frequent tendency for drug effects to become more manifest with lengthy procedures or over trial blocks or testings within a procedure. To date there is no compelling evidence that stimulant drugs have beneficial effects on problem-solving, reasoning, nonrote learning, or actual school achievement.

4. *Stimulant drugs and adult performance (paradoxical drug effect?)*. Until recently it was common practice to describe the effects of stimulant drugs on children with behavior problems as paradoxical. The implica-

tion is that while amphetamines or Ritalin "stimulate" adults and normal children, they have instead a "calming" effect with hyperactive children, while sedatives do not (Lourie 1964; Pincus and Glaser 1966; Sainz 1966). Such a notion is readily challenged. First, it is inappropriate to speak of *a* drug response. As discussed in various parts of this paper, drug effects depend on dosage level, situational factors, subject expectation, and the particular dependent measures employed. Second, only one experiment has been reported in which children described as normal have been given stimulant drugs, so the response of such a sample is not known.[1] Finally, as discussed below, the findings with human adult subjects and those with behavior-problem children are fully consistent.

The literature on stimulant drug effects on adult performance is extensive and has been the subject of two comprehensive reviews by Weiss and Laties (Weiss and Laties 1962; Laties and Weiss 1967). The results have been quite consistent and generally indicate that a wide range of behaviors are "enhanced" by amphetamines, with intellectual tasks being a "notable exception" (Weiss and Laties 1962). When inconsistencies do occur, generally they can be reconciled by consideration of dosage levels or the time lag between drug administration and testing, which have been parametrically manipulated in studies with adults. A consideration of some of the details of this literature will point up the striking parallels between effects reported for adults and those reported for children labeled as hyperactive or behavior-disordered.

With adults amphetamines decrease both simple and discriminative reaction time, even in nonfatigued subjects. They increase motor steadiness, with the possible exception that fine tremor may be increased. They also improve motor coordination, including pursuit motor and other tracking tasks.

Closely related to the tracking tasks are tasks involving "monitoring" or vigilance. A number of these studies have involved a simulated airplane cockpit situation, and the results have been uniformly quite posi-

---

[1] The single experiment found in which control children were given stimulant drugs is that of Shetty (1971). Both control children *and* hyperkinetic children showing a favorable drug response showed an increase in alpha activity following drug administration. It is usually maintained that drug studies with normal children would be unethical (Eisenberg 1971). In light of the increasing number of studies in which children are selected merely on the basis of teacher referral, without neurological or psychological examination (Conners, Eisenberg, and Barcai 1967), such an objection is becoming meaningless. If we cannot do some key drug experiments with "normal" volunteers, perhaps our own children, how can we continue to prescribe these drugs to thousands of children or experiment with heterogeneous samples of referred children? Labeling a behavior problem as medical does not make drug administration ethical. Such a judgment can only be made after a careful weighing of the child's needs and the benefits of the research for human welfare.

tive (Payne and Hauty 1955). Amphetamines overcome the deterioration in performance that occurs with prolonged tasks, oxygen depletion, or other physiologically stressful conditions and also improve performance above base levels. For example, the vigilance procedure used by Mackworth (1950) is similar to procedures used with children and produced parallel results. When adults on placebo were asked to monitor movements of a pointer, pressing a key when infrequent "double-steps" occurred (twelve times in a half hour), performance deteriorated strikingly after the first half hour. With amphetamine, however, errors of omission remained constant and response latencies were reduced. Amphetamines also enhance performance on other tasks requiring attentiveness, such as typing (speed and accuracy), crossing out randomly distributed letters within a matrix, and simple arithmetic problems, especially over time.

Well-controlled studies using measures of general intelligence, problem-solving (syllogisms or anagrams), and short-term memory (Crow and Bursill 1970) have been negative. Again, however, amphetamines can overcome the effects of fatigue on such intellectual measures. There are few data on learning, with the exception that amphetamines appear to hasten conditioning and increase the rate at which motor-skill proficiency is achieved.

In reviewing this literature, Weiss and Laties (1962) reached the following conclusions: (1) in many studies much of the effect of stimulant drugs has to do with arresting the decline in proficiency as a session progresses; (2) effects are sometimes due to the overcoming of subject-state variables (fatigue, oxygen depletion) which can cause performance deterioration; (3) some of the effect is due to improved attitude toward the task and increased desire for work; yet, (4) stimulant drugs seem to enhance performance beyond these attitude or fatigue effects, since scores on the drug are often higher than the best prior scores of well-motivated subjects. In summary, both attitude and performance appear to be enhanced by short-term administration of stimulant drugs. Whether such effects persist or whether tolerance develops remains open to question.

Thus, the effects of stimulant drugs with adults are fully congruent with those found in studies of behavior-problem children. Moreover, even within the literature on behavior-problem children, it is clear that the drug response of these children is not paradoxical. First, these drug-treated children are not sedated; for example, they are more active in a free-field situation and they remain vigilant longer than placebo-control subjects. Second, a number of the studies reviewed were based on heterogeneous groups of children, in some cases defined only by teacher referral for behavior problems. Other investigators report positive effects for problem children defined as *either* "organic" or "non-organic" (Knights and Hinton

1969), or for those defined only as delinquent or emotionally disturbed (Conners et al. 1964; Conners et al. 1971). Therefore, even with only one experiment using children defined as "normal," one begins to question whether the reported stimulant drug effects are restricted to children with a unique behavioral syndrome (see footnote 1 above).

Summary

1. There are difficult methodological problems in child psychopharmacology, with even adequate research designs having both disadvantages and advantages.

2. Still, research makes it clear that sedatives and tranquilizers are contraindicated in treating children with behavior problems; sedatives because they may exacerbate symptoms and tranquilizers because of undesirable side effects.

3. Stimulant drugs do seem to produce short-term improvement of both performance and behavior in many children.

4. However, results achieved with stimulant drugs are similar to findings with adults and animals in crucial ways, calling into question the notion of an atypical drug response.

5. Finally, important questions remain concerning the meaning of the drug effects, whether the short-term effects persist, and whether there are undesirable consequences of stimulant drug treatment.

THE SCIENCE OF CHILD PSYCHOPHARMACOLOGY
CURRENT STATUS

Stimulant drug effects are legion, but the meaning of the numerous findings reported above is far from clear. Integration of these data around meaningful physiological models or behavioral constructs which do more than provide names for poorly understood phenomena, has proceeded far more slowly and less successfully than has the accumulation of empirical findings. Sprague and Werry (1971) presented the analogy of a man trying to fix a radio by shaking it, to describe this nearly total empiricism. Which of the numerous effects reported may be primary and which secondary is only now beginning to be specified, and such specifications have been routinely outside of efforts at model building. If we are to have a science of child psychopharmacology, such conceptual integration is necessary.

The Psychological Locus of Stimulant Drug Effects

Concern about model formation or psychological theory has not been clearly apparent in child drug studies to date. Only a single study was found in which negative as well as positive drug findings were predicted (see below), and experiments employing multiple measures of the same construct are extremely rare. Clearly, such studies are crucial for construct validation and theory formulation.

Even when studies do have multiple measures of constructs, or at least measures of multiple constructs, there is a *consistent failure to report intercorrelations among change scores* following drug administration. Some investigators speak of "correlations" among drug effects to refer to the fact, for example, that both clinical and laboratory measures are routinely affected by drugs (Werry 1970). Others attempt to unify sets of findings with constructs like attention (Conners and Rothschild 1968; Conners et al. 1969). However, such interpretations typically have been made without evidence that the various measures are in fact changing together, as one would expect if a common process were involved (see Douglas 1972*a*, for a recent exception). An example will be instructive. The study by Sprague et al. (1970) is exemplary in that type of drug and drug-dosage level were varied, and a central task feature was manipulated along a dimension. A Sternberg-type delayed recognition task was used in which a slide containing one, two, or three pictures was exposed for two, four, or six seconds, respectively. After a four-second interval, a single stimulus was presented, and the child indicated a judgment of "same" or "different" by pressing one of two panels. In addition to accuracy and latency of responses, movement during the task was objectively and quantitatively assessed using a stabilimetric cushion. Moreover, independent of these measures, classroom observations were made on these same subjects. In keeping with the review presented above, Sprague et al. found that Mellaril (thioridazine, a tranquilizer) produced negative or nonsignificant effects while Ritalin treatment led to uniformly positive results, increasing accuracy and reducing latency, movement during the task, and "nonattentive" behavior and isolation periods (punishment) in the classroom. This is an impressive convergence of measures. Unfortunately, it is not reported whether reduced activity during task performance correlated with increased attentiveness at school, or whether the child whose activity was most reduced during the delayed recognition task had shorter latencies or was more accurate. In defense of Sprague et al. (1970), the sample here was small (n = 12) and negative findings would have been ambiguous because of sizeable error variance. Still, such results should be reported, even if based only on rank orderings. Similarly, Conners and Rothschild (1968) included two vigilance tasks, two paired-associate learning tasks, two memory tasks, other psychometric tasks, and parent and teacher ratings, and they report no relationships among change scores in the drug-treated children.

Such examples could be extended considerably, since failure to intercorrelate change scores is the rule throughout this literature, even in studies using large batteries of measures. One begins to suspect that such relationships are not reported because they consistently have failed to yield significant results. Sroufe et al. (1973, see below) and Denhoff, Davis, and Hawkins (1971) have reported such negative findings. Conners (1972b) also reported low change-score intercorrelations among the 32 variables he used, with values seldom greater than .20 or .30. He went on to argue, however, that factor-analyzing these change scores clarifies the nature of the changes which are occurring together. The results of his analysis will be presented in the section on prediction of drug response.

1. *Research derived from models.* The literature has not been completely without attempts at psychological conceptualization. Three experiments will be described that suggest directions for future research. While not without limitations, each of these studies utilized measures chosen because of their presumed relationship to a model of attention.

If we are to assume that children participating in drug evaluation studies have an attention problem, then the extensive empirical and conceptual work on attention in adults and children should be of value in suggesting assessment strategies. Sykes (1969), for example, based his important doctoral thesis on Broadbent's model of attention, with some revisions to accommodate more recent work by Neisser, Machworth, and others (see also Sykes et al. 1971, 1972). Centering on the problem of selectivity in attention (the limited capacity for dividing attention), Sykes deduced that factors such as duration of task and experimenter versus self-pacing would have an important influence on stimulant drug effects with hyperactive children. Therefore, he selected three tasks varying on these dimensions: (1) a choice reaction-time (RT) task with a warning signal so that only brief periods of attention were required, (2) a serial RT task which was of long duration but self-paced (a new stimulus automatically came on following each response), and (3) a continuous performance test (detecting certain letters presented serially), which was both long and experimenter-paced. A major prediction was that there would be drug effects only on the last two tasks. Hyperactive children were not different from control children on choice reaction-time *prior* to drug treatment. However, as our review would lead one to predict, Ritalin affected performance on all three tasks, including choice reaction-time. Moreover, Sykes found a drug group X period interaction only on the continuous performance task (CPT), not on both CPT and serial RT task as predicted. Still, the greater drug-placebo difference on the CPT over time supports Sykes's conclusion that hyperactive children are prone to lapses of attention. This conclusion was corroborated by Sykes's records of "non-observing" responses during the CPT. Though Sykes's results were not completely consistent, and intercorrelations among change scores were not reported, this study provides an excellent example of theory-derived child psychopharmacology.

A recent paper by Sroufe et al. (1973) describes the effect of Ritalin on the relationship between heart rate (HR) deceleration in the foreperiod of a reaction-time task and median RT, both of which have been suggested to be indices of attention by a large number of investigators. In studies with adults and children, significant within- and between-subjects correlations between speed of response and magnitude of HR deceleration just prior to the reaction stimulus have been reported (see Sroufe et al., [1973] for references). Sroufe et al. reported the following results based on these measures: (1) in agreement with Sykes (1969), Ritalin speeded simple reaction-time more than did placebo, even though the hyperactive and control samples were not initially different on median RT; (2) Ritalin significantly increased the average HR deceleration in anticipation of the reaction stimulus more than did placebo; (3) only Ritalin affected the *relationship between* RT and HR deceleration. Before drug treatment, RT and HR deceleration did not correlate for the hyperactive sample, whereas they did for control subjects; that is, nonhyperactive subjects who had larger average HR decelerations had faster median RTs. After Ritalin treatment such a between-subjects correlation was also significant for hyperactive children, whereas following placebo it was not. Again, with the small samples used, the data are not completely consistent. Within-subject correlations between the two variables (that is, trial-by-trial pairings of HR deceleration and RT) were not significant, the change scores on these two measures were not significantly correlated (n = 11), and neither set of change scores correlated with reduction in activity during psychological testing. Still, such studies of drug effects on the relationships between measures purporting to tap the same construct will be far more informative than a continued accumulation of simple drug effects. As suggested earlier, stimulant drugs may affect any routinized performance task.

Finally, there is one exception to the absence of studies in which there are model-based predictions of both positive and negative drug effects. The study is unpublished (described in Sprague et al. 1969), was based on a small sample, and failed to find significant results. Nonetheless, the research strategy is laudable. A standard discrimination learning paradigm was utilized, in which there was an irrelevant dimension (form) during original learning (e.g., red vs. green). If stimulant drugs influence selective attention (that is, allow attention to be focused on the relevant dimension), then drug subjects should take *longer* than placebo subjects on the transfer task when the previously irrelevant dimension becomes relevant.

Although only a tendency in the predicted direction was found, such a procedure and other incidental learning paradigms merit further work. A problem with such procedures is that if original learning is to criterion, placebo subjects may get more exposure to the irrelevant dimension, since treated children should learn the original problem faster; but if there are a fixed number of trials, drug subjects would have more time to attend to the irrelevant dimension after learning the original task. Incidental learning measures obtained outside of learning tasks may provide a solution to this problem.

These examples are not intended as prototype experiments but rather as illustrations of the type of conceptualization that has been lacking in child psychopharmacology to date. Stimulant drugs typically have been expected to produce positive results; that is, to overcome the deficits of these children. However, under specified conditions, any well-developed behavioral model of positive drug effects would certainly have to predict either nonsignificant or negative findings as well. If attention is postulated to become more "focused" with stimulant drugs, then drug-treated subjects may be at a disadvantage on tasks requiring "wide-ranging" attention (broad utilization of cues).

2. *The construct of attention.* Despite certain limitations in the existing data, it is useful to attempt an integration of the findings on stimulant drug effects around an attention construct. As reviewed earlier, stimulant drugs have been associated with reduced activity during task performance and more focused activity in school and in the playroom, all of which suggest increased concentration. Also, an examination of the results on paired associate learning (PAL) and of the findings for IQ, achievement, and other psychological tests reveals that *performance* on these tasks rather than ability per se is affected. As examples, PAL performance change and continuous performance test (vigilance) improvement both load high on the same factor, which Conners (1972*b*) labels "attentional," and achievement test scores, especially arithmetic, sometimes improve sharply in just a few weeks. Moreover, test subscales, which seem heavily dependent on concentration, such as WISC digit symbol and Frostig figure-ground, are most consistently affected by stimulant drugs. And a detailed analysis of motor performance (e.g., on a stylus maze) has shown that scores are improved because of a rapid correction of errors (careful monitoring) rather than flawless performance. Finally, numerous studies find increased accuracy of perceptual judgments, fewer errors of omission on vigilance tasks, shortened reaction-time and decreased reaction-time variability, especially over trials. All of these results are consistent with the notion of increased maintenance of attention following stimulant drug administration. (Both Conners 1972*a*, and Douglas 1972*b*, have

similarly concluded that the host of findings with hyperactive children are best interpreted in terms of an inability to focus and sustain attention.)

There are two major problems with the preceding analysis. One concerns the simplistic notion of implied attention deficit. As discussed in the preceding section, it is frequently assumed that hyperactive children have a general attention deficit, which is overcome with stimulant drugs. For example, hyperactive children, like young children, are posited to have a short "attention span" (Boydstun et al. 1968). The inadequacy of such a general deficit model is readily apparent from observations of children. Distractible as young children and infants are, in many instances, under some circumstances they remain attentive for long periods of time (Moyer and Gilmer 1955; Horowitz, Paden, Bhana, and Self 1972). Piaget (1953) has observed this in infants, and we have confirmed the same thing with preschool children through observation and telemetered heart-rate records of orienting behavior (unpublished data). When engaged in a self-selected puzzle, for example, three- and four-year-olds essentially cannot be distracted. Are there situations in which hyperactive children attend appropriately? Because of a deficit model, our research effort has been unfortunately narrow. To date, we can only conclude with reasonable certainty that hyperactive children *do not* (not *cannot*) maintain attention on routinized, extrinsically motivated tasks. Until we determine the circumstances in which hyperactive children do attend adequately, we will not understand the nature of any attention problem they may have. The research strategy of manipulating situational variables until behavioral similarity is achieved would seem to be fully applicable here (see chapter 11 in this book). Likewise, until we determine the negative effects of stimulant drugs on aspects of attention and behavior, we will not fully understand the positive effects that have been reported.

The second problem with the attention interpretation concerns the difficulty of separating attention from motivation constructs. For example, speed of response and increased vigilance have become standard indices of heightened drive. Also, the greater drug-placebo differences as task duration increases and the increased deliberateness on stimulant drugs suggested by several studies are congruent with a motivation interpretation. Finally, clinical reports and rating studies clearly indicate that feelings of well-being and attitude toward tasks to be performed are altered by short-term trials of stimulant drugs. A motivation interpretation is supported by the factor analytic study of Conners et al. (1967), which suggests that something like "need for achievement" (an "assertiveness" factor) is improved with Dexedrine. An intellectual ability factor, freed from this "motivation" variance, did not show a Dexedrine effect.

Two possible ways to separate attention from motivation would be to use short or exceptionally engaging tasks or to vary incentive parametrically. As an example of the former, Sroufe et al. (1973) used a very short reaction-time task (fifteen trials) and still found drug effects on median RT and heart-rate deceleration prior to the reaction stimulus. While incentive or other motivational manipulations have not been reported in drug studies surveyed, Elliott (1970) has used incentive manipulations to tease apart factors influencing the well-known age changes in reaction time.

There are difficulties in validating a construct like attention, and it may not be separable from motivation (Douglas 1972*b*). Still, testing model-derived hypotheses and generating formulations which integrate existing data will probably be more fruitful than a continued accumulation of empirical findings.

The Physiological Basis of Stimulant Drug Effects

1. *The concept of minimal brain dysfunction.* Much of the rationale for drug treatment of children rests on the assumption of underlying central nervous system impairment. Since it has not been possible to demonstrate frank brain damage in more than a minority of behavior-problem or hyperactive school children, *minimal* brain damage or dysfunction has been postulated (Birch 1964; Clements 1966; Laufer and Denhoff 1957; Minde, Webb, and Sykes 1968; Stewart, Pitts, Craig, and Dieruf 1966; Wender 1971; Werry 1972). The U.S. Department of Health, Education and Welfare (Clements 1966) has defined minimal brain dysfunction as follows:

the "minimal brain dysfunction syndrome" refers to "children of near average, average, or above average general intelligence with certain learning or behavioral disabilities ranging from mild to severe, which are associated with deviations of function of the central nervous system. These deviations may manifest themselves by various combinations of impairment in perception, conceptualization, language, memory, and control of attention, impulse or motor function. . . . During the school years, a variety of learning disabilities is the most prominent manifestation . . ." (pp. 9–10).

This statement is commonly accepted and is similar to those of the American Psychiatric Association and World Health Organization.

At the outset it is important to note that this definition is totally behavioral. Birch (1964), Rutter, Graham, and Yule (1970), and Werry (1968*a*, 1968*c*) have been persuasively critical of using behaviors such as those outlined above as proof of brain damage or dysfunction in the neurological sense.[2] Birch (1964) underscored the point that the adjective *minimal* "does not increase the descriptive accuracy of the term or add to either its scientific validity or its usefulness. Regardless of any adjectives, we have the overriding obligation to demonstrate . . . that the multiplicity of aberrant behaviors we now attribute to 'minimal brain damage' are, in fact, the result of damage to the brain" (p. 5).

The concept of an MBD syndrome rests on four assumptions, each of which can be challenged: (1) that there is a syndrome—that is, that the behaviors subsumed under this rubric form a unitary cluster; (2) that the syndrome can be related to underlying neuropathology or "dysfunction"; (3) that indices of neuropathology can be utilized to predict drug response; and (4) that a positive response to stimulant drugs is itself indicative of underlying neuropathology or dysfunction (Laufer and Denhoff 1957; Lourie 1964; Sainz 1966; Solomons 1965; Wender 1971). Since the logic underlying the fourth proposition is patently circular (see, for example, Eisenberg 1959, on reasoning from effects to causes) and is clearly contradicted by our review of the adult and child literature, we will focus our discussion on the first three assumptions.

2. *Relationships among variables subsumed under the MBD label.* While clustering of variables such as hyperactivity, impulsivity, underachievement, and the like is generally assumed, very few relevant data are available. Multiple measures of these constructs are seldom utilized and intercorrelations are almost never reported (Boydstun et al. 1968; Clements 1966; Laufer and Denhoff 1957; Stevens, Boydstun, Dykman, Peters, and Hinton 1967). Studies which do not force clustering through subject selection fail to find much support for a syndrome. For example, when Palkes and Stewart (1972) compared children selected for overactivity and distractibility with control children matched for socioeconomic status, they did find differences in tested IQ. However, they did not find differences on standard perceptual-motor tasks or on achievement tests after IQ was partialled out; that is, underachievement (learning disability) and perceptual-motor problems could not be predicted from activity-distractibility status.

Even children with known or probable brain damage, or those selected to meet the criteria of "minimal brain dysfunction," fail to exhibit a uni-

[2] To illustrate his point concerning the mutual contamination of behavior and neurological disciplines, Birch (1964) related the story of a remarkable concordance between the sounding of a village clock and a rifle volley at a nearby garrison. The sergeant explained that he could be so precise because he set his watch every day by the village clock. The clockmaker, in turn, explained his precision by explaining that each day at 5:00 sharp there was a rifle volley, and he adjusted his clock accordingly.

form pattern of behaviors (Birch 1964; Ernhart, Graham, Eichman, Marshall, and Thurston 1963; Graham, Ernhart, Thurston, and Craft 1962; Kaspar, Millichap, Backus, Child, and Schulman 1971; Pond 1961; Werry 1968c). Werry (1972) gave a good review of this literature and in another paper (1968c) reported the most relevant and crucial study for our consideration. First, he intercorrelated sixty-seven neurological, psychometric, performance, and rating variables on a large sample selected for meeting the criteria of MBD. Then, from these intercorrelations *ten orthogonal factors* were derived. The variance was rather evenly distributed across these ten factors, with the first factor accounting for *only* 16 percent. The first factor was almost purely neurological (impaired rapid-finger movements, finger flexion extension, standing or hopping on one foot), with other independent factors reflecting history of perinatal complications, cognitive abilities, figure-drawing ability and so forth. This is clearly not the pattern of results predicted by the notion of an MBD syndrome. Schulman, Kaspar, and Throne (1965) reached a similar conclusion from their factor-analytic study with retarded children. Hyperactivity, distractibility, emotional lability, inconsistency, and so on, all operationally defined and measured, failed to intercorrelate, and only distractibility could be related to neurological or EEG measures. Even factor analyses of parent or teacher ratings, which are, of course, not based on independent measures, have failed to yield much evidence of a syndrome (Conners 1969; Conners 1970b).

As Birch (1964), Werry (1968c), and Stewart (Stewart and Olds, in press) have concluded, there is apparently not *a* MBD child but a large variety of children with learning or behavioral problems. This is in accord with the great heterogeneity in both symptomatology and drug response of behavior-problem children reported in virtually all drug studies surveyed (Conners 1971d; Knights and Hinton 1969). Finally, in a recent chapter to be discussed more fully below, Conners (1972b) was able to make firm predictive statements about drug response only after dividing his sample of behavior-problem children into seven distinct groups.

3. *Underlying neuropathology and neurological predictors of drug response.* As suggested above, only a minority of children designated as having MBD show clearly abnormal EEGs or neurological signs of brain damage (Clements 1966; Stewart et al. 1966). Given the failure to tie hyperkinesis or behavior problems to frank brain damage, proponents of the MBD concept argue that the abnormalities involved are mild, borderline, or subclinical (Clements 1966). Thus, clinical studies have claimed that children with MBD have a greater prevalence of "equivocal" or "soft" neurological signs (e.g., choreiform movements, poor fine or gross visual-motor coordination, general awkwardness) and *minor* EEG dys-

rhythmias, and more often have medical histories suggestive of CNS impairment (Burks 1960; Clements 1966; Clements and Peters 1962; Paine 1962; Prechtl and Stemmer 1962; Sainz 1966; Strauss and Lehtinen 1947; Weiss, Minde, Werry, Douglas, and Nemeth 1971).

However, most of the studies on EEG and neurological "soft" signs fail to use standardized criteria and often lack necessary control groups; that is, the judgments of abnormality are subjective and not independent of knowledge of behavior problems. In a well-known study, for example, Prechtl and Stemmer (1962) reported that many hyperkinetic children exhibit choreiform movements (slight, jerky, irregular movements in various muscles) and that such children have reading and other achievement problems. However, in a study utilizing a control group, Rutter, Graham, and Birch (1966) found choreiform movements to be quite unreliable and to exhibit no correlation with behavioral status (reliably assessed) or complications of pregnancy. Similarly, most studies finding order within the minor dysrhythmias of the ambiguous EEG lack adequate controls. Controlled studies sometimes find differences between hyperactive and control children (Burks 1960) and sometimes do not (Werry, Weiss, and Douglass 1964). There is a tendency for investigators reporting positive findings to give less information about rating criteria and steps taken to ensure blindness of ratings. It should also be pointed out that if certain equivocal neurological signs or minor EEG abnormalities are shown to discriminate between behavior-problem children and controls (Satterfield, Lesser, Saul, and Cantwell, in press; Weiss et al. 1971), the meaning of such signs will still be unclear. The EEG, for example, is notably unreliable (even in coarse judgments), fails to correlate with neurological status in well-controlled studies, is highly unstable, and is frequently abnormal in both normal and psychiatrically-ill children (Werry 1972). Also, EEG dysrhythmias and neurological "soft" signs may represent a psychophysiological reaction to the testing procedure rather than physiological dysfunction (Werry 1972).

Attempts to tie hyperkinesis or behavior problems to historical antecedents suggestive of neurological impairment are also inconclusive. A large number of investigators have reported a high incidence of pre- and perinatal complications in the history of these children, but these studies are based on maternal report and fail to include control groups (Burks 1960; Laufer et al. 1957; Prechtl and Stemmer 1962; Strauss and Lehtinen 1947). In a study based on actual medical records, Minde et al. (1968) found no evidence for a differential frequency of complications in pregnancy or delivery (e.g., anoxia) which might produce brain damage. They also found that information from mothers was quite inaccurate, with mothers of hyperactive children erring in the direction of overstating the degree and amount of difficulty. Thus, they concluded that earlier positive findings, including one report by their own group (Werry et al. 1964), were artifactual. Also, in an important *prospective* study, Graham et al. (1962) found that anoxia and other perinatal complications did lead to greater cognitive deficit and neurological impairment than was true for control subjects. However, such complications were not associated with hyperactivity (parent questionnaire) and did not produce a particular behavior-disorder syndrome. The important epidemiologic study by Rutter et al. (1970) similarly failed to find evidence for an association between a particular behavior disorder and organic brain dysfunction. As Werry (1972) concluded from both the neurological comparisons and the birth-history data, it seems that "the better the study methodologically, the smaller the effect observed."

Like attempts to relate children's behavior problems to underlying neuropathology, prediction of stimulant drug response on the basis of neurological status has, at best, produced inconsistent results. Typically, when investigators have divided their sample into "organic" or "nonorganic" groups or have correlated drug response with individual neurological or EEG indices, stimulant drugs have not been found to be differentially effective for "organic" subjects (Burks 1964; Knights and Hinton 1969; Knobel et al. 1959; Weiss et al. 1971; Werry 1968; Werry and Sprague, in press; Zrull et al. 1966). The many studies finding positive stimulant drug effects with heterogeneous groups of children, sometimes selected only on the basis of teacher referral, also have suggested that neurological status is irrelevant to the outcome of stimulant drug treatment (Conners et al. 1967; Conners and Rothschild 1968). While occasional studies have reported successful prediction of drug response with neurological, EEG, or other physiological indices (Conrad and Insel 1967; Rapoport, Lott, Alexander, and Abramson 1970; Satterfield et al. 1972, in press; Steinberg et al. 1971), no single neurological index or neurological battery has been established through cross-validation to have predictive utility.

4. *Arousal level and catecholamines as predictors of drug response.* Recently there has been growing interest in the use of biochemical measures and autonomic and EEG indices or arousal to predict positive responses to stimulant drugs. Considered individually, some of the theoretical and empirical work in this area is intriguing. Taken as a whole, however, the picture that emerges is quite unclear.

High arousal. Some investigators have theorized that hyperactive or MBD children are overaroused, with stimulant drugs decreasing arousal level (Laufer et al. 1957; Wender 1971), while others have suggested that they are underaroused (Conners 1971*b;* Satterfield and Dawson 1971; Satterfield et al. 1972). Arousal level would certainly seem to be a relevant consideration in studying children presumed to be abnormal with respect to activity level. The work of two of these investigators, Wender and Satterfield, can be used as a framework for a discussion of the research findings in this very active area.

Based on observations from his clinical practice, Wender (1971) has presented one of the few comprehensive theories concerning stimulant drug effects with children. He bases his formulation on the following assumptions about children he believes may suffer from "minimal brain dysfunction": (1) they are typically higher in arousal than normal children; (2) they have defective reward mechanisms in that they are not influenced by rewards and punishment; (3) paradoxically, they are calmed by stimulant drugs in low to moderate doses (stimulants lower arousal and do not produce euphoria); and (4) excited by high doses of stimulants. From these assumptions and a review of the animal literature, Wender explained the "paradoxical" drug effect, using a two-component model which includes an excitatory system and an inhibitory system in the lower brain. Essentially, Wender postulated that the typical MBD child has low cortical norepinephrine levels and thus a deficient inhibitory system. Amphetamines, being chemically quite similar to the catecholamines epinephrine and norepinephrine (NE), substitute for the NE, acting on both the inhibitory and excitatory systems. Since the curvilinear inhibitory function is more steeply sloped near the zero point, the net effect for these low-arousal children is an increase in inhibitory capacity (Wender 1971, p. 187). As discussed in various parts of this chapter, the assumptions listed above are either currently without clear support or are contradicted by the current research evidence. Still, the model is not implausible, and the speculations on NE levels may be valid even if the assumptions made are without clear basis.

While Wender himself failed to find differences in monoamine (including catecholamine) production between MBD and control children (Wender, Epstein, Kopin, and Gordon 1971), Rapoport et al. (1970) did report data which they felt were consistent with Wender's notion. While hyperactive and control children were again not significantly different on predrug urinary NE levels, there was a significant negative correlation between NE level and objectively measured playroom activity before treatment. Also, low predrug NE level was associated with a greater reduction in playroom activity following amphetamine treatment, though it is not clear what the magnitude of the correlation would have been with predrug activity partialled out. A major problem in relating these data to Wender's theory is that the relationship between urinary and CNS NE levels is not clear and is not necessarily positive. Kornetsky (1970) presented some evidence that the relationship is negative and further suggested that "hyperkinesis" is due to an *increase* in the synthesis or turn-over rate of NE in the CNS, which is counteracted by amphetamine. (The data on the relationship between amphetamine action and brain catechola-mines is quite complicated [Costa and Garattini 1970], so that it is diffi-cult to reconcile or choose between these two positions at present.)

The picture is further clouded by the data of Epstein et al. (1968). Using a very small sample of hyperactive children, they reported that an organic subgroup with rather clear indications of CNS damage showed a more positive response to amphetamine on some measures. Further, the organic group tolerated larger doses of the drug and excreted greater amounts, though this may have been due to their greater urinary volume. Again, it is difficult to relate this finding to Wender's theory, and Wender himself failed to do so. The greater tolerance of these children for am-phetamines seems to square with the idea of "depleted stores" of NE, but why would children excreting more drug show a more positive response?

A classic study by Laufer et al. (1957) may also be interpreted as sup-port for the high-arousal position. Laufer et al. demonstrated that low photo-Metrazol thresholds (the amount of titrated Metrazol per mg/body weight required to produce an EEG burst and myoclonic jerking of the forearms in response to a strobe light) distinguished hyperkinetic from nonhyperkinetic children, and that amphetamine administration signifi-cantly increased this threshold in the hyperactive sample. With some evidence, they interpreted their findings as indicative of diencephalon (subcortex) dysfunction. Specifically, they hypothesized lowered synaptic resistance in the diencephalon, with the consequence that incoming stim-uli irradiate diffusely, flooding the cortex. As a result these children are hypertonic (aroused) and unable to inhibit or delay responses. Ampheta-mine increases synaptic resistance, reducing the "storm" of impulses from the diencephalon. Shetty (1971) has recently reported data similar to those of Laufer et al. Eleven of thirty-six hyperkinetic children initially exhibited photic driving (EEG frequencies which were fundamentals or harmonics of a photic flicker frequency). Seven of these eleven children were given injections of d-amphetamine or methylphenidate, and six of these seven no longer showed photic driving, while all four subjects in-jected with saline continued to show such a response. Unfortunately, from Shetty's study it cannot be concluded that hyperkinetic children show a higher frequency of photic driving than normal children or that the drug response of these children is atypical, because only adults selected for having photic driving were used as control subjects. Wender does not try to incorporate the data of Laufer et al. into his scheme, though such an integration would be possible merely by assuming that low NE levels in the diencephalon would lower synaptic resistance.

Low arousal. Turning now to the low-arousal position, Satterfield and Dawson (1971) reported that hyperactive children have lower basal skin conductance and less nonspecific GSR activity. Both of these findings indicated lower autonomic arousal and both were unexpected by the authors. Since amphetamines are sympathomimetic drugs, it is not surprising that they tended to raise arousal level in this and other studies (see "Physical Side Effects" below). Satterfield and Dawson speculated that overactivity in these children is secondary to low arousal and serves a stimulus-generating function. Further, stimulant drugs lower activity and "calm" hyperactive children by *raising* mid-brain RAS (reticular activating system) excitability. As is the case with Wender's theory, many of the key assumptions here do not have empirical support; for example, as presented earlier, free-field activity of hyperactive children increases following stimulant drug medication. Also, no other investigator has found evidence for lower autonomic arousal in hyperactive or MBD children, and the weight of the evidence appears to be counter to this position (Boydstun et al. 1968; Cohen et al. 1971; Stevens et al. 1968). In a more recent study Satterfield himself found *higher* skin conductance levels in children diagnosed as MBD, though he points to differences in the testing situation to explain the discrepancy (personal communication).

CNS measures. In light of the inconsistent results with autonomic indices, investigators have been turning to CNS measures. Both Satterfield and Conners have reported EEG (power spectrum analyses) and/or evoked potential data that could be interpreted in terms of a low-arousal hypothesis. In a study to be discussed later, Conners (1972b) found that predrug differences in latency and amplitude of visual evoked potentials distinguished his seven distinct groups of problem children, who subsequently showed different patterns of change in response to stimulants. In one of Satterfield's studies (Satterfield et al. 1972, and in press) children "diagnosed independently by two child psychiatrists as MBD" showed more amplitude attenuation and slower latency of the cortical evoked response than control subjects. Satterfield et al. pointed to the frequent slow dysrhythmias in the EEGs of the MBD children and the evoked potential data in concluding that MBD children have delayed maturation of the CNS, and that high drug-responders are low in arousal before treatment. In the 1972 report, low skin conductance level, high amplitude of the resting EEG, and high amplitude of the auditory evoked response (with slow recovery), all assessed prior to treatment, distinguished the six best (of thirty-one) from the five worst responders to Ritalin, based on teacher ratings. However, these autonomic, EEG, and evoked potential data have not yet been related to each other, and none of the individual findings here have been replicated. Also, some of the findings reported are quite confusing. Satterfield et al. (in press) has reported that the evoked potential amplitude of MBD children is lower than that of control subjects; yet, in the 1972 paper, high amplitude predicted better drug response.

Contradictory findings. Until there is convergence of these measures, or at least replication, one hesitates to conclude that these physiological measures are useful in predicting drug response. In this regard, Satterfield's findings cannot be considered a replication of Conners' published evoked potential study (1971*b;* 1972*b*). Conners found attenuation and longer latency of the *later* components of the *visual* evoked potential. Satterfield et al. (1972, and in press) reported findings for earlier components of the *auditory* evoked potential. In fact, Satterfield et al. may have found shorter latencies for the portion of the wave suggested by Conners to have longer latency. There is clearly a need for replication of these studies.

The low-arousal hypothesis suggested by Satterfield and Dawson (1971) seems in direct opposition to the theory of Laufer (Laufer et al. 1957), which suggests greater subcortical excitability in hyperactive children. In their photo-Metrazol study Laufer et al. did not obtain autonomic measures, and the correlation between photo-Metrazol threshold, other EEG indices, and autonomic arousal is not known. Perhaps lower photo-Metrazol threshold does not indicate higher basal arousal but rather greater reactivity. Unfortunately, the data on reactivity are also inconsistent, with differences in autonomic responsiveness not being found in most studies comparing hyperactive or MBD children with control subjects. The habituation study of Conners and Rothschild (1969), described earlier, can be interpreted as indicating greater reactivity to stimuli in hyperactive children, but other studies have not found habituation differences. And in their own study Satterfield and Dawson (1971) reported *lower* responsivity in the hyperactive sample, which is in agreement with the finding that hyperactive children have shown less increase in skin conductance than controls upon becoming engaged in a reaction-time task (Cohen and Douglas 1972).

In sum, what we have here are contradictory theories and inconsistent or as yet unreplicated experimental findings. One way out of the dilemma is to suggest that some MBD or behavior-problem children are overaroused (hyper*active*) and others are underaroused (hyper*reactive*); that is, variability of arousal level is greater in these children. This seems to be an increasingly popular notion (Satterfield et al. 1972) and agrees with the clinical impression that some hyperactive children seem to become settled in unintrusive stimulus environments, while others do not. The problem is that this post-hoc interpretation does not readily account for the significant differences reported. Also, if future research consistently reveals greater variability in arousal (extreme highs and lows) in hyperactive or MBD samples, this would probably be best interpreted as contrary to the notion of a syndrome; that is, more variability in arousal might well be found in the clinical sample because such samples are often heterogeneous. Since the clinical samples are referred and diagnosed in a variety of ways and are not volunteers, such groups probably include retarded, brain-damaged, emotionally disturbed, and normal children, some of whom would be highly anxious, others of whom would be poorly motivated, and so forth. Sampling differences would then account for the occasional significant differences in one direction or another. To establish that such high variability is due to the presence of two or more types of hyperactive children rather than to sample heterogeneity, consistent intercorrelations across studies must be obtained, and predictors of drug response must be cross-validated. This will, no doubt, be the subject of a great amount of continuing research.

5. *The sum of the evidence.* It is, of course, not being argued that the brain does not affect behavior, that stimulant drugs do not affect the central nervous system, or that some hyperactive children do not have CNS impairment. It is merely being argued that, to date, there is no compelling evidence that brain damage or dysfunction produces a single behavioral syndrome or that, as a group, the children labeled hyperactive, hyperkinetic, or MBD have underlying neuropathology or dysfunction. As Birch (1964) has concluded, "all of our designations of nervous system damage, whether they be described as minimal, diffuse, or as non-focal, remain presumptive" (p. 5). Similarly, the neurological examination is apparently unrelated to diagnosis of these children (Kenny, Clemmens, Hudson, Lentz, Cicci, and Nair 1971), and the "relevance of organic factors in the prognosis and treatment of hyperactive children has not yet been demonstrated" (Werry 1968*b*, p. 183). Research should continue aimed at specifying the mechanisms underlying stimulant drug effects and isolating the small subset of children who may show a dramatic response to stimulant drugs. At present, there is a clear need for replication studies, especially those that would relate autonomic and EEG measures of arousal and catecholamine levels. However, on the basis of the work to date, it is difficult to conclude that we are on the threshold of a major breakthrough in our understanding of either behavior and learning problems or the effects of stimulant drugs with children. Clearly, proposals for massive screening of school children on the basis of neurological, physiological, or biochemical measures are premature, at best.

Summary

1. The development of psychological or physiological models to account for the multitude of stimulant drug effects is proceeding slowly.

2. While many of the existing data can be integrated around an attention concept, much work needs to be done to make such a formulation precise.

3. Physiological models have primarily revolved around the concept of "minimal brain dysfunction."

4. The concept of MBD is in large part a tautology, being frequently defined in terms of a positive drug response.

5. Independent of drug response, there is little evidence that behaviors subsumed under the MBD label cluster together or that children called MBD or hyperactive constitute a homogeneous entity.

6. Currently, considerable research is aimed at discovering biochemical or physiological predictors of drug response.

7. However, to date, no biochemical, physiological, or neurological index, test, or test battery has been established through cross-validation to predict drug response.

Problems in Evaluating Drug Treatment of Children

Despite the consistency in the data on short-term effects of stimulant drugs with children, a number of problems arise in attempting to utilize these data in evaluating current medical practice. Two sets of problems will be considered here: (1) those related to limitations in the existing data, that is, what is *not known* about the effects of stimulant drugs with children; and (2) those concerning extradrug factors which influence drug effects. Then, alternative intervention strategies will be considered since such a discussion is necessary to evaluate fully drug treatment.

Limitations in the Existing Data

1. *Absence of long-term drug studies: behavioral effects.* Perhaps the most glaring deficiency in the child pharmacotherapy literature is the absence of long-term controlled experiments with objective measures. Only one study with a drug trial longer than eight weeks has been conducted (Conrad, Dworkin, Shai, and Tobiessen 1971); the typical drug trial in this review was four weeks or less. To evaluate the practice of medicating large numbers of children over a span of several years we *must* know whether the behavioral and/or negative side effects of stimulant drugs persist. The necessary information is simply not available.

Logistically, such long-term evaluations would be quite difficult because of subject attrition and the washing out of drug effects due to uncontrolled environmental or developmental changes. The latter problem is, of course, part of the point. If objective drug effects are not powerful enough to emerge despite changes in curriculum, teaching competence, the family situation, and the like, one must question the utility of such medication. To date, evidence on this point is meagre and largely tangential. Knights and Hinton (1969), for example, in their well-controlled six-week drug study, had a number of pre-measures that were obtained five and a half months prior to the start of their experiment. They concluded that the general lack of results with these measures was due to tutoring and parental counseling which had intervened, washing out the drug effects. In a four-to-six-month study, Conrad et al. (1971) found drug-placebo differences only on Frostig subtests and ratings data (discussed below), not on a number of cognitive and clinical measures. In addition, Zimmerman and Burgemeister (1958), who also utilized a lengthy drug trial (six months), reported very limited effects over this period following amphetamine administration. This study is merely suggestive, however, because there was no placebo-control group and no statistical analysis of results.

The argument has been made by a number of clinicians and researchers that behavioral effects with children will persist over several years because children, unlike adults, do not develop tolerance for stimulant drugs and do not exhibit habituation (Conners 1972a; Eisenberg 1972). The argument that children generally do not develop tolerance for stimulant drugs is in part circular; that is, it is based on the presumed persistence of drug effects. As just discussed, this assumption is supported by little experimental evidence. It should be pointed out that the deterioration of performance reported when children are temporarily withdrawn from medication does not demonstrate the persistence of positive drug effects but may rather be interpreted as evidence of behavioral drug dependence. Work with animals suggests a deterioration in performance following withdrawal of amphetamines, even after a maintenance dosage has been achieved (Thompson and Pickens 1971). In addition to long-term assessments, studies are needed in which children are gradually shifted from drug to placebo so that such behavioral withdrawal can be minimized.

A second argument concerning the lack of tolerance, and therefore persistence of effects, has to do with the ease of establishing a "maintenance" dosage with children. However, there is no evidence that children differ from adults in this respect. It is not legitimate, as is frequently done, to compare a child under physician's care to a "speed" abuser who controls his own intake of amphetamine, using large amounts of drug within a period of hours for the purpose of experiencing a "rush." Adults, carefully monitored, would also be expected to maintain dosage levels of amphetamine (Office of Child Development Report 1971), as is the case with many of the heroin addicts maintained on methadone. Also, cessation of stimulant drug intake is *not* associated with physical withdrawal symptoms in children, but this is the case with adults as well (Gillespie 1970). Adults do often exhibit lethargy and increased need for sleep following stimulant drug withdrawal, but, as reported by Small, Hibi, and

Feinberg (1971), this may also be the case with children. They reported that 20 mg of Dexedrine given in the morning delayed sleep onset and onset of REM sleep in three hyperactive-children studied. Also, *during amphetamine withdrawal* the children were sleepier during the day and slept more deeply at night.

Summarizing here, there is nothing in the literature, to date, that suggests an atypical amphetamine response in children; that is, that children, unlike adults, fail to show tolerance for stimulant drugs. Whether adaptation to the effects of stimulant drugs occurs within the drug regimens typically utilized remains an empirical question. At least one experienced clinician feels that stimulant drugs, especially Ritalin, lose their effectiveness over time (Stewart 1970: Stewart and Olds, in press).

2. *Absence of long-term studies: physical side effects.* Despite the substantial number of drug studies with children and the widespread use of stimulant drugs in medical practice, there has been little systematic research on short-term physical side effects and almost no adequate research on long-term effects. As is the case with adults, the most frequent initial side effects of both Ritalin and the amphetamines are loss of appetite and sleeplessness (Conners 1971*a;* Conners and Eisenberg 1963; Epstein et al. 1968; Laufer and Denhoff 1957; Small et al. 1971). Sadness of expression, unhappiness, and irritability are also frequently reported (Conners 1971*a;* Laufer et al. 1957; Stewart and Olds, in press). Epstein et al. (1968), for example, reported that nine out of ten of their subjects cried without provocation during the first few days of amphetamine treatment. Physical complaints such as headaches, stomachaches, jitteriness, and anxiety are apparently infrequent, although Conners and Eisenberg (1963) found a significant increase in nail biting (and a trend for stomachaches) on Ritalin as compared to placebo. At least two studies with Ritalin reported increases in heart rate, blood pressure, and/or skin conductance (Cohen et al. 1971; Knights and Hinton 1969). Finally, Werry and Sprague (in press) have found side effects with Ritalin, principally weight loss and stomachaches, to be a direct function of dosage up to 1.0 mg/kg, the highest dosage studied.

It is important to point out that these side effects generally last only a few days (sleeplessness, irritability, tearing) or weeks (appetite, autonomic reactions). It almost never happens that a child must be withdrawn from an experiment because of severe adverse effects. Children, like adults, may develop tolerance for the side effects of stimulant drugs.

Although there is only one report of physical harm from long-term drug treatment in the literature (Safer, Allen, and Barr 1972), it is probably too early to know in detail about possible long-term effects of stimulant drugs. Widespread use of these drugs with children is quite recent, so that the effects of several years of drug treatment on, for example, kidney function in adult life cannot be known. The fact that in an eight-week study Dexedrine produced "no hematologic, liver, kidney, or cardiovascular effects of consequence" (Conners 1971*a*) cannot really be reassuring on this point, though it is valuable information. Similarly, parent questionnaire responses following twelve to sixteen months of stimulant drug treatment are not sufficient basis for the conclusion that "it is safe to employ these chemical aids for a year or more, if necessary (Comley 1971)." In the single study alluded to above, Safer et al. (1972) reported suppression of weight increase for children treated with stimulant drugs compared to other hyperactive children not given drugs because of parental objection. This drug effect persisted for more than two years. Safer et al. also reported that thirteen children taken off medication during the summer showed a rebound weight increase, gaining significantly more weight than seven children remaining on medication. The data also suggested greater effects for Dexedrine or large (30–40 mg) doses of Ritalin as compared to smaller (20 mg) Ritalin dosages. While this study was based on heterogeneous samples, and control children in each sample could be systematically different from "experimental" subjects (there was not random assignment), the data are nonetheless disconcerting.

In summary, there is only modest evidence to date that Ritalin or Dexedrine produce harmful physical effects, even over several years with daily dosages larger than those employed in experiments with adults (up to 40 mg of Dexedrine, 75 mg of Ritalin). However, it certainly has not been demonstrated that these drugs are safe or that the effects with the developing child are similar to the effects with adults (Ghent 1959; Kornetsky 1970). "What is given briefly at a particular developmental period may have unforeseen long-term consequences," and "the available data urge caution upon us" (Eisenberg 1971, p. 373).

3. *Limitations in variables assessed.* As discussed earlier, a serious limitation in the existing information on stimulant drug effects with children derives from the homogeneous nature of the tasks employed. The tasks used in typical drug-evaluation studies are repetitious, relatively unengaging, and/or of long duration. While the routinized measures commonly employed may represent proper analogues of skills required in school, information with regard to reasoning, concept learning and other cognitive skills should be available before considering long-term treatment of children, especially in light of the failure to find changes in academic achievement (Conrad et al. 1971). To determine whether positive drug effects are limited to routinized tasks, studies should be done in which engagingness of task is manipulated. Studies with adults (above) certainly suggest that routinization of task and subject motivation are important

parameters in stimulant drug research. Note that it is not being argued that stimulant drugs take the curious child and dull his senses, but only that there is a notable lack of information concerning core human abilities and the range of stimulant drug effects in terms of the nature of the task.

4. *Predicting drug response.* As discussed earlier, information is currently not sufficient to enable the clinician to predict from neurological or physiological variables which children will show the most favorable drug response. Even when certain indices have yielded significant results, relationships are far from perfect. For example, Satterfield et al. (in press) found that abnormal EEG and/or neurological status predicted teacher ratings of improved behavior. Still, in the group with neither abnormal EEG nor neurological status, 60 percent of the subjects were rated as clearly improved. A similar generalization can be made about prediction from psychological test data or other nonmedical information (Knights and Hinton 1969). While findings with certain physiological or psychological measures have been provocative, at present no single index, test, combination of tests, or test battery has been established as a valid predictor of drug response (Report of the Office of Child Development 1971).

A paper by Conners (1972b) represents the most comprehensive and suggestive work to date on the problem of predicting drug response. This paper has underscored the problems of prediction that remain to be solved. Beginning with the argument that inconsistencies within and across drug studies may be due to subject diversity. Conners factor-analyzed predrug scores on thirty-two measures and subjected the factor scores to a profile analysis. Seven distinct groups emerged, and these groups exhibited different patterns of drug response as measured by six independent "gain" factors derived from a factor analysis of change scores. (Conners argued that such gain factors are logically more powerful than separate measures, and he reports high multiple-correlations between combinations of predrug measures and these gain factors.) Some groups changed on one set of gain factors, some on others, and one group (20 percent of the total sample) showed no drug response on any of the factors. While the "logic" behind the different patterns of change for the various groups is difficult to perceive, except that there is generally improvement where initial performance was suppressed, and while the group structure and the relationship to gain factors must be cross-validated, the results are probably not due simply to capitalizing on chance. The seven groups were distinguished in terms of latencies and amplitudes of late components (Wave VI) of the visual evoked potential and in terms of hemispheric dominance, and these measures were not included in the original factor analysis. The seven groups also differed in terms of change on some of the evoked potential measures following drug treatment.

It is important to point out that what was being predicted in Conners's study was group improvement on particular factors, which is sometimes accompanied by lowering of performance on other factors. Whether a particular child would show drug improvement and whether the overall improvement would be sufficient to outweigh possible costs remains at present a matter of clinical judgment. And, of course, this set of findings, including the evoked potential data, must be replicated before firm conclusions can be reached. Still, the attempt to specify discrete groups of children who show particular types of response will probably be more profitable than efforts to show that stimulant drugs are uniquely beneficial for behavior-problem children taken as a whole.

Nonchemical Factors Influencing Drug Effects

1. *Placebo effects.* Placebo effects are well known in psychopharmacology, both in terms of extent and range of effects. In stimulant drug studies with children, for example, significant placebo effects have been reported on both standard psychological tests and ratings of activity (Conners and Rothschild 1968; Finnerty, Greaney, Soltys, and Cole 1971; Knights and Hinton 1969; Millichap et al. 1968; Rapoport et al. 1971; Werry et al. 1966). Estimates of the percentage of children who will improve on placebo center around 35 percent, but range up to 70 percent (Beecher 1955; Freed 1962; Freeman 1966; Knights and Hinton 1969), apparently depending on the subjectivity of the instrument and the degree of blindness of the evaluators. The chlorpromazine study of Werry et al. (1966) is typical. More than half of the placebo subjects showed improvement (on ratings of activity), and *none* became worse. The authors concluded: "Both the doctors' and the mothers' expectations of a positive therapeutic result are sufficient to produce some change in an overwhelming majority of children" (p. 309). So ubiquitous are placebo reactions that Eisenberg (1968) advised readers to be suspicious of any study *failing* to find such effects.

The range of placebo effects is also impressive; for example, thirty-five "toxic" effects (e.g., dermatitis) of placebos have been catalogued (Beecher 1955). Also, placebos have been found to suppress a range of physical ailments, including asthma and coughing, and cases of placebo dependence and withdrawal symptoms have been reported (Trouton 1957). A tic was exacerbated by placebo in one of our subjects (Sroufe et al., 1973) but it "responded" to a lowering of dosage. As Freedman has concluded, practically any effect can be obtained with a placebo (in Fisher 1959, p. 44). (For general references to placebo effects see DeLong 1972; Freed 1962; Freeman 1966.)

It must be understood that placebo effects—that is, effects due merely to subject or evaluator expectations—are likely to be greater with active drugs than inert substances. If the active drug produces tachycardia, flushing, or other clear side effects, belief in the potency of the drug is likely to be enhanced (Cole 1968; Eisenberg 1968).

2. *Set and expectation.* The particular placebo effect that is obtained following drug administration depends to a large extent on the expectation of the child (or parent) concerning the drug. As Trouten (1957) has pointed out, placebo effects tend to resemble effects expected from the drug; for example, placebos may have either stimulant or depressant properties. The power of set or expectation in determining the subject's response to a drug is well illustrated by the work of Schachter (1964). In perhaps his most striking experiment (see Schachter 1964), depending on the cognitive set created, adult subjects became either euphoric *or angry* following administration of epinephrine (adrenalin: a sympathomimetic amine similar to amphetamine), *and the effect of set was greater for active drug than placebo.* Schachter explained this interaction between subject expectation and physical drug effects in the following way: "Given this state [of physiological arousal] . . . for which an individual has no immediate explanation, he will label this state . . . in terms of cognitions available to him" (p. 167).

A study by Fisher (1962) is similar to Schachter's work and is also relevant here. Fisher found that subjects given "correct" expectations concerning Dexedrine showed more drug effect than subjects not so set. The difference between set conditions was greater for drug subjects than for the two comparable placebo groups.

Other work on the nonspecificity of drug action (Lennard, Epstein, Bernstein, and Ransom 1970) and the general literature on the effects of experimenter expectation (Rosenthal and Rosnow 1969) cannot be discussed here. Unfortunately, none of this work has been done with children. Still, it is reasonable to assume that young subjects would be influenced by factors of set and expectation at least as much as adult subjects. If this is the case, reports that children do not get high (euphoric) on stimulant drugs, if true, can be readily explained. The children are not set to experience a high; rather, they are authoritatively led to believe that the drugs will help them control their activity (calm them down), improve their ability to concentrate, and generally help them do better in school. These are the effects that occur. Bradley's (1937) subjects, not set to be calmed by stimulants, did report euphoric experiences ("I have joy in my stomach!").

3. *Contextual factors: behavioral pharmacology.* As stressed previously, it is a serious misconception to think of drug effects as specific or unitary. The effect of a drug is a function not only of dosage level and

subject expectation but a variety of contextual factors, including prior history of the organism, organismic state, environmental contingencies, and the nature of the response being assessed (Dews and Morse 1961; Kornetsky 1970; Thompson and Schuster 1968). Behavioral pharmacologists (Thompson and Schuster 1968) have stressed that drug effects can be meaningfully evaluated only subsequent to an operant analysis of the behavior to be assessed.

While behavior pharmacological studies to date have been done almost exclusively with animals, this approach will suggest implications for evaluating drug studies with children. For example, animals reinforced for the first response made following a fixed time period (fixed interval schedule) typically have a low response rate. An effective dose of Dexedrine *increases* this rate of responding. If, however, the animals are on a fixed ratio schedule (that is, receiving a reinforcement after a fixed number of responses), they show a high rate of responding, which is *decreased* by stimulant drug treatment. Other studies show differential drug effects depending on the nature of the response being learned (e.g., conditioned discrimination versus simple discrimination), the drive state of the animal, and the animal's early experience (Kornetsky 1970; Thompson and Schuster 1968). It is important to note the unsystematic way in which behaviors to be evaluated in child drug studies are selected and how little is known about what in the environment maintains and influences children's problem behavior (Chess, Thomas, Rutter, and Birch 1963).

The stimulant drug effects reviewed earlier are probably not due merely to expectations and other extradrug factors. Many of the specific effects reported would require extensive post-hoc reasoning to be explained in this way. However, placebo effects are quite powerful and may be exceptionally strong in the presence of genuine drug effects which are consonant with the expectations created. These suppositions concerning the influence of extradrug factors are bothersome largely because of the absence of careful long-term evaluations. Until such studies exist, we cannot know the extent to which genuine drug effects fade, being increasingly replaced by behavior based on the expectations of the child, parent, and teacher. McDermott (1965) reports a case in point. The child's parents misinterpreted medication instructions and discontinued Dexedrine treatment. Still, the long-term effects they expected from short-term treatment—dramatic improvement in school performance and behavior—persisted for six months. Neither do we know whether stimulant drugs have immediate effects on the child's belief in his capacities or child-parent or child-teacher interaction patterns, which then contribute to any change in behavior that persists. Currently, thousands of children receive stimulant medication for a period of years. We need the information pertinent to these questions in order to evaluate this practice. At present, it is only a matter of belief that beneficial drug effects persist; that is, that children develop tolerance only with regard to the negative effects of stimulant drugs, not the positive effects.

Alternatives to Drug Treatment

Several physicians who are well versed in nonmedical intervention techniques have concluded that medication may be the least effective form of treatment for hyperactive children (Werry 1968a; Stewart 1970). To evaluate fully drug effectiveness and the assumptions underlying drug treatment, it is necessary to consider whether there are alternatives which have been demonstrated to alter the problem behaviors leading to referral, as well as to examine whether in many cases aspects of the environment should be manipulated rather than intervening with the child. Our discussion will focus on behavior modification, since reports concerning other intervention techniques are scattered and largely anecdotal. Behavior modification with children is discussed extensively elsewhere in this book (see chapter 8) and has been the subject of several reviews (O'Leary and Drabman 1971; Werry and Wollersheim 1967).

1. *Psychological intervention (behavior modification)*. In our laboratory it is standard procedure to spend two minutes with a handcounter, shaping the child to sit still. The child is merely given points for sitting quietly, first for five seconds, ultimately for fifteen, and he is told that the points can be traded for candy at the end of the hour. Forty-two children, referred for hyperactivity and behavior problems, and diagnosed as MBD by a pediatric neurologist, have been tested using this procedure. With only an occasional requirement for reinstating instructions, each of these children has remained sufficiently still for forty-five minutes of physiological recording. The point is not that school problems can be solved with two minutes of behavioral shaping, but that children, including an overwhelming majority of those diagnosed as MBD, are readily responsive to clear instructions backed up by tangible rewards.

Experimental investigations have shown behavior techniques to be quite successful in modifying problem behavior. Disruptive behavior, aggressive behavior, tantrum behavior, and overactivity have been dramatically altered by manipulating parent or teacher responses or by introducing rewards (Bernal, Duryee, Pruett, and Burns 1968; Brown and Elliott 1965; O'Leary and Drabman 1971; Patterson, Jones, Whittier, and Wright 1965; Thomas, Becker, and Armstrong 1968; Wahler, Winkel, Peterson, and Morrison 1965). Within the classroom, specific behaviors have been altered, such as lack of visual orientation to the teacher (Quay, Werry, McQueen, and Sprague 1966) and being out of seat or talking without raising the hand (O'Leary and Becker 1967). These are just the behaviors that typically exhaust the teacher's patience and lead to referral for medical evaluation and treatment. There are also reports that school attendance (that is, attitude toward school) and school work are improved (O'Leary, Becker, Evans, and Saudargas 1969) and that school achievement can be improved over periods as long as a year (Hewett, Taylor, and Artuso 1969). Such are the stated goals of drug treatment programs.

It is also informative to consider characteristics of the subjects and therapeutic setting in these studies. While behaviorists are inclined to describe their subjects in terms of specific behaviors, many of the children in these studies would be defined as hyperactive, learning-disabled, or MBD (O'Leary and Becker 1967; Patterson 1964; Quay et al. 1966). In some instances the children have actually been diagnosed as MBD (Stern 1972; Toffler, in Novack 1971) or as having clearly demonstrable brain damage (Patterson et al. 1965). Also, programs have been administered in the home with the parent as reinforcing agent and in the school classroom (O'Leary et al. 1969; Wahler, Winkel, Peterson, and Morrison 1965). There have been "token economy" programs administered by a single teacher with an entire classroom of children with adjustment problems (O'Leary and Becker 1967). Thus, nonmedical treatments can be applied to children with "suspected" or clear "organicity" and with entire classrooms. Neither diagnosis of the child nor numbers of children to be treated would seem to dictate the use of drugs.

Two additional psychological intervention studies with hyperactive children are important because they involved training in self-instruction on the one hand (Palkes, Stewart, and Kahana 1968) and the interaction of reward with situational characteristics on the other (Stern 1972). In the Palkes et al. study, hyperactive children who experienced two half-hour training sessions showed dramatic improvement on the Porteus mazes. Briefly, experimental subjects were trained to instruct themselves to "stop," "listen," "look," and "think" before responding to subtasks on three well-known psychological tests (matching familiar figures, embedded figures, trailmaking). Following such training, both Porteus IQ and qualitative scores were changed significantly more than was the case for control subjects. Some of the most striking changes involved fewer cut corners or line crossings, lifting the pencil less, and threading the maze with fewer irregular lines. Since these behaviors had not been specifically trained, Palkes et al. argued that the children were generally exhibiting greater care and less impulsivity during the testing. It is important to note that most of these children would be considered MBD, some of them having been temporarily withdrawn from drugs to participate in the study. Others have successfully used similar procedures, sometimes with filmed models, to reduce impulsive responding in children (Meichenbaum and Goodman 1971; Ridberg, Parke, and Hetherington 1971). As Palkes et al. concluded, "hyperactive children are receptive and eager to be taught control of their own behavior" (p. 826).

In the study by Stern (1972) hyperactive (MBD) and control children were tested on a coding task in distracting and standard conditions. The clinic sample performed more poorly in both situations, and performance of *both* groups deteriorated in the distracting situation, which included both visual and auditory distractions. Most significantly, however, the introduction of rewards into the distracting situation improved performance beyond the nondistraction level for both groups, and with reward there was no longer a significant difference between groups. An important addition to this research program would be studies in which the nature of the task was manipulated along with distraction and reward.[3]

2. *Educational intervention.* In light of the fact that learning and other school problems are a major reason for referral for hyperactive children, it is unfortunate that little systematic research has been done on educational approaches with these children. Numerous clinical recommendations can be found in the literature, which usually center on firm, consistent handling and restructuring of the educational environment (Glasser 1968; Stewart 1970; Werry 1968*a*). Special classrooms with specially trained teachers have also been suggested (Office of Child Development Report 1971). Finally, a number of critics have argued that children's problem behavior would be best ameliorated by structural changes in the schools, primarily along lines of reducing the rigidity of rule systems, deemphasizing memory-fact education, and altering the sedentary nature of most classrooms (Holt 1964; Silberman 1970). While there are anecdotal reports that "open" classrooms or other contemporary educational alternatives benefit children with learning problems (Kohl 1967), to date there is no experimental evidence pertinent to this question.

One current educational practice requires comment. It is apparently common to minimize visual (e.g., decorations) or auditory stimuli in the hyperactive child's learning environment (Cruickshank, Bentzen, Ratzeburg, and Tannhauser 1961; Pincus and Glaser 1966) or to actually have the child work in a study carrel without windows and stripped of all stimulation (Gallagher 1970). There is currently no research evidence to support such a practice (Douglas, in press; Meyer 1968). In fact, there is some evidence that performance of both "normal" and distractible chil-

---

[3] In a similar study by Lee Marcus (unpublished dissertation, University of Minnesota), reaction-time differences between "externalizing" children and controls were eradicated in conditions of high incentive or short preparatory (attention maintenance) interval.

dren is improved with background stimulation (Reger 1963; Turnure 1970, 1971).

3. *Interaction of drug treatment with other intervention strategies.* One conclusion of the panel convened by the Office of Child Development (1971) was that medicine does not cure hyperactive children "but the child may become more accessible to educational and counseling efforts." Currently, this conclusion is difficult to support with research data. There are crucial questions here concerning whether psychological or educational treatment efforts are enhanced or impeded by stimulant drug treatment or whether drug effects are washed out by nonmedical interventions.

No published study on the interaction of drug treatment and behavior modification was found, though questions concerning such interaction would seem to be more important than those concerning the efficacy of either technique in isolation. An unpublished study by Christensen (in Sprague 1972) is of little value since in this experiment the behavior modification program apparently had no effect with either the drug or placebo group, and drug-placebo differences in activity level (the dependent measure) were due primarily to increases in the placebo group.

One study on the interaction of stimulant drug treatment and tutoring has provided quite interesting results (Conrad et al. 1971). Groups of poor children, selected by their teacher for "hyperkinesis," were treated in the following four ways: Dexedrine alone, placebo alone, Dexedrine plus tutoring, and placebo plus tutoring. The tutors were adult volunteers, trained through twenty ninety-minute lectures, and then supervised weekly. A large number of measures were obtained before and after four to six months of treatment, including the WISC, Frostig, Bender, reading and arithmetic achievement, behavior ratings by parents and teachers, and clinical judgments of activity, coordination, and distractibility. Most relevant for our consideration are the drug versus tutoring comparisons and the drug plus tutoring versus placebo plus tutoring comparisons. Only the behavior ratings by parents (not teachers) indicated significantly greater improvement by the Dexedrine group without tutoring compared to the tutoring group given placebo. None of the cognitive, achievement, or perceptual-motor measures yielded significant differences in this comparison, suggesting little advantage of the drug treatment. The Dexedrine group tended to be superior on certain WISC subscales, such as coding, digit span, and similarities, and on some Frostig subscales. The tutored group tended to be superior on the information, picture-arrangement, and block-design subscales of the WISC. Again, these latter differences were not significant. Therefore, in this study, there is little evidence that drug treatment is superior to tutoring by semi-trained volunteers. However, does stimulant drug treatment enhance the effects of tutoring? Both parent and teacher ratings suggested more improvement for the Dexedrine plus tutoring group compared to the placebo plus tutoring group. But again, no perceptual-motor, cognitive, or achievement measures were significant.

Behavior modification is one nonmedical intervention technique that has proved highly successful with problem children. There have not yet been adequate demonstrations of generalization of effects across situations or time (O'Leary and Drabman 1971); reports are often based on short-term case studies, and changes in behavior observed may or may not be congruent with an incremental learning model; that is, the behaviors in question often seem to change suddenly upon instigation of the reward procedures. Still, dramatic effects seem easily achieved with behavioral techniques, even with children having suspected or known organic impairment. Also, reward is powerful enough to overcome deleterious effects of distraction and to eradicate initial differences between hyperactive (MBD) children and control subjects. Reinforcement techniques, like stimulant drugs, can affect behaviors which typically are the basis for referral of hyperactive children. When the problem lies in an unengaging curriculum or ineffective teaching, of course, neither medication nor behavior modification is appropriate.

At the present time there is little evidence that medication is superior (or inferior) to behavior modification or tutoring, or that drugs enhance the effects of other intervention techniques. This is clearly a research area of great need. As suggested earlier, an entire research discipline has developed to investigate drug effects as they occur in conjunction with behavior defined in terms of schedules of reinforcement and other contextual factors. It has been argued that drug effects can *only* be interpreted from within such a framework (Thompson and Schuster 1968); yet not a single behavior pharmacological study with children can be found in the literature.

Summary

1. The great many unknowns concerning stimulant drugs pose problems for evaluating the practice of drug treatment.

2. There is little evidence concerning the persistence of the behavioral effects of stimulant drugs, the long-term physical side effects, or the effects on higher cognitive skills such as reasoning and concept formation.

3. It is not known to what extent expectations of parent, child, and physician, and other nonchemical factors account for reported drug treatment effects, especially over time.

4. Finally, little is known about how drug treatment interacts with other intervention strategies, such as behavior modification.

THE PRACTICE OF DRUG TREATMENT

Current and Future Medical Practice

The preceding discussion of the literature on drug treatment of behavior-problem children can be summarized as follows: first, there is no evidence that more than a minority of the large number of children currently labeled as "hyperactive," "hyperkinetic," or "minimal brain dysfunction syndrome" have underlying CNS impairment or a medical history conducive to brain damage. In fact, it seems clear that there is great heterogeneity in this group of children and that they probably do not make up a medical entity at all (Stewart and Olds, in press). Second, no diagnostic index, test, or test battery has been established as a valid predictor of drug response (or response to an alternative intervention), and clinicians typically rely on the child's response to the drug to establish the medical nature of the problem (Report of the Office of Child Development 1970). There is a problem with using drug response as a diagnostic tool, however. While the response of some children to stimulant drugs is dramatic and distinctive, generally it would be difficult to distinguish the response of the child with a medical problem from that of the typical child. Most children would be expected to show improved concentration and persistence on routinized tasks common in the school situation. Similarly, attitude toward work, motor skill, and other aspects of performance would be expected to improve. All of this follows from the literature on adult performance and the results with heterogeneous groups of problem children. Placebo effects, omnipresent in drug research, would add to any actual chemical effects, especially in the context of therapeutic expectations of the physician, parent, and teacher.

Finally, there are important gaps in our knowledge about the effects and effectiveness of stimulant drugs. We have little information concerning stimulant drug effects on important types of learning, reasoning, problem-solving or other aspects of cognitive development, including actual academic achievement. Moreover, given the lack of long-term controlled experiments and adequate follow-up studies, conclusions cannot be reached concerning the persistence of the behavioral and performance effects that are reported in short-term studies, or the possibility of serious adverse physical effects in later life. Further research may clarify a number of these issues, but at present, stimulant drug treatment of an individual child involves a complex clinical judgment.

1. *Guidelines for medical practice.* Partly in response to this situation, a number of important papers on drug treatment of children have proposed guidelines for appropriate medical practice (Eisenberg 1968, 1971, 1972;

Solomons 1965, 1972; Stewart and Olds, in press; Office of Child Development 1970). Each of these papers has emphasized a conservative, discriminate use of medications with behavior-problem children, suggesting that drugs be used *only* when necessary and only as long as necessary. Stewart and Olds (in press) perhaps represent the most cautious position.

If, after this time (3 to 6 months), things seem just as bad as ever—no matter how they (the parents) have changed the pressures at home or at school, no matter how they have rewarded their child's efforts to improve, no matter how they have dealt with the school and with professional consultants—then it may be time to think about medication.

Similarly, there is agreement that the decision to employ medication is between parent and physician, and "under no circumstances should any attempt be made to coerce parents to accept any particular treatment" (Office of Child Development Report, p. 6). Finally, each paper stressed that there must be careful monitoring and follow-up of drug-treatment cases and that medication must be only the beginning of a total treatment program which includes parent counseling, teacher conferences, and the like.

Unfortunately, there is reason to suspect that these guidelines frequently are not followed in actual medical practice. Probably because of an uncritical belief in the safety and effectiveness of stimulant drugs, and heavy patient loads, monitoring of drug treatment is often not adequate. One leading proponent of drug treatment, for example, counseled that diagnosis is easy based on drug reaction, and that the physician's total time-commitment to the MBD child need be only three hours, and that much only the first year (Wender 1971). It has also been reported that physicians sometimes prescribe medication without seeing the child at all or following a single brief interview with mother and child (Browder 1972). It is not surprising, then, to find children being kept on medication when either no effects or negative effects occurred, or to find adolescents who have been on stimulant drugs for six years without a trial withdrawal (all reported by Stewart and Olds, in press). Unhappily, these impressions concerning inadequate practice recently have been confirmed in a survey of physicians (Solomons 1972). Solomons found that even with the support of a concerned, active university clinic, 45 percent of the children being treated by individual practitioners were not being monitored adequately, including nineteen of twenty-eight patients (parents) allowed to "juggle" dosage on their own discretion. It is important to note that the criterion of "adequate" monitoring was merely two patient contacts within six months. Clearly, for many children currently being given stimulant drugs, the medication is being given longer than necessary, when not helpful, without proper concern for monitoring and follow-up, and as the total treatment rather than the starting point for a comprehensive intervention program.

Similarly, there is reason to suspect that many parents experience pressure concerning medication for their children. These pressures may be explicit or implicit. One physician, because of his belief in the efficacy of stimulant medication, has suggested that "parents must be sometimes seduced into accepting it" (Wender 1971, p. 114). Also, there are individually documented cases of school personnel putting direct pressure on parents to seek medication, or even making school attendance contingent on such treatment (Browder 1972; Gallagher 1970; Ladd 1971; Richard 1972; Stewart and Olds, in press). For example, one parent reported being told that her child had to remain away from school until put on stimulant drug medication and, ultimately, that he would be sent to reform school unless medicated (reprinted from *The Challenge,* in the *Clinical Child Psychology Newsletter* 1971, *10,* 5; see also Mrs. Young's testimony in Gallagher 1970). Moreover, in a recent survey, 60 percent of the parents of forty-seven hyperactive children said that medication had originally been suggested by a school official (Stewart and Olds, in press).

Parents also experience indirect pressure from school officials and physicians. The child has "minimal brain dysfunction" or "special learning disability," and these drugs will help him overcome *his* handicaps and be more successful in school. The effectiveness of such suggestions can be inferred from the high volunteer rate reported in drug studies. In the study by Steinberg et al. (1971), one-fifth of an entire elementary school population was selected by teachers for "behavior disorders" and "difficulty concentrating." The parents of these children were told of the possible side effects of Dexedrine and that the drug "might help their children behave better and do better school work." Sixty-four percent of these parents agreed to participate in the drug study, even though their children had not previously had psychiatric referral and were not initially evaluated by any medical professional. In a similar study of poor, black, behavior-problem children referred by teachers, Conners et al. (1967) had a volunteer rate of 97 *percent,* even though each parent was contacted individually, told of the school problems and the proposed treatment program, and given the opportunity to decline participation (Eisenberg, personal communication). Parents want their children to be successful in school, and if school officials or physicians say drugs may be the solution, they will try them.

2. *The expansion of stimulant drug treatment.* It seems likely that problems such as inadequate monitoring, nonsupplemented drug treatment, and pressure on parents, which may exist mostly in isolated cases now, will increase dramatically as the concepts of "minimal brain dysfunc-

tion" and "special learning disability" become widely accepted and drug treatment of children accelerates. A great deal of evidence, including the testimony of government health officials, suggests that the number of children treated with stimulants is increasing rapidly (see Gallagher 1970). Recently, it was reported that an overwhelming majority of child psychiatrists and pediatricians in the Washington, D.C., area and in Chicago (Stephen, Sprague, and Werry, unpublished) has already prescribed drugs, mostly stimulants, for hyperactive children (Greenberg and Lipman 1971). It can be expected that general practitioners will likewise be influenced by the persuasive advertisements and positive reports which are in virtually every journal. Medical journal advertisements cite government panels concerning the high prevalence (10 percent) of MBD and the proven effectiveness of stimulant drugs in government-sponsored research. Papers critical of drug treatment seldom appear; for example, an entire issue of the *Journal of Learning Disabilities* (November 1971) was devoted to drug treatment, and critical comments could be found in only two articles, one a two-page paper by an educator. Instead, studies discussed critically in various parts of this paper were presented as conclusive evidence that stimulant drugs are both safe and effective.

Wender's (1971) book will also influence the practitioner. Wender not only diversified the definition of MBD (Sroufe 1972) and suggested "giving all children a trial of medication" (p. 127) where the diagnosis of MBD is "suspected," he also stated that not treating such children with drugs may constitute medical malpractice. Moreover, citing important follow-up studies which showed that hyperactive children often continued to have problems (Mendelson, Johnson, and Stewart 1971; Menkes, Rose, and Menkes, 1967; Robins 1972; Weiss et al. 1971), Wender urged continued drug treatment *through adolescence.*[4]

Parents and teachers are likewise being flooded with information about the presumed prevalence of MBD and "special learning disabilities" at PTA meetings and in the media. A recent television ad described the symptoms of MBD and counselled parents to see their physician if their child might be afflicted. Studies already show that 50 percent of mothers surveyed see their boys as unusually active (Lapouse and Monk 1958) and that teachers see 40 to 50 percent of their male students as impulsive, *hyper*active, excessively distractible, or having an unusually short attention-span. Since these are the behaviors that prompt referral, the practi-

---

[4] It may be the case that children labeled early as "hyperactive" continue to have problems. However, it is important to point out that most children studied by Mendelson et al. (1971) had been in a drug treatment program. Still, they had behavioral difficulties as adolescents, similar to those described by Robins (1972) and others. The problems may not be transient, but the efficacy of drug treatment is not yet demonstrated.

tioner's case load will increase markedly as the behaviors become associated with an organic pathology model.

Increasingly, then, pediatricians and general practitioners will be confronted with problem-children cases. The parent says the child is "impossible," and the report card suggests that schoolwork is poor but could be better "if he were not so active and distractible." The EEG or neurological evaluation, if done at all, is likely to be ambiguous, and there is not time to actually examine the home or school situation. Parents and teachers wonder about a trial of medication, and it seems worth a try. Sometimes the child will not respond. Sometimes the response will be dramatic, and some of these children may actually have required medication. Many more children, because of placebo and actual drug effects, may show the expected normal stimulant drug response of improved concentration and diligence. However, using medication to produce such effects in children without unquestionable medical need may have serious negative consequences.

Potential Consequences of the Drug Solution

It is often pointed out that stimulant drug treatment has the general positive effect of breaking up the vicious cycle of failure, reprimand, unhappiness, and failure. The child begins having success-experiences, parents and teachers like him better and believe in him more,‘and school becomes a positive rather than a dreaded situation. This is no doubt true in some cases. But there are other possible consequences of the drug solution as well, including effects on the child's self-concept, abdication of responsibility by parents, and deflection of attention from important educational and social problems.

The child learns that he cannot really control himself, that there is something wrong with his brain or body. He needs medical help in order to learn normally. Internalizing this medical solution, the child can say, "I can't help being bad today. I haven't had my pill" (Stewart and Olds, in press). Or, as cited by Wender (1971, p. 123), the child can come to believe in "my magic pills that make me into a good boy and make everybody like me." That is, it may be that drug treatment actually prevents the child from learning to cope with his disability, many aspects of which may remain following short-term drug treatment (Douglas 1972b).

Likewise, the drug solution may often allow teachers and parents to abdicate their responsibility towards the child. Teachers may ask if the child "had his pill" on a troublesome day and have even been quoted as saying, "Peter will be sent home if he doesn't take his pill" (Stewart and Olds, in press). One parent was recently overheard asking his child if he had "taken his human pill today."

The consequences for educational practice can be equally serious. The distractibility and impulsivity of *some* children seriously restrict their freedom, creativity, and learning ability, which sometimes suggests the need for dramatic intervention (Eisenberg 1972). Some children cannot be managed by teachers without special training, especially within a large classroom. But *most* children respond to effective teaching. The educational process is the child learning how to learn and the teacher learning how to help him learn. Educator John Holt has pointed out that the drug solution may mean fitting the child to a generally unhealthy school situation, steering around the problem of education. Referring to the overly sedentary nature of most school classrooms, Holt remarked: "Children have a great deal of energy; they like to move about; they live and learn with their bodies and muscles, not just their eyes and ears" (Gallagher 1970, p. 33). Quickly turning to the drug solution for any child who presents a problem, will clearly jeopardize the educational process and will delay the development of more effective educational procedures.

Drug treatment can also be misused as a solution for important social problems. A high prevalence of "minimal brain dysfunction" has been suggested as central in the school dropout-delinquency problem and the special problems of many children from poverty areas (Gallagher 1970; Tarnopol 1970; Wender 1971). The MBD label and widespread drug treatment suggests an individual basis for what are largely sociological problems and, thus, deflect attention from the genuine needs of these children. Some of these children may, of course, have organic problems, or may respond dramatically to stimulant drugs, just as would be true for some middle-class children. Often, though, drugs may merely mask the problem. Stimulant drugs can overcome the performance decrement shown by oxygen-depleted or overly fatigued adults (Weiss and Laties 1962), and they probably can improve the performance of malnourished, poorly rested, and poorly motivated children as well. Eisenberg (1971) has clearly stated the inappropriateness of treating hypoglycemia ("in a child who is malnourished and regularly has no breakfast") with stimulant drugs rather than food.

In sum, stimulant drugs may work *too* well. They can be an overly simplistic solution to complex social, educational, and intrafamilial problems. The decision to use drugs to "tide the child over" the difficult years of his childhood, rather than attempting to meet the challenges which his development pose for home and school, must be made only after the most careful evaluation. Drugs "can make a child pliant enough to conform to undesirable child-rearing or teaching practices. They can sacrifice the child's optimal development to the parent's or teacher's convenience. These dangers must be recognized and conscientiously avoided in any medication program" (Stewart and Olds, in press).

Drug Treatment in American Society

Drug treatment of children cannot be separated from the larger social context. That we are a drug-oriented culture needs no further documentation, since drugs are viewed as a solution for nearly every social and personal problem. Media advertisements inform the consumer that drugs are not only aids for relaxation or sleep but also can be used to promote interpersonal relationships, to project a sophisticated image, and to help cope with everyday problems. Catchy ads fill the medical journals suggesting antidepressants to improve communication and cooperation, or minor tranquilizers (e.g., Librium} for the college freshman faced with "exposure to new friends" and the need to "re-evaluate herself and her goals" or for the child soon to see the dentist (Lennard et al. 1970). Medication is even suggested for abusers of hallucinogens (*JAMA* editorial, January 18, 1971, p. 475)! Partly as a result of this media barrage and current standards of medical practice, Americans consume enormous quantities of medications, often in the absence of clear physical need; for example, of 1.1 billion prescriptions filled in 1967, costing 3.9 billion dollars, 178 million prescriptions were for amphetamines (Graham 1972).

Massive pharmacological treatment of children not only follows from our society's preoccupation with a drug solution for problems, it could possibly contribute to the perpetuation of both legal and illegal drug abuse. It is clear, for example, that amphetamines are grossly overproduced by American pharmaceutical companies and that these "legally" produced drugs are the principal source for illegal amphetamine traffic (Graham 1972). Since stimulant drug treatment of narcolepsy and behavior problems in children are probably the *only* valid medical uses of amphetamines (their use for adult weight-control having been discredited), widespread use of these drugs for children would help legitimize overproduction, whereas cautious, discriminate prescription for those rare cases clearly justifying medical treatment would help strip the industry of its "legitimate" base.[5]

5. In the recent congressional hearings on drug abuse, the following facts came to light: (1) Drug companies constitute a multihundred-million-dollar industry, with advertising budgets to match; (2) 8–10 billion amphetamine tablets are legally produced each year, with at least 50 percent of these being "diverted" to illegal use; (3) 92 percent of the illegally consumed amphetamines were manufactured legally; and (4) 99 percent of the amphetamines prescribed are for weight control, but the evidence clearly indicates their lack of utility for this purpose; for example, only one of fifty-three medical school deans and health organizations surveyed by Congressman Pepper's committee felt that stimulants were of any use in the control of obesity. Graham (1972) provides a good source for information concerning amphetamine overproduction and the political clout of the pharmaceutical industry.

More relevant for our consideration is the potential contribution of drug treatment to individual drug abuse by children and youth. One must be concerned about markedly increasing the availability of these widely abused drugs for elementary schoolchildren. Drug abuse is not restricted to the postpuberty years. While government agencies are unable to provide any information on the matter, a month of interviewing revealed that drug use is now occurring among elementary schoolchildren in both urban and rural communities (unpublished data). Expert opinion currently suggests that most treated children view their pills as "medication" rather than "drugs" (Gallagher 1970). But as the drug movement moves into the elementary school, it seems all too likely that the treated children, or their friends, will discover that three or four days' medication, ingested at one time, can produce a drug experience similar to the hallucinogens.

To date, there is no adequate information on misuse of stimulant drugs by children during treatment or on the potential of the drugs for later abuse. The single relevant study in the literature is grossly deficient methodologically. In this study (Laufer 1971), parents of one hundred formerly treated children were surveyed by mail questionnaire. Only sixty-six responses were received, and not all of these parents answered all questions. Virtually no drug abuse was reported, but this information is hardly reassuring. There was no control group, and the return rate was not adequate for this type of survey. Also, parents of drug-treated children cannot be considered unbiased or objective. In fact, it is doubtful that many parents had much information at all, since the median age of the former patients was twenty, not an age at which young people are known to confide in their parents concerning drug-taking practices. At present, then, it is not possible to conclude that drug treatment increases, decreases, or does not affect later drug abuse.

Finally, our efforts to educate and rehabilitate youthful drug-abusers lose force in light of the obvious double standard of the physical and mental-health professions. Young people are told that drugs are not the solution to problems, but stimulant medication is becoming the "treatment of choice" for children's behavior problems. American Medical Association literature refers to drugs such as marijuana as the "chemical cop-out." Problems are to be faced, and development comes through meeting life's challenges; yet stimulant drugs are justified for children because they provide an easy, practical (inexpensive) solution. Finally, youth are told not to experiment with marijuana because "the evidence is just not in," but drug treatment of hundreds of thousands of children can be justified because there is little evidence to date that these drugs are harmful.

Summary

1. Adequate guidelines for the conservative use of medication in treating behavior and learning problems can be found in the literature.

2. However, it is doubtful that such guidelines concerning care in treatment and follow-up are being followed in many cases.

3. If drug treatment expands rapidly, it seems likely that an even greater percentage of children will be treated inappropriately.

4. Treating hundreds of thousands of children with stimulant medication in the absence of *clear* medical need, would have serious negative consequences.

CONCLUSIONS

The lack of critical analysis uncovered by this review is the most disconcerting feature of the literature on drug treatment of children. The unquestioning acceptance of the atypical drug-response notion and the general deficit model has clearly slowed the development of meaningful integrative models of drug effects with problem children. The consequences for medical practice have been even more unfortunate. Existing information concerning the effects of stimulant drugs on cognitive development, the persistence of behavioral effects, and the long-term physical and psychological consquences of these drugs is simply too limited to justify the current level of drug treatment.

It is likely that there are some children for whom stimulant drug medication is appropriate. These children may be having great difficulties at home and at school, and their problems may be unusually unresponsive to educational or other nonmedical intervention. Parents and teachers without special training may be unable to cope with these children, the net result being a great deal of unhappiness for all concerned. It is probable that in some of these cases a dramatic, atypical response to stimulant medication outweighs the possible costs involved. It is even possible that a subset of these children makes up a genuine medical entity, perhaps deriving from nonfocused minimal brain dysfunction. However, identifying these children will always be a difficult clinical judgment, because of the diagnostic ambiguity of this disorder, its behavioral base, and its close resemblance to normal extreme variation. It seems likely, therefore, that for many of the one hundred fifty to two hundred thousand children currently being treated with stimulant drugs, medication is not appropriate.

It is now being suggested that three to ten percent of the school population suffers from "special learning disability" or "minimal brain dysfunction" (Gallagher 1970; Wender 1971). It is said that these 1.5 to 4 million healthy school children are not amenable to educational efforts and re-

quire medication. Drug treatment on this scale would have extremely negative consequences for many thousands of individual children, the American
educational system, and our society.

REFERENCES

Baker, R. R. The effects of psychotropic drugs on psychological testing. *Psychological Bulletin*, 1968, *69*, 377–387.

Beecher, H. K. The powerful placebo. *Journal of the American Medical Association*, 1955, *159*, 1602–1606.

Bernal, M. E., Duryee, J. S., Pruett, H. L., Burns, B. J. Behavior modification and the brat syndrome. *Journal of Consulting and Clinical Psychology*, 1968, *32*, 447–455.

Birch, H. G. *Brain Damage in Children*. New York: Williams & Wilkens, 1964.

Blum, B., Stern, M., & Melville, K. A comparative evaluation of the action of depressant and stimulant drugs on human performance. *Psychopharmacologia*, 1964, *6*, 173–177.

Boydstun, J. A., Ackerman, P. T., Stevens, D. A., Clements, S. D., Peters, J. E., & Dykman, R. A. Physiologic and motor conditioning and generalization in children with minimal brain dysfunction. *Conditional Reflex*, 1968, *3*, 81–104.

Boyle, R. H., Dykman, R. A., Ackerman, P. T. Relationships of resting autonomic activity, motor impulsivity, and EEG in children. *Archives of General Psychiatry*, 1965, *12*, 314–323.

Bradley, C. The behavior of children receiving benzedrine. *American Journal of Psychiatry*, 1937, *94*, 577–585.

Browder, J. A. Appropriate use of psychic drugs in school children. *American Journal of Diseases of Children*, 1972, *124*, 606–607.

Brown, P. & Elliot, R. Control of aggression in a nursery school class. *Journal of Experimental Child Psychology*, 1965, *2*, 103–107.

Burks, H. F. Effects of amphetamine therapy of hyperkinetic children. *Archives of General Psychiatry*, 1964, *11*, 604–609.

————. The hyperkinetic child. *Exceptional Children*, 1960, *27*, 18–26.

Campbell, S., Douglas, V. I., & Morgenstern, G. Cognitive styles in hyperactive children and the effect of methylphenidate. *Journal of Child Psychology and Psychiatry*, 1971, *12*, 55–67.

Chassan, J. B. *Research Design in Clinical Psychology and Psychiatry*. New York: Appleton-Century-Crofts, 1967.

Chess, S., Thomas, A., Rutter, M., & Birch, H. G. Interaction of temperament and environment in the production of behavioral disturbances in children. *American Journal of Psychiatry*, 1963, *120*, 142–148.

Clements, S. D. Minimal Brain Dysfunction in Children: Terminology and Identification. Phase one of a three-phase project. U.S. Department of Health, Education, and Welfare, Public Health Service Publication No. 1415, 1966.

Clements, S. & Peters, J. Minimal brain dysfunction in the school-age child. *Archives of General Psychiatry*, 1962, *6*, 185–197.

Cohen, N. J. Psychophysiological concomitants of attention in hyperactive children. Doctoral thesis, McGill University, 1970.

Cohen, N. J. & Douglas, V. I. Characteristics of the orienting response in hyperactive and normal children. *Psychophysiology*, 1972, *9*, 238–245.

Cohen, N. J., Douglas, V. I., & Morgenstern, G. The effect of methylphenidate on attentive behavior and autonomic activity in hyperactive children. *Psychopharmacologia*, 1971, *22*, 282–294.

Cohen, S. Theoridazine (Mellaril): recent developments. *Journal of Psychopharmacology,* 1966, *1,* 1–15.

Cole, J. O. Peeking through the double blind. In Daniel H. Efron, ed., *Psychopharmacology: A Review of Progress 1957–1967.* Washington, D. C.: U. S. Government Printing Office, 1968, 979–984.

Comly, H. H. Cerebral stimulants for children with learning disorders? *Journal of Learning Disabilities,* 1971, *4,* 484–490.

Conners, C. K. A teacher rating scale for use in drug studies with children. *American Journal of Psychiatry,* 1969, *126,* 152–156.

————. Stimulant drugs and cortical evoked responses in learning and behavior disorders in children. Paper presented at the Second Annual Cerebral Function Symposium, Denver, 1970a.

————. Symptom patterns in hyperkinetic, neurotic, and normal children. *Child Development,* 1970b, *41,* 667–682.

————. Comparative effects of stimulant drugs in hyperactive children. Paper presented at the Thirteenth International Congress of Pediatrics in Vienna, August 29-September 4, 1971a.

————. Cortical visual evoked response in children with learning disorders. *Psychophysiology,* 1971b, *7,* 418–428.

————. The effect of stimulant drugs on human figure drawings in children with minimal brain dysfunction. *Psychopharmacologia,* 1971c, *19,* 329–333.

————. Recent drug studies. *Journal of Learning Disabilities,* 1971d, *4,* 476–483.

————. Pharmacotherapy of psychopathology in children. In H. C. Quay and J. S. Werry, eds., *Psychopathological Disorders of Childhood.* New York: John Wiley, 1972a.

————. Stimulant drugs and cortical evoked responses in learning and behavior disorders in children. In W. L. Smith, ed., *Drugs, Development and Cerebral Function.* Springfield, Ill.: Thomas, 1972b.

Conners, C. K. & Eisenberg, L. The effects of methylphenidate on symptomatology and learning in disturbed children. *American Journal of Psychiatry,* 1963, *120,* 458–464.

Conners, C. K., Eisenberg, L., & Barcai, A. Effect of dextroamphetamine on children: studies on subjects with learning disabilities and school behavior problems. *Archives of General Psychiatry,* 1967, *17,* 478–485.

Conners, C. K., Eisenberg, L., & Sharpe, L. Effects of methylphenidate (Ritalin) on paired associate learning and Porteus Maze performance in emotionally disturbed children. *Journal of Consulting Psychology,* 1964, *28,* 14–22.

Conners, C. K., Kramer, R., Rothschild, G. H., Swartz, L., & Stone, A. Treatment of young delinquent boys with diphenylhydantoin sodium and methylphenidate: a controlled comparison. *Archives of General Psychiatry,* 1971, *24,* 156–160.

Conners, C. K. & Rothschild, G. H. Drugs and learning in children. In J. Hellmuth, ed., *Learning Disorders.* Vol 3. Seattle, Washington: Special Child Publication, 1968, 191–224.

————. The effect of dextroamphetamine on habituation in peripheral vascular response in children. Presented to the Society for Psychophysiological Research, Monterey, California, October, 1969.

Conners, C. K., Rothschild, G. H., Eisenberg, L., Swartz, L., & Robinson, E. Dextroamphetamine sulfate in children with learning disorders: effects on perception, learning and achievement. *Archives of General Psychology,* 1969, *21,* 182–190.

Conrad, W. G., Dworkin, E. S., Shai, A., & Tobiessen, J. E. Effects of amphetamine therapy and prescriptive tutoring on the behavior and achievement of lower class hyperactive children. *Journal of Learning Disabilities,* 1971, *4,* 509–517.

Conrad, W. G. & Insel, J. B. Anticipating the response to amphetamine therapy in the treatment of hyperkinetic children. *Pediatrics,* 1967, *40,* 96–98.

Costa, E. & Garattini, S. *International Symposium on Amphetamines and Related Compounds.* New York: Raven Press, 1970.

Crow, T. J. & Bursill, A. E. An investigation into the effects of methamphetimine on short-term memory in man. In E. Costa & S. Garattini, eds., *International Symposium on Amphetamines.* New York: Raven Press, 1970.

Cruickshank, W. M., Bentzen, F. A., Ratzeburg, F. H., & Tannhauser, M. T. *A Teaching Method for Brain Injured and Hyperactive Children.* Syracuse: Syracuse University Press, 1961.

DeLong, A. R. What have we learned from psychoactive drug research on hyperactives? *American Journal of Diseases of Children,* 1972, *123,* 177–180.

Denhoff, E., Davids, A., & Hawkins, R. Effects of Dexedrine on hyperkinetic children: a controlled double blind study. *Journal of Learning Disabilities,* 1971, *4,* 27–34.

Dews, P. B. & Morse, W. H. Behavioral pharmacology. *Annual Review of Pharmacology,* 1961, *1,* 145–174.

Douglas, V. I. Stop, look and listen: the problem of sustained attention and impulse control in hyperactive and normal children. *Canadian Journal of Behavioral Science,* 1972a, *4,* 259–282.

———. Differences between normal and hyperkinetic children. Paper presented at the Symposium on the Clinical Use of Stimulant Drugs in Children, Key Biscayne, Florida, May, 1972b.

———. Sustained attention and impulse control: implications for the handicapped child. In J. A. Swets & L. L. Elliot, eds., *Psychology and the Handicapped Child,* in press.

Eisenberg, L. The basic issues in drug research with children: opportunities and limitations of a pediatric age group. In S. Fisher, ed., *Child Research in Psychopharmacology.* Springfield, Ill.: Thomas, 1959, 21–47.

———. The management of the hyperkinetic child. *Developmental Medicine and Child Neurology,* 1966, *8,* 593–598.

———. Psychopharmacology in childhood: a critique. In E. Miller, ed., *Foundations of Child Psychiatry.* Oxford: Pergamon Press, 1968, 625–641.

———. Principles of drug therapy in child psychiatry with special reference to stimulant drugs. *American Journal of Orthopsychiatry,* 1971, *41,* 371–379.

———. Symposium: behavior modification by drugs. III. The clinical use of stimulant drugs in children. *Pediatrics,* 1972, *49,* 709–715.

Eisenberg, L. & Conners, C. K. Psychopharmacology in childhood. In N. B. Talbot, J. Kagan, & L. Eisenberg, eds., *Behaviorial Science in Pediatric Medicine.* Philadelphia: W. B. Saunders, 1971.

Eisenberg, L., Conners, C. K., & Sharpe, L. A controlled study of the differential application of outpatient psychiatric treatment for children. *Japanese Journal of Child Psychiatry,* 1965, *6,* 125–132.

Elliott, R. Simple reaction time: effects associated with age, preparatory interval, incentive-shift, and mode of presentation. *Journal of Experimental Child Psychology,* 1970, *9,* 86–107.

Epstein, L. C., Lasagna, L., Conners, C. K., & Rodriguez, A. Correlation of dextroamphetamine excretion and drug response in hyperkinetic children. *Journal of Nervous and Mental Diseases,* 1968, *146,* 136–146.

Ernhart, C., Graham, F., Eichman, P., Marshall, J., & Thurston, D. Brain injury in the preschool child: some developmental considerations. II. Comparison of brain-injured and normal children. *Psychological Monographs,* 1963, *77,* 17–33.

Finnerty, D., Greaney, J., Soltys, J., & Cole, J. The use of d-amphetamine with hyperkinetic children. *Psychopharmacologia,* 1971, *21,* 302–308.

Fish, B. Problems of diagnosis and the definition of comparable groups: a neglected issue in drug research with children. *American Journal of Psychiatry,* 1969, *125,* 900–908.

Fisher, S. On the relationship between expectations and drug response. *Clinical Pharmacology and Therapeutics,* 1962, *3,* 125–126.

Fisher, S., ed., *Child Research in Psychopharmacology.* Springfield, Ill.: Thomas, 1959.

Freed, H. *The Chemistry and Therapy of Behavior Disorders in Children.* Springfield, Ill.: Thomas, 1962.

Freeman, R. D. Drug effects on learning in children—a selective review of the past 30 years. *Journal of Special Education,* 1966, *1,* 17–37.

Gallagher, C. C. Federal involvement in the use of behavior modification drugs on grammar school children. Hearing before a subcommittee of the Committee of Government Operations, House of Representatives, September 29, 1970.

Garfield, S. L., Helper, M. M., Wilcott, R. C., & Muffly, R. Effects of chlorpromazine on behavior in emotionally disturbed children. *Journal of Nervous and Mental Diseases,* 1962, *135,* 147–154.

Ghent, L. Some neuropsychological problems relevant to chemical intervention in the growing organism. In S. Fisher, ed., *Child Research in Psychopharmacology.* Springfield, Ill.: Thomas, 1959.

Gillespie, D. G. *Drugs and Law Enforcement.* St. Louis: Washington University Social Science Institute,1970.

Glasser, W. *Schools Without Failure.* New York: Harper & Row, 1968.

Graham, F., Ernhart, C., Thurston, D., & Craft, M. Development three years after perinatal anoxia and other potentially damaging newborn experiences. *Psychological Monographs,* 1962, *76,* 1–53.

Graham, J. M. Drugs and politics: amphetamine politics on Capitol Hill. *Transaction,* 1972, *9,* 14–22.

Greenberg, L. M. & Lipman, R. S. Pharmacotherapy of hyperactive children: Current practices. *Clinical Proceedings,* Children's Hospital, Washington, D.C., 1971, *27,* 101–105.

Hartlage, L. C. Effects of chlorpromazine on learning. *Psychological Bulletin,* 1965, *64,* 235–245.

Helper, M. M., Wilcott, R. C., & Garfield, S. L. Effects of chlorpromazine on learning and related processes in emotionally disturbed children. *Journal of Consulting Psychology,* 1963, *27,* 1–9.

Hewett, F. M., Taylor, F. D., & Artuso, A. A. The Santa Monica Project: evaluation of an engineered classroom design with emotionally disturbed children. *Exceptional Children,* 1969, *35,* 523–529.

Holt, J. *How Children Fail.* New York: Pitman, 1964.

Horowitz, F. D., Paden, L., Bhana, K., & Self, P. An infant-control procedure for studying infant visual fixations. *Developmental Psychology,* 1972, *70,* 90.

Kaspar, J. C., Millichap, J. G., Backus, R., Child, D., & Schulman, J. L. A study of the relationship between neurological evidence of brain damage in children and activity and distractibility. *Journal of Consulting and Clinical Psychology,* 1971, *36,* 329–337.

Kenny, T. J., Clemmens, R. L., Hudson, B. W., Lentz, G. A., Cicci, R., & Nair, P. Characteristics of children referred because of hyperactivity. *The Journal of Pediatrics,* 1971, *79,* 618–622.

Knights, R. M. & Hinton, G. The effects of methylphenidate (Ritalin) on the motor skills and behavior of children with learning problems. *Journal of Nervous and Mental Diseases,* 1969, *148,* 643–653.

Knobel, M., Wolman, M. B., & Mason, E. Hyperkinesis and organicity in children. *Archives of General Psychiatry,* 1959, *1,* 310–318.

Kohl, H. *36 Children.* New York: New American Library, 1967.

Kornetsky, C. Psychoactive drugs in the immature organism. *Psychopharmacologia,* 1970, *17,* 105–136.

Ladd, E. Disciplinary principles and behavior-changing drugs. *Inequality in Education,* 1971, *8,* 2–10.

Lapouse, R. & Monk, M. A. An epidemiologic study of behavior characteristics in children. *American Journal of Public Health,* 1958, *48,* 1134–1144.

Laties, V. G. & Weiss, B. Performance enhancement by the amphetamines: a new appraisal. In H. Brill, ed., *Neuropsychopharmacology.* Amsterdam: Excerpta Medica Foundation, 1967.

Laufer, M. W. Long-term management and some follow-up findings on the use of drugs with minimal cerebral syndromes. *Journal of Learning Disabilities,* 1971, *4,* 55–58.

Laufer, M. W. & Denhoff, E. Hyperkinetic behavior syndrome in children. *Journal of Pediatrics,* 1957, *50,* 463–474.

Laufer, M. W., Denhoff, E., & Solomons, G. Hyperkinetic impulse disorders in children's behavior problems. *Psychosomatic Medicine,* 1957, *19,* 38–49.

Lennard, H., Epstein, L. J., Bernstein, A., & Ransom, D. C. Hazards implicit in prescribing psychoactive drugs. *Science,* 1970, *169,* 438–441.

Lindsley, D. B. & Henry, C. E. The effect of drugs on behavior and the electroencephalograms of children with behavior disorders. *Psychosomatic Medicine,* 1941, *4,* 140–149.

Lourie, R. S. Psychoactive drugs in pediatrics. *Pediatrics,* 1964, 34, 691–693.

Mackworth, N. H. Researches on the measurement of human performance. Medical Research Council, Special Report No. 268. H. M. Stationery Office, London, 1950.

Maynard, R. Omaha pupils given "behavior" drugs. *Washington Post,* June 29, 1970.

McDermott, J. F. A specific placebo effect encountered in the use of Dexedrine in a hyperactive child. *Case Reports,* March, 1965.

Meichenbaum, D. H. & Goodman, J. Training impulsive children to talk to themselves: a means of developing self-control. *Journal of Abnormal Psychology,* 1971, *77,* 115–126.

Menkes, M. M., Rose, J. S., & Menkes, J. H. A twenty-five-year follow-up study on the hyperkinetic child with minimal brain dysfunction. *Pediatrics,* 1967, *39,* 393–399.

Meyer, W. J. Cerebral dysfunction. In C. O. Johnson & H. D. Blank, eds., *Exceptional Children Research Review.* Washington: Council for Exceptional Children, 1968.

Mendelson, W., Johnson, N., & Stewart, M. Hyperactive children as teenagers: a follow-up study. *Journal of Nervous and Mental Diseases,* 1971, *153,* 273–279.

Millichap, J. G. Drugs in management of hyperkinetic and perceptually handicapped children. *Journal of the American Medical Association,* 1968, *206,* 1527–1530.

Millichap, J. G., Aymot, F., Sturgis, L. H., Larsen, K. W., & Egan, R. A. Hyperkinetic behavior and learning disorders. III. Battery of neuropsychological tests in controlled trial of methylphenidate. *American Journal of Diseases in Childhood,* 1968, *116,* 235–244.

Millichap, J. G. & Boldrey, E. E. Studies in hyperkinetic behavior. II. Laboratory and clinical evaluations of drug treatments. *Neurology,* 1967, *17,* 467–472.

Minde, K., Webb, G., & Sykes, D. Studies on the hyperactive child. VI. Prenatal and paranatal factors associated with hyperactivity. *Developmental Medicine and Child Neurology,* 1968, *10,* 355–363.

Minde, K. K. & Weiss, G. C. The assessment of drug effects in children as compared to adults. *Journal of the American Academy of Child Psychiatry,* 1970, *9,* 124–131.

Moyer, K. E. & Gilmer, B. V. H. Attention spans of children for experimentally designed toys. *Journal of Genetic Psychology,* 1955, *87,* 187–201.

Novack, H. S. An educator's view of medication and classroom behavior. *Journal of Learning Disabilities,* 1971, *4,* 43–44.

Office of Child Development report on the conference on the use of stimulant drugs in the treatment of behaviorally disturbed young school children. Sponsored by the Office of Child Development and the Office of the Assistant Secretary for Health and Scientific Affairs, Department of Health, Education, and Welfare, Washington, D.C., January 11-12, 1971. Reprinted in *The National Elementary Principal,* 1971, *50,* 53–59.

O'Leary, K. D. & Becker, W. C. Behavior modification of an adjustment class: a token reinforcement program. *Exceptional Children,* 1967, *33,* 637–642.

O'Leary, K. D. & Drabman, R. Token reinforcement programs in the classroom: a review. *Psychological Bulletin,* 1971, *75,* 379–398.

O'Leary, K. D., Becker, W. C., Evans, M. B., & Saudargas, R. A. A token reinforcement program in a public school: a replication and systematic analysis. *Journal of Applied Behavior Analysis*, 1969, *2*, 3–13.

Paine, R. S. Minimal chronic brain syndrome in children. *Developmental Medicine and Child Neurology*, 1962, *4*, 21–29.

Palkes, H. & Stewart, M. Intellectual ability and performance of hyperactive children. *American Journal of Orthopsychiatry*, 1972, *42*, 35–39.

Palkes, H., Stewart, M., & Kahana, B. Porteus Maze performance of hyperactive boys after training in self-directed verbal commands. *Child Development*, 1968, *39*, 817–826.

Patterson, G. R. An application of conditioning techniques to the control of a hyperactive child. In L. P. Ullman & L. Krasner, eds., *Case Studies in Behavior Modification*. New York: Holt, Rinehart & Winston, 1964.

Patterson, G. R., Jones, R., Whittier, J., & Wright, M. A. A behavior modification technique for the hyperactive child. *Behavior Research and Therapy*, 1965, *2*, 217–226.

Payne, R. B. & Hauty, G. T. Factors affecting the endurance of psychomotor skill. *Journal of Aviation Medicine*, 1955, *25*, 382.

Piaget, J. *The Origins of Intelligence in the Child*. London: Routledge & Kegan Paul, 1953.

Pincus, J. H. & Glaser, G. H. The syndrome of 'minimal' brain damage in childhood. *New England Journal of Medicine*, 1966, *275*, 27–35.

Pond, D. Psychiatric aspects of epileptic and brain-damaged children. *British Medical Journal*, 1961, *2*, 1377–1382, 1454–1459.

Prechtl, H. F. R. & Stemmer, C. J. Choreiform syndrome in children. *Developmental Medicine and Child Neurology*, 1962, *4*, 119–127.

Quay, H. C., Werry, J. S., McQueen, M., & Sprague, R. L. Remediation of the conduct problem child in the special class setting. *Exceptional Children*, 1966, *32*, 509–515.

Rapoport, J., Abramson, A., Alexander, D., & Lott, I. Playroom observations of hyperactive children on medication. *Journal of the American Academy of Child Psychiatry*, 1971, *10*, 524–533.

Rapoport, J. L., Lott, I. T., Alexander, D. F., & Abramson, A. U. Urinary noradrenaline and playroom behavior in hyperactive boys. *Lancet*, 1970, *2*, 1141.

Reger, R. Stimulating the distractible child. *The Elementary School Journal*, 1963, *64*, 42–48.

Richard, R. Drugs for children—miracle or nightmare? *Providence Sunday Journal*, February 6, 1972.

Rickels, K., Lipman, R. S., Fisher, S., Park, L. C., & Uhlenhuth, E. H. Is a double-blind clinical trial really double-blind? A report of doctor's medication guesses. *Psychopharmacologia*, 1970, *16*, 329–336.

Ridberg, E. H., Parke, R. D., & Hetherington, E. M. Modification of impulsive and reflective cognitive styles through observation of film-mediated models. *Developmental Psychology*, 1971, *5*, 369–377.

Robins, L. N. Follow-up studies of behavior disorders in children. In H. C. Quay and J. S. Werry, eds. *Psychopathological Disorders of Childhood*. New York: John Wiley, 1972.

Rosenthal, R. & Rosnow, R. L. *Artifact in Behavioral Research*. New York: Academic Press, 1969.

Rutter, M., Graham, P., & Birch, H. Interrelations between the choreiform syndrome, reading disability, and psychiatric disorder in children of 8–11 years. *Developmental Medicine and Child Neurology*, 1966, *8*, 149–159.

Rutter, M., Graham, P., & Yule, W. A neuropsychiatric study in childhood. *Clinics in Developmental Medicine*, 1970, *35/36*.

Safer, D. J. Drugs for problem school children. *The Journal of School Health*, 1971, *41*, 491–495.

Safer, D., Allen, R., & Barr, E. Depression of growth in hyperactive children on stimulant drugs. *New England Journal of Medicine*, 1972, *287*, 217–220.

Sainz, A. Hyperkinetic disease of children: diagnosis and therapy. *Diseases of the Nervous System*, 1966, *27*, 48–50.

Satterfield, J. H., Cantwell, D. P., Lesser, L. I., & Podosin, R. L. Physiological studies of the hyperkinetic child: I. *American Journal of Psychiatry*, 1972, *128*, 1418–1424.

Satterfield, J. H. & Dawson, M. E. Electrodermal correlates of hyperactivity in children. *Psychophysiology*, 1971, *8*, 191–197.

Satterfield, J. H., Lesser, L. I., Saul, R. E., Cantwell, D. P. EEG aspects in the diagnosis and treatment of minimal brain dysfunction. *Annals of the New York Academy of Sciences*, in press.

Schachter, S. The interaction of cognitive and physiological determinants of emotional state. In P. H. Leiderman & D. Shapiro, eds., *Psychobiological Approaches to Social Behavior*. Stanford: Stanford University Press, 1964, 138–173.

Schulman, J. L., Kaspar, J. E., & Throne, F. M. *Brain Damage and Behavior: A Clinical Experimental Study*. Springfield, Ill.: Charles C. Thomas, 1965.

Shetty, T. Photic responses in hyperkinesis of childrood. *Science*, 1971, *174*, 1356–1357.

Silberman, C. E. *Crisis in the Classroom*. New York: Random House, 1970.

Small, A., Hibi, S., & Feinberg, I. Effects of dextroamphetamine sulfate on EEG sleep patterns of hyperactive children. *Archives of General Psychiatry*, 1971, *25*, 369–380.

Solomons, G. Drug therapy, initiation and follow-up. Paper presented at the Conference on Minimal Brain Dysfunction, New York, March, 1972.

———. The hyperactive child. *Journal of the Iowa Medical Society*, 1965, *55*, 464–469.

Sprague, R. L. Minimal brain dysfunction from a behavioral viewpoint. Paper presented at the Conference on Minimal Brain Dysfunction, New York, March, 1972.

Sprague, R. L., Barnes, K. R., & Werry, J. S. Methylphenidate and thioridazine: learning, reaction time, activity, and classroom behavior in disturbed children. *American Journal of Orthopsychiatry*, 1970, *40*, 615–628.

Sprague, R. L., & Werry, J. Methodology of psychopharmacological studies with the retarded. In N. Ellis, ed., *International Review of Research in Mental Retardation*. Vol. 5, New York: Academic Press, 1971.

Sprague, R. L., Werry, J., & Davis, K. Psychotropic drug effects on learning and activity level of children. Paper presented at the Gatlinburg Conference on Research and Theory in Mental Retardation, March, 1969.

Spring, C., Greenberg, L., Scott, J., & Hopwood, J. Effect of Ritalin on two components of reaction time in children with severe learning problems. Unpublished paper.

Sroufe, L. A. The diversification of 'minimal brain dysfunction.' Review of P. H. Wender, Minimal brain dysfunction in children. *Contemporary Psychology*, 1972, *17*, 264–266.

Sroufe, L. A., Sonies, B. C., West, W. D., & Wright, F. S. Anticipatory heart rate deceleration and reaction time in children with and without referral for learning and behavior disorders. *Child Development*, 1973, *44*, 267–273.

Steinberg, G. G., Troshinsky, C., & Steinberg, H. R. Dextroamphetamine responsive behavior disorder in school children. *The American Journal of Psychiatry*, 1971, *128*, 174–179.

Stephen, K. V., Sprague, R. L., & Werry, J. S. Drug treatment of hyperactive children in Chicago. Manuscript.

Stern, J. A. Personal communication, 1972.

Stevens, D. A., Boydstun, J. A., Ackerman, P. T., & Dykman, R. A. Reaction time, impulsivity, and autonomic ability in children with minimal brain dysfunction. *Proceedings*, Seventy-sixth Annual Convention, American Psychological Association, 1968, 367–368.

Stevens, D. A., Boydstun, J. A., Dykman, R. A., Peters, J. E., & Hinton, D. W. Presumed minimal brain dysfunction in children, relationship to performance on selected behavioral tests. *Archives of General Psychiatry,* 1967, *16,* 281–285.

Stewart, M. A. Hyperactive children. *Scientific American,* 1970, *222,* 94–98.

Stewart, M. A., & Olds, S. W. *Raising a Hyperactive Child.* New York: Harper & Row, 1973.

Stewart, M. A., Pitts, F., Craig, A., & Dieruf, W. The hyperactive child syndrome. *American Journal of Orthopsychiatry,* 1966, *36,* 861–867.

Strauss, A. A. & Lehtinen, L. E. *Psychopathology and Education of the Brain Injured Child.* New York: Grune and Stratton, 1947.

Sykes, D. H. Sustained attention in hyperactive children. Doctoral dissertation, McGill University, 1969.

Sykes, D. H., Douglas, V. I., & Morgenstern, G. The effect of methylphenidate (Ritalin) on sustained attention in hyperactive children. *Psychopharmacologia,* 1972, *25,* 262–274.

Sykes, D. H., Douglas, V. I., Weiss, G., & Minde, K. K. Attention in hyperactive children and effect of methylphenidate (Ritalin). *Journal of Child Psychology and Psychiatry,* 1971, *12,* 129–139.

Tarnopol, L. Delinquency and minimal brain dysfunction. *Journal of Learning Disabilities,* 1970, *3,* 200–207.

Thomas, D. R., Becker, W. C., & Armstrong, M. Production and elimination of disruptive classroom behavior by systematically varying teachers' behavior. *Journal of Applied Behavior Analysis,* 1968, *1,* 35–45.

Thompson, T. & Pickens, R. *Stimulus Properties of Drugs.* New York: Appleton-Century-Crofts, 1971.

Thompson, T. & Schuster, C. R. *Behavioral Pharmacology.* Englewood Cliffs, N. J.: Prentice-Hall, 1968.

Trouton, D. S. Placebos and their psychological effects. *Journal of Mental Science,* 1957, *103,* 344–354.

Turnure, J. E. Children's reaction to distractors in a learning situation. *Developmental Psychology,* 1970, *2,* 115–122.

————. Control of orienting behavior in children under five years of age. *Developmental Psychology,* 1971, *4,* 16–24.

Wahler, R. G., Winkel, G. H., Peterson, R. F., & Morrison, D. C. Mothers as behavior therapists for their own children. *Behavior Research and Therapy,* 1965, *3,* 113–124.

Weiss, B. & Laties, V. G. Enhancement of human performance by caffeine and the amphetamines. *Pharmacological Review,* 1962, *14,* 1–36.

Weiss, G., Minde, K., Werry, J. S., Douglas, V., & Nemeth, E. Studies on the hyperactive child. VIII. Five-year follow-up. *Archives of General Psychiatry,* 1971, *24,* 409–414.

Wender, P. H. *Minimal Brain Dysfunction in Children.* New York: John Wiley, 1971.

Wender, P. H., Epstein, R. S., Kopin, I. J., & Gordon, E. K. Urinary monoamine metabolites in children with minimal brain dysfunction. *American Journal of Psychiatry,* 1971, *127,* 1411–1415.

Werry, J. S. Developmental hyperactivity. *Pediatric Clinics of North America,* 1968*a, 15,* 581–599.

————. Diagnosis, etiology, and treatment of hyperactivity in children. *Learning Disorders.* Vol. 3. Washington, D. C.: Special Child Publication, 1968*b,* 171–190.

————. Studies of the hyperactive child. IV. An empirical analysis of the minimal brain dysfunction syndrome. *Archives of General Psychiatry,* 1968*c, 19,* 9–16.

————. Some clinical and laboratory studies of psychotropic drugs in children: an overview. In W. L. Smith, ed., *Drugs and Cerebral Function.* Springfield, Ill.: Thomas, 1970.

————. Organic factors in childhood psychopathology. In H. C. Quay & J. S. Werry, eds., *Psychopathological Disorders of Childhood.* New York: John Wiley, 1972.

Werry, J. S. & Sprague, R. L. Methylphenidate in children—effect of dosage. *New England Journal of Medicine,* in press.

————. Some issues in the design of psychopharmacological studies in children. Paper presented at the meeting of the American Psychiatric Association, San Francisco, May, 1970.

Werry, J. S., Weiss, G., & Douglas, V. Studies on the hyperactive child. I. Some preliminary findings. *Canadian Psychiatric Association Journal,* 1964, *9,* 120–130.

Werry, J. S., Weiss, G., Douglas, V., & Martin, J. Studies on the hyperactive child: the effect of chlorpromazine upon behavior and learning ability. *Journal of the Academy of Child Psychiatry,* 1966, *5,* 292–312.

Werry, J. S. & Wollersheim, J. P. Behavior therapy with children: a broad overview. *American Academy of Child Psychiatry Journal,* 1967, *6,* 354–370.

Witter, C. Drugging and schooling. *Transaction,* 1971, *8,* 31–34.

Zedler, E. Y. Screening underachieving pupils for risk of neurological impairment. In J. Hellmuth, ed., *Learning Disorders.* Vol. 3. Seattle: Special Child Publication, 1968.

Zimmerman, F. T. & Burgemeister, B. B. Action of methylphenidylacetate (Ritalin) and reserpine in behavior disorders in children and adults. *American Journal of Psychiatry,* 1958, *115,* 323–328.

Zrull, J. P., Westman, J. C., Arthur, B., & Rice, D. L. A comparison of diazepam, D-amphetamine and placebo in the treatment of the hyperkinetic syndrome in children. *American Journal of Psychiatry,* 1964, *121,* 388–389.

8 Behavior Modification As an Educational Technique

JAMES A. SHERMAN and
DON BUSHELL, JR.
University of Kansas

INTRODUCTION

EACH YEAR, classroom teachers greet a new group of children. Generally, it is expected that, by the end of the year, the children will have developed new abilities and attitudes as a result of the teacher's instruction. In short, one of the important responsibilities of a teacher is to change (develop) the behavior of students.

Although we might find general agreement about the responsibility of a teacher to change the behavior of students, there is little immediate hope of substantial agreement on *how* this is to be accomplished. Quite independent of any particular theoretical persuasion about child development, some teachers are far more effective than others. The "good" teacher is remembered as a wise counselor and eulogized in narrative accounts of "The Most Unforgettable Person I Ever Met"; others are less affectionately recalled with harsh limericks and rhymes of "no more teacher's dirty looks." Whatever it is that distinguishes the "good" teacher, it cannot yet be predictably taught in any teacher training program. Consequently, "good" teaching remains an *art,* appreciatively recognized but difficult to replicate.

By definition, artistry cannot be mass-produced. It might, however, be possible to distill some of the essential ingredients of effective teaching into specified procedures that could be accurately reproduced by the great majority of practicing teachers. The application of behavior modification procedures to the classroom is one attempt to develop an empirically based set of techniques that can be used by all teachers who seek to change the behavior of their students.

Behavior modification as an educational technique is a descendant of

Preparation of this paper was supported, in part, by Program Project Grant HD 00870 to the Bureau of Child Research, University of Kansas, and by Grant OEG–0–8–522422–4433 from the United States Office of Education to the University of Kansas Support and Development Center for Follow Through.

the laboratory science called "the experimental analysis of behavior." The kinship of each to the other is reflected in some characteristics that are common to both. Like its parent discipline, behavior modification focuses particular attention on: precisely specified (replicable) procedures that can be applied to alter behavior; and objectively measured behaviors. The goal is to relate the two so that reliably measured changes in behavior are demonstrated to be a direct function of controlled changes in the environment, that is, a function of a specific procedure.

Historically, the experimental analysis of behavior has devoted considerable attention to the way in which behaviors are altered by their consequences. Correspondingly, most behavior modification techniques have emphasized procedures for arranging consequences that will alter behavior in desirable ways. Indeed, the emphasis on consequences has been so great that common usage often equates behavior modification with contingency management. It is an emphasis that may be slightly misplaced.

It is our opinion that, in the long run, the convention of measuring the behavioral effects of specified procedures is of paramount importance. The objective and systematic measurement of the effects of a procedure builds a self-corrective feedback system that progressively improves and refines that procedure. The resulting procedure and its associated measurement techniques enable more certain, and therefore more widespread, replication by others. A familiar behavioral maxim states that "behavior is a function of its consequences." In the development of improved educational techniques it may be timely to add a new maxim that states "measurement is fundamental."

As classroom behavior modification techniques have been successfully developed, it has become popular to label a variety of procedures (including drug prescriptions) as behavior modification. Consequently it was necessary to establish some criteria that could be used to separate those reports of classroom research that should be included in this review from those that should not be included. We have chosen to include those reports published prior to September, 1972, that:

1. provided for the direct observation and measurement of an overt classroom behavior,

2. clearly specified the procedure used to alter the environmental consequences of the behavior in question, and

3. demonstrated an explicit relationship between environmental events and behavior by directly manipulating those events.

Further, because of the large number of studies available, the review is limited to those studies that have immediate relevance to elementary and secondary classrooms, including some special educational environments. For previous reviews of the use of behavior modification procedures in classrooms and other settings, see Baer and Sherman (1970), Hanley (1970), Kazdin and Bootzin (1972), O'Leary and Drabman (1971), Risley and Baer (1973), and Sherman and Baer (1969).

Regardless of the type of behavior under investigation, many of the studies reviewed in this chapter have attempted to provide definitions of the behaviors measured, a description of the measurement system, and some estimate of the degree to which independent observers agreed on the occurrence or nonoccurrence of the behaviors measured. One measurement method has been to have observers count the number of times a particular behavior occurs (frequency counts) or record the total amount of time the behavior is exhibited (duration measure).

In most cases, the reliable observation and recording of academic responses is easier than the observation and recording of social behaviors. Many academic responses leave physical evidence of their occurrence and correctness. The student's answers to math problems, the accuracy of responses to a spelling test, the style and content of his or her narrative prose, and the accuracy of reading comprehension are all likely to be represented by marks on paper that can be examined after the fact. These behaviors do not require direct and continuous observation.

For behaviors which do not leave physical traces, such as social behaviors, a common type of measurement system involves breaking an observation period down into a consecutive series of small time intervals of, say ten seconds in length. In each ten-second interval an observer records whether or not the behavior of interest occurred. At the end of the observation period, the number or percentage of intervals in which the behavior occurred is calculated, thereby providing a measure of the amount of behavior observed. A variation of this interval-by-interval measurement system is one in which observers watch for, say, twenty seconds, record for ten seconds, observe for twenty seconds, record for ten seconds, and so on. Typically, this variation is employed when there are a large number of different behaviors to record. Occasionally, a time-sample method has been used in which observers simply look and at the end of a fixed time-period, say ten seconds, record what behaviors are occurring at that moment in time.

Interval-by-interval recording procedures can be used to record the behaviors of individual students and teachers or to record the behaviors of several students. In the latter case, the observer might observe and record the behavior of one student for one interval, then the behavior of the next student for an interval, and so on until all students have been observed. Alternatively, the observers might watch the behavior of all of the students, and, if any member of the class displayed the behavior, the interval would be scored for that behavior.

The primary advantage of using interval systems of recording are that they provide a convenient way of evaluating the reliability of the recording system. Each interval scored by two independent observers can be compared for agreement on the scoring of the occurrence or nonoccurrence of a particular behavior. A high degree of interval-by-interval agreement suggests that the definitions of the behavior and the recording system are explicit enough to allow other researchers to replicate them. However, the interval method of recording sacrifices some completeness since an interval containing, say, five instances of behavior is scored the same as an interval containing one or two instances.

Using the criteria for inclusion stated at the outset, three major areas of research on behavior modification in educational settings will be reviewed in this chapter. They involve the work on social behaviors, academic behaviors and, finally, the teaching of behavior modification techniques. The last section of this chapter is devoted to a discussion of basic issues that require the consideration of enthusiasts and thoughtful critics alike.

SOCIAL, DISRUPTIVE AND ATTENDING BEHAVIORS

The largest number of classroom studies have been concerned with what used to be called deportment: increasing the amount of time students spend attending to or looking at the teacher or study materials during individual work periods, and reducing student behaviors that may interfere with their work behaviors or may disrupt others (talking, wandering around the room, throwing objects, looking out the window). The techniques of behavior modification have also been used to produce changes in other behaviors important for the development of the child. These changes include increasing cooperative play and work with other students during group activities, improving school attendance, developing motor skills such as walking and active play with materials, and reducing crying and tantrum behaviors during class periods and aggressive behaviors during group activities.

Types of Consequences Used

The research on modifying children's social behaviors in the classroom can best be reviewed by looking at the consequences used.

1. *Teacher attention.* Perhaps the most commonly used behavior modification technique in the classroom has involved changing the ways teachers provide their praise and disapproval for student behaviors. In most studies teachers have been taught to increase the amount of praise delivered for appropriate or desirable behaviors of the students. Very often this procedure has been combined with additional techniques that rapidly

reduce undesirable behaviors or behaviors that compete with those the teacher wishes to increase. These additional techniques include ignoring undesirable or incompatible behaviors or delivering reprimands following these undesirable behaviors.

A series of pioneering studies done in preschool settings exemplifies the combined use of praise for desirable behavior and the ignoring of undesirable or incompatible behaviors to change the behaviors of individual children. These changes included the development of a greater amount of interaction with other children (Allen, Hart, Buell, Harris, and Wolf 1964); increased walking and decreased crawling (Harris, Johnston, Kelley, and Wolf 1964); reduction in crying (Hart, Allen, Buell, Harris, and Wolf 1964); and the development of more active motor skills (Johnston, Kelley, Harris, and Wolf 1966). The use of very similar techniques has continued to the present time in preschool settings to produce, for example, reductions in aggressive and disruptive behaviors (Allen, Turner, and Everett 1970; Brown and Elliott 1965); increases in outdoor play (Buell, Stoddard, Harris, and Baer 1968); increased cooperative play (Hart, Reynolds, Baer, Brawley, and Harris 1968); increased social interactions (Sibley, Abbott, and Cooper 1969; Harris and Miksovic 1972; Scott, Burton, and Yarrow 1967); and increased time spent with play materials (Allen, Henke, Harris, Baer, and Reynolds 1967).

The early preschool studies, by clearly showing the possibility of developing desirable student behaviors through the use of teacher attention and by clearly specifying the techniques by which this was accomplished, provided a model for the use of similar techniques in elementary and secondary classrooms. An example of the use of teacher attention to affect the behavior of an entire class of students in an elementary school has been provided by Hall, Panyan, Rabon, and Broden (1968). In this study thirty students in a sixth grade had high rates of disruptive and other nonstudy behaviors. During an initial baseline period, the level of study behavior of these students was simply recorded each day for thirty minutes using a version of an interval recording system. After a number of days of baseline, the teacher was asked to increase the frequency with which he made positive comments to the students for their appropriate study behaviors. The results are shown in figure 1. The top set of axes displays the percent of intervals scored for student study behavior for the entire class, and the bottom set of axes the number of intervals scored for teacher attention following student study behavior. Instructions to the teacher to increase the frequency of positive comments for study behavior (labeled reinforcement[1] on figure 1) seemed to produce a higher number of these comments and a corresponding increase in student study behavior

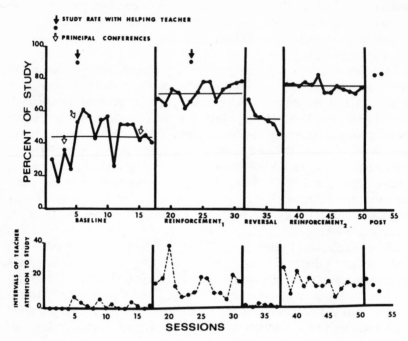

Fig. 1. A record of class study behavior and teacher attention for study behavior during reading period in a sixth-grade classroom: Baseline—before experimental procedures; Reinforcement₁—increased teacher attention for study; Reversal—removal of teacher attention for study; Reinforcement₂—return to increased teacher attention for study; Post—follow-up checks up to twenty weeks after termination of experimental procedures. (From Hall, Panyan, Rabon and Broden 1968.)

over baseline. Next, there was a return to a condition in which the teacher no longer provided the higher frequency of positive comments for appropriate study behaviors (labeled "reversal" on figure 1). Student study behavior declined, but again increased when the teacher once more provided a higher frequency of positive comments for study behavior (reinforcement₂). During the last nine sessions of the reinforcement₂ condition, the teacher was told to continue providing positive comments to students for appropriate study but to discontinue making any comments for nonstudy behavior. (Up to this time nonstudy behaviors occasionally produced comments from the teacher, usually reprimands, at a frequency of 12 intervals per observation period.) As can be seen, there was no marked effect from this in spite of the fact that teacher comments following nonstudy behavior declined to an average of 4.5 intervals scored per observation period. Finally, postcheck observations taken one, three, and five months later indicated that the teacher was maintaining a relatively high frequency of positive comments for study behavior and that the study behavior also remained at a high level.

Several features of this study seem noteworthy. First, the investigators showed the effects of increasing the teacher's comments for study behavior by taking baseline observations and then systematically increasing, decreasing, and again increasing the frequency with which the teacher provided positive comments for studying. The fact that the amount of study behavior increased and decreased reliably with changes in teacher behavior, indicates that it was the teacher's behavior and not other variables that were responsible for changes in amount of study behavior. Second, the investigators presented measures of both student behavior and teacher behavior. This seems very important in studies that attempt to alter student behaviors by changing teacher behavior, since any changes in student behavior are only clearly interpretable if accompanied by corresponding changes in teacher performance. Third, the fact that students' level of study behavior did not change when the frequency of comments (usually reprimands) following nonstudy behaviors was decreased, suggests that these types of consequences were not functional for the maintenance of study behavior. Finally, the investigators provided some indication of what happened after the formal termination of the study, by including postcheck measures.

The study by Hall et al. (1968) was chosen to display the ways in which attention from a teacher, properly arranged to follow appropriate study behaviors of students, can produce desirable changes in those behaviors. However, there are a number of additional studies that could also be cited to exemplify the use of similar procedures to increase study, on-task, and desirable social behaviors (Breyer, Calchera, and Cann 1971; Broden, Bruce, Mitchell, Carter, and Hall 1970; Broden, Hall, Dunlap, and Clark 1970; Hall and Broden 1967; Hall, Lund, and Jackson 1968; Lates, Egner, and McKenzie 1971; Peterson, Cox, and Bijou 1971; and Wasik, Senn, Welch, and Cooper 1969) and to decrease undesirable or disruptive behaviors such as talking out, making noise in class, tantrums, and aggression (Becker, Madsen, Arnold, and Thomas 1967; Hall, Fox, Willard, Goldsmith, Emerson, Owen, Davis, and Porcia 1971; Lates et al. 1971; McAllister, Stachowiak, Baer, and Conderman 1969; Madsen, Becker, and Thomas 1968; Thomas, Nielsen, Kuypers, and Becker 1968; Ward and Baker 1968; Wasik et al. 1969; Zimmerman and Zimmerman 1962). In each of these studies, with individual students or with entire classrooms of students, teachers praised and attended to desirable or appropriate student behaviors (and in some cases also allowed students to play games contingent on appropriate behaviors). Undesirable behaviors were commonly ignored but in some instances produced reprimands from the teacher or brief periods of social isolation.

Thus, there is a wide range of evidence to indicate that careful use of praise and attention from teachers can produce desirable changes in student behaviors. However, the practice of combining praise for appropriate behaviors with other procedures designed to simultaneously reduce undesirable behaviors, makes it difficult to specify exactly what components of the procedure were functional for changed student behaviors. In some cases, such as when the component procedures are easy to implement and involve little cost, there may be little reason to analyze their functions separately. In other cases, particularly when one component of a treatment package is difficult to use, when it may be aversive to students and teachers, or when it may work against the changes desired, it seems important to begin to analyze its specific function. Some of the research on the use of teacher reprimands and disapproval for undesirable student behavior may represent such a case. Although there is evidence to indicate that reprimands alone can reduce behavior such as pinching and biting (Hall, Axelrod, Foundopoulos, Shellman, Campbell, and Cranston 1971) and various disruptive behaviors (O'Leary and Becker 1968; O'Leary, Kaufman, Kass, and Drabman 1970), several qualifications are required. First, the studies by O'Leary and Becker (1968) and O'Leary et al. (1970) suggest that soft reprimands, audible only to the particular student who is engaged in the disruptive behavior, are more functional in producing reductions in disruptive behavior than loud reprimands audible to the entire class. Second, the results of a study by Thomas, Becker, and Armstrong (1968) indicate that for some students frequent statements of disapproval for disruptive behavior, in the absence of praise for appropriate behavior, may produce an increase in disruptive behavior. These results, as well as results obtained by Madsen, Becker, Thomas, Koser, and Plager (1968), suggest that attention from teachers, whether of an "approving" or "disapproving" form, may act as a positive reinforcer to increase the behaviors it follows. Thus, a great deal of care needs to be exercised by a teacher when providing social consequences for undesirable student behaviors.

2. *Prizes and special activities.* The contingent award of prizes and access to special activities has also been extensively used to produce changes in classroom deportment. These consequences have involved a wide range of reinforcers such as candy, toys, money, and access to special activities like extra recess, gym periods, movies, stories, and trips; and punishing events such as being required to remain after school and loss of recess or free time. Prizes and special activities seem to be used in those cases where teacher attention and praise do not appear to be effective or, in the estimate of the teacher, are not likely to be successful

in changing student behavior. However, it should be noted that in many cases use of prizes and special activities is combined with systematic teacher attention as well.

Perhaps the simplest way to arrange for the use of tangible and activity consequences is to make them contingent upon specific behaviors and to inform the students of the contingency. Two studies provide examples of this with entire classrooms. Osborne (1969) markedly reduced the out-of-seat behaviors of deaf students by providing five minutes of free time for students who remained seated during instructional periods. Wasik (1970) provided play periods contingent upon desirable classroom behaviors such as engaging in self-directed activities, sharing materials, and following directions; and reduced play time for inappropriate behaviors such as aggression and "resisting authority." Under these contingencies, desirable behaviors were increased somewhat and inappropriate behaviors were reduced. Direct use of activity consequences or loss thereof with individual students was effective in changing out-of-seat behavior (Hall et al. 1971), the time required for a girl to get dressed in the morning (Hall, Axelrod, Tyler, Grief, Jones, and Robertson 1972), and time spent in clarinet practice, on a Campfire Girls project and on a reading project (Hall, Cristler, Cranston, and Tucker, 1970). In one study (Meichenbaum, Bowers, and Ross 1968) money given for work and study behaviors increased these behaviors.

A somewhat more complex system for arranging the contingency between desirable behaviors and positive reinforcers such as prizes and special activities is through the use of a contracting system. Although this procedure has not received a great deal of experimental attention, it has been used in at least two studies. MacDonald, Gallimore, and MacDonald (1970) negotiated "deals" between individual high school students and the mediators of their reinforcers such that attendance at school resulted in events such as access to a pool hall, time with a girl friend, money, and weekend privileges. Another report (Cohen, Keyworth, Kleiner, and Libert 1971) described the negotiation of contracts between students and their parents whereby money and record albums were provided for appropriate school behaviors. In each of these studies, desirable behavior increased. The use of such contracting systems may be more frequent where individual teachers do not have control over powerful positive reinforcers for students. In such cases it may be necessary to enlist the help of the student in specifying his or her own reinforcers and those outside the school system who control these reinforcers.

Similar control over reinforcers outside the classroom situation was attained in studies by Bailey, Wolf, and Phillips (1970) and Hawkins, Sluyter, and Smith, in press. In these studies students took home notes or daily report cards from the teacher. These were used as a basis by which the students gained or lost privileges in the home.

Perhaps the most systematic use of tangible items and access to special events as consequences for classroom behavior has been provided through the use of token or point systems. (See Axelrod 1971, and O'Leary and Drabman 1971, for reviews of token systems in classroom situations.) In most token or point systems, appropriate student behaviors produce relatively immediate, saveable consequences in the form of a token or points. These points or tokens may then be exchanged at some later time for the student's choice of various "back-up" reinforcers such as candy, money, toys, and special events and privileges. Usually an assortment of such back-up reinforcers is provided, and different point or token costs are assigned to the prizes or activities, depending upon their desirability. Thus, a student who earns more points or tokens typically has a wider assortment of back-up reinforcers from which to choose. Because tokens are discriminative for a number of different reinforcers they may, over time, come to function as generalized reinforcers (Skinner 1953).

There are a number of good examples of the use of point or token systems to change social, disruptive, and attending behavior of students. O'Leary, Becker, Evans, and Saudargas (1969) measured the disruptive behavior of seven second-grade children who were wandering around the room, hitting, kicking, or striking other students, and making noises or talking to other students when it was not appropriate. The initial attempt to reduce disruptive behavior included specifying the classroom rules to the students by telling them to sit in their seats, not to talk out of turn, and to work hard. Following this, the classroom was restructured to contain four different thirty-minute academic periods to evaluate the effects that a structured program might have. Next, in addition to providing the classroom rules and the structured program, the teacher praised appropriate classroom behavior and ignored disruptive behaviors. The results of these conditions are shown in figure 2, which displays the average percent of intervals scored for disruptive behavior of the seven students. Rules, classroom structure, praising appropriate behavior, and ignoring disruptive behavior had little effect on the average amount of disruptive behavior displayed. Next, a token or point system was employed: four times each afternoon the students received points reflecting the extent to which they followed the classroom rules, showed improvement from day to day, participated in class discussions, and were accurate in their work in arithmetic or spelling. Points could be exchanged for back-up reinforcers such as candy, pennants, dolls, comic books, and the like. Initially points were exchanged for back-up events each day, then points were saved and exchanged at the end of every other day and then

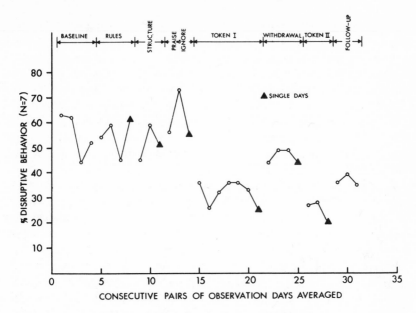

Fig. 2. Average percentage of combined disruptive behavior of seven children during the afternoon over the eight conditions: Base, Rules, Educational Structure, Praise and Ignore, Token I, Withdrawal. Token II, Follow-up. (From O'Leary, Becker, Evans and Saudargas 1969.)

at the end of each third day. The average percent of intervals scored for disruptive behavior declined when the token system was first used ("Token I"), then increased when the token system was withdrawn ("Withdrawal"), and again declined when the token system was reinstated ("Token II"). After the second use of the token system, a modified token system was introduced in which students received stars for good behavior, and these stars produced candy at the end of the week. The data for this period, labeled "follow-up" on figure 2, showed maintenance of a relatively low level of disruptive behavior although a somewhat higher one than that obtained during the Token II period.

Similar types of token or point systems have been employed to increase the amount of time individual students or entire classrooms of students spend in appropriate classroom behaviors such as writing, reciting to the teachers, attending to and working with appropriate academic materials (Bushell, Wrobel, and Michaelis 1968; Broden et al. 1970; Ferritor, Buckholdt, Hamblin, and Smith 1972; Sulzer, Hunt, Ashby, and Krams 1971) as well as to reduce the amount of disruptive, deviant, and aggressive behaviors of students (Carlsen, Arnold, Becker and Madsen 1968; Kuypers, Becker, and O'Leary 1968; O'Leary and Becker 1967; Perline and Levinsky 1968; Schwarz and Hawkins 1970; Walker and Buckley 1968). Desirable behavioral changes have also been produced through the use of modified token systems in which lights, visible to the students, provided immediate feedback for performance corresponding to the amount or number of back-up reinforcers students received (Craig and Holland 1970; Quay, Sprague, Werry, and McQueen 1967; Surrat, Ulrich, and Hawkins 1969). In another study (Ramp, Ulrich, and Dulaney 1971), the disruptive classroom behavior of a boy was reduced by flashing a light upon each occurrence of the behavior, with each light-flash signifying loss of free time.

The previously cited studies have attempted to modify social, disruptive, or attending behaviors of students by arranging consequences on an individual basis. That is, the consequences for an individual student were directly related only to his or her own performance. However, a number of studies have provided consequences for an entire group of students depending upon the performance of only one student or the combined performance of a few students in the group. The consequences provided typically have been candy, prizes, and access to special privileges, often mediated by various forms of point or token systems. An exception is McAllister et al. (1969), where the group consequences provided were praise and disapproval for appropriate and inappropriate classroom behaviors.

In one of the earliest uses of group consequences, Patterson (1964) arranged a box on the desk of a hyperactive boy which flashed a light and accumulated counter points contingent upon the student's attending behavior in class. Counter points were exchanged for candy to be divided up among the entire class at the end of each session. This procedure was associated with a reduction in the student's hyperactive behaviors, such as talking to other students, and pushing and hitting other students. Very similar techniques were employed by Patterson, Jones, Whittier, and Wright (1965) and by Coleman (1970) to reduce disruptive classroom behavior and to increase work behaviors.

A variation of group consequence procedures used in several studies has provided that performance measures which potentially reflect the behavior of any or all students in the class or group is used to determine whether all members of the class or group receive consequences. An example of this type of group consequence procedure is provided by Schmidt and Ulrich (1969). In this study, a sound-level meter was used to measure the noise level (in decibels) of a fourth-grade classroom during free-study periods. The consequences were arranged as follows. A timer was set at ten minutes. If the timer ran down to zero, a buzzer sounded, signifying that the students received two extra minutes added to the gym period and a two-minute break to do whatever they wished before the next ten-minute period. However, if the noise level of the room became too great (established at 42 decibels or above), then a whistle was blown and the timer was reset to ten minutes and allowed to start again. Figure 3 presents the average sound reading for each session when there were no consequences for classroom noise (sessions labeled "baseline" and "reversal") and when the consequences were in effect (sessions labeled "Phase 1" and "Phase 2"). On this figure, each data point represents the average sound-meter reading for a session, and the vertical lines running through the points represent the mean deviations within a session. The use of the consequences during Phase 1 and Phase 2 was associated with a marked reduction in the noise level of the classroom compared to the no-consequences condition. Similar group consequences depending upon the combined performance of students in a class or classroom-like situation have been used alone or in combination with other procedures (Graubard 1969; Hall et al. 1970; Herman and Tramontana 1971; Medland and Stachnik 1972; Packard 1970; and Sulzbacher and Houser 1968) to increase attending and other appropriate classroom behaviors and to decrease disruptive behaviors, to reduce disputing and talking-out behaviors, to reduce inappropriate behaviors during rest times, to increase

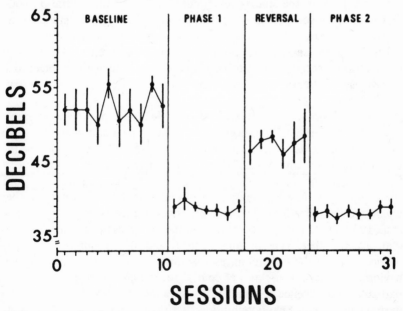

Fig. 3. The effects of sound-control procedures on the classroom noise level. Each point represents the average sound-level reading for one session with vertical lines denoting the mean deviation. (From Schmidt and Ulrich 1969.)

attending behaviors, and to reduce the frequency with which students made an obscene gesture.

Another variation of group consequence procedures involves possible competition between groups of students, as exemplified in a study by Barrish, Saunders, and Wolf (1969). In this study, students in the classroom were divided into two groups. If any member of a group engaged in disruptive behavior (such as talking to classmates, wandering around the room or making loud noises), that student's team received a point. At the end of each session, the members of the team with the fewer number of marks received special privileges such as being first in the lunch line, receiving stars to be placed on a chart, and being allowed to wear victory tags. Thus, the two groups competed against each other. However, there was an additional contingency that allowed students in both groups to receive the special privileges: if any team scored less than a fixed number of marks, all members of the team would be allowed access to the special privileges whether or not they had a greater number of marks than the other team. The use of these group consequences reliably produced large decreases in disruptive behavior.

Discussion and Evaluation

On the basis of the studies reviewed, there seems to be little question that a variety of social, disruptive, and attending behaviors of students can be changed by careful, systematic use of consequences in various classroom situations ranging from preschool to secondary school. However, if consequence procedures are to be widely used to change the social, disruptive, and attending behavior of students, several issues deserve discussion.

First, not all of the systems were always effective in producing desirable changes in student performance. This seemed to be a particularly difficult problem with the use of teacher attention and praise. It simply may be the case that attention and praise from the teacher are not sufficiently powerful reinforcers for some students to affect their behavior, particularly for students who display extremely deviant behavior. In cases where teacher attention is not effective or is minimally effective (see examples by Broden et al. 1970 and O'Leary et al. 1969), it may be necessary to go to systems that provide other types of consequences and to gain control of consequences outside the classroom, as was done in the studies involving behavioral contracts. There are, of course, several additional reasons that a particular consequence system may not have the effects desired or reported in previous studies. One possibility is that the system was not adequately implemented. For example, in a number of studies in which teachers have been instructed to use attention and praise as consequences for desirable behavior, little or no data have been presented as to whether the teachers actually changed their behavior to correspond to the instructions. Obviously, if a particular procedure is not implemented with precision, there is little reason to presume that the behavior of students will change. Another possibility is that all of the relevant or important parts of the procedures are not described in the published research and, thus, are not used by other investigators when attempting to replicate or extend the findings of previous research. This issue has been discussed by Kuypers et al. (1968) in the context of application of token systems.

Second, there is the question of whether the kinds of behaviors changed in the studies reviewed in this section are appropriate ones for teachers to change. (See O'Leary 1972b; comments by Reviewer A and B 1972; and Winett and Winkler 1972, for an extensive discussion of this issue.) Most teachers, principals and parents would agree that it is desirable to teach a nursery school student to walk rather than crawl, and to reduce the frequency with which a fourth-grade boy hits, kicks, and bites his peers. However, there may not be such agreement on the need to reduce the frequency of students' talking and wandering around the room during individual study times and to increase the amount of time a student sits quietly looking at the teacher or his study materials. Perhaps an alternative approach is to increase the teacher's tolerance for classroom noise and other so-called "deviant" behavior of children, as exemplified in studies reported by Graubard, Rosenberg, and Miller (1971). One common rationale for attempting to reduce disruptive behaviors and to increase the amount of time students spend sitting quietly attending to the teacher or to study materials is that it is assumed that this will produce beneficial effects on their responses to curriculum materials by, for example, increasing the frequency of correct responses. Improved performance on curriculum materials and improved grades have been anecdotally reported in several studies in which study and attending behaviors have been increased. However, no clear, consistent relationship has been found across those few studies that have attempted to analyze experimentally the possible relationship between attending behaviors, disruptive behaviors, and performance on curriculum materials (Ferritor et al. 1972; Kirby and Shields 1972; Sulzer et al. 1971).

Third, in most of the studies cited that have attempted to change the social, disruptive, and attending behaviors of students, individual consequences depended on the behavior of the individual student. However, in several studies group consequences were employed that depended upon the combined performances of the students in the group. When using such group consequences, it is possible that the desirable behavior of an individual student may not be reinforced because all of the other members of the group have displayed inappropriate behaviors. A frequently cited rationale for the use of group consequences is that the combined performance of a group is often easier to monitor and provide consequence for than are the behaviors of a number of individual students. Also it can be argued that the use of group consequences brings into play various forms of peer reinforcement and influence that facilitate and maintain desirable behaviors. For example, Hamblin, Hathaway, and Wodarski (1971) used group consequences for the academic performance of fifth-grade students and found increases in the proportion of time students spent tutoring each other as an increasing proportion of the consequences were determined by the performance of the four students scoring the lowest in the group. Herman and Tramontana (1971) compared the effects of group and individual consequences with an entire classroom of students and found that both types of consequences, in combination with a clear specification of the rules, were equally effective in controlling inappropriate behaviors during rest periods. However, the results obtained with one student in a study of Wolf, Hanley, King, Lachowicz, and Giles (1970) indicated that individual consequences for performance were not as effective in reducing out-of-seat behavior in the classroom as was a procedure in which the student's behavior resulted in consequences for both the student and her peers. Because of the relatively few studies available at this time, the behavioral effects of group consequences on peer interactions and the relative effects of individual and group consequences cannot be clearly specified.

Fourth, a frequently raised question is whether the desirable changes produced by a procedure generalize so the behavior of students is similarly improved in other situations or at a later time when the procedure is not in effect. Although some of the studies cited in this section have reported postcheck or follow-up measures of student performance after formal termination of the study (Allen et al. 1964; Hall et al. 1968; O'Leary et al. 1969; Osborne 1969; Schwarz and Hawkins 1970; Surrat et al. 1969; Wasik et al. 1969) and these have often indicated maintenance of the desirable behavioral changes (see Surrat et al. 1969 for an exception), the maintenance of the changes was frequently under conditions that were very similar to the original treatment conditions in that consequences were still provided for appropriate behaviors. Further, a large number of studies have found that removal of the treatment procedure is associated with a reversal, or at least reduction, of the desirable changes produced by the treatment program. In fact, this ability to change or reverse the desirable behaviors is important in demonstrating the function of the treatment program.

Studies by Kuypers et al. (1968), O'Leary et al. (1969), and Schwarz and Hawkins (1970) offer some of the few formal evaluations of the possible generalized effects of producing desirable changes in one situation on behavior in a similar situation where the treatment program was not in effect.

In the study of Schwarz and Hawkins (1970), decreased face-touching, better posture, and increased loudness of voice were produced by showing a sixth-grade girl videotapes of her behaviors recorded during a math period and by making tokens, exchangeable for back-up reinforcers, contingent on improved performance. The procedure improved these behaviors during math periods and also during spelling periods where the procedures were never used.

Kuypers et al. (1968) and O'Leary et al. (1969) used token systems to reduce disruptive behavior in the afternoon. Observations taken on a sample of the same students in the morning, when no tokens were used, showed no reduction in disruptive behavior. Similarly, Broden et al. (1970) found that increases in study behavior produced by the use of a token system in one class period did not transfer to other periods of the day for the same students, although such increases in study behavior could be produced throughout the classroom day by additional utilization of the token system. Thus, the available research suggests that behavioral changes produced in one situation do not automatically generalize to other situations where the treatment program is not in effect, nor are they necessarily maintained once the treatment program is entirely removed. However, if generalization to other situations is not achieved, it would seem reasonable that the treatment procedures could be correspondingly used in these situations if such generalization is deemed important. Similarly, if the behavioral changes are not maintained upon the withdrawal of the treatment procedures, it may be most reasonable to continue their use. It does not seem surprising that students stop displaying high amounts of desirable behaviors if there are not appropriate consequences for these behaviors or, worse yet, if the environment is arranged to maintain high amounts of undesirable behavior. Thus, the primary issue may not be the maintenance of beneficial changes once the treatment program is removed but rather restructuring the typical classroom setting so that appropriate consequences always support desirable behavior. One possible problem arises when the treatment procedures employ relatively immediate consequences for behavior. It may be unreasonable to expect that "real life" situations will always provide appropriate consequences with such immediacy. In this case, the principal issue is how to teach students to be influenced by consequences relatively remote in time from the occurrence of the behavior. This is an important area for additional research, although at least one study (O'Leary et al. 1969) has indicated some possible ways in which this might be done within the context of a token system.

Summary

1. A number of studies have shown that attention and praise from teachers as consequences for student behaviors can increase desirable social behaviors, such as working or studying quietly, and decrease undesirable social behaviors, such as wandering around the classroom and disrupting others.

2. Occasionally, the use of attention and praise has not been successful. In these cases, and in many others, tokens, exchangeable for prizes and special activities, have been used to increase desirable social behaviors and decrease undesirable social behaviors.

3. Although it appears that many social behaviors of students can be affected in a desirable way by the use of attention and praise and with token procedures, there is little clear evidence that the academic performance of the students is thereby improved.

ACADEMIC BEHAVIOR

There is not a clear line to be drawn between investigations of classroom social and disruptive behaviors and those that concentrate on academic performance. Several investigators have indicated that their objective is to minimize behavior that competes with effective learning. Others have worked with deportment problems in response to specific requests of classroom teachers. In these latter cases, it is difficult to know if the teacher's concern was for academic achievement or her own tranquility. Even though it may be an arbitrary distinction, the purposes of this paper seem best served by providing a separate treatment of those analyses that treat some form of academic behavior as their principal dependent variable.

In comparison with the relatively large number of studies that deal with conduct and deportment, the number of studies of academic behaviors is small. The proportionately small representation of academic studies can probably be attributed to a number of factors. Historically, behavior modification has been developed more by those who are clinically oriented than by educators. Politically, the behavior modification consultant or researcher has been an invited guest of the classroom teacher. That teacher's role presumed a degree of sophistication in academic and curriculum issues not shared, and perhaps not to be shared, by others. Most important, however, it is probable that the somewhat lagging development of academic procedures reflects some serious scientific problems of measuring responses that are not uniform.

The specific and discrete responses appropriate to several academic areas are not of uniform difficulty. Unlike a "talk-out" which is similar to most other "talk-outs," an arithmetic response may be to a simple addition problem or to a time-consuming story problem. In addition to the constantly shifting response requirement of academic materials, the problem of nonuniform responses is further confounded by the constantly changing skill of the child. A given response is more difficult for some children than for others, depending on their past learning history, and a given response may be more difficult for any given child at one point in time than at a later point in time. It can be a formidable task to establish that any observed change in behavior is a function of altered contingencies rather than a function of shifting problem difficulty or changing skill.

In spite of these difficulties, a growing body of academic research is indicating that the development of children's academic skills can be appreciably improved by systematically redesigning the conditions and the consequences of academic behavior.

Out-of-Class Analyses of Individual Performance

The experimental analysis of academic behavior has its roots in a series of studies conducted by Staats and his colleagues at the Arizona State University in the early 1960s. Staats, Staats, Schutz, and Wolf (1962) opened the issue with an experiment that evaluated the effects of tangible reinforcers in a beginning reading sequence for four-year-old children. Six children were individually taken through an instructional sequence that began with a picture-matching task and progressed to a sight-vocabulary training procedure. Three of the children began the sequence under a condition which only provided praise statements for their responses. In less than two forty-five-minute sessions each child indicated that he wanted to quit. At the point when tangible reinforcers (trinkets and candy) were introduced, each of the children elected to continue as willing and productive students through a total of eight forty-five-minute sessions. An alternate sequence of conditions for the other three children confirmed the motivational effectiveness of the reinforcement procedure.

In subsequent work along the same lines, Staats, Minke, Finley, Wolf, and Brooks (1964) refined the method of presenting stimulus materials to individual children with an experimental apparatus that displayed the reading stimuli and dispensed marbles for correct responses. The marbles served as tokens that could be deposited in one of four containers of different sizes. A different toy was associated with each container, and a full container of marbles could be exchanged for that toy.

At the time of their work, Staats and his associates may have been most interested in the progress they were making in developing a highly refined technology for the experimental analysis of reading behavior. In retrospect, however, their work appears to have been most influential as a model for the elaboration of classroom token systems.

Whitlock (1966) and Whitlock and Bushell (1967) replicated and extended the work by Staats and his colleagues to improve the reading performance of first-grade children who were individually tutored in a procedure that was demonstrated to be effective because of its use of tokens backed up by child-selected materials and activities.

More recently, the strategy of working with individual children outside their regular classroom setting has been used by Lovitt and his colleagues at the University of Washington. In general, these more sophisticated analyses have served to increase the refinement and precision of information about the effects of various contingencies on academic performance. Lovitt and Curtiss (1969) found that the academic performance of a twelve-year-old girl was higher when she set her own reinforcement contingencies than when the contingencies were specified by the teacher.

Lovitt and Esveldt (1970) found that the reinforcement value of free time was enhanced when it was available according to a complex adjusting-ratio schedule rather than a single ratio of, for example, one minute of free time for every twenty correct math problems. The rate of responding essentially doubled under an arrangement that provided more free time per response as the number of responses increased (for example, sixty problems in a session yielded three minutes of free time, but twice as many problems yielded five times as many minutes of free play).

Lovitt, Eaton, Kirkwood, and Pelander (1971) reported a series of experiments that demonstrated how various contingencies influenced various aspects of reading behavior. When contingencies were focused on errors, errors were reduced although the rate of correct responding was not correspondingly increased. When contingencies were established on both correct and incorrect rates, both were influenced, and, in every case, children exposed to reinforcement contingencies improved more in their reading than comparison children who were not exposed to contingencies.

The discussion thus far has been devoted to the benefits resulting from the contingent delivery of reinforcing consequences. Another form of behavior analysis is illustrated by Lovitt and Curtiss (1968), who, without manipulating any behavioral consequences, obtained reliable and repeated improvements in the accuracy with which an eleven-year-old boy solved subtraction problems. They followed the simple practice of requiring the boy to recite aloud the problem to be solved before writing his answer on the paper. Each time this practice was initiated, accuracy increased.

Classroom Analyses of Individual Performance

The strategy of ameliorating a child's academic problem by removing him to a special situation outside his regular classroom has been helpful in developing prototype procedures, but it may not always be the best practice. Experimental analysts have concentrated on explicating the relationships between behaviors and their consequences. Consequently, they have a preference for treating a behavior problem in the situation where it occurs most frequently. It may be possible to correct a behavior problem in a special situation that has specially arranged contingencies, but if these improved contingencies are not also a part of the regular classroom environment, there would be no reason to expect behavioral improvement in that setting. A variety of studies have demonstrated techniques for arranging special contingencies for the academic performance of a single child in a classroom that does not otherwise use systematic contingency management.

Tyler (1967) attached points to the daily and weekly performance of a sixteen-year-old delinquent boy in an institutional classroom. The accumulated points, up to thirty per day, could be exchanged for clothing items, a special mattress for his bed, cigarettes, and money for Christmas gifts. The procedure seemed to be helpful, but there were some indications that the boy found ways to get the back-up items even when he was short on points, and the analysis was inconclusive.

Reynolds and Risley (1968) used a very different procedure to increase the talking rate of an excessively quiet four-year-old preschool girl. Her rate of talking to the teacher and to other children increased markedly when a contingency was arranged that required her to ask for toys and objects. Each request set the occasion for the teacher to provide extended attention in the form of questions, praise, and assistance. After a series of careful experimental manipulations, the authors concluded that it was only when teacher attention mediated access to materials that it functioned as a reinforcer for this girl's talking. When the materials were presented noncontingently, the attention of the teacher did not reinforce talking.

Evans and Oswalt (1968) used a somewhat unorthodox strategy in an attempt to improve the quiz performance of four individual children in different classes. Two of the children were in fourth-grade classes, the other two were sixth-graders. The target child was asked a single question from a quiz that had just been taken by the entire class. If the child answered correctly, the entire class received extra recess time or the teacher read them a story. The procedure proved to be quite effective in the fourth grade that had a cooperative teacher and showed no effects in the sixth grade where the teacher was doubtful about the whole procedure.

Goetz and Baer (1971) worked with individual children in an ongoing preschool program to examine the role of teacher attention as a reinforcer for "creative" block-building. They classified twenty elements of form that proved to be a reliable measure of the various patterns contained in the children's constructions. Following baseline, the teacher began a program of responding "with enthusiasm, interest, and delight" each time the child produced a new form. Throughout this condition the amount of form diversity increased above baseline for every child. The effect was shown to be reversible and recoverable, demonstrating the responsiveness of even very complex behavior to differential teacher attention.

The rather poorly understood relationship between attending behavior and academic performance was investigated by Kirby and Shields (1972) by working with a single boy in a regular seventh-grade classroom. Their baseline records indicated both low accuracy and a low percentage of attending behavior when the boy was given twenty minutes to do multiplication problems that were scored and returned the next day. When the procedure was changed so that he brought the assignment to the teacher as soon as it was done and she scored it immediately with praise for his correct answers, accuracy increased and the proportion of time he spent attending to the task rose nearly to the 100 percent level. The interesting point is that the greatest behavioral effect was on attending behavior even though feedback was only attached to academic performance.

The practice of conducting experimental analyses of academic performance with individual students either in or out of their regular classroom will undoubtedly continue. To the extent that a large proportion of classroom problems are generated by the behavior of a few children, this is a strategy that offers practical benefits to teachers and school psychologists. If, on the other hand, Hamblin et al. (1971) are correct in their contention that teachers need procedures that improve the academic performance of "at least half of the class," individual procedures need to be complemented with whole-class procedures.

Classroom Analyses of Group Performance

Some of the individual-child procedures described in the preceding paragraphs are easily translated for use with larger groups. Hart and Risley (1968), for example, used a procedure very similar to that described by Reynolds and Risley (1968) to increase the use of descriptive adjectives by fifteen preschool children during their free-play periods. In both cases, talking increased when materials were provided contingent on elaborated verbal interaction at the time of the request.

Lovitt, Guppy, and Blattner (1969) demonstrated that a simple procedure could improve the spelling performance of thirty-two fourth-grade

children in the same class. During baseline a traditional spelling instruction technique provided the children with the week's word list on Monday,
study time and drill periods through the week, and a graded quiz on Friday.
In the altered procedure, the children were given the word list as usual but
they could take the quiz during any spelling period that followed. If they
passed the test at the next available period, they had free time during
the spelling periods for the balance of the week. The rate of perfect
spelling papers rose from twelve during baseline to twenty-five as a result
of this procedure, and increased to thirty during the final phase of the study
which provided, in addition to free time, fifteen minutes of listening to the
radio if all children received 100 percent on any given testing day.

An intensely practical demonstration of the use of teacher attention
as a reinforcer was provided by Schutte and Hopkins (1970) in a rural
kindergarten classroom. Ten routine instructions were given to this class
of five girls each day during baseline. In very typical classroom circum-

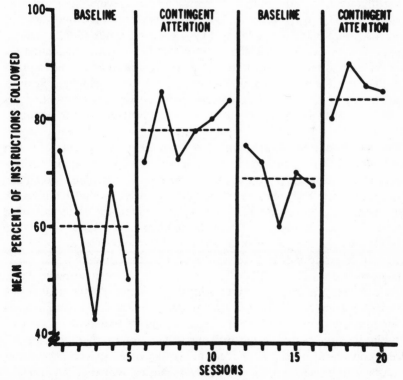

Fig. 4. The daily mean percent of instructions followed by all subjects for each
session. The horizontal dashed line under each condition shows the mean percent of
instructions followed for all observations within that condition. (From Schutte and
Hopkins 1970.)

stances, the teacher's instructions were compiled with 60 percent of the time (number of children × number of opportunities = 100 percent). In the next phase of the analysis the teacher differentially attended to each child who complied with an instruction within fifteen seconds after it was given. This change resulted in instruction following 78 percent of the time. After an experimental reversal, differential teacher attention brought instruction following above 80 percent. Moreover, individual data showed that each child was similarly influenced by the procedure.

When the behavior under consideration is speech (Hart and Risley 1968; Reynolds and Risley 1968) or following instructions in kindergarten, there is little alternative to the direct monitoring of the behavior as it occurs. When the emphasis shifts to behavior that is represented by marks on paper some observation problems are eliminated.

Allowing children access to self-selected activities contingent on appropriate or improved performance has a long history in behavior modification literature extending from Homme, deBaca, Devine, Steinhost, and Ricket (1963) to the present. It is the basis of the procedure used by Nolen, Kunzelmann, and Haring (1967), Lovitt et al. (1969), and of those used by Jacobson, Bushell, and Risley (1969), who increased the handwriting of Head Start children by requiring the completion of a printing task as a ticket to enter any of several activity areas. Hopkins, Schutte, and Garton (1971) used a similar technique with the handwriting behavior of two groups of children in a combined classroom. Fourteen first-grade children printed about 194 letters each day, and the ten second-grade children in the same room wrote approximately 259 cursive letters each day. When the first-grade children completed their copying assignment, they took their papers to the teacher to be checked and scored and then returned to their seats to wait until everyone had completed his work and had it checked. Under this baseline condition, the children copied about six letters per minute. Later, the children were allowed to go to an area known as the playroom as soon as their work was complete and checked; the rate increased to nearly eight letters per minute. In subsequent conditions the total length of the handwriting period was gradually reduced from the original fifty to thirty-five minutes. As the total period became shorter, the children needed to complete the copying assignment more quickly in order to have the same amount of time in the playroom. By the time the period length was thirty-five minutes, these first-graders were copying at a rate 90 percent above the baseline level. Moreover, accuracy improved, even though no contingencies were attached to errors. The performance improvements of the second-graders replicated those of the first-graders.

The teacher in this study was able to monitor the children's behavior with an after-the-fact procedure. Even that task became an excessive burden, however, when a teacher has thirty or more children in a single class. A recent study by Salzberg, Wheeler, Devar, and Hopkins (1971) may provide some excellent suggestions toward the solution of that problem. Following a recommendation by Lindsley (1958), Salzberg et al. randomly selected half of the handwriting papers of six kindergarten children for grading each day. The children could not know if their paper would be graded on any given day, but when it was graded they would have to meet an individual accuracy criterion before they were released for free play. Children whose work was not selected for grading were released to play as soon as they completed their assignment. Consequently, an individual child was on an intermittent schedule of contingent acess to free play. This intermittent contingency produced very substantial increases in the printing accuracy of all the children. When the intermittent grading procedure produced only descriptive feedback (e.g., "You got four wrong"), accuracy remained at baseline levels.

Classroom Analyses of Token Reinforcement Procedures

The majority of classroom experiments dealing with the academic behavior of groups of children have utilized some form of token reinforcement system. An early and very influential report of the benefits of a classroom token system was presented by Birnbrauer, Wolf, Kidder, and Tague in 1965. Their system provided tokens (marks in booklets) for both the social and academic behavior of fifteen retarded children in a special institutional classroom. The children exchanged their accumulated tokens at the end of each class period for an array of edibles, inexpensive toys, and school supplies or they could save them toward a shopping trip to the nearby town. Though experimentally inconclusive, the Birnbrauer et al. report provided other researchers with an excellent procedural description for the operation of a token system.

Some of these suggestions were adapted by Tyler and Brown (1968), who used token procedures to improve the performance of fifteen institutionalized delinquent boys on daily quizzes over the evening television newscast. Clark, Lachowitz, and Wolf (1968) used tokens backed up by money to obtain significant improvement in the achievement test scores of five Neighborhood Youth Corps girls who had dropped out of school. McKenzie, Clark, Wolf, Kothera, and Benson (1968) used grades as tokens which were exchanged at home for weekly allowances provided by parents. The children in this study were enrolled in a learning disabilities class. Prior to the introduction of the allowance-for-grades contingency, a number of other contingencies were found to be less effective: contingent recess, contingent free time, special privileges, the opportunity to eat lunch with classmates, teacher attention and praise. None of these was as effective in supporting academic behavior as was the use of weekly grade reports backed up by allowances.

One of the most frequently cited examples of classroom applications of behavior modification procedures is Wolf, Giles, and Hall (1968). Their report described the effects of an after-school remedial classroom program that made very extensive use of token reinforcement procedures. The fifteen sixth-graders and one fifth-grader who attended this class were at least two years behind reading norms, chronic low achievers in school, and predominately from welfare families without fathers. Nevertheless, these children showed pre- to post-test gains of 1.5 years on the Stanford Achievement Test while a matched comparison group gained 0.8 during the same period. Total program effects of this magnitude recommend a closer look at some of the details of the procedure.

The token system constructed by Wolf et al. (1968) was described as resembling a trading stamp plan. Every child kept a booklet of different-colored pages that were divided into one hundred squares. Marks entered in the squares could be redeemed for different categories of back-up reinforcers that corresponded to the different-colored pages. One set of back-ups consisted of weekly field trips; another was a daily snack of sandwich, milk, fruit, and cookie; another was canteen items such as candy and small novelties and toys; and still another was made up of long-range purchases worth two dollars or more. The points were earned for work that was completed in regular school and brought to the after-school class (e.g., 100 points for an A grade on a school assignment); for homework assignments and remedial work completed in the remedial classroom; and for report-card grades each six weeks.

A number of experimental analyses were conducted within the remedial classroom during the course of the year. A brief summary of one will serve to illustrate how the functional role of the tokens was established in repeated instances. Figure 5 displays the number of reading units completed in each session by two children (a unit consisted of a two-hundred-word story and twelve to thirteen comprehension and vocabulary questions). On the two occasions when the point value of reading units was decreased, KT nearly stopped reading. When the point value of reading doubled for AS, he broke a month-long tradition and began to read.

More recently, reports of classroom token systems have been coming out of regularly operating classroom situations rather than from the variety of "special" situations represented through 1968. Miller and Schneider (1970) reported the successful use of token procedures to support the beginning handwriting training of Head Start children. Glynn (1970) conducted a complex analysis of the effects of various token procedures with

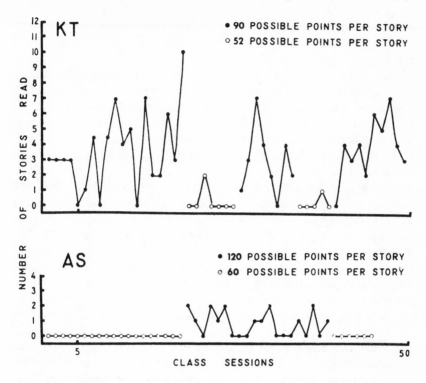

Fig. 5. A record of completing reading units by two students, KT and AS. Each dot represents the number of units completed during a class session. (From Wolf, Giles and Hall 1968.)

128 "well-motivated" students in four ninth-grade classes. Glynn attached tokens to the performance of the students on history and geography quizzes and backed them up with a variety of inexpensive souvenir items. Somewhat after the pattern of Lovitt and Curtiss (1969), Glynn compared students' performance with no tokens, with experimenter-determined token rates, with student-determined token rates, and with chance-determined token rates. Unlike Lovitt and Curtiss (1969), he did not find that subject-determined token rates produced higher performance levels than experimenter-determined rates, but he did find that experimenter-determined and student-determined rates were comparable and that both were superior to chance-determined rates or no tokens.

Sulzer, Hunt, Ashby, and Krams (1971) and Ferritor, Buckholdt, Hamblin, and Smith (1972) have examined the question of whether social behavior can be improved when contingencies are provided only for academic behavior or whether academic behavior can be improved by contingencies for conduct. The ambiguity of the data compiled on this issue thus far probably recommends that those wishing to improve a specific behavior would do best by providing consequences for that specific behavior.

Two recent studies deserve special attention because they have made such substantial advances in demonstrating the practical advantages of classroom token systems. The first report by Chadwick and Day (1971) described a summer program that was conducted for twenty-five underachieving minority-group children who ranged from eight to twelve years of age. The eleven-week program, conducted by a teacher and two aides, was divided into three phases: baseline, tokens and social reinforcement, and social reinforcement only. The token system, as in Wolf, Giles, and Hall (1968), used different-colored pages of marks that could be exchanged for different categories of back-ups: green for lunch, yellow for canteen items, and red for weekly field trips. The points were earned for both appropriate conduct and for academic performance. Following a three-week baseline period, the introduction of this reinforcement system produced significant improvement in three major dependent variables: the children worked longer, faster, and more accurately than before. Further, the improvements were statistically significant (.001) in every one of the seven academic subjects that made up the program's curriculum. In addition Chadwick and Day found that, when the reinforcement system was introduced, there were increases in the approving and supportive statements of the teacher and aides and decreases in their disapproving statements and in their rate of giving instructions.

For the final two weeks of the program the token system was eliminated. During the short time available to continue monitoring the students' performance, it was noted that the percent of time they spent working returned to baseline levels but that the rate and accuracy of their work remained high. During the eleven weeks of the program, the children gained an average of .42 years in grade placement on the California Achievement Test. A program that could maintain that rate of gain for a single year would bring these children up to normative achievement levels.

The Chadwick and Day study is noteworthy for the thoroughness of the authors in utilizing a variety of relevant measures. They measured the three indicators of academic performance (work time, rate of output, and accuracy); they measured and reported changes in teacher behavior (rates of approval, disapproval, and instruction); and they measured the collateral changes in achievement test performance.

The final study of particular importance is by McLaughlin and Malaby (1971). McLaughlin is a public-school teacher with daily responsibility for thirty fifth-grade students. His 1971 report describes the product of three years of work intended to develop a classroom token system that is (1) effective, (2) cost-free, (3) used with an entire class, and (4) can be managed by a single teacher without outside help. The system is elegantly straightforward.

To identify the students' reinforcers, he asked them what they were. He then assigned point values to the named activities in order of the students' preferences. All of the activities were indigenous to regular public-school classrooms. He listed the behaviors he wanted the students to display and assigned point values to them according to their importance (his list included thirteen different academic and social behaviors), and he specified the number of points to be lost for engaging in six unacceptable behaviors. With ingenuity and some training, the students were taught to do most of the observation and recording.

Using a series of procedural variations, McLaughlin and Malaby illuminate many of the functional properties and additional practical aspects of this economical system. The results are shown in figure 6.

The "baseline" period shown in figure 6 consisted of traditional classroom procedures that depended on the usual array of appeals and threats characteristic of most fifth-grade classrooms. During the Token I phase the token system was in effect. At the beginning of each week, a fifteen-minute period allowed the children to exchange the points they had accumulated during the preceding week for the privileges they wished or could afford for the ensuing week. Each available back-up was "sold" by a different student, who made appropriate records of each transaction and turned them over to the teacher. The procedure also included a sav-

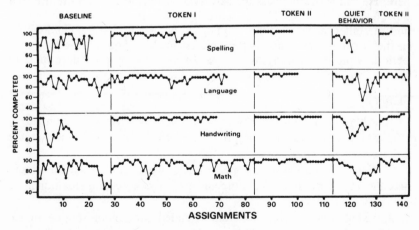

Fig. 6. Percent of assignments completed in four subject areas as a function of experimental conditions for a class of thirty students. (From McLaughlin and Malaby 1971.)

ings plan. Those who wished could set aside points to be used at some future time. Then, if a student were ill and did not have the opportunity to earn points, the student could draw on his or her savings for the weekly exchange period. The number of assignments completed in the four subjects approached 100 percent during this condition. Even further improvement resulted with one additional change. The Token II condition was similar to Token I except that exchange periods occurred at unpredictable intervals (two to seven days apart) rather than on the fixed schedule of every Monday morning.

During the period labeled "Quiet Behavior," the students received the same number of points for being quiet as they had previously received for correct answers in their assignments. During this condition there were no points for completed assignments, and the rate of completing assignments dropped back into baseline levels.

Additional comment on the McLaughlin and Malaby (1971) study seems superfluous. For the research-oriented, the data are clean and convincing. For the practically oriented, the procedures are exemplary. Those with an historical bent will find almost every procedure previously discussed in this section assembled into a single system. It seems somehow appropriate to close this section with McLaughlin and Malaby's own comments about some of the unmeasured benefits of their system, and to hope that similar commentaries can be made by more and more teachers in the future.

The senior author is the homeroom teacher in all of the work reported here. He can leave the class for extended periods of time and return to a quiet and orderly room. He can send his class to the restrooms unattended and the other teachers in the building do not know that the children are in the corridors. His class is the quietest in the school during the lunch period. More importantly, under the token economy procedure most of the students do most of their work most of the time (p. 40).

Summary

1. Although somewhat slower to develop, an increasing number of studies have attempted to improve the academic performance of the children.

2. Early studies of academic performance were conducted in laboratory settings that used token reinforcement to teach reading to individual children.

3. Later, similar techniques were extended into schools, but continued to be used more with individual children who had special learning problems.

4. The effectiveness of these early phases led to work emphasizing

techniques and procedures specifically designed to facilitate the academic performance of entire classes of children in regular school programs.

5. Procedures have been developed to improve the rate and the accuracy of children's reading, handwriting, arithmetic, spelling, and a growing variety of other academic skills. As the effectiveness of procedures like token systems and contingent access to activities continues to be documented, it is becoming more appropriate to speak of an instructional technology.

TEACHING OTHERS TO USE BEHAVIORAL TECHNIQUES

Inevitably, the existence of useful behavior techniques for improving classroom management and academic performance is stimulating interest in teaching people to use them. With some notable exceptions, the overwhelming majority of studies discussed thus far have been designed, executed, and reported by research scientists, not practicing classroom teachers. In point of fact, behavior analysis in education is only *potentially* an "applied" science. However elegant, the combined set of procedures that are the product of experimental research will not be genuinely applied until a substantial proportion of the school population benefits from these procedures at the hands of teachers, administrators, school psychologists, and other support personnel who face the daily task of making the schools work.

A number of conditions need to be met before practicing educators can be expected to make extensive use of behavioral teaching techniques. A list of such conditions might be expected to include three kinds of demonstrations: (a) a demonstration that a given procedure makes a desirable difference in the classroom, (b) a demonstration that the procedure can be implemented by someone other than a research psychologist, and (c) a demonstration that it is possible to teach teachers how to incorporate the procedure into their regular classroom operations.

The preceding sections of this paper provide encouragement that the first demonstration is well under way. An expanding array of helpful procedures is accumulating through the efforts of a growing company of researchers. There have also been several demonstrations that helpful procedures can be implemented, completely or in part, by people who are not research psychologists. Following the early work of Hawkins, Peterson, Schweid, and Bijou (1966), the aid of parents has been enlisted to provide contingent back-up reinforcers by Martin, Burkholder, Rosenthal, Tharp, and Thorne (1968); McKenzie et al. (1968); Cantrell, Cantrell, Huddleston, and Woolridge (1969); and Bailey et al. (1970).

Following the suggestions of Tharp and Wetzel (1969), MacDonald et al. (1970) reduced truancy by enlisting support from parents, grandparents, mother of a girl friend, uncles, adult friends, a spouse, and a pool-hall proprietor, all of whom were contacted by a nonprofessional attendance aide. Surrat et al. (1969) even demonstrated that observation procedures can be reliably used by a fifth-grader, and McLaughlin and Malaby (1971) used sixth-grade observers.

These are promising demonstrations. Nevertheless, they have used strategies that require minimal training of the nonprofessional, and they have also required a degree of willing cooperation that may not be generally available. Most important, none of these studies indicated that the nonprofessional gained any generalized skill as a result of participating in these investigations. In the optimum situation adults who learned how to dispense back-up reinforcers contingent on the presentation of a favorable report from school would, as a consequence, begin to make better use of reinforcement contingencies in their routine interactions with their child.

Because there is no practical way to design training programs that specifically treat every possible application of a behavioral procedure, ways must be found to teach the use of a procedure across a wide range of appropriate situations. A teacher who is taught to deliver her approving attention contingently in a handwriting lesson has not profited greatly unless this skill generalizes to reading, arithmetic, recess, and the lunch-room. Unfortunately, the available research clearly indicates that generalization should not be expected to occur unless it is specifically programmed into a training sequence.

Demonstrations that it is possible to teach teachers how to incorporate behaviorial procedures into their regular classroom operations are limited, and they have only recently begun to confront the issue of generalization. Until very recently, it was a more common practice to teach paraprofessional aids how to use tutorial procedures in remedial or supplementary sessions with children outside the classroom. One of the early reports in this vein was provided by Ellson, Barber, Engle, and Kampwerth (1965), and similar strategies were followed in a series of three investigations by Staats and his colleagues.

Staats, Minke, Goodwin, and Landeen (1967) used high school seniors and adult volunteers to extend the benefits of a reading program first reported by Staats and Butterfield (1965), who improved the reading skill of a single under-achieving delinquent. Staats et al. (1967) had eighteen tutors work with eighteen junior high students who displayed reading problems. The tutors were given two ninety-minute training sessions on the use of the remedial procedure, and they received periodic observation after they began to work. Although the behavior of these tutors was never directly measured, in seventeen of eighteen cases they appeared to have succeeded in improving the skills of their students. In one case a tutor was dismissed for nagging a child, and the authors concluded that the use of paraprofessional helpers could be effective if supported by the supervision of a "specialist." There remains, of course, the possibility that improvements in the training and in the measurement of the tutor's behavior may correspondingly reduce the need for subsequent supervision. This possibility seems to have been recognized in the subsequent report by Ryback and Staats (1970) which provided four hours of training for each of four parents who used the procedure to tutor their children. Again, however, the absence of measures of the tutors' behavior makes it difficult to determine the precise function of the training procedure.

The use of trained paraprofessional tutors is certainly a demonstration that behavior techniques can be implemented by someone other than a research psychologist, but it falls short of demonstrating that teachers can incorporate such techniques into their own routines. A few very recent reports, moreover, served notice that this third, and most critical, kind of demonstration has begun.

Training Programs

Andrews (1970) sought to provide eleven elementary (K–4) teachers with basic behavior modification skills that would free them from being dependent on the school psychologist for the solution of classroom behavior problems. He conducted four ninety-minute weekly training sessions that considered reinforcement principles and their application to the classroom situation. Andrews did not report any specific changes in teaching behavior as a result of these training sessions, but data provided by the teachers did describe the reduction of problem behaviors within their classes.

Improvements in both teacher behavior and class behavior were reported by Breyer et al. (1971) who used M.A.-level students as consultants to a fifth-grade teacher who was experiencing difficulty in controlling her class. These consultants observed in the classroom and provided the teacher with information, suggestions, and feedback concerning the use of various reinforcement techniques. Although the specific training procedures were not evaluated directly, a four-week delayed follow-up did show that the experimental improvements were subsequently maintained. Some degree of generalization did seem to have occurred. Breyer et al. saw these results as suggestive of the possibility that a consultative system could provide practical, economical training and psychological services to entire school systems.

McKenzie, Egner, Knight, Perelman, Schneider, and Garvin (1970) have, in fact, designed and implemented a very large-scale consulting-teacher program based at the University of Vermont. This is a two-year program leading to a Masters of Education Degree which emphasizes behavioral principles, measurement procedures, parent and teacher training, research skills, curriculum construction, and behavior management. Although no systematic analyses of the program's training procedures have been reported, its general effectiveness is supported indirectly by the behavioral improvements brought about by the consulting teachers (Knight, Hasazi, and McNeil 1971; Lates et al. 1971; Hanley and Perelman 1971).

The problem of developing generalized behavior modification skills in teacher aides has been investigated by Wetzel (1970). In his four-week training program, Wetzel emphasized a learning-by-doing strategy that put trainees in direct contact with children for the bulk of the training period. The steps in this training sequence were: (1) observation of children, (2) observation of teaching models, (3) corrective feedback, and (4) daily staff discussions. The third step, corrective feedback, was direct and immediate. If a trainee engaged in incorrect behavior, a trainer told her it was incorrect. The trainee was then either told or shown the correct behavior and asked to try it again. When the behavior was corrected, the trainee was praised. There was no attempt to analyze the relative effectiveness of the various aspects of this complex training procedure, but pre-post evaluations did confirm desired improvements in the classroom behavior of the trainees and in their attitudes toward reinforcement procedures.

Another large teacher-training program based at Florida State University is represented in the work of Madsen, Madsen, Saudargas, Hammond, Smith, and Edgar (1970). The Madsen et al. strategy emphasized in-service workshops for professional teachers. In this instance thirty-two teachers from two elementary schools were taught the RAID system (Rules, Approval, Ignore, Disapprove) with discussions, role play, videotape, demonstrations, and lectures. Following the two-week workshop, observations were obtained on these teachers and on comparison teachers who had not received workshop training. Those who attended the workshop were observed to use more approval, less disapproval, and enjoyed fewer inappropriate student behaviors from children who had been specifically identified as "problem children." The data presented suggested that the workshop participants had acquired some generalized management skills, but there was no attempt to identify what aspect(s) of this training was responsible for the observed effects.

Responsive Teaching is the name that Hall and his associates have given to their teacher-training system based at the University of Kansas. The Responsive Teaching Model (Hall and Copeland 1971) emanates from a one-semester, three-hour graduate-level course with enrollments as high as seventy. Graduate students lead discussion groups of about ten people that examine recording and measurement procedures, applied research designs, learning principles, and research studies. These discussion sessions are supplemented by lectures and films, and the course content is based on three of Hall's published booklets (1971). As a part of this course, several students have conducted applied experiments in both classroom and home settings. Hall et al. (1970) reported three multiple baseline studies by students from the Responsive Teaching course. Each study adhered to strict rules of evidence and experimental control as it effectively dealt with typical behavior management problems. One used a reinforcement procedure for reducing tardiness after recess; a second used an avoidance procedure to improve low quiz grades; the third used a response-cost procedure to increase music practice and studying at home. Hall et al. (1971) presented six additional experiments by teachers who conducted their own studies to reduce "talking out" disruptions in a variety of classroom situations. Hall et al. (1972) described four successful studies done by parents in their own homes.

As with the other training systems, it is difficult to know what aspects of the Responsive Teaching program are most critical in producing the participant's new skills. It also remains for future research to determine what, if any, general or specific benefits flow to the children who are taught by teachers who have mastered the skill of conducting experimental research. For the most part the teaching procedures of these training systems appear to reflect the learning experiences of their designers. Hall, McKenzie, and Andrews utilize relatively traditional academic practices that are generally assumed to correlate with the development of rather generalized skills. Madsen et al. (1970) and Breyer, Calchera, and Cann (1971) retained some of the academic components but reported a greater emphasis on classroom performance in practicum, or on-the-job, situations. Of those examined, the training program described by Wetzel is the least academic and the most direct in dealing with the specific classroom behaviors he seeks in the performance of his trainees. Solid rationales can be developed to support either academic or practicum training strategies. It is too early, however, to ask which approach is empirically superior, since neither has presented sufficient evidence to establish that it leads to a generalized use of behavioral teaching techniques.

Research on Teacher Training

Only a limited number of citations are possible under the heading of "research on training procedures" in behavior modification, and all of them are relatively recent. It has been noted that several categories of "helpers" have stretched the reach of academicians, but the greater promise for the development of a practical applied technology seems to be contained in the growth of "training systems." The premise of any training system is that there exists a useful set of procedures, based on a unified collection of principles. The training system seeks to teach the use of these procedures and their underlying principles so that those responsible for the daily development of children's skills can be more effective.

There is no need to survey the variety of socialization practices that have developed to meet similar needs. The present requirement is for experimental analyses that will progressively accumulate empirical evidence that describes the functional relationship between specific training procedures and equally specific teacher performances. Even though it is not set in a school situation, the work of Panyan, Boozer, and Morris (1970) is noteworthy precisely because it presents an experimental analysis of a straightforward training technique.

When a teacher is instructed in the use of a particular procedure, it is for the purpose of having that technique used in the teacher's classroom. It is difficult to assert that the training is effective if the procedure is never used following training. The empirical question is: what procedures can maximize the subsequent use of skills acquired in a training program? Panyan et al. (1970) asked this question following a four-week training program for the adult staff of four living units for profoundly and severely retarded children who lacked basic self-care skills. During their training the adult attendants had to be taught to conduct training sessions in self-feeding, handwashing, dressing, bathing, and toileting. They were then instructed to conduct daily sessions and keep performance records on each child in training. Even though the attendants had the skill and the opportunity to conduct these daily sessions for the children, they failed to do so nearly 75 percent of the time unless a feedback procedure was introduced. This conclusion was drawn after the introduction of a feedback procedure in each hall at different intervals following initial training. After four weeks of baseline in one hall where the number of sessions conducted dropped to a low of 20 percent, the feedback procedure sessions conducted rose to a high of 99 percent. Similar effects were observed in other halls with baseline periods of different lengths.

The procedure is elegant in its simplicity. Each Monday the record sheets were collected from each hall showing the number of sessions conducted the previous week. During baseline, that was the end of it. Under the feedback condition, the psychologist returned an analysis of the reported data showing total sessions possible, number of sessions conducted, the names of the adults who had conducted sessions, and the percent of sessions conducted in each hall. The unit psychologist reviewed this information with the staff members on duty at that time and then posted

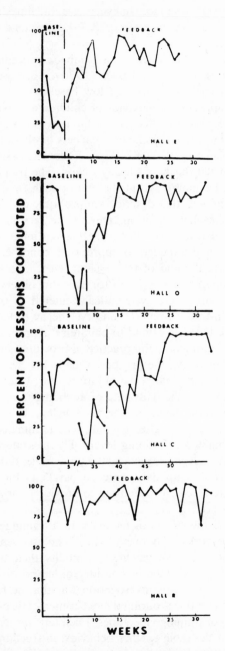

Fig. 7. Percent of requested training sessions conducted by the staff on Halls E, O, C, and R. (From Panyan, Boozer, and Morris 1970.)

the analysis in a conspicuous place. In every case, the introduction of this procedure resulted in an increase of nearly 70 percentage points in the conduct of the sessions.

A second analysis of the effects of a feedback procedure has been provided by Cooper, Thomson, and Baer (1970). Their work was with two Head Start teachers who displayed low baseline rates of attending to the situationally appropriate behavior of children around them in the classroom. Cooper et al. eliminated the preliminary training course used by Panyan et al. and worked with the two teachers on-the-job in a fashion similar to that advocated by Wetzel (1970). Following baseline, training sessions were conducted during each day's class. The training consisted of reviewing, at the beginning and at the end of each two-hour training session, a list of definitions that described appropriate and inappropriate child behavior and teacher attention. During the session, an observer spoke briefly to the teacher (Teacher A) every ten minutes, telling her how many times she had attended to appropriate child behavior during that interval. Then, at the end of the session, the teacher was told her rate of attending to appropriate behavior for the entire observation period. The feedback procedures were systematically altered as training progressed. On the eighth training day the observer began to tell the teacher how many times she failed to attend to children's appropriate behavior, and on the ninth day terminated the practice of providing success reports at ten-minute intervals. Next, the practice of daily reviews of the definitions were eliminated, and, finally, the failure reports were discontinued. Throughout this sequence, the daily rate of attending to appropriate behavior rose to nearly 40 percent from the baseline level below 10 percent. In a follow-up check a week after training was terminated, the newly trained behavior remained at training levels. The procedure was essentially replicated with a second teacher with comparable, though less dramatic, results. The follow-up data were encouraging, but the authors pointed out that more research is required to provide information on the durability of the observed effects.

A third analysis of the effects of feedback in a training situation has been provided by the work of Thomas (1971), who used teachers' videotape observations of their own teaching to modify their behavior. For research purposes, Thomas would be considered the trainer in this study, but an interesting aspect of his investigation was that he had no direct contact with any of the trainees during the experiment. His procedure was built around a series of training videotapes. Each tape presented a definition of a category of desirable teacher behavior, instructions on how to record and graph that behavior, some examples of the behavior, and a five-minute teaching segment for practice in recording. Using a very convincing research design, Thomas established that when a teacher observed and graphed her own behavior by observing a ten-minute videotape a few minutes after teaching, the frequency of that behavior changed. Questions about the durability of these effects need further research, but the results were clean and the implications for practical (economical) in-service training programs are considerable.

It is appropriate to draw a distinction between experimental analyses of training procedures presented by Panyan et al. (1970), Cooper et al. (1970), and Thomas (1971) and analyses that describe setting events or ecological factors that influence teacher behavior. The former category of concerns is clearly linked to the total process of teaching a teacher to utilize behaviorial teaching techniques. The latter seeks to evaluate the conditions under which specific teacher behaviors are more probable, even when no training occurs. The second category is illustrated by the work of Sanders and Hanson (1971) who found that if children moved from the regular classroom into a play area as soon as they completed an assignment, the more skillful children left earlier than the less skillful. This resulted in a redistribution of the teacher's attention, providing more to the slower children who were in the regular classroom longer and less to those who left sooner. This altered the pattern observed during baseline, where it was observed that children who completed their assignments first subsequently received more attention in the form of extra assignments and more individualized work.

Similarly, following the work of Rosenthal and Jacobson (1968), Meichenbaum, Bowers, and Ross (1969) systematically varied the amounts of positive and negative teacher attention given to students by merely advising the teacher that certain individuals could be "expected" to demonstrate superior or inferior capabilities.

A final example of this category is provided by Mandelker, Brigham, and Bushell (1970), where the rates of teacher attention were found to be systematically higher to children in a handwriting group who received response-contingent tokens than to those who received noncontingent tokens.

While studies such as these may have future implications for the content of teacher training programs, they are not systematic analyses of training procedures that seek generalized behavioral teaching skills.

Discussion and Evaluation

There is a serious shortage of demonstrations that systematic training procedures can provide classroom teachers with useful management and teaching skills. The approximations that appear to be most effective are not supported by data identifying their most salient or critical procedures.

The gap between existing knowledge of effective classroom procedures and existing knowledge of how to build an effective delivery system for those procedures must be closed.

There are probably a number of factors that are inhibiting the development of empirically based training procedures. One is surely a question of maturity. The experimental analysis of classroom behavior is a very young dicipline. Until the past few years there has not been an obvious need for special training procedures because there was not an impressive list of techniques available for teachers to use. At the current rate of development in the field, time alone should solve any problems of maturity. A second inhibiting factor can be brought into focus by noting that work with teachers has not followed the pattern of successful work with children.

Almost without exception, when behavior modifiers have improved the academic performance or the classroom conduct of children, they have designed powerful contingencies that provide reinforcing *consequences* for improvement. Studies such as Salzberg et al. (1971) have indicated that simple feedback is not a strong consequence unless that feedback is discriminative for subsequent reinforcement. Nevertheless, simple feedback is the only procedure that has been used to modify the behavior of teachers through training. Assuming that future research will demonstrate that contingent reinforcement is more effective than simple feedback in developing improved teaching skills, it may still be difficult to put that procedure into operation.

Differential reinforcement in the form of salary is now paid to teachers on the basis of college credits and length of classroom service. Professional teacher organizations have at various times taken firm stands against other forms of incentive (e.g., "merit pay"); given the state of the art in measuring teaching performance without bias, their posture may be extremely reasonable. The problem will not be easy to solve, but it surely deserves the disciplined attention of careful research. O'Leary (1972a) has urged investigators to remain aware of the need for reinforcement not only for the children but for the teachers, the principal, and the school board as well. It is probably advice that will have to be followed before effective training and support programs for teachers are a reality.

Summary

1. There have been only a few demonstrations of systematic training procedures that can increase useful management and teaching skills of teachers.

2. Simple feedback has been the only procedure used in such studies.

3. Much more remains to be done, both in the area of increased system-

atic analyses as well as in the use of more powerful reinforcement conditions.

DISCUSSION

Reviewing the brief history of behavior modification in education illuminates the progress which is turning the science of behavior to the task of dealing with the practical "realities" of classroom behavior. It also suggests that some issues need closer attention.

Issues for Research

One list of issues is addressed primarily to those working as behavior modification researchers. The fact that the issues on this list are technical does not remove their practical implications, but it may restrict the ranks of those who are interested in resolving them. One such issue can be headed, simply, "replication."

The studies that have been examined throughout this paper have used a variety of more or less well-described procedures to bring about improvements in the classroom behavior of children and teachers. The phrase "more or less" needs to be taken rather literally, because there is room to doubt that experimenter B can, in all cases, replicate experimenter A's procedures from the published description. Only a minority of studies reviewed, for example, presented measures of teacher behavior in those cases where it was the independent variable used to modify students' behavior. Consider the description of an experimental manipulation of this sort: "The teacher was then instructed to ignore out-of-seat behavior and increase the amount of praise given to those who were seated appropriately." The stylistic variations possible in implementing such instructions are so great that a failure to reproduce the effects of the original study should be anticipated as the norm rather than the exception. If classroom investigations do not increase the specificity of their procedural descriptions, the result must certainly be an increase in the number of failures to replicate.

It is also possible for an attempted replication to fail when the procedures *are* faithfully and completely reproduced. This possibility calls for a distinction between a replication of procedures and a replication of effects. Suppose, for example, an investigator found that well-timed contingently delivered praise and approval from a teacher did *not* serve as a reinforcer for the behavior to which it was attached. This could be an extremely instructive finding if it focused attention to the need for a clearer grasp of the conditions under which praise is a reinforcer. Future classroom studies will undoubtedly be paying more attention to precise descriptions of the conditions under which a given consequence functions as a reinforcer: conditions such as the reinforcement history of the child, the timing of the delivery of reinforcement, and the nature of competing contingencies.

A second issue concerns the establishment of shaping of new behaviors and the design of procedures to insure that these behaviors will persist in environments less favorable than those in which the behaviors were initially taught or established.

A commonly used technique in many behavior modification studies with children who have severe behavioral deficits is that of shaping. Shaping is typically used to establish behaviors that children do not already exhibit. In shaping, reinforcement is often delivered initially only for behaviors that may be distant approximations to the desired behavior. Gradually, over time, the requirements are changed so that only behaviors that more and more closely resemble the desired behavior are reinforced. Finally, only the desired behavior is reinforced. Although shaping is an extremely useful procedure for establishing new behaviors, there has been relatively little use of this procedure in the classroom studies reviewed (see Allen et al. 1964; Harris et al. 1964; and Johnson et al. 1966, for exceptions). Part of the reason for this is because, in most of the studies cited, students already exhibited instances of desirable classroom behaviors for which consequences could be directly applied. Thus, the initial establishment of these behaviors was not necessary. But, if behavior modification procedures are to be used more extensively to improve the academic capabilities of students, particularly those with severe academic deficits, it would appear that increased attention needs to be given to procedures such as shaping, that teach students new skills as well as increase or decrease the behaviors already present in their repertoires.

In part, an emphasis on developing new skills has been approximated in those studies that have used shifting reinforcement criteria as behavior progressively approaches a (perhaps theoretical) terminal goal. For example, Hopkins et al. (1971) required successive increases in the rate and accuracy of children's handwriting before the consequences were available, and Herman and Tramontana (1971) gradually increased the amount of desirable student behaviors required for the delivery of the consequences. Similarly, the arrangement of most token systems is such that increases in desirable behaviors automatically produce more tokens and thus the ability to purchase a larger variety of back-up reinforcers.

Another aspect of teaching "new skills" is to insure that desirable student behaviors, once established and increased to an acceptable level under certain conditions, are maintained or persist in spite of less favorable support. Although the ability to "reverse" behavior by withdrawal of behavioral consequences is often necessary to show experimentally the function of the consequences, this may not be fully appreciated by teachers and parents who are likely to be more interested in the development of enduring improvements in children that are resistant to, rather than responsive to, temporary alterations in the environment. Nevertheless, as was noted earlier, it is probably unrealistic to expect that desirable behaviors can be maintained in the total absence of desirable consequences for these behaviors. Thus, within the technology of behavior modification, this seems to require the development of procedures to insure that student behavior be influenced by positive consequences relatively remote in time from the occurrence of the behavior. The study by O'Leary et al. (1968) suggests one way in which this might be done—by gradually shifting from relatively immediate consequences for desirable behavior to consequences more remote in time and requiring longer sequences of behavior. Similarly, Cooper et al. (1970), within the context of a teacher-training situation, faded out the trainer in gradual steps, leaving behind a new pattern of interaction between a teacher and her students.

Issues of Acceptance

Quite obviously the continued development of behavior modification techniques for education depends on the "acceptability" of the recommendations and procedures of these techniques. The problem is not unique to behavior modification, but it may be more pointed for any science whose laboratories are the operating classroom of a community's schools. Collectively, the introduction and discussion sections of reports by classroom investigators make it clear that their behavior is being shaped by some heavy and very practical constraints. Although it has several dimensions, the basic issue is summarized by the label "cost-effectiveness."

In its early history, behavior modification research arose out of laboratory situations or out of total institutions (hospitals and "special" classroom settings). In those situations, elaborate instrumentation, observational help, and grant support fostered the development of techniques that couldn't make the leap to the budget-bound public-school classroom. Now, as more and more work is ongoing in regularly operating schools, some new contingencies have been attached to the behavior of behavior modifiers. McLaughlin and Malaby (1971) exemplify the trend in their quest for a token system that is (1) effective, (2) cost-free, and (3) easy for a single teacher to manage in a large class.

The schools will not long indulge a researcher who cannot adapt to the constraints of cost-effectiveness. Further, it may be possible to anticipate some of the limits and some of the pressures that are probable for those who would work in the schools. First, there is not likely to be a vigorous market for procedures that require the teacher to make an abrupt departure from accustomed practice. The reinforcement, management, or recording procedure that demands extensive restructuring of the classroom is likely to produce the type of extinction that is technically known as "ratio strain" because it requires more behavior from the teacher than can be supported by available reinforcers.

As a guest in the schools, the behavioral researcher will probably increase his attention to the problem of generalization during the next few years. It has already been pointed out that many of the procedures reported in the literature have not made explicit provisions for engineering the control of appropriate behavior beyond the confines of the experimental situation. If a procedure improves conduct in the experimental hour but not in the hours that precede and follow, the teacher and the principal are likely to have some predictable discussions with the researcher. As difficult as the problem of generalization is, it appears that the "natural" contingencies of the school environment are ideally arranged for its solution.

As those who conduct the research that produces new classroom procedures come inevitably under greater and more immediate control of the school situation, we will no longer need to worry that critical issues are being neglected. The researcher will learn to respond effectively to the needs that the school considers critical or he or she will decide to follow some other career. Apparent differences in philosophy between behavioral scientists and practicing educators will dissolve as each becomes more accustomed to the rhetoric of the other, and as each learns more of the other's skills. In sum, the second decade of behavior modification work in education ought to be even more productive than the first, providing the researcher is not seduced away from the data by becoming an educational fad, and providing that his or her graphs are not fashioned into a protective cloak of mysterious expertise.

Ethical Issues

It is common in reviews of behavior modification techniques and research to discuss the ethical issues involved in the use and implementation of these techniques, whether in the classroom, in hospital wards, homes, or clinics. There are several of these discussions that consider the general ethical issues associated with any technique which influences, controls, or has demonstrable effects on human behavior and the more specific issues concerned with the use of particular techniques (Baer 1970; Bandura 1969; Harris 1972; Krasner 1968; Risley and Baer 1973). We do not intend to repeat the various arguments and counterarguments here since they have already been adequately discussed. Instead, we start with several assumptions related to the use of behavior modification techniques or, for that matter, any effective teaching technique in our schools. The first assumption is that the primary function of our schools and the teachers is to produce changes in student performance—to teach specifiable skills considered desirable by society. The second assumption is that there are a variety of procedures available to teach or influence the acquisition of desirable skills, some of which include techniques referred to as behavior modification. Further, since many of the techniques are based on the ways in which teachers "normally" or "usually" interact with students, we assume that the procedures for changing or affecting student performance are already often used in classrooms by teachers, although, perhaps, not as systematically or for as explicit a purpose as they might be.

Given these assumptions, it seems to us that a primary ethical question is, who is to decide what kinds of student performances are to be considered desirable and what kinds or types of techniques are to be used to teach them?

At the present time, public-school educators and school boards (elected representatives of the community) decide what is to be taught and, very generally, how it is to be taught. It is often argued that these decisions reflect the general values or represent the consensus of most members of our society. However, not everyone agrees that this is the case. More important, these decisions are almost invariably made without systematic, direct input from those members of society, other than the students themselves, who are most directly affected by the decisions, the parents of the students. It seems to us that one (and it is only one) of the important considerations in whether certain goals and the use of specific procedures to accomplish these goals are ethical, is the degree to which those directly affected by them have consented to or have influence over the decisions.

There are several possible mechanisms for allowing parents of students to participate, directly or indirectly, in decisions about the goals and the use of teaching techniques to accomplish these goals. One is to establish a committee or series of committees composed of educators and parents of students who will attempt to state explicitly what the educational goals of the schools will be and to judge or "certify" as acceptable certain types of teaching procedures to accomplish these goals. However, it is not immediately clear how this mechanism differs greatly from the present system, in which educators and elected community representatives make the relevant decisions. Further, the degree to which individual parents, other than those few on the committees, can participate in the decision-making process is limited. A second mechanism is one in which teachers and principals of each school present to the parents of the students information about the alternative skills that could be taught, the rationale for teaching these skills, the procedures by which the skills might be taught, and whatever relevant data are available that show the effectiveness of these alternative procedures. The parents then, collectively, might participate with the teachers and principals in the relevant decisions. This mechanism provides a possible public mechanism for deciding on the goals and procedures of the school that potentially can reflect the values of the teachers and parents directly concerned. However, effective use of this method depends upon adequate presentation of information to parents and probably the ability of parents to evaluate some technical information in a relatively sophisticated manner. A third mechanism is to allow and encourage schools to develop goals and teaching procedures which may vary considerably from school to school. Parents could then choose which of several available school programs they would have their children attend. This alternative would allow parents some choice, on an individual basis, as to the educational goals and teaching procedures. However, its usefulness depends upon adequate descriptions of objectives, procedures, and data concerning the outcome of these procedures for each available school program, as well as availability of enough schools with enough variability to provide meaningful alternatives.

Although implementation of any of these alternatives, or even others, would involve a large number of practical problems, they might provide a greater degree of parent participation in setting educational goals and deciding on teaching procedures than now exists. A central notion in each of these alternatives is that schools be publicly accountable to the parents of the students, for what they do and how they do it. This in turn seems to require at least two features. One is that parents be provided clear, objective statements of educational goals and data to evaluate student progress toward these objectives. This feature does not currently exist, even at an individual level. It is true that most schools periodically provide report cards to students to take home to their parents. However, report cards as they are currently used, typically state neither what kinds of objective performances or skills are to be taught for a particular student nor the degree to which the student is being taught these performances or skills. A second feature of public accountability is that there be methods of providing incentives for schools to establish teaching goals with which parents are in agreement and that these incentives be awarded to the degree to which the schools accomplish these goals. An obvious candidate for an incentive system involves the monies available to school districts from state governments. At the present time, much of the money school districts receive is allocated on the basis of average daily student attendance. If instead, monies were made available to the extent to which schools publicly stated and accomplished their educational goals, at a minimum this information would become publicly available. Further, the potential would then exist for parents, through the usual political channels, to affect these requirements and thereby to affect the goals and the teaching accomplishments of our schools.

REFERENCES

Allen, K. E., Hart, B. M., Buell, J. S., Harris, F. R., and Wolf, M. M. Effect of social reinforcement on an isolate behavior of a nursery school child. *Child Development,* 1964, *35,* 511–518.

Allen, K. E., Henke, L. B., Harris, F. R., Baer, D. M., and Reynolds, N. J. Control of hyperactivity by social reinforcement of attending behavior. *Journal of Educational Psychology,* 1967, *58,* 231–237.

Allen, K. E., Turner, K. D., and Everett, P. M. A behavior modification classroom for Head Start children with problem behaviors. Experiments 1–3. *Exceptional Children,* 1970, *37,* 119–127.

Andrews, J. K. The results of a pilot program to train teachers in the classroom application of behavior modification techniques. *Journal of School Psychology,* 1970, *8,* 37–42.

Axelrod, S. Token reinforcement programs in special classes. *Exceptional Children,* 1971, *37,* 371–379.

Baer, D. M. A case for the selective reinforcement of punishment. In C. Neuringer and J. L. Michael, eds., *Behavior Modification in Clinical Psychology.* New York: Appleton-Century-Crofts, 1970, 243–249.

Baer, D. M. and Sherman, J. A. Behavior modification: clinical and educational applications. In H. W. Reese and L. P. Lipsitt, eds., *Experimental Child Psychology.* New York: Academic Press, 1970, 643–672.

Bailey, J. S., Wolf, M., and Phillips, E. L. Home-based reinforcement and the modification of pre-delinquents' classroom behavior. *Journal of Applied Behavior Analysis,* 1970, *3,* 223–233.

Bandura, A. Ethical issues of behavioral control. *Principles of Behavior Modification.* New York: Holt, Rinehart and Winston, 1969, chapter 2.

Barrish, H. H., Saunders, M., and Wolf, M. Effects of individual contingencies for group consequences on disruptive behavior in a classroom. *Journal of Applied Behavior Analysis,* 1969, *2,* 119–124.

Becker, W. C., Madsen, C. H., Jr., Arnold, C. R., and Thomas, D. R. The contingent use of teacher attention and praise in reducing classroom behavior problems. *Journal of Special Education,* 1967, *1,* 287–307.

Birnbrauer, J. S., Wolf, M. M., Kidder, J. D., and Tague, C. E. Classroom behavior of retarded pupils with token reinforcement. *Journal of Experimental Child Psychology,* 1965 *2,* 219–235.

Breyer, N. L., Calchera, D. J., and Cann, C. Behavioral consulting from a distance. *Psychology in the Schools.* 1971, *8,* 172–176.

Broden, M., Bruce, C., Mitchell, M. A., Carter, V., and Hall, R. V. Effects of teacher attention on attending behavior of two boys at adjacent desks. *Journal of Applied Behavior Analysis,* 1970, *3,* 199–203.

Broden, M., Hall, R. V., Dunlap, A., and Clark, R. Effects of teacher attention and a token reinforcement system in a junior high school special education class. *Exceptional Children,* 1970, *36,* 341–349.

Brown, P. and Elliott, R. Control of aggression in a nursery school class. *Journal of Experimental Child Psychology,* 1965, *2,* 103–107.

Buell, J., Stoddard, P., Harris, F. R., and Baer, D. M. Collateral social development accompanying reinforcement of outdoor play in a preschool child. *Journal of Applied Behavior Analysis, 1968, 1,* 167–173.

Bushell, D., Wrobel, P. A., and Michaelis, M. L. Applying "group" contingencies to the classroom study behavior of preschool children. *Journal of Applied Behavior Analysis, 1968, 1,* 55–63.

Cantrell, R. P., Cantrell, M. L., Huddleston, C. M., and Wooldridge, R. L. Contingency contracting with school problems. *Journal of Applied Behavior Analysis, 1969, 2,* 215–220.

Carlson, C. S., Arnold, C. R., Becker, W. C., and Madsen, C. H. The elimination of tantrum behavior of a child in an elementary classroom. *Behaviour Research and Therapy, 1968, 6,* 117–119.

Chadwick, B. A. and Day, R. C. Systematic reinforcement: academic performance of underachieving students. *Journal of Applied Behavior Analysis, 1971, 4,* 311–319.

Clark, M., Lachowicz, J., and Wolf, M. M. A pilot basic education program for school dropouts incorporating a token reinforcement system. *Behaviour Research and Therapy, 1968, 6,* 183–188.

Cohen, S. I., Keyworth, J. M., Kleiner, R. I., and Libert, J. M. The support of school behaviors by home-based reinforcement via parent-child contingency contracts. In E. A. Ramp and B. L. Hopkins, eds., *A New Direction for Education: Behavior Analysis 1971.* Lawrence, Kansas: Support and Development Center for Follow Through, 1971.

Coleman, R. A conditioning technique applicable to elementary school classrooms. *Journal of Applied Behavior Analysis, 1970, 3,* 293–297.

Cooper, M. L., Thomson, C. L., and Baer, D. M . The experimental modification of teacher attending behavior. *Journal of Applied Behavior Analysis, 1970, 3,* 153–157.

Craig, H. B. and Holland, A. L. Reinforcement of visual attending in classrooms for deaf children. *Journal of Applied Behavior Analysis, 1970, 3,* 97–109.

Ellson, D. G., Barber, L., Engle, T. L., and Kampwerth, L. Programmed tutoring: a teaching aid and a research tool. *Reading Research Quarterly, 1965, 1,* 77–127.

Evans, G. W. and Oswalt, G. L. Acceleration of academic progress through the manipulation of peer influence. *Behaviour Research and Therapy, 1968, 6,* 189–195.

Ferritor, D. E., Buckholdt, D., Hamblin, R. L., and Smith, L. The noneffects of contingent reinforcement for attending behavior on work accomplished. *Journal of Applied Behavior Analysis, 1972, 5,* 7–17.

Glynn, E. L. Classroom applications of self-determined reinforcement. *Journal of Applied Behavior Analysis, 1970, 3,* 123–132.

Goetz, E. M. and Baer, D. M. Descriptive social reinforcement of "creative" block building by young children. In E. A. Ramp and B. L. Hopkins, eds., *A New Direction for Education: Behavior Analysis 1971.* Lawrence, Kansas: Support and Development Center for Follow Through, 1971.

Graubard, P. S. Utilizing the group in teaching disturbed delinquents to learn. *Exceptional Children, 1969, 36,* 267–272.

Graubard, P. S., Rosenberg, H., and Miller, M. B. Student applications of behavior modification to teachers and environments or ecological approaches to social deviancy. In E. A. Ramp and B. L. Hopkins, eds., *A New Direction for Education: Behavior Analysis 1971,* Lawrence, Kansas: Support and Development Center for Follow Through, 1971.

Hall, R. V. Behavior management series. *Part I. The Measurement of Behavior, Part II. Basic Principles, Part III. Applications in School and Home.* Merriam, Kansas: H & H Enterprises, Inc., 1971.

Hall, R. V., Axelrod, S., Foundopoulos, M., Shellman, J., Campbell, R. A., and Cranston, S. The effective use of punishment in modifying behavior in the classroom. *Educational Technology, 1971, 11,* 24–26.

Hall, R. V., Axelrod, S., Tyler, L., Grief, E., Jones, F. C., and Robertson, R. Modification of behavior problems in the home with a parent as observer and experimenter. *Journal of Applied Behavior Analysis*, 1972, *5*, 53–64.

Hall, R. V. and Broden, M. Behavior changes in brain-injured children through social reinforcement. *Journal of Experimental Child Psychology*, 1967, *5*, 463–479.

Hall, R. V. and Copeland, R. E. The responsive teaching model: a first step in shaping school personnel as behavior modification specialists. A paper presented at the Third Banff International Conference on Behavior Modification, April, 1971.

Hall, R. V., Cristler, C., Cranston, S., and Tucker, B. Teachers and parents as researchers using multiple baseline designs. *Journal of Applied Behavior Analysis*, 1970, *3*, 247–255.

Hall, R. V., Fox, R., Willard, D., Goldsmith, L., Emerson, M., Owen, M., Davis, F., and Porcia, E. The teacher as observer and experimenter in the modification of disputing and talking-out behaviors. *Journal of Applied Behavior Analysis*, 1971, *4*, 141–149.

Hall, R. V., Lund, D., and Jackson, D. Effects of teacher attention on study behavior. *Journal of Applied Behavior Analysis*, 1968, *1*, 1–12.

Hall, R. V., Panyan, M., Rabon, D., and Broden, M. Instructing beginning teachers in reinforcement procedures which improve classroom control. *Journal of Applied Behavior Analysis*, 1968, *1*, 315–322.

Hamblin, R. L., Hathaway, C., and Wodarski, J. Group contingencies, peer tutoring and accelerating academic achievement. In E. A. Ramp and B. L. Hopkins, eds., *A New Direction for Education: Behavior Analysis 1971*. Lawrence, Kansas: Support and Development Center for Follow Through, 1971.

Hanley, E. M. Review of research involving applied behavior analysis in the classroom. *Review of Educational Research*, 1970, *40*, 597–625.

Hanley, E. M. and Perelman, P. F. Research resulting from a model cities program designed to train paraprofessionals to aid teachers in elementary school classrooms. In E. A. Ramp and B. L. Hopkins, eds., *A New Direction for Education: Behavior Analysis 1971*. Lawrence, Kansas: Support and Development Center for Follow Through, 1971.

Harris, F. R., Johnston, M. K., Kelley, C. S., and Wolf, M. M. Effects of positive social reinforcement on regressed crawling of a nursery school child. *Journal of Educational Psychology*, 1964, *55*, 35–41.

Harris, M. B. and Miksovic, R. S. Operant conditioning in social interaction in preschool children. In M. B. Harris, ed., *Classroom Uses of Behavior Modification*. Columbus, Ohio: Charles E. Merrill, 1972, 37–46.

Harris, M. B. Conducting and evaluating behavior modification projects. In M. B. Harris, ed., *Classroom Uses of Behavior Modification*. Columbus, Ohio: Charles E. Merrill, 1972, 19–32.

Hart, B. M., Allen, K. E., Buell, J. S., Harris, F. R., and Wolf, M. M. Effects of social reinforcement on operant crying. *Journal of Experimental Child Psychology*, 1964, *1*, 145–153.

Hart, B. M., Reynolds, N. J., Baer, D. M., Brawley, E. R., and Harris, F. R. Effect of contingent and non-contingent social reinforcement on the cooperative play of a preschool child. *Journal of Applied Behavior Analysis*, 1968, *1*, 73–76.

Hart, B. M. and Risley, T. R. Establishing use of descriptive adjectives in the spontaneous speech of disadvantaged preschool children. *Journal of Applied Behavior Analysis*, 1968, *1*, 109–120.

Hawkins, R. P., Sluyter, D. J., and Smith, C. D. Modification of achievement by a simple technique involving parents and teacher. *Journal of Learning Disabilities*, in press.

Hawkins, R., Peterson, R., Schweid, E. S., and Bijou, S. Behavior therapy in the home: amelioration of problem parent-child relations with the parent in a therapeutic role. *Journal of Experimental Child Psychology*, 1966, *4*, 99–107.

Herman, S. H. and Tramontana, J. Instructions and group versus individual reinforcement in modifying disruptive group behavior. *Journal of Applied Behavior Analysis,* 1971, *4,* 113–119.

Homme, L. E., deBaca, P. C., Devine, J. V., Steinhost, R., and Ricket, E. J. Use of the Premack principle in controlling the behavior of nursery school children. *Journal of the Experimental Analysis of Behavior,* 1963, *6,* 544.

Hopkins, B. L., Schutte, R. C., and Garton, K. L. The effects of access to a playroom on the rate and quality of printing and writing of first- and second-grade students. *Journal of Applied Behavior Analysis,* 1971, *4,* 77–87.

Jacobson, J., Bushell, D., Jr., Risley, T. Switching requirements in a Head Start classroom. *Journal of Applied Behavior Analysis,* 1969, *2,* 43–47.

Johnston, M. K., Kelley, C. S., Harris, F. R., and Wolf, M. M. An application of reinforcement principles to development of motor skills of a young child. *Child Development,* 1966, *37,* 379–387.

Kazdin, A. E. and Bootzin, R. R. The token economy: an evaluative review. *Journal of Applied Behavior Analysis,* 1972, *5,* 343–372.

Kirby, F. D. and Shields, F. Modification of arithmetic response rate and attending behavior in a seventh-grade student. *Journal of Applied Behavior Analysis,* 1972, *5,* 79–84.

Knight, M. F., Hasazi, S. E., and McNeil, M. E. A home-based program for the development of reading skills for preschoolers. In E. A. Ramp and B. L. Hopkins, eds., *A New Direction for Education: Behavior Analysis 1971.* Lawrence, Kansas: Support and Development Center for Follow Through, 1971.

Krasner, L. Behavior modification: Values and training. In C. M. Franks, ed., *Assessment and Status of the Behavior Therapies.* New York: McGraw-Hill, 1968, 537–566.

Kuypers, D. S., Becker, W. C., and O'Leary, K. D. How to make a token system fail. *Exceptional Children,* 1968, *35,* 101–109.

Lates, B. J., Egner, A. N., and McKenzie, H. S. Behavior analysis of the academic and social behavior of first grade children or what happens when educators turn on. In E. A. Ramp and B. L. Hopkins, eds., *A New Direction for Education: Behavior Analysis 1971.* Lawrence, Kansas: Support and Development Center for Follow Through, 1971.

Lindsley, O. R. Intermittent grading. *The Clearing House: A Journal for Modern Junior and Senior High Schools,* 1958, *32,* 451–454.

Lovitt, T. C. and Curtiss, K. A. Effects of manipulating an antecedent event on mathematics response rate. *Journal of Applied Behavior Analysis,* 1968, *1,* 329–333.

———. Academic response rate as a function of teacher and self-imposed contingencies. *Journal of Applied Behavior Analysis,* 1969, *2,* 49–54.

Lovitt, T., Eaton, M., Kirkwood, M., and Pelander, J. Effects of various reinforcement contingencies on oral reading rate. In E. A. Ramp and B. L. Hopkins, eds., *A New Direction for Education: Behavior Analysis 1971.* Lawrence, Kansas: Support and Development Center for Follow Through, 1971.

Lovitt, T. C. and Esveldt, K. A. The relative effects on math performance of single-versus multiple-ratio schedules: a case study. *Journal of Applied Behavior Analysis,* 1970, *3,* 261–270.

Lovitt, T. C., Guppy, T. E., and Blattner, J. E. The use of a free-time contingency with fourth-graders to increase spelling accuracy. *Behaviour Research and Therapy,* 1969, *7,* 151–156.

McAllister, L. W., Stachowiak, J. G., Baer, D. M., and Conderman, L. The application of operant conditioning techniques in a secondary school classroom. *Journal of Applied Behavior Analysis,* 1969, *2,* 277–285.

MacDonald, W. S., Gallimore, R., and MacDonald, G. Contingency counseling by school personnel: an economical model of intervention. *Journal of Applied Behavior Analysis,* 1970, *3,* 175–182.

McKenzie, H. S., Clark, M., Wolf, M., Kothera, R., and Benson, C. Behavior modification of children with learning disabilities using grades as token reinforcers. *Exceptional Children*, 1968, *34*, 745–752.

McKenzie, H. S., Egner, A. N., Knight, M. F., Perelman, P. F., Schneider, B. M., Garvin, J. S. Training consulting teachers to assist elementary teachers in the management and education of handicapped children. *Exceptional Children*, 1970, *37*, 137–143.

McLaughlin, T. F. and Malaby, J. E. Development of procedures for classroom token economies. In E. A. Ramp and B. L. Hopkins, eds., *A New Direction for Education: Behavior Analysis 1971*. Lawrence, Kansas: Support and Development Center for Follow Through, 1971.

Madsen, C. H., Becker, W. C., and Thomas, D. R. Rules, praise and ignoring: elements of elementary classroom control. *Journal of Applied Behavior Analysis*, 1968, *1*, 139–151.

Madsen, C. H., Jr., Becker, W. C., Thomas, D. R., Koser, L., and Plager, E. An analysis of the reinforcing function of "sit-down" commands. In R. Parker, ed., *Readings in Educational Psychology*. Boston: Allyn and Bacon, 1968, 265–278.

Madsen, C. H., Jr., Madsen, C. K., Saudargas, R. A., Hammond, W. R., Smith, J. B., and Edgar, D. E. Classroom RAID (rules, approval, ignore, disapproval): a cooperative approach for professionals and volunteers. *Journal of School Psychology*, 1970, *8*(3), 180–185.

Mandelker, A. V., Brigham, T. A., and Bushell, D. The effects of token procedures on a teacher's social contracts with her students. *Journal of Applied Behavior Analysis*, 1970, *3*, 169–174.

Martin, M., Burkholder, R., Rosenthal, R. L., Tharp, R. G., and Thorne, G. L. Programming behavior change and reintegration into school milieux of extreme adolescent deviates. *Behaviour Research and Therapy*, 1968, *6*, 371–383.

Medland, M. B. and Stachnik, T. J. Good Behavior game: a replication and systematic analysis. *Journal of Applied Behavior Analysis*, 1972, *5*, 45–51.

Meichenbaum, D. H., Bowers, K. S., and Ross, R. R. Modification of classroom behavior of institutionalized female adolescent offenders. *Behaviour Research and Therapy*, 1968, *6*, 343–353.

———. A behavioral analysis of teacher expectancy effect. *Journal of Personality and Social Psychology*, 1969, *13*, 306–316.

Miller, L. K. and Schneider, R. The use of a token system in Project Head Start. *Journal of Applied Behavior Analysis*, 1970, *3*, 213–220.

Nolen, P. A., Kunzelmann, H. P., and Haring, N. G. Behavior modification in a junior high learning disabilities classroom. *Exceptional Children*, 1967, *34*, 163–168.

O'Leary, K. D. Establishing token programs in schools: issue and problems. In M. B. Harris, ed., *Classroom Uses of Behavior Modification*. Columbus, Ohio: Charles E. Merrill, 1972a, 373–378.

———. Behavior modification in the classroom: a rejoinder to Winett and Winkler. *Journal of Applied Behavior Analysis*, 1972b, *5*, 505–511.

O'Leary, K. D. and Becker, W. C. Behavior modification of an adjustment class: a token reinforcement program. *Exceptional Children*, 1967, *33*, 637–642.

———. The effects of the intensity of a teacher's reprimands on children's behavior. *Journal of School Psychology*, 1968, *7*(1), 8–11.

O'Leary, K. D., Becker, W. C., Evans, M. B., and Saudargas, R. A. A token reinforcement program in a public school: a replication and systematic analysis. *Journal of Applied Behavior Analysis*, 1969, *2*, 3–13.

O'Leary, K. D. and Drabman, R. S. Token reinforcement programs in the classroom. *Psychological Bulletin*, 1971, *75*, 379–398.

O'Leary, K. D., Kaufman, K. F., Kass, R. E., and Drabman, R. S. The effects of loud and soft reprimands on the behavior of disruptive students. *Exceptional Children,* 1970, *37,* 145–155.

Osborne, J. G. Free time as a reinforcer in the management of classroom behavior. *Journal of Applied Behavior Analysis,* 1969, *2,* 113–118.

Packard, R. G. The control of "classroom attention"; a group contingency for complex behavior. *Journal of Applied Behavior Analysis,* 1970, *3,* 13–28.

Panyan, M., Boozer, H., and Morris, N. Feedback to attendants as a reinforcer for applying operant techniques. *Journal of Applied Behavior Analysis,* 1970, *3,* 1–4.

Patterson, G. R. An application of conditioning techniques to the control of a hyperactive child. In L. Ullmann and L. Krasner, eds., *Case Studies in Behavior Modification,* 1964, 370–375.

Patterson, G. R., Jones, R., Whittier, J., and Wright, M. A. A behavior modification technique for the hyperactive child. *Behaviour Research and Therapy,* 1965, *2,* 217–226.

Perline, I. H. and Levinsky, D. Controlling maladaptive classroom behavior in the severely retarded. *American Journal of Mental Deficiency,* 1968, *73*(1), 74–78.

Peterson, R. F., Cox, M. A., and Bijou, S. W. Training children to work productively in classroom groups. *Exceptional Children,* 1971, *37,* 491–500.

Quay, H. C., Sprague, R. L., Werry, J. S., and McQueen, M. M. Conditioning visual orientation of conduct problem children in the classroom. *Journal of Experimental Child Psychology,* 1967, *5,* 512–517.

Ramp, E., Ulrich, R., and Dulaney, S. Delayed timeout as a procedure for reducing disruptive classroom behavior: a case study. *Journal of Applied Behavior Analysis,* 1971, *4,* 235–239.

Reviewer A and B. Current behavior modification in the classroom: reviewers' comments. *Journal of Applied Behavior Analysis,* 1972, *5,* 511–515.

Reynolds, N. J. and Risley, T. R. The role of social and material reinforcers in increasing talking of a disadvantaged preschool child. *Journal of Applied Behavior Analysis,* 1968, *1,* 253–262.

Risley, T. R. and Baer, D. M. Operant behavior modification: the deliberate development of behavior. Chapter 5 in B. Caldwell and H. Ricciuti, eds., *Review of Child Development Research,* vol. 3. Chicago: University of Chicago Press, 1973.

Rosenthal, R. and Jacobson, L. *Pygmalion in the Classroom: Teacher Expectation and Pupils' Intellectual Development.* New York: Holt, Rinehart and Winston, 1968.

Ryback, D. and Staats, A. W. Parents as behavior therapy-technicians in treating reading deficits (dyslexia). *Journal of Behavior Therapy and Experimental Psychiatry,* 1970, *1,* 109–119.

Salzberg, B. H., Wheeler, A. A., Devar, L. T., and Hopkins, B. L. The effect of intermittent feedback and intermittent contingent access to play on printing of kindergarten children. *Journal of Applied Behavior Analysis,* 1971, *4,* 163–171.

Sanders, R. M. and Hanson, P. J. A note on a simple procedure for redistributing a teacher's student contacts. *Journal of Applied Behavior Analysis,* 1971, *4,* 157–161.

Schmidt, G. W. and Ulrich, R. E. The effects of group contingent events upon classroom noise. *Journal of Applied Behavior Analysis,* 1969, *2,* 171–179.

Schutte, R. C. and Hopkins, B. L. The effects of teacher attention on following instructions in a kindergarten class. *Journal of Applied Behavior Analysis,* 1970, *3,* 117–122.

Schwarz, M. L. and Hawkins, R. P. Application of delayed reinforcement procedures to the behavior of an elementary school child. *Journal of Applied Behavior Analysis,* 1970, *3,* 85–96.

Scott, P. M., Burton, R. V., and Yarrow, M. R. Social reinforcement under natural conditions. *Child Development,* 1967, *38,* 53–63.

Sherman, J. A. and Baer, D. M. Appraisal of operant therapy techniques with children and adults. In C. M. Franks, ed., *Assessment and Status of the Behavior Therapies.* New York: McGraw-Hill, 1969, 192–219.

Sibley, S. A., Abbott, M. S., and Cooper, B. P. Modification of the classroom behavior of a disadvantaged kindergarten boy by social reinforcement and isolation. *Journal of Experimental Child Psychology,* 1969, *7,* 203–219.

Skinner, B. F. *Science and Human Behavior.* New York: Macmillan, 1953.

Staats, A. W. and Butterfield, W. H. Treatment of non-reading in a culturally deprived juvenile delinquent: an application of reinforcement principles. *Child Development,* 1965, *36,* 925–942.

Staats, A. W., Minke, K. A., Finley, J. R., Wolf, M. M., and Brooks, L. O. A reinforcer system and experimental procedure for the laboratory study of reading acquisition. *Child Development,* 1964, *35,* 209–231.

Staats, A. W., Minke, K. A., Goodwin, W., and Landeen, J. Cognitive behavior modification: "motivated learning" reading treatment with subprofessional therapy-technicians. *Behaviour Research and Therapy,* 1967, *5,* 283–299.

Staats, A. W., Staats, C. K., Schutz, R. E., and Wolf, M. M. The conditioning of textual responses using "extrinsic" reinforcers. *Journal of the Experimental Analysis of Behavior,* 1962, *5,* 33–40.

Sulzbacher, S. I. and Houser, J. E. A tactic to eliminate disruptive behaviors in the classroom: group contingent consequences. *American Journal of Mental Deficiency,* 1968, *73*(1), 88–90.

Sulzer, B., Hunt, S., Ashby, C. K., and Krams, M. Increasing rate and percentage correct in reading and spelling in a fifth grade public school class of slow readers by means of a token system. In E. A. Ramp and B. L. Hopkins, eds., *A New Direction for Education: Behavior Analysis 1971.* Lawrence, Kansas: Support and Development Center for Follow Through, 1971.

Surrat, P. R., Ulrich, R. E., and Hawkins, R. P. An elementary student as a behavioral engineer. *Journal of Applied Behavior Analysis,* 1969, *2,* 85–92.

Tharp, R. G. and Wetzel, R. J. *Behavior Modification in the Natural Environment.* New York: Academic Press, 1969.

Thomas, D. R. Preliminary findings on self-monitoring for modifying teaching behaviors. In E. A. Ramp and B. L. Hopkins, eds., *A New Direction for Education: Behavior Analysis 1971.* Lawrence, Kansas: Support and Development Center for Follow Through, 1971.

Thomas, D. R., Becker, W. C., and Armstrong, M. Production and elimination of disruptive classroom behavior by systematically varying teacher's behavior. *Journal of Applied Behavior Analysis,* 1968, *1,* 35–45.

Thomas, D. R., Nielsen, L. A., Kuypers, D. S., and Becker, W. C. Social reinforcement and remedial instruction in the elimination of a classroom behavior problem. *Journal of Special Education,* 1968, *2,* 291–306.

Tyler, V. O. Application of operant token reinforcement to academic performance of an institutionalized delinquent. *Psychological Reports,* 1967, *21,* 249–260.

Tyler, V. O. and Brown, G. D. Token reinforcement of academic performance with institutionalized delinquent boys. *Journal of Educational Psychology,* 1968, *59*(3), 164–168.

Walker, H. M. and Buckley, N. K. The use of positive reinforcement in conditioning attending behavior. *Journal of Applied Behavior Analysis,* 1968, *1,* 245–250.

Ward, M. and Baker, B. Reinforcement therapy in the classroom. *Journal of Applied Behavior Analysis,* 1968, *1,* 323–328.

Wasik, B. H. The application of Premack's generalization on reinforcement to the management of classroom behavior. *Journal of Experimental Child Psychology,* 1970, *10,* 33–43.

Wasik, B. H., Senn, K., Welch, R. H., and Cooper, B. R. Behavior modification with culturally deprived school children: two case studies. *Journal of Applied Behavior Analysis,* 1969, *2,* 181–194.

Wetzel, R. J. Behavior modification techniques and the training of teacher's aides. *Psychology in the Schools,* 1970, *7,* 325–330.

Whitlock, C. Note on reading acquisition: an extension of laboratory principles. *Journal of Experimental Child Psychology,* 1966, *3,* 83–85.

Whitlock, C. and Bushell, D., Jr. Some effects of "back-up" reinforcers on reading behavior. *Journal of Experimental Child Psychology,* 1967, *5,* 50–57.

Winett, R. A. and Winkler, R. C. Current behavior modification in the classroom: be still, be quiet, be docile. *Journal of Applied Behavior Analysis,* 1972, *5,* 499–504.

Wolf, M. M., Giles, D. K., and Hall, R. V. Experiments with token reinforcement in a remedial classroom. *Behaviour Research and Therapy,* 1968, *6,* 51–64.

Wolf, M. M., Hanley, E. M., King, L. A., Lachowicz, J., and Giles, D. K. The timergame: a variable interval contingency for the management of out-of-seat behavior. *Exceptional Children,* Oct. 1970, 113–117.

Zimmerman, E. H. and Zimmerman, J. The alteration of behavior in a special classroom situation. *Journal of the Experimental Analysis of Behavior,* 1962, *5,* 59–60.

9 Parent-Child Relations

BARCLAY MARTIN
University of North Carolina

INTRODUCTION

AT THE MOMENT OF BIRTH, parent and child begin an interactive drama
that will evolve its own unique character and destiny. Affection, joy,
antagonism, openness, withdrawal, demands, and acquiescence will be
interchanged according to each dyad's own pattern—a pattern that is likely
to vary considerably according to circumstances and over time. How these
different styles of interaction develop and how they are related to certain
child behaviors outside the parental relationship, such as dependency,
internalization, achievement, aggression, and withdrawal will be the main
focus of this chapter.

In 1964 Wesley Becker wrote a chapter entitled "Consequences of
Parental Discipline" for the first volume in this series. The present chapter
represents an up-dating of that chapter, with a shift of focus to a view
of the parent-child relation as an interactive system rather than one in
which child behavior is a consequence of parental behavior, and also with
a considerable broadening of coverage. Recent work, for example, on
infant-mother attachment and the experimental research on factors affecting internalization of adult standards of behavior represent major addi-
tions.

Despite some lip service to the role of genetic and constitutional factors,
research in the area of parent-child relations was conceived for a long
time as the study of the effect of certain parental behaviors or attitudes
upon the child. Thus, the finding that parents of adolescent delinquents
were rejecting or hostile tended to be interpreted as evidence that delinquency was caused by rejecting parents. The empirical finding, however,
may well result in part because parents find it difficult to accept antag-
onistic, rebellious, antisocial delinquents. Almost any association of a
given type of parent behavior with a given type of child behavior can be
interpreted in terms of the parent influencing the child or the child influencing the parent, and, of course, what is actually going on in most

cases is some degree of mutual influence. Conceptualizing parent-child relations as an interactive process is not a particularly recent idea, but it has been rather slow to influence psychological thinking and research strategy. Bell (1968), Gewirtz (1969), and Rheingold (1969a) have made particularly strong pleas for this point of view.

The parent-causation model may have persisted for so long, in part, because of the character of the data being studied. Usually, the child has been designated as belonging in a certain category, for example, delinquent, or clinic case, or possessing a certain trait, for example, aggressiveness, and information about the parents' behavior was frequently obtained separately by interview or questionnaire. It is easy to miss the interactive quality of the relationship when this approach is used. On the other hand, imagine observing the following sequence: Tommy begins to tease his baby sister; mother says, "Don't do that"; Tommy continues to tease; mother, somewhat louder, "Tommy, stop that"; Tommy continues to tease; baby sister starts to cry; mother yells loudly and slaps Tommy; Tommy stops teasing baby sister. These kind of data almost force one to think interactively. Tommy is "teaching" his mother to escalate her response to yelling and slapping; the mother is providing a model of aggressive behavior and perhaps, somewhat paradoxically, providing reinforcement for his teasing by her dramatic display of attention. The question of causation now becomes one of trying to understand the circumstances that maintain recurring interactions of this kind, or perhaps of seeking out the historical circumstances surrounding the beginnings of this kind of interaction, which may turn out to be different from those currently maintaining it.

An extensive experimental literature has blossomed over the last decade in which variables thought to parallel features of parental behavior, such as punishment and nurturance, were manipulated. In almost all of these studies features of the adult experimenter's behavior were varied and the effects upon the child were measured—reflecting a continuing preoccupation with the parent side of the dyad. There is almost no experimental research in which parents were randomly assigned to conditions where children provided the distinctive experimental manipulations. From a practical standpoint such research would be difficult, but logically it should be as important as the traditional approach in understanding dyadic interaction.

In this chapter, then, wherever possible research will be considered in an interactive framework. Unfortunately, much of the research was not conceived in this way, and it is necessary to present it in the more traditional format of parental child-rearing correlates of certain child behaviors. The focus in this review will be generally on the intact family. The correlates of fatherless families are reviewed by Herzog and Sudia in volume three of this series and in Hetherington and Deur (1971).

The Domain of Parent Behaviors

The early impetus for the study of parent-child relations derived from research on the child-rearing characteristics of parents of delinquents and emotionally disturbed children. Parents of delinquents, for example, were frequently reported to be rejecting (hostile, lacking in warmth, punitive), and lax or erratic in the application of discipline (Burt 1929; Glueck and Glueck 1934, 1950; Healy and Bronner 1926). Rejection was also found to be prominent in many parents of children attending child guidance clinics (Hewitt and Jenkins 1946; Newell 1936; Symonds 1939). Symonds (1939), after reviewing studies to that time, proposed two major dimensions of parent behavior, acceptance-rejection and dominance-submission—dimensions which have withstood the test of time rather well. Using data from the longitudinal study conducted by the Fels Research Institute, Baldwin, Kalhorn, and Breese (1945, 1949) intercorrelated ratings of maternal behavior based on home observations carried out over two and one-half years, starting when the child was one month of age. Three clusters of highly intercorrelated variables were extracted by inspection: affection (acceptance, affectionateness, and rapport); indulgence (babying, protective, and solicitousness); democracy (justification of policy, democracy of policy, clarity of policy, noncoercive suggestion, readiness of explanation, and understanding).

Schaefer (1959) provided a nice integration of work in this area as well as an important conceptual contribution. He analyzed data gathered by the University of California Institute of Child Welfare in another longitudinal study (Jones and Bayley 1941). Mothers were rated on eighteen behaviors related to child interaction from sets of notes made by a testing examiner during some ten to twenty child testing sessions conducted when the child was between one month and three years of age. Guided by Guttman's (1954) conceptions about circumplex ordering, Schaefer showed that these eighteen maternal behaviors could be arranged in a systematic circular order. Correlations between adjacent variables were high, but taking any one variable as a starting point and moving along the circumplex ordering, the correlations between that variable and the other variables began to decrease, then became negative, and finally became positive and high again when the circle was completed. A factor analysis of these same data substantiated the notion that these behaviors could be conceptualized in a two-dimensional space. The circumplex ordering of the specific eighteen variables, based on factor loadings, is shown in figure 1. Clearly, the variables do not conform perfectly to the circumplex model; there is, for example, a large gap in the upper right quadrant. By pointing to such an unfilled area, however, the model suggests a search for additional measures which might fill this space. Schaefer also showed that a similar circumplex ordering was obtained for ratings made when the same children were nine to fourteen years of age, and for the maternal behavior ratings in the Fels study (Baldwin et al. 1945). A hypothetical circumplex of maternal behavior concepts derived from these empirical findings was proposed by Schaefer and is shown in figure 2.

The main advantage of this model over the factor analytic models is that it is not necessary to select any particular orientation of the spatial axes as representing the "true" dimensions of parent behavior. Basically, it is a method of portraying relationships among a number of variables; those variables which appear close to one another on the circumplex are likely to have similar values for a given mother. The particular arrangement of the axes in figures 1 and 2 is arbitrary, although it does happen to conform to the dimensions of acceptance-rejection (horizontal axis) and control or dominance (vertical axis) as proposed by Symonds (1939) and later by Roe (1957) and Slater (1962). But the axes in Figure 1 could be rotated so that emotional involvement and ignoring would become ends of an equally meaningful dimension. Becker and Krug (1964) showed that a similar two-dimensional circumplex ordering could be obtained for both father- and mother-ratings with respect to both male and female children; and Peterson and Migliorino (1967) found much the same two-dimensional space for ratings of Sicilian mothers as for American mothers.

Schaefer (1965) and Siegelman (1965) have also reported factor analyses of children's reports of parental behavior, and both investigators found that three dimensions were necessary to account for the intercorrelations of the subscales used. The new dimension in these analyses seemed to primarily involve harshness, or punitiveness of punishment.

In subsequent sections of this chapter the dimensions of acceptance-rejection and permissiveness-restrictiveness will be referred to frequently, and it should be useful to define them briefly at this point.

Acceptance-rejection or warmth-hostility. The nonaccepting parent is dissatisfied with the child, inclined to be critical and derogatory of many of his abilities or personality characteristics, does not seek out the child or enjoy his company, does not provide much positive reinforcement, and is likely to be insensitive to the child's needs and point of view. The accepting parent is characterized by the opposite attitudes and behaviors.

Permissiveness-restrictiveness. The permissive parent does not clearly state the rules or the consequences for violations, does not firmly or consistently enforce rules, and is likely to give in to the child's coercive demands. The restrictive parent does the opposite. The factor analytic

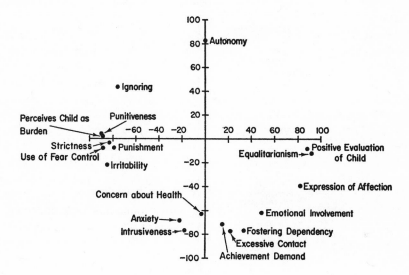

Fig. 1. A circumplex of maternal behavior ratings. (Reprinted by permission of the American Psychological Association from E. S. Schaefer, A circumplex model for maternal behavior, *Journal of Abnormal and Social Psychology*, 1959, *59*, 226–235. Copyright © 1959 by the American Psychological Association.)

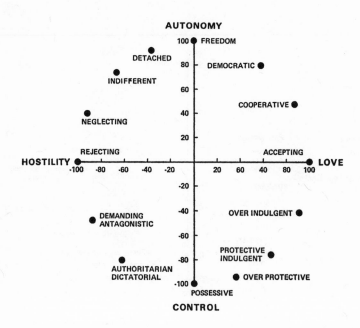

Fig. 2. A hypothetical circumplex of maternal behavior concepts. (Reprinted by permission of the American Psychological Association from E. S. Schaefer, A circumplex model for maternal behavior, *Journal of Abnormal and Social Psychology,* 1959, *59,* 226–235. Copyright © 1959 by the American Psychological Association.)

studies imply that permissiveness-restrictiveness might reasonably be conceptualized as independent of acceptance-rejection, that is, a parent can be accepting *and* restricting, or rejecting *and* restricting, and likewise for the permissive end of the dimension. In the actual measurement of this dimension, however, some authors (or raters) have probably not maintained this independence. Kagan and Moss (1962), for example, reported a correlation of about .50 between ratings of restrictiveness and hostility. This is not surprising when one considers the definition of restrictiveness used by these authors: "mother's attempts to force the child, through punishment or threat, to adhere to her standards . . . without regard for his abilities or interests" (p. 205). Baumrind (1967, 1971), on the other hand, prefers the term "control," and his definition is essentially the same as the present definition of permissiveness-restrictiveness. Unfortunately, one cannot always be sure how a given investigator (or rater) defines the variable; and some of the inconsistencies in results are probably attributable to variations in definition.

The Domain of Child Behaviors

Becker and Krug (1964) found that ratings of child behavior that were derived from parent interviews conformed rather well to a two-dimensional circumplex model with reference dimensions labeled "Extroversion-Introversion" and "Emotional Stability-Emotional Instability" (or "Love-Hostility"). Ratings of child behaviors in preschool or classroom settings have also been fitted to the circumplex model (Becker and Krug 1964; Schaefer 1961). The relationship between parent and child circumplex orderings will be considered later in the chapter, in the section on comprehensive models.

Some Methodological and Conceptual Considerations

What are the implications of the above research for the study of parent-child relations? Certainly, mapping the domain of child-rearing behaviors has value in providing a broad perspective of the area and in indicating which parental behaviors are likely to be correlated. A major drawback, however, to much of this research is the indirect character of the data. Measures derived from interviews with parents are especially subject to this criticism. By the time the actual parent-child interaction has been filtered through the parent's memory and capacity for verbal articulation, the interviewer's skill in eliciting relevant descriptions, and the judgment processes of the raters, one can at best expect to see only the broad outlines of the phenomena of interest. Ratings based on notes made by home observers, or questionnaires filled out by parents or children likewise introduce unknown degrees of distortion into the data.

Generally speaking, it would seem desirable to use relatively direct measures of parent-child interaction and thus eliminate some of the intervening sources of error. Another advantage of a more direct approach is that it usually permits a more fine-grained analysis of the interaction than is possible with global ratings. Direct behavioral measures, however, present their own set of problems: the unknown effects of the presence of the observer, the representativeness of the sample of interaction observed, and the coding of the flow of interaction into units for analysis. Lytton (1971) provides a more detailed critique of different approaches to the measurement of parent-child interaction than can be given in this chapter. All methods have shortcomings, and perhaps most confidence should be put in findings supported by several sources of data.

A second problem usually associated with the data used in factor analytic studies, and with any other study which assumes that parents or children possess general traits such as acceptance or aggressiveness, is that little, if any, account is taken of situational variables. Thus, a mother's behavior probably varies in important respects as a function of whether father, grandparents, siblings, or guests are present; the child is sick or well; the setting is home or a restaurant; the other stresses present in her life; and, most important, the immediately preceding child behavior. With respect to the last, a parent's severity of punishment, for example, is likely to vary a great deal depending upon the nature of the infraction and the number of warnings or mild punishments previously given. Interview or questionnaire measures usually reflect some kind of subjective averaging process across these and other situations; this may not provide a very accurate picture of how the parent behaves in any one situation. Gewirtz (1969) used the phrase "one-sided summary variables" to refer to measures of this kind which not only ignore situational influences but focus on only one side of what is really a two-way interaction.

A substantial proportion of this chapter is devoted to research on the relation of parent-child interaction to child characteristics or traits measured outside the family context. An example is aggression displayed at nursery school. Child aggression at nursery school is significantly affected by what happens at nursery school, as Patterson, Littman, and Bricker (1967) have demonstrated; and one can expect at best that correlations between parent-child measures and extrafamilial measures will be modest. In this chapter, however, attention will be directed primarily to the parent-child interaction measures, and little if any consideration will be given to all of the other factors that influence a child's behavior away from home. Whenever possible, responses directed toward the parent will be considered separately from those occurring elsewhere.

Another problem specifically associated with the factor analytic approach is that it is usually possible to drastically affect the number of factors extracted by varying the specificity of the ratings made or the questions asked. Thus, Sears, Maccoby, and Levin (1957) and Becker et al. (1962) rated relatively specific aspects of child-rearing behavior such as permissiveness toward aggression, toward sex, toward table manners, toward toilet training, and so on, and factor analyses yielded five to ten factors, respectively. Specificity in these examples can be seen as a special kind of situational variable, that is, permissiveness with respect to different kinds of child behaviors. A second-order factor analysis based upon the intercorrelation of a first set of factors will sometimes reduce to a two- or three-dimensional solution but again at the price of increasing the level of abstraction of the obtained dimension. It is hard to escape the conclusion that the "basic" dimensions derived from factor analyses are influenced to a considerable degree by the number, variety, and specificity of measures that a given investigator somewhat arbitrarily decides to include.

Despite the various criticisms raised, topological surveys of the domain of parent-child interactions would still seem to serve a useful purpose. Further consideration of these comprehensive schemes and some suggestions for future research will be given in a later section.

ATTACHMENT AND DEPENDENCY IN INFANTS

No important theoretical distinction will be made between attachment and dependency in the first year of life. Attachment has been the more popular term used in recent years to apply to young infants, human and nonhuman, and dependency has traditionally been more often applied to older children and adults. The specific behaviors and their functional meaning are the important considerations to keep in mind as these phenomena are followed developmentally from infancy to older children.

Infants of many animal species show attachment to a specific adult, usually the mother, manifested by tendencies to seek physical contact or proximity, maintain visual and auditory contact, and show distress at forced separation. The human infant is no exception, and numerous behaviors have been proposed as indicative of attachment. Ainsworth (1963, 1964) proposed thirteen behaviors as criteria for attachment: differential (more to the specific object of attachment than to others) smiling, vocalization, visual-motor orientation, following, "scrambling" over mother, burying face in mother's lap, exploration from mother as a secure base, clinging, lifting arms in greeting, clapping hands in greeting, approaching through locomotion, crying when held or comforted by another person, and crying when mother departs. These criteria emphasize the specificity of attachment, that is, the differential response to a specific person such as the mother versus other people. The very young infant shows many of these reactions (smiling, vocalization, visual-motor orientation) rather indiscriminately to different people as well as to a variety of nonsocial stimuli. The differential attachment to mother usually develops between five and fourteen months of age and is associated with a wide range of individual differences in age of onset (Ainsworth 1967; Ainsworth, Bell, and Stayton 1971, in press; Fleener and Cairns 1970; Schaffer and Emerson 1964; Spitz 1965; Tennes and Lampl 1964; Yarrow 1967).

The different measures thought to be indicative of attachment are only moderately correlated with each other. Coates, Anderson, and Hartup (1972) examined the intercorrelations among four measures of attachment with mother present (visual regard, vocalizing, touching, and proximity) and four measures obtained when mother was temporarily absent (crying, looking at the door, touching the door, and proximity to door). Correlations within each of these groups of four measures were generally significant and moderate in magnitude, falling mainly in the range from .40 to .70. Vocalization showed the least tendency to correlate with the other measures. For the measures obtained during separation, only crying correlated consistently with the measures, other than vocalization, obtained with mother present. Although leaving ample room for individual variation and situational determinants, these correlations do suggest some basis for a unitary concept of attachment. Maccoby and Feldman (1972), however, obtained repeated measures of attachment on an older sample of children at ages two, two and one-half, and three, and found no correlation between proximity-seeking behavior and measures of visual regard or vocalization. Proximity-seeking did correlate with crying when left with a stranger. With increasing age, proximity-seeking and protest over separation may come to be functionally different from the visual regard and vocalizing variables. This possibility will be considered further in the next section.

Once some degree of attachment has developed, much of the young infant's behavior, aside from satisfying homeostatic needs for nourishment and sleep, can be seen as reflecting somewhat incompatible tendencies to seek proximity and contact with the primary caretaker and to explore, by distance receptors or by locomotion and manipulation, the surrounding environment. The evolutionary significance of both attachment and exploratory behavior is reasonably obvious; the mother-infant attachment system insures a degree of protection and caretaking that is essential for survival in species whose young are relatively helpless, and exploratory behavior insures that the infant will progressively learn more about the world in which he will some day have to live without his mother's aid.

Some Theoretical Differences

Attempts to explain attachment behavior might be grouped under three headings: psychoanalytic, learning, and ethological-evolutionary theories.

Psychoanalytic formulations of attachment phenomena have centered around the concept of *object relations*. As a result of the mother's special role in gratifying the infant's instinctual needs, she becomes a differentiated part of the environment and becomes positively "cathected." Early learning-theory approaches, using different terminology, also emphasized the importance of the association between gratification (primary reinforcement) and other aspects of the mother—her physical appearance, sounds, smells, and so on. Thus, the presence of the mother was considered to become a powerful secondary or learned reinforcer because of the repeated pairing of her presence with primary reinforcers such as feeding and discomfort reduction (Sears, Whiting, Nowlis, and Sears 1953). Infants would thus strive to be near mother because the stimuli associated with mother had developed learned reward value.

Gewirtz (1969), working within a more purely behavioral and Skinnerian framework, further elaborated the learning approach to attachment behavior. Attachment, in his view, is not seen as a unitary trait, underlying structure, or drive, but is seen rather as a loose classification of behaviors, each being controlled by its own set of discriminative stimuli and reinforcement contingencies. He has continued to emphasize the learned or conditioned reinforcement value of certain of the mother's characteristics. Discriminative stimuli which signal to the infant that he can *do* something to obtain primary reinforcements are especially likely to become strong conditioned reinforcers. Although there may be some "instinctual" or unlearned response tendencies to certain stimuli, Gewirtz has emphasized the operant learning of most attachment behaviors: the infant learns to seek proximity, make visual contact, and so on, because these responses are reinforced by either learned or unlearned reinforcers. He further stresses the interactive nature of attachment. Many responses on the part of the infant, for example, smiling, vocalizing, and clinging, are reinforcing to the mother, and thus the infant reinforces the mother for reinforcing him with her smiles, vocalization, physical contact, and kinesthetic stimulation. The phenomenon of attachment, then, becomes a characteristic of dyadic interaction, not a hypothetical state that resides inside one person.

Bowlby (1958, 1969) and Ainsworth (1969) have taken an ethological-evolutionary view of attachment and have suggested that the young of most animal species are born with certain instinctive tendencies which promote the development of attachment to the primary adult caretaker. Thus, in the human neonate behaviors such as rooting, sucking, grasping, following with the eyes, and crying all tend to achieve contact with the mother, and the mother's response in turn, according to Bowlby, may be partly instinctual; for example, her response to the infant's cry. An interactive system thus develops, and the infant's initial primitive responses are further shaped by this interaction. Bowlby emphasizes the role of environmental feedback as part of a control system which mediates attachment behavior. This position is presented in a more elaborated form by Ainsworth in her chapter on attachment in volume 3 of this series (Ainsworth 1973).

What Infants Bring to the Relationship

Early mother responsiveness to the infant may promote attachment, but likewise infants who are responsive to mothers' initial overtures may "train" their mothers to provide more stimulation than less responsive infants. There is considerable evidence that individual differences in infant temperament exist very early in life and probably have some genetic basis. Scarr (1969) found six- to ten-year-old identical twin girls to be substantially more alike on measures of sociability (friendliness, lack of social apprehension) than a similar sample of fraternal twins. Freedman, D. G. (1965) took motion pictures of the behavior of nine identical and eleven fraternal twins during the first year of life and had different judges rate each twin in a given pair. Identical twins showed greater similarity on responsiveness to people and objects, goal directedness of behavior, attention span, reactivity to stimuli, and fearfulness in new situations. Methodologically, this is one of the most impressive twin studies, since there is no way that the judges could have been influenced in their rating of one twin by knowledge of the other twin; additionally, the young age of the twins should have limited the effects of environmental influence. There is little research that demonstrates how these genetically influenced characteristics affect parental response, but it is a plausible hypothesis that such is the case.

Thomas, Chess, and Birch (1968) found relatively stable individual differences during the first five years of life on such characteristics as activity level, rhythmicity (regularity of sleeping, eating, bowel movements), approach-withdrawal to new stimuli, and adaptability with repeated exposure to new situations. These authors strongly advocate that parent-child relations depend on how parents respond to the temperamental differences in the child, and give a number of case examples of how, on the one hand, children with similar temperaments develop different relations with parents because parents reacted differently to the same trait, and how, on the other hand, children with different temperaments developed similarly because of similar parental responses. This study, however, does not get beyond the case-example stage in this particular area, since standard procedures were not used for assessing parental reactions to specific child characteristics. Yarrow (1963) has also reported interesting examples of the same foster mother responding quite differently to infants assigned to her at different times.

On the basis of mothers' reports, Schaffer and Emerson (1964) concluded that some babies very early in life actively sought out physical contact with people and that other babies actively resisted such contact. Selecting extreme groups of infants on this dimension and calling them cuddlers and noncuddlers, respectively, they found that the noncuddlers were generally more restless and active and at six months had higher scores on the Cattell Infant Scale, which largely measures motor development at that age. There was a trend for mothers of noncuddlers to prefer nonphysical kinds of interactions, but the difference was not statistically significant. However, mothers of cuddlers showed about equal preference on their part for physical handling as opposed to nonphysical means of stimulation and contact. Schaffer and Emerson have leaned to a genetic explanation for the cuddling differences in the infants, and the dimension sounds similar in some respects to activity level (noncuddlers being more active), but the data from their study were basically inconclusive on this issue. Thus, although it seems quite likely that individual differences in the newborn affect parental responses, the evidence remains somewhat indirect and anecdotal in nature.

The sex of the infant and any sex-related biological or temperamental characteristics may also affect the parental response. Moss (1967) found that three-week-old and three-month-old boys slept less and were more fussy and irritable than girls, and the mothers responded by holding the male infants more and generally providing more stimulation. These differences in maternal response disappeared when differences in irritability level were statistically controlled, indicating that temperament rather than sex per se was affecting the mothers' responses. Reports that one-year-old boys (Goldberg and Lewis 1969) and two-year-old boys (Maccoby and Feldman 1972) have been found to attack a frustrating barrier more vigorously than girls may be related to irritability differences. Differences of this kind may also evoke different parental responses, but such responses were not measured in these two studies.

With respect to the specific response of vocalization, Moss (1967) reported that mothers vocalized more to infant girls; Thoman, Leiderman, and Olson (1972) found greater maternal vocalization only to firstborn girls, with a slight opposite trend for later-born children; and Lewis

(1972) found that mothers were more likely to respond in some fashion to boys' vocalizations, but when the mother did respond her response was more likely to be vocal if the child was a girl. There is, then, some indication that mothers respond vocally to girls more than boys, but the evidence is by no means clear-cut.

What Mothers Bring to the Relationship

Moss (1967) found an interview measure of "acceptance of nurturant role" obtained prior to birth predicted directly observed maternal responsiveness when the infant was three weeks old; Robson, Pedersen, and Moss (1969) found "interest in affectionate contact" measured before birth to correlate with frequency of mother-infant mutual gazing at one month; and Moss, Robson, and Pedersen (1969) reported that ratings of animation in a mother's voice obtained prior to birth correlated with the amount of stimulation she provided the infant at one and three months of age. These researches document only a small part of maternal characteristics present before birth which are likely to influence the parent-child relationship. Clearly, both participants begin their encounter with behavioral dispositions that can make a big difference in the resulting interaction.

Developmental Antecedents of Attachment

Schaffer and Emerson (1964a) followed the development of attachment during the first eighteen months of life and also made certain ratings of the mother's behavior, both kinds of measures being derived from interviews with the mothers conducted every four weeks over the first year and again at eighteen months. Attachment, in this case, was inferred from the amount of protest associated with the infant's separation from mother. There was no relation between the strength of attachment and schedule of feeding, age or duration of weaning, age or severity of toilet training, or the amount of time the mother spent with the child. The ratings of responsiveness of the mother to the infant's crying and the total amount of stimulation provided were both related positively to the infant's attachment at eighteen months. There was a tendency (nonsignificant) for attachment to be greater for infants cared for exclusively by the mother. The age of onset of attachment was not related to any maternal variables.

Other studies have generally borne out these findings. Attachment was found by Caldwell (1962) to be greater for infants cared for exclusively by the mother than for those with multiple caretakers. Maccoby and Feldman (1972), however, found relatively little indication that American children were more attached to their mothers than kibbutz-reared Israeli children, as might be expected on the basis of the greater number of caretakers utilized in the kibbutz. In these kibbutz studies the mother was the chief caretaker for the first six months of life, and this may have reduced the magnitude of the difference between these rearing conditions.

The importance of stimulation, especially stimulation that is contingent upon the infant's signals, has been further verified by longitudinal studies employing direct measures of mother-child interaction (Ainsworth 1964; Ainsworth and Bell 1969; Caldwell, Wright, Honig, and Tannenbaum 1970). Ainsworth and Bell, for example, directly observed twenty-two white, middle-class mothers interacting with their infants for four-hour periods every three weeks from birth until the infants were fifty-four weeks of age. A classification system was developed for categorizing different patterns of mother-child interaction associated with feeding. At approximately one year of age measures of attachment and exploratory behavior were made of the infant in a series of standardized situations involving the presence of the following combinations of people: mother and infant; mother, stranger, and infant; stranger and infant; mother and infant; infant alone; stranger and infant; mother and infant. All nine infants who responded to the strange situation with strong indications of attachment but who could also use the presence of mother as a "secure base for exploration" fell in the feeding interaction pattern in which the mothers were most sensitive to the demands and rhythms of the infant, permitting the infant to play an active part in determining the timing, pacing, and termination of feeding. Twelve of fourteen infants who either lacked interest in regaining or maintaining contact with their mothers when reunited, or intermingled contact-seeking behavior with rejection of the mother (e.g., angry pushing-away) had mothers who had been relatively insensitive and unresponsive to them in the early feeding situation. Ainsworth did not provide statistical analyses of these data, but a chi-square computed by the present author indicated a significant effect (p .05) for these relationships. The measure of sensitivity in the feeding situation used in this research is not exactly synonomous with the well-studied characteristic of demand versus scheduled feeding; for example, a mother rated sensitive might be moving the infant toward a regularly scheduled feeding time but doing so with flexibility and responsiveness to the infant's signals. Perhaps this characteristic of the feeding interaction will prove to be more predictive of future mother-child relations or other child behaviors than the generally inconclusive results (Caldwell 1964) for the demand versus scheduled feeding variable.

More general ratings of the mothers' sensitivity to the infants' needs, made during the first three months and again during the nine- to twelve-month period, were also similarly related to the strange-situation behavior (Ainsworth, Bell, and Stayton 1971). Attachment-exploration behavior observed in the home was compared with that shown in the standardized strange-situation test, and a strong relationship was found. All of the infants who fell in the category of home behavior characterized as a "smooth balance between exploratory and attachment behavior" were in the similar category for the strange-situations test.

The configural approach to classifications used by Ainsworth and her colleagues is both a strength and a weakness. The strength lies in the possibility that this feature of mother-child interaction is indeed a configuration that is not wholly captured by additive combinations of more specific behaviors. The weakness lies in the difficulty of specifying the proper weightings for the different components of the configuration and generally objectifying its measurement. Good agreement was obtained between independent judges in placing infants in the categories associated with the strange-situation procedure, but interjudge reliability was not reported for the other classification systems.

Cross-sectional studies at one age level have likewise shown a kind of reciprocity in mother-child interaction in which the mother's involvement and stimulation correlates positively with the child's social responsiveness to the mother (Beckwith 1972; Bell 1970; Stern, Caldwell, Hersher, Lipton, and Richmond 1969). Beckwith, for example, found that the more the mothers ignored their seven- to ten-month-old babies' signals or criticized their behavior, the less the infants were found to orient to them and maintain contact with them. The quantity of available social contact with the mothers, however, was not related to the infants' social behavior. All of the white, middle-class mothers in the sample seemed to be spending a reasonable amount of time in caretaking activities, so that the range of variation on this variable was limited. The results suggest that the contingent nature of the mothers' response is more important than the absolute amount of time spent with the infant, assuming that some reasonable minimum of the latter is present.

Attachment to fathers apparently has not been studied directly, although Pedersen and Robson (1969), using reports from mothers' interviews, found sons', but not daughters', attachment behavior to fathers (in the form of "greeting behavior") to be correlated with the extent of the fathers' caretaking behavior and the level of the fathers' stimulation via play.

Overall, then, research suggests that both the general level of stimulation and the response-contingent nature of the stimulation (that is, the sensitivity of the mother to the infant's signals) are important factors in the development of mother-child attachment. The general level of stimulation has also been found to be associated with infant development much more broadly than just in the mother-child relationship (Beckwith 1971; Casler

1961; Pedersen, Yarrow, and Rubenstein 1972; and Yarrow 1963). Yarrow, for example, found correlations in the .50s between measures of mothers' physical and social stimulation and infants' IQ scores at six months. Other investigators have emphasized the importance of contingent stimulation in the general development of the infant. Lewis and Goldberg (1969) proposed that the capacity of the infants to habituate (to show a "response decrement" in their terminology) attentional responses to repeated presentations of a novel stimulus is affected by the amount, variety, and contingency of past stimulation. In line with this theory they found that directly observed maternal stimulation (amount of touching, looking, holding, and smiling) of twelve-week-old infants in the laboratory correlated positively with the tendency of the infants' attentional response to habituate to several presentations of a blinking light. The percentage of times each mother responded to the infant's crying or vocalizing, a measure of contingent stimulation, was also correlated with rapidity of habituation. According to Lewis and Goldberg, contingent stimulation by the mother or others helps to create a generalized expectancy on the part of the infant that he can *do* something to obtain rewards or avoid distress. More detailed examinations of the relation of social learning experiences to the development of cognitive and intellectual competencies can be found in other chapters in this volume (chapters 3 and 11).

In studying mothers and infants in naturalistic settings the general level of maternal stimulation and the degree of contingency of this stimulation are likely to be correlated, making it difficult to assess their relative importance. That the human infant tends to seek both contingent and noncontingent stimulation has been underestimated. There are by now many studies demonstrating the capacity of the young infant, even neonate, to show operant learning if provided with reinforcement that is contingent on a particular response: for example, eye contact with smiling (Etzel and Gewirtz 1967); vocalizations (Rheingold, Gewirtz, and Ross 1959), and visual fixation (Watson 1969). What is of special interest is the joy and delight that the infant seems to take in learning to manipulate his environment. Watson and Ramey (in press) have reported intriguing results of a study in which eight-week-old infants were given the opportunity to make a colored mobile rotate by moving their heads in their cribs at home. Infants in the contingency mobile group clearly learned to make the head-moving response relative to infants in a noncontingency mobile control group. More relevant to the present point, infants in the contingency mobile group were reported by the mothers to show obvious signs of enjoyment and interest in the task, manifested specifically by a marked increase in smiling and cooing during the ten minutes per day in which they were exposed to the mobile. These authors suggested that the responsiveness of the human infant to the adult face may not develop so much because of innate reactions to the facial stimulus itself (Fantz 1961), or by secondary reinforcement resulting from associations of the face with rewarding caretaking activities (Gewirtz 1965), or by association with distance receptor stimulation itself (Walters and Parke 1965) but rather as a result of responsiveness (perhaps unlearned) to response-produced changes in stimulation. The experience, in other words, of *making* the environment provide changes in stimulation is more rewarding to the infant than passively experiencing such changes. The mother's face is especially likely to become the focus of such interest, with accompanying signs of delight such as smiling and cooing, because it is a stimulus capable of much variation in appearance that can to a large degree be brought under control of the infant's responses. Of course, once the infant begins to smile, coo, and show other signs of delight, the mother's responsive behavior is further reinforced and a strong dyadic system maintained by mutual reinforcement is likely to develop.

The authors have also suggested that contingency learning in the young infant may not be possible for relationships that involve a delay of longer than about seven seconds between infant response and environmental effect (Watson 1967). Accordingly, they have proposed that many of the major caretaking contingencies, for example, crying-brings-comfort, or kicking-brings-food, may not be effective for operant learning. Various "interactional games" between mother and infant do meet these temporal requirements and are more likely to play a role in the development of this kind of social interaction; for example, the mother may react almost simultaneously to the baby's facial or motor responses with vocal, tactile, or visual responses of her own.

Ramey, Hieger, and Klisz (1972) have also reported the use of *synchronous reinforcement* in modifying vocalization responses in two maternally deprived infants who were showing "failure-to-thrive." Synchronous reinforcement involved a situation in which any vocalization would simultaneously produce a brightly colored geometric figure. Vocalizations were indeed increased by this procedure, and these generally withdrawn and apathetic infants began to show more normal responsiveness to the environment outside of the experimental situation. One infant showed a 21 point increase on the Cattell Infant Intelligence Scale. These results are generally consistent with the notion that a lack of contingent maternal stimulation produces the failure-to-thrive syndrome and that the provision of a contingent reinforcement experience can begin to reverse this process. The findings of Ramey et al. (1972) as well as those of Watson and Ramey need further verification, and, in the latter case, a more direct measure of the infant's smiling and cooing would be desirable, but the results thus far are most provocative.

It has been well demonstrated that infant exploration of an unfamiliar environment is facilitated and signs of distress and fearfulness are decreased by the presence of the mother (Arsenian 1943; Cox and Campbell 1968; Rheingold 1969). Infants who have developed some degree of attachment, when placed in an unfamiliar setting *without* their mother, tend to show inhibition of exploratory and manipulatory behavior and manifest behaviors oriented toward reestablishing contact with the mother, such as crying and moving toward the place of the mother's disappearance. Mother's presence seems to reduce the fear of the unfamiliar, and the infant can then proceed with his exploration, intermingled with occasional visual or physical contacts with mother. It is of interest to note that Morgan and Ricciuti (1969) found that fear of strangers for eight- to twelve-month-old infants was considerably stronger when infants were separated from their mothers by only four feet than when held on the mother's lap—a further demonstration that the occurrence and intensity of the fear response to strangeness is apparently modulated by the mother's presence. Exploratory behavior and low fear of the unfamiliar would also seem to be associated with high levels of varied maternal stimulation (Moss, Robson, and Pedersen 1969; Robson, Pedersen, and Moss 1969; Rubenstein 1967).

Summary

1. Genetically influenced individual differences, especially those involving social responsiveness, contact-seeking, and fearfulness, probably affect the subsequent course of attachment development.

2. Mothers likewise bring to the relationship qualities which may foster or inhibit the development of attachment, especially the two characteristics listed under numbers 3 and 4 below.

3. Higher levels of maternal stimulation (auditory, visual, touch, and kinesthetic) are related to greater infant attachment.

4. The extent to which the mother's stimulation is contingent upon the infant's responses, her sensitivity to the infant's signals, would seem to be an especially important factor in facilitating attachment.

5. The same factors that facilitate attachment may also contribute to the development of the infant's general intellectual and social competencies.

6. Fear of the unfamiliar is less if mothers in the past have provided the infant with a high level of varied stimulation and also is less if the mother is present.

ATTACHMENT AND DEPENDENCY BEYOND INFANCY

Relationships among Different Measures of Dependency

Despite the fact that different measures of attachment are only moderately intercorrelated, conceptually, at least, infant attachment seems to be a reasonably unitary phenomenon. Attachment or dependency in older children becomes a much more fragmented concept, and a greater diversity of behaviors become subsumed under this heading. When these various behaviors (e.g., negative attention-seeking, reassurance-seeking, positive attention-seeking, touching and holding, being near, and help-seeking) are measured by frequency counts from direct observation in preschool settings, the intercorrelations are frequently low and nonsignificant (Emmerich 1964; Heathers 1955; Rosenthal 1965; Sears, Rau, and Alpert 1965). On the other hand, when ratings of different kinds of dependency are made by teachers or observers, the intercorrelations tend to be of moderate size (Beller 1959; Emmerich 1966) probably reflecting, in part, consistency derived from the imposition of the raters' own cognitive structures upon the observations.

Some authors have distinguished between different clusters of dependency behaviors: for example, affectional versus instrumental dependency (Kagan and Moss 1962), and proximity- or contact-seeking versus attention-seeking dependency (Rosenthal 1965). Heathers (1955), Maccoby and Feldman (1972), and Maccoby and Masters (1970), in a re-analysis of the data from Sears et al. (1965), all obtained results supporting Rosenthal's finding of no correlation between proximity- or affection-seeking and attention-seeking measures. Heathers (1955) and Maccoby and Masters (1970) also reported that, although attention-seeking toward adults correlated with attention-seeking toward children, there was no correlation between proximity- or affection-seeking toward adults and toward children. Both Becker and Krug (1964) and Baumrind and Black (1967) related the results of factor analyses of kindergarten and preschool children's behavior to Schaefer's circumplex model, and proximity- or contact-seeking was associated with relatively passive, submissive characteristics, whereas attention-seeking was located in the opposite quadrant and was related to active, extroverted, and aggressive behaviors.

In summary, then, various behaviors subsumed under the label of dependency do not correlate highly for the two- to five-year-old child. It may be especially important to distinguish the cluster of behaviors involving proximity-seeking and protest at separation from those behaviors oriented toward attention-seeking.

Some evidence for the persistence and generalization of the proximity-seeking variety of dependency was reported by Maccoby and Feldman

(1972), who found that two-year-old children who were high on this cluster of dependency measures showed a relatively high level of inter-action with, and sought proximity to, their nursery-school teachers at three years of age. Specificity of target was also shown in that these mea-sures of attachment to mother at age two did not predict dependency behavior toward other children in the nursery school.

Rewarding and Punishing Dependency

When specifically defined child dependency responses are studied exper-imentally or in the context of directly observed mother-child interaction, some consistent findings emerge. Nelson (1960) and others (Maccoby and Masters 1970) have shown that dependency responses can be in-creased by rewards and decreased by punishments given by an adult experimenter; and Yarrow, Waxler, and Scott (1971) have shown that a somewhat broader manipulation of nurturance versus nonnurturance had a similar effect on children's attention-seeking behavior. Thus, de-pendency responses like most other behaviors are affected by the reward-ing or punishing consequences which follow them. The application of this seemingly simple principle to the study of parent-child relations has frequently led to confusing results—largely because detailed knowledge about the previous learning history of this dyadic system has not been available to the investigators.

One empirical finding is reasonably clear. If the mother of most two- to five-year-olds ignores or mildly punishes the child's bid for attention in a specific experimental situation, the child is likely to increase the in-tensity and frequency of his demands. Sears, Rau, and Alpert (1965) compared child dependency responses when mother was busy filling out a questionnaire to when she was attentive to and helping the child while he was solving a puzzle. Child dependency was much higher when the mother was busy. Smith (1958) reported a negative correlation ($-.36$) between mother rewarding behavior (attention, affection, praise) and child dependency, and positive correlations ($.51$ and $.40$) between mother ignoring and punishing, respectively, and child dependency. Similar results have been obtained from mother-interview ratings (Sears, Maccoby, and Levin 1957; Yarrow, Campbell, and Burton 1968). In both of these studies it was found that the more the mothers reported that they reacted to the child's dependency behavior with irritable scolding or impatient pulling-away the more generally dependent he was likely to be ($r = .28$ for Sears et al.).

It would be misleading to conclude from findings of this kind that current child dependency has been produced primarily by parental punish-ment of dependency, or that the more a parent has rewarded dependency in the past the less dependent the child will be in the future. It makes more sense to assume that the child has already learned to respond with bids for attention, help, or closeness in certain situations because in the past the schedule of rewards and punishments favored such learning. In the present situation, mother's temporary nonresponse or mild punishment simply evokes redoubled efforts to achieve her attention. It is the contrast, in other words, between the mother's immediate punishment and the child's expectancy of dependency satisfaction based on past reinforcements that is related to the child's increase in dependency behavior. The dependency response is maintained because sooner or later the mother probably does reward it—perhaps after a certain intensity of child demandingness occurs. It is of interest in this respect that Sears et al. (1953) found that the correlation of maternal punishment of dependency with child dependency increased when computed only for dyads where dependency was most highly rewarded (r = .39). Or, put otherwise, the highest percentage of dependent children was associated with mothers who were both highly rewarding and highly punishing of dependency.

In one of the rare studies which focused on the effects of child behavior on adult behavior, Yarrow, Waxler, and Scott (1971) demonstrated some strong effects of the child's dependent behavior on the adult's nurturant behavior. Thus, children, boys especially, who engaged more frequently in attention- or help-seeking behavior received more nonnurturance from adults. It was also shown that if a child responded positively to a contact initiated by an adult, then the adult was likely to initiate a subsequent contact with the child more quickly than if the child had been nonresponsive on the first occasion. The adult's social behavior, in other words, was being shaped by the child's response. Of course, both participants influence subsequent behavior, and as previously noted it was also found in this study that the children's attention-seeking was lower with adults instructed to be nonnurturant than with those instructed to be nurturant.

Warmth-Hostility and Child Dependency

1. *Parent-directed dependency.* To the extent that warmth is defined as sensitive responsiveness to the infant's signals and the provision of a high level of general stimulation (touching, holding, smiling, talking to, and so on), then the previously reviewed research on attachment suggests that warmth in infancy is related to infant attachment. Several studies using direct observation of children in the two- to five-year age-range interacting with their mothers have found correlations that suggest reciprocity in the interchange of maternal and child warmth (Antonovsky 1959; Hatfield, Ferguson, Rau, and Alpert 1967; Kogan, Wimberger, and Bobbitt 1969; Stern, Caldwell, Hersher, Lipton, and Richmond 1969). Thus, Stern et

al. (1969) found mothers who were high in involvement, visual contact, and play had children who were loving and involved with the mother, and Hatfield et al. (1967) found rated maternal warmth to correlate .52 with rated child warmth. At this age conceptions of dependency seem to diverge from conceptions of infant attachment, so that, although "warm," responsive behavior on the part of the one-year-old may be considered one indication of attachment, it is not likely to be considered an indication of dependency at age three. The behaviors usually labeled dependent at this older age, attention-seeking or proximity-seeking, tend to be viewed as undesirable, immature, and different from a friendly, positive interest in social interaction. For example, in the Hatfield et al. (1967) study, ratings of child warmth did not correlate with ratings of child dependency obtained during the same interaction. Thus, these studies showing a reciprocal interchange of warmth should not be taken to mean that parental warmth is related to child dependency.

When the more usual measures of parent-directed dependency are measured in two- to five-year-old children, studies have generally failed to find any consistent relationship to parental warmth. Hatfield et al. (1967) and Yarrow et al. (1968) have reported modest but significant positive correlations between these variables for preschool boys but not for girls. Smith (1958) found a positive relationship for preschool girls but not for boys. No clear relationship among various measures of parental warmth and dependency emerged in the studies of five-year-olds by Sears et al. (1957) and Becker et al. (1962).

Nor have investigators found a consistent relationship between parental hostility-rejection, measured separately from warmth, and parent-directed dependency in preschool children (Becker et al. 1962; Hatfield et al. 1967; Kagan and Moss 1962; Sears et al. 1957; Smith 1958; Yarrow et al. 1968). The emphasis here is on the word *consistent*; an occasional significant correlation, usually for only one sex, occurs in these studies but not with enough consistency to warrant even tentatively stated conclusions.

2. *Dependency toward peers and adults other than parents.* For boys there is a tendency in several studies for parental rejection or low parental warmth to correlate positively with dependency toward peers and adults other than parents (McCord, McCord, and Verden 1962; Sears et al. 1953; Sears et al. 1965; Siegelman 1966; Winder and Rau 1962). In the McCord et al. study (1962) extensive data from the Cambridge-Somerville Youth Study were used to identify a group of dependent nine- to seventeen-year-old lower-class boys and as a basis for rating parental behavior. Highly dependent boys, relative to a control group of moderately (that is, within the normal range) dependent boys, were found to have a higher proportion of rejecting mothers and rejecting fathers.

Permissiveness-Restrictiveness and Child Dependency

Considering results for preschool children first, Sears et al. (1965) found general maternal permissiveness to be related to the negative attention-seeking (toward other children and teachers) variety of dependency in both boys and girls, but not to be consistently associated with the more passive kinds of dependency (seeking reassurance, being near, seeking contact) in either sex. The importance of the distinction between attention-seeking and contact-seeking dependency and the former's relation to general aggressiveness is further emphasized by their findings. However, Kagan and Moss (1962) did not find maternal restrictiveness to be related to the child's emotional or instrumental dependency on mother at age three to six, nor did Yarrow et al. (1968) find any relation between general maternal restrictiveness and ratings of dependency toward either mother or teacher in three- to six-year-olds.

More consistency appears with older children. Maternal restrictiveness measured both at ages three to six and at ages six to ten correlated positively with emotional dependence on adults (but not instrumental dependence) as measured in the child at ages six to ten for boys and girls (Kagan and Moss 1962). Winder and Rau (1962) reported peer-rated dependency on other children and teachers in nine- to twelve-year-olds to be related to both maternal and paternal restrictiveness (measured by parent questionnaire). In both Kagan and Moss, and Winder and Tau, studies, restrictiveness correlated substantially with parental rejection so that these findings may reflect the same relationship of dependency to parental rejection referred to in the previous section. The McCord et al. (1962) study is especially valuable because the authors also divided their group of dependent boys into those who were (1) dependent upon adults but not peers, (2) dependent upon peers but not adults, and (3) pervasively dependent upon peers and adults. The adult-dependent group had a higher proportion of parents who made many demands, were strict in supervision, and were restrictive in an authoritarian manner than the peer-dependent or the control groups. The peer-dependent boys had a higher proportion of parents who showed a total lack of supervision, were low on demands, and were emotionally indifferent than did the adult-dependent or the control boys.

The relationship of parent-child measures to child dependency might be considerably clearer if there were a few additional studies that distinguished between the targets of dependency (parent, peer, other adult) and the emotional or proximity-seeking and the attention-seeking varieties of dependency. The data at this time suggest, though, that adult-directed dependency of the emotional kind is likely to be associated with parental restrictiveness of an authoritarian kind administered without much warmth or acceptance. Peer-directed dependency, perhaps with more emphasis on the attention-seeking kind, is likely to be associated with parental laxity or permissiveness, occurring in an atmosphere lacking in warmth or acceptance. The strong relationship of the attention-seeking type of dependency to aggression suggests that the parental correlates of aggression should be similar to those for this kind of dependency, and that indeed is the case, as will be seen in the section on aggression.

Maternal Protectiveness and Dependency

Maternal protectiveness as defined by Kagan and Moss (1962) assessed the degree to which the mother rewarded dependent overtures, encouraged the child to become dependent on her, and showed overconcern when the child was ill or in danger. In the Kagan and Moss study this variable did not correlate with maternal restrictiveness, tended to have a small negative correlation with maternal hostility, and was associated with mother-directed dependency and passivity at ages three to six for both boys and girls. Smith (1958) found similar results for preschool girls but not for boys. Levy (1943) divided a sample of overprotective mothers seen at a child guidance clinic into two categories, the indulgent type and the dominating type. At home the children of the former were aggressive, disrespectful, and disobedient; the children of the latter were submissive, dependent, and timid. And Watson (1957) found mothers who were warm and restrictive (perhaps protective by the present definition) had children who were highly dependent on adults. The kind of dependency involved in these studies was probably of the emotional or proximity-seeking variety rather than the more aggressive, attention-seeking kind.

These findings with respect to maternal protectiveness suggest that dyadic systems develop in which mother and child mutually reinforce each other to maintain closeness. In such a system separative tendencies on the part of the child may be experienced as aversive by the mother, and her attempts to restore the closeness may be reinforced by a reduction of this distress. The child, at the same time, may also experience forced separations as aversive, and returning to mother may be reinforced by the reduction of his distress. Whatever the originating circumstances, both participants work at maintaining the system—a system that is roughly revealed by the correlation between the one-sided summary variables of maternal protectiveness and child dependency. When the system becomes especially strong and the negative affect associated with separation becomes intense, the phenomena of separation anxiety and school phobia may then appear (Eisenberg 1958; Waldfogel 1957).

Summary

1. Behavioral measures of dependency in the two- to five-year-old child are not highly correlated. Two clusters of measures would seem to be especially important and have different functional meanings: (a) proximity-seeking and protest-at-separation behaviors, and (b) attention-seeking behaviors. The former would seem to be more related to passive-fearful-introverted characteristics and the latter to aggressive-extroverted features.

2. Experimental studies show that dependency responses can be increased by rewards or decreased by punishments administered by adult experimenters. However, correlations between measures of maternal punishment of dependency and child dependency are usually positive. This apparent contradiction probably reflects the child's redoubled efforts to obtain dependency gratification after parental frustration, assuming that dependent behaviors have already been learned on the basis of past rewards.

3. The one-sided summary variables of warmth and hostility show no clear or consistent relationships to parent-directed dependency, but parental hostility may have some positive relationship to dependency directed at peers or other adults.

4. Parental restrictiveness combined with parental hostility (or low warmth) shows some relationship to adult-directed dependency.

5. Parental laxity or permissiveness combined with parental hostility (or low warmth) is related to peer-directed dependency.

6. Adult-directed dependency of an emotional or proximity-seeking type is positively related to maternal overprotection.

INTERNALIZATION: EXPERIMENTAL RESEARCH

Much of the parent-child relationship is devoted to socialization, the transmission of the prohibitions, proscriptions, and associated values and beliefs of the surrounding culture. The features of socialization that seem to exert the greatest strain upon parent-child relations are those in which the child is required to forego, postpone, or modify some strongly motivated activity, as in toilet training, waiting for mealtimes, inhibiting aggression, and sharing desirable toys. Most children do learn to inhibit or regulate these impulses, and to the extent that such self-denial is performed when there is no apparent likelihood that external rewards or punishments will be forthcoming, the child is said to have internalized the cultural prohibition. There is, of course, no way to rule out completely the possibility that external consequences may affect the behavior. Internalization is nevertheless a useful concept if seen as a relative matter, as an indication of the extent to which a person will not give in to temptation in situations where the probability of apprehension and punishing external consequences is low. Internalization is closely related to the concept of superego in psychoanalytic theory and in more everyday language to the concept of conscience. Experimental studies of internalization will be surveyed first, followed by a consideration of more naturalistic studies of parents and children.

Reward

A great deal of the young child's social behavior is controlled by external rewards, but to what extent do these external rewards play a role in the development of internalized constraints? In learning to wait for desired outcomes, that is, to choose more attractive rewards at some future time as opposed to less attractive immediate rewards, children are affected by their general expectation that the future will indeed be forthcoming, and this is undoubtedly influenced by their experiences of delayed rewards actually materializing, of promises being kept (Mischel 1966; Mischel and Grusec 1967; Mischel and Staub 1965). Aronfreed (1968, pp. 130–31) reported a study in which children in one group were rewarded with verbal approval ("Good!") and candy as soon as the child's hand reached for an unattractive toy, and given no reward when he or she reached for an attractive toy. Another group was treated similarly except that the reward was given after the child had already picked up the toy. Later, when left alone with the toys, the children who had been rewarded immediately upon reaching for the unattractive toy picked up the toy more quickly than those rewarded after picking up the toy. These results not only indicate the effect of the early-late variable but more generally show that rewards may have some effect on self-denying behavior. How long the effects lasted was not investigated.

Punishment

1. *Timing, intensity, and cognitive structure.* Research has shown that resistance to deviation in young children is increased if punishment (usually in the form of a verbal reprimand or a noxious noise) is given early rather than late in a transgression sequence (Aronfreed and Reber 1965; Cheyne 1971a; Cheyne and Walters 1967; Parke 1969; Parke and Walters 1967; Walters, Parke, and Cane 1965), if high-intensity rather than low-intensity punishment is used (Cheyne 1971a; Parke 1969; Parke and Walters 1967), and if high cognitive structure in the form of a clear statement of the rule, reasons for the rule, and consequences of deviation are provided (Aronfreed 1966, 1968; Cheyne 1971a; Cheyne and Walters 1967; Liebert, Hanratty, and Hill 1969; O'Leary 1967; Parke 1969).

Parke's (1969) study provides a good example of research in this area. During training trials the child was presented with pairs of toys—one attractive and one unattractive—and each time the child selected the attractive toy he was punished. The child was then left alone with the prohibited toys, after having been instructed not to touch them, and unbeknownst to the child an observer behind a one-way mirror recorded the latency, number, and duration of times that he touched the prohibited toys. The experimental design was such that comparisons could be made among two timing-of-punishment conditions (high and low), two levels of cognitive structure (high and low), and two nurturance conditions (high and low). Children in the early punishment condition were punished just before they touched the attractive toy, and late punishment children were punished after they had picked up and held the attractive toy for two to three seconds. Children in the low cognitive-structure group were told that they should not touch or play with some of the toys and that if they picked an incorrect one, a buzzer would sound. On punished trials, these children heard only the buzzer—no verbal remark accompanied the noise. Children in the high cognitive-structure group were told:

Some of these toys you should not touch or play with because I don't have any others like them. And if they were to get broken or worn out from boys playing with them, I wouldn't be able to use them anymore. So for that reason I don't want you to touch or play with some of these toys. And if you pick one of the toys you're not supposed to touch or play with, I'll tell you and you'll hear a buzzer.

High-intensity punishment consisted of a noxious buzzer (96 db) and low-intensity punishment of a milder buzzer (65 db). In the high cognitive-structure condition all punishments were accompanied by the verbal statement, "No, that one might get broken."

Timing, intensity, and cognitive structuring all had significant effects in the directions described above. In addition there were some interesting interactions among these variables. Early punishment was significantly more effective than late punishment only under low cognitive structure, and like-wise high-intensity punishment was significantly more effective than low-intensity punishment only in the low cognitive-structure condition. These trends, generally consistent with those of other investigators (e.g., Cheyne and Walters 1967), suggest that cognitive structuring tends to dilute the effects of timing and intensity of punishment. In other words, the internal thought processes of the child, what the child may be telling himself when faced with temptation, begin to control the child's behavior more than some of the external characteristics of the punishing stimulus. Another interesting finding of Parke's was that the average duration of deviations showed a steady increase over the test period under low cognitive structure but remained constant under high cognitive structure, a finding suggesting that the mediating cognition was continuing to maintain control over the tendency to deviate while the effects of the physical punishment were beginning to wear off.

One might expect that mediating cognitions would play a less important role in the young child than in the older child, and this is, indeed, what Cheyne (1971*b*) found—that kindergarten children were less influenced by reasoning than children in the third grade. Luria (1961) at a more general level has also shown that the capacity of words to acquire control over behavior increased with age. Cheyne (1971*a*) also reported some evidence that punishment accompanied by cognitive structuring was less likely to generalize to nonpunished responses than punishment without cognitive structuring. In other words, with cognitive structuring one can pinpoint the effects of punishment to a specific response and run less risk of producing generalized response inhibition. And Aronfreed (1966) showed that adding cognitive structuring which focused on the child's intentions ("No, you should not have *wanted* to pick up that thing") to a late-timed punishment made it as effective as an early-timed punishment without cognitive structuring.

2. *Relationship with the agent of punishment.* The nature of the relationship between the agent and the recipient of punishment would seem to be a factor that would influence the effectiveness of any punishments. A punishment, even when physical in nature, tends to carry with it a message of disapproval and withdrawal of affection. The explicit or implicit withdrawal of approval, so the argument goes, will be most influential when the child has come to expect a generally high level of approval or affection. In fact, attempts to study the effects of nurturance experimentally have yielded mixed results.

Parke (1969), in the study just described, found that resistance to deviation was not affected by a high-low nurturance manipulation. (Before the administration of punishment, children in the high-nurturance condition were engaged by the experimenter in friendly play in which he freely helped the children and expressed approval for their efforts.) There was, however, a significant interaction between nurturance and cognitive structuring. Under low cognitive structure, high nurturance was associated with more resistance to deviation than under low nurturance; whereas under high cognitive structure the reverse was true. Again cognitive structure seemed to override the effects of other variables, in this case, nurturance. In an earlier study conducted generally with little cognitive structure Parke and Walters (1967) found that a prior condition of high nurturance was associated with increased resistance to deviation. If there is an effect of the preceeding level of nurturance, it would seem to be most apparent under conditions of low cognitive structure.

3. *The context of punishment.* One important implication of laboratory research is that a given punishment is not always a punishment, and a reward is not always a reward. The punishing or rewarding character of a given event is greatly influenced by the sequential flow of events in which it is embedded.

Parke (1967) studied the effect of prior nurturance withdrawal on resistance to deviation when children were threatened with future nurturance withdrawal if they deviated, and promised a reinstatement of nurturance if they did not deviate. Children in the nurturance withdrawal group experienced five minutes of nurturant interaction followed by five minutes of nurturance withdrawal; children in the other group received ten minutes of continuous nurturance. All children were then placed in the resistance-to-deviation situation and told that, if they conformed to the requested prohibition, the experimenter would play with them upon returning. Nurturance withdrawal was associated with more resistance to deviation, more so for girls than boys and most of all for girls with a female experimenter. Burton, Maccoby, and Allinsmith (1961), however, found that nurturance withdrawal was associated with *more* deviation (cheating) in four-year-old boys and showed no effects for girls. Cheating is an achievement-oriented task, however, and is quite different from Parke's measure of deviation; the cheating might have reflected an attempt on the part of these young boys to regain the nurturance of the experimenter. Saadatmand, Jensen, and Price (1970) repeated Parke's procedure and found that four-year-olds showed greater resistance to deviation following nurturance withdrawal, but found a reverse tendency in six-year-olds and no effects with eight-year-olds. Thus, the effects of preceding nurturance withdrawal on resistance to deviation remain somewhat unclear.

Another series of researches has shown that the reinforcing value of adult attention and approval can be increased if preceded by a brief period of social isolation (Gewirtz and Baer 1958a, 1958b; Lewis 1965; Walters and Parke 1964a). And in a related vein Crandall (1963) and Crandall, Good, and Crandall (1964) have demonstrated that adult silence which followed adult approval served as a punishment, whereas adult silence which followed adult disapproval functioned as a reward. Rather simple learning tasks were used to measure the rewarding or punishing effects in these studies, and thus the full implication for resistance to deviation remains to be tested.

Verbal punishments in the form of scolding, nagging, and yelling do not always produce their intended effect of response suppression, at least from a longer time-perspective. Madsen, Becker, Thomas, Koser, and Plager (1968) demonstrated experimentally that the more a teacher said "Sit down" the more the children stood up! The initial response to the command to sit down was frequently compiled with, but a few minutes later the child was up again. The mild reuke, in fact, seemed to be serving as a positive reinforcer for standing-up behavior. Gallimore, Tharp, and Kemp (1969) have also demonstrated the positive reinforcing effect of negative attention. Thus, the labeling of certain parental reactions as "negative" does not necessarily mean that they will function as punishments; whether they do or not will depend upon the history of these responses in past interactions.

The consistency with which punishment is used or the mixture of rewards and punishments for the same response are factors thought to be of considerable importance in child-rearing. Martin (1963), after reviewing animal and human research concluded that under certain conditions a response which had been both rewarded and punished was more resistant to extinction than a response which had been rewarded only. Paradoxically, the addition of punishment seems to increase the strength of the response, a possibility which would seem to have important implications for parent-child relations. Deur and Parke (1970), using children as subjects, provide some further empirical support for this notion. A 50 percent reward—50 percent punishment (noxious buzzer) condition was associated with greater persistence of an aggressive response (hitting a Bobo doll) in six- to nine-year old boys after all rewards and punishments were stopped (extinction) than did a 100 percent reward condition. A 50 percent reward—50 percent no-reward condition produced an intermediate amount of resistance to extinction. Similar results were obtained for groups of boys who were given the same learning conditions but who were subsequently tested under a condition of 100 percent punishment. Katz (1971) has found similar facilitating effects of mixtures of rewards and punishments on hitting responses in first-grade boys. Research with animals and with adult human subjects (Deur and Parke 1968) has shown that the effect is not specific to aggressive responses, although as yet this has not been clearly shown with young children. Several explanations have been offered for this kind of effect: when punishment is mixed with reward the punishment may come to serve as a signal that a reward will be forthcoming if the child continues to make the response; or if the agent ceases to reward and begins to punish 100 percent of the time, the child who had previously been experiencing intermittent punishment would have more difficulty discriminating the new conditions of punishment than one who had had no prior experience of punishment.

Conditioned Emotional Responses

Aronfreed (1968) has proposed that learned empathic emotional responses play an important role in internalization processes. According to this view, positive and negative emotional reactions become conditioned to social cues which carry information about the emotional experience of other people. Thus, it is presumed likely that generally positive emotional states on the part of a parent are more likely than not to be paired with generally positive emotional states in the infant; and generally negative emotional states in the parent are more likely to be paired with generally negative emotions in the child. The evidence on reciprocity of interchange of positive and negative reactions referred to in the section on attachment and dependency is consistent with this proposition, although more data are needed to provide additional support for the assumption. Such a rough pairing of emotional experiences would provide the basis for conditioning in which the overt expressive cues of the parent (smiling, frowning, tone of voice) become conditioned stimuli eliciting emphatic reactions. Thus, verbal expressions of emotion by the parent (I am upset, afraid, angry), cognitive representations of the effects of observed environmental events (images or words conveying the idea that, when a person bumps his head, it hurts), and eventually verbal descriptions of situations not directly observed by the person (being told that someone was hurt) can all supplement the overt expressive cues as elicitors of empathic responses.

Aronfreed and Paskal (1965) reported an ingenious study with six- to eight-year-old children in which a positive emphatic response was conditioned to expressive cues from the experimenter. These results showed that the explicit pairing of the child's positive emotional reaction with the experimenter's expressive cues resulted in greater altruism (the child was willing to forego candy in order to elicit the experimenter's expressive cues of pleasure) than was the case with children in various control conditions. Midlarsky and Bryan (1967) repeated the essential findings of Aronfreed and Paskal but also showed that a backward conditioning procedure was about as effective as the usual forward conditioning procedure. In commenting on the study, Aronfreed (1968) proposed that children of this age have already learned to use cognitive mediators and can thus cognitively represent the association between the expressive cues and their effective reaction regardless of the exact timing of the sequence.

Aronfreed and Paskal (1966) also studied the role of learned empathic responses on sympathetic behavior in seven- to eight-year-old girls. In this study, expressive cues indicative of a negative emotional reaction in the experimenter were conditioned to a negative emotional reaction in the child, the negative reaction being produced by a noxious noise. Girls who were given appropriate conditioning trials were subsequently found to be more sympathetic, making responses which terminated distress cues in another girl of the same age, than did girls in various control conditions. These studies generally support the notion that conditioned emotional reactions to cues (or cognitive representations) associated with other people's emotional responses may play a role in the internalization of altruistic, sympathetic, and other self-denying or self-controlling behaviors. Of course, within this context the behavior is not really self-denying since it results in a positive emotional reaction or the avoidance of a negative emotional reaction. The question of whether a conditioned emotion is, in fact, empathic in the sense of being similar to that of the other person is not particularly relevant to the basic issue here. Children, for example, may well learn conditioned emotional reactions of shame, fear, and unspecifiable blends of negative affect to expressive cues associated with parental anger, disapproval, or withdrawal. And eventually these emotional reactions may be elicited by mediating cognitions involving anticipations of parental approval or disapproval. The unpleasant anticipatory negative emotion could be reduced by resisting deviation; the anticipatory positive emotion could also be sustained or enhanced by resisting or performing some altruistic act. Once learned, these conditioned emotions and their associated cognitions could provide a powerful mechanism for controlling behavior in the absence of external agents—a mechanism that is clearly the essence of what is usually referred to as conscience. Similar emotional reactions could also become conditioned to actual transgressions and might motivate behavior aimed at reparation, confession, and punishment-seeking, another set of reactions usually subsumed under the heading of conscience. These comments remain largely speculative at this time, and additional research is clearly needed to further clarify the role of conditioned emotional reactions in internalization.

Modeling

Observing another person engaged in some form of self-control has been shown to increase similar self-control behavior on the part of the observing child (Bandura and Kupers 1964; Bandura and Mischel 1965; Bandura and Whalen 1966; Mischel and Liebert 1966). Similar modeling effects have been shown for self-criticism (Grusec 1966; Mischel and Grusec 1966). Models perceived as powerful (controlling resources) relative to models perceived as nonpowerful facilitate more altruistic behavior (Grusec 1971) and delay of gratification (Mischel and Grusec 1966). Observation of the rewarding or punishing consequences to a model's self-denying behavior tends also to enhance or suppress, respectively, imitative behavior by the observing child (Bandura, Grusec, and Menlove 1967; Rosekrans and Hartup 1967; Walters, Leat, and Mezei 1963; Walters and Parke 1964b; Walters, Parke, and Cane 1965).

The role of the model's nurturance has not been so clearly demonstrated. For incidental behavior or behavior which involves no cost or self-denial on the part of the subject, it would appear that nurturant models produce more imitation than nonnurturant models (Bandura and Huston 1961; Bandura, Ross, and Ross 1963). On the other hand, Rosenhan and White (1967) and Grusec and Skubiski (1970) found no relationship between levels of nurturance and imitation of altruistic behavior; and Mischel and Grusec (1966) reported no effects of model-nurturance on the imitation of delay of gratification. Bandura, Grusec, and Menlove (1967) found that children were *less* likely to imitate a stringent level of self-reward for performance when observing a nurturant than a nonnurturant model, and Grusec (1971) reported a similar trend for sharing behavior. Nurturance apparently either has no general effect on imitation of self-denying behaviors or, if it has an effect, it is negative, producing less self-denial. Nurturance tends to be dispensed noncontingently in these studies; thus the child is perhaps being taught that it is not necessary to exert any effort or otherwise engage in self-denying behavior in order to earn the nurturance. Grusec (1966), on the other hand, did find more imitation of self-critical responses with a nurturant than a nonnurturant mode, implying that verbalization of self-criticism involves little cost to the person and perhaps further implying that self-criticism will not be associated necessarily with resistance to deviation or other behavioral manifestations of internalization.

Mediating cognitions

The human child is a thinking organism. With imagery and language the child learns to formulate internal representations of rules and moral principles, and of anticipated consequences for various courses of action. It is difficult to study the exact role of mediating cognitions because one always has to rely on indirect manipulation and measurement of these unobservable events. Nevertheless, their importance in controlling behavior is undoubtedly great, as was indicated in the previous review of the punishment literature.

Cognitions play a much broader role in internalization than just as a supplement to punishments. Even the simplest rewards and punishments, administered with no cognitive structuring, cannot be divorced from the effect of cognitive activity in the human child. Mediating cognitions, then, are involved not only in simple physical punishment situations but in formulating expectations about probable future rewards and punishments (Mischel 1966), as elicitors of conditioned emotional reactions (Aronfreed 1968), and as an essential mechanism in observational learning (Bandura 1969).

Another line of research that has implications for the role of cognitive processes in internalization derives from the theory of cognitive dissonance

(Festinger 1957). The relevant aspect of this theory is the proposition that the smaller the external reward (or punishment to be avoided) that affects one's decision the more positive will be one's evaluation of the behavioral choice. The principle is illustrated by the experiment of Aronson and Carlsmith (1963). The experimenter left preschool children in a room after telling them that they could play with all but one toy, previously judged to be attractive. The prohibition was supported by either a mild or severe threat of future punishment if they disobeyed. Covert observation revealed that no children in either condition played with the forbidden toy. Subsequently, children who had experienced the mild threat showed a significantly greater decrease in their attractiveness rating than did children in the high-threat condition, who, in fact, tended to increase their evaluation. Other investigators have replicated and extended this finding (J. L. Freedman 1965; Pepitone, McCauley and Hammond 1967). In both of these studies it was also demonstrated that children under a mild-threat condition actually played less with the designated toy when the prohibition was lifted at a later time (one month later in Freedman's study). The theory of cognitive dissonance explains these findings by saying that resistance to deviation under mild threat creates conflicting cognitions—the mildness of the threat is out of line with the behavioral act of nondeviation. In order to resolve this contradiction the child devalues the object of temptation ("It was not such a good toy after all") and thereby makes it reasonable that a mild threat is a sufficient deterrent. Whether or not this particular interpretation is correct, the phenomenon seems to be real and would seem to imply that milder, nonthreatening approaches to discipline would be associated with greater internalization.

Bandura and Perloff (1967) found that seven- to ten-year-old children will choose stringent criteria for themselves when permitted to have complete control over the evaluation and reward of their performances, even though they have been given no direct training or exposure to models, and Metzner (1963) found that children will more frequently make voluntary choices of delayed reward when their own performance controls the eventual reward than when the rewards are determined externally. Perhaps findings of this kind indicate that belief in control over eventual rewards produces more self-restraint in the present than believing that one has no control. The implication is that giving children clear responsibility for determining whether or not certain rewarding consequences occur enhances internalization.

Summary

1. External rewards for self-control enhance internalization. How persistent the effect is when external rewards are withdrawn is problematic.

2. External punishment (physical or verbal) for deviation increases resistance to deviation. Early as opposed to late punishment, intense as opposed to mild punishment, and cognitive structuring associated with punishment increase its effectiveness. Cognitive structuring overrides the effects of timing and intensity. A nurturant relationship with the agent of punishment seems to increase the effectiveness of punishment, but the evidence for this is not strong.

3. The place of a punishment in the sequential flow of events determines its effectiveness. Punishments which are mixed with rewards for the same response may, in fact, increase rather than decrease the strength of the response.

4. Conditioned emotional responses elicited by cognitive anticipations of deviation, or resisting deviation, may motivate the child to resist deviation in order to reduce the negative conditioned emotion and increase the positive conditioned emotion. Similar emotional reactions which become associated with actual transgressions may motivate behavior aimed at reparation, confession, and punishment-seeking. There is only preliminary experimental evidence for these conclusions.

5. Observing a model engage in self-control increases the likelihood of self-control on the part of the observer. The power (control over resources) of the model and the observed rewarding or punishing consequences to the model's behavior affect the observer's response. Nurturance of the model increases imitation of incidental and noneffortful responses but does not increase, and may decrease, imitation of self-restraining behavior.

6. Mediating cognitions contribute to the effectiveness of all the above factors in promoting internalization. Cognitive activity with respect to decision-making, as in cognitive dissonance resolution, may also further internalization.

INTERNALIZATION AND PARENT-CHILD INTERACTION

Parental Warmth, Power-Assertion, and Cognitive Structuring

Some of the relationships suggested by the experimental research have their counterparts in the findings of more naturalistic studies of parent-child interaction; some relationships have not been confirmed; and others have not been tested.

Stayton, Hogan, and Ainsworth (1971) propose that the human in-infant's socialization is facilitated by genetic predispositions and that, given an ordinary expectable social environment, the infant will acquire the appropriate self-restraints and internalization without specialized training procedures. As part of their research on attachment, these authors obtained some data bearing on this hypothesis from measures of mother-infant interaction during the first year. They found that compliance to commands and internalized controls were correlated with the general level of maternal sensitivity to the infant's needs and with general acceptance of the infant but were not correlated with specific attempts to teach prohibitions, such as the frequency of verbal commands or physical interventions. These results suggest that general maternal sensitivity-acceptance is more important than specific training procedures in achieving obedience in young infants and that perhaps, as many parents intuitively know, for some infants obedience and internalization seem to develop "naturally" without any special effort on the parents' part. For other infants socialization is a very difficult process, no matter how much time, energy, and sophistication go into the training regimens (Thomas et al. 1968).

A measure of infant IQ (a measure which does not relate highly to later measures of IQ) also correlated significantly with internalized controls as well as with the maternal variables of sensitivity and acceptance. Causation is undoubtedly bidirectional in the dyads: the mother's sensitivity-acceptance may well facilitate the development of internalized controls, but the inclinations and capacities (including infant IQ, perhaps) of the infant for internalized controls will affect how easy it is for the mother to be sensitive and accepting.

1. *Reactions to transgressions.* Yarrow et al. (1968) presented a summary of results of four studies with preschool children using similar methodologies: their own study, additional analysis of data collected by Burton (1959), Sears et al. (1957), and Sears et al. (1965). Data for both mother and child were obtained from mother interviews, and the measures of conscience were in all cases ratings based on mother-reported reactions to transgression, especially tendencies to confess and blame one's self after deviation. In all four studies there was a positive correlation between maternal warmth and son's conscience, and no relationship between these variables for daughters. In three of four studies there were negative correlations between maternal use of physical punishment and conscience for both boys and girls. In one case, Sears et al. (1965), the negative correlation for boys was not significant (−.14). Although use of praise correlated positively with conscience in all four studies for both boys and girls, the correlations were significant in only three out of eight instances. Maternal use of withdrawal of love as a punishment showed no consistent relationship to conscience, and although the correlations between maternal reasoning and child conscience were in all cases positive, only one reached statistical significance. An intuitively appealing relationship reported by Sears et al. (1957), in which maternal use of withdrawal of love as a

disciplinary technique was found to relate to the strength of child conscience only under conditions of high maternal warmth, was unfortunately
not borne out in the two studies in which a similar comparison was made.

Two dimensions of parental discipline have commonly been used in
studies of internalization. The first has been called "love-oriented" by
Sears et al. (1957) and Becker (1964) and "induction" by Aronfreed
(1961). There are two major components in this dimension which have
not been treated separately in many studies: (1) *cognitive structuring* or
reasoning in which the parent clearly describes what is expected, explains
why a rule should be obeyed (usually with an emphasis on abstract principles of right and wrong), and describes long-term consequences, including negative consequences to others; (2) using the *affective relationship*
as a basis for either withdrawing love contingent on undesirable behavior
or for making the child feel badly by emphasizing how badly (hurt, dis-
appointed) the child's misbehavior makes the parent or others feel. This
latter strategy would seem to rely heavily on learned emphatic emotional
reactions in the child. The second dimension of parental discipline, sometimes considered a polar opposite to the love-oriented dimension, has been
labeled "power-assertion" by Hoffman (1960) and "sensitization" (to
external consequences) by Aronfreed (1961). This kind of disciplinary
punishment is intense and frequently physical (hitting, slapping, spank-
ing), usually involves verbal abuse and loss of parental temper, and would
include unreasonable deprivations of privileges. It is likely to be administered abruptly, involving a crude display of parental power.

There is considerable consistency in a number of studies in which guilt
and internalized orientations (accepting responsibility for a transgression
and for making reparation; moral belief that one should resist deviation
because it is wrong rather than because of external consequences) following transgressions were assessed by a story-completion projective technique (or, in one case, by interview with the child), and parental disciplinary behaviors were assessed either by interview or by children's reports
(Allinsmith 1960; Allinsmith and Greening 1955; Aronfreed 1961;
Heinicke 1953; Hoffman and Saltstein 1967; Unger 1962). Love-oriented
approaches to discipline were associated with high expressions of guilt and
an internal orientation to deviation. The love-withdrawal component of
this dimension, when treated separately, does not show a consistent relationship to these reactions to transgression (Hoffman 1970). Power-
assertive approaches to discipline were associated with low expressions
of guilt and an external orientation to transgression (concern about being
caught, and so on). Maccoby (1961) found that children in the Sears et
al. (1957) study who had warm *and* restrictive mothers at age five
obtained higher scores on a self-report measure of rule enforcement at

age twelve. These children said, for example, that if they witnessed a rule violation by another child, they would attempt to enforce the rule. Lower-class families have been found to employ more power-assertive techniques than middle-class families (Allinsmith 1960; Aronfreed 1961; Hoffman and Saltstein 1967), and in two of these studies (Allinsmith 1960; Hoffman and Saltstein 1967) the relationship between parental discipline and child guilt did not hold for the lower-class families.

2. *Resistance to deviation.* Studies that have related parental disciplinary techniques obtained by interview to measures of resistance to deviation based on direct observation of young children have shown no clear pattern of results (Burton et al. 1961; Grinder 1962; Sears et al. 1965). One set of positive findings from Sears et al. in which both the mother's and the child's responses were derived from directly observed behavior (in separate situations) should perhaps be weighted most heavily. Mother's pressure for the daughter's independence, mother's responsiveness to the daughter, and mother's use of reasoning all correlated substantially with the daughter's resistance to temptation. The relationship did not hold for boys, however. Different specific measures of resistance to temptation have only modest correlations with one another (Sears et al. 1965), and it should not be surprising that parental correlates of any given measure of resistance to deviation are low or nonexistent. When ratings of self-control are based on many months of nursery-school observation, such correlates may emerge. Thus, Baumrind (1967) found that nursery-school children who were rated high on self-control had parents who made extensive use of reasoning in a generally nurturant and nonpunitive atmosphere, rewarded self-controlling behavior, and firmly enforced rules. This pattern includes the cognitive structuring feature of love-oriented discipline but does not necessarily include use of the effective relationship to make the child feel badly. There is also considerable evidence, which will be summarized in the next section, that one form of deviation, antisocial aggression, is associated with power-assertive parental discipline, low warmth, and low use of cognitive structuring.

Bronfenbrenner (1961) had teachers rate tenth-grade students on responsibility and obtained descriptions of parental characteristics from the students. Students rated very low on responsibility reported parental rejection, neglect, and low affiliative companionship. Some interesting sex differences were associated with measures of disciplinary control. For boys the *lack* of firm discipline by fathers was associated with low responsibility; for girls it was the *presence* of strong paternal discipline that was related to low responsibility. Bronfenbrenner suggested that these and other similar trends indicate that firm, strong discipline creates a risk of over-socialization in girls, with consequent inhibition and passivity; whereas for boys the greater risk is undersocialization as a result of discipline that is not firm enough. There is, in fact, considerable research support for the proposition that young girls accept the demands of socialization more readily than boys. Thus, girls were found at twenty-seven months to obey a first maternal command more often than boys (Minton, Kagan, and Levine 1971), at four to five years of age to show more adult role-behavior and self-control (Sears et al. 1965), to be more obedient at nursery school (Baumrind 1971), and at elementary school age to show greater resistance to deviation (Stouwie 1971) and to show a greater *decrease* in deviation following nurturance withdrawal (Parke 1967). The long-term differential effects on over- or undersocialization of various parent-child relationships on boys and girls, however, has not been pursued to any extent since Bronfenbrenner's proposals were made.

There is, in conclusion, some indication that parental warmth and an approach to discipline that emphasizes cognitive structuring and use of the affective relationship are associated with guilt and internalized reactions to transgression, whether measured by mothers' reports or projective techniques. The relation of these parental characteristics to specific measures of resistance to deviation has not been so clearly demonstrated. However, when resistance to deviation is measured in a broader context, such as by Baumrind (1967) or in the research on antisocial aggression, then similar relationships appear.

Parental warmth might contribute to the development of these various aspects of internalization in several ways. A warm or accepting parent is a reliable source of positive reinforcement or reward, and such should be a more effective teacher of internalized attitudes and behaviors than a nonaccepting parent. Expressions of disapproval by a generally accepting parent may be more effective than similar expressions by a nonaccepting parent; in the former case the child has more to lose if approval is withdrawn. An additional possibility is that emotional reactions conditioned to expected or imagined parental approval or disapproval may be stronger for a warm parent, with the result that guilt and other internalized reactions would occur more often after a transgression. An important component of warmth, suggested by the results of Stayton et al. (1971) with infants, may be the extent to which the parent's responsiveness is contingent on signals from the child. This component, however, has not been measured separately or particularly emphasized in research with older children.

Cognitive structuring also contributes to internalization. Conditions which aid in the development of mediating cognitions—rules and expectations about consequences—would seem to help the child control his behavior. The speculations in the previous section about conditioned emotional responses are relevant to the use of the affective relationship in producing internalization. Circumstances in the early parent-child relation that would facilitate the development of conditioned emotional reactions (empathic or otherwise) to parental expressions of approval, disapproval, disappointment, or hurt would make it possible for parents subsequently to use the affective relationship as a powerful instrument for internalization—perhaps too powerful in some cases, with crippling neurotic inhibitions resulting. Since warmth, cognitive structuring, and use of the affective relationship are likely to be positively correlated, especially the first two, it is usually not possible to know the extent to which the separate variables are contributing to the development of internalization.

Parental Modeling of Internalization

The general finding that parents of aggressive children are also overtly aggressive (see section on aggression, for references) is consistent with the results of experimental studies indicating the potency of modeling in relation to self-control or, in this case, its lack. Likewise the results of McCord, McCord, and Gudeman (1960), that mothers of sons who subsequently became alcoholic were more likely to react to crisis situations by evasion, retiring to their rooms, becoming sexually promiscuous, drinking excessively, or ignoring the crisis, suggest a modeling influence.

Consistent with the experimental literature, several studies using direct observation indicate that children will show more imitation of incidental responses that involve no self-denial if parents are nurturant than if they are nonnurturant (Hetherington and Frankie 1967; Mussen and Parker 1965), but there are no studies using direct measurement that have assessed the effects of parental nurturance on imitation of parental resistance to deviation or other forms of self-control. The experimental research using nonparents as models suggests that noncontingent nurturance would be less important than whether the parent is seen as powerful. Hetherington (1965) and Hetherington and Frankie (1967) have shown that children tended to imitate the dominant parent, but again the measures did not involve resistance to deviation.

Summary

1. For infants there is some evidence that maternal sensitivity-acceptance is more highly related to the rudimentary development of obedience and internalization than are more specific disciplinary techniques. Infant characteristics contribute to this relationship as well as maternal characteristics.

2. Internalized reactions to transgressions (self-blame, guilt, and moral

conceptions of right and wrong) in children are correlated with maternal warmth (more strongly for boys than girls) and with disciplinary practices characterized by cognitive structuring (clear statements of expectations, abstract moral principles, and consequences, especially negative consequences to others) and use of the affective relationship (making the child feel badly by describing how badly he is making others feel). Withdrawal of love is not related to internalization. Power-assertive techniques of discipline are associated with an external orientation to transgression in which the child is more concerned about getting caught and punished than with internal reactions. These findings have been demonstrated primarily for middle-class families, and it is difficult to assess the independent contribution of these variables.

3. Resistance to deviation as measured in specific experimental contexts does not relate consistently with parental variables. When considered in a broader context such as ratings in nursery school or as reflected in research on antisocial aggression, the findings are similar to those for reactions to transgressions.

4. Young girls accede to the demands of socialization more readily than boys and may be more subject to oversocialization than boys, but this proposition and its implications need further research.

5. Parental modeling of internalization contributes to the development of internalization in children. Only a few studies provide data on this conclusion.

INDEPENDENCE AND ACHIEVEMENT

Independence

Independence usually includes such characteristics as initiative, self-reliance, and the unaided striving for goals. A person low in independence would be described as conforming, suggestible, and help-seeking. Low independence is not necessarily synonomous with high dependency, although there is clearly some overlap between these two concepts. A child, for example, who is lacking in independence and conforms rather than risk peer or adult disapproval would not necessarily show the attention- or contact-seeking behavior associated with high dependency.

Maternal restrictiveness was found to be related to compliant, submissive, and nonindependent behavior in children by Baldwin et al. (1949), Kagan and Moss (1962), and Watson (1957). Levy (1943) found overprotecting mothers of a dominating type to have nonindependent children. Baumrind (1967, 1971) and Baumrind and Black (1967), however, reported that such variables as maturity demands and firm, consistent control relate positively to independent, self-reliant behavior. This contradiction in results probably reflects, once again, differences in the definition and measurement of restrictiveness. Baumrind's definition is relatively independent of the warmth-hostility dimension, although, as it turned out, the group of parents who had independent children were also warm and accepting, implementing their control with sensitivity to the child's needs, providing explanations, and generally being reasonable in their expectations. Another factor that should be taken into account is that the degree of maternal restrictiveness in Levy's study was extreme, much beyond what is ordinarily found in studies of normal samples.

Since Baumrind (1967) used both direct observation and interview measures, gave some attention to interactional sequences, and reported several dimensions of both parent and child behavior, her study will be described in some detail at this time and will be referred to in subsequent sections because of its relevance to various topics. Three groups of children were selected from a larger group of 110 three- to four-year-old nursery-school children on the basis of fourteen weeks of observation. The six girls and seven boys in group I were rated higher than either of the other two groups on each of the following characteristics: self-reliance, approach to novel or stressful situations with interest and curiosity, confidence, self-control in situations requiring some appropriate restraint, energy level, achievement orientation, cheerful mood, and friendly peer relations. Group II children (seven girls, four boys) when compared to group III children (three girls, five boys) were more passively hostile, guileful, unhappy in mood, vulnerable to stress, and did more careful work. Group III children were more purely impulsive and lacking in self-discipline; they were more cheerful and recovered from expressions of annoyance more quickly than children in group II. Thus, although children in both groups II and III were aggressive and unfriendly toward peers, group II children were inclined to express their aggression more indirectly and were not able to get over their unhappy mood state so readily.

Parent behavior was assessed in three ways: a three-hour unstructured home observation; a forty-minute structured observation (mother only); and father and mother interview. Frequencies of different types of interaction sequences were counted in the home observations, for example, how the parent and child responded to demands from the other person or, more specifically, the number of times the parent was coerced into complying by the child's whining or crying. Data from all three sources were generally in agreement. Parents of group I children (friendly, self-reliant), relative to parents in both other groups, exerted more general control over the child's behavior and did not succumb to the child's "nuisance value"; made more demands for mature, age-appropriate behavior; engaged in more open communication with the child in which reasons were given, the child's opinion was solicited, and open rather than disguised means of influence were used. They were also more nurturant as indicated by a greater use of positive reinforcement and lesser use of punishment, and by the fact that a greater percentage of child-initiated response sequences resulted in satisfaction for the child. Thus the parents' exercise of control and demands for maturity occurred in a context in which the parents encouraged verbal give-and-take, listened to the child's point of view, and occasionally retracted a demand on the basis of the child's expression and provided a generous measure of affection and approval which was to some extent contingent on the child's performance.

Parents of group III children (impulsive, not self-reliant) relative to parents of group II children (unhappy, passively hostile) generally exerted less control and more specifically were less persistent in enforcing demands in the face of the child's opposition and succumbed more to the child's nuisance value. Group III parents also provided fewer maturity demands and showed a trend to be more nurturant (not statistically significant).

Many features of this study were replicated in a subsequent study (Baumrind 1971). In that research, rather than identify groups of children and look for parental correlates, the author identified groups of parents according to a-priori patterns and reported associated characteristics of the children. Some of the main groupings were: authoritarian (arbitrary control administered without consideration of child's point of view), authoritative (firm control but administered in a rational manner, with encouragement of verbal give-and-take with child, generally similar to group I parents in previous study), permissive, and rejecting-neglecting. Boys of authoritative parents, relative to all other boys, were more friendly, cooperative, and achievement-oriented; girls of authoritative parents tended to be more dominant, achievement-oriented, and independent. It is well to keep in mind what Baumrind's studies showed is that a *pattern* of parental characteristics were associated with a *pattern* of child characteristics. One cannot be sure of the relative contribution of the individual parental measures; for example, would high parental control be associated with independence if the parent did not also communicate more openly, solicit the child's opinion, use more positive reinforcement and less punishment, and so on?

Achievement

Achievement involves more than just independent behavior. The person is not merely performing an action without assistance but is trying to do well with respect to a standard of comparison. Achievement behavior involves some degree of internalization of external standards, and one might expect that many of the features thought to facilitate internalization would also be related to an achievement orientation. This seems to be the case, as the following research suggests.

Experimental research has demonstrated that achievement standards in children can be influenced by direct reinforcement and modeling (Bandura and Kupers 1964; Mischel and Liebert 1966). Correspondingly, parental demands and reinforcement of achievement behavior have been shown to be related to various measures of children's achievement motivation. Winterbottom (1958) identified high and low achievement-motivated eight-year-old boys by scoring achievement imagery in stories told to pictures. Mothers of high-achievement boys reported that they had expected various behaviors indicative of both independence and achievement at a younger age, and also that they gave larger and more frequent reinforcements when their sons performed independently and successfully. Rosen and D'Andrade (1959) measured achievement motivation in the same way in nine- to eleven-year-old boys and directly observed parental responses to their sons when the latter were working on achievement tasks. They found parents of high-achievement boys to have higher expectations for their sons; the mothers, especially, of high-achievement boys were more likely to give approval when performance was good and criticize when performance was substandard.

Turning to studies which attempted to measure actual achievement behavior, one finds considerable support for the conclusion that high-achievement behavior is associated with explicit maternal training in such behavior (Baumrind 1967, 1971; Crandall, Preston, and Rabson 1960; d'Heurle, Mellinger and Haggard 1959; Kagan and Moss 1962). Chance (1961), studying a group of intellectually superior first-grade children in a small university community, found the opposite: mothers who reported an earlier age for the Winterbottom independence and achievement items had boys and girls who showed *less* achievement in reading and arithmetic than would be expected in terms of their Stanford-Binet IQ. It is difficult to know what to make of Chance's results. Perhaps other parent-child variables that were not measured would have thrown light on this puzzling finding. At any rate the otherwise consistent trend in a number of studies is that maternal attempts to accelerate developmental skills with appropriate rewards and punishments is associated with achievement motivation and behavior.

Crandall and Battle (1970) reported childhood correlates of two types of adult achievement behavior—academic effort and intellectual effort. The former referred strictly to course-work at school or college and the latter to self-chosen intellectual pursuits outside of school. Adult academic effort was related to help-seeking and proximity-seeking dependency from birth to six years of age. Intellectual effort was not associated with childhood dependency but was positively correlated with maternal independence training at three to six years of age. And for females, adult intellectual effort was associated with low levels of maternal protectiveness and babying at three to ten years of age and high rejection by father reported when the subjects were young adults. Crandall's distinction between academic and intellectual effort is probably an important one, and her findings suggest that school-oriented academic achievement may be more related to needs to obtain adult approval by getting good grades than is the case for the more self-initiated intellectual effort.

There is additional evidence that high achievement may be related to relatively low levels of parental acceptance, especially for girls (Crandall, Dewey, Katkovsky, and Preston 1964; Drews and Teahan 1957; Kagan and Moss 1962). It may not be necessary for mothers to be nurturant in order to be effective models of achievement behavior, a conclusion that is quite consistent with experimental findings reported in the section of internalization. Radin (1971), on the other hand, in an observational study of lower-class mothers and their four-year-old children reported that maternal warmth correlated .46 with a rating of motivation while taking the Stanford-Binet. This correlation was not computed separately for boys and girls, and variation in IQ scores was held constant by partial correlation.

If directly tested sex differences should show that high achievement in girls is related to less nurturant and accepting parental behavior than is the case for boys, one interpretation of such a finding would be that loving, accepting parents have socialized their daughters to accept the prevailing norm and *not* be competitive and achievement-oriented. Daughters of less accepting parents may have had to find rewards through achievement as a substitute for parental acceptance, or perhaps their relatively "unmotherly" mothers were very achievement-oriented themselves and thus provided their daughters with a model. Cultural norms for achievement in women are changing, however, and the relationships between parent-child variables and achievement may change before empirical support for the above relationships can be clearly demonstrated.

Summary

1. The most convincing evidence at this time indicates that independent behavior is associated with a pattern of parent-child interaction in which the parent demands age-appropriate behavior; enforces rules firmly and consistently; encourages, listens to, and is occasionally influenced by communications from the child; and provides a generous measure of affection and approval. It is not possible to assess the relative contribution of these characteristics from the published researches.

2. Achievement behavior in children is related to direct attempts on the part of parents to demand such behavior and to reinforce it.

3. High achievement in girls may be associated with lower than usual levels of parental acceptance.

AGGRESSION

Aggression is behavior whose aim is to hurt or injure a person or object. The injury may be accomplished physically or verbally, as with insults.

Individual differences in activity level which show some stability from early infancy to later childhood have been reported by several authors (Escalona and Heider 1959; Fries and Woolf 1953; Kagan and Moss 1962), and such differences in temperament have frequently been proposed as contributing to the later development of variations in aggressive behavior. Consistent with this data, Thomas, Chess, and Birch (1968) found that children identified as "difficult" in the first two years were more likely than other children subsequently to develop conduct disorders with aggressive features. Prominent characteristics of children labeled difficult were: (1) biological irregularity, especially with respect to sleep, feeding, and elimination cycles; (2) withdrawal and associated expressions of distress to new stimuli, for example, to the first bath or new foods; (3) slow adaptability to change, taking many exposures to new situations before overcoming the initial negative reaction; and (4) a predominance of negative mood, involving a greater readiness to fuss and cry.

Environmental conditions thought to promote the development of aggressive behavior in children are: arbitrary frustrations—especially, perhaps, pain-inducing physical punishments; models of aggressive behavior, especially if the models are powerful and if they are rewarded for their aggression; and the rewards and punishments which follow aggressive responses. See Feshbach (1970) for a comprehensive theoretical and empirical review of the experimental literature bearing on these propositions. Many of the factors previously discussed with respect to internalization are also likely to affect aggressive behavior insofar as learned inhibitions modulate its expression.

Power-Assertive, Punitive Discipline and Child Aggression

Harsh, punitive, power-assertive punishment by parents has been found to be a frequent correlate of aggression in children: in delinquent adolescent males (Andry 1960; Bandura and Walters 1959; Burt 1929; Glueck and Glueck 1950; Hetherington, Stouwie and Ridberg 1971; Jenkins 1966; McCord, McCord, and Zola 1959; Wittman and Huffman 1945); in delinquent adolescent females (Burt 1929; Hetherington et al. 1971; Wittman and Huffman 1945); in preadolescent children (Becker, Peterson, Hellmer, Shoemaker, and Quay 1959; Eron, Walder, Toigo, and Lefkowitz 1963; Martin and Hetherington 1971; McCord, McCord, and Howard 1961; Rosenthal, Finkelstein, Ni, and Robertson 1959; Rosenthal, Ni, Finkelstein, and Berkwits 1962; Siegelman 1966; Winder and Rau 1962); in preschool children (Baumrind 1967, 1971; Becker, Peterson, Luria, Shoemaker, and Hellmer 1962; Hoffman 1960, Sears et al. 1957; Sears et al. 1953). These results held for middle-class as well as lower-class families. Two studies using mother interview data with preschool children failed to find this relationship (Burton, as reported by Yarrow et al. 1968; Sears et al. 1965).

There is a great deal of variation in these studies with respect to measurement procedures (interview, direct observation, peer ratings, ratings from case notes), the number of different measures of aggression used, toward whom aggression was directed (parents, siblings, peers at school, teachers, society in general), the range of aggressiveness and severity of parental punishment, the sex of the children, whether sex groups were analyzed separately, and whether measures were obtained for one (usually mother) or both parents. Statistically significant findings were not always obtained for all measures, both sex groups, or for both parents. Nevertheless, overall this body of research provides impressive evidence that harshness of parental punishment is likely to be associated with child aggression. This conclusion is somewhat more strongly supported for boys than girls. First, there are simply more studies with separate analyses for boys, and, second, some studies have yielded rather complicated results for girls; for example, both Sears et al. (1953) and Becker et al. (1962) found ratings of maternal punitiveness to be related in a curvilinear fashion to girls' aggression in nursery school or kindergarten.

These results support the theoretical contention that punitive parental discipline serves both as a frustrating instigation to aggression and as an aggressive model. It is of some interest that the empirical relationship tends to hold even when the parental punishment is directed toward aggressive responses, suggesting that the frustration and modeling effects outweigh the strictly punishing effects. The point is worth emphasizing. In naturalistic studies it is difficult to control for other parental characteristics that are correlated with punitiveness of punishment for aggression; for example, harshness of punishment for other behaviors; parental modeling of aggression toward spouse, siblings, and others; low parental acceptance; and the low use of cognitive structuring. Punishment for aggression, then, may be positively correlated with aggression because the effects of these correlated features outweigh the suppressive effects of the punishment. In contrast to the findings in naturalistic studies within the limited confines of the experiment, punishment has been shown to be an effective inhibitor of aggression (Cowan and Walters 1963), even though the frustration and modeling effects are presumably present in that situation too.

Aggressive child behavior, especially if directed toward the parent, is likely to evoke more severe parental responses, so that the observed correlations between the one-sided summary variables probably represent dyadic systems in which there is a reciprocal interchange of aggressivity.

Acceptance-Rejection and Child Aggression

A positive relation between parental nonacceptance and aggression was found in almost all of the studies of delinquents referred to previously and in most of the studies of preadolescent and preschool children where nonacceptance or hostility was measured separately. In addition, studies by Kagan and Moss (1962) and Lesser (1952) (which were not included previously because punitiveness of punishment was not measured) found substantial correlations between maternal rejection and child aggression.

Parental rejection may have some aggression-producing qualities because it is associated with frustrations—the rejecting parent may ignore the young child's expressions of discomfort and thwart his needs for nurturance. Also, as mentioned in the section on internalization, nonacceptance probably means that the parent is a poor source of positive reinforcements or rewards, which should result in the parent being less effective as a teacher of self-restraint, whether for the control of aggression or for any other socially disapproved behavior. And the other side of the coin—aggressive, disobedient children are not as "likeable" as more well-behaved children and are likely to elicit more critical reactions.

Permissiveness-Restrictiveness and Child Aggression

For adolescent delinquents the research findings are reasonably clear: parents of delinquents are likely to be lax, meaningful, and inconsistent in providing supervision and discipline (Bandura and Walters 1959; Glueck and Glueck 1950; McCord et al. 1959). All of these authors, however, report that for some families a pattern of lax discipline by mothers is paired with rigid, overly restrictive discipline by fathers. For preadolescents (six to thirteen years of age) there is some overall support for the relationship (Lesser 1952; Levy 1943; McCord et al. 1961; Rosenthal et al. 1959) but with a few inconsistencies. Thus, McCord et al. (1961) found either maternal undercontrol or overcontrol to be associated with aggression in sons; Becker et al. (1959) found lax enforcement by father, but not by mother, to be correlated with aggression; Martin and Hethering-ton (1971) found only a nonsignificant trend for mothers of aggressive boys to be more permissive than mothers of nondeviant boys and no trends for fathers of boys or for either parent of girls.

At the preschool level the results provide less support for a relationship between parental permissiveness and aggression. Yarrow et al. (1968) in their summary of four studies that used similar methodology with preschool children (their study; their analysis of Burton's [1959] data; Sears et al. 1957; Sears et al. 1965) show that various forms of parental permissive-ness measured by parent interview show only spotty and generally in-significant relationships to child aggression directed at various targets. Nor did Baumrind and Black (1967) find any clear relationship between parent-interview measures of restrictiveness and child aggression. On the other hand, Baumrind (1967, 1971) in two independent studies found parental permissiveness (based on direct observation) to be associated with hostile, resistive, and aggressive behavior in a mixed sample of boys and girls in the first study and for boys only in the second study. As described previously, in the latter two studies extreme groups defined by certain patterns of either child or parental behaviors were used; whereas in the Baumrind and Black study, correlations between pairs of variables were reported for the entire sample.

In conclusion, some relationship between permissiveness and aggression at the older age-levels seems likely, but the evidence is not so clear for the preschool ages. Most of the negative findings at this age level occur in studies in which parental permissiveness is measured by interview, and child aggressiveness and parental permissiveness are not extreme. Further-more, the stability over time of measures of child aggressiveness at this age level is questionable. Some inconsistency probably also results from variations in the definition of permissiveness-restrictiveness, although re-sults from two studies were not included (Becker et al. 1962; Kagan and Moss 1962) because there was clear internal evidence that restrictive-ness correlated substantially with parental hostility. The strongest relation-ship between parental permissiveness and aggression at the preschool age occurs in Baumrind's studies (1967, 1971), which suggests that it is only when permissiveness occurs in combination with other parental characteristics such as low acceptance, low use of cognitive structuring, and high punitiveness that one finds a strong relationship to aggression.

Configurations of Parental Variables and Child Aggression

In most studies of parent-child relations one variable is analyzed at a time; a more promising approach may be to search for configurations of several parental variables that may be more strongly related to a given child characteristic than any single variable. The term "configuration," as used here, does not refer to a profile of means computed separately for a series of variables; rather it means that mothers, for example, are selected to represent a given configuration because *each* mother scored high on each of two variables. Sears et al. (1957) provided a configural analysis of maternal permissiveness for child aggression toward parents. The highest percentage of aggressive children (41.7 for boys and 38.1 for girls) was associated with mothers who were *both* highly permissive *and* highly punitive, and the lowest percentage of aggressive children (3.7 for boys and 13.3 for girls) had mothers who were both low on permissiveness and low on punitiveness. These findings were replicated in a study by Burton (in Yarrow et al. 1968) and replicated for maternal questionnaire measures but not for maternal interview measures by Yarrow et al. (1968). Similar configural results have been obtained for mothers and nine- to twelve-year-old boys by Martin and Hetherington (1971); but results were not significant for mothers and girls, or for fathers with children of either sex. Baumrind did not identify this particular configuration in her 1971 study; and in her 1967 study configurations were determined by child rather than parental characteristics. Nevertheless, the 1967 study suggests indirectly that permissiveness combined with either low acceptance or punitive punishment is associated with child aggressiveness.

Configurations between parents have also been explored. McCord et al. (1959) rated parental characteristics of five- to thirteen-year-old boys from extensive information gathered in the Cambridge-Somerville Youth Study. The percentages of boys *later* convicted of crimes as a function of a four-fold classification of mother and father, loving and rejecting, were: loving mother and loving father, 32 percent; loving mother and rejecting father, 36 percent; rejecting mother and loving father, 46 percent; rejecting mother and rejecting father, 70 percent. These results suggest that one loving parent (especially if it is mother) can considerably counteract a rejecting parent. The effect of rejection does not appear to be additive in this data: two rejecting parents appear to have more than twice the effect of one rejecting parent. Likewise, if father was rated as neglecting and mother was rated as loving, 47 percent of the boys were subsequently convicted of crimes, but if father was neglecting and mother was non-loving, 80 percent were so convicted.

McCord et al. (1961) reported configural analyses in their study of aggressive (but nonconvicted), assertive, and nonaggressive boys. Fifty-four percent of the aggressive boys had a family in which both parents imposed low demands (permissive), and one parent was punitive and the other was not; whereas 14 percent of the nonaggressive boys had a family configuration of this kind.

Configurations based on two or, at most, three variables were used in the above studies. Martin and Hetherington (1971) performed a cluster-analytic procedure (McQuitty 1967) using twelve ratings obtained from interviews with fathers and mothers on a sample of seventy-three boys composed of subsamples of aggressive, withdrawn, mixed (aggressive *and* withdrawn), and nondeviant boys as determined by peer and teacher ratings. A four-group cluster solution yielded one group which was composed of 59 percent of the aggressive boys. This group, relative to the group in which the largest percentage (63) of the nondeviant boys fell, was characterized by punitive punishment for both father and mother, inconsistency of punishment for both father and mother, low acceptance by mother only, and high reported aggression toward father, mother, and peers.

A further clustering led to a subdivision of this cluster into one which was characterized by *high* father acceptance and otherwise average ratings for father, mothers who were low on rule enforcement (permissive), punitive and inconsistent in punishment, and nonaccepting. The boys in this cluster were reported to be highly aggressive toward mother but not toward father. This configuration suggests a family in which the mother-son dyad is largely involved in the maintenance of the son's aggression, perhaps with some general acceptance of aggressive behavior by a friendly father. In the other cluster resulting from the subdivision of the first cluster, both parents were clearly involved in the dynamics of aggressive interaction: father and mother were both nonaccepting, punitive, and inconsistent in punishment; and the son was highly aggressive toward both parents. The potential value of the configural approach is illustrated by these findings. In single-variable analyses fathers of aggressive sons had a mean rating on acceptance only slightly and nonsignificantly lower than fathers of nondeviant boys. The configural analyses suggest that low paternal acceptance is associated with aggression in some boys, and high paternal acceptance is associated with aggression in other boys. This latter possibility is consistent with results of Winder and Rau (1962), who used a similar peer-rating procedure on the same age group and found that fathers of aggressive boys were high on demonstration of affection and expectation of fulfillment of a masculine role as measured by a parent self-report questionnaire.

Parental Modeling of Aggression

Aggressive parents tend to have aggressive children. Bandura and Walters (1959) and Becker et al. (1959) reported that parents of aggressive children were themselves given to explosive expressions of anger. And Glueck and Glueck (1950) and McCord and McCord (1958) report a high incidence of crime and antisocial behavior in the siblings and parents of adolescent delinquents. Interparental conflict, another source of modeled aggression, has also been found to be high in parents of delinquents (Bennett 1960; Glueck and Glueck 1950; McCord, McCord, and Gudeman 1960; Nye 1958).

Hetherington and Frankie (1967) assessed parental conflict, dominance, and warmth in a modified revealed-differences test, and measured the child's imitation of the mother's and father's behavior in a game-playing session. Children tended to imitate a dominant, hostile parent when the home was high in conflict and when both parents were low in warmth. If either interparental conflict was low or the other parent was warm, the imitation of the hostile, dominant parent decreased. Imitation of a hostile, dominant parent occurred more frequently in boys than girls and more frequently for boys if the hostile, dominant model was the father. Although the responses imitated in this experiment were not aggressive in nature, the results do indicate conditions under which an aggressive parent is more likely to be imitated generally, and would probably include the imitation of aggressive responses.

Summary

1. Individual differences in early infancy in activity level and general irritability may predispose the young child toward the development of aggressive behavior. The extent to which this happens will depend, in part, on the character of the parent-child interaction.

2. Parental punitiveness and nonacceptance have consistently shown a positive relationship to child aggression at all age levels. These relationships probably reflect dyadic systems in which there is a reciprocal interchange of aggression.

3. Parental permissiveness or laxity is generally related to aggression in adolescents and six- to twelve-year-olds, but the relationship is less clear for preschool children. The occasional association of aggression with parental overcontrol may occur when the parent is also high on hostility and administers the control in a rigid, insensitive fashion.

4. Configural studies may yield insights into the family dynamics of aggression not obtained by single variable analyses. Configurations which combine permissiveness and punitiveness either within the same parent or between parents are especially likely to be associated with aggression. Child aggression may be maintained largely by mother-child interaction in one family but by both mother-child and father-child interaction in another family. The relation of parent-child variables to child aggression may be obscured if these family configurations are ignored by an averaging process which lumps all families together.

5. Aggression is likely to be modeled by parents of aggressive children in the form of antisocial acts and interparent conflict.

WITHDRAWN-NEUROTIC BEHAVIOR

In this section parent-child interaction correlates of withdrawn-inhibited behavior and to a lesser extent of neurotic and psychosomatic symptoms will be considered. It is not meant to be a comprehensive survey of all forms of psychopathology.

Permissiveness-Restrictiveness and Withdrawal

Several studies have found that withdrawn-inhibited, or neurotic children experience greater and more consistent parental restrictiveness than aggressive or delinquent children (Bennett 1960; Hewitt and Jenkins 1946; Lewis 1954; McCord et al. 1961; Rosenthal et al. 1959; Rosenthal et al. 1962). There have been a number of exceptions. Becker et al. (1959) and Becker et al. (1962) did not find parental restrictiveness to correlate with child personality problems; Bandura (1960) found no difference in parental obedience demands and restrictiveness between six- to ten-year-old inhibited and aggressive boys; and Martin and Hetherington (1971) found no relationship between ratings of restrictiveness for either parent and withdrawal in nine- to twelve-year-old boys or girls. In the latter study a special attempt was made to have ratings of restrictiveness be independent of parental hostility. Horowitz (1944), using the same data pool as Hewitt and Jenkins, failed to replicate their findings when greater control was introduced over such factors as low intelligence and physical disability. With the exception of McCord et al. (1961), the studies with positive results did not include a control group of normal or nondeviant children; so that even in the older studies with positive results there was little direct evidence that parents of withdrawn-neurotic children were more restrictive than parents of nondeviant children. To the extent that Baumrind's (1967) unhappy, passively hostile group of children included a substantial proportion of children destined to become inhibited-neurotic (a rather tenuous assumption), the findings of that study point in the opposite direction: parents of such children were *less* restrictive than were parents of well-adjusted children.

Acceptance-Rejection and Withdrawal

Findings in several of the above studies suggest that the parents, especially the father of the withdrawn child, are critical and nonaccepting of the child and frequently are somewhat withdrawn or neurotic themselves (Becker et al. 1959; Hewitt and Jenkins 1946; Rosenthal et al. 1962).

The role of parental acceptance in personality disorders is further shown in studies of children with psychosomatic disorders. Garner and Wenar (1959) compared directly observed mother-child interaction of a group of children suffering from a variety of psychosomatic disorders (bronchial asthma, rheumatoid arthritis, ulcerative colitis, peptic ulcer, and atopic eczema) with another group in which the children suffered from a chronic illness (polio, congenital cardiac disease, nephrosis, or hemophilia). Interaction in the psychosomatic group was characterized by a general climate of negative entanglement and irritability in which neither person could leave the other alone. The mother tended to compete with and dominate the child. Interaction in the chronic illness group was generally more positive. The use of this kind of control group increases the confidence with which one can conclude that the mothers' reactions in the psychosomatic group were not just secondary responses to a chronically incapacitated child.

Block, Jennings, Harvey, and Simpson (1964) reported rather similar characteristics for mother-child interaction for asthmatic children who had low allergic predisposition relative to a comparison group in which the children had a high allergic predisposition to asthma. The results thus suggest that when allergic predisposition is low, parent-child relations contribute more to the development of asthma than when it is high, and that maternal criticism and rejection are prominent in the interaction.

Low self-esteem is a frequent accompaniment of neurotic-inhibited behavior. Coopersmith (1967) studied maternal correlates of self-esteem in sons by means of an interview and a questionnaire. Mothers of high-esteem boys were found to have high self-esteem themselves, be more satisfied with the father's child-rearing practices, have less conflict with the father, have a more friendly, mutually satisfying relationship with her son, demand higher standards of performance, enforce rules and demands with consistency and firmness, use reasoning and discussion instead of arbitrary, punitive discipline, and use more rewards and less punishment in training the child.

High self-esteem children were also found to have higher IQs, to be more well-formed and physically coordinated, to come less often from broken homes, and to have a strong but nonsignificant tendency to come from higher socioeconomic backgrounds. All of these factors may well have contributed to self-esteem and are thus confounded with the mother-child measures. Nevertheless, the results are of considerable interest, especially since the findings involving firm and consistent rule-enforcement parallel similar characteristics found by Baumrind (1967) in mothers of well-adjusted preschool children. Most of the other characteristics are generally indicative of a lack of maternal acceptance of the child with low self-esteem. This particular maternal correlate of low self-esteem was also found by Sears (1970); namely, low maternal warmth when the children (boys or girls) were age five predicted low self-esteem at age twelve.

A relationship between sex of parent and nonacceptance of the withdrawn boy was shown in a recent study by Martin and Hetherington (1971). Fathers of withdrawn nine- to twelve-year-old boys were found to be less accepting than fathers of either nondeviant or aggressive boys; mothers, on the other hand, were as accepting of withdrawn boys as they were of nondeviant boys and were least accepting of aggressive boys. Mothers of withdrawn girls were less accepting than mothers of nondeviant girls, and fathers showed no difference in relative acceptance. These results suggest that low acceptance by the same sex parent and at least average acceptance by the opposite sex parent accompany withdrawal in children. Perhaps dislike by the same sex parent exerts an especially crippling effect on the self-confidence and assertiveness of children.

The correlation between parental nonacceptance and child withdrawal no doubt reflects an interactive process. The child's withdrawn, inhibited behavior may provoke dislike in the parent, especially in the case of fathers of withdrawn boys. How parental nonacceptance, a loose term that covers a variety of critical behaviors, and child responses interact in a developmental sequence to produce the observed associations with personality disorders has not been studied in any detail.

High Restrictiveness-Low Acceptance and Withdrawal

Becker (1964), in his previous review of the literature, concluded that restrictiveness on the part of an accepting parent was associated with submissive nonaggressiveness; whereas restrictiveness by a nonaccepting parent was associated with more conflicted and neurotic child behavior. The first relationship would seem to be contraindicated by Baumrind's (1967) finding of high restrictiveness and high acceptance being related to independence and appropriate assertiveness. As indicated in an earlier section, parental overprotection combined with acceptance does seem to be associated with submissive and dependent child behavior. In addition, Jenkins (1966) and Rosenthal et al. (1959) found anxious, phobic, and obsessional children to have a higher proportion of infantilizing and protective mothers than was the case for comparison groups of aggressive or delinquent children. Overprotection, however, probably includes an anxious involvement and concern about the child's welfare and a tendency to reward dependency overtures not subsumed under high restrictiveness. Sears (1961) provided some partial support for the second relationship. Mothers, rated from interviews as both restrictive and punishing when their sons were age five, had sons at age twelve who reported themselves to be inclined toward self-aggression (self-punishment, suicidal tendencies, and accident-proneness). However, Sears did not report on the relationship between low maternal warmth (as distinguished from punishing) combined with restrictiveness and later self-aggression. And Martin and Hetherington (1971) did not find a configural pattern of high parental restrictiveness and low parental acceptance to be associated with withdrawal in children.

That low acceptance should be associated with low restrictiveness in aggressive children and with high restrictiveness in neurotic children is an intuitively appealing hypothesis, and it is puzzling that research does not provide more support for the idea. The most that the evidence seems to suggest is that a configuration of low acceptance and intermediate control (higher than for parents of aggressive children but lower than for parents of normal children) is characteristic of the parent of the neurotic-inhibited child. Again, perhaps one is asking too much of the noninteractively oriented methodology. Parents of neurotic-inhibited children may wind up with low ratings on restrictiveness because their inhibited child is conforming, obedient, and does not test limits. The parent, accordingly, reports that he rarely has to set or enforce rules.

Mother Dominance and Withdrawal in Boys

Hetherington (1965) and Hetherington and Frankie (1967) have shown that children are more likely to imitate the dominant parent regardless of the sex of the parent. The boy who imitates or identifies with a dominant mother may thus acquire some of the passivity associated with femininity in our society. Hetherington et al. (1971) did find high mother-dominance accompanied by no conflict with mother and some conflict with father for neurotic-delinquent males, and father dominance for male delinquents who were free of neurotic conflict. Martin and Hetherington (1971) likewise found withdrawn nine- to twelve-year-old boys to come from mother-dominant homes more often than nondeviant or aggressive boys. A cluster analysis of the Martin and Hetherington data yielded a cluster which included 67 percent of the withdrawn boys. This cluster was characterized by mother dominance, low father-acceptance, and *low* restrictiveness by both parents but especially father. For boys, these results suggest that at least one form of withdrawal is associated with a close and relatively warm relationship with a dominant mother and a lack of closeness with a critical, nonaccepting, and somewhat remote or uninvolved father.

Power-Assertive Versus Love-Oriented Discipline and Withdrawal

It is a common assumption, especially within the framework of psychoanalytic theory, that many neurotic individuals have an especially severe conscience or superego. Since love-oriented approaches to discipline have been found to be associated with guilt and internalized reactions to transgression, one might expect that parents of neurotic-inhibited children would more often use this approach, or would *less* often use power-assertive techniques. Actually, there is not much support for such a relationship. Although several studies have found that parents of aggressive or delinquent boys used more power-assertive forms of discipline than parents of boys with personality disorders, the lack of a normal control group in these studies renders interpretation difficult. Hetherington et al. (1971) did include a normal control group and found parents of neurotic delinquents to be *more* power-assertive than parents of nondelinquents and not to be different from parents of psychopathic or social delinquents in this regard. To the extent that use of physical punishment is an important component of power assertion, then the study of Becker et al. (1959) does not support the expected relationship. And for fathers, Becker et al. (1962) found the opposite—positive correlations between measures of paternal use of physical punishment and measures of personality problems and hostile-withdrawal for both boys and girls. When the cluster extracted from the Martin and Hetherington data composed primarily of withdrawn boys was further subdivided, a cluster emerged that was characterized by a punitive (power-assertive), inconsistent, nonaccepting, and permissive father and a very nonpunitive, dominant mother. Research, then, does not support a negative relationship between parental power assertion and withdrawn-neurotic behavior; if anything, the opposite may be true. One interpretation of these results is that guilt and internalized reactions to transgressions are not such common accompaniments of the neurotic-inhibited pattern as commonly assumed.

Summary

1. Despite earlier conclusions to the contrary, parental restrictiveness shows no consistent relationship to withdrawn-neurotic behavior.

2. Parental nonacceptance shows a generally strong relationship to withdrawn-neurotic behavior and to psychosomatic disorders in children. Fathers are more likely to be nonaccepting of withdrawn boys than are mothers.

3. A combination of high restrictiveness and low acceptance was not found to be consistently related to withdrawn-neurotic behavior.

4. Withdrawn-neurotic boys are likely to come from mother-dominant homes. A common pattern, then, for withdrawn boys may be a remote and unaccepting father and a dominant mother with whom he has a relatively close relationship.

5. Love-oriented discipline was not found to be related to withdrawn-neurotic behavior, as might be expected if one assumes high guilt and an

internalized orientation in these disorders. In fact, in a few studies there was an opposite trend—parental power-assertive discipline was positively related to withdrawn-neurotic behavior.

COMPREHENSIVE MODELS

Despite some attempt to deal with multivariate findings, the organization of this chapter has led to a piecemeal approach in which much of the research has been presented in terms of a single child-variable and a single parent-variable. Becker and Krug (1964), using the same data reported by Becker et al. (1962), brought together parental and child behaviors in one comprehensive scheme. They did this by ordering both their measures of child behavior (five-year-olds) and parent behavior into two different circumplexes and then correlating these two sets of circumplex-ordered variables with each other. Three sources of child behaviors were treated separately: teacher ratings, mother ratings, and father ratings. The circumplex-ordered variables and their intercorrelations for the interview-based ratings of parental behaviors for boys are shown in table 1, and for the son's behavior derived from parent interviews are shown

TABLE 1. CORRELATIONS AMONG CIRCUMPLEX-ORDERED MOTHER AND FATHER VARIABLES FOR BOYS

Parent Variables	Parent Variables				
	1	2	3	4	5
1. Childrearing anxiety[a]		58	45	22	30
2. Hostility	22		53	19	24
3. Physical punishment	24	49		−16	32
4. Strictness[b]	05	38	71		16
5. Restrictiveness (routines)	11	42	36	56	

NOTE: Correlations are above the diagonal for mothers and below for fathers. (Adapted from Becker and Krug, 1964.)

[a] Includes such characteristics as child-rearing anxiety, high disciplinary friction, little concern for child's welfare, and low parent self-esteem.

[b] This variable is called "strictness" with respect to sex and "aggression" for mothers, and "coercive-strictness" for fathers.

in table 2. Two contrasts between the mother and father data are apparent: for fathers, strictness and restrictiveness are more highly correlated with hostility and physical punishment than for mothers (table 1); and fathers are more likely than mothers to perceive and rate their more withdrawn sons as also more distrusting (not loving, guilt-ridden, maladjusted) and to a lesser extent as more defiant-hostile (table 2).

The correlations between the parental and the child variables are presented in table 3. The potential value of this kind of presentation is that it permits one to see variations in relationships as a function of gradations

TABLE 2.   CORRELATIONS AMONG CIRCUMPLEX-ORDERED SONS'
VARIABLES DERIVED FROM MOTHER AND
FATHER INTERVIEWS

	Son Variables				
Son Variables	*1*	*2*	*3*	*4*	*5*
1. Calm-compliant vs. emotional-rebellious		51	01	—37	—73
2. Submissive vs. dominant	—27		59	10	—36
3. Withdrawn vs. sociable	—31	74		69	25
4. Distrusting vs. loving	—44	59	82		72
5. Defiant-hostile vs. cooperative-responsible	—62	33	56	73	

NOTE: Correlations are above the diagonal for mothers' ratings and below for fathers'. (Adapted from Becker and Krug, 1964.)

TABLE 3.   CORRELATIONS BETWEEN CIRCUMPLEX-ORDERED
PARENTAL AND SONS' VARIABLES

	Mother Ratings of Son				
Mother Variables	*Calm-Compliant*	*Sub-missive*	*With-drawn*	*Distrust-ing*	*Defiant-Hostile*
Childrearing anxiety	—47	—50	—22	13	36
Hostility	—45	—24	04	22	38
Physical punishment	—29	—34	—02	18	31
Strictness	02	—15	—10	—07	—02
Restrictiveness	—03	—03	—20	—20	—34
Father Variables	*Father Ratings of Son*				
Child-rearing anxiety	—32	14	31	34	34
Hostility	—31	04	30	42	46
Physical punishment	—21	23	47	51	31
Strictness	03	21	46	42	21
Restrictiveness	23	—17	17	04	—08

NOTE: Adapted from Becker and Krug, 1964.

in both parental and child behaviors and not to be limited to the myopic view of one parent-variable with one child-variable. Thus, both mother and father hostility can be seen to relate more and more positively to child behavior that becomes more uninhibitedly aggressive and defiant. Restrictiveness shows some tendency to be increasingly negatively correlated with the more direct expressions of aggression for mothers but not for fathers. Withdrawal in boys is found to be related to fathers' hostility and physical punishment but not to mothers' ratings on these variables—a trend also found by Martin and Hetherington (1971) and described in the previous section. This is where the broader picture provided by the circumplex orderings in tables 1 and 2 aids interpretation. The fathers' hostile reactions to their withdrawn sons is consistent with their ratings of these sons as relatively distrusting and defiant, and the correlation between the fathers' strictness and their sons' withdrawal should take into account the fact that paternal strictness correlated .71 with physical punishment. If for fathers their sons' withdrawal is associated with greater distrust and defiance, whether in reality or in terms of the fathers' perceptions, and the same relationship does not hold for mothers, then it is not surprising that withdrawal is associated with punitiveness by fathers but not by mothers.

Overall, the correlations between parental and child variables are low in absolute magnitude; and a similar portrayal of correlations between circumplex-ordered parent and child variables by Baumrind and Black (1967) produced an even weaker and less consistent pattern of relationships. All of the shortcomings of the one-sided summary variable approach discussed at the beginning of the chapter probably contribute to the lack of power in these schemes. Also, correlations computed separately between pairs of variables may not detect configurations of variables that might be related to child behaviors.

An approach to a comprehensive scheme that should provide a more powerful and fine-grained analysis and also should avoid some of the pitfalls of the one-sided summary variable approach, would be one in which the units of measurement and their associated variables were defined in interactional terms (e.g., frequency of parental power-assertive punishment associated with certain preceding and following child responses). Different samples could be used to control for such moderator or situational variables as sex and age of child, family size, sibling position, and social class. Measures need not be limited to just one parent and the child but could include interactional measures involving the three possible dyads in the mother-father-child triad. Thus, dominance and marital discord in the mother-father dyad might enter importantly into some family configurations. A given sample could be analyzed in two ways: (1) a cluster-analytic procedure would indicate the occurrence of naturally occurring configurations of families (not variables) and would not assume that variables were linearly related to one another. Measures of extrafamilial child behavior could either be included as variables in the cluster analyses or the obtained configurations could be related to such measures. (2) For purposes of estimating the separate contribution of various measures of parent-child interaction to extrafamilial child behavior, various statistical procedures could be used, stepwise regression analyses or analyses of covariance, both of which do assume linear relationships among variables.

SEX OF CHILD—SEX OF PARENT

Sex differences have been referred to in the contexts of specific researches previously reviewed. In almost all areas it is common to find a significant association between a parent and a child variable for one sex and not for the other, but, unless a direct test has been made, the temptation should be resisted to conclude from such findings that the sexes differ. A moderate number of such directly tested sex differences can be found sprinkled throughout the literature, but frequently these differences have not been replicated, or differences in the opposite direction have been found in other studies. Under the circumstances many of these differences may well reflect chance effects resulting from testing many dependent variables across a number of studies.

One finding does appear with considerable consistency: young girls seem more amenable to the demands of socialization; they are more obedient and more self-controlled (see the section on internalization, for references). The widespread finding that boys at almost all ages are more aggressive than girls (Mischel 1970, provides a survey of these results) may reflect part of this same pattern.

But what parent-child interactions are related to this difference? There is some evidence that boys receive more physical punishment than girls (Minton et al. 1971; Newson and Newson 1968), and perhaps related to this is the finding that male infants are handled more roughly than girls by mothers (Moss 1967; Yarrow and Pedersen 1971). Although the lesser use of physical punishment suggests that girls may experience more love-oriented socialization techniques, which might account for the earlier development of the internalized responses, sex differences in other aspects of love-oriented discipline have not been consistently found. With respect to maternal affection and warmth, for example, Baumrind (1971), Hatfield et al. (1967), Moss (1967), and Yarrow and Pedersen (1971) reported no sex differences.

Kagan and Moss (1962) found greater consistency in aggressiveness from early childhood to adulthood in boys than girls and proposed that differential acceptance and social reinforcement of aggression in boys relative to girls might account for this difference in consistency. It has, however, been difficult to document differential *parental* responses to aggression in boys and girls. Sears et al. (1957) found that mothers permitted more peer-directed and mother-directed aggression in boys than in girls. But Lambert, Yackley, and Hein (1971), in a study of French-

Canadian and English-Canadian parents, and Minton et al. (1971) found the opposite; Sears et al. (1965) found no differences between the sexes. A more precise examination of parent-child interaction might clarity this issue. If boys, indeed, are generally more extreme in their aggressivity, then they may provoke more extreme parental responses. Sex differences in parental response should be examined in terms of responses to the *same* degree of child provocation. It may also be that the greater aggressiveness and resistiveness to the socialization process on the part of boys is determined as much by genetically influenced differences in temperament as by differences in social learning experiences.

Trends in the data of several studies that used either parent questionnaires or children's reports suggest that, although mothers are generally seen as showing more affection, the opposite sex parent is seen as more benevolent, less strict, and more autonomy-granting than the same sex parent (Droppleman and Schaefer 1963; Emmerich 1959a, b; Kagan 1956; Kagan and Lemkin 1960). This sex of child by sex of parent interaction has been confirmed by a study in which direct measurement of parental responses to tape-recorded presentations of various kinds of child expressions were obtained (Rothbart and Maccoby 1966). Thus, fathers of nursery-school-age boys were more likely to refuse comfort-seeking requests from boys than girls, and vice versa for mothers. The same kind of interaction was found for refusing to meet dependency demands, siding with a baby versus the child, and not permitting aggression toward the parent. Lambert, Yackley, and Hein (1971), using the same procedure as Rothbart and Maccoby, found similar results for French-Canadian parents. Fathers accepted insolence from daughters more readily than from sons, and if a child got into an argument with a guest, the father would tend to take his daughter's side but not his son's. The reverse was true for mothers. Oedipus and Electra are alive and doing reasonably well in the family picture. Of course, a less psychoanalytic explanation in terms of parents conforming to culturally prescribed role-expectations about their relationships with their sons and daughters might apply equally well.

ORDINAL POSITION

The parent-child relationship is likely to be affected by the position of the child in the sibling sequence, with accompanying effects on the child's personality. There is some indication that firstborn females are more likely than later-born females to seek an affiliative relationship with other people when stressed or made anxious (Gerard and Rabbie 1961; Schachter 1959). MacDonald (1969) has argued that the important correlate of being a firstborn is a tendency toward adult-directed dependency with associated tendencies to conform and generally accede to the social expectations of others; his empirical results generally support this interpretation. In studies which have more carefully controlled for family size and sex of sibling by using two-child families, these findings have been extended and also qualified. Thus, when all eight possible sibling combinations in two-child families (firstborn boy with brother, firstborn boy with sister, secondborn boy with brother, and so on) have been compared, it has been shown with some consistency that firstborn boys and firstborn girls with younger brothers are more dependent, conforming, and affiliative than children representing other ordinal position-and-sex-of-sibling combinations (Koch [1955] with six-year-olds, Sampson and Hancock [1967] with adolescents, and Bragge and Allen [1966] with college students). The interaction of later-born siblings with earlier-born may also affect their development. With respect to conformity, for example, both boys and girls who have older sisters may tend to imitate her sex-role-related conformity and thus minimize the more general tendency for secondborns to be less conforming.

These differences associated with ordinal position may result in part from differences in parental response. Thus, Thoman, Leiderman, and Olson (1972) found that mothers of firstborns more generally stimulated and talked to their forty-eight-hour-old infants in the breast feeding situation and were more interfering with their infants' feeding than were mothers of later-borns. At somewhat older age-levels mothers of firstborns have been found to be more attentive (Koch 1954) and more directing (Lasko 1954; Hilton 1967).

In Hilton's study mother-child interaction was directly observed for twenty only children, twenty firstborns, and twenty later-borns. Half of these four-year-olds were boys and half girls, and the firstborns and later-borns were all from two-child families with siblings of the same sex. In a series of puzzle-solving tasks mothers of only and firstborn children were found to be more interfering and directing (e.g., giving twice as many suggestions as mothers of later-borns), to express more overt, physical affection, and to more distinctively associate demonstrations of love with success relative to failure. Only and firstborn children also showed more proximity-seeking and help-seeking dependency toward their mothers than later-borns. These results are consistent with the relation found between maternal overprotection and dependency described in the section on dependency. The greater intrusive directiveness of mothers of only and firstborn children may contribute to their children's dependency (and perhaps to conformity and affiliative needs under stress) by depriving them of the opportunity to develop self-determined goals and practice self-initiated behavior. Likewise the mothers' greater display of affection in association with "correct" behavior may also contribute to the strength of the dependency disposition and to an orientation toward pleasing others rather than pleasing oneself. Interestingly, the four-year-old later-borns in this study praised themselves more than did the firstborns.

SOCIAL CLASS

A more comprehensive review of the literature on social class and child development can be found in the chapter by Deutsch in volume three of this series. Social-class distinctions are usually based on the prestige and income associated with the parents' occupation and the level of parental education. Earlier research, based largely on parent interviews, indicated that middle-class parents showed more warmth, used more reasoning and love-oriented approaches to discipline, and were more permissive. Lower- or working-class parents were more likely to use ridicule, shouting, or physical punishment with their children (Bronfenbrenner 1958; Kohn 1963; Kohn and Carroll 1960; Miller and Swanson 1960; Sears, Maccoby, and Levin 1957). Davis and Havighurst (1946), and Littman, Moore, and Pierce-Jones (1957), however, reported a number of inconsistencies with the above conclusions. More recently, several studies using direct observations of parent-child interaction have generally borne out the findings of the parent-interview studies: white mothers (Minton, Kagan, Levine 1971; Tulkin and Kagan 1972); black mothers (Brophy 1970; Hess and Shipman 1965; Kamii and Radin 1967); mixed sample of lower-class white and black mothers (Bee, Van Egeren, Streissguth, Nyman, and Leckie 1969); and white fathers (Radin 1972). Noteworthy in these observational studies is the strong tendency for a middle- or upper-class mother to verbalize more with her child; to use more complex syntax, longer sentences, and qualifying modifiers; and generally to be more efficient in her teaching strategies.

These class-associated characteristics would seem to be similar to many of the features of parent-child interaction found to be correlated with internalization of parental or social standards. Lower-class families, with their tendency to use power-assertive disciplinary techniques and a minimum of verbal give-and-take, would thus seem to be promoting an external orientation to transgressions and consequences. Such an orientation probably mirrors in part the reality that their lives are more affected than those of middle-class parents by external circumstances over which they have little control. Although there is reason to expect that contemporary American society may be heading toward greater homogenization of values and behaviors as a result of increased mobility and more commonality of experience fostered by such ubiquitous influences as television and movies, these quite consistent research findings indicate that this equalizing process is by no means complete at this time.

AN OVERVIEW

Summary statements of specific empirical findings have been included at the end of each section in the chapter and will not be repeated here. Instead, some broad implications derived from viewing the research as a whole will be presented.

To what extent can the professional reader apply the findings surveyed in this chapter to his or her own work with parents and children? There is, of course, no simple answer to this question. Some of the more strongly supported conclusions will come as no surprise to many readers; other and perhaps more recent findings may at least alert the reader to issues and possible relationships that had not been considered previously.

Several findings served the latter purpose for this reviewer. For example, parental stimulation which is contingent upon the infant's response would seem to be an important contributor to the development of an appropriate balance between attachment and exploration. The interactional "games" that mothers and infants play (mother approaches, infant smiles, mother smiles and vocalizes, infant vocalizes, and so on) may be especially significant in this regard and also for the broader intellectual and social development of the infant. The mother's behavior in this kind of interaction is clearly part of what traditionally has been called maternal warmth. (See chapter 3 of this volume for extended discussion of infant development.)

The quality of the mother-infant interaction during the first year no doubt has some influence on the course of parent-child relations in the next few years, although not enough short-term longitudinal studies have been performed to give much substance to this proposition. It is clear, however, when one picks up the study of parent-child relations at older age-levels that the one-sided summary variable of parental warmth (or acceptance) continues to be a variable of exceptional importance. Non-acceptance is related both to withdrawn-neurotic behavior and to antisocial aggression across a wide age-range. And, acceptance appears to be part of the love-oriented approach to discipline that is associated with internalization. When one considers the severe methodological handicaps associated with the one-sided summary variable approach, the consistency of these empirical findings on acceptance are a tribute to the magnitude and pervasiveness of the role that this aspect of interaction must play in parent-child relations.

This has not been a "how-to-do-it" chapter aimed at instructing either parent or professional consultant in the art of child-rearing. There continues to be a sizable outpouring of books of that kind. Some of the more prominent in recent years have been *Living with Children* by Patterson and Gullion (1968), *Parents Are Teachers* by Becker (1971), *Parents/Children/Discipline* by Madsen and Madsen (1972)—all three of these taking a behavioral or social-learning point of view. *Parent Effectiveness Training* by Gordon (1970) and *Between Parent and Child* by Ginott (1965) derive from a more traditional therapeutic orientation that emphasizes the way feeling expressions are interchanged between parents and children and conflicts are verbally resolved. These books were not considered in the research review because they are not research; that is, they do not provide systematic evidence to support the particular theories and techniques that are presented. Nevertheless, it is of interest that the two somewhat different themes emphasized by these two approaches find a rough parallel in the research literature. The theme of reinforcement management and rule enforcement as a basis for "well-behaved" and "well-adjusted" children emphasized in the social-learning approaches find support in Baumrind's (1967) findings. Sensitivity in responding to the child's needs and the honest expression of the parent's feelings without continual nagging and criticism, as emphasized in the approaches of Gordon and Ginott, is supported by the almost universally found correlation of parental acceptance with the child's general adjustment. It is reassuring to see a growing congruence between research findings and popular, contemporary child-rearing literature.

References

Ainsworth, M. D. S. The development of infant-mother interaction among the Ganda. In B. M. Foss, ed., *Determinants of Infant Behavior*. Vol. 2. London: Metheun; New York: John Wiley, 1963.

———. Patterns of attachment behavior shown by the infant in interaction with his mother. *Merrill-Palmer Quarterly*, 1964, *10*, 51–58.

———. *Infancy in Uganda: Infant Care and the Growth of Love*. Baltimore: Johns Hopkins University Press, 1967.

———. Object relations, dependency, and attachment: a theoretical review of the mother-infant relationship. *Child Development*, 1969, *40*, 969–1025.

———. The development of infant-mother attachment. In B. Caldwell and H. Ricciuti, eds., *Review of Child Development Research*. Vol. 3. Chicago: University of Chicago Press, 1973.

Ainsworth, M. D. S. & Bell, S. M. Some contemporary patterns of mother-infant interaction in the feeding situation. In J. A. Ambrose, ed., *Stimulation in Early Infancy*. London: Academic Press, 1969.

Ainsworth, M. D. S., Bell, S. M., & Stayton, D. J. Individual differences in strange-situation behavior of one-year olds. In H. R. Schaffer, ed., *The Origins of Human Social Relations*. London: Academic Press, 1971.

Ainsworth, M. D. S., Bell, S. M., & Stayton, D. J. Individual differences in the development of some attachment behaviors. *Merrill-Palmer Quarterly,* in press.

Allinsmith, W. Moral standards: II. The learning of moral standards. In D. R. Miller & G. E. Swanson, eds., *Inner Conflict and Defense.* New York: Holt, Rinehart, and Winston, 1960.

Allinsmith, W. & Greening, T. C. Guilt over anger as predicted from parental discipline: a study of superego development. *American Psychologist,* 1955, *10,* 320 (abstract).

Andry, R. G. *Delinquency and Parental Pathology.* London: Metheun, 1960.

Antonovsky, H. F. A contribution to research in the area of the mother-child relationship. *Child Development,* 1959, *30,* 37–51.

Aronfreed, J. The nature, variety, and social patterning of moral responses to transgression. *Journal of Abnormal and Social Psychology,* 1961, *63,* 223–240.

————. The internalization of social control through punishment: experimental studies of the role of conditioning and the second signal system in the development of conscience. *Proceedings of the Eighteenth International Congress of Psychology,* Moscow, 1966.

————. *Conduct and Conscience.* New York: Academic Press, 1968.

Aronfreed, J. & Paskal, V. Altruism, empathy, and the conditioning of positive affect. Manuscript, University of Pennsylvania, 1965 (also described in Aronfreed, 1968.

————. The development of sympathetic behavior in children: an experimental test of a two-phase hypothesis. Manuscript. University of Pennsylvania, 1966 (also described in Aronfreed, 1968).

Aronfreed, J. & Reber, A. Internalized behavioral suppression and the timing of social punishment. *Journal of Personality and Social Psychology,* 1965, *1,* 3–16.

Aronson, E. & Carlsmith, J. M. Effect of the severity of threat on the devaluation of forbidden behavior. *Journal of Abnormal and Social Psychology,* 1963, *66,* 584–588.

Arsenian, J. M. Young children in an insecure situation. *Journal of Abnormal and Social Psychology,* 1943, *38,* 225–249.

Baldwin, A. L. The effect of home environment on nursery school behavior. *Child Development,* 1949, *20,* 49–61.

Baldwin, A. L., Kalhorn, J., & Breese, F. H. Patterns of parent behavior. *Psychological Monograph,* 1945, *58,* No. 3.

————. The appraisal of parent behavior. *Psychological Monograph,* 1949, *63,* No. 4.

Bandura, A. Relationship of family patterns to child behavior disorders. Progress Report, 1960, Stanford University, Project No. M-1734, U. S. Public Health Service.

————. *Principles of Behavior Modification.* New York: Holt, Rinehart and Winston, 1969.

Bandura, A., Grusec, J. E. & Menlove, F. L. Some determinants of self-monitoring reinforcement systems. *Journal of Personality and Social Psychology,* 1967, *5,* 449–455.

Bandura, A. & Huston, A. C. Identification as a process of incidental learning. *Journal of Abnormal and Social Psychology,* 1961, *63,* 311–318.

Bandura, A. & Kupers, C. J. The transmission of patterns of self-reinforcement through modeling. *Journal of Abnormal and Social Psychology,* 1964, *69,* 1–9.

Bandura, A. & Mischel, W. Modification of self-imposed delay of reward through exposure to live and symbolic models. *Journal of Personality and Social Psychology,* 1965, *2,* 698–705.

Bandura, A. & Perloff, B. Relative efficacy of self-monitored and externally imposed reinforcement systems. *Journal of Personality and Social Psychology,* 1967, *7,* 111–116.

Bandura, A., Ross, D., & Ross, S. A. Imitation of film-mediated aggressive models. *Journal of Abnormal and Social Psychology,* 1963, *66,* 3–11.

Bandura, A. & Walters, R. H. *Adolescent Aggression.* New York: Ronald, 1959.

Bandura, A. & Whalen, C. K. The influence of antecedent reinforcement and divergent modeling cues on patterns of self-reward. *Journal of Personality and Social Psychology,* 1966, *3,* 373–382.

Baumrind, D. Child care practices anteceding three patterns of preschool behavior. *Genetic Psychology Monographs,* 1967, *75,* 43–83.

————. Current patterns of parental authority. *Developmental Psychology Monograph,* 1971, *4* (no. 1, part 2).

Baumrind, D. & Black, A. E. Socialization practices associated with dimensions of competence in preschool boys and girls. *Child Development,* 1967, *38,* 291–327.

Becker, W. C. Consequences of parental discipline. In M. L. Hoffman and L. W. Hoffman, eds., *Review of Child Development Research.* Vol. 1. New York: Russell Sage Foundation, 1964.

————. *Parents Are Teachers.* Champaign, Ill.: Research Press, 1971.

Becker, W. C. & Krug, R. S. A circumplex model for social behavior in children. *Child Development,* 1964, *35,* 371–396.

Becker, W. C., Peterson, D. R., Hellmer, L. A., Shoemaker, D. J., & Quay, H. C. Factors in parental behavior and personality as related to problem behavior in children. *Journal of Consulting Psychology,* 1959, *23,* 107–118.

Becker, W. C., Peterson, D. R., Luria, Z., Shoemaker, D. J., & Hellmer, L. A. Relations of factors derived from parent-interview ratings to behavior problems of five-year-olds. *Child Development,* 1962, *33,* 509–535.

Beckwith, L. Relationships between attributes of mothers and their infants' IQ scores. *Child Development,* 1971, *42,* 1083–1097.

————. Relationships between infants' social behavior and their mothers' behavior. *Child Development,* 1972, *43,* 397–411.

Bee, H. L., Van Egeren, L. F., Streissguth, A. P., Nyman, B. A., & Leckie, M. S. Social class differences in maternal teaching strategies and speech patterns. *Developmental Psychology,* 1969, *1,* 726–734.

Bell, R. Q. A reinterpretation of the direction of effects in studies of socialization. *Psychological Review,* 1968, *75,* 81–95.

Bell, S. M. The development of the concept of object as related to infant-mother attachment. *Child Development,* 1970, *41,* 291–311.

Beller, E. K. Exploratory studies of dependency. *Transactions of New York Academy of Science,* 1959, *21,* 414–426.

Bennett, I. *Delinquent and Neurotic Children: A Comparative Study.* New York: Basic Books, 1960.

Block, J., Jennings, P. H., Harvey, E., & Simpson, E. Interaction between allergic potential and psychopathology in childhood asthma. *Psychosomatic Medicine,* 1964, *26,* 307–320.

Bowlby, J. The nature of the child's tie to his mother. *International Journal of Psycho-Analysis,* 1958, *39,* 350–373.

————. *Attachment and loss.* Vol. I, *Attachment.* London: Hogarth: New York: Basic Books, 1969.

Bragge, B. W. E. & Allen, V. L. Ordinal position and conformity. Paper presented at the meeting of the American Psychological Association, New York, September, 1966.

Bronfenbrenner, U. Socialization and social class through time and space. In E. E. Maccoby, T. M. Newcomb, & E. L. Hartley, eds. *Readings in Social Psychology.* York: Holt, Rinehart and Winston, 1958.

————. Some familial antecedents of responsibility and leadership in adolescents. In L. Petrullo & B. M. Bass, eds., *Leadership and Interpersonal Behavior.* New York: Holt, Rinehart and Winston, 1961.

Brophy, J. E. Mothers as teachers of their own preschool children: the influence of sociometric status and task structure on teaching specificity. *Child Development,* 1970, *14,* 79–97.

Burt, C. *The Young Delinquent.* New York: Appleton, 1929.

Burton, R. V. Some factors related to resistance to temptation in four-year-old children. Doctoral dissertation, Harvard University, 1959.

Burton, R. V., Maccoby, E. E., & Allinsmith, W. Antecedents of resistance to temptation in four-year-old children. *Child Development*, 1961, *32*, 689–710.

Caldwell, B. M. Mother-infant interaction in monomatric and polymatric families. *American Journal of Orthopsychiatry*, 1962, *32*, 340–341.

———. The effects of infant care. In M. L. Hoffman & L. W. Hoffman, eds., *Review of Child Development Research*. Vol. 1. New York: Russell Sage Foundation, 1964.

Caldwell, B. M., Wright, C., Honig, R., & Tannenbaum, J. Infant day care and attachment. *American Journal of Orthopsychiatry*, 1970, *40*, 397–412.

Casler, L. Maternal deprivation: a critical review of the literature. *Monographs of the Society for Research in Child Development*, 1961, *26*, no. 2.

Chance, J. E. Independence training and first graders' achievement. *Journal of Consulting Psychology*, 1961, *25*, 149–154.

Cheyne, J. A. Some parameters of punishment affecting resistance to deviation and generalization of a prohibition. *Child Development*, 1971a, *42*, 1249–1261.

———. Punishment and reasoning in the development of self-control. In R. D. Parke, ed., *Recent Trends in Social Learning Theory*. New York: Academic Press, 1971b.

Cheyne, J. A. & Walters, R. H. Timing of punishment, intensity of punishment and cognitive structure in resistance-to-deviation. *Journal of Experimental Child Psychology*, 1967, *7*, 231–244.

Coates, B., Anderson, E. P., & Hartup, W. W. Interrelations in the attachment behavior of human infants. *Developmental Psychology*, 1972, *6*, 218–230.

Coopersmith, S. *The Antecedents of Self-Esteem*. San Francisco: Freeman, 1967.

Cowan, P. A. & Walters, R. H. Studies of reinforcement of aggression: I. Effects of scheduling. *Child Development*, 1963, *34*, 543–551.

Cox, F. N. & Campbell, D. Young children in a new situation with and without their mothers. *Child Development*, 1968, *39*, 123–131.

Crandall, V. C. Reinforcement effects of adult reactions and nonreactions on children's achievement expectations. *Child Development*, 1963, *34*, 335–354.

Crandall, V. C. & Battle, E. S. The antecedents and adult correlates of academic and intellectual achievement effort. In J. P. Hill, ed., *Minnesota Symposia on Child Psychology*. Vol. 4. Minneapolis: University of Minnesota Press, 1970.

Crandall, V. C., Good, S., & Crandall V. J. The reinforcement effects of adult reactions and nonreactions on children's achievement expectations: a replication study. *Child Development*, 1964, *35*, 485–497.

Crandall, V. J., Dewey, R., Katkovsky, W., & Preston, A. Parents' attitudes and behaviors and grade school children's achievement development. *Journal of Genetic Psychology*, 1964, *104*, 53–66.

Crandall, V. J., Preston, A., & Rabson, A. Maternal reactions and the development of independence and achievement behavior in young children. *Child Development*, 1960, *31*, 243–251.

Davis, A. & Havighurst, R. J. Social class and color differences in child-rearing. *American Sociological Review*, 1946, *11*, 698–710.

Deur, J. L. & Parke, R. D. Resistance to extinction and continuous punishment in humans as a function of partial reward and partial punishment training. *Psychonomic Science*, 1968, *13*, 91–92.

———. Effects of inconsistent punishment on aggression in children. *Developmental Psychology*, 1970, *2*, 403–411.

Deutsch, C. P. Social class and child development. In B. M. Caldwell and H. N. Ricciuti, eds., *Review of Child Development Research*. Vol. 3. Chicago: University of Chicago Press, 1973.

d'Heurle, A., Mellinger, J., & Haggard, E. Personality, intellectual, and achievement patterns in gifted children. *Psychological Monographs*, 1959, 73 (whole no. 483).

Drews, E. M. & Teahan, J. E. Parental attitudes and academic achievement. *Journal of Clinical Psychology*, 1957, *13*, 328–332.

Droppleman, L. F. & Schaefer, E. S. Boys' and girls' reports of maternal and paternal behavior. *Journal of Abnormal and Social Psychology*, 1963, *67*, 648–654.

Eisenberg, L. School phobia: a study in the communication of anxiety. *American Journal of Psychiatry*, 1958, *114*, 712–718.

Emmerich, W. Parental identification in young children. *Genetic Psychology Monographs*, 1959a, *60*, 257–308.

———. Young children's discriminations of parent and child roles. *Child Development*, 1959b, *30*, 404–420.

———. Continuity and stability in early social development, *Child Development*, 1964, *35*, 311–332.

———. Continuity and stability in early social development: II. Teacher's ratings. *Child Development*, 1966, *37*, 17–27.

Eron, L. D., Walder, L. O., Toigo, R., & Lefkowitz, M. M. Social class, parental punishment for aggression, and child aggression. *Child Development*, 1963, *34*, 849–867.

Escalona, S. K. & Heider, G. *Prediction and Outcome*. New York: Basic Books, 1959.

Etzel, B. C. & Gewirtz, J. L. Experimental modification of caretaker-maintained high-rate operant crying in a 6- and 20-week-old infant (Infans tyrannotearus): extinction of crying with reinforcement of eye contact and smiling. *Journal of Experimental Child Psychology*, 1967, *5*, 303–317.

Fantz, R. L. The origin of form perception. *Scientific American*, 1961, *204*, 66–72.

Feshbach, S. Aggression. In P. H. Mussen, ed., *Carmichael's Manual of Child Psychology*. New York: John Wiley, 1970.

Festinger, L. *A Theory of Cognitive Dissonance*. Stanford: Stanford University Press, 1957.

Fleener, D. E. & Cairns, R. B. Attachment behavior in human infants. *Developmental Psychology*, 1970, *2*, 215–223.

Freedman, D. G. Heredity control of early social behavior. In B. M. Foss, ed., *Determinants of Infant Behavior*. Vol. 3. New York: John Wiley, 1965.

Freedman, J. L. Long term behavioral effects of cognitive dissonance. *Journal of Experimental Social Psychology*, 1965, *1*, 145–155.

Fries, M. E. & Woolf, P. J. Some hypotheses on the role of the cogenital activity types in personality development. *Psychoanalytic Study of the Child*, 1953, *8*, 48–62.

Gallimore, R., Tharp, R. G., Kemp, B. Positive reinforcing function of "negative attention." *Journal of Experimental Child Psychology*, 1969, *8*, 140–146.

Garner, A. M. & Wenar, C. *The Mother-Child Interaction in Psychosomatic Disorders*. Urbana: University of Illinois Press, 1959.

Gerard, H. B. & Rabbie, J. M. Fear and social comparison. *Journal of Abnormal and Social Psychology*, 1961, *62*, 586–592.

Gewirtz, J. L. The course of infant smiling in four child-rearing environments in Israel. In B. M. Foss, ed., *Determinants of Infant Behavior*. Vol. 3. New York: John Wiley, 1965.

———. Levels of conceptual analysis in environmental-infant interaction research. *Merrill-Palmer Quarterly*, 1969, *15*, 7–47.

Gewirtz, J. L. & Baer, D. M. The effect of brief social deprivation on behaviors for a social reinforcer. *Journal of Abnormal and Social Psychology*, 1958a, *56*, 49–56.

———. Deprivation and satiation of social reinforcers as drive conditions. *Journal of Abnormal and Social Psychology*, 1958b, *57*, 165–172.

Ginott, H. *Between Parent and Child*. New York: Macmillan, 1965.

Glueck, S. & Glueck, E. T. *One Thousand Juvenile Delinquents*. Cambridge, Mass.: Harvard University Press, 1934.

———. *Unraveling Juvenile Delinquency*. Cambridge, Mass.: Harvard University Press, 1950.

Goldberg, S. & Lewis, M. Play behavior in the year-old infant: early sex differences. *Child Development*, 1969, *40*, 21–32.

Gordon, T. *Parent Effectiveness Training*. New York: Wyden, 1970.

Grinder, R. E. Parental childrearing practices, conscience, and resistance to temptation of sixth grade children. *Child Development*, 1962, *33*, 803–820.

Grusec, J. E. Some antecedents of self-criticism. *Journal of Personality and Social Psychology*, 1966, *4*, 244–252.

————. Power and the internalization of self-denial. *Child Development*, 1971, *42*, 93–105.

Grusec, J. E. & Skubiski, S. L. Model nurturance, demand characteristics of the modeling experiment, and altruism. *Journal of Personality and Social Psychology*, 1970, *14*, 352–359.

Guttman, L. A new approach to factor analysis: the Radex. In P. F. Lazarfeld, ed., *Mathematical Thinking in the Social Sciences*. Glencoe, Ill.: The Free Press, 1954.

Hatfield, J. S., Ferguson, P. E., Rau, L., & Alpert, R. Mother-child interaction and the socialization process. *Child Development*, 1967, *38*, 365–414.

Healy, W. & Bronner, A. F. *Delinquents and Criminals: Their Making and Unmaking*. New York: Macmillan, 1926.

Heathers, G. Emotional dependence and independence in nursery school play. *Journal of Genetic Psychology*, 1955, *87*, 37–57.

Heinicke, C. M. Some antecedents and correlates of guilt and fear in young boys. Doctoral dissertation, Harvard University, 1953.

Herzog, E. & Sudia, C. E. Children in fatherless families. In B. Caldwell and H. Ricciuti, eds., *Review of Child Development Research*, Vol. 3, Chicago: University of Chicago Press, 1973.

Hess, R. D. & Shipman, V. C. Early experiences and socialization of cognitive modes in children. *Child Development*, 1965, *36*, 869–886.

Hetherington, E. M. A developmental study of the effects of sex of the dominant parent on sex-role preference, identification, and imitation in children. *Journal of Personality and Social Psychology*, 1965, *2*, 188–194.

Hetherington, E. M. & Deur, J. L. The effects of father absence on child development. *Young Children*, 1971, *26*, 233–248.

Hetherington, E. M. & Frankie, G. Effects of parental dominance, warmth, and conflict on imitation in children. *Journal of Personality and Social Psychology*, 1967, *6*, 119–125.

Hetherington, E. M., Stouwie, R. J., & Ridberg, E. H. Patterns of family interaction and child-rearing attitudes related to three dimensions of juvenile delinquency. *Journal of Abnormal Psychology*, 1971, *78*, 160–176.

Hewitt, L. E. & Jenkins, R. L. *Fundamental Patterns of Maladjustment: The Dynamics of Their Origin*. Chicago: State of Illinois, 1946.

Hilton, I. Differences in the behavior of mothers toward first and later born children. *Journal of Personality and Social Psychology*, 1967, *7*, 282–290.

Hoffman, M. L. Power assertion by the parent and its impact on the child. *Child Development*, 1960, *31*, 129–143.

————. Moral development. In P. H. Mussen, ed., *Carmichael's Manual of Child Psychology*. New York: John Wiley, 1970.

Hoffman, M. L. & Saltstein, H. D. Parent discipline and the child's moral development. *Journal of Personality and Social Psychology*, 1967, *5*, 45–57.

Horowitz, E. A study of overinhibited and unsocialized aggressive children. Part I: A quantitative analysis of background factors. *Smith College Studies of Social Work*, 1944, *15*, 121–122.

Jenkins, R. L. Psychiatric syndromes in children and their relation to family background. *American Journal of Orthopsychiatry*, 1966, *36*, 450–457.

Jones, H. E. & Bayley, N. The Berkeley growth study. *Child Development*, 1941, *12*, 167–173.

Kagan, J. The child's perception of the present. *Journal of Abnormal and Social Psychology*, 1956, *53*, 257–258.

Kagan, J. & Lemkin, J. The child's differential perception of parental attributes. *Journal of Abnormal and Social Psychology*, 1960, *61*, 440–447.

Kagan, J. & Moss, H. A. *Birth to Maturity*. New York: John Wiley, 1962.

Kamii, C. K. & Radin, N. L. Class differences in the socialization practices of Negro mothers. *Journal of Marriage and the Family*, 1967, *29*, 302–310.

Katz, R. C. Interactions between the facilitative and inhibitory effects of a punishing stimulus in the control of children's hitting behavior. *Child Development*, 1971, *42*, 1433–1446.

Koch, H. L. The relation of "primary mental abilities" in five- and six-year-olds to sex of child and characteristics of his sibling. *Child Development*, 1954, *25*, 209–223.

————. The relation of certain family constellation characteristics and the attitudes of children toward adults. *Child Development*, 1955, *26*, 13–40.

Kogan, K. L., Wimberger, H. C., & Bobbitt, R. A. Analysis of mother-child interaction in young mental retardates. *Child Development*, 1969, *40*, 799–812.

Kohn, M. L. Social class and parent-child relationship: an interpretation. *American Journal of Sociology*, 1963, *68*, 471–480.

Kohn, M. L. & Carroll, E. E. Social class and the allocation of parental responsibilities. *Sociometry*, 1960, *23*, 372–392.

Lambert, W. E., Yackley, A., & Hein, R. N. Child training values of English-Canadian and French-Canadian parents. *Canadian Journal of Behavioral Science*, 1971, *3*, 217–236.

Lasko, J. K. Parent behavior toward first and second children. *Genetic Psychology Monographs*, 1954, *49*, 97–137.

Lesser, G. S. Maternal attitudes and practices and the aggressive behavior of children. Doctoral dissertation, Yale University, 1952.

Levy, D. M. *Maternal Overprotection*. New York: Columbia University Press, 1943.

Lewis, H. *Deprived Children*. London: Oxford University Press, 1954.

Lewis, M. Social isolation: a parametric study of its effect on social reinforcement. *Journal of Experimental Child Psychology*, 1965, *2*, 205–218.

————. State as an infant-environment interaction: an analysis of mother-infant interactions as a function of sex. *Merrill-Palmer Quarterly*, 1972, *18*, 95–122.

Lewis, M. & Goldberg, S. Perceptual-cognitive development in infancy: a generalized expectancy model as a function of mother-infant interaction. *Merrill-Palmer Quarterly*, 1969, *15*, 81–100.

Liebert, R. M., Hanratty, M., & Hill, J. H. Effects of rule structure and training method on the adoption of a self-imposed standard. *Child Development*, 1969, *40*, 93–101.

Littman, R. A., Moore, R. C. A., & Pierce-Jones, J. Social class differences in child rearing: a third community for comparison with Chicago and Newton. *American Sociological Review*, 1957, *22*, 694–704.

Luria, A. R. *The Role of Speech in the Regulation of Normal and Abnormal Behavior*. New York: Liveright, 1961.

Lytton, H. Observation studies of parent-child interaction: a methodological review. *Child Development*, 1971, *42*, 651–684.

Maccoby, E. E. The taking of adult roles in middle childhood. *Journal of Abnormal and Social Psychology*, 1961, *63*, 493–503.

Maccoby, E. E. & Feldman, S. S. Mother-attachment and stranger-reactions in the third year of life. *Monographs of the Society for Research in Child Development*, 1972, *37* (1, serial no. 146).

Maccoby, E. E. & Masters, J. C. Attachment and dependency. In P. H. Mussen, ed., *Carmichael's Manual of Child Psychology*. New York: John Wiley, 1970.

MacDonald, A. P., Jr. Birth order and religious affiliation. *Developmental Psychology*, 1969, *1*, 628.

Madsen, C. H., Becker, W. C., Thomas, D. R., Koser, K., & Plager, E. An analysis of the reinforcing function of "Sit Down" commands. In R. K. Parker, ed., *Readings in Educational Psychology*. Boston: Allyn and Bacon, 1968.

Madsen, C. K. & Madsen, C. H. *Parents/Children/Discipline*. Boston: Allyn and Bacon, 1972.

Martin, B. Reward and punishment associated with the same goal response: a factor in the learning of motives. *Psychological Bulletin*, 1963, *66*, 91–94.

Martin, B. & Hetherington, E. M. Family interaction and aggression, withdrawal, and nondeviancy in children. Progress Report, 1971, University of Wisconsin, Project No. MH 12474, National Institute of Mental Health. (For copies write first author at Psychology Department, University of North Carolina, Chapel Hill.)

McCord, J. & McCord, W. The effects of parental models on criminality. *Journal of Social Issues*, 1958, *14*, 66–75.

McCord, W., McCord, J., & Gudeman, J. *Origins of Alcoholism*. Stanford: Stanford University Press, 1960.

McCord, W., McCord, J., & Howard, A. Familial correlates of aggression in nondelinquent male children. *Journal of Abnormal and Social Psychology*, 1961, *62*, 79–93.

McCord, W., McCord, J., & Verden, P. Familial and behavioral correlates of dependency in male children. *Child Development*, 1962, *33*, 313–326.

McCord, W., McCord, J., & Zola, I. K. *Origins of Crime*. New York: Columbia University Press, 1959.

McQuitty, L. L. A novel application of the coefficient of correlation in the isolation of both typal and dimensional constructs. *Educational and Psychological Measurement*, 1967, *27*, 591–599.

Metzner, R. Effects of work requirements in two types of delay of gratification situations. *Child Development*, 1963, *34*, 809–816.

Midlarsky, E. & Bryan, J. H. Training charity in children. *Journal of Personality and Social Psychology*, 1967, *5*, 408–415.

Miller, D. R. & Swanson, G. E. *Inner Conflict and Defense*. New York: Holt, Rinehart and Winston, 1960.

Minton, C., Kagan, J., & Levine, J. A. Maternal control and obedience in the two-year-old. *Child Development*, 1971, *42*, 1873–1894.

Mischel, W. Theory and research on the antecedents of self-imposed delay of reward. In B. A. Maher, ed., *Progress in Experimental Personality Research*. Vol. 3. New York: Academic Press, 1966.

———. Sex-typing and socialization. In P. H. Mussen, ed., *Carmichael's Manual of Child Psychology*. Vol. 2. New York: John Wiley, 1970.

Mischel, W. & Grusec, J. Determinants of the rehearsal and transmission of neutral and aversive behaviors. *Journal of Personality and Social Psychology*, 1966, *3*, 197–205.

———. Waiting for rewards and punishments: effects of time and probability on choice. *Journal of Personality and Social Psychology*, 1967, *5*, 24–31.

Mischel, W. & Liebert, R. M. Effects of discrepancies between observed and imposed regard criteria on their acquisition and transmission. *Journal of Personality and Social Psychology*, 1966, *3*, 45–53.

Mischel, W. & Staub, E. Effects of expectancy on working and waiting for larger rewards. *Journal of Personality and Social Psychology*, 1965, *2*, 625–633.

Morgan, G. A. & Ricciuti, H. N. Infants' responses to strangers during the first year. In B. M. Foss, ed., *Determinants of Infant Behavior*. Vol. 4. London: Methuen, 1969.

Moss, H. A. Sex, age, and state as determinants of mother-infant interaction. *Merrill-Palmer Quarterly*, 1967, *13*, 19–36.

Moss, H. A., Robson, K. S., & Pedersen, F. Determinants of maternal stimulation of infants and consequences of treatment for later reactions to strangers. *Developmental Psychology*, 1969, *1*, 239–246.

Mussen, P. H. & Parker, A. L. Mother nurturance and girls' incidental imitative learning. *Journal of Personality and Social Psychology,* 1965, *2,* 94–97.

Nelson, E. A. The effects of reward and punishment of dependency on subsequent dependency. Manuscript, Stanford University, 1960. (Also described in Maccoby and Masters, 1970.)

Newell, H. W. A further study of maternal rejection. *American Journal of Orthopsychiatry,* 1936, *6,* 576–588.

Newson, J. & Newson, E. *Four Years Old in an Urban Community.* Middlesex, England: Penguin Books, 1968.

Nye, F. I. *Family Relationships and Delinquent Behavior.* New York: John Wiley, 1958.

O'Leary, K. D. The effects of verbal and nonverbal training on learning and immoral behavior. Paper presented at the meeting of the American Psychological Association, Washington, D. C., 1967.

Parke, R. D. Nurturance, nurturance withdrawal and resistance to deviation. *Child Development,* 1967, *38,* 1101–1110.

———. Effectiveness of punishment as an interaction of intensity, timing, agent nurturance, and cognitive structuring. *Child Development,* 1969, *40,* 211–235.

Parke, R. D. & Walters, R. H. Some factors influencing the efficacy of punishment training for inducing response inhibition. *Monographs of the Society for Research in Child Development,* 1967, *32* (no. 2, serial no. 109).

Patterson, G. R. & Gullion, M. E. *Living With Children.* Champaign, Ill.: Research Press, 1968.

Patterson, G. R., Littman, R. A., & Bricker, W. Assertive behavior in children: a step toward a theory of aggression. *Monographs of the Society for Research in Child Development,* 1967, *32,* no. 5 (serial no. 113).

Pedersen, F. A. & Robson, K. S. Father participation in infancy. *American Journal of Orthopsychiatry,* 1969, *39,* 466–472.

Pedersen, F. A., Yarrow, L. J., & Rubenstein, J. L. Tactile and kinesthetic stimulation in infancy. Paper presented at the Southeastern Conference on Research in Child Development, Williamsburg, Va., April, 1972.

Pepitone, A., McCauley, C., & Hammond, P. Change in attractiveness of forbidden toys as a function of severity of threat. *Journal of Experimental Social Psychology,* 1967, *3,* 221–229.

Peterson, D. R. & Migliorino, G. Pancultural factors of parental behavior in Sicily and the United States. *Child Development,* 1967, *38,* 967–991.

Radin, N. Maternal warmth, achievement motivation, and cognitive functioning in lower-class preschool children. *Child Development,* 1971, *42,* 1560–1565.

———. Father-child interaction and the intellectual functioning of four-year-old boys. *Developmental Psychology,* 1972, *6,* 353–361.

Ramey, C. T., Hieger, L., & Klisz, D. Synchronous reinforcement of vocal responses in failure-to-thrive infants. *Child Development,* 1972, *43,* 1449–1455.

Rheingold, H. L. The social and socializing infant. In D. A. Goslin, ed., *Handbook of Socialization Theory and Research.* Chicago: Rand McNally, 1969*a*.

———. The effect of a strange environment on the behavior of infants. In B. M. Foss, ed., *Determinants of Infant Behavior.* Vol. 4. London: Metheun, 1969*b*.

Rheingold, H. L., Gewirtz, J. L., & Ross, H. W. Social conditioning of vocalizations in the infant. *Journal of Comparative and Physiological Psychology,* 1959, *52,* 68–73.

Robson, K. S., Pedersen, F. A., Moss, H. A. Developmental observations of diadic gazing in relation to the fear of strangers and social approach behavior. *Child Development,* 1969, *40,* 619–627.

Roe, A. Early determinants of vocational choice. *Journal of Counseling Psychology,* 1957, *4,* 212–217.

Rosekrans, M. A. & Hartup, W. W. Imitative influence of consistent and inconsistent response consequences to a model on aggressive behavior in children. *Journal of Personality and Social Psychology,* 1967, *7,* 429–434.

Rosen, B. & D'Andrade, R. The psychosocial origins of achievement motivation. *Sociometry*, 1959, *22*, 185–252.

Rosenhan, D. & White, G. M. Observation and rehearsal as determinants of pro-social behavior. *Journal of Personality and Social Psychology*, 1967, *5*, 424–431.

Rosenthal, M. K. The generalization of dependency behaviors from mother to stranger. Doctoral dissertation, Stanford University, 1965.

Rosenthal, M. J., Finkelstein, M., Ni, E., & Robertson, R. E. A study of mother-child relationships in the emotional disorders of children. *Genetic Psychology Monographs*, 1959, *60*, 65–116.

Rosenthal, M. J., Ni, E., Finkelstein, M., & Berkwits, G. K. Father-child relationships and children's problems. *Archives of General Psychiatry*, 1962, *7*, 360–373.

Rothbart, M. & Maccoby, E. E. Parents' differential reactions to sons and daughters. *Journal of Personality and Social Psychology*, 1966, *4*, 237–243.

Rubenstein, J. Maternal attentiveness and subsequent exploratory behavior in the infant. *Child Development*, 1967, *38*, 1089–1100.

Saadatmand, B., Jensen, L., & Price, A. Nurturance, nurturance withdrawal, and resistance to temptation among three age groups. *Developmental Psychology*, 1970, *2*, 450.

Sampson, E. E. & Hancock, F. T. Ordinal position, socialization, personality development, and conformity. *Journal of Personality and Social Psychology*, 1967, *5*, 398–407.

Scarr, S. Social introversion-extroversion as a heritable response. *Child Development*, 1969, *40*, 823–832.

Schachter, S. *The Psychology of Affiliation.* Stanford: Stanford University Press, 1959.

Schaefer, E. S. A circumplex model for maternal behavior. *Journal of Abnormal and Social Psychology*, 1959, *59*, 226–235.

———. Converging conceptual models for maternal behavior and for child behavior. In J. C. Glidewell, ed., *Parental Attitudes and Child Behavior*. Springfield, Ill.: C. C. Thomas, 1961.

———. Children's reports of parental behavior: an inventory. *Child Development*, 1965, *36*, 413–424.

Schaffer, H. R. & Emerson, P. E. The development of social attachments in infancy. *Monographs of the Society for Research in Child Development*, 1964, *29*, no. 3 (serial no. 94).

———. Patterns of response to physical contact in early human development. *Journal of Child Psychology and Psychiatry*, 1964b, *5*, 1–13.

Sears, R. R. The relation of early socialization experiences to aggression in middle childhood. *Journal of Abnormal and Social Psychology*, 1961, *63*, 466–492.

———. Relation of early socialization experiences to self-concepts and gender role in middle childhood. *Child Development*, 1970, *41*, 267–289.

Sears, R. R., Maccoby, E. E., & Levin, H. *Patterns of Child Rearing.* Evanston, Ill.: Row, Peterson, 1957.

Sears, R. R., Rau, L., & Alpert, R. *Identification and Child Rearing.* Stanford: Stanford University Press, 1965.

Sears, R. R., Whiting, J. W. M., Nowlis, V., & Sears, P. S. Some child rearing antecedents of dependency and aggression in young children. *Genetic Psychology Monographs*, 1953, *47*, 135–234.

Siegelman, M. Evaluation of Bronfenbrenner's questionnaire for children concerning parental behavior. *Child Development*, 1965, *36*, 163–174.

———. Loving and punishing parental behavior and introversion tendencies in sons. *Child Development*, 1966, *37*, 985–992.

Slater, P. E. Parental behavior and the personality of the child. *Journal of Genetic Psychology*, 1962, *101*, 53–68.

Smith, H. T. A comparison of interview and observation measures of mother behavior. *Journal of Abnormal and Social Psychology,* 1958, *57,* 278–282.

Spitz, R. A. *The First Year of Life.* New York: International Universities Press, 1965.

Stayton, D. J., Hogan, R., & Ainsworth, M. D. S. Infant obedience and maternal behavior: the origins of socialization reconsidered. *Child Development,* 1971, *42,* 1057–1069.

Stern, G., Caldwell, B., Hersher, L., Lipton, E., & Richmond, J. A factor analytic study of the mother-infant dyad. *Child Development,* 1969, *40,* 163–181.

Stouwie, R. J. Inconsistent verbal instructions and children's resistance-to-temptation behavior. *Child Development,* 1971, *42,* 1517–1531.

Symonds, P. M. *The Psychology of Parent-Child Relationships.* New York: Appleton-Century-Crofts, 1939.

Tennes, K. H. & Lampl, E. E. Stranger and separation anxiety in infancy. *Journal of Nervous and Mental Diseases,* 1964, *139,* 247–254.

Thoman, E. B., Leiderman, P. H., & Olson, J. P. Neonate-mother interaction during breast-feeding. *Developmental Psychology,* 1972, *6,* 110–118.

Thomas, A., Chess, S., & Birch, H. G. *Temperament and Behavior Disorders in Children.* New York: New York University Press, 1968.

Tulkin, S. R. & Kagan, J. Mother-child interaction in the first year of life. *Child Development,* 1972, *43,* 31–42.

Unger, S. M. Antecedents of personality differences in guilt responsivity. *Psychological Reports,* 1962, *10,* 357–358.

Waldfogel, S. The development, meaning, and management of school phobia. *American Journal of Orthopsychiatry,* 1957, *27,* 754–780.

Walters, R. H., Leat, M., & Mezei, L. Inhibition and disinhibition of responses through empathetic learning. *Canadian Journal of Psychology,* 1963, *17,* 235–243.

Walters, R. H., & Parke, R. D. Social motivation, dependency, and susceptibility to social influence. In L. Berkowitz, ed., *Advances in Experimental Social Psychology.* Vol. 1. New York: Academic Press, 1964*a.*

———. Influences of response consequences to a social model on resistance to deviation. *Journal of Experimental Child Psychology,* 1964*b, 1,* 269–280.

———. The role of the distance receptors in the development of social responsiveness. In L. P. Lipsitt and C. C. Spiker, eds., *Advances in Child Development and Behavior.* Vol. 2. New York: Academic Press, 1965.

Walters, R. H., Parke, R. D., & Cane, V. A. Timing of punishment and the observation of consequences to others as determinants of response inhibition. *Journal of Experimental Child Psychology,* 1965, *2,* 10–30.

Watson, G. Some personality differences in children related to strict or permissive parental discipline. *Journal of Psychology,* 1957, *44,* 227–249.

Watson, J. S. Memory and "contingency analysis" in infant learning. *Merrill-Palmer Quarterly,* 1967, *13,* 55–76.

———. Operant conditioning of visual fixation in infants under visual and auditory reinforcement. *Developmental Psychology,* 1969, *1,* 508–516.

Watson, J. S. & Ramey, C. T. Reactions to response-contingent stimulation in early infancy. *Merrill-Palmer Quarterly,* in press.

Winder, C. L. & Rau, L. Parental attitudes associated with social deviance in preadolescent boys. *Journal of Abnormal and Social Psychology,* 1962, *64,* 418–424.

Winterbottom, M. The relation of need for achievement in learning experiences in independence and mastery. In J. Atkinson, ed., *Motives in Fantasy, Action and Society.* Princeton, N. J.: Van Nostrand, 1958.

Wittman, M. P. & Huffman, A. V. A comparative study of developmental adjustment, and personality characteristics of psychotics, psychoneurotics, delinquent, and normally adjusted teen-aged youths. *Journal of Genetic Psychology,* 1945, *66,* 167–182.

Yarrow, L. J. Research in dimensions of maternal care. *Merrill-Palmer Quarterly,* 1963, *9,* 101–114.

———. The development of focused relationships during infancy. In J. Hellmuth, ed., *Exceptional Infant.* Vol. 1. Seattle: Special Child Publications, 1967.

Yarrow, L. J. & Pedersen, F. A. Dimensions of early stimulation: differential effects on early development. Paper presented at meeting of Society for Research in Child Development, Minneapolis, April, 1971.

Yarrow, M. R., Campbell, J. D., & Burton, R. V. *Child Rearing.* San Francisco: Jossey-Bass, 1968.

Yarrow, M. R., Waxler, C. Z., & Scott, P. M. Child effects on adult behavior. *Developmental Psychology,* 1971, *5,* 300–311.

10 Intellectual Development during Adolescence

EDITH D. NEIMARK

Douglass College, Rutgers—The State University of New Jersey

ADOLESCENCE is generally regarded as a time of special developmental significance and, regardless of one's theory of development, an easily identifiable one since it marks the penultimate stage prior to the attainment of adult status and abilities. From a physical standpoint, it is a period of rapid growth culminating in the attainment of adult height and sexual maturity. From a sociocultural standpoint, it is the period of admission to adult status with all its privileges and responsibilities; frequently a formal ceremony or rite marks this admission. On a more personal level, it is a period of breaking parental ties and of forming intense new peer relationships. From an intellectual standpoint, it is marked by the appearance of more abstract, powerful modes of thought and, in some individuals, of intense intellectual exploration and creativity made possible by these new modes. These advances in cognitive skills, in turn, have a profound effect upon many aspects of behavior with respect to other individuals and to the world at large. In short, the world of the adolescent is qualitatively different from the world of the child; it is far bigger, richer, and more complex. It is, in many respects, like the world of the adult except that much of it is new, and the adolescent does not yet have relevant experience to bring to bear upon it.

In surveying the current status of knowledge concerning adolescent intellectual development, one is struck first by the paucity of systematic evidence, by the limited generality of what evidence there is, and by the almost complete failure to relate intellectual development to other concomitant developmental changes which mark this period. The review which follows, will therefore, summarize not only current theory and relevant evidence but also will attempt to identify major unanswered questions and suggest directions for future research.

The first section of this chapter is given over to a brief explication of Piaget's theory of cognition. The reader who is familiar with Piagetian theory may wish to skip this section. The novice, on the other hand, may

541

wish to read the section carefully or resort to supplementary readings to get a full understanding of the theory.

PIAGET'S THEORY OF FORMAL OPERATIONS

The Theory

There is at present but one theoretical description of the nature and organization of adolescent thought: Piaget's elegant and comprehensive treatment of formal operations (Inhelder and Piaget 1958). For a full understanding of Piaget's treatment there is no substitute for careful reading (and rereading) of the 1958 Inhelder and Piaget volume, especially of chapter 17 in which is given a closely reasoned account of formal operations structures and their development in relation to data from illustrative experiments presented in the first two sections. Briefer accounts appear in Piaget and Inhelder (1969) and Piaget (1970). For a brief introduction there are several excellent summaries: by far the best is Flavell's (1963) chapter 6, but Ginsburg and Opper (1969) is good for a start. For the benefit of readers with little or no background, a brief and superficial summary of Piaget's theory of cognitive development and formal operations follows.

1. *Operative and figurative aspects of cognition, and their development through earlier stages.* The term "cognition" has traditionally been used to encompass all mental activity through which knowledge of the outside world is attained: perception, learning and memory, as well as thought. Piaget uses the term in its traditional sense. He starts from a central focus upon the development of knowledge within an individual—genetic epistemology—and emphasizes that from birth on the development of understanding is an ongoing and active process. Experience does not, as the British empiricists would have us believe, leave its mark willy-nilly upon a *tabula rasa*; rather, from earliest infancy the individual is actively engaged in the construction of his world in accord with the level of his abilities at the time of construction.

It might be useful to view the constructive process from the standpoint of an analogy to the computer for purposes of understanding Piaget's distinction between the operative and figurative aspects of cognition. The term "operative" refers to activities through which the individual attempts to transform reality. These activities are analogous to the program of a computer: a set of steps, or transformational procedures, applicable to a wide variety of data. For example, the possessor of an adding program can apply it for the summation of digits, algebraic unknowns, or aggregations of objects; adding is a very general procedure whose nature is not limited by the conditions of its application. The term "figurative," by contrast, refers to "the activities which attempt only to represent reality as it appears without seeking to transform it: (a) perception, (b) imitation, in a broad sense (including graphic imitation or drawing) and (c) pictorial representations in mental imagery" (Piaget 1970, p. 717). In accord with the computer analogy, the figurative aspect of cognition corresponds to the computer language, the form in which data are presented and processed.

During the first months of life all information impinging upon the infant comes from its immediate external or internal environment. The infant begins developing organized behavioral patterns, *schemes,* to deal with the information. The first schemes, e.g., sucking, are reflex-based, but they are elaborated and refined through the action of two processes: the functional invariants of assimilation and accommodation. Through *assimilation* a scheme is expanded to encompass new objects and contexts, while *accommodation* is reflected in modification of component behaviors as required to deal with the new objects and contexts. For example, sucking is initially evoked by tactile stimulation of the lip or cheek. The infant learns to feed efficiently whether sucking at a bottle or the breast (accommodation); it also sucks its thumb, its toys, its blanket, and practically every portable object in the vicinity (assimilation). Other examples of early schemes are grasping, attending (e.g., looking, listening), kicking, and so on. Each new scheme is an accomplishment; when the infant has mastered a repertoire of schemes he can begin to combine them and direct them toward exploration of the environment. By the second year of life the infant is an accomplished perceiver and learner with a working practical understanding of his world. Such are the cognitive accomplishments of the sensorimotor period. It would be inaccurate, however, to describe the two-year-old as a thinker, because thinking, by definition, is a process of acting upon or transforming the world at a symbolic level.

Both the figurative and operative modifications prerequisite for true thought develop during the next major stage of cognitive development: the stage of *concrete operations* (see table 1 for a brief summary of stages and their approximate age equivalents). Discussion of concrete and formal operations here will be exclusively concerned with the development of thought (to the exclusion of the other cognitive processes). The figurative prerequisites of thinking are satisfied by the development of the *semiotic function*: a repertoire of symbols and signs (arbitrary conventionalized symbols) for the representation of absent, remembered, or anticipated reality. These representations, all of which initially derive from imitation, develop through the activities of deferred imitation, play, drawing, mental imagery, and language.

TABLE 1. THE PIAGETIAN STAGES, THEIR DEFINING CHARACTERISTICS, AND AVERAGE AGE OF APPEARANCE

STAGES	Average age of appearance	Kind of operation available	CHARACTERISTICS		
			Status of semiotic functions	Elements of thought	Organizational structure of operations
Sensorimotor	0–1½ or 2	None—motor schemes, which are not reversible, serve in lieu of operations. They are practical but not logical, e.g. sucking, throwing, looking.	No representation as such except where an internalized scheme or imitation serves this function, e.g. closing eyes and lying down as a sleep symbol.	No real thought, hence no basis of distinguishing its elements.	
Concrete operations Preoperational subperiod	2–7		Development of imagery and symbolization thru play, drawing, mental-imagery language.	Tend to be objects and individuals in context.	
Concrete operation subperiod	7–11	Concrete operations, e.g. classification (single and multiple), seriation, conservation.	Further refinement in forms and functions of language and of imagery, i.e. appearance of anticipatory imagery in addition to reproductive imagery.	Properties and relations	Eight *groupements:* four parallel classes for dealing with operations on properties and four for operations relations.
Formal operations Subperiod of organization	11–15	Formal operations, e.g. deduction, permutation correlation.	Not studied. Presumably further refinements in and abstractions of imagery and language over those attained in concrete operations.	Propositions	The four-group, or INRC group. The complete combinatorial scheme.
Subperiod of achievement	15–				

NOTE: Based upon Piaget (1970).

Although most persons assume that the thought of the young child is rich in pictorial imagery, studies by Piaget and Inhelder (1971) show that the young child's imaginal abilities may be limited. The child can reproduce (by drawing or mental imagery) a stimulus array which is physically present or recently removed; this is called *reproductory imagery*. But simple adjustments cannot be visualized through *anticipatory imagery* in advance of their occurrence. For example, if three balls—red, yellow, and blue—are inserted in a tube in that order, the five- or six-year-old child can correctly recall the order of insertion; he cannot, however, correctly predict order of emergence when the tube is rotated through an arc. The development of anticipatory imagery appears to require the prior development of the appropriate concrete operation; that is, there is evidence of an effect of operative developmental events upon figurative ones. This conclusion is supported by results of a long-term memory experiment reported by Inhelder (1969).

Operations differ from schemes along at least three dimensions: (a) the level of activity through which they are manifest (schemes are overt physical manipulations or interiorizations thereof, whereas operations can be conducted mentally); (b) the elements to which they are applied (schemes are applied to entities, whereas operations are applied to abstractions from entities and, in the case of concrete operations, to properties and relations); and (c) the nature of their organization into higher-order structures. The last two distinctions will be explained in greater detail in elaborating the distinction between concrete and formal operations. Piaget (1970, p. 705) defines operations as "interiorized actions [e.g., addition, which can be performed either physically or mentally] that are reversible [addition requires an inverse in subtraction] and constitute set-theoretical structures [such as the logical additive "grouping" or algebraic groups]."

2. *The difference between concrete and formal operations.* With the development of concrete operations during roughly the seven- to eleven-year age range, the child develops adultlike reasoning skills of great generality. One of the foremost such skills is *classification*. Classification involves the ability to set up classes and hierarchies of classes on the basis of defining properties (and ignoring other irrelevant properties). A class is always defined with respect to a larger universe: all members that possess the defining property are members of the class; others lacking the defining property are not members of the class. For example, the universe of animals (to be symbolized B) can be divided into two major classes. Animals which have a backbone are class A, and those which do not have a backbone are class "not A" or $\bar{A}$, or the complement of class A. We can represent this in an equation: $B = A + \bar{A}$. This equation is a

proper equation. An equation is a "proper equation" if for all classes so defined (regardless of their size, the nature of the defining property, and so on) it is true that $A = B - \bar{A}$, and $\bar{A} = B - A$. In other words, the process of logical addition has an *inverse*—namely, subtraction—by means of which the operation of addition can be reversed.

Moreover, since classes are defined in terms of *properties,* in order to classify one must be able to focus upon properties that are relatively independent of the objects bearing those properties. This ability represents a higher level of abstraction over dealing with objects as unique entities or classes only in terms of the behavior toward them. It also makes for greater flexibility in the sense that any given object can be a member of many different classes at the same time. For example, my cat, Big Red, is simultaneously a cat, a pet, a red quadruped, a resident of my house, and so on. One can pose and unpose classes depending on the property— or combination of properties—selected, and one can order classes into hierarchies. To summarize the foregoing discussion in Piagetian terms, classification is an important skill that develops during the concrete operational period. Classification is an operation that (a) can be performed on any set of property elements and (b) has a definite logical structure. Piaget further described the structure in terms of four groupings, or "groupements" which will not be described here (see Piaget 1970, pp. 723–26; or Flavell 1963, pp. 168-201).

There are other skills that develop during the period of concrete operations. One of these is the operation of *seriation*. This is an operation that orders items in terms of their relational elements such as larger, lower, harder, prettier, son of, and so on. This ordering operation is, once again, reversible, but in this case reversal takes the form of shift in direction of ordering (smaller, higher, softer, uglier, parent of). The reversal here is described as a "reciprocal" rather than an "inverse."

Another widely studied concrete operation is that of *conservation*. For example, all children agree that two corresponding rows of, let us say, ten equally spaced objects "have the same number of objects." If one row is then spread out relative to the other and the child is asked, "Now does one row have more than the other, or do they both have the same number?" the child who can "conserve" will know, without counting, that the rows remain equal with respect to number. Prior to this period, the child will claim that the longer row now has *more* objects. Although several theoretical explanations have been offered for the development of conservation, descriptively it is clear that the conserving child is responding on the basis of logic rather than the experienced perceptual transformation. In effect, he can reverse the transformation of spreading out and realize that two rows identical in number to begin with remain unchanged in number when one row is made longer relative to the other.

The operations of seriation and conservation, as compared with the operation of classification, are both reversible, but they differ with respect to the form of the reversibility (reciprocal rather than inverse) and in the elements to which they are applied (relations rather than properties). They also differ with respect to organizational structure; the organization of operations upon relations are described by four *groupements* closely paralleling but differing from the *groupements* of operations on properties.

It should be clear that the development of concrete operational thought represents an enormous advance over the sensorimotor period in power, complexity, and abstraction. Not only is the child now capable of thought, but also he can use the result of his thought processes to override the data of his senses (as in the conservation experiment). The concrete-operational child is freed of the tyranny of the here and now and of his behavior with respect to it. It might appear that no additional skills as a thinker are possible or desirable. However, Piaget distinguishes a higher level of thought which he calls "formal operations." Formal operations differ from concrete operations along the same dimensions by which concrete operations differ from sensorimotor schemes: (a) level of abstraction, (b) elements, and (c) structure of organization.

First it should be noted that formal operations, like concrete operations, are *operations* (reversible mental transformations). They apply at a higher level of abstraction, however, and represent a higher level of generality than concrete operations. Where concrete operations had to be described in terms of two types of operations, each with its own appropriate element (properties or relations) and organizational structure (the eight *groupements*), for formal operations there is but one element (propositions) and one organizational structure (the four-group, or INRC group). The last two points will be expanded in greater detail following clarification of differences in level of abstraction.

Although the properties and relations at issue during the concrete operational stage are abstract in the sense of being derived from objects and events, they are still dependent upon specifics of the objects and events from which they derive; that is, they are empirically based abstractions rather than pure abstractions. In this sense the elements of concrete operational thought are "concrete" rather than "abstract" or "formal." On the other hand, propositions, the elements of formal operational thought, are abstract in the sense that the truth value of a statement can be freed from a dependence upon the evidence of experience and, instead, determined logically from the truth values of other propositions to which it bears a formal, logical relationship. This type of reasoning, deriving from the form of propositions rather than their content, is new in the development of the child: deductive rather than inductive thought. Inductive thought proceeds from the specific (experienced events) to the general through a summative process of accumulating instances and correspondences. Final conclusions are only as good as the evidence upon which they are based; for example, the child who has never seen a Great Dane or a Saint Bernard might conclude that dogs are small animals. Inescapable generalizations based upon logical necessity, on the other hand, are generally arrived at deductively. Moreover, since the truth or falsity of a deduced conclusion is not dependent upon the empirical content of the premises, it is possible to reason from premises contrary to normal experience or never before experienced (e.g., to assume that the trajectory of an object is not constrained by gravity, or that there are living organisms whose respiratory cycle is based upon hydrogen). This kind of hypothetico-deductive reasoning is characteristic of formal operations.

3. *The complete combinatorial scheme.* Piaget has characterized the shift in level of abstraction which accompanies the shift from concrete to formal operations as reasoning from the possible to the actual. To some extent this is a result of the shift from inductive to deductive thought, but it is also the result of a changed outlook on the nature of the universe and one's experience thereof. *"Possibility* no longer appears merely as an extension of an empirical situation or of actions actually performed. Instead, it is *reality* that is now secondary to *possibility"* (Inhelder and Piaget 1958, p. 251). The real world is but one actualizaton of the set of possible worlds.

In order to reason from the possible it is first necessary to be able to generate it; this is accomplished through the use of the complete combinatorial scheme, which may be regarded as a higher-order combinatorial scheme, or a combination of combinations. In the discussion of the concrete operation of classification it was noted that the child has a scheme for dealing with combinations of *properties.* This scheme is the rectangular matrix. For example, let us define two property classes B and H where B = the class of all mammals which walk on two feet, that is, bipeds (its complement, $\bar{B}$ = the class of all mammals which do not walk on two feet, that is, quadrupeds); and H = the class of all mammals which feed exclusively on plants (its complement, $\bar{H}$ = the class of all mammals which do not feed exclusively on plants, that is, carnivores and omnivores). The concrete operational child can generate the four new classes defined by the combination of those two properties: BH, B$\bar{H}$, $\bar{B}$H, and $\bar{B}\bar{H}$, but he is not able to deduce a correlation or causal relation between the two properties as a result of observations of occurrence and nonoccurrence of various combinations of these four combinations. To put it another way, the concrete operational child can operate upon property classes multi-

TABLE 2. THE COMBINATORIAL SYSTEM

Name	Symbol	Combination*	Name of Complement	Symbol	Combination
Complete Affirmation	$(p*q)$	$BH+\bar{B}H+B\bar{H}+\bar{B}\bar{H}$	· Negation	(ϕ)	
Incompatibility	(p/q)	$\bar{B}H+B\bar{H}+\bar{B}\bar{H}$	· Conjunction	$(p \cdot q)$	BH
Disjunction	(pvq)	$BH+\bar{B}H+B\bar{H}$	Conjunctive negation	$(\bar{p} \cdot \bar{q})$	$\bar{B}\bar{H}$
Implication	$(p \supset q)$	$BH+\bar{B}H+\bar{B}\bar{H}$	· Nonimplication	$(p \cdot \bar{q})$	$B\bar{H}$
Reciprocal Implication	$(q \supset p)$	$BH+B\bar{H}+\bar{B}\bar{H}$	· Negation of reciprocal implication	$(\bar{p} \cdot q)$	$\bar{B}H$
· Equivalence	$\left(p \underset{\cup}{\subset} q \right)$ or $(p=q)$	$BH+\bar{B}\bar{H}$	Reciprocal exclusion or exclusive disjunction	$(p\overline{v}q)$	$\bar{B}H+B\bar{H}$
Affirmation of p	$p[q]$	$BH+B\bar{H}$	Negation of p	$\bar{p}[q]$	$\bar{B}H+\bar{B}\bar{H}$
Affirmation of q	$q[p]$	$BH+\bar{B}H$	Negation of q	$\bar{q}[p]$	$B\bar{H}+\bar{B}\bar{H}$

* NOTE: to shift from property combinations to propositional combination, $B=p$, $\bar{B}=\bar{p}$, $H=q$, $\bar{H}=\bar{q}$, $+=v$

plicatively to form a matrix of property combinations, but he cannot operate upon the product of his operations to generate all possible propositional combinations of the four possible property combinations.

To continue with the example, in order to decide whether there is a relation between mode of locomotion and nature of diet in mammals it is necessary to get all combinations of the four basic property combinations taken zero at a time, one at a time (that is, the four property combinations themselves), two at a time ($BH + B\overline{H}$, $BH + \overline{B}H$, $BH + \overline{B}\overline{H}$, and so on, for all six possible two-pair sums), three at a time ($BH + \overline{B}H + B\overline{H}$, $\overline{B}H + B\overline{H} + \overline{B}\overline{H}$, and so on, for all four possible three-pair sums), and four at a time ($BH + \overline{B}H + B\overline{H} + \overline{B}\overline{H}$), and consider the logical implications of each propositional combination. All sixteen possible combinations of the four basic property combinations are summarized in table 2 in the form of eight complementary pairs. In the first column of the table is given the name of the propositional combination followed by its traditional symbolic notation. The letters B and H have been used to refer to property combinations; it would be as correct (and more accurate for present purposes) to refer to propositional combinations, in which case B and H (and their complements, $\overline{B}$ and $\overline{H}$) would be replaced by p and q (and their complements, $\overline{p}$ and $\overline{q}$) respectively, and + would be replaced by v (the logical symbol for the conjunction "or"). For example, suppose we observe $\overline{B}H + B\overline{H}$ (line 6, column 2 of table 2 which is labeled "reciprocal exclusion" or "exclusive disjunction") and never observed $BH + \overline{B}\overline{H}$ (line 6, column 1, "equivalence," which is the denial of reciprocal exclusion, and vice-versa). In this case we would conclude that bipedalism and herbivorousness (and their complements, nonbipedalism and nonherbivorousness) never co-occur; thus, they appear to be negatively correlated, or incompatible. In common English, people are not grass-eaters and animals are. Had we, on the other hand, observed $B\overline{H} + \overline{B}H + \overline{B}\overline{H}$ and never observed BH (line 2 of table 2) then we would conclude that bipedalism is incompatible with herbivorousness, that is, people are not cud-chewers—a conclusion which must be abandoned on discovery of one negative instance of a human cud-chewer.

The formal operational thinker is able not only to generate all sixteen possible combinations of binary propositions but also to utilize them in his reasoning. That is not to say that he is consciously aware of the existence of these combinations or even that he can generate them on command; rather, he engages in a variety of forms of thought which would be impossible without the combinatorial scheme or some functional equivalent thereof. To quote Piaget (Inhelder and Piaget 1958, p. 310), "The deliberate and reasoned use of these combinations is as foreign to the subject who begins to reason formally as are the laws of harmony to the child or to the popular singer who retains a melody or whistles an improvised tune."

4. *The INRC group of transformations.* Operations have already been defined as reversible internalized transformations. Furthermore, it was noted that the negation of operations upon properties is inversion, whereas the negation of operations upon relations is reciprocity. In other words, there are two kinds of operations upon two different kinds of elements (properties or relations), each with its own structure of rules; there is no single means of encompassing and integrating the separate sets of rules. The great advance in both power and parsimony of formal operations over concrete operations is the development of a fully flexible structure of four transformations: Identity, Negation, Reciprocal, and Correlative, fondly summarized INRC. An INRC structure has all the requisite properties of the mathematical structure known as the "group": the properties of a "group" are composition, associativity, identity, and inverse. *Composition* is said to exist when an operation upon two or more elements of a set yields a new element that is itself an element of the set. Composition is also referred to in terms of openness or closedness of a set under an operation. For example, the set of real numbers is closed under multiplication (and other operations as well) in that the product of any two real numbers is a real number. With respect to the group of transformations as will be seen shortly, $RC = N$, $RN = C$, $CN = R$. *Associativity* exists when the product of a series of transformations is independent of their order of application: $2 \times 4 \times 6 = 4 \times 2 \times 6 = 48$; similarly, $RNC = CNR = NRC = I$. *Identity* refers to a transformation which, when applied to any element, yields the element itself (such as multiplication by 1, or addition of 0 in arithmetic). For the four-group, that identity is I; $IN = N$, $IR = R$, and so on. Finally for each element there is an *inverse* —for the four-group the element itself, which transforms the element into the identity element (e.g., adding $-n$ to $n = 0$ or dividing n by $n = 1$ in arithmetic; for the four-group $NN = I$, $CC = I$, and so on).

The four transformations and the structure of their relations to each other are illustrated in table 3 with two types of elements: an algebraic quantity, *x,* and a propositional quantity *p v q.* The algebraic applications are obvious, the propositional ones will be discussed in greater detail. The identity transformation, I, leaves whatever element to which it is applied unchanged. The reciprocal, R, changes the sign of each element but leaves the form of the connective unchanged. For example, the reciprocal of $\bar{p}{\cdot}q$ is $p{\cdot}\bar{q}$. The correlative, C, on the other hand, changes the form of the connective ("and" to "or" and vice versa: $\cdot$ to v and v to $\cdot$ while leaving the sign of the element unchanged. For example, the correlative of $\bar{p}{\cdot}q$ is $\bar{p}$ v q. Finally, negation, N, changes both the sign of each element and the

TABLE 3.   THE GROUP OF INRC TRANSFORMATIONS

Name	Example	Name	Example
Identity	$I(x) = x$ $I(pvq) = pvq$	Negation	$N(x) = -x$ $N(pvq) = \bar{p} \cdot \bar{q}$
Reciprocal	$R(x) = 1/x$ $R(pvq) = \bar{p}v\bar{q}$	Correlative	$C(x) = -1/x$ $C(pvq) = p \cdot q$

Reciprocal (vertical label, left margin)

Correlative

← Negation →

form of the connective, e.g., the negative of $\bar{p} \cdot q$ is $p \vee \bar{q}$. The composition of the table suggests the relationship among the transformations: each member of the top row bears the same relation, R, to its corresponding number in the bottom row $(R(I) = R, R(N) = C$ or $R(C) = N)$; similarly, each entry in the right column is the negative of its counterpart to the left $(N(I) = N, NR = C$ or $NC = R)$. As an additional test of his understanding of table 3, the reader may want to prove that IRC = N, NRC = I, and so on. This is somewhat more easily done with the algebraic example before proceeding to the propositional one.

This abstract description of the four-group of transformations may have left the reader wondering what all that has to do with thinking by real adolescents. It may help to consider one of the experiments. A child is given a balance with the arms marked off in equal-unit intervals and a number of unit weights. The length of the arms or the combination of weights is varied by the experimenter to tip the balance, and the child must return it to equilibrium and explain why his solution worked. The three- to five-year-old typically intervenes directly by pressing down on the lighter side or pushing up the heavier with the expectation that the correction so induced will remain when his hand is removed. There is no awareness of length of arm or of weight as relevant variables, although dawning appreciation of the role of the weights is reflected in the child's readiness to add weight (often to the heavier side). He does not, however, spontaneously think to subtract weight. The five- to seven-year-old, on the other hand, is aware of the role of the weights and freely adds or subtracts them in his attempts at equalization. He may even note the relevance of length of arm, but at this age its role is not formulated. The young concrete-operations child of seven to nine is aware of the importance of both weight and length, and he can achieve balance by manipulation of one or the other of these variables. However, when both are varied simultaneously, successful correction is a matter of trial and error. The older concrete-operations child, nine to eleven, copes with simultaneous variation through a system of quantitative correspondences such as fixed pairing of heavy weight with short-arm length, light weight with long-arm length, and so on. Here, in effect, the child has produced an amalgam of two variables which may be treated as one in a direct adjustment. He does not appreciate the reciprocal relationship among variables and has no notion of producing equilibrium in a system through compensatory adjustment of opposing forces. In other words, although he can balance with respect to weight by adding or subtracting weights (inversion), and balance with respect to length by adjusting distance of weight from the fulcrum (reciprocity), he has no mechanism for integrating the independent compensatory schemes. With the appearance of formal operations at adolescence and the development of an INRC structure, it is possible not only to integrate negation and reciprocity but also to formulate a quantitative relationship expressed in terms of proportions.

5. *Formal operational concepts.* Piaget distinguishes a group of concepts which are developed as a result of formal operational thinking and which have three identifying characteristics: (a) they have such generality as to serve as operational schemata, (b) they are not discoverable in objects but must be deduced from operations, (c) they are related to and dependent upon the combinatorial and INRC structures discussed earlier. There are eight formal concepts which meet these criteria. 1. *Combinatorial operations.* General systematic procedures for generating such things as all possible distinguishable pairs of n colors (combinations), or all possible orderings on n objects (permutations). For example, with three letters there are six permutations of them: ABC, ACB, BCA, BAC, CAB, CBA. The number of permutations of n objects is $n!$ (n factorial $= n \cdot n - 1 \cdot n - 2 \cdot$ to $n - (n-1)$). 2. *Proportions.* Ability to deal with the equality of two ratios, $x/y = x'/y'$, as in the balance experiment or in solving an equation, is a formal operations development. 3. *Coordination of two systems of reference,* as, for example, in dealing with the problem of the mountain climber who ascends during one day in h hours and descends the following day in the same time and by the same route. Is there one spot on the route which is occupied at the same clock time in both the ascending and descending route? Yes, as may be easily verified by imagining two climbers traveling in opposite directions at the same time. They must meet somewhere along the way. The ability to coordinate disparate referential systems underlies all relativistic thinking. 4. *The concept of mechanical equilibrium.* For example, the principle of equality of action and reaction. Equilibrium is obviously closely related to proportion. 5. *The concept of probability.* Probability is defined as a proportion the numerator and denominator of which generally require calculation of combinations. Clearly, then, a concept of probability presupposes the first two concepts listed. 6. *The concept of correlation,* which is partially an

extension of the notion of probability. 7. *Multiplicative compensations,* as
reflected, for example, in conservation of volume which involves three
dimensions and which, unlike most one- or two-dimensional conservations such as number, space, mass, and so on, is an attainment of formal
operations. 8. *Forms of conservation,* which go beyond direct empirical
discovery or verification, as, for example, notions of inertia, energy,
valence.

The Experiments

Protocols from fifteen experimental tasks in the form of simple physical
demonstrations which the child must explain, have been discussed within
the framework of Piaget's theory (Inhelder and Piaget 1958, chaps. 1–
15). In each case, children in a wide age-range (five to fifteen) are tested,
and three qualitative levels of performance are described. (In most
instances two substages, A and B, are distinguished in the later levels, II
and III. These levels correspond to concrete and formal operations respectively.) The first six experiments are designed primarily to assess
the development of propositional thought as reflected, e.g., in identifying
variables and formulating and testing of hypotheses as to their effects. In
the remaining nine experiments, the role of formal operational structures
(the combinatorial scheme and the INRC group) is clarified, and the
development of some of the formal concepts discussed above (specifically,
proportions, hypothetical forces, probability, and correlation) is traced.

Generally, in each of the tasks three levels of performance clearly
emerge, corresponding to the preoperational, concrete-operational, and
formal-operational stages of Piaget's theory. Moreover, although the
details of performance and explanation proposed by subjects vary with
the context of the individual task, there are clear similarities in performance across tasks which are well illustrated in the balance experiment
described earlier. The preoperational child does not think like a scientist
at all; he focuses upon the goal and uses direct action to attain it (as in
pushing down the lighter balance pan); effects are explained by analogy
to his own action. He is not analytic in approach to the task, nor is he
accurate in his description of it. Often the child may offer multiple or
even mutually contradictory explanations for the same phenomena (as
in the experiment of floating bodies). The concrete operational child,
on the other hand, is both more analytic and more objective than the
preoperational child. He can identify relevant variables and appreciates
the nature of their effect; he does recognize contradiction and is troubled
by it. But, he goes only so far as concrete operations can take him. Having
mastered the skills of classification and seriation, he can and does apply
them with increasing spontaneity and effectiveness. These skills, however,

can get him only to the establishment and enumeration of empirical correspondences. They do not enable him to formulate a theoretical law or
to establish by compelling logical inference what cannot be directly
observed. That level of mastery is attained only by the formal operational
child. Not only does the adolescent proceed in a more systematic fashion,
but he also approaches the whole task in a different manner. He considers
possible alternatives, formulates hypotheses, and proceeds to test them.
Having reached a tentative conclusion, he spontaneously verifies it to see,
for example, if this is a unique solution. In short, the hypothetico-deductive reasoning of scientific procedure appears along with such fundamental methodology as the use of controls, or holding other variables
constant while systematically varying an independent variable.

1. *The transition from concrete to formal operations.* The wealth of
protocols nicely illustrates the transition from concrete to formal operations and the causal factors producing the transition. One necessary precondition is that the child must be well-practiced in the use of concrete
operations in a variety of contexts so that he uses them spontaneously
and skillfully. Only when he is proficient in a mode of thought can the child
recognize its failure for what it is. A second precondition is that the child
encounter a variety of situations in which (a) his concrete approaches
and skills are inadequate to produce success and (b) the shortcomings are
evident. In the course of casting about to eliminate difficulties, the child
must become more analytic; he has to identify relevant factors and to control them through elimination or neutralization. As a result, he encounters
new possibilities which must be dealt with by the mechanisms at hand,
such as creation of classes of classes, which leads to a full combinatorial
scheme and the shift from focus on properties and relations to the use
of propositions. Propositions are either true or false (rather than in correspondence or noncorrespondence with experience). Once the child operates at a propositional level and with the aid of a combinatorial structure,
(a) the structure of INRC transformations follows (an assumption which
Lunzer [1965] questions), and (b) he is freed from reliance upon direct
physical experience and able to function at the abstract level of logic.
Piaget is not explicit as to the details of this crucial transition, the assumed
nature of which is based more upon inference than evidence. However,
once the transition has begun it is clear that it has self-perpetuating properties. By virtue of its intrinsic power and efficacy, a logical approach
must work better than other alternative approaches; thus, formal-operations thinking creates the occasion of its own reinforcement (which, to be
sure, is not a word Piaget uses to describe the process of strengthening
and consolidation). As the adolescent becomes more proficient at logical
thought, he applies it more broadly and more proficiently, eventually orga-

nizing at the new and different equilibrium level of formal operations.

It seems quite reasonable that different cultures or subcultures within a culture may be differentially effective in providing both the precipitating conditions for transition to and the occasions for reinforcement of formal operational thought. Thus, one should expect to find cultural, class, and even sex differences in both the frequency of occurrence of formal-operations thought and the rate of its development. Although environmental influences are of obvious importance, genetic factors are not necessarily ruled out. The maturation of the nervous system may also play a role, although at this stage of knowledge the details of that role are by no means clear. Finally, although the abstract logical thought of formal operations constitutes an a priori optimal state of final equilibrium, it is clear that this final state may not be attained in practice. The prior stages of development are, in effect, forced upon every normal human being by virtue of the structure of the physical world and the conditions of human existence. The final stage, on the other hand, may be a refinement of advanced civilization rather than a necessary condition of survival.

Summary

1. After a very general characterization of adolescence, some of the concepts of Piaget's theory of cognitive development were introduced and developmental stages were described in terms of: (a) their characteristic operations; (b) the elements to which operations are applied; and (c) the structure or coordination among operations.

2. Adolescent, or formal operational, thought was then characterized in greater detail in terms of two features of the structure of operations (the combinatorial scheme and the INRC group of transformations) and the higher-level concepts whose attainment is made possible by these structures.

3. The fifteen experiments used by Inhelder and Piaget to support their theory were briefly introduced and the transition from concrete to formal operations was recapitulated in terms of behavior exhibited in the experimental tasks rather than in theoretical terms.

EXPERIMENTAL EVIDENCE

Verifications, Extensions, and Tests of Generality

Although Inhelder's formal-operations tasks are widely used for assessment of adolescent thought, it is surprising how few replications have been reported and how few authors attempt to answer the obvious questions which arise from *The Growth of Logical Thinking*. One objection which is constantly raised about the Geneva studies is concerned with the "clinical method" of questioning a child about his performance and with the mode of reporting results. Most of the studies selected for discussion below, therefore, employ a more rigid procedure for testing (e.g., with a series of fixed questions and task orders for all subjects), and report group means or frequency distributions as well as statistical tests of group differences, correlations, and so on. The Inhelder tasks which have been used in reported research are summarized in table 4. In general, with the exception of the flexibility of rods and pendulum tasks, the tasks designed to assess development of propositional logic as reflected in the identification of variables are much less frequently used than tasks for the assessment of development of operational schemes for combination, proportion, and so on. Two tasks (equality of angles of incidence, and reflection and centrifugal force) have not been used at all; four other tasks have been used by only one investigator: law of floating bodies, and communicating vessels by Jackson (1965); and falling bodies on an inclined plane, and equilibrium in the hydraulic press by Lovell (1961a). These six tasks which are rarely or never used have been excluded from table 4. Some studies still in preparation for publication have been included.

TABLE 4. SUMMARY OF STUDIES EMPLOYING
THE INHELDER TASKS

---

1. *Development of propositional logic*
   Flexibility of rods: Lovell (1961a); Tomlinson-Keasey (1972); Schwebel (1972)
   Pendulum: Lovell (1961a); Jackson (1965); Lovell & Shields (1967); Bart (1971); Tomlinson-Keasey (1972); Jones (1972); Kuhn et al. (1972)
   Invisible magnetization: Lovell (1961a); Weitz, Bynum, Thomas & Steger (1972)
2. *Operational schemata of formal logic*
   Chemical combination of colorless liquids: Lovell (1961a); Lovell & Shields (1967); Dale (1970); Neimark (1970a); Stephens, McLaughlin & Mahaney (1971); Tomlinson-Keasey (1972); Schwebel (1972); Kuhn et al. (1972)
   Conservation of motion on a horizontal plane: Lovell (1961a); Jackson (1965); Bart (1971)
   Equilibrium in a balance: Lovell (1961a); Jackson (1965); Lovell & Shields (1967); Bart (1971); Lee (1971); Tomlinson-Keasey (1972); Jones (1972); Schwebel (1972)
   Hauling weight on an inclined plane: Tomlinson-Keasey (1972); Schwebel (1972)
   Projection of shadows: Lovell (1961a); Bart (1971); Lee (1971); Schwebel (1972)
   Correlation: Lovell (1961a); Neimark (1970a); Kuhn et al. (1972)

---

1. *Direct verification.* In only two studies have a variety of tasks over a broad age-range been used to determine replicability of the Inhelder and Piaget findings: Lovell (1961a) used a heterogeneous assortment of persons from age eight to adult and ten of the Inhelder tasks (each subject did four of them); Jackson (1965) administered the same six tasks to normal children aged five to fifteen years and ESN (educable low-IQ) children aged seven to fifteen. Both authors found that level of perform-

ance for normals improves with age, that there is a shift around the age of eleven to twelve from concrete to formal level, and that performance continues to improve through late adolescence. The ESN children showed little evidence of formal operations. Both investigators reported frequency distributions of performance level which indicated wide group variability within a given age or ability level, as well as the shift with age in central tendency. However, both investigators found relatively few of the oldest subjects to be at the higher level, IIIB, of formal operations. In general, at all age levels, performance appears to be below the qualitative levels obtained in Geneva. This, as will be seen, is a common finding in most other studies as well (Dale 1970; Tomlinson-Keasey 1972). Both Jackson and Lovell have provided some detail as to the ways performance on each task varied from the Geneva findings. Dale (1970) has provided an extensive analysis for the chemical combinations task. Neimark (1970*a*) suggested that this task did not bring forth logic in her subjects.

As a result of their analysis of the *Gou* protocol reported by Inhelder and Piaget (1958), Bynum, Thomas, and Weitz (1972) question whether any normal subject ever displays many of the sixteen propositional combinations in analyzing the magnetization task (or any of the other Inhelder experiments). In a repeat of the invisible magnetization task with nine-, twelve-, and sixteen-year-old children, Weitz, Bynum, Thomas, and Steger (1972) found that 80 percent of all children tested immediately identified the magnet solution with no prior reasoning at all. Those who did display reasoning relied almost entirely upon conjunction and implication. Nor was there a change with age in the frequency or type of combination used, although the authors reported a greater "sophistication and complexity" in the usage of combinations employed.

Although one gets the impression that Inhelder's original subjects were probably run on more than one problem, no evidence was reported on individual consistency in performance across problems. Both replications addressed this problem. Jackson found only 10 percent of his normal subjects performed all tasks at the same substage level, while 60 percent spanned two substages and 4 percent spanned four substages. On the other hand, Kuhn, Langer, Kohlberg, and Haan (1972), using only three tasks (pendulum, chemicals, and correlation) reported much more intra-individual variation and clear evidence of differential task difficulty (in the order listed). Neimark (1970*a*) also found the correlation task to be more difficult than the chemicals task.

Lovell reported his data in terms of coefficients of concordance, suggesting that eight tasks were of equivalent difficulty while two, correlation and projection of shadows, were discrepant, with the latter being clearly of greater difficulty. Lee (1971), however, reported very similar developmental trends for the balance and projection of shadows tasks over the five- to seventeen-year age range and a correlation of .85 between the two tasks. Bart (1971) reported a factor analysis of a battery of four Inhelder tasks (pendulum, motion on a horizontal plane, balance, and projection of shadows) along with a vocabulary and several reasoning tasks administered to bright thirteen- to nineteen-year-olds. He found that all Inhelder tasks loaded on a single factor. Lovell and Butterworth (1966) and Lovell and Shields (1967) also reported this single factor. The shadow and balance tasks were correlated .78 (comparable to Lee's value), while motion on a horizontal plane was least correlated with the other three tasks. Thus, although there is some evidence for a common factor among formal operations tasks and for homogeneity of difficulty among tasks, the evidence is skimpy and not altogether clear-cut. Much more work on intra-individual difficulty and possible difference among tasks in age mastery (horizontal decalages) is needed. Incidentally, none of these investigators who tested for sex differences found them except Dale. Schwebel (1972), using three Inhelder tasks, also found sex differences in favor of males for college freshmen.

Finally, it should be noted that all of the developmental literature cited is cross-sectional. Although some longitudinal data have been collected by Inhelder (Shard, Inhelder, Noelting, Murphy, and Thomae 1960), and by Hughes (1965), the material is not readily available. Two studies in which one-year retests for selected tasks were reported may be available shortly (Kuhn et al. and Schwebel). At present, the correspondence between longitudinal and cross-sectional development on the Inhelder tasks is very much of an open question.

2. *Development of the formal concepts.* The fifteen Inhelder tasks, while most closely associated with the assessment of formal operations, have a number of disadvantageous features: they involve special equipment which must work accurately if the experiment is to be of value; each task yields only one measure of performance, a rating on a three- or five-point scale; there is no good theoretical rationale for selecting among the tasks; nor is there evidence on which to base generalization from the tasks to other specific component skills. Many investigators have chosen to focus upon one of the eight formal concepts listed earlier as representative of formal operational thought and to use one of the assessment tasks developed earlier by Piaget and his associates which are less open to the objections above.

a. Conservation of volume. One Piagetian assertion which is now well supported by research is the order of development of conservations: mass, then weight, then volume, with about two years between the appearance of each and with volume conservation appearing at the time of formal operations (Uzgiris 1964). Elkind (1961*a*), testing for the three conservations in school children in kindergarten through sixth grade, found that most sixth-graders conserved mass and weight but that only 25 percent of them conserved volume. Among 469 junior and senior high-school students (Elkind 1961*b*), volume conservation increased over the twelve to nineteen age-range, and significant sex differences appeared. In a repetition of this experiment with two groups of college students, Elkind (1962) found that only 58 percent of the college students conserved volume and that there were large sex differences (74 percent of the boys and 52 percent of the girls). Towler and Wheatley (1971) repeated the experiment with college girls and found volume conservation in only 61 percent of the group. Higgins-Trenk and Gaite (1971), using high-school students as subjects, found that percent of conservers increased with age from thirteen to seventeen years but found no sex differences. Lovell and Shields (1967), working with very bright (IQ 140) eight- to ten-year-olds, suggested that volume conservation precedes formal level performance on three Inhelder tasks. Stephens, McLaughlin, and Mahaney (1971) reported 66 percent or more of their normals showed simple volume conservation at age thirteen and more sophisticated volume conservation only at age seventeen (retardates, on the other hand, failed to evidence even simple volume conservation by age eighteen).

The concept of volume is, of course, a complex one with several possible levels of abstraction involved (Piaget, Inhelder, and Szeminska 1960; Vinh Bang 1967). For example, interior volume (e.g., conserving the number of unit cubes in a three-dimensional structure over changes in component dimensions) appears before conservation of occupied volume (e.g., volumes of water displaced by equal-sized clay balls, one of which is transformed in shape). A short, simple discussion of these differences is given in Lovell (1961*b*). Lunzer (1960) has compared several manifestations of the volume concept, as have Lovell and Ogilvie (1961). A more sophisticated step in this direction is Brainerd's (1971*a*) comparison of judgments of solid volume, liquid volume, and density, showing density to be the last attained. Elsewhere, Brainerd (1971*b*) provides a nice discussion of the difference between concrete and formal conservations.

b. Combinatorial operations. Piaget makes a distinction between the complete combinatorial scheme of sixteen propositional combinations as a hypothesized structure underlying formal thought and a subject's actual use of a systematic general procedure for generating all possible combinations or orderings of a set of elements. The chemicals experiment provides one technique for assessing the development of a systematic procedure. Two simpler and more direct means were employed earlier by Piaget and Inhelder (1951) in their *combinations* and *permutations* tasks. Still a third procedure, closer in form to the chemistry experiment, has been employed by Elkind, Barocas, and Rosenthal (1968), who presented four poker chips differing in color and requested all possible combinations of chips taken n at a time. They found that most fourteen- to fifteen-year-olds ignored the 0 possibility. The remaining fifteen combinations (see table 2) were successfully generated by 52 percent of their normal group.

The combinations task requires a child to make all possible pairs of n colors (generally six are used), disregarding order, and yields scores for comprehensiveness of the generating scheme as well as understanding of the principle and ability to generalize it. Piaget and Inhelder (1951) reported that development of a systematic combination procedure appeared early in formal operations, whereas a comparable scheme for permutations appeared much later. Recent work by Neimark (1972) supported this conclusion with respect to a generating system. When her subjects were asked to predict the number of combinations for sample values of n colors, no fourth-grader could answer correctly, and only two of twenty-three fifth- and sixth-graders did so. Two years later, half of the fourth- (now sixth-) graders answered correctly for combinations, but only two out of twenty could perform the same feat for permutations.

Several Piagetian tasks are simply administered and readily adapted for use cross-culturally or with the deaf (Furth and Youniss 1971). Goodnow (1962) administered the combinations task along with conservation of space, weight, and volume tasks to a variety of groups in Hong Kong: European school children, Chinese children in Anglo-Chinese schools with and without science courses, Chinese school children in poorer Chinese schools, relatively unschooled children, and dockworkers. For the conservation tasks, there was little evidence of increase in success with age, and overall level of attainment was below Genevan levels. The combination task, on the other hand, showed an effect not only of age but also amount and quality of schooling. In a subsequent paper, Goodnow and Bethon (1966) compared the Chinese data with data for normal and dull American school children. The unschooled Chinese boys did as well as American and European children on the conservation tasks but much more poorly on the combination task, where their performance was comparable with that of dull children. Further evidence of the role of education (or general social milieu) upon formal operations tasks is pro- vided by Peluffo (1962, 1967) who reported that only 20 percent of illiterate Sardinian adults solved the combinations task successfully. Peluffo also compared three groups of eight- to ten-year-olds (urban resi- dents, immigrants with three years of urban residence, and new immigrants) on an ingenious test of proportionality notions and found clear between-group differences. The new immigrants did not show improvement with age, whereas the other groups did. By age ten, the percent correct solution was 90, 50, and 8 for longest to shortest urban residence, respectively.

For the permutation task (where the subject is required to produce all possible orders of four objects taken once each), several objective scoring procedures for evaluation of the generating scheme have been developed by Leskow and Smock (1970). They asked twelve-, fifteen-, and eighteen-year-olds in Gary, Indiana, to do four versions of the task, each with a different type of material. They found both age and sex differences (in favor of boys), as well as a type of material effect. Any evidence that quality of performance is affected by the nature of the material suggests that a truly general scheme has not yet been attained. Neimark (1972), using New Jersey school children and a procedure which placed no demands upon memory, found a parallel age trend. These more advantaged children consistently showed better performance than the Leskow and Smock subjects. That performance on this task may be subject to improvement through training is suggested by the results of two experiments, one with American tenth-graders (DeSciora 1971) and one with Rumanian children in grades four, six, and eight (ten- to fifteen-year-olds) (Fischbein, Pampu, and Mânzat 1970a). The Rumanian study employed a step-by-step procedure designed to promote generalization. Only the oldest subjects reached the last, most difficult step.

c. Proportionality, probability, and correlation. All three concepts share a simple arithmetic operation, the setting up of a ratio or, in the case of proportionality, the equating of two ratios. Multiplication and division are typically taught to school children in second and third grades in the United States and elsewhere and are generally well mastered as rote skills during the period of concrete operations. The three concepts, however, seem quite clearly to be formal operational attainments and, at least in the case of correlations, among the very latest attainments at that. The obstacle to early attainment in all cases seems to be awareness that a ratio is required and appreciation of the quantities to be included in that ratio. A priori, one would expect attainment of these concepts to be influenced by mathematics and science teaching—an influence that is not always beneficial. A number of investigators have commented on the interfering effects of confusions arising from poor teaching (Lunzer and Pumfrey 1966; Szeminska 1965; Goodnow 1962; Woodward 1969).

The development of proportionality concepts from ages five to fifteen has been examined by Lunzer and Pumfrey (1966) and Pumfrey (1968) through use of three tasks (which are not intercorrelated once MA is partialed out): building a wall of Cuisenaire rods, a pantograph task, and the balance task. Development in all three tasks is reflected by replacement of additive strategies by multiplicative ones. Proportionality as a spontaneously employed scheme does not appear much before age fourteen.

Experimental attempts at assessing the child's understanding of probability are difficult to compare because authors have differed in their criteria for "having" a concept. The tasks used by Piaget and Inhelder (1951) led to the conclusion that the young child responds to absolute number rather than to ratio of "favorable cases" to all outcomes. However, the Piaget and Inhelder tasks required the child to remember two sets of instances previously seen prior to judging. As will be seen shortly, the memory of the young child is fallible. Other evidence on the role of memory and question context is available in Hale, Miller, and Stevenson (1967). A more recent replication with similar tasks where the material was present at the time of judging (Hoemann and Ross 1971) has shown that children did well where little more than perceptual judgment was required but foundered when prediction based on probability was required. This finding may account for earlier results (Davies 1965; Goldberg 1966; Yost, Siegel, and Andrews 1962), showing that in some situations even preschoolers demonstrate a comprehension of probability. For a more extended critical discussion of this point see Flavell (1970a, p. 1008–9). Research by Fischbein, Pampu, and Mânzat (1970b) suggests that third-graders can profit from instruction in learning to choose "through comparison of quantitative ratios." On the other hand, there is also evidence showing that even adults have a shaky command of probability concepts. For example, Ross (1966) and Ross and Levy (1958) showed that susceptibility to the "gambler's fallacy" increased with age.

In the correlation task, a subject is presented with varying numbers of four types of instances (AB, $\overline{A}$B, A$\overline{B}$, and $\overline{A}\overline{B}$, where A and B refer to property classes) and is asked if A and B are related or go together. Inhelder and Piaget used hair- and eye-color for this task; other investigators have used the relation of disease to symptom (Smedeslund, 1963), cause (Neimark 1970a, 1972), or cure (Seggie and Endersby 1972). Smedslund lists three criteria for successful performance: in situations requiring a selective strategy, the subject with a concept of correlation will order the data into four categories and count the frequency in each; in situations requiring a receptive strategy, the subject distributes attention equally over four categories; estimates will be based on estimates of the ratio of the sum of two diagonal cell frequencies (AB + $\overline{A}\overline{B}$) to the sum of the counterdiagonal ($\overline{A}$B + A$\overline{B}$). The third criterion, which is necessary and sufficient, presupposes the first two. In two experiments employing student nurses, there was little evidence of understanding of correlation (one-third of the nurses in Experiment II said they didn't even understand the task). Neimark (1972), using a procedure similar to Smedslund's Experiment II with children, found that although many youngsters did better than Smedslund's nurses in sorting the data and were quite accurate in assigning a probability to one of the events (e.g., having the disease), they were poor at assessing the correlation of presence of green germs and the disease. When asked to "make up a deck showing that green germs cause the disease" they tended to give only one cell (e.g., AB or $\overline{AB}$, rather than both); when asked for a deck showing no relation whatsoever, no child created a deck showing equal instances of all four combinations.

d. Other formal concepts. To the author's knowledge there are no systematic investigations involving the coordination of two systems of reference (relativity) other than the work of Piaget (1946), or forms of conservation which go beyond empirical verification. One would expect both to be difficult concepts attained late in the period of formal operations, if they are attained at all.

Other Indices of Adolescent Thought

The foregoing discussion has been concerned with research issues arising directly from Piagetian theory. There are investigators, working within different frameworks or on empirical bases, who have noted other areas in which adolescent thought differs qualitatively from the thought of the secondary school child. A few of these areas will be reviewed briefly.

1. *Classification and concept attainment.* For Piaget, classification is one of the major concrete operations. On this basis, one might not expect much difference between the classification concepts of adolescents or adults and those of fourth- or fifth-graders (except where formal concepts are involved). Other theorists, however, e.g., Vygotsky (1962), have emphasized that adult concepts are formulated at a higher level of abstraction than child concepts. A number of investigators report a shift with age in basis, or criterion, of classification from perceptual properties and functions to categorical classification (Bruner, Olver, and Greenfield 1966; Reichard, Schneider, and Rapaport 1944; Sigel 1953). Elkind (1966) has shown that adolescents are more flexible in shifting criterion and less influenced by mode of stimulus representation than children (Elkind, Barocas, and Johnsen 1969; Elkind, Medvene, and Rockway 1969). All of these findings are compatible with the assumption of a shift to higher levels of abstraction in adolescene.

Another approach to the study of concept attainment is one in which the subject is told the rule being used to identify the class and is required to identify the defining attribute over a series of instances (where instances may be controlled by the experimenter or the subject). Earlier work was modeled on the procedure used by Bruner, Goodnow, and Austin (1956). More recent work tends to follow the more carefully controlled blank-trials procedure of Levine (1966). All of these approaches lead to an examination of the subject's utilization of information from prior instances as determinants of his response to present instances, that is, his strategy. For most procedures the most efficient strategy is one of focusing (holding one attribute constant and varying others systematically). Yudin (1966), using a modified Bruner procedure, found an increase in focusing over the twelve to sixteen age-range as well as a strong effect of IQ. Eimas (1969) and Ingalls and Dickerson (1969) both employed the Levine procedure in comparing the performance of children over a fairly wide age-range with performance of college students. Both found an increase in focusing with age, with only college students approximating a perfect focusing strategy. Gholson, Levine, and Phillips (1972) presented comparable findings along with an analysis of the systems employed by children in grades two to six on blank trials: Relative preference among systems was essentially stable throughout this range, with dimension checking, a slightly less efficient system than focusing, preferred by all children. Eimas (1970) reported that even very young children adopted a focusing strategy when a previous outcome remained visible. These results suggest that whatever difficulties young children have in efficient information processing stem largely from problems of storing information in memory. This conclusion was also suggested by earlier evidence from Huttenlocher (1964).

2. *Memorization procedures.* Psychologists have long appreciated that immediate memory span lengthens with age; span forward and backward is one of the more durable items of the Stanford-Binet. Only recently, however, has there been evidence showing that memory is not a passive process of "beating in" traces through repetition but, rather, an active process of information transformation which bears many similarities to problem-solving and which shows a developmental course paralleling other aspects of cognitive development. Smirnov and Zinchenko (1969) were among the first to study developmental changes in memory systematically. Piaget (1968) and Inhelder (1969) examined the changes wrought in figurative aspects of memory by development of concrete operations, but no comparable studies have yet appeared concerning changes in memory coding wrought by development of formal operations.

Much of the recent American work on the development of memorizing skills has been aptly summarized by Flavell (1970b). In general it reflects: an increasing awareness with age of the difference between perceiving and storing in memory (Appel, Cooper, McCarrell, Sims-Knight, Yussen, and Flavell 1972); an increasingly accurate appraisal with age by the individual of his own memory capacities and limitations (Flavell, Friedrichs, and Hoyt 1970); and development of increasingly sophisticated and efficient mnemonic schemes (Mandler and Stephens 1967; Moely, Olson, Halwes, and Flavell 1969; Neimark, Slotnick, and Ulrich 1971). The concrete operational child does label instances and even classifies them into categories, but he or she still relies heavily upon rehearsal (Hagen 1971). Neimark (1971) has speculated that increasingly heavy demands placed upon limited "storage space" force the adult to utilize his formal operational skills to create schemes for avoiding the use of rehearsal, wherever possible, by developing a succinct principle or mnemonic scheme with which to generate the needed information. Concomitant with these changes and reflective of them, is a change in the nature of the mnemonic code that takes the form of a shift from literal reproduction to "chunking" and increasingly abstract labeling (Belmont and Butterfield 1969, 1971, Wapner and Rand 1968). An especially clear example of the development of mnemonic coding is provided by Lehman and Goodnow (1972), who asked children in kindergarten and grades two, four, and six to reproduce a pattern of pencil taps. Young children (55 percent of kindergarten) reported that their recall derived from "hearing it in their head" (a literal trace); older children assigned a number to each tap (e.g., 123, 12) while still older children (33 percent of grade six) simply noted the number of taps in each grouping (e.g., 32). Late adolescents and adults (who were not run in this study) undoubtedly seek still more efficient compression (e.g., an algebraic formula of the series).

3. *Problem-solving.* Many investigators have raised methodological objections to Piaget's tasks on a number of grounds: the clinical method of questioning places a premium on the verbal facility of the child and probably puts the younger child at a disadvantage for this reason; many tasks, and most especially the formal-operations tasks, involve special knowledge and may reflect schooling as well as general level of cognitive development; the finding of relatively discrete qualitative stages in development may be an artifact of the rating-scale scoring system. To circumvent these objections, Neimark used a diagnostic problem-solving task in which the subject was given an answer sheet with n different patterns of k binary elements and a problem board in which one of the n patterns was concealed by a movable shutter over each of the k elements. The subject was instructed to identify the concealed pattern by uncovering as few of its elements as possible. Since the task is a paradigm of all diagnostic problem-solving, it presumably provides a basis for generalization. On the other hand, it is pretty much language-free and novel to all subjects. In addition, it is possible to obtain a number of objective measures of the individual's information-gathering strategy as well as a qualitative rating of the

subject's strategy based upon his or her own description of it. The major quantitative measure in this task is a "strategy score" summarizing the mean expected informational outcome of a series of shutter openings. It is measured on a continuous logarithmic scale with a maximum of unity reflecting optimal performance. The comparable qualitative rating of the subject's strategy is a four-point scale ranging from 0 for no system whatsoever, through 1 for a limited local rule (generally for the last move), 2 for a collection of local rules (for the last move plus the first or the next-to-last), to 3 for a fully general rule (halve the number of alternatives with each shutter opening).

In a cross-sectional study, using bright and normal IQ children over a wide age-range, the strategy score was shown to be a smooth negatively accelerated function of MA (Neimark and Lewis 1967). A one-year retest of another group of children (Neimark and Lewis 1968) revealed that the qualitative rating of the child's described strategy reflected a stepwise course of development: the intermediate ratings, 1 and 2, appeared to reflect transition states whereas 0 and 3 were relatively stable levels of performance. When magnitude of change in strategy score over a one-year period was compared for two groups, one of which showed an increase in qualitative rating and one of which did not, only the group with a rating increase showed a statistically significant increase in strategy score. Thus, stepwise improvement was not an artifact of the rating-scale measure. Moreover, rating-scale score was closely correlated with strategy score and had as high a retest reliability over time as the objective measure. These findings have been replicated and extended in a subsequent longitudinal study in which children were retested repeatedly over a period of three to four years (Neimark 1972) with no apparent practice gain when compared with control groups. The pattern of change over time as a function of MA for individual longitudinal subjects was comparable to results obtained in the earlier cross-sectional study. Finally, it was assumed at the outset that level-3 performance on this task corresponded to formal operations as assessed in the traditional Piaget procedures (that is, at this level the subject is operating in terms of an abstract combinatorial scheme and working from possible to actual rather than at the concrete level of performing manipulations and being governed by their consequences). The assumption was borne out by the finding of significant positive correlations with a number of Piaget's formal-operations tasks (Neimark 1970a, 1972) and even with a task to assess memorization strategy.

4. *Logical reasoning.* Since formal operational thought is characterized as logical thought utilizing propositions as its elements and a full combinatorial system as a keystone of the structure of its operations, one would

expect to find logical reasoning, in the narrowly defined sense, to develop during adolescence. One of the most popular tasks for the assessment of logical reasoning is the transitive inference task: Given $A > B$ and $B > C$ one logically infers that $A > C$. In a sense, such inference is related to seriation of relations, which is a concrete operation (Murray and Youniss 1968). The major difference is that the ordering proceeds at a purely symbolic level. The fact that inference with concrete examples proceeds in à parallel course to inference for verbal material over the age range of eight to eighteen, but with verbal lagging behind concrete at all ages, is illustrated by the data of Glick and Wapner (1968).

In his early work, Piaget (1964*a*) used a modified version of one of Burt's inference tests: Edith is fairer than Suzanne; Edith is darker than Lili. Which is the darkest, Edith, Suzanne, or Lili? Even thirteen-year-olds seem to have great difficulty with this problem (perhaps, as Hunter suggests, because it is especially misleading in French), a difficulty which in the early stages is attributable to inadequate memory of the component relations. Bryant and Trabasso (1971), in an elegantly controlled experiment involving inference of stick length, showed that when component information is clearly in memory, preschoolers make the correct logical inference. Of course, these experimenters utilized concrete instances, and Glick and Wapner (who did ensure that subjects remembered the component information for verbal problems) have shown a superiority of concrete over verbal forms. Change in performance as a result of variation of material or of form of questioning suggests that a skill is not perfectly mastered.

Perhaps the best evidence of developing imperviousness to surface variation is provided by Hunter (1957), who compared performance of eleven- and sixteen-year-olds on four forms of the inference problem and with two types of relations (height and happiness). He found consistent age differences which suggested that only the older children were responding to the structural characteristics of the problem per se, treating each problem as a representative of a class of problems. There is a growing literature (Clark, 1969*a*, *b*, DeSoto, London, and Handel 1965; Huttenlocher 1968) showing that the more transformation of presented information is required, the longer it takes adults to reach a correct inference. Although interpretations of the meaning of these data vary, it is interesting to note that many adults attempt to convert the abstract problem to a concrete analogue (Handel, Desoto, and London 1968).

Perhaps the best illustration of the methodological pitfalls in the study of logical thinking in children is provided in a dissertation (1960) in which Hill purported to show logical inference in six- to eight-year-olds given items of sentential logic, classical syllogism, and logic of quantification, all to be answered "Yes" or "No" (that is, the stated conclusion is or is not correct). Hill's items were repeated by O'Brien and Shapiro (1968), Shapiro and O'Brien (1970), initially with first- to third-graders and later with children in grades one to eight. In addition to Hill's items, they included thirty-three items in which no necessary conclusion followed and added a third alternative answer ("can't say"). O'Brien and Shapiro replicated Hill's findings of significantly better than chance performance and no improvement with age on the items originally used by Hill. However, with the items for which there was no necessary conclusion, there was highly significant improvement with age. With these items, the frequency of correct response was *below* chance through grade four, and the mean proportion correct did not equal the level reported by Hill for six-year-olds until age thirteen (at which time accuracy was still well below 100 percent).

There is a considerable literature showing that syllogistic inference in adults is subject to error (Chapman and Chapman 1959; Henle 1962; Sells 1936; Woodworth and Sells 1935). Ceraso and Provitera (1971) have suggested, without providing a completely convincing case for their argument, that adults reason logically but that errors arise from a misunderstanding of the premises. Even if one accepts their conclusion, the old question of why adults reason incorrectly is merely replaced by a new question: why do adults so consistently misinterpret the meaning of certain premises? The answer to that question may well turn out to lie in imperfect knowledge of the language of logic, specifically the meaning of some logical quantifiers and connectives. With respect to quantifiers, there is little developmental evidence, but work in progress by Chapman and Neimark (1973) suggests, as one would expect, that the chief culprit is "some."

With respect to connectives, on the other hand, there is a good deal of developmental evidence (Furth and Youniss 1965; Peel 1967; Suppes and Feldman 1971; Youniss and Furth 1964). Although these studies differ with respect to procedure, materials, and age groups tested, there is consistency in the finding that some terms and forms are much more difficult than others and that, although even young children do well with some instances, the more difficult items are beyond the concrete operational child. An especially thorough examination of development of understanding of the connectives "and" and "or" in kindergarten and grades two, four, six, and eight under a variety of conditions was reported by Nitta and Nagano (1966) and partially replicated by Neimark and Slotnick (1970). All the data have shown that understanding of class inclusion and exclusion, and of class intersect ("and") are attained early —certainly within the early years of concrete operations. Understanding of inclusive class union ("or"), however, was not fully attained by the oldest groups investigated (eighth- and ninth-graders). A subsequent study (Neimark 1970c) showed rapid development of comprehension of inclusive interpretation of union throughout the high-school age range.

Despite the sketchiness of this review of logical reasoning and the heterogeneity among experiments covered, a consistent picture emerges: abstract logical reasoning in the formal sense and with respect to a reasonably demanding criterion for "reasoning" begins to appear during adolescence. Under some conditions and with some types of material, young children in the early elementary grades reason logically, but the accuracy of their performance is very much situation-specific. Logical reasoning, as reflected in consistent performance across a broad class of instances, does not appear until adolescence and even at that age is by no means a universal attainment of all adolescents. Thus, logical reasoning seems to require the use of formal operations. However, a systematic examination of the relation between formal operational skills and performance on logic tasks remains to be done.

5. *Thinking in other types of tasks.* There are several studies done in a variety of contexts and addressed to a great variety of problems that shed some peripheral light on the development of adolescent thought. They are, however, too scattered and heterogeneous to provide much by way of clear generalization. Some authors (Dennis 1953; Maurer 1970) have suggested that animistic thought persists into adolescence and adulthood. Simmons and Goss (1957) attempted to discover if frequency of animistic response among college students was influenced by context of questioning or background factors such as sex, religion, or extent of scientific training; they found it was not. Another persistence of childish thought that has been noted is egocentrism, the peculiarly adolescent aspects of which have been discussed by Elkind (1967) in a very perceptive paper.

Some investigators report an increase in comprehension, organization, and level of abstraction in the adolescent period. These have included: analogies (Lunzer 1965), interpretation of proverbs (Freides, Fredenthal, Grisell, and Cohen 1963), verbal comprehension of subject matter (Case and Collinson 1962), use of future time perspective (Monks 1968), notions of law (Adelson, Green, and O'Neil 1969), and the tendency to integrate discrete stimuli within a uniform framework (Schnall 1968; Schnall and Kemper 1968). Collis (1971), in a mathematics test given to school children from ten to seventeen years of age, independently varied level of abstraction of structure of the problem and the elements involved and found that increase in level of abstraction of elements produced a concomitant increase in difficulty only for the youngest subjects. Abstract structures, on the other hand, were difficult even with concrete elements.

Summary

1. In this section, experimental evidence concerning intellectual development during adolescence was differentiated with respect to the experimental task employed, according to those studies employing tasks introduced by Piaget and his collaborators and those employing other tasks.

2. The number of replications of the fifteen Inhelder experiments is surprisingly small; what few replications do exist, generally employ only one or two of the tasks.

3. Although improvement in performance with increasing age is generally reported in all the replication studies, the level of performance is generally lower than reported for comparable ages in Genevan subjects, and specific details of the Inhelder findings often are not replicated.

4. Experiments using tasks to assess the formal operational concepts have fared much better with replication. Volume conservation is the most frequently studied concept, and it has been consistently found to differ from other conservation tasks in being attained much later. Conservation of volume is attained, if at all, during adolescence. Parallel findings have been obtained for the formal operational concepts of proportionality, probability, correlation, and for combinatorial operations; all are attained during adolescence, but they are not universally attained by all adolescents.

5. Although classification is a concrete operation, studies of free classification among adolescents find them to be more likely to use abstract sorting criteria and more flexible in shifting criterion as compared with children. When a concept identification procedure was employed, adolescents were found to use more efficient strategies than children in both collection and utilization of information.

6. Comparable changes in the direction of increasing efficiency in coding, storage, and retrieval of information have been reported for adolescent performance on memory tasks. Furthermore, increasing age appears to be accompanied by increased awareness of the demands of memory tasks and of the memorizer's own ability relative to them. With respect to problem-solving, the review dealt with data and procedures from a diagnostic problem-solving task which may provide an alternative to the Inhelder tasks for assessing the onset of a formal operational approach to problems.

7. Direct investigations of the development of logical reasoning, as exemplified in traditional tasks of formal logic, have yielded a number of consistent findings with respect to transitive inferences and reasoning

with sentential logic or the classical syllogism; adequate performance of these forms of reasoning appears for the first time at the adolescent level. Studies of the sources of errors in formal logic point to differential comprehension of key logical terms: quantifiers and connectives.

8. All of the research reviewed supports the validity of formal operational thought as an empirical phenomenon distinct from concrete operations and demonstrates that age-related improvements in performance occur during adolescence. The research does not, however, shed much light upon the precise nature of the changes or the variables which affect them. It is difficult, therefore, to come forth with a firm generalization other than that adolescent thought develops from, but is different than, child thought.

QUESTIONS: ANSWERED, UNANSWERED, AND UNRAISED

What Is an Answer?

Flavell (1970a) raises the provocative question (pp. 1032–34) of what it means to say that a child "has a concept." Parallel questions may be raised with respect to formal operations: what does it mean to say that an individual "has" formal operations, and when can one say it? Perhaps the best answer was provided by one of Piaget's (1964b) subjects, a boy of five who had been apportioning beads equally into two glasses and judging the quantity in each glass to be equal. When asked if there would still be equal amounts if he continued adding beads all day and all night and all the next day, he replied, "Once you know, you know for always" (p. 17). In other words, this is not an arbitrary association which can be made or unmade under appropriate training conditions. Rather, it has the compelling conviction of inescapable logic. Such, presumably, is the quality of operational structures. Unfortunately, very few investigators have attempted to determine if this identifying characteristic, or other alternative ones, applies to the subject's behavior in a given situation.

Before considering the data that have been collected and before deciding what is known about adolescent thought and what remains to be discovered, it is first essential to consider some methodological issues. Specifically, a critical examination is needed of the requirements of an appropriate experiment; alternatively, what constitute acceptable data?

1. Methodological issues. It is not possible to pose a set of independent questions to be ticked off one by one; the issues are too complexly interrelated. For example, the question of acceptable response measures cannot be considered to be independent of the experimental task in which they are obtained or of the original questions they were gathered to answer. If one starts with the question, "Is it possible to arrange conditions

under which a subject will reliably display precocious behavior?" the answer is presumed to be "yes"; only patience and ingenuity are required to obtain it. But what does such evidence mean, and to what extent can one generalize beyond it? In order to provide data relevant to a given theory it is necessary to work within the framework of that theory. In the case of research addressed to Piaget's theory of formal operations, this means that, as a minimum, one selects dependent variable measures that are valid indices of formal operations. This, in turn, requires careful consideration not only of the measures to be obtained but also of the appropriateness of the task and the representativeness of the groups employed. Each of these issues will be considered in turn.

a. Response measures. Flavell and Wohlwill (1969) proposed a competence/automata version of the psycholinguists' competence/performance distinction which is reminiscent of Hull's learning (habit)/performance distinction or Lewin's borrowing of the genotype/phenotype distinction. The essence of all these dichotomies is the distinction between fundamental defining properties and characteristics of a state (competence) versus the defining properties being inferred from the effects of specific experimental conditions (performance). Formal operations, by virtue of definition as an organized structure of general transformations, are to be coordinated to the competence side of the dichotomy. Criteria for inferring the presence of this competence must, of course, be specified, but clearly no single behavioral measure of performance can provide an index of competence. It is impossible to determine from only a single measure whether one is dealing with general competence or with situation-specific performance.

There has been a good deal of discussion in the literature concerning response criteria for Piagetian research. Most often discussion has centered on whether an objective response alone, e.g., a judgment in a conservation task, is required or whether adequate justification of the response is required as well. In some instances (Papalia 1972), addition of justification does not appreciably change the pattern of results; but it is more often the case that it has a profound effect on conclusions (e.g., in the studies of probability concepts). In principle, adequate justification is necessary for assessment of operational status. In practice, however, it may constitute an inappropriate or impossible demand (in work with the deaf, the illiterate, or members of other cultures). In those cases, there are alternative means to establish the generality of a response or the extent to which it is impervious to variation of conditions: use of several versions of the task with different material or use of several correlated tasks, retest after a short interval, test of transfer to a novel context, or test of resistance to argument and counterexample. Most authors are

insufficiently concerned with response generality and do not employ procedures to assess it.

Another and a related concern has to do with psychometric properties
of the response. Many investigators are uneasy about use of the coarse-
textured and subjective Piaget rating scale. While most investigators still
their uneasiness by determining interrater reliability, the finding of a high
correlation is not an altogether satisfactory solution. Presumably these
high correlations are at least partially attributable to uniform instruction
of the raters, including use of specific protocols as examples. This device
does not guarantee use of uniform criteria across investigators. Without
uniform criteria within a broader psychological community, comparison
across experiments, or pooling of findings into a single functional relation,
is not possible. Thus, in attempting to generalize over assembled published
evidence, one often wonders whether discrepant findings are to be attributed to variation in subject populations, experimental procedures, discrepancies in rating criteria, or some combination of two or more of
these factors.

An alternative solution is to use additional, preferably objective and
quantitative, measures of the major dependent variable. The measures of
permutation strategy employed by Leskow and Smock (1970) are a
good example of this solution. Through the use of such additional measures, Neimark (1972; Neimark and Lewis 1968) was able to demonstrate that ratings are more psychometrically sound than might have
been expected.

Another interpretive complication arises from the hypothesized existence of qualitative stages and transition levels between stages. Some good
techniques for the assessment of stages are described in Flavell and
Wohlwill (1969, pp. 98ff). They require the use of additional measures
of response generality as well as comparison of performance within age
levels. One of the simplest approaches, proposed by Wohlwill (1970),
is careful scrutiny of frequency distributions. Wherever clear stages do
exist, one should be unlikely to find normal distributions at the extreme
age-levels. Still another analytic device (Neimark and Lewis 1968) is to
form subgroups on the basis of one response measure (e.g., rating) for
between-group comparison with respect to another response measure
(e.g., change in strategy score). Of course, the most direct solution is to
work with longitudinal data. Once again, use of these more searching
techniques of data analysis is rare in published research.

b. Task selection. Another objection to much published research concerns selection of the experimental task. In many instances it appears to
be largely arbitrary or dictated by convenience rather than by a priori
analysis of demands of the problem itself. As indicated earlier, a subset

of the Inhelder tasks is commonly used. Although Piaget and Inhelder have managed to distill a good deal of developmental insight from use of these tasks, other investigators have been less imaginative and resourceful. It is this author's personal conviction that the Inhelder tasks are of limited general utility for a number of reasons, among which are: paucity of measures yielded, importance of good apparatus (inadequate apparatus and procedures lead to a lot of noisy variability), demands upon the experimenter's skill as a probing, clinical questioner. The use of formal-operation concept tasks, especially where additional quantitative measures of response quality are available (as in the case of the Leskow and Smock scoring of permutations) appears preferable. Alternatively, one might use a task designed specifically to tap presumed underlying determinants of behavior if its properties are well established (e.g., the Neimark problem-solving task).

c. Subject selection. A final methodological objection has to do with subject selection. Many authors have reported studies in which small groups were sampled from a parent population whose characteristics are described inadequately, if at all. As a result extent of possible generalization is indeterminant and power of statistical tests is reduced by large error variance. With respect to the second point, all the "noise" attributable to poorly controlled procedures or inadequate scoring criteria goes into group variability, as does variation in known contributory factors that are not assessed or controlled. The most prominent among such factors is mental age (which is a better basis for constituting homogeneous groups than chronological age, especially when working with small Ns). Other possible contributory factors are sex differences (where known to operate) and several individual-difference variables (which will be discussed in greater detail in the next section).

2. Variations on Piaget's theory. As noted at the outset, there is only one comprehensive theory of cognitive development, Piaget's. All other contenders are so deeply influenced by and derivative from the work of Piaget as to be better classified as shifts in focus or extension. Two shifts in focus are also heavily influenced by information-processing approaches. Gyr, Brown, and Cafagne (1967) have a computer analogue which generates qualitative stages but is rather impoverished with respect to empirical correlates and links to psychological processes. To date it has generated only one experimental investigation (Gyr and Fleisher 1967). Neimark (1970b) has proposed an information-processing analysis which closely parallels Piaget for the first two stages and differs only with respect to treatment of formal operations (and only for the operative aspects of them). In her view, the requirement of a complete combinatorial system and the INRC group of transformations is unduly restrictive. She proposes

that the essence of formal operations lies in organization and compression of information (as represented in terms of more abstract figurative aspects) for more efficient storage, retrieval, and utilization. This type of informational organization is reflected not only in performance on the traditional formal operational tasks but also in, for example, deliberate creation of mnemonics, spontaneous imposition of order on discrete instances and events (as in the formulation of explicit generalizations as well as in experimental tasks such as employed by Schnall and Kemper 1968), and in a great variety of heuristics for planning and organizing daily activities, such as scheduling of chores, outlining an argument prior to presenting it, and so on (common types of behavior about which there is no research evidence whatsoever).

Perhaps the most extensive and imaginative extension of Piaget is that of Pascual-Leone (1972), which has some features in common with the Flavell and Wohlwill (1969) general model for analysis of stages but is elaborated in greater detail and has already led to some specific research (Pascual-Leone, 1972). Pascual-Leone treats cognitive development as the resultant of the operation of five factors identified by the letters *I, M, L, F* and *B*. The *I* factor consists of a repertoire of schemes for operating directly upon input from the environment. The remaining four factors (*M, L, F* and *B*) operate upon activated schemes. The *M* factor is a multichannel central processor which coordinates the information transformed by the *I* operator. The *M* factor corresponds to Piaget's treatment of intelligence. Its central processing space (that is, the number of schemes which can be integrated in a single act) is assumed to grow in discrete linear fashion as a function of age. This *M* factor is similar to the P_a parameter of Flavell and Wohlwill. *L* is a logical or structural learning factor which operates in the creation of superordinate schemes or relational structures. The *F* operator refers to field effects associated with the particular task and experimental conditions which affect the probability of activation of schemes. It is proportional to salience of input features and demands of the required response. This factor appears to correspond to the P_b factor of Flavell and Wohlwill. The last factor, *B*, refers to individual-difference response biases, most especially Witkin's field-dependence and field-independence. This factor is similar to the *k* factor proposed by Flavell and Wohlwill. Whether one uses a single factor, or three, or five—or *n*—to describe cognitive development, there is evidence to suggest that an individual-difference factor is both relevant and needed, as will be seen in the next section.

What do we know?

In view of the preceding comments concerning inadequacy of data, methods, and formulation of research questions, it should be clear that

"What do we know?" must be taken to mean "know in a general sense." Most of the tentative conclusions that follow are based upon consistent findings, but they are consistent relative to a narrow data base of heterogeneous studies. Moreover, the best one can obtain in many instances are conclusions about general trends or identification of relevant independent variables. Specific details as to the nature of the effect of a variable, or the reasons for the effect, often remain to be spelled out by future research. Some of the major unanswered questions will be discussed in the concluding section.

1. *Is there a level of intellectual functioning above concrete operations?* At this stage of discussion the question is largely rhetorical, although it logically precedes the questions that follow. There is little doubt, at least in this author's mind, that there is a stage of development beyond concrete operations and that formal operations, as described by Piaget and Inhelder, provide a good first approximation for studying it, although some modification of the original formulation now appears to be in order.

2. *How universal and how stable is this stage?* There seems to be almost universal agreement in results of studies done with older adolescents and adults in Western cultures that not all individuals attain the level of formal operations. For example, Jackson (1965) found that among his oldest group (thirteen to fifteen years), only seven of sixteen adolescents attained the IIIB level: five on the pendulum problem, and one each on the balance and communicating vessels. Far fewer than 75 percent of Dale's (1970) fifteen-year-olds successfully performed the chemistry experiment. For the conservation of volume task, there seems to be close agreement (Elkind 1962; Towler and Wheatley 1971) that only about 60 percent of college students show conservation. Somewhat lower figures are reported by Papalia (1972), who found a precipitous drop in volume conservation among sixty-five- to eighty-two-year-olds. Similarly, Tomlinson-Keasey (1972) found only a little over 50 percent of her middle-aged women subjects attained formal operations (less than 20 percent if IIIB was used as the criterion). Thus, it seems very clear that, although there is a higher level, not all adults among the educated members of technologically advanced societies attain formal operations when assessed for such competence on formalized tasks. Piaget's (1972) reconsideration, in light of recent evidence, focused upon three alternative explanations: there is a slowing in the rate of attainment primarily as a result of environmental factors; there is a failure of attainment because of diversification of abilities with age ("in other words, our fourth period can no longer be characterized as a proper stage, but would already seem to be a structural advancement in the direction of specialization"); or, all individuals attain formal operations, not at a fixed age, but in different areas according to their aptitudes and their professional specialization. Of these three

alternatives, Piaget favors the last one. He further considers the possibility that the Inhelder tasks are not appropriate for general use and that other simpler and more general tasks may have to be developed.

a. Generality across cultures. There have been several good recent reviews of cross-cultural research (Vernon 1969; Dasen 1972), as well as chapter 11 in this volume. Although most research has been directed toward development of concrete operations, there seems to be clear evidence of retardation of development and even failure of attainment in most non-Western groups. Relatively little work has been done with formal operations, doubtless (at least in part) because of the difficulty of getting meaningful results from societies so unfamiliar with the materials or even the kinds of formal responses required by the tasks. A number of investigators comment on the difficulty of overcoming the African tendencies to immediate and impulsive responding (Richelle 1966) or to imitate what the experimenter has just done (Heron 1968). Quite often the Kohs blocks subtest of the WAIS is used, and this seems uniformly to produce poor performance among Africans (Jahoda 1956; Kellaghan 1968), although Eskimos appear to do well as Westerners (Berry 1966).

Some investigators have examined possible contributory effects of variables which might produce cultural differences: linguistic structure (Cole, Gay, Glick, and Sharp 1969) appears to have no effect on transposition performance; amount and kind of schooling does have an effect on combinations (Goodnow 1962), as does length of residence in an urban milieu (Peluffo 1962). There is even evidence that familiarity with clay affects conservation performance (Price-Williams, Gordon, and Ramirez 1969). A study by Jahoda (1969) on understanding the mechanism of bicycles, repeated after a thirteen-year interval in Accra and Glasgow, showed interesting interactions of culture, sex, and time of testing: African boys (especially older one of fourteen or fifteen) did much better at the later time.

b. Stability across the life span. There is remarkably little evidence about stability of formal operational thought through adulthood and into old age, and none of the evidence is based upon longitudinal data (as it should be to provide a fully valid answer). All of the available evidence has been summarized by Papalia (1972), who found some evidence for deterioration with advanced age. Her own data (based on very small groups at each age range) showed a sharp decline in conservation of volume after sixty-five, as well as a lesser decline for conservation of weight and substance. The pattern of decline was such as to suggest a generalization that the last-acquired is the first to go. Conservation of number is shown by all subjects through the range tested.

c. Generality within a culture. Although it has recently become fashionable to include socioeconomic status as a variable in all sorts of research, there is no evidence concerning its effect upon the development of formal operational thought. One would be very surprised if an effect were not found, especially with the use of the Inhelder tasks; but what such a finding would mean is not at all clear. In view of evidence to be reviewed shortly about the relation of performance to IQ and education, one would want to be sure that these variables are eliminated as contributory factors. In practice this may not be feasible.

With respect to sex differences, the picture is totally confusing; some investigators find them (Dale 1970; Elkind 1962; Graves 1972; Schwebel 1972) and others do not (Jackson 1965; Lovell, 1961a). There is some suggestion that sex differences are more likely to be reported for college students than for younger adolescents and for formal-operations concept tasks as opposed to Inhelder tasks.

3. *How consistent is performance across tasks?* If, as hypothesized, formal operational thinking reflects an organized structure of operations, one would expect to find a basic consistency in level across tasks, but one would also expect to find increases with age (that is, as the operations become integrated into a structural unity). The prediction, of course, is predicated upon assumptions which may not obtain in practice: that the tasks are of equivalent difficulty, and/or that there are no horizontal decalages. Available data are totally inadequate to answer this question. Only one investigator (Jackson 1965) has reported a comparison of rankings across tasks for individuals, and he finds only 10 percent to be at a uniform level across all tasks, although scores of 60 percent span only two substages. The few who have attempted factor analysis tend to find a single factor (Bart 1971) or a limited number of meaningful factors when a wide variety of concrete and formal-operations tasks are included along with ability and achievement measures (Stephens, McLaughlin, Miller, and Glass 1972). Nassefat (1963) used a battery of concrete and formal-operations tasks and performed Guttman as well as Loevinger scaling at each age level. He found consistency highest at the age level at which the discriminative power of each item category is maximal. Other investigators report Pearson product-movement correlations (generally without partialling out chronological age) over varying age ranges and number and type of tasks. The magnitude of the resulting r values varies considerably. Not surprisingly, the highest correlations have been reported for broad age-ranges (Lee 1971). Nevertheless, it is almost invariably the case that statistically significant positive correlations are reported among formal operational tasks. This appears to constitute weak evidence that all of them are measuring a common property of behavior.

4. *What other variables are related to performance on formal-opera-*

tions tasks? The answer to this question starts with persistent individual characteristics and proceeds to more transitory ones and to environmental factors. Practically every investigator who has computed it reports a high positive correlation of level-of-task performance with mental age and in many instances with IQ as well (Jackson reports a correlation of .86 with the Raven Progressive Matrices score). Another interesting test of the role of general intelligence is provided by an examination of performance of groups at the extremes of the IQ distribution. Several studies have been reported in which dull normals in the 60–80 IQ range were used as subjects (Inhelder 1966; Jackson 1965; Stephens et al. 1971). In no instance is there any evidence that these subjects attain formal operational thought. At the opposite extreme, there is less evidence and it is less consistent: Lovell and Shields (1967) found little evidence of formal operations among their eight- to ten-year-olds with IQs greater than 140; on the other hand, Neimark (1972) and Neimark and Lewis (1967) have reported that very bright children performed at the same level as normals of equivalent mental age; in some instances (in deriving a formula for permutations) they were superior.

Although intelligence is part of the story of cognitive development, it is by no means the whole story. Every investigator who works with normals within a restricted IQ range (generally 90–110) has found a distribution of performance at every age range. Clearly, other sources of variability are operating. Pascual-Leone (1973) suggested cognitive style as a factor, and he reported significant differences between field-dependent and field-independent subjects (in favor of the latter), especially on those tasks where field factors were more prominent. Neimark (1972) also found superior performance on field-independents on her problem-solving task and on the permutations task, as well as a significant correlation of Embedded Figures Test (EFT) score and performance on cognitive tasks. In addition, she found an effect of reflection-impulsivity: children who scored reflective on Kagan's Matching Familiar Figures (MFF) Test showed a higher-level strategy on problem-solving, permutations, and organization for memorization. Correlations of MFF score and performance on cognitive tasks were significant but of somewhat lower magnitude than EFT. Clearly "cognitive style" factors, which have been relatively neglected heretofore in studies of formal operations, merit closer scrutiny in the future. For whatever it is worth, Eskimos, who tend to stand up well in cross-cultural comparisons of cognitive performance, are likely to be field-independent with no sex differences on EFT (MacArthur 1967).

Education is an interesting variable: massive differences in amount do have an effect (Goodnow 1962; Peluffo 1962, 1967); Papalia (1972) found consistent low positive correlations ($r = .25$ to $.30$) between volume conservation and amount of schooling for her three adult groups, but Graves (1972) found an effect of amount of education among minimally educated adults only for conservation of mass (not volume). On the other hand, specifics of educational content appear not to have an effect: Dale (1970), Lovell (1961a), Simmons and Goss (1957), Schwebel (1972), and Goodnow (1962) have all reported no effect of amount and kind of science training. Hall (1972) has reported a relation for Colombian schoolchildren between amount of schooling and how information is processed for memory storage. This kind of finding may provide a good lead to understanding the nature of the effects of schooling.

One might also ask whether formal operation development can be advanced by specific training. Only two authors have addressed themselves to this question: Tomlinson-Keasey (1972) found significant improvement on a specific task but little evidence of generalization of the effects of training; Schwebel (1972) reported evidence of effects of more prolonged and generalized training, but it was not resoundingly impressive. Lathey (1970), with the more limited goal of producing volume conservation in eleven-year-olds, had no success. In view of preliminary evidence on the role of cognitive style, a profitable training strategy might include attempts at modification of cognitive style.

Important Unanswered Questions

In each of the preceding sections, almost as many questions were raised as were answered. At this point, it appears that formal operations constitute a genuine developmental stage which, however, is not universally attained by all adults. There still remains a great deal to be discovered about the components of formal operations, the nature of their structuring, the course of their development and the variables which affect it. Perhaps the most urgent need is for good longitudinal evidence about the development of formal operations from the ages of ten to twenty. This is certain to be a lengthy and enormously expensive project that is unlikely to repay the effort unless it is carefully planned and directed by an insightful formulation of theoretical issues. Careful formulation, in turn, will require more specific information than is currently available. Needed information will be discussed below with respect to three general areas of potential research.

1. *Task considerations.* A first need is for good tasks which yield objective scores as well as ratings, and whose procedures are well standardized to ensure greater comparability of findings. The author's personal candidates for future test batteries include combinations, the problem-solving board, permutations, and volume conservation (including occupied volume and specific gravity). Some additional tasks might well be

developed to get more directly at the extent to which a subject is thinking formally (in terms of propositional form and language rules). In addition, for one who really uses Piaget's theory, there must be more direct assessment of the use of a combinatorial system with propositions (the thirty-three additional items developed by O'Brien and Shapiro [1968] might serve as a start) and the INRC group of transformations (no obvious candidate comes to mind). Some Wechsler (WAIS) items, especially from the performance battery, might also prove to be of value. The Kohs block subtask is already widely used in cross-cultural research. Even some items on "planning ahead" and organizing alternatives in a variety of contexts might be of value.

For traditionalists who feel more comfortable with the Inhelder experiments, a good standardization of procedures and scoring is in order, followed by a thorough scaling of the items for differential difficulty and possible horizontal decalages. Research by Martorano (1973) may fill this need. With respect to the question of differential difficulty, the available data are not altogether consistent. There is some suggestion that the pendulum, balance, and rods tasks are relatively easier and that correlation and projection of shadows are among the most difficult. The combining of chemicals task seems to be of intermediate difficulty. The remaining tasks lack sufficient data for placement. Whatever tasks are ultimately employed, their psychometric properties need to be better established; for example, in all the research reviewed, only one author (Neimark 1972) examined retest reliabilities. Finally, as noted earlier, there is need for greater concern with establishing the consistency of performance across tasks for a given individual to better determine whether the individual is at a transitional, early, or relatively advanced stage in consolidation of formal operations. Without prior evidence about differential task difficulty, it is impossible to know whether discrepant performance reflects incomplete consolidation or noncomparable items.

2. *Course of development and stability throughout the life span.* It has been assumed throughout that formal operations is a qualitatively different stage from concrete operations, but relatively little support for a stage view is provided in published research. For the most part, there are not even any attempts to examine stagelike properties. One major cause of this shortcoming is probably the shortage of analytic techniques for identification of stage properties. Flavell and Wohlwill (1969) have proposed some, and others are suggested in this chapter. It is hoped that still more refined analysis will appear in the future.

Another urgent need repeatedly noted in this chapter is the almost total absence of longitudinal data. Once again, the absence of good statistical techniques for analysis of longitudinal data has been an obstacle, as are the obvious practical problems of conducting such research. From personal experience with longitudinal research on the development of formal operations, it is abundantly clear to the author that one should not stop at the age of fourteen or fifteen. There appears to be a good deal of development beyond early adolescence. Adequate research requires the use of high-school and college-age subjects.

At present, longitudinal research appears to offer the best promise not only for clarifying the course of the transition to and the development of formal operations but also for answering questions concerning sequencing of component skills and the nature of their integration. Research on this question is rare for the well-worked field of concrete operations (but see Kofsky 1966; Brainerd 1972); for formal operations it is yet nonexistent. Another question that might profitably be raised in the context of longitudinal research involves determining which, if any, component skills are the best predictors of future performance. The technique of cross-lagged panel analysis (Crano, Kenny, and Campbell 1972) provides a useful tool for this purpose.

Almost all investigators whose research has been reported here tested students in junior and senior high school and in college: With higher grade-levels, the population probably becomes more highly selected. Thus, it is conceivable that group mean-improvement with age may reflect the higher proportion of brighter students rather than genuine age changes. Work with garden-variety humanity is badly needed, especially in the middle-age ranges from late twenties to fifties. Longitudinal work with the aged is also needed to determine if formal operations do, in fact, decline with age.

3. *Closer examination of the variables affecting formal operational development.* The contributory roles of intelligence and individual-difference factors have already been noted. However, the available evidence is skimpy, and a good deal is needed to spell out the nature of the effects of these factors. For example, it is quite possible that there is a lower bound on IQ below which formal operations do not appear; work in progress by H. Spitz suggests this to be the case. Similarly, there may be an upper IQ bound beyond which mental age equivalence does not apply (that is, IQ no longer compensates for additional years of life experience). With respect to other individual-difference variables, field dependence/independence and reflection/impulsivity have already been shown to have an effect. It is quite possible that other factors of the sort usually employed in studies of creativity, or even some of the variables identified by Guilford as dimensions of intelligence may be worth investigation as well.

One variable (or, more accurately, one set of variables) of fundamental importance which has been almost totally neglected is the figurative aspect of formal operational thought. In this connection the role of language comes most immediately to mind. One strategy that has been employed is to use the deaf for evidence of effects of extreme language deficiency, although assessment of formal operations with this group poses many problems. Pettifor (1968) has reported that the deaf were significantly less abstract on a conceptual sorting task than matched hearing controls, but her deaf group was too young to provide conclusive evidence of deficit rather than delay. On the other hand, Furth and Youniss (1971), using relatively language-free tasks like combinations, reported finding formal operations among their deaf subjects. However, their data, as reported, were not especially convincing. Another strategy which may be employed to assess the role of language is to use some relatively pure "language" measure (e.g., vocabulary, sentence or paragraph comprehension, or some measure of productive fluency) to identify groups for comparative or correlational analysis with respect to formal operations. One report in this vein (Jones 1972) showed no difference between matched groups differentiated on the basis of use of tentative statements, but these may not be the most sensitive measures of verbal skills. Of course, the Piagetian position is that language skills per se have no effect upon operational development. It is, however, difficult to prove the null hypothesis.

Language is by no means the only vehicle of representation in abstraction; imagery, in some form or other, undoubtedly plays a role, one which is largely neglected by research. There is, for example, the repeated suggestion in the mental-testing literature of a relation between spatial visualization and abstract thought. Whether this relationship applies to formal operations is still an open question. Piaget and Inhelder (1971) have shown that anticipatory imagery is a relatively late development. Unfortunately, in all of their research they utilized preadolescent children. Whether the development of mental imagery continues into and/or throughout adolescence remains to be determined. A very spotty literature on chess players (Binet 1966) and lightning calculators (Bousefield and Barry 1933; Hunter 1962), for example, suggests that the role of unusually developed representational skills might affect the development of formal operations in interesting ways (for better or worse—Luria 1968). But we have yet to know what imagery in normal adolescents is like and how its development is related to the operational aspects of formal thought.

Each reader, no doubt, has favorite variables of his own to nominate for more intensive investigation. A few of them have been noted earlier. One of the more surprising gaps in reported research concerns what Piaget has called "the American question": the possibility of accelerating development through specific training. When more is known about the course of normal development and the variables which affect it, it is quite likely that sophisticated training research will begin in earnest. Piaget's prediction would be that all such attempts are doomed to failure.

A final area of research that might be mentioned concerns the relation of formal operational development to the development of other aspects of behavior: conceptual development, intelligence in the mental test sense, moral and social development, and so on. Some work on relation of formal operations to moral development has been reported (Lee 1971), and more is in process (Kuhn et al. 1972). There is already evidence that development of communication skills continues on into adolescence (see chapter 6 in this volume), and it is quite likely that it is related to formal operations.

Summary

Much of the difficulty in deriving meaningful generalizations from the research reviewed in the preceding section arises from wide variation among investigators in their fastidiousness with respect to theoretical and methodological issues. This section has examined the theoretical and methodological issues in detail in the hope that future research may be better focused and better formulated as a result.

Some major methodological shortcomings stem from the failure to treat "formal operations" as a stage of development rather than a response characteristic. To assess the existence of formal operations it is necessary to measure several aspects of performance in more than one task and to determine consistencies among measures. This is rarely, if ever, done in existing research.

Despite the methodological shortcomings of existing research, it does provide some basis for the following tentative generalizations:

1. There is a stage of thinking beyond and different from concrete operations.

2. That stage is not universally attained by all individuals and may not even be stable within an individual over time.

3. Differences among cultures in proportion of the society's members attaining the level of formal operations undoubtedly exist. Identification of the causal variables responsible for these differences (differences in cultural emphases, education, life-experience, and so on) remains a question for future research to answer.

4. Within-culture differences undoubtedly exist, also. Here, again, research is needed to identify causal factors such as class, caste, and the like. Existing evidence with respect to obvious variables, such as amount and kind of education, is totally ambiguous.

5. Among individual-difference variables, general level of intelligence appears to be an important factor. It is probable that a minimal level of intelligence, in terms of mental age, is a prerequisite for the attainment of formal operational thought.

6. Individual-difference variables as assessed on such continua as field dependence/independence or reflection/impulsivity appear to account for some variation in rate of development and final level of attainment.

7. The effect of specific training procedures is largely unexplored and remains problematic.

A host of questions—in addition to those raised above—remains to be answered. Are there systematic changes continuing into adolescence with respect to nature of mental imagery or to levels of language usage and comprehension? What is the course of cognitive development during middle- and old-age? Does formal operational thinking decline, or disappear, with advancing old-age? Can the development of formal operational thought be promoted or advanced by specific training? If so, what kind of training? Are developmental aspects of formal operational thought more predictive of adult intellectual attainment than scores on standard intelligence and achievement tests?

If these and similar questions are attacked only at an empirical level, it is unlikely that satisfactory answers will ever result. There is need for an integrative theory to direct the formulation and interpretation of research. Although Piaget's treatment of formal operations provides a promising theoretical framework, its utility at present is hampered by lack of coordination of theoretical constructs to experimental operations. Some of the requisites for providing the needed coordination were discussed.

Finally, one should consider the practical value and potential implications of an adequate understanding of the development of thought in adolescence. At present we know relatively little about adolescent thought or about the adult thought of which it is the immediate precursor. Ignorance is not a state to be cherished. With respect to practical applications, it is obvious, for example, that a sound understanding of adolescent thought can provide the basis for educational practice at the high-school and college levels. At both levels a good deal of dissatisfaction exists on the part of educators, students, and the taxpaying public. There is much popular concern with the "youth culture," and many popular writers attempt to "explain" adolescent behavior. Many such explanations treat adolescents as a group molded by social and environmental forces. To do so is to lose sight of the fact that the group is composed of individual members whose behavior is also influenced and directed by individual thought-processes. Many aspects of adolescent behavior from fads and foibles to rebellion against parents and institutions can be considerably clarified by an understanding of the thought processes that underlie and direct them.

At this age, under favorable conditions of freedom from social demands or family responsibilities, and exposure to an institutional environment (school) supposedly designed to promote and direct intellectual growth, the adolescent can devote full time and energy to perfecting his developing skills: physical, social, and intellectual. As a formal operational thinker, he is freed from the bonds of personal experience and present time to explore ideas, ideals, roles, beliefs, theories, commitments, and all sorts of possibilities at the level of thought. At the level of thought, the adolescent, aware of the arbitrariness of practices and institutions, can create more desirable alternatives for himself and for society. There is more than a little egocentrism in this high-flown thought, but the adolescent perforce achieves a "decentering" through interaction with peers, elders, and—increasingly—with the assumption of adult roles and responsibilities. "The focal point of the decentering process is the entrance into the occupational world or the beginning of serious professional training. The adolescent becomes an adult when he undertakes a real job" (Inhelder and Piaget 1958, p. 346). And so the weight of the world gradually transforms adolescent flights of fancy into adult anxieties.

REFERENCES

Adelson, J., Green, B., & O'Neil, R. Growth of the idea of law in adolescence. *Developmental Psychology*, 1969, *1*, 327–332.

Appel, L. F., Cooper, R. G., McCarrell, N., Sims-Knight, J., Yussen, S. R., & Flavell, J. H. The developmental acquisition of the distinction between perceiving and memorizing. *Child Development*, 1972, *43*, 1365–1381.

Bart, W. M. The factor structure of formal operations. *British Journal of Educational Psychology*, 1971, *41*, 70–77.

Belmont, J. M. & Butterfield, E. C. The relations of short-term memory to development and intelligence. In L. P. Lipsitt & H. W. Reese, eds., *Advances in Child Development and Behavior*. Vol. 4. New York: Academic Press, 1969, 30–82.

———. What the development of short-term memory is. *Human Development*, 1971, *14*, 236–248.

Berry, J. W. Temne and Eskimo perceptual skills. *International Journal of Psychology*, 1966, *1*, 207–229.

Binet, A. Mnemonic virtuosity: a study of chess players. Translated by M. Simmel & S. Barron. *Genetic Psychology Monographs*, 1966, *74*, 127–162.

Bousefield, W. A. & Barry, H., Jr. The visual imagery of a lightning calculator. *American Journal of Psychology*, 1933, *45*, 353–358.

Brainerd, C. J. Continuity and discontinuity hypotheses in studies of conservation. *Developmental Psychology*, 1970, *3*, 225–228.

———. The development of the proportionality scheme in children and adolescents. *Developmental Psychology*, 1971, *5*, 469–476.

————. Structure of thought in middle-childhood: recent research of Piaget's concrete-operational groupements. Paper delivered at third annual meeting on structural learning, Philadelphia, 1972.

Bruner, J. S., Goodnow, J. J., & Austin, G. A. *A Study of Thinking*. New York: John Wiley, 1956.

Bruner, J. S., Olver, R., & Greenfield, P. *Studies in Cognitive Growth*. New York: John Wiley, 1966.

Bryant, P. E. & Trabasso, J. Transitive inferences and memory in young children. *Nature*, 1971, *232*, 456–458.

Bynum, T. W., Thomas, J. A., & Weitz, L. J. Truth-functional logic in formal operational thinking: Inhelder & Piaget's evidence. *Developmental Psychology*, 1972, *7*, 129–132.

Case, D. & Collinson, J. M. The development of formal thinking in verbal comprehension. *British Journal of Educational Psychology*, 1962, *32*, 103–111.

Ceraso, J. & Provitera, A. Sources of error in syllogistic reasoning. *Cognitive Psychology*, 1971, *2*, 400–410.

Chapman, L. J. & Chapman, J. P. Atmosphere effect re-examined. *Journal of Experimental Psychology*, 1959, *58*, 220–226.

Chapman, R. H. & Neimark, E. D. Age changes in interpretation of local quantifiers: "All" and "Some." Paper read at meeting of the Society for Research in Child Development, Philadelphia, 1973.

Clark, H. H. Influence of language on solving three-term series problems. *Journal of Experimental Psychology*, 1969a, *82*, 205–215.

————. Linguistic processes in deductive reasoning. *Psychological Review*, 1969b, *76*, 387–404.

Cole, M., Gay, J., Glick, J., & Sharp, D. Linguistic structure and transposition. *Science*, 1969, *164*, 90–91.

Collis, K. F. A study of concrete and formal reasoning in school mathematics. *Australian Journal of Psychology*, 1971, *23*, 289–296.

Crano, W. D., Kenny, D. A., & Campbell, D. T. Does intelligence cause achievement? A cross-lagged panel analysis. *Journal of Educational Psychology*, 1972, *63*, 258–275.

Dale, L. G. The growth of systematic thinking: replication and analysis of Piaget's first chemical experiment. *Australian Journal of Psychology*, 1970, *22*, 277–286.

Dasen, P. R. Cross-cultural Piagetian research: a summary. *Journal of Cross-Cultural Psychology*, 1972, *3*, 23–39.

Davies, C. M. Development of the probability concept in children. *Child Development*, 1965, *36*, 779–788.

Dennis, W. Animistic thinking among college and university students. *Science Monographs*, 1953, *76*, 247–250.

DeSciora, A. M. Permutation strategies of high IQ tenth graders. Douglass College Senior Honors Thesis, 1971.

DeSoto, C. B., London, M., & Handel, S. Social reasoning and spatial paralogic. *Journal of Personality and Social Psychology*, 1965, *2*, 513–521.

Eimas, P. D. A developmental study of hypothesis behavior and focusing. *Journal of Experimental Child Psychology*, 1969, *8*, 160–172.

————. Effects of memory aids on hypothesis behavior and focusing in young children and adults. *Journal of Experimental Child Psychology*, 1970, *10*, 319–336.

Elkind, D. Childrens' discovery of mass, weight, and volume: Piaget replication study II. *Journal of Genetic Psychology*, 1961a, *98*, 219–227.

————. Quantity conceptions in junior and senior high school students. *Child Development*, 1961b, *32*, 551–560.

————. Quantity conceptions in college students. *Journal of Social Psychology*, 1962, *57*, 459–465.

————. Conceptual orientation shifts in children and adolescents. *Child Development*, 1966, *37*, 493–498.

———. Egocentrism in adolescence. *Child Development,* 1967, *38,* 1025–1034.

Elkind, D., Barocas, R., & Johnsen, P. Concept production in children and adolescents. *Human Development,* 1969, *12,* 10–21.

Elkind, D., Barocas, R., & Rosenthal, R. Combinatorial thinking in adolescents from graded and ungraded classrooms. *Perceptual and Motor Skills,* 1968, *27,* 1015–1018.

Elkind, D., Medvene, L., & Rockway, A. Representational level and concept production in children and adolescents. *Developmental Psychology,* 1969, 85–89.

Fischbein, R., Pampu, I., & Mânzat, I. Effect of age and instruction on combinatory ability in children. *British Journal of Educational Psychology,* 1970a, 261–270.

———. Comparison of ratios and the chance concept in children. *Child Development,* 1970b, *41,* 377–389.

Flavell, J. H. *The Developmental Psychology of Jean Piaget.* Princeton: Van Nostrand, 1963.

———. Concept development. In P. H. Mussen, ed., *Carmichael's Manual of Child Psychology.* Vol. 1. New York: John Wiley, 1970a, 983–1059.

———. Developmental studies of mediated memory. In L. Lipsitt & H. W. Reese, eds., *Advances in Child Development and Behavior.* Vol. 5. New York: Academic Press, 1970b.

Flavell, J. H., Friedrichs, A. G., & Hoyt, J. D. Developmental changes in memorization processes. *Cognitive Psychology,* 1970, *1,* 324–340.

Flavell, J. H. & Wohlwill, J. F. Formal and functional aspects of cognitive development. In D. Elkind & J. H. Flavell, eds., *Studies in Cognitive Development.* New York: Oxford University Press, 1969, 67–120.

Freides, D., Fredenthal, B. J., Grisell, J. L., & Cohen, B. D. Changes in two dimensions of cognition during adolescence. *Child Development,* 1963, *34,* 1047–1055.

Furth, H. G. & Youniss, J. The influence of language and experience on discovery and use of logical symbols. *British Journal of Psychology,* 1965, *56,* 381–390.

———. Formal operations and language: a comparison of deaf and hearing adolescents. *International Journal of Psychology,* 1971, *6,* 49–64.

Gholson, B., Levine, M., & Phillips, S. Hypotheses, strategies, and stereotypes in discrimination learning. *Journal of Experimental Child Psychology,* 1972, *13,* 423–446.

Ginsburg, H. & Opper, S. *Piaget's Theory of Intellectual Development: An Introduction.* Englewood Cliffs, N.J.: Prentice-Hall, 1969.

Glick, J. & Wapner, S. Development of transitivity: some findings and problems of analysis. *Child Development,* 1968, *39,* 621–638.

Goldberg, S. Probability judgments by preschool children: task conditions and performance. *Child Development,* 1966, *37,* 157–167.

Goodnow, J. J. A test of milieu differences with some of Piaget's tasks. *Psychological Monographs,* 1962, *76,* no. 36, whole no. 555.

Goodnow, J. J. & Bethon, G. Piaget's tasks: the affect of schooling and intelligence. *Child Development,* 1966, *37,* 573–582.

Graves, A. J. Attainment of conservation of mass, weight, and volume in minimally educated adults. *Developmental Psychology,* 1972, *7,* 223.

Gyr, J. W., Brown, J. S., & Cafagne, A. C. Quasi-formal models of inductive behavior and their relation to Piaget's theory of cognitive states. *Psychological Review,* 1967, *74,* 272–289.

Gyr, J. W. & Fleisher, C. Computer-assisted studies of Piaget's three-stage model of cognitive development. *Psychological Reports,* 1967, *20,* 165–166.

Hagen, J. W. Some thoughts on how children learn to remember. *Human Development,* 1971, *14,* 262–271.

Hale, G. A., Miller, L. K., & Stevenson, H. W. Developmental changes in children's concepts of probability. *Psychonomic Science,* 1967, *9,* 229–230.

Hall, J. W. Verbal behavior as a function of amount of schooling. *American Journal of Psychology,* 1972, *85,* 277–289.

Handel, S., DeSoto, C. B., & London, M. Reasoning and spatial representations. *Journal of Verbal Learning and Verbal Behavior,* 1968, *7,* 351–357.

Henle, M. On the relation between logic and thinking. *Psychological Review,* 1962, *69,* 366–378.

Heron, A. Studies of perception and reasoning in Zambian children. *International Journal of Psychology,* 1968, *3,* 23–30.

Higgins-Trenk, A. & Gaite, J. H. Elusiveness of formal operations thought in adolescents. *Proceedings,* Seventy-ninth Annual Convention, APA, 1971, 201–202.

Hill, S. A. A study of logical abilities of children. Ph.D. dissertation, Stanford University, 1960.

Hoemann, N. W. & Ross, B. M. Children's understanding of probability concepts. *Child Development,* 1971, *42,* 221–236.

Hughes, M. M. A four-year longitudinal study of the growth of logical thinking in a group of secondary modern schooling. Master's thesis, University of Leeds, 1965.

Hunter, I. M. L. The solving of 3-term series problems. *British Journal of Psychology,* 1957, *48,* 286–298.

———. An exceptional talent for calculative thinking. *British Journal of Psychology,* 1962, *53,* 243–258.

Huttenlocher, J. Development of formal reasoning on concept formation problems. *Child Development,* 1964, *35,* 1233–1242.

———. Constructing spatial images: a strategy in reasoning. *Psychological Review,* 1968, *75,* 550–560.

Ingalls, R. P. & Dickerson, D. J. Development of hypothesis behavior in human concept identification. *Developmental Psychology,* 1969, *1,* 707–716.

Inhelder, B. Cognitive development and its contribution to the diagnosis of some phenomena of mental deficiency. *Merrill-Palmer Quarterly,* 1966, *12,* 299–319.

———. Memory and intelligence in the child. In D. Elkind & J. H. Flavell, eds., *Studies in Cognitive Development.* New York: Oxford University Press, 1969, 337–364.

Inhelder, B. & Piaget, J. *The Growth of Logical Thinking from Childhood to Adolescence.* New York: Basic Books, 1958.

Jackson, S. The growth of logical thinking in normal and subnormal children. *British Journal of Educational Psychology,* 1965, *35,* 255–258.

Jahoda, G. Assessment of abstract behavior in a non-western culture. *Journal of Social Psychology,* 1956, *53,* 237–243.

———. Understanding the mechanism of bicycles: a cross-cultural study of developmental change after 13 years. *International Journal of Psychology,* 1969, *4,* 103–108.

Jones, P. A. Formal operational reasoning and the use of tentative statement. *Cognitive Psychology,* 1972, *3,* 467–471.

Kellaghan, T. Abstraction and categorization in African children. *International Journal of Psychology,* 1968, *3,* 115–120.

Kofsky, E. A scalogram study of classificatory development. *Child Development,* 1966, *37,* 191–204.

Kuhn, D., Langer, J., Kohlberg, L., & Haan, N. S. The development of formal operations in logical and moral judgement. Manuscript, 1972.

Lathey, J. W. Training effects and conservation of volume. *Child Study Center Bulletin.* Buffalo, New York: State University College, 1970.

Lee, L. C. The concomitant development of cognitive and moral modes of thought: a test of selected deductions from Piaget's theory. *Genetic Psychology Monographs,* 1971, 93–146.

Lehman, E. B. & Goodnow, J. Memory of rhythmic series: age changes in accuracy and number coding. *Developmental Psychology,* 1972, *6,* 363.

Leskow, S. & Smock, C. D. Developmental changes in problem-solving strategies: permutations. *Developmental Psychology,* 1970, *2,* 412–422.

Levine, M. Hypothesis behavior by humans during discrimination learning. *Journal of Experimental Psychology*, 1966, *71*, 331–338.

Lovell, K. A follow-up study of Inhelder and Piaget's *The Growth of Logical Thinking*. *British Journal of Psychology*, 1961a, *52*, 143–153.

————. *The Growth of Basic Mathematical and Scientific Concepts in Children*. London: University of London Press, 1961b, 119–126.

Lovell, K. & Butterworth, I. B. Abilities underlying the understanding of proportionality. *Mathematical Teaching*, 1966, *37*, 5–9.

Lovell, K. & Ogilvie, E. The growth of the concept of volume in junior high school children. *Journal of Child Psychology and Psychiatry*, 1961, *2*, 118–126.

Lovell, K. & Shields, J. B. Some aspects of a study of the gifted child. *British Journal of Educational Psychology*, 1967, *37*, 201–208.

Lunzer, E. A. Some points of Piagetian theory in the light of experimental evidence. *Journal of Child Psychology and Psychiatry*, 1960, *1*, 191–202.

————. Problems of formal reasoning in test situations. *Society for Research in Child Development Monographs*, 1965, *30*, 19–46, serial no. 100.

Lunzer, E. A. & Pumfrey, P. D. Understanding proportionality. *Mathematics Teaching*, 1966, *34*, 7–12.

Luria, A. M. *The Mind of a Mnemonist*. New York: Basic Books, 1968.

MacArthur, R. Sex differences in field dependence for the Eskimos. *International Journal of Psychology*, 1967, *2*, 139–140.

Mandler, G. & Stephens, D. The development of free and constrained conceptualization and subsequent verbal memory. *Journal of Experimental Child Psychology*, 1967, *5*, 86–93.

Martorano, S. C. The development of formal operations thinking. Paper read at meeting of the Society for Research in Child Development, Philadelphia, 1973.

Maurer, A. Maturation of concepts of life. *Journal of Genetic Psychology*, 1970, *116*, 101–111.

Moely, B. M., Olson, F. A., Halwes, J. G., & Flavell, J. H. Production deficiency in young children's clustered recall. *Developmental Psychology*, 1969, *1*, 26–34.

Monks, F. Future time perspective in adolescents. *Human Development*, 1968, *11*, 117–123.

Murray, J. P. & Youniss, J. Achievement of inferential transitivity and its relation to serial ordering. *Child Development*, 1968, *39*, 1259–1268.

Nassefat, M. *Etude Quantitative sur l'evolution des Operations Intellectuelles*. Neuchatel: Delachaux et Niestle, 1963.

Neimark, E. D. A preliminary search for formal operations structures. *Journal of Genetic Psychology*, 1970a, *116*, 223–232.

————. Model for a thinking machine: an information processing framework for the study of cognitive development. *Merrill-Palmer Quarterly*, 1970b, *16*, 345–368.

————. Development of comprehension of logical connectives: understanding of "or." *Psychonomic Science*, 1970c, 217–219.

————. An information processing approach to cognitive development. *Transactions New York Academy of Sciences*, 1971, *33*, 516–528.

————. Longitudinal development of formal operations thought. Report no. 16, 1972.

Neimark, E. D. & Lewis, N. The development of logical problem-solving strategies. *Child Development*, 1967, *38*, 107–117.

————. Development of logical problem-solving: a one-year retest. *Child Development*, 1968, *39*, 527–536.

Neimark, E. D. & Slotnick, N. S. Development of the understanding of logical connectives. *Journal of Educational Psychology*, 1970, *61*, 451–460.

Neimark, E. D., Slotnick, N. S., & Ulrich, T. Development of memorization strategies. *Developmental Psychology*, 1971, *5*, 427–432.

Nitta, N. & Nagano, S. Basic logical operations and their verbal expressions. *Research Bulletin of the National Institute for Educational Research*, 1966, no. 7.

O'Brien, T. C. & Shapiro, B. J. The development of logical thinking in children. *American Educational Research Journal*, 1968, *5*, 531–542.

Papalia, D. E. The status of several conservation abilities across the life-span. *Human Development*, 1972, *15*, 229–243.

Pascual-Leone, J. A mathematical model for the transition in Piaget's developmental stages. *Acta Psychologica*, 1972.

———. *Cognitive Development and Cognitive Style*. Lexington, Mass.: Lexington Books (D. C. Heath & Co.), 1973.

Peel, E. A. A method for investigating children's understanding of certain logical connectives used in binary propositional thinking. *British Journal of Mathematical and Statistical Psychology*, 1967, *20*, 81–92.

Peluffo, N. Culture and cognitive problems. *International Journal of Psychology*, 1967, *2*, 187–198.

———. The notions of conservation and causality in children of different physical and socio-cultural environments. *Archives de Psychologie*, 1962, *38*, whole no. 151, 275–291.

Pettifor, J. L. The role of language in the development of abstract thinking: a comparison of hard-of-hearing and normal-hearing children on levels of conceptual thinking. *Canadian Journal of Psychology/Revue Canadian de Psychologie*, 1968, *22*, 139–156.

Piaget, J. *Les notions de mouvement et de vitesse chez l'enfant*. Paris: Presses Universitaires de France, 1946, chapters 5, 8. Ballantine Books, 1970.

———. *Judgment and Reasoning in the Child*. Paterson, N. J.: Littlefield, Adams & Co., 1964*a*.

———. Development of learning. In R. E. Ripple and V. N. Rockcastle, eds., *Piaget Rediscovered*, Cornell, 1964*b*, 7–19.

———. *On the Development of Memory and Identity*. Barre, Mass.: Clark University Press, 1968.

———. Piaget's theory. In P. Mussen, ed., *Carmichael's Manual of Child Psychology*. Vol. 1. New York: John Wiley, 1970, 703–732.

———. Intellectual evolution from adolescence to adulthood. *Human Development*, 1972, *15*, 1–12.

Piaget, J. & Inhelder, B. *La Genese de l'idée de hazard chez l'enfant*. Paris: Presses Universitaires, 1951.

———. *The Psychology of the Child*. New York: Basic Books, 1969.

———. *Mental Imagery in the Child*. New York: Basic Books, 1971.

Piaget, J., Inhelder, B., & Szeminska, A. *The Child's Conception of Geometry*. New York: Basic Books, 1960.

Price-Williams, D., Gordon, W., & Ramirez, M., III. Skill and conservation: a study of pottery-maker's children. *Developmental Psychology*, 1969, *1*, 769.

Pumfrey, P. The growth of the scheme of proportionality. *British Journal of Educational Psychology*, 1968, *38*, 202–204.

Reichard, S., Schneider, M., & Rapaport, D. The development of concept formation in children. *American Journal of Orthopsychiatry*, 1944, *14*, 156–162.

Richelle, M. Etude génétique de l'intelligence manipulatoire chez des enfants africains a l'aide des dispositifs de Rey. *International Journal of Psychology*, 1966, *1*, 273–287.

Ross, B. M. Probability concepts in deaf and hearing children. *Child Development*, 1966, *37*, 917–927.

Ross, B. M. & Levy, N. Patterned predictions of chance by children and adults. *Psychological Reports*, 1958, *4* (Monograph Supplement 1), 87–124.

Schnall, M. Age differences in integration of progressively changing visual patterns. *Human Development*, 1968, *11*, 287–295.

Schnall, M. & Kemper, T. Modes of organizing progressively changing stimulation: a developmental study. *American Journal of Psychology,* 1968, *81,* 375–383.

Schwebel, M. Logical thinking in college freshman. Final report, Project No. 0–B–105, Grant No. OEG–2–7–0039 (509), April, 1972.

Seggie, J. L. & Endersby, H. The empirical implications of Piaget's concept of correlation. *Australian Journal of Psychology,* 1972, *24,* 3–8.

Sells, S. B. The atmosphere effect: an experimental study of reasoning. *Archives of Psychology,* 1936, *29,* 3–72.

Shapiro, B. J. & O'Brien, T. C. Logical thinking in children ages 6 through 13. *Child Development,* 1970, *41,* 823–829.

Shard, A. G., Inhelder, B., Noelting, G., Murphy, L. B., & Thomae, H. Longitudinal research in personality development. In H. David & J. C. Brengelman, eds. *Perspective in Personality Research.* London: Crosby Lockwood & Son, 1960.

Sigel, I. E. Developmental trends in the abstraction ability of young children. *Child Development,* 1953, *24,* 131–144.

Simmons, A. J. & Goss, A. E. Animistic responses as a function of sentence contexts and instructions. *Journal of Genetic Psychology,* 1957, *91,* 181–189.

Smedslund, J. The concept of correlation in adults. *Scandinavian Journal of Psychology,* 1963, *4,* 165–173.

Smirnov, A. A. & Zinchenko, P. I. Problems in the psychology of memory. In M. Cole & I. Maltzman, eds., *A Handbook of Contemporary Soviet Psychology,* New York: Basic Books, 1969, 452–502.

Stephens, B., McLaughlin, J. A., & Mahaney, E. J. Age at which Piagetian concepts are achieved. *Proceedings,* APA, 1971, 203–204.

Stephens, B., McLaughlin, J. A., Miller, C. K., & Glass, G. V. Factorial structure of selected psycho-educational measures and Piagetian reasoning assessments. *Developmental Psychology,* 1972, *6,* 343–348.

Suppes, P. & Feldman, S. Young children's comprehension of logical connectives. *Journal of Experimental Child Psychology,* 1971, *12,* 304–317.

Szeminska, A. The evolution of thought: some applications of research findings to educational practice. *Monographs of the Society for Research in Child Development,* 1965, *30,* 47–57.

Tomlinson-Keasey, C. Formal operations in females from eleven to fifty-four years of age. *Developmental Psychology,* 1972, *6,* 364.

Towler, J. O. & Wheatley, G. Conservation concepts in college students: a replication and critique. *Journal of Genetic Psychology,* 1971, *118,* 265–270.

Uzgiris, I. C. Situational generality of conservation. *Child Development,* 1964, *35,* 831–841.

Vernon, P. E. *Intelligence and Cultural Environment.* London: Methuen, 1969.

Vinh Bang. Methode d'apprentissage des structures operatoires. *Psychologie,* 1967, *26,* 107–124.

Vygotsky, L. S. *Thought and Language.* Cambridge, Mass.: MIT Press, 1962.

Wapner, S. & Rand, G. Ontogenetic differences in the nature of organization underlying serial learning. *Human Development,* 1968, *11,* 249–259.

Weitz, L. J., Bynum, T. W., Thomas, J. A., & Steger, J. A. Piaget's system of 16 binary operations: an empirical investigation. *Journal of Genetic Psychology,* in press.

Wohlwill, J. F. Methodology and research strategy in the study of developmental change. In R. Goulet and P. Baltes, eds., *Life-Span Developmental Psychology.* New York: Academic Press, 1970, 149–207.

Woodward, D. H. Teaching science in Ethiopia. *American Scientist,* 1969, *57,* 338A–344A.

Woodworth, R. S. & Sells, S. B. An atmosphere effect in formal syllogistic reasoning. *Journal of Experimental Psychology,* 1935, *18,* 451–460.

Yost, P. A., Siegel, A. E., & Andrews, J. M. Non-verbal probability judgments by young children. *Child Development,* 1962, *33,* 769–780.

Yudin, L. W. Formal thought in adolescence as a function of intelligence. *Child Development,* 1966, *37,* 697–708.

Youniss, J. & Furth, H. G. Attainment and transfer of logical connectives in children. *Journal of Educational Psychology,* 1964, *55,* 357–361.

————. The role of language and experience in the use of logical symbols. *British Journal of Psychology,* 1967, *58,* 435–443.

11 Cognitive Development in Cross-Cultural Perspective

JOSEPH GLICK

City University of New York Graduate Center

INTRODUCTION

THE STUDY of cognition and its development is a difficult undertaking under any circumstances. Adding the cross-cultural dimension makes the problem even more difficult. Yet this addition may be well worth it, for a cultural dimension in psychological enquiry can serve to broaden the base of the field and, as well, provide a new perspective on old achievements.

Accordingly, the focus throughout this chapter is on the unique perspective provided by considerations of culture. In some cases this led to greater selectivity than a review chapter usually reflects. The hope was that the growing field of the study of cognitive development in cultural perspective would be better served, at this point, by a prolegomenon than by a summation.

The Study of Cognition

The study of cognition is the study of the means by which an individual comes to have organized knowledge of the world, and of the way in which that knowledge is used to guide behavior. Yet "having knowledge" is not an uncomplicated topic of inquiry, since many things may be meant by the term "knowledge." In one sense, "knowledge" can mean something akin to "detection" of environmental features. Here the focus would be on the potential information that the environment can supply, and questions asked about how acutely the human can detect important features of that information. How finely can seemingly similar events be discriminated? How astutely are these detected and discriminated features used to guide behavior? The model of cognition involved in this formulation is that of the thinker as a detective finding clues; the more sharp-eyed he is, the better the chance for solution of the crime.

To focus exclusively on this model of cognition, however, would in-

volve a paradox; a paradox which has been well started by Bruner, Goodnow, and Austin (1956):

> We begin with what seems a paradox. The world of experience of any
> normal man is composed of a tremendous array of discriminably different
> objects, events, people, impressions. There are estimated to be more
> than 7 million discriminable colors alone, and in the course of a week
> or two we come in contact with a fair proportion of them. No two people
> we see have an identical appearance and even objects that we judge to
> be the same object over a period of time change appearance from mo-
> ment to moment with alterations in light or in the position of the viewer.
> All of these differences we are capable of seeing, for human beings have
> an exquisite capacity for making distinctions. But were we to utilize fully
> our capacity for registering the differences in things and to respond to
> each event encountered as unique, we would soon be overwhelmed by the
> complexity of our environment (p. 1).

Accordingly, a new level must be introduced, a level that deals with the
ability of man to override the diversity of the environment and its detected
features by organizing this diversity into categories.

The category or concept describes an organizational feature of cognitive
process whereby objectively discriminable stimuli are treated as being
similar. This has the adaptive consequence of reducing the amount of
complexity that must be dealt with and the psychological consequence of
involving a level or organization that overrides and organizes discriminative abilities.

Concept behavior thus becomes a central part of the treatment of cognition. Not only must one know the manner in which information is
"extracted," one must also know how people organize that information
into handleable units. The detective must not only have a rich source of
clues but must, as well, have the means to organize those clues and reduce
their diversity.

While the extraction and organization of empirical information are
adaptively central, the cognitive processes encompass activities of a different sort as well. Not only is the world found out, but also actions are
planned within it and attempts at achieving coherent theories of the
significance of detected features and organizations are proposed. Therefore, to the array of cognitive processes must be added those that have
to do with the formation of plans of behavior (Miller, Galanter, and
Pribram 1960) and those that have to do with theories about the world
(Werner and Kaplan 1963).

The planning of action is well allied with information extraction and
classification, since all of these have to do with behavior that is adaptive
with respect to the physical world. The consideration of theoretical knowl-

edge or "objects of contemplation" introduces a new possibility, however. Cognitive processes can be described which can apply to either the real world or to the world as conceived in thought, and whose relationship to the real world is problematic. Many advanced forms of thinking have precisely this characteristic. Their relationship to empirical knowledge is uncertain. Logical systems, mathematical systems, religious systems—all deal with the organization of thoughts with respect to each other and do not necessarily derive from empirical knowledge. Piaget (1970) has reinforced this point by distinguishing between figurative aspects of cognition, which represent reality as it appears, and operative aspects of cognition, which give logical structure to experience.

This brief attempt to identify what is encompassed by the area of cognition suggests several dimensions or levels at which to attempt to understand development. One can be concerned with the manner in which information is extracted from incoming stimulation, the manner in which that information is conceptualized, the manner in which it is used, and, finally, the processes by which thought is organized to consider things real on the one hand and things theoretical on the other.

The Study of Development

The developmental psychologist views the development of cognitive structures from a dual perspective: that of a description of the particular processes involved at different age levels and that of identifying specific etiological factors which determine their development.

1. *The descriptive aim.* That one can identify aspects of cognitive function in adults does not tell much about the structure of the behavior involved, nor does it tell about cognitive organization at earlier developmental levels. For both of these reasons, the study of the development of cognition provides useful information. On the one hand, it tells something of the different types of structures that can be used to fulfill various cognitive functions, and, on the other, it can provide information about the organization of the cognitive processes by looking at their developmental sequencing.

The descriptive aim of developmental psychology is fulfilled by a research methodology that uses age comparisons as its primary technique. Either children of different ages (cross-sectional comparison) or the same children at different points in their development are compared (longitudinal comparison). Some task or series of tasks is designed to reflect the type of cognitive process in question (e.g., classification). Children of different ages are compared as they perform on that task. The resultant data yield a picture of the ontogenetic course of the achievement in question. Further, experiments may be designed that test interpretations of the kind of functioning observed. The resultant age comparison lays out a progression of behaviors which yield data on the development of cognitive processes. Many of the important questions ask whether various features of behavior, such as classification, show a succession of "forms" or "types" that follow one another in regular order. Similarly, questions are asked about whether various features regularly succeed one another so that the extraction of information always reaches a certain point of efficiency before conceptualization occurs, or so that conceptualization reaches a certain point of efficiency before theorizing occurs.

The finding of such regularities, or rules of succession, then becomes a source of theorizing about both the nature of development and the nature of cognitive processes. Typically, this theorizing involves consideration of etiology, or the factors that underlie and determine development.

2. *The etiological aim and cross-cultural research.* According to Piaget (1966) and Dasen (1972*a*) there are four kinds of factors that can be considered as determinants of development:

a. biological factors
b. interactions with the physical environment
c. interactions with the social environment
d. sociocultural factors such as language and education.

While there are few theorists who claim exclusive determination of development by any of these factors, there are theoretical differences in the relative degree of importance assigned to one form of "causation" or another.

Many of the theoretical divisions derive from differences in analytic orientation (e.g., rationalist approaches vs. empiricist approaches—see Chomsky 1966 or Cassirer 1953) and hence are not really open to empirical information. Yet, a strong case can be made for the possibility that many theoretical divisions derive from the fact that studies performed within a single culture and theories derived from an acultural standpoint are incapable of obtaining clear-cut evidence that would allow for theoretical decisions concerning the relative importance of biological, interactional, and cultural factors in determining development.

In order to gain empirical information relevant to decisions about the relative contribution of these factors, two requirements must be fulfilled. First, there must be variability within each factor that contrasts between different values of a factor may be compared; second, there must be separability of factors, in such a way that the factors do not always co-vary but may be pitted against one another.

Neither of these conditions is easy to fulfill in studies that make use of only one national grouping.

Variability. With respect to the question of variability, it should be clear that there is less intracultural variation than there is cross-cultural variation. On the biological level, differences between gene pools are attenuated by the increased possibilities of interbreeding that national or tribal membership and, hence, physical proximity afford. Other biological factors such as nutritional history are likely to be more similar in nations that share a common material culture than in those which do not. Similarly, at the other end of the spectrum, it is self-evident that sociocultural factors such as language, or educational differences, and often the mere fact of education, are more pronounced in a cross-cultural than in an intracultural comparison.

Cross-cultural studies may also allow for greater precison in the specification of variables that we might wish to deal with. This advantage does not derive merely from the ability to make a comparison between cultures but derives, as well, from certain features of non-Western, nonindustrial cultures considered in themselves. Industrialized societies are often marked by a great degree of social mobility. Associated with this, there is often an increased tendency to break many of the implicit or explicit rules that govern such things as intermarriage or interbreeding. More traditional societies, however, tend to maintain patterns of intermarriage in keeping with a rather restrictive set of selection rules that determine who may be married to whom. Traditional societies may differ from industrialized societies not only in social mobility but in geographical mobility as well. Absence of transportation systems, lack of good reasons to leave (such as going to the city to work) tend to maintain a situation of greater geographical isolation among various groups. For these and a number of related reasons, cross-cultural studies have been seen as important tools for the developmental psychologist interested in the etiology of behavior.

The analytic advantages of cross-cultural comparison have been exploited from a number of different directions. The precision gained by being able to identify and thereby scale environmental inputs, has led to investigations of the manner in which information is extracted from the environment within environments of definably different types. For example, Segall, Campbell, and Herskovitz (1966) have examined the way in which perceptual information is obtained in environments that have been ranked in terms of their "carpenteredness" (the degree to which structures in that environment are organized in terms of rectilinear coordinates such as vertical and horizontal). In like manner, DeLemos (1969) and Dasen (1972a) have been able to construct research designs that compare "full breeds" and "half-breeds" among Australian aborigine groups on a number of Piagetian measures.

Separating confounded variables. In addition to the value of finding variation and defining variables, cross-cultural comparisons may help to separate variables which in industralized societies often overlap. For example, there is the question of the degree to which development is influenced by biological maturation or schooling. Most industrialized societies have a system of formal education that is pervasive. It is likely that there will be schools in all areas of the country and that the bulk of the school-candidate population will attend. The assessment of the impact of the relative contributions of such confounded variables as maturational development and education requires a research design where not all children of the same age are in school. Ideally, one would like to compare children of the same age groups who differ only in whether they have attended formal schools or not. Many societies provide the possibility for such contrasts. There are areas where formal education is available but where not all children of school age attend such schools. A design that made use of this feature has been employed by Greenfield (1966) in her studies of cognitive development in Senegal. By carefully selecting from the available instances of natural cultural variation in important determinant variables, Greenfield was able to independently examine the effects of age, schooling, language, and degree of urban experience. To do such a study in the United States would be next to impossible and contingent on abnormal sets of circumstances (see Mermelstein and Shulman 1967, for a study of this sort that made use of the unusual circumstance of the closing down of schools in Prince Georges County, Maryland, after attempts to implement the school desegregation order).

Thus, cross-cultural study may be used as an important tool for separating and analyzing factors that are important to development. One can treat this study in a manner analogous to a classical laboratory study (Strodtbeck 1964; LeVine 1970). Where natural variations exist, one may seek to measure their impact on some aspect of cognition. Should variations in performance concordant with variations in a relevant variable be found (whether it be genetic, environmental, or cultural), one can assign importance to that variable. In a similar manner, should a candidate variable not yield measurable differences, its importance can be downgraded.

3. *Problems of interpretation.* The etiological relevance of cross-cultural study involves the investigator in a search for whether there are "universal" features of behavior (related presumably to biological characteristics of man as a "species") or whether a variety of conditioning factors, such as specific heredities, environmental variations and/or cultural variations, act in such a manner as to introduce more variability into human behavior than the "man as a species" view would maintain. It is

at this juncture that one must be very careful about the way in which inferences are made and conclusions drawn. The problem of universals and differentia in human performance is by no means straightforward and has been the subject of considerable controversy.

The problem of universals of human cognition. While one may wish to search for the differences that culture and heredity make in the determination of human development, one must be clear at the outset about what is to be considered as evidence that some factor does make a difference.

A useful distinction has been proposed within the context of linguistic theory. Chomsky (1965) distinguished between substantive universals and formal universals. A substantive universal implies that the judgment of sameness or difference can be characterized in terms of a selection of some particular feature from a constrained set of alternatives. In linguistics the most common example is the selection of "distinctive phonological features." All phonological systems may be characterized by positive or negative positions on a set of twenty-six such features (Halle 1967). On a grammatical level, there are claims that all languages must have noun-phrase and verb-phrase components, and so on. Formal universals, on the other hand, make no claims about the particular features. Rather, they describe certain abstract conditions that must be met by any number of particular realizations (Chomsky 1965). The issue is whether we are looking for universal contents of mind or universal modes of minding. Levi-Strauss has attempted to show, for example, that though the surface features of mythological and scientific thought are apparently different, the underlying rules generating the system are fundamentally similar (Levi-Strauss 1966).

These distinctions are particularly important to keep in mind in cross-cultural psychology, since investigators are often led to postulate wide differences on the basis of *surface features* which may, in fact, disappear when underlying formal and functional questions are raised. Thus, it is not as important to know whether a given set of peoples possesses a certain set of "advanced ideas" as it is to know whether they have the formal capabilities of generating these ideas under conditions of adequate input.

An additional argument related to this problem has been advanced by Piaget (1952) in his discussions of the relationship between psychological accounts of cognitive development and philosophical accounts as embodied in Kant's postulation of a set of a priori categories of experience. Piaget is led to distinguish between two ways of conceiving of hereditary structures. On the one hand they can be looked at in substantive terms—as a set of structures which are innate and which maturationally become revealed in the course of development. Piaget discounts this sort of notion and posits that the human infant starts with an extremely limited set of structural universals (e.g., sucking and grasping reflexes).[1] Universal laws of functioning governing the active use of a small set of inbuilt structures will lead to a progressive structural elaboration that will be universal but only because of the organizational or functional modes that are characteristic of the species.

Accordingly, one should be cautious in reviewing a literature that purports to talk of universals. Some investigators seek substantive universals (Berlin and Kay 1969; Jung 1956), others may search for formal universals, and others are unsure of the kinds of universals they expect to discover. The distinction between formal and substantive universals is quite relevant to the conclusions we might wish to make about the impact of environmental variables. Consider, for the moment, the inferential status of the demonstration of an environmental impact of some sort. One might wish to claim that since the demonstration of an environmental impact has been shown, etiological factors of a cultural or interactional nature apply, therefore, and human universals are not apparent. A counterclaim would be that the arguing about issues on the level of the substantive impact of some particular variable does not touch on the question of formal universals. A universalist might claim that the variable —leading to a superficially different product—nonetheless reflected an identical underlying form of operation.

It is reasoning very much like this that has made linguistics a current center for the search for universals (Greenberg 1966). There is nothing so obvious as the fact that people "learn" the language of the group within which they are reared. But, the question is whether this obvious fact of learning is merely a superficial coloration, hiding the basic fact that all different languages are learned in essentially the same way and, in fact, share deep similarities. Although this issue will be explored in later sections of this chapter, we would do well to keep it in mind here as we consider the claims made for cross-environmental studies.

Some Methodological and Conceptual Considerations

Beyond the level of abstractness with which we view behavior are the problems having to do with the gathering of data, on any level of abstractness, in a cross-cultural context. The methodological difficulties involved in cross-cultural research are varied and complex. Often they may outweigh the advantages that have been claimed for the cross-cultural method

[1] This has been well exemplified in Jungian psychology by the search for universally human symbols of determined shape, and so on, and has been used to support such notions as a collective unconscious (Jung 1956—see also Fingeston 1971, for a critical discussion).

in clarifying etiological questions. As has been suggested earlier, cross-cultural methodology allows for the testing of the impact of variables that cannot be manipulated in intracultural studies. However, as soon as inter-cultural studies are undertaken, variables are introduced that pose severe problems for the investigator. In some cases these variables are recognized and considered in the design and interpretation of the study; in other cases they may remain unknown.

The logic of comparative study involves the testing of different peoples in a comparable manner. Yet, when different cultural groups with different cultural experience, with different languages and different views of appropriate activities, are involved, the establishment of comparability becomes difficult. Three threats to comparability will be discussed here—familiarity problems, communication problems, and problems of motivation.

1. *Familiarity problems.* If one wants to compare two or more cultural groups in order to gauge their relative ability to perform some cognitive act, one wants to be sure of two things: that a cognitive act is involved in the task demands and that any differences which are found in perform-ance are not due to such simple factors as differential "familiarity" with materials.

Several studies in the literature have compared performance with materials that were "familiar" vs. those which were "unfamiliar" and have found that classification abilities were better with the familiar materials (Okonji 1971; Irwin and McLaughlin 1970; Kellaghan 1968; Greenfield, Reich, and Olver 1966). Greenfield (1972), however, pointed out that the term "familiarity" can mean a number of different things and that dif-ferent bases of familiarity must be distinguished.

Mode of representation of materials. Many standard tests of cognitive ability rely upon two-dimensional representations of three-dimensional objects (many perceptual illusion tasks involve two-dimensional informa-tion; many classification tasks use such things as cards representing geo-metrical shapes). It has been claimed by some (Hudson 1960; Biesheuval 1949) that the unfamiliarity of this mode of representation may preclude recognition of the materials in the task. Some studies that have compared familiar and unfamiliar materials inadvertently confuse familiarity of objects and mode of representation. For example, Irwin and McLaughlin (1970), in their study of classification abilities among the Mano of Liberia, contrasted classification abilities as applied to two-dimensional representations of geometrical figures which varied in number, color, and shape (unfamiliar materials) with classification of bowls of rice (familiar materials) which varied in size, type of rice, and cleanliness of rice. The contrast between these two types of materials involved more than just a contrast of familiarity of objects; it involved mode of representation (two-dimensional cards vs. three-dimensional objects) and the dimensions of classification as well.

The obtained results of better sorting behaviors with the familiar materials might derive either from their familiarity or their three-dimensionality (familiar objects vs. familiar mode of representation). Less confounded support for the influence of mode of representation has been represented by Deregowski and Serpell (1971) who compared sorting performance of Zambian and Scottish children with objects and with pictures of the objects. They found that sorting with real objects yielded no differences between the two cultural groups, while sorting with pictures of the objects showed more classificatory ability for the Scottish group.

Familiarity of objects and dimensions. As mentioned above, in reference to the Irwin and McLaughlin study, the familiarity of objects may also be a factor in determination of performance. In a study that directly investigated this factor, Okonji (1971) found evidence of superiority of sorting behavior at older age-levels for an African (Ibusa) group of subjects over a Scottish group when the materials to be sorted were more familiar to the African group. No differences were obtained when objects which were equally familiar were employed.

A dimension may be considered to be familiar when it is used to label distinctions. The evidence for dimensional familiarity may derive from linguistic analysis where a category label (size) is used to distinguish objects differing in terms of some featural contrast (large vs. small). Thus, familiar objects presented in the appropriate mode of representation may not be enough to guarantee familiarity if the dimension involved is one which finds no place in the language of the group to be tested.

Familiarity of the application of a dimension to a domain. Collections of natural objects are frequently the subject of classificatory operations. Some collections of objects are typically analyzed in terms of certain dimensions, although the same dimension may not be appropriate when applied to a different domain (though it may be familiar in terms of the linguistic criteria discussed above). Thus, there is the possibility of unfamiliar concordance between the two (as would be the case in our culture, for example, if one were asked to sort psychologists in terms of their weight rather than their competence).

In a study that carefully obeyed all of the distinctions discussed above, Greenfield (1972) compared sorting behaviors in a familiar domain (with familiar dimensions applicable to that domain available) with sorting behaviors in an unfamiliar domain. Subjects were asked to classify and reclassify cut flowers, an activity and type of material familiar to the Mexican groups with whom Greenfield worked. The classification of cut flowers was contrasted with classifications of sticks of various sizes, colors, and so on.

Greenfield (1972) found no effect of any form of familiarity, although three-dimensional real objects were used throughout. In fact, she found some evidence that familiarity with a domain and important distinctions within it could be a hindrance to some classificatory operations. Younger subjects, in particular, seemed resistant to break up functionally adequate sorts, based upon habitually applied principles, in order to fulfill some classificatory criterion which countermanded the dictates of "good sense."

Greenfield's results raise one of the more difficult points in cross-cultural comparison. There seems to be little doubt that it is more reasonable to use materials with known properties that are equally familiar, yet there may be hidden dangers in the use of this technique. The dangers hinge on the first requirement of cross-cultural comparability; the ability to reasonably assume that a cognitive operation is in use with respect to the materials at hand. Most of the time the argument is made that familiar materials allow for the use of more advanced operations (Okonji 1971; Price-Williams 1961, 1962), as if this was a self-evident proposition. However, findings such as those presented by Greenfield (1972) raise some doubts about this assumption. The basic problem is this: to be able to study a cognitive operation, one must be sure that the task demands the use of that operation and that the solution of the task reflects that operation and none other.

For example, when a psychologist is interested in people's abilities to reason syllogistically, this process is seen as a logical process of combining premises in such a way as to reach a conclusion. The logical operation is assumed to be independent of the content of the premises to be formally combined. Thus, if one had syllogisms that were factual (all men are mortal, Socrates is a man, therefore Socrates is mortal) or that were counterfactual (all men are green, Socrates is a man, therefore Socrates is green), the syllogisms would be formally equivalent, although one of them yields an assertion of utter nonsense. From the point of view of diagnosing the logical ability to solve syllogisms, one would be interested in both the factual and the counterfactual cases, since a correct conclusion in the factual case alone could not be distinguished from factual truth which does not have logical support. Luria (1971) and Cole, Gay, Glick, and Sharp (1971) have presented evidence that culturally familiar proverbs and problems of syllogistic form can be "solved" readily by peoples who do not live in cultures which have either developed technologies or explicitly logical rules. However, when counterfactual, and hence necessarily unfamiliar, premises are to be dealt with, logical conclusions are not made by the groups. Interestingly, Wason (1965) has shown the influence of familiarity with context on judgments of presumably logical form for Western groups as well. However, this influence does not seem to be as extreme as in the cases reported in nontechnological societies.

Considerations such as those presented above suggest a danger in the uncritical use of familiar materials in cross-cultural cognitive testing. Too much familiarity may not allow the psychologist to distinguish between the formal and the empirical aspects of the cognitive operations under study. Too little familiarity, on the other hand, may threaten comparability as well.

There is no easy methodological prescription on this point. One solution might be to use materials of equal *un*familiarity in different cultural settings. However, an etiological variable such as schooling can be seen as practice in the use of unfamiliar organizations of materials, or in the application of familiar dimensions to unfamiliar domains. Accordingly, this is likely to increase the probability of finding differences in performance based upon the schooling factor. These differences may, in fact, be related more to the "familiarity" of the *task* to the schooled group than to any cognitive impact of schooling.

A second possibility may be more reasonable. One might adopt a research strategy where familiar materials are chosen for study but where prior research suggests that there is no strong tendency in the "folk wisdom" of the culture to treat those familiar materials in certain proscriptive ways. In this manner one might be able to establish comparability, by choosing carefully domains which have similar degrees of familiarity with no compelling cultural structure, which at the same time allow for the investigation of cognitive operations in their proper sense, unconfounded by overlearned or proscriptive cultural formulations.

2. *Communication problems.* Problems of cross-cultural communication, particularly vis-à-vis experimental test items or instructions, have received considerable attention in the literature. Werner and Campbell (1970), Brislin (1970), Sechrest, Fay, and Zaidi (1972) have given serious attention to the centrality of the problem for cross-cultural research and have provided a number of useful distinctions among types of translation problems. Additionally, several techniques have been suggested for the achievement of appropriate translations.

While full justice to this sort of work cannot be done in the context of a review paper, some flavor of the type of problems to be dealt with can be given. Sechrest, Fay, and Zaidi (1972) indicate four sources of translation problems in experimental work.

Translation specific to tasks or measures. Even tasks requiring nonverbal responses usually use a verbal introduction. Problems of linguistic and developmental comparability of task instructions must be dealt with. Greenfield (1966) provides a particularly important instance of this sort of problem in discussing research on conservation. The study of conservation typically involves presentation of two quantities which are equal, e.g., water in two similar glasses. A transformation is then applied to one of the quantities—the water is poured into a taller, thinner glass. The subject is then asked to judge the equality or inequality of the original and the transformed quantities. If one looks for an exact translation of the term "equal" into Wolof (the group studied by Greenfield) there are two words, "tolo" and "Yem." Both, however, have a double sense, referring to "equal perceptible level" of things or "equal amounts." Since solution of conservation problems (continuous quantity) critically depends upon the separation of these two sorts of "equality," the linguistic problem is paramount in this case. Eventually an elaborate paraphrase was constructed which adult speakers of Wolof agreed would unambiguously define equality of amount. Yet, considered from the point of view of cross-cultural comparability, the instructions used for Western and Wolof children would be nonidentical (word for word) translations.

Dialect problems. A third class of problems concerns the overall strategy of presentation of verbal instructions or materials. Means of address may be formal or informal, one may use scholarly vs. vernacular forms, and so on. Little is known about the effects of phrasing instructions and defining contexts in these ways. Should there be an impact of these factors it would be of interest to know whether they operate alike in different cultural groups. Clearly, this unexamined factor could bias the comparability of test results in different cultures and also could affect the relationship between different kinds of tests given in the same culture.

Response translation. Whenever verbal responses are elicited, as, for example, in eliciting justification for categorizations or justification for conservation judgments, translation problems can exist. Word-for-word translation may do an injustice to the response in question for much the same reasons offered above. Little is known about this issue at present.

Considerations of the above four factors should give some indication of the tremendous difficulty of establishing cross-cultural equivalence of verbal material and, possibly, definitions of testing situations. The reader is referred to Werner and Campbell (1970) and Sechrest et al. (1972) for a more detailed analysis of the multitude of problems that exist. For an attempt to evaluate the effectiveness of various techniques of establishing equivalence, Brislin (1970) should be consulted.

3. Motivational problems. Biesheuval (1949) indicated that the establishment of motivational equivalence is a difficult one for cross-cultural research. If cultures differ, for example, in such factors as competitiveness, then it should be difficult to assure equal motivation in different samples (see Madsen 1971; Kubany, Gallimore, and Buell 1970).

Although investigators in the United States (Zigler and Butterfield

1968) have shown that test performances may vary quite widely dependent upon motivational conditions, only one cross-cultural or cognitive-functioning study has considered this factor and employed procedures to deal with it (Lloyd 1971).

It would seem important to explore this dimension of confounded cross-cultural contrast quite seriously. It may be the case, for example, that contrasts between schooled and unschooled populations may vary not only on the dimension of degree of schooling but on degree of motivation to perform on school-like tasks. Several investigators have noted, moreover, that the quality of motivation may vary widely between cultures. Schools in many developing areas (particularly where there are wide tribal linguistic differences) may often stress processes of rote memorization and strict obedience to the authority of the teacher (Gay and Cole 1967). This may lead to a rather restrictive approach to problems if these problems are treated as being "school-like" or an adult tester is involved. This motivational factor may be of considerable importance when tests requiring exploratory rather than answer-oriented styles of response are employed.

Similar observations have been made by Greenfield and Bruner (1969), who offered an explanation in terms of cultural value systems (collective vs. individualistic). This suggests the possibility that what has been discussed here in terms of a methodological nuisance of equating motivation in a particular situation may have deeper cultural roots in systems of socialization.

Summary

1. Methodological difficulties exist for the cross-cultural investigator in three areas: establishing comparable familiarity of materials when different groups are employed; establishing equivalences of communication and translation when different language groups are used; and establishing motivational comparability among differently motivated and oriented groups.

2. Familiarity problems apply with respect to the mode of representation of materials, familiarity of materials themselves, familiarity of dimensions applied to materials, and relationship between materials and dimensions.

3. There are dangers in using materials which are too familiar, since one may be unable to distinguish between rote performances with respect to these materials and cognitive processes applied to them.

4. Communication problems exist in introducing tasks, establishing clear communication of instructions, esablishing clear translation of responses, and choosing an idiom or dialect which may establish unintended attitudes toward the task.

5. Motivational problems may be heavily involved in determining people's performances on cognitive tasks. These may be of two types, motivation to work on some problem, and motivational direction to work on the problem versus working to please the experimenter.

CROSS-CULTURAL STUDIES OF PERCEPTUAL DEVELOPMENT

The plan of this review of the literature is to follow the model of cognitive processes outlined in the previous section and to consider the types of etiological factors of concern to developmentalists with regard to this model. Some areas are included which may seem to belong more properly to other reviews (e.g., perceptual development) and others are excluded which may seem properly to belong to the domain of cognitive development (e.g., studies of "Intelligence" as dealt with by IQ-testing approaches). The underlying basis for these inclusions and exclusions is that a broad view is taken of cognition as a process of information extraction and organization. Perceptual development studies can aid in understanding that process, while IQ studies, which typically use a potpourri of subitems bearing on different sorts of things, yield little in the way of direct information about the processes of cognition.

Three main theoretical views have dominated the treatment of perceptual development in Western psychology. The first view holds that perceptual processes detect environmental information. Perception is assumed to reflect directly the information present in the environment. Perceptual development is seen as the increasing differentiation of the detection of information (Gibson 1969). It is not clear exactly what role experiential differences may play although it is clear that differentiations occur in areas where there is focal interest, and this may be culturally determined. A second view holds that perception is a judgmental process which involves the evaluation of different cues in terms of their reliability in reflecting objective states of affairs, and the weighing and evaluation process depends strongly on learning to assess the validity of the cue as an index of the environment. The process of "unconscious inference" computes the past meanings and confirmations and disconfirmations of various cues (Brunswick 1956). This view has been elaborated cross-culturally in terms of the "carpentered-world hypothesis" (Segall et al. 1966), which holds that since ecologies differ in terms of the degree of rectilinearity that is habitually encountered, this should lead to different weighings of rectilinear cues in different ecologies. Accordingly, perceptual processing should vary with the type of environment habitually encountered. This view of perception stresses interactional factors and the importance of past history.

A third view of perception argues for a cultural impact on perceptual process but a cultural impact of a more sociocultural than an interactional sort. The major sociocultural factor that has been examined is language structure. This view, known as the Sapir-Whorf hypothesis, holds that the structure of language influences the manner in which things are perceived (Brown and Lenneberg 1954; Whorf 1956). Differences in language structure might be expected to be related to the way in which perceptual distinctions are made.

The focus of cross-cultural empirical work has been on those areas of study where explicitly cross-cultural hypotheses have been proposed. For this reason the review of evidence will focus first on those areas where these concerns have been most developed.

Perception and Interactional Determinants:
The Carpentered-World Hypothesis

People from Western societies are exposed to an ecological environment that is differentially structured from environments in many other parts of the world. One important dimension of this difference is the degree of "carpenteredness" of the environment. Western houses are typically constructed on rectilinear principles, with walls being perpendicular to one another, and so on. Similarly, roads, railroad tracks, and the like are organized in terms of straight-line principles. Environments in other parts of the world deviate from this rectilinearity in a number of ways. Houses may not be rectilinear, some have curved walls (round houses) and curved roofs (made of thatch). While an environment cannot be characterized as being absolutely carpentered or absolutely not carpentered (some roads curve, some houses in the West are curved, some in other areas are rectilinear), it is possible to classify ecologies by relative degrees of "carpenteredness." If this is the case, then it might also be the case that environmental cues relative to carpenteredness assume greater or lesser importance depending on the degree of carpenteredness of the environment.

Segall et al. (1966), in a study elaborately constructed to deal with the methodological difficulties in cross-cultural research, investigated the question of whether rectilinearity of the environment was related to use of rectilinear cues in perception. They made use of illusion figures such as the Muller-Lyer illusion and the horizontal-vertical illusion. The Muller-Lyer illusion consists of two line segments of equal length. The lines are, however, surrounded by arrowheads which point toward the end of the line segments or away from the ends, as in figure 1. Subjects are asked to judge the equality or inequality of the two line segments. Since these segments are equal to begin with, a judgment of inequality would mean that the surrounding arrowheads have influenced the perception of line length. By using additional figures where the line segments are unequal,

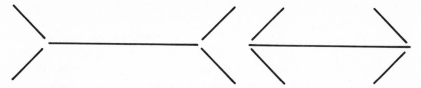

Fig. 1. An example of a Muller-Lyer illusion figure. (From Segall, Campbell and Herskovitz 1966.)

one can measure the strength of the illusion by seeing what degree of inequality is judged as being equal. The horizontal-vertical illusion consists of a horizontal line joined to a vertical line of equal length. Again, the illusion consists in the judgment of one of the lines as being longer than the other. The vertical line is usually judged as longer.

Segall et al. (1966) argued that the Muller-Lyer illusion effect depends on the interpretation of the two-dimensional figures as representations of three-dimensional figures. The arrowheads function as perspective cues which lead to the illusion. This depends upon inferences from the use of rectilinear cues. Thus, it might be expected that people who make use of rectilinear cues should be more illusion-prone than those who do not. The horizontal-vertical illusion, on the other hand, which is formed of a horizontal and vertical line, is presumed to be based on cues which are more fostered in open environments where the vertical is seen to be receding into space. This illusion should be related to the "openness" of environments. In the study, Segall et al. (1966) employed a large number of samples (eighteen) from a diverse array of environments that were rated on degree of carpenteredness and reported results in conformity with the notions of environmental openness. The Muller-Lyer illusion was strongest in groups from carpentered environments, the horizontal-vertical illusion was strongest in groups from open environments. Overall, however, the Muller-Lyer illusion decreased with age in those groups where it was found to be prevalent. The result is puzzling for the view of the problem which relies only on the factor of experience with carpenteredness or noncarpenteredness. If experience alone is the answer, then illusion effects should increase with more experience and therefore with age. At the least, a two-factor interpretation taking into account degree of carpenteredness and other changes associated with age is required. These results seem to argue strongly for the environmentalist view that differences in ecology make for differences in perceptual inference processes which are reflected in perceptual experience.

The environmentalist interpretation has been challenged by Pollack (1972), who has amassed a considerable amount of evidence to suggest that findings with respect to the Muller-Lyer illusion could be better explained on biological grounds. Pollack noted that the groups employed by Segall et al. (1966) not only varied in carpenteredness of their environments but in their skin color as well. Skin coloration is related to coloration of the fundus oculi (Silvar and Pollack 1967). Moreover, susceptibility to the Muller-Lyer illusion is related to the pigmentation of the fundus oculi (Pollack and Silvar, 1967), with Muller-Lyer susceptibility being lower when pigmentation is higher. Finally, pigmentation of the fundus oculi increases with age (Coren and Girgus, 1972). Putting all of this together, Pollack argued that a one-factor interpretation of the Muller-Lyer illusion *is* possible, one which moreover reduces both the cultural and the age differences to differences in optical pigmentation.

Experimental evidence of Pollack's thesis in a cross-cultural context has been provided by both Berry (1971) and Jahoda (1971). Berry, for example, examined conjointly the variables of degree of carpenteredness of environments and an index related to skin pigmentation as they affected Muller-Lyer susceptibility in ten different samples. He found that both carpenteredness and pigmentation were strongly related to Muller-Lyer susceptibility. However, carpenteredness and pigmentation are themselves strongly related. When the relationship between carpenteredness and pigmentation was statistically controlled, the pigmentation factor was much more strongly related to Muller-Lyer susceptibility than was carpenteredness. Jahoda (1971) further explored Pollack's notions and extended them to tests of spatial abilities based upon map-reading skills. The pigmentation factor operates on short wavelengths (blue end of spectrum) to a greater degree than on long wavelengths. Jahoda compared Scottish and Malawi subjects on Muller-Lyer susceptibility when the illusion figures were presented in red, against when they were presented in blue. This should have held constant figural processes bearing on the carpentered-world hypothesis. In accordance with expectation, Jahoda found that there was no difference between red and blue presentation for Scottish subjects, while there was a significant difference for Malawi subjects. However, Jahoda found overall greater Muller-Lyer susceptibility for the Malawi subjects, which contradicts just about everybody. In an interesting extension of Pollack's notions, Jahoda noted that topological maps make use of red and related colors for land areas and blue and related colors for water areas. He predictably found that Malawi subjects made more errors when dealing with water regions than with land topography, while Scottish subjects performed about the same in both areas when they were tested for map-reading skills.

Although this evidence is impressive, it is not clear at this time whether any position that supports a single-factor theory can be unequivocally supported, whether that factor is ecological or retinal. There are studies that have attempted to replicate the Pollack findings which have not succeeded (Armstrong, Rubin, Stewart, and Kuntner 1970, cited in Jahoda 1971). Further, there are inconsistencies such as Jahoda's finding that Malawi subjects were more subject to the Muller-Lyer, which confute both Pollack and Segall et al. Finally, there are enough inconsistencies in the cross-cultural literature on illusions to suggest that any single-factor interpretation may be difficult to maintain (see, for example, Berry 1968; Gregor and McPherson 1965; Jahoda 1966; Jahoda and Stacy 1970). In particular, Jahoda (1966) presents evidence that the horizontal-vertical illusion does not follow the hypothesized course of increase with "openness" of environment. Moreover, it is unclear how a "retinal" interpretation would deal with the horizontal-vertical illusion.

Perception and Sociocultural Determinants:
Picture Perception and Education

   One of the major problems met with by those who wish to use Western-style tests with peoples from nontechnological societies is that many of these tests make extensive use of pictorially representative materials. Biesheuval (1949, reprinted in Price-Williams 1970) in an essentially methodological review, pointed to problems in the use of either representational or abstract two-dimensional presentation with non-Western populations.

   Hudson (1960) tested several subcultural groups in Africa on a test designed to explore the ability to perceive depth cues in two-dimensional representations. He presented to the subjects cards which depicted a hunting scene: a hunter holding a spear, an elephant, a mountain, an antelope. The antelope was drawn to be bigger than the elephant and was placed lower in the picture, while on some cards the elephant was placed on the mountain toward the upper part of the picture. The hunter was also drawn large and near the bottom. The arrangement of the pictorial cues should suggest that the elephant was further away than the antelope, the hunter and the antelope being on the same plane. By questioning subjects about the relative arrangements of the figures in the picture (Can the hunter see the antelope? Which animal is he hunting? and so on) information concerning the perception of depth relationships would be obtained. Hudson (1960, 1967) reported that younger children, both white and black, had difficulty seeing three-dimensionality in the drawings. However, with schooling, the white sample increased (from 17 percent in lowest primary to 72 percent in highest) in their ability to see depth while the black groups did so minimally. This was reported to be the case even for university-trained subjects.

Mundy-Castle (1966), repeated the Hudson experiment with Ghanaian students and found almost no response to depth cues in children ranging in age from five to ten years. In an analytic study that attempted to distinguish various reasons for the lack of the depth response, Mundy-Castle reported that the critical perspective giving elements of the picture were often misinterpreted. For example, the horizon line in the Hudson pictures was seldom recognized as such and was often interpreted as any of the following: "stick, line, rope, ruler, path, thread, hill, mound, tape, spear, heavens" (from Mundy-Castle 1966, table 1).

It is difficult to say much about the effects of formal schooling, or the absence of the effects of formal schooling, since training in pictorial depth perception is often not given in school—it is rather assumed. However, both Mundy-Castle and Hudson do point to informal schooling as an important source of the ability to interpret pictorial depth. An exemplary quote:

The hypothesis that cultural stimulus is critical for the development of pictorial depth perception is supported by the present results. Surveys undertaken in the communities and homes of all the children studied revealed no evidence of activities such as reading, drawing, painting, looking at pictures, pattern-making or playing with construction toys, and it was exceptional for a child to have used a pencil prior to going to school. . . . The opportunity for informal pictorial experience was, therefore, negligible" (Mundy-Castle 1966, p. 129).

It is difficult to understand how formal education experience, which does involve many of the activities described in the above quote, could fail to produce increased pictorial depth perception. This is particularly puzzling in the light of findings reported by Dawson (1967*a*), using laborers, apprentices, and secondary-school students in Sierra Leone, that three-dimensional pictorial depth perception is readily trainable within a three-month period of eight one-hour sessions. However, Dawson (1967*a*, *b*) argued instead that the determining factor is not experience but, rather, "cognitive styles" of field dependence and field independence (see next section) which limit the possible influence of learning.

One approach to the dilemma presented by these results is to assume that pictorial depth perception may be a rather complicated process involving far more than the familiarity with two-dimensional depth cues. A recent experiment by Leibowitz and Pick (1971), investigating the Ponzo illusion, serves to indicate some of the complexities involved. The Ponzo illusion involves the presentation of two lines which to Westerners look like railroad tracks that converge at the horizon (upper part of drawing). A horizontal bar placed across these lines close to their apex will be judged to be larger than a bar placed at the open end of the lines. The magnitude of the illusion depends on the misuse of the perspective depth cue of convergence at the horizon. Leibowitz and Pick compared susceptibility to the illusion of four different groups: Pennsylvania college students, Uganda college students, Guam college students, and Ugandan villagers. The Ugandan villagers showed almost no illusion effect, while the other groups showed effects of up to 30 percent overestimation. Leibowitz and Pick pointed out that two factors determined the Ugandan villagers' response. The first factor is the by now familiar lack of familiarity with pictorial depth cues. A second factor determining lack of illusion response depends on the very nature of two-dimensional representation—that it is two-dimensional. In the presentation of a two-dimensional stimulus, there are ample cues to the fact that the stimulus is two-dimensional, and these cues must be suppressed in order to interpret the picture three-dimensionally. It may be the case that unfamiliarity with the representational use of two-dimensional surfaces for three dimensional purposes influences the ability to suppress cues to two-dimensionality as much as it does the ability to recognize cues to three-dimensionality.

This analysis of the problem suggests that the subject is always presented with a dilemma in approaching a task of the type that has been used to study pictorial depth perception. The dilemma involves the sets of cues that confront an individual and the cues to which he or she should respond—the cues to two-dimensionality or the cues to three-dimensionality. It may be the case that training specific to making that decision is effective and is not normally provided in formal schooling.

There is evidence in the literature that when response conditions are set up so that a three-dimensional response is clearly called for, uneducated subjects can provide three-dimensional responses, albeit with some distortion. Deregowski (1968), for example, presented subjects with two-dimensional drawings representing three-dimensional objects and required his subjects to build a model out of clay that would correspond to the depicted object. Three-dimensional figures were constructed, although there were distortions in the production. It seems that the response constraint—to make a three-dimensional figure—was sufficient to bring out three-dimensional interpretations of the stimulus.

Accordingly, there is some support for the view that pictorial depth perception involves a conflict situation where objective cues to flatness must be suppressed in order to participate in the cultural convention that flat pictures really *represent* nonflat situations. In a major sense, the subject must suppress his perception of the way things *are,* in order to respond to things as they *were intended to be.* The latter should be maximally susceptible to cultural convention.

Unfortunately for the neatness of this sort of interpretation, the evidence is not clear-cut. Deregowski and Byth (1970), in a study of three-dimensional perception of Hudson's pictures under conditions that might be expected to suppress cues to flatness, still found evidence of two-dimensional perception in Zambian subjects and suggested that, in addition to any cultural convention or familiarity effects, there were real perceptual difficulties. Additionally, Deregowski (1971) presented evidence that difficulties in orientation which lead to increased three-dimensional perception in Scottish samples did not do so for Zambian groups. However, his study did show that older Zambian subjects gave a considerable number of three-dimensional responses and that, in some conditions, their performance was indistinguishable from the Scottish comparison groups. It appears from this study that a considerable amount of three-dimensional responding was possible for the Zambians, but there was an insensitivity to the orientational conditions that tended to increase three-dimensional responses for the Scottish group. Does this mean that Zambians are different in their perception of orientation as well? Serpell (1971) has found that preferences for orientations of two-dimensional figures were alike in Zambian and American groups. He concluded that "intrinsic perceptual features of abstract shapes give rise independently of cultural background to consistent preferences for certain specific orientations of these shapes." Even the orientation evidence is mixed.

Perception and Sociocultural Determinants:
Socialization Practices and Field Dependence

Witkin and his colleagues (1962) developed the concept of psychological differentiation with respect to American groups. The basic notion is that people differ in the degree to which they are able to extract an item from its context. Some people are presumed to be field independent and others to be field dependent. The former are more analytic and able to separate an item from its context. For example, one task used to separate field independent and field dependent people is the embedded figures test (EFT). In this test the subject is shown a shape and is asked to find it when it is hidden among a number of lines which "camouflage" it. Measures are taken of the speed with which an identification is made. Those taking more time presumably have more difficulty in separating the figure from its confusing context. This sort of ability may be centrally involved in many tests of perceptual functioning (picture perception and illusion perception among them) and may, moreover, be maximally susceptible to cultural influence. Witkin et al. (1962) related the different perceptual styles to intracultural differences in socialization practices—practices, moreover, that have wide intercultural differences. Lack of differentiation is presumably related to restrictiveness of child-rearing practices. Often harsh punishment practices are used to produce conformist children, and this may lead to a lack of skills related to visual analysis. Less punitive, more exploration-oriented child-rearing practices are presumed to lead to more analytic, independent-minded perceptual types.

There has been a good deal of experimentation with this hypothesis. Dawson (1967a, b) was the first to apply field independence theory to cross-cultural phenomena. Working in Sierra Leone, he compared performances of male members to the two dominant tribal groups, the Temne and Mende. These tribal groups differed in their socialization practices. The Temne mother is presumed to be domineering and to maintain a very strict home discipline—conditions that are related to the development of a field-dependent style. The Mende people, contrastingly, are assumed to have less severe socialization practices and a home atmosphere where individual initiative is encouraged to a greater extent than occurs in the Temne home.

Dawson tested both groups with measures of field dependence (such as the embedded figures test), measures of pictorial depth perception (some figures borrowed from Hudson), and directly measured strictness of socialization practices. The hypotheses tested were (a) that the differences in attributed socialization practices would be found in measures of strictness of parents, (b) that strictness would be related to field dependence, and (c) that trainability for 3-D perception would be related to degree of field dependence. All of these hypotheses were confirmed. A very strong relationship was found between degree of field dependence and degree of improvement in pictorial depth perception due to training.

Similar findings have been reported by Berry (1966), who found marked differences between Temne and Eskimo subjects on measures of field dependence and other sorts of perceptual discriminative and spatial functioning. Both cultural groups differed on socialization practices and in ecological environments as well. While a contrast is not clear-cut when such confounded variation exists, these results, taken with others which are within the same type of ecologies (e.g., the Dawson study), lend support to finding a field-dependence, socialization-practice relationship. An additional interesting feature of Berry's results was that in contrast to most studies of field dependence where sex differences have been found (females being more field independent than males) no such differences were found for the Eskimo groups. This finding has been replicated by MacArthur (1967). A reason offered for this finding is that Eskimo females are given the same sort of independence training as males. Accordingly, sociocultural, rather than biological factors, may be at the heart of the sex differences reported in other studies. A rather extensive review of this literature has been provided by Witkin (1967).

There are methodological difficulties involved in the testing of "field dependence" in other cultures. Wober (1967) has suggested that different cultures may have differential sensitivity to some of the sensory systems involved in the standard measures. However, the overall pattern of findings suggests that this dimension is an important one, and one, moreover, which may account for some puzzling phenomena (such as the experience effects in pictorial depth perception [Dawson 1967a, b]).

These findings, however, must be interpreted carefully in the light of our prior discussions of human universals and differentia. On the one hand, the cognitive-style literature suggests that there are substantive differences between the perceptual performances of diverse cultural groups. On the other hand, the same factors that have been found to be operative intra-culturally operate cross-culturally as well. In this sense, then, the finding of cultural differences corresponding to variations in socialization practice is as strong an argument for universality as it is for differences among cultural groups. The particular performances may be found to vary but the constellation of factors influencing those performances may be very much the same in different cultures.

It should be noted that there is a generic relationship between the concept of psychological differentiation as used by Witkin and the notion of differentiation proposed as a criterion of development by Werner (1957). Werner posited developmental "primitivity" as a lack of differentiation and has been interpreted by some to mean that "primitivity" is a biological attribute of nontechnological peoples (Werner and Kaplan 1956). This was not Werner's attempt, and he might have found Witkin's formulation of the determinants of "lack of differentiation" applied to a cross-cultural context compatible with his developmental position.

Perception and Sociocultural Determinants:
The Sapir-Whorf Hypothesis

Sociocultural determinants of the development of perception have received a good deal of attention in the cross-cultural literature. Perhaps the boldest position linking sociocultural factors and perceptual processes has been embodied in those investigations bearing on what is known as the Sapir-Whorf hypothesis (based on the original work of Sapir [1921] and extended by Whorf [1952, 1956]).

The basic notion involved in this hypothesis is that language structure is related to the structure of perceptual experience. B. L. Whorf (1952, 1956), guided in part by his insurance investigation work in Connecticut, noted that many of the causative factors in accidents had to do with people "mislabeling" a situation and responding to the situation in terms of the wrong label applied. For example, flammable materials which are stored in solid form are often responded to with behaviors appropriate to things solid (like rocks) and not to things flammable (like gasoline). Accidents occur when one is cavalier about the use of matches and lighted cigarettes in the proximity of "rocks" which are really flammable.

Whorf extended his investigations to the study of languages of southwestern Indian tribes and found that the linguistic encoding of fundamental categories of perceptual experience, such as space and time (see also Hallowell 1951), differed widely among languages. His hypothesis was that in much the same way as mislabelings are at the root of many insurance claims, so too might the structure of language in different groups lead to fundamental differences in the way in which they experienced the world. Whorf restricted much of his investigation to language and did not directly investigate the implications of linguistic differences in behaviorial terms. However, many psychologists have been influenced by the implications of Whorf's work and have attempted such studies.

Many of the studies investgating the Sapir-Whorf hypothesis have employed the physical domain of color and have looked for the influence of the paucity or richness of different linguistic groups' color terminology on various aspects of behavioral functioning. The choice of color as a domain seemed at the onset to be a uniquely well-constructed one, since, on the one hand, various colors exist on a physical continuum with different labels (color names) being applied to differentiate between areas of that continuum, and, on the other hand, various languages of the world seem to vary widely in the lexicon of color names used (Berlin and Kay 1969).

Early studies dealt with the Sapir-Whorf hypothesis in intralingual and intracultural designs (Greenfield and Bruner 1969). Brown and Lenneberg (1954), for example, investigated the relationship between the "codability" (ease, speed, and simplicity of naming) of a color stimulus and the accuracy with which that stimulus would be recognized in a larger stimulus array. They found evidence for the codability factor, with the more easily coded colors being more easily recognized. Lantz and Stefflre (1964) and Stefflre, Castillo-Vales, and Morley (1966) demonstrated a similar relationship and, moreover, showed a strong relationship between recognition accuracy and communication accuracy for color stimuli.

While these studies suggest an impact of the linguistic factor, it is not clear whether that influence is on a perceptual process or some other kind of process, such as memory.

Greenfield and Bruner (1969), in surveying much of the literature bearing on this topic, cite an unpublished review by McNeill (1965) which concluded that the majority of studies indicate that language influences are found only when memory tasks are involved and are not found when the stimuli to be dealt with are actually present. For example, Lenneberg (1961) studied the relationship between color terminology and perceptual discrimination errors on the one hand, and recognition memory on the other. He found that perceptual errors were influenced by color terminology in Zuni children but not in adults. In contrast, effects of linguistic factors on memory were found for both children and adults.

Greenfield and Bruner, however, presented some evidence for their own studies of the Wolof (in Senegal) which suggested that, when perceptual discrimination errors were made, they were made in terms which were consonant with linguistic determinants. The task that they used involved presenting triads of pictures that were constructed in such a way that two of the pictures could be related on the basis of their color, two on the basis of their form, and two on the basis of their function. Several triads, however, had the additional property of contrasting colors which are accorded the same name in the Wolof language. Thus, in a triad where color grouping involved a contrast between two pictures that are red with a third that is orange, the Wolof subject is presented a task where the colors are all named "Honka." Under these conditions, one might expect that, if a color grouping is made, there is a high likelihood of error, since two of the three possible "Honka" pairs would involve a crossing of a red with an orange stimulus. Although such errors were relatively infrequent, when they did occur they were in accord with linguistic factors.

A study of Cole, Gay, and Glick (1969) presented some evidence relative to the problems of evaluating the effects of linguistic factors on perceptual functioning. In this study a methodological distinction was made between perception and memory in terms of whether stimuli were present or not at the time of experimental testing. Working among the Kpelle tribe of Liberia, they constructed a task of the following form. Two subjects were seated across from one another at a table with identical sets of playschool blocks. The blocks differed both in form and color. A barrier was interposed between the subjects so that they had to communicate verbally to each other about the blocks, without being able to see what each other was doing or being able to use such devices as pointing. One subject was told to verbally instruct the other to pick out the same block as the experimenter had pointed to. Among the blocks were several that would be assigned the same color name by the lexical organization of the language. What would a subject do when faced with two identically shaped blocks, one orange, one red, when his language presented him with only one term for both? They found that subjects could invent apt paraphrases of the following form, "see the two red ones, pick the one that is most red"—or, when presented with two shades of green, "pick the one that is like the X tree leaf."

Findings of this sort suggest that lexical characterization may not be fully determined by the population of nouns in a language. Accordingly, the contrasts used in cross-language study may actually be dealing with a more sophisticated relationship than that of mere presence or absence of terms—rather, they may be dealing with factors that influence the *ready* "availability" of some distinctions. From this vantage point, it is not surprising that a good amount of evidence suggests that, when present perceptual materials are to be dealt with, linguistic limitations may be overcome, especially if subjects are given time to invent and use interesting functional paraphrases. Yet, when tasks are involved which call for economical means of codification or the use of a clear designation, evidence for linguistic influence may be found.

This conclusion is in accord with the formulation offered by Greenfield and Bruner (1969), who pointed to the necessity of analyzing the demands of the experimental situation that will govern whether linguistic coding is necessary to the solution of a particular task. One might expect linguistic coding to be necessary when information must be stored over time or when the temporal demands of a situation require immediate response. When subjects are given time to analyze and overcome their linguistic barriers, they may do so by the pat invention of paraphrase or by the use of nonlinguistic processes of analysis, whatever these might be.

Even this assertion is not unequivocal, since work by Heider and Olivier (1972), using a multidimensional analysis of the "structure" of color *memory,* suggested a great similarity in structure between color memory of the Dani of New Guinea, who use a two-word color lexicon ("dark" and "light") based on brightness, and the memory structure of English-speakers, who possess a more elaborate color terminology based on hue. These studies, while not directly contradicting those studies which have shown an effect of language on memory, do suggest that the particular manner in which the Whorfian hypothesis is operationalized may greatly influence the kinds of conclusions suggested.

A formulation such as the one above suggests the possibility that, although different languages seem to have different lexicons for physical domains such as color, there may be underlying humanly universal perceptual processes that allow for linguistic difficulties to be overcome.

Berlin and Kay (1969), using foreign students in the United States, elicited the basic color terms in the informant's native language. The informant was then asked to pick the "best example" of each of his basic color names from an array of all hues and brightness values at maximum saturation from the Munsell book of color. They found that languages differed in the number of basic color terms available but that color terminologies across different languages fall into an "evalutionary" pattern. Level 1 languages have available only two primary terms, black and white. At a second level, red is added to the available lexicon. At level 3, either green or yellow is added to the available terminology, and succeeding stages are defined by the addition of yellow (green), level 4; blue, 5; brown, 6; and finally, in a bunch, purple, pink, orange, and grey, level 7. Using techniques borrowed from historical linguistics, Berlin and Kay attempted to show that the more advanced color terminologies acquired additional terms in an historical order which parallels the order of levels described above.

Despite the wide concurrent differences in linguistic coding of the color domain, Berlin and Kay found that the "best examples" of the available color names were quite similar across language groups, so that a "green" in level 3 language is best exemplified by the same sort of "green" in a level 5, 6, or 7 language.

Berlin and Kay (1969) concluded:

Perhaps we have here in the domain of semantics a finding analogous to some phenomena recently recorded in the area of syntax and phonology. Chomsky (1965) . . . argued that the complexities of language structures, together with known limitations of human neurophysiology, imply that human language cannot be considered simply a manifestation of great general intelligence. Rather, it must be recognized as a species-specific ability ultimately based on species-specific biomorphological structures. What the particular linguistic function may be is not possible to say at this time in any detail. The study of the biological foundations of the most peculiarly and exclusively human set of behavioral abilities—language— is just beginning (Lenneberg 1967), but sufficient evidence has already accumulated to show that such connections must exist for the linguistic realms of syntax and phonology. The findings reported here concerning the universality and evolution of basic color lexicon suggest that such connections are also to be found in the realm of semantics (pp. 109– 110).

Heider (1972b, in press), in an interesting series of studies, further investigated the universality and functional properties of basic color terms. She found, in accord with much of the literature previously reviewed, that there are "universal" foci of color terms (best examples) and that these focal areas were most easily codable and best remembered. She concluded:

Given the attributes of focal colors—their occurrence as examples of basic color names, their linguistic codability across languages, and their superior retention in short and long term memory—it would seem most economical to suppose that these attributes are derived from the same underlying factors, most likely having to do with the physiology of primate color vision. In short, far from being a domain well suited to the study of the effects of language on thought, the color space would seem to be a prime example of the influence of underlying perceptual-cognitive factors on the formation and reference of linguistic categories (p. 24).

Heider (1972*a,* in press) has extended the argument to the domain of form perception, where early results indicate the existence of basic forms which serve as the center of form categories and which may, moreover, be universal. Findings such as these again suggest that, amidst the many cultural differences that seem to be apparent, there may be universal modes of human perception.

The research on the Sapir-Whorf hypothesis as it is specified with respect to perception seems to present incompatible findings which are related to different research and analytic strategies. One tradition of research which has focused upon perceptual categorization and memory suggests an influence of linguistic structure, at least on memory operations. The second tradition of research (Berlin and Kay 1969; Heider 1972*a, b,* in press) has focused on the internal structure of categories and looked at the problem from the point of view of seeing perceptual operations providing a central focus of experience (the basic or best example of a color or form). This tradition of research seems to find few perceptual differences related to linguistic or other cultural factors, either in perception or in memory.

Summary

In this section we have reviewed the cross-cultural evidence about perceptual development. We can draw the following conclusions.

1. There is evidence for the operation of ecological weighings of cues as determining perception of illusion figures. Yet, there are biological factors themselves, possibly due to ecological factors (such as the degree of ultraviolet light in daylight in different areas of the world), which are strong determinants of perceptual processes dependent upon contour detection.

2. Considered from the point of view of universals of cognitive processing, it seems to be the case that illusion perception may reflect universal processes insofar as the influence of brightness on illusion perception operates in a similar way in different cultural groups. The measured differences between cultural groups may have to do simply with peripheral factors such as retinal and crystalline lens pigmentation which serve to

make cross-cultural comparisons of differently pigmented groups under "standard" illumination conditions noncomparable because of the different filtering properties of the optical systems.

3. There are enough unexplained sources of variance to leave one unconfident about any grand conclusion. The lack of specification of such factors as the brightness of illumination of various illusion figures leads to the suspicion that much of the inconsistency may have to do with such "incidental" features of cross-cultural experiments as the use of unspecified stimulus presentation conditions which vary across experiments, and, more important, between groups with different physiological constitutions.

An additional feature of difficulty stems from the reliance of many studies of illusion on two-dimensional representations of three-dimensional relationships. There is a considerable literature, reviewed in the next section, which suggests that this mode of presentation of materials affects the perceptual processes.

4. A brief review of the literature on pictorial depth perception suggests that there do seem to be differences between cultural groups in the degree to which three-dimensional responding to two-dimensional materials occurs. However, the perceptual basis for this is not clear, since there has been little work to separate and specify the independent contributions of cues to flatness and conventions of depth representation. There is some evidence to suggest that specific features of the response task, as well as features of stimulus presentation, may act to produce or minimize cultural differences. Given the contradictory evidence, the best conclusion may be that suggested by Hagen (1972*a, b*). Not enough is known about the factors that determine pictorial perception. Accordingly, any specific cross-cultural comparisons bearing on the contribution of various etiological factors are premature.

5. There is some impressive evidence of the relationship of socialization practices to the degree of analytic style in perceptual functioning. This dimension is related, in particular, to the trainability of subjects in interpreting two-dimensional pictures three-dimensionally. Sex differences, which are typically found in studies of field dependence, are not found where socialization practices stress independence for both males and females.

6. A review of the role of language in perceptual development suggests that linguistic factors seem to be operative in tasks which involve memory and which are sensitive to perceptual categorization. Universal forms of perception are found when the center of perceptual categories are evaluated. The universal aspects of experience may be utilized in some situations—where ample time is given to analyze stimulus input—to circumvent any limitations which may be introduced by linguistic factors.

However, much of the research has been limited to the domain of color perception and there have been doubts raised about the adequacy of this domain for studying linguistic influence.

CROSS-CULTURAL STUDIES OF CONCEPTUAL DEVELOPMENT

Not only do men detect features of their environments, they organize these features in classes or categories. The adaptive necessity of such organizational abilities has been discussed earlier. Yet there is no unanimity on whether classification abilities are similar in different human groups (questions of adaptive necessity aside). The cross-cultural literature has investigated questions of two different sorts. On the one hand there have been investigations of the attributes of objects that different people select for classification (e.g., do people classify more in terms of the color of things, their form, their function, and so on); this class of problems may be technically termed the "intentional" aspects of concept formation. Additionally, one may ask questions concerning the structure of concepts that have been formed. Are they exhaustive classes making use of all objects sharing the same attribute? Are classes hierarchically arranged in such a manner that membership in a subordinate class implies membership in a class which superordinates it? Can classes be additively and multiplicatively combined (additive classification—cars and trucks are both vehicles; multiplicative classification—blue things and automobiles combine to define a blue automobile). The two questions, substantive and structural, may be separated for purposes of review and have, in some instances, been separated in experimental work as well. However, it should be noted that the substantive and structural aspects of concept formation are integrally related.

Two types of studies of the attributes used for classification have been pursued in the literature. There are studies that use artificially constructed materials that have known "conceptual properties" and that can be unambiguously defined as possessing a set of attributes. For example, if one were interested in whether form or color is used for classification, one might construct a set of materials which vary only on those dimensions (a red and blue triangle and a red and blue square). A subject's response in this sort of situation would be easy to identify—he either uses color or form or neither. However, such artificially constructed stimuli may not do justice to subjects' classification abilities since the very strangeness of materials may limit performance. Accordingly, there is another tradition of research that uses natural objects, found in the subject's environment, as a basis for classification studies. Since on a priori grounds one might expect a difference between these types of studies, they will be reviewed separately.

Studies Using Artificial Materials

In Western industrialized schooled samples, it is generally found that children show a preference for sorting on the basis of color at early ages and later shift toward form-responding (Brian and Goodenough 1929; Corah 1964). From these intracultural studies it is difficult to know whether this shift represents some maturational change, some direct effect of either formal or informal education, or some other sociocultural factor. Accordingly, several studies have used cross-cultural comparison in order to evaluate the impact of sociocultural factors. The bulk of the studies have investigated the impact of schooling and/or westernization, while some studies have investigated this area from the familiar grounds of the Sapir-Whorf hypothesis.

1. *Educational effects.* The basic finding of a number of studies has been that unschooled groups of subjects tend to maintain a preference for sorting on the basis of color. Studies in Nigeria (Suchman 1966) and Zambia (Serpell 1969), using colored geometric forms, have all demonstrated color preference. This appears to be maintained even in older groups. However, there are some conflicting reports. Gay and Cole (1967) found number and color both being used over form, although a later replication by Cole et al. (1971), did report color dominance. Several of these studies involved a contrast between schooled or westernized groups and unschooled, unwesternized counterparts. Serpell (1969) found an increase in form preference for his schooled subjects, as did Schmidt and Nzimande (1970). Moreover, Schmidt and Nzimande found that both degree of literacy and degree of urbanization (presumably related to westernization) related to the use of the form dimension in sorting. They found, as well, results similar to those found by Gay and Cole (1967). When subjects were asked to re-sort the materials on the basis of some other attribute, about 60 percent were able to do so but were unable to extend the basis of sorting any further.

Corah (1964) has suggested that the use of color is really a preference for using color, rather than an inability to use form. The ability of Gay and Cole's and Schmidt and Nzimande's subjects to perform re-sorts of the materials (at least 60 to 66 percent of the unschooled population could do so) would tend to lend some support for this notion. Corah's notion is that Western-style education directs attention toward the use of form by involving the student in tasks that require form discriminations to be made. While the bulk of the results seem to support this conclusion, there is some countervailing evidence. Suchman (1966), for example, was unable to find an impact of the schooling variable.

What is clearly required at this point is some job analysis of what it is about schooling or westernization that is effective. Many explanations which point to the effects of schooling do so in global terms. At present, a good candidate for the effective factor in schooling is training in reading. As Gibson, Gibson, Pick, and Osser (1962) have shown, training in reading alters the manner in which form discriminations are made and may, in fact, significantly affect the tendency to pay attention to form in a situation where there are a number of possible bases of classification.

It is surprising that color, which is often poorly encoded in languages (Berlin and Kay 1969), should be so dominant in unschooled subjects' approach to classification tasks. Greenfield et al. (1966), citing Bruner and Rigney, suggested the possibility that color is a dimension that requires a minimum of cognitive activity when used in a sorting task. Comparison of shapes requires several features of the stimulus to be simultaneously compared; color usage requires only one thing to be kept in mind at a time.

2. *Linguistic effects: Sapir-Whorf hypothesis revisited.* Carroll and Casagrande (1958), in a classic study bearing on the linguistic determinants of color-form preference, studied such preferences in a linguistic group whose language is sensitive to form distinctions. In Navajo, the verb for "handling" differs, depending upon the object to be handled.

Thus, if I ask you in Navajo to hand me an object, I must use the appropriate verb stem, depending on the nature of the object. If it is a long flexible object, such as a piece of string, I must say sanleh; if it is a long rigid object, such as a stick, I must say santiih; if it is a flat flexible material such as paper or cloth, I must say saniicoos, and so on (p. 27).

This feature of Navajo suggested to Carroll and Casagrande that, if linguistic features were important in determining the bases of classification preferred by speakers of different languages, one might expect that Navajo speakers would show a greater proclivity than English-speaking children to use form as a basis of classification.

To test this hypothesis, they employed an object-triads test in which three objects were presented and the child was to tell which two went best together. For example, the child might be shown a yellow stick and a blue rope of the same size. The child would then be shown a piece of yellow rope and asked which of the two other objects it went with. The expectation was, since Navajo was particularly sensitive to things like stick and rope differences, that this dimension might be used as the basis of pairing rather than the color similarity.

Two groups of children were compared, Navajo children who were English dominant and Navajo children who only spoke Navajo. Both groups showed the increasing saliency of form over color as age increased, but the shift was faster for the Navajo-dominant speakers. The Navajo-only group used form more than the English-dominant group, though this difference tended to lessen with increasing age. These results lend support to the linguistic hypothesis formulated by Carroll and Casagrande (1958). However, when other English-speaking children are compared, they respond on the test more like the Navajo-speakers than like the English-speaking Navajos. This would suggest that the linguistic factor is but one of many in determining color-form preferences. Several of the other candidate factors have been discussed above.

It is unfortunate that little is known about the nature of obligatory grammatical distinctions for the variety of cultural groups that have been tested on color-form or on other attribute-sorting tests. We cannot know if there may be, in these groups as well, some grammatical predilection for responding to the color dimension or not responding to the form dimension. It does not seem likely that this is the case, since so many linguistic groups have a sparse terminology for color. However, second-order relationships, such as the determiners of verb forms on the basis of object attributes, remain unexplored.

The study of the influence of linguistic factors on the handling of arbitrary materials has not been limited to color and form. Cole, Gay, Glick, and Sharp (1969) studied the case of the Kpelle language, which has an interesting anomaly (vis-à-vis English) in that one can encode size comparison in increasing order (A is big past B), but one *cannot* perform the same comparison in reverse (B is small past A). A test of the impact of this linguistic variable was constructed using the transposition task. In this task a subject is taught that when presented with a pair of stimuli which differ in size (e.g., a two-inch vs. a four-inch square), one of the sizes is "correct" (e.g., the four-inch square). The subject is then asked to select the correct stimulus from a second pair of stimuli (e.g., a four-inch square and an eight-inch square), and his transfer to this pair is observed. There is an ambiguity in the presentation of the second pair in that either the identical stimulus could be chosen (e.g., the four-inch square in the example given) or the relationally similar stimulus could be chosen (e.g., the four-inch square was the larger stimulus in the first pair, and the eight-inch square would be the larger stimulus in the second pair). Needless to say, this same experimental paradigm can be used to test relationships either in ascending order of magnitude (as in the example given) or in order of decreasing magnitudes (if the two-inch square was rewarded in the first pair, and the second pair consisted of a two-inch and a one-inch square).

Although results in the transposition paradigm are not, even within Western psychology, fully understood, there has been some agreement that transposition-responding shifts from an absolute to a relative basis and that this shift may involve the use of verbal mediational mechanisms.

Returning now to the Kpelle linguistic feature of being able to encode size relationships of increasing order but having to paraphrase relationships of a descending-size order, one might expect that Kpelle subjects would show relational responding on transposition of a relationship in an increasing magnitude direction and be either inconsistent or absolute responders on the inverse arrangement. Comparisons of younger (four- to five-year-old) and older (six- to eight-year-old) African children with (three- to five-year-old) American children showed few differences between the groups. The only effects of the linguistic asymmetry on performance occurred in a slightly higher probability for the African subjects to choose the larger stimulus on the first trial of training. A rather high percentage of children in all groups performed the transposition response, in both the up and down directions, even when the occurrence of transposition should have been minimal for these age groups (a "far" transposition test).

There was, however, a rather interesting effect of the linguistic variable on the subject's ability to verbalize the basis for his performance. Fifty percent of the Kpelle subjects were able to provide relevant verbalizations on the basis for their transposition up responses (e.g., "I chose the one that was big past the other"), but 71 percent were unable to verbalize a rationalization for their transposition down responses that corresponded with the task demands ("God told me," "My Kpelle sense told me").

This set of results indicates that the linguistic variable may have been operative but in ways that were unexpected. Linguistic factors may have served to limit the degree to which a communicable reason could be given for some performance, but that performance itself was relatively unaffected by the linguistic factor.

These findings make suspect many of the reports of differences between cultures that have been largely based on reading implications about cognitive abilities from an analysis of linguistic material (Werner 1957; Cassirer 1953). What people say and what people do may be quite different things. We do not as yet fully understand the relationship between the two. Both of the studies reviewed here yield weak and equivocal evidence for the operation of linguistic factors in determining conceptual performance.

3. *Studies of classificatory structure: concreteness and abstractness.* In addition to questions that may be raised about the various bases of classifications, one may ask whether classes are structured in the same manner in different cultures. When studies using artificial materials are employed, the structural question is usually asked in either of two forms.

First, is the subject "stuck" with an initially-made basis of classification? That is, can he re-sort a collection of materials that have already been sorted and use a different basis of sorting on demand? Second, one can ask whether the relationship between classifications of materials follows logical rules of class addition and multiplication.

The former question bears on an important, but somewhat different, issue in studies of cross-cultural cognition. Price-Williams (1962) identified the re-sorting question with the issue of whether non-Western thought is "concrete" or "abstract." Abstract thought presumably regards objects as being defined by a number of attributes—which have the status of being applicable to objects but not of being "inherent" in the objects. Accordingly, the ability to apply a multitude of classificatory operations to an aggregate of objects would index the ability to separate attribute and object. Price-Williams (1962) reviewed a number of the studies that had been used to support the contention that "primitive" peoples have concrete thought. We have already reviewed studies by Gay and Cole (1967) and Schmidt and Nzimande (1970) which indicate that re-sorting is possible in African groups (Kpelle of Liberia and Julus) but that it is not as extensive as in Western groups. Ciborowski and Cole (1971), Cole et al. (1971), and Cole, Gay, and Glick (1968) investigated issues bearing on classificatory structure using learning paradigms. In those studies, the approach taken was to use learning tasks that are highly dependent on subjects' abilities to classify and reclassify stimulus materials. Intensive experimental analyses of learning behaviors in these tasks can then reveal the type of classificatory structures used. Since this strategy involves experiments that are done in series and that make use of complex systems of data analysis, they defy description in a review article. The point made by these studies, however, is that Kpelle and American subjects can be shown to be either quite similar or quite dissimilar depending upon the particular experimental arrangements which were used.

A second sort of structural question has been asked, using as a model the kinds of logical operations with classes that Inhelder and Piaget (1964) have described for Western groups. DeLacey (1970), for example, employed tests of addition and multiplication of classes. Using materials identical to those used by Inhelder and Piaget (1964), he presented small blocks of wood, red or blue squares or circles, and asked questions of the following sort: Are all the circles blue? Are all the red ones square? and so on. Additionally, tests of classification and reclassification (similar to those discussed in the preceding section) were used, as well as tests involving hierarchical classification. DeLacey tested high and low socioeconomic-status Europeans and high- and low-contact Australian aborigines and reported that for all tests the order of achievement was high SES

Europeans, low SES Europeans, high-contact aborigines, low-contact aborigines. For all groups, performance increased with age but with the relative ordering of groups maintained. Although DeLacey has made some rather provocative speculations concerning the reasons for the differences (ranging from different brain cell populations to cultural deprivation), the results obtained show rather slight differences among the groups and considerable near-overlap in the curves plotting percentages of subjects showing more "advanced" classificatory abilities.

Similar tasks have been employed by Lloyd (1971) but her results are not reported in a way that reveals much about classificatory abilities.

In sum, though some studies suggest cultural differences in concept structure, the differences found have been minimal. Other studies that have intensely investigated various experimental arrangements have found that similarities or differences between African and Western groups depend greatly on the particular experimental arrangement used.

Studies Using Natural Materials

There are several reasons for separating studies based on natural and artificial materials. We have already discussed some of the differences between these two types of materials under the heading of "familiarity." However, beyond noting that familiarity of materials is an important issue, there are other issues that underlie the separation of artificial and natural materials. Two of the major reasons to be dealt with here are (a) the relationship between the mundane use of classifications of natural objects and their use for purposes of classification studies, and (b) the relationship between classification criteria imposed by a cross-cultural investigator and those normally employed by the subject of that investigation.

1. *Effects of urban experience and schooling.* Maccoby and Modiano (1966) and Greenfield et al. (1966) have studied the bases of classification in a variety of cultural settings (Mexican, Eskimo, and Senegalese subjects were used) and have employed materials which are "natural" to the groups tested. The technique employed in these studies is to present items in a series (e.g., banana, peach, potato, meat, milk, water, air, germs, stones). The child is asked of the first pair of objects, "How are these alike?" The next item is then presented and the child is asked, "How is this different from the others?" "How are they all alike?" This is carried out until all of the items have been used. Analyses were carried out with respect to two features of the childrens' responses, the attributes used for judging similarity and differences and (in the case of the Greenfield et al. study) the structure of the groupings obtained.

Five bases of similarities and differences were distinguished: perceptual bases (e.g., shape, color); functions of objects (what it can do or what can be done with it); moral or affective labels (e.g., "These are both good"); nominal characteristics (e.g., "These are all solids," "These are all fruits," and so on); and, finally, groupings not by attribute but by decree ("They are alike because I say they are").

Maccoby and Modiano (1966) studied the responses of Mexican and North American children. They found that the youngest children (six to eight) were best able to specify differences between the objects and had difficulty with the task of finding similarities. The basis of differentiation was in terms of perceptible attributes, color or form for the youngest children.

When older children were compared, cultural differences became more manifest. The older Mexican children persisted in the use of perceptible attributes while the older North American children began to use more abstract concepts of use as principles of organization. It seemed as if the Mexican children used finer and finer perceptual classifications, while the North American children shifted their bases of classification.

In further studies contrasting rural and urban Mexican children, the urban children were found to perform more like their North American counterparts, while the rural children lagged behind in their abilities to make equivalence groupings and continued to use perceptible characteristics to buttress their difference judgments.

The authors summarize the significance of their findings as follows:

A city child coming from an industrial society starts by dealing with objects in terms of their perceptible, concrete characteristics. He soon comes to consider them in the light of what he can do with them. In time, he is led to more abstract formulations as to how things are, how they are alike and different. Some go so far that they lose the sense of the concreteness of things and become buried in a dry nominalism. . . .
Peasant children do not change that much. They are much more similar to their older brothers: they both look. The older one looks at things more closely and considers more concrete ways to use them. While the older peasant child can say how things are alike, he feels more at home with their differences, for that is where reality lies for him. He does not think in generalities. . . .
Essentially, such cognitive styles reflect the demands of a culture. The modern industrialized world demands abstractions. . . . What is demanded of the peasant, on the other hand, is that he pay attention to his crops, the weather, and the particular people around him (p. 268).

Greenfield et al. (1966) extended studies of the type discussed above to other cultural groupings such as Eskimo subjects from Anchorage and various Senegalese (Wolof) groups. In addition, they distinguished between several forms of the structure of an equivalence grouping: "superordinate groupings" where a group is formed on the basis of one or more attributes common to the group's members, and "complexive groupings" based on several different attributes, none common to all of the group's members. Since all of the children involved in this study, both white and Eskimo, were urban, of various degrees of acculturation, results paralleling the urban results reported above might be expected. An analysis of both the content of similarity and difference judgments and the form of those judgments showed for both groups a decrease in perceptually based groupings and an increase in superordinate forms of grouping. Though there was a slight lag, with the Eskimo groups attaining the same level as the white groups at a somewhat later age, the overall pattern of results for these two urban groups was similar.

The above results seem to argue for the effect of urbanness on various aspects of grouping behavior. Greenfield, working among the Wolof, further investigated factors bearing on classificatory behavior, making use of a distinction between her subjects in terms of their relative degree of urbanness and the extent of their schooling as well. She contrasted the performance of three groups of children, classified according to their urban experience and their schooling. One group consisted of children who had *neither schooling nor urban experience* at three age levels (six to seven, eight to nine, eleven to thirteen years of age). A second group was composed of children who had schooling but lived in a rural village. The third group consisted of first-, third-, and sixth-graders from an urban school in Dakar.

On an initial test she found that the degree to which unschooled children made superordinate groupings increased linearly with age, although almost all sortings (in a free sorting experiment where the bases of sorting could be on the attribute of color, form, or material) were based on color. The application of "superordinate linguistic structure" was not frequent. It appeared that a single basis of classification was used and that this basis was seen as inhering in the object itself and was not seen as the product of an act of classification.

Further experimental studies using a classification test that employed triads of items, two of which could be grouped either on the basis of color, form, or function, revealed major differences between the schooled and unschooled populations. Superordinate reasons for grouping increased linearly with age in the schooled group while nonsuperordinate "accidental" properties of objects were used as the basis for grouping in the unschooled "bush" groups. For the unschooled groups, no developmental trend was obtained. When the content basis of grouping was examined (color, form, or function), color grouping increased with age for the unschooled groups, while form reasons correspondingly increased for the schooled groups. Moreover, the urban schooled groups showed an increase in the use of function groupings.

Additional considerations of the language within which superordinate classification is expressed, suggested to Greenfield, Reich, and Olver that one of the main effects of schooling was to increase the use of linguistically hierarchical devices that a language contains. They demonstrated a relationship between flexibility of conceptual behavior (ability to use a number of alternative bases for grouping) and use of a more abstract linguistic structure (e.g., labeling a class as based on "color," as opposed to labeling the class as based on a particular attribute, e.g., "yellow"). Additionally, one of the major differences between schooled and unschooled populations concerned this dimension. Older schooled subjects used sentences to express the basis for grouping ("These are the same colors"), while the unschooled subjects used labels ("yellow"). Summarizing these results and those involving subanalyses of bilingual and monolingual subjects, Greenfield, Reich, and Olver (1966) concluded:

the positive results . . . lead to the hypothesis that the school is acting on grouping operations through the training embodied in the written language. . . . The written language . . . provides an occasion in which one must deploy language out of the immediate referential context. . . . Writing, then, is a training in the use of linguistic contexts that are independent of the immediate referents. . . . The implications of this fact for the manipulation of concepts are great: linguistic contexts can be turned upside-down more easily than real ones can. Indeed, the linguistic independence of context achieved by certain grammatical modes appears to favor the development of the more self-contained, superordinate structure used by the school children (p. 310).

The reasoning behind this formulation is powerful: conceptual behavior involves the ability to take a conceptual stance toward material and to recognize categorization as an imposition of order by the conceptualizer. This, in turn, depends upon the freeing of the thinker from the immediate context of the things thought about. This is an integral feature of written communication, which is communication in absence of the immediate context of things. Similar formulations have been provided by Vygotskii (1962), Werner and Kaplan (1963) Luria and Yudovich (1959), and Goody and Watt (1962).

Although conceptually powerful, this formulation depends upon the regular association of inflexibility and primitiveness of conceptual behavior with absence of a written language. Further, it depends upon the written language as being the only carrier of such decontextualized information transmission. The latter assumption is questionable since cultures may provide many alternative forms whereby some decision about the real properties of things is challengeable. Many cultures have highly ritualized and formally participated-in occasions for the confrontation of different viewpoints about some state of affairs. It may be the case that some of these forms of argumentation can fulfill the same function as written language in "decontextualizing" thought.

The relationship between conceptual sophistication and written language, however, can be empirically investigated. The evidence in support of the Greenfield et al. position is by no means clear-cut, though Luria (1971) has presented some evidence parallel to that presented above.

Price-Williams (1962) reported little influence of schooling on the ability of Tiv (Nigerian) children to make conceptually hierarchical classifications. According to Price-Williams, schooling did not affect the kinds of attributes that children used to classify an array of plants, and even unschooled children were able to make use of a functional grouping rule.

Some of the difficulties of researching this area have been well demonstrated by Cole et al. (1971) and by Glick (1968, 1969). Their general approach was to elicit a taxonomic classification system from the cultural group within which their experiments were performed and to utilize various features of that classification system to make predictions about the way in which objects so classified would be used in a variety of cognitive tasks.

As a result of various elicitation and checking techniques (Cole et al. 1971, chap. 3), a list of twenty objects was compiled which could be seen as five representatives of each of four culturally relevant categories. The basic question posed in a number of their studies was whether these linguistically organized and elicited categories would influence the way in which people organize their performance.

The tests employed included sorting tests where the twenty objects were randomly mixed and subjects asked to put the ones together that go together; tests of organization in memory, where object names were presented in systematically randomized fashion and subjects asked to recall the presented names; and a number of similar measures of organizational learning. The initial run-through of the measures, given in ways that are standard in the Western literature, yielded almost unequivocal evidence of nonuse of linguistic categories, even for the memory task.

Yet the first run-through was not the last. And when a series of experiments were performed, results seemed to change. For example, in the sorting task, twenty items representing five types of food, five types of clothing, and five types of cooking utensils were heaped on a table in front of a Kpelle subject. When the subject had finished sorting, what was present were ten categories composed of two items each—related to each other in a functional, not a categorical, manner. Thus, a knife might have been placed with an orange, a potato with a hoe, and so on. When asked, the subject would rationalize the choice with such comments as, "The knife goes with orange because it cuts it." When questioned further, the subject would often volunteer that a wise man would do things in this way. When an exasperated experimenter asked finally, "How would a fool do it," he was given back sorts of the type that were initially expected—four neat piles with foods in one, tools in another, and so on.

In further studies of this problem (Glick 1969; Cole et al. 1971), a variety of manipulations were found that could alter the manner in which subjects performed in this problem. In similar fashion, Cole et al. (1971) found that the use of categories as an organizational device for free recall could be varied from nonuse to almost full use by changing the manner in which the task was presented. One manipulation that was successful was embedding the to-be-remembered items in the context of a culturally familiar folk-story framework.

These results indicate that, as yet, we understand very little of the way in which people perform on classification tasks. It is quite possible that the various tasks employed by different groups of experimenters yield radically different pictures of people's abilities. Maccoby and Modiano (1966) and Greenfield et al. (1966) have found situations where there seem to be cultural differences depending on such etiological factors as education and urbanization. Cole et al. (1971) found evidence for variation in performances *within groups* which raised serious questions about cross-group comparisons.

It may be the case that these two sets of data may not stand in opposition to one another. Performance on a classification task may depend on two sets of factors—cognitive capacity and availability of cognitive capacities for application to particular testing situations. The effects of etiological variables may be such as to alter either of these two factors. It seems at the present time more likely that the factors most subject to cultural influence are those that determine the conditions of application of cognitive abilities to particular tests of them.

If this proves to be the case, it may be that the use of mundane objects may be a biasing factor in experimental tests of conceptual activities. It seemed in the Cole et al. (1971) studies that people, when confronted with objects which have known and useful properties vis-à-vis one another, interpret their task to be one of exposing the rationality of their relationship.

Classification of these objects is unreasonable for the tasks as construed. Under these conditions it takes a rather elaborate cueing system to guarantee that a reasonable, pragmatic approach is not to be preferred in a task which the experimenter intends to be conceptual. Recent evidence, reported by Greenfield (1972), supports this claim. She showed that familiar propeties of objects used in a classification task often interfered with the ability to reconceptualize the familiar objects. Similar arguments may apply to the Greenfield et al. data. It seems arbitrary to ask of a subject who is confronted with a present context to choose modes of thinking about the items presented in that context which are acontextual. Part of the communication system surrounding a classification task involves an implicit instruction to "be conceptual—not merely effective in the here and now." This may require special communicative devices for those unfamiliar with schoollike environments, and may be part of the implicit rules of the game for people familiar with school.

About the only thing that is crystal clear at this point is that much more needs to be known about the relationship between performance and cognitive competence (Mehler and Bever 1968) before rational arguments about the etiological factors in conceptual development can be pursued.

In sum, several studies have shown major effects of both urbanization and of schooling on a variety of measures of conceptual functioning. These differences are seen in the use of perceptual attributes in relating various objects to one another and in the development of formal devices for relating various instances. Such effects may be due to the effects of having a written language or the ability to transcend the immediate features of objects in order to use more abstract means of classification. There are studies, though, which do not show the effects of schooling and urbanization. These studies suggest that a critical feature of the analysis of conceptual behavior is the factors which govern the application of a particular sorting strategy to a set of objects. Variations in task structure which call out more sophisticated strategies are successful in attentuating initially observed cultural differences.

2. *"Emic" and "etic" categorization.* The foregoing discussion raised the problem of the relationship between the subject's criterion of rational behavior and the experimenter's judgment of rational behavior with respect to the communicational demands of a classification experiment. Much the same kind of argument can be raised about the classification structures that are employed in experimentation.

Western experimenters generally employ materials that are categorizable to them and ask whether subjects from other cultures use the same kind of classification system. This strategy of experimentation can be regarded as being "centered" (Werner and Campbell 1970; Wober 1969) in one culture. Recently, voices have been raised which call into question the wisdom and meaning of this sort of research strategy.

The basic point raised by these investigators is that the use of a classification system determined from "outside" the culture of the subjects
confounds ability to classify with ability to use arbitrary and unnatural
systems of classification. They insist that what is needed prior to cross-
cultural tests of conceptual abilities is the application of discovery procedures to find out what systems of classification are naturally used within
the culture. The impetus for this type of approach has been mainly within
the field of anthropology; a flavor for the insights gained and problems
involved with it can be gleaned from two important volumes in the area
(Romney and D'Andrade 1964; Tyler 1969). A major theoretical work
dealing with the distinction between "emic" approaches (those which
seek to work within the category system particular to a culture) and "etic"
approaches (those which seek to compare different cultures on common
measurement tasks) has been published by Pike (1954). Applications
of the emic approach to classificatory behavior have been presented
by investigators who have explored "ethnoscientific" procedures (Conklin 1955; Frake 1962) for discovering naturally used classification
systems.

There are, as yet, few studies that have systematically explored the
use of "natural classifications" in relationship to measured conceptual
abilities, although the work of Cole et al. (1971) is a beginning in that
direction. Romney and D'Andrade (1964) have performed some experiments attempting to relate natural categorization systems such as kinship
systems to conceptual operations measured in behavioral terms, with some
degree of success. The application of this approach to etiological questions (schooling, urbanization, and so on) has not, as yet, been developed.

3. *Cross-cultural Piagetian research.* The work of Jean Piaget in detailing the various stages of cognitive development has provided a powerful
stimulus to cross-cultural research. Throughout his work, he has attempted to describe the succession of structures that link elementary forms
of activity that infants perform with respect to objects (sensorimotor activity) to the most abstract theoretical conceptualizations that scientific
and logical thought entail.

For a more extended discussion of Piaget's formulations, three excellent
sources exist. Flavell (1963) has given a comprehensive view of much of
the factual material generated by the Piagetian school. Furth (1969) gave
an excellent description of the conceptual intent of Piagetian theory and,
for the undaunted, Piaget (1970) has summarized himself.

Piaget sees cognitive development as being composed of four major
periods: the sensorimotor, the preoperational, the concrete operational,
and the formal operational stages. During the sensorimotor stage, which
encompasses the first two years of life, the child is seen as learning about

the world mainly through the elaboration of his sensorimotor schemes for handling and manipulating his physical surroundings. At first the schemes of action are limited and uncoordinated, but by constant application they become more differentiated, more elaborated, and more coordinated with one another. This manipulative interaction occurs naturally and is not the product of specific educational efforts by adults. During the preoperational period, the action schemes become "interiorized," and the child learns to deal with the world via representations of those schemes. He comes to exercise symbolic activities which allow him to experience the world via symbolic systems such as language. As yet the interiorized actions are not organized with respect to one another, so that the child's thought has a rather disorganized character. Around the seventh year of life, the action schemes become organized and the child begins to show evidence of coherent logical thought. During this concrete operational period, he is able to reason about the world and to guide his behavior by means of that reasoning. As yet this logical organization is limited to dealing with things in the physical here and now. By about the eleventh year, the child begins to be able to reason logically about things that are not concretely present. This marks the beginning of the formal operational period during which the capability for hypothetical, systematic, scientific thought is developed.

Piaget sees these developments in the context of a theory of knowledge acquisition that views the child as his or her own teacher, learning about the world through the extension of his or her own activities and deriving logical knowledge from the structuring of those activities. Since all human groups exist in a world governed by common physical principles, one might therefore expect that cultural differences in fundamental forms of thought would be minimal. At the least, exploration of different cultures would serve to elaborate the theory of detailing those elements of development which are determined by the biological aspects of humans vis-à-vis the nature of the physical world and those which are more sensitive to cultural differences.

There has been a growing body of literature concerned with cross-cultural tests of Piaget's formulations. This movement has resulted in the publication of a newsletter called *An Inventory of Cross-Cultural Piagetian Research,* edited by Dasen and Seagrim at the University of Montreal and the Australian National University, Canberra. In addition, a number of review articles have appeared (e.g., Dasen, 1972a). Chapter 10 in this volume provides a full review of the research on the period of formal operations, with some special attention to cross-cultural evidence.

It would be fruitless to re-review an area already excellently reviewed by Dasen and others. Accordingly, this section will provide an overview of the complexity of findings obtained, some of the author's notions of the difficulties of interpretation in the area, and will dwell on some studies that have attempted seriously to cope with these difficulties.

As Dasen (1972*a*) has pointed out, most cross-cultural investigators have focused on the transition from preoperational to concrete operational thought. A few studies (Golden and Birns 1968; Dasen 1972*b*) of sensori-motor development as conceptualized within Piaget's system have reported little in the way of cultural or racial differences. LeVine (1970), however, reviewed a number of studies of sensorimotor development based on other measurement systems, which suggested some degree of difference in sensorimotor acquisitions.

Similarly, there has been little work on formal operational thought as conceived of in Piaget's system. Dasen (1972*a*) cited studies by Peluffo, Goodnow, Were, and Kelly, which suggested that formal operations may not be universally found and that, where found, their presence may depend on schooling and urban experience. However, Dasen suggested that a conclusion at this point would be premature.

In his review, which focussed on the bulk of studies dealing with achievement of concrete operations, Dasen (1972*a*) distinguished between several possible types of findings. Four protypical findings that can occur in testing Piaget's theory cross-culturally are represented by the curves in figure 2.

Curve X may be taken to represent the typical proportions of attainment of concrete operations in a standard European or American population. The three other curves represent hypothetical findings that show a developmental lag in acquisition (curve c attains the same points as

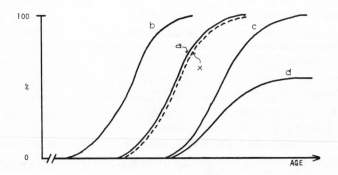

Fig. 2. Percentage of subjects attaining the concrete operational stage as a function of age. (From "Cross-Cultural Piagetian Research: A Summary," by Pierre R. Dasen, *Journal of Cross-Cultural Psychology, 3,* no. 1 (March 1972), p. 27. By permission of the publisher, Sage Publications, Inc.)

curve X at a later age), a developmental precocity of attainment (curve b reaches the points of curve X at an earlier age), a differential leveling off point (some members of a comparison group never attain concrete operations in curve d). A fourth curve (a) would represent a matching of the European and American group by the target group of subjects.

Not surprisingly, Dasen reported that, in the extensive literature, cases of all types of curves have been found. (See Dasen [1972a] for a citation of the particular studies involved). Perhaps it is not mysterious that there would be a wide variation in findings in such indices of concrete operational development as conservation (which has been the focus of a number of these investigations). There has, on occasion, arisen within the source literature (European and American studies) conflicts concerning ages of acquisition.

The conservation task has been used by a number of investigators as a primary index of the acquisition of concrete operations. This task requires the child to pit his reasoning abilities against the distortions that perceptual arrangements may introduce. For example, the task of conservation of continuous quantity involves the child in judging the equality of the quantity of water in two identically shaped beakers. After an initial equivalence is established to the child's satisfaction, the water in one of the beakers is poured into another beaker which might be much taller and thinner than the original beaker. The level of water in the new beaker would be much higher than it was in the old one. Yet the child must countervail this perceptual distortion and reason that since no water has been added or taken away by the pouring there must be the same amount. Conservation tasks have been devised for other physical quantities in a manner quite similar to that exemplified here for continuous quantity.

Some hint of the complexities involved in this sort of research has been provided by Greenfield and Bruner (1966). They paid unusual attention to the linguistic problems involved in posing a conservation task to Wolof (Senegalese) children. Their efforts in this regard have been discussed earlier. It is important to note here that much of the primary data reviewed by Dasen does not demonstrate such care in translation—most reports simply give an English "gloss" or rough translation of instructions and leave it at that—producing interpretational difficulties far beyond the substantive ones often claimed.

The data obtained by Greenfield and Bruner (1966) indicated that (a) conservation does develop among both rural- and urban-schooled Wolof children, but (b) bush Wolof children reach asymptote (about 50 percent) at age eight to nine and show only slight upward shifts in proportions of conservers between nine and thirteen years of age.

Greenfield and Bruner (1966) identified several possible sources of difficulties that the unschooled Wolof children may have had in the conservation task. One source corresponds to a widespread difficulty of relying on perceptual cues (such as water level) when attention to conserving and nonconserving transformations is demanded. A second source of difficulties was determined to be more potent to the bush Wolof—the tendency to interpret events in terms of action-magic. Children would often justify a nonconservation response by saying "there is more in that glass because you poured it."

Recognizing these as possible sources—and especially the latter as a culturally potent one—Greenfield derived techniques to test out the impact of these features. The upshot of a variety of experimental procedures was that elimination of perceptual distractions (the screening procedure) had negligible effects in improving conservation performance, while directly combating action-magic, by having the child himself do the pouring in a conservation task, produced marked shifts in conservation performance (from 50 percent to 82 percent attaining concrete operations).

These findings suggest that the curve of findings in general may be susceptible to factors which are of a specific cultural nature—but which have little to do with conservation itself. The action-magic variable, while certainly limiting conservation performance, can be exorcised by appropriate procedures.

An interesting case in the literature, perhaps revealing the "state of the art" is presented by Dasen (1972c), who replicated one of the major studies in the field which had presented some of the more challenging sorts of data. DeLemos (1969) tested full-blooded and half-blooded aboriginal children on one of the major tests of concrete operations—the ability to conserve a quantity under irrelevant changes (e.g., pouring a glass of water from a normal glass into a thin tall one). DeLemos administered tasks of conservation of number, quantity, length, weight, area, and volume, and reported three major findings bearing on Piaget's theory. First, the order of performances within each of the tasks followed the order found by Piaget; however, many subjects failed to achieve full conservation. Second, across tasks, the normal finding that conservation of continuous quantity precedes the acquisition of the conservation of weight was reversed, with more aboriginal children conserving weight than quantity. Third, full-blooded aborigine children showed markedly worse conservation than half-blooded children, although both lived in "identical" physical and social environments.

Dasen attempted to replicate DeLemos's findings and in so attempting probed various aspects of DeLemos's procedures that may have contributed to some of the anomalies found. In general, Dasen failed to replicate the major features of DeLemos's results, finding no differences between part- and full-blooded aborigines, finding no reversal of quantity and weight conservation (perhaps because the Dasen replication used the original Genevan materials while DeLemos used culturally relevant ones) although the Dasen study reported a reversal of two other sorts of conservation. Where the studies do agree, however, is in their finding of a large number of subjects who did not achieve conservation. Moreover, when Dasen extended his study to include adults, they showed less conservation than fifteen- to sixteen-year-olds.

Needless to say, there is considerable variation among the various studies. The assignment of importance to this or that study has, as yet, no firm grounding in research. For each type of finding, some counterpart can be found.

The upshot of these considerations is that there is a considerable amount of "noise" lurking beneath neatly presented findings. Most often, detailed analyses of the behaviors involved serves to reveal many difficulties which serve to make attribution of "presence" or "absence" of some cognitive structure, or "potency" or "irrelevance" of some etiological factor, impossible.

In sum, the few studies of sensorimotor development suggest that the substages of this period do not vary much between cultures. However, the findings are, as yet, too sparse to be conclusive. The evidence on the transition from preoperative to concrete operational thought presents every conceivable type of finding. It is clear that much more remains to be learned.

Anthropological Cross-Cultural Experimentation

There is an increasingly impressive body of data, gathered both cross-culturally and intraculturally, which suggests that performance of a cognitive nature involves determinants of two sorts: capacity determinants (what people can do) and performance determinants (factors which determine whether a capacity will be applied). Cole and Bruner (1971), Cole et al. (1971), Flavell (1970), Garfinkel (1967), Glick (1968, 1969), Goffman (1971), Goodnow (1969, 1970, 1972), Labov (1970), Mehler and Bever (1968), and many others have pointed to the "strategic" aspects of human performance. They have shown in a variety of ways that a critical problem in analyzing human capacities involves an understanding of both the capacities and the myriad of factors which determine whether that capacity will be used on a given occasion. What must be understood is that human performance is, in fact, a *performance* for an audience, which critically involves decisions about what to present to that audience. In some cases, the decisions will be of the sort described by Goffman (1971) and Garfinkel (1967)—a reading of the implicit rules of the game and a performance in accord with those rules. In other cases, there may be real capacity limitations which govern when and how a skill can be applied (Goodnow 1970; Flavell 1970). Some skills may be too embedded in ongoing activities and may require special experiences, or a lot of practice (Goodnow 1970; Mandler 1962) to get disembedded and applied to a variety of other areas.

The critical point here is that we do not know much about the conditions which govern the applicability of skills to experimental or other contexts. Until we know about these, we can make little progress in asking questions about etiology or capacity.

The modeling of cross-cultural experimentation on the laboratory model of experimental psychology has limited our perspective on these problems. In the laboratory experiment we constrain the types of cognitive abilities that people may display to just those we believe we are testing. Moreover, the use of a single artificial occasion for the display of cognitive abilities confounds rules of application of abilities with the having of abilities.

It may be time to explore seriously a different approach to cross-cultural study. One such approach would be to conceive of cross-cultural study as a form of experimental anthropology (Cole 1972; Cole et al. 1971; Strodtbeck 1970; LeVine 1970). The anthropological approach involves an appreciation of behavior *as it occurs* in its natural context. The analysis of this behavior provides clues to the kind of cognitive abilities that people might be expected to display. Experimental studies can then be performed to test out the implications of the anthropological analysis.

Such an approach might be useful, at the least, in exposing the incompatabilities of different orders of data; useful, at the most, in deepening our understanding of human behavior.

A fruitful area for application of this approach would be that of incompatabilities between the descriptions of cognitive capacity garnered from experimental work and those descriptions derived from an analysis of the use of cognitive abilities in context. In the area of classification abilities, particularly, psychologists' claims that perceptual bases of classification are used by people with a certain level of schooling conflict with anthropologists' study of "natural" systems of classification, where it is more often the case that sophisticated strategies of classification, based on deeper and often more abstract principles of organization, have been involved (Tyler 1969; Maranda and Maranda 1971; Horton 1967*a, b*; Levi-Strauss 1963, 1966; Wilson 1970).

In a rather remarkable book, Gladwin (1970) introduced an analysis of the navigational system of Puluwat islanders in terms of the problem of the analysis of cultural deprivation. Gladwin argued with some force that, until analyses of behavior in context are performed, misleading data will be produced. Following his own lead, Gladwin analyzed the achievement of Puluwat islanders in navigating over long stretches of sea, with no visual landmarks. These people, who do not have many signs of advanced technology or elaborate formal schooling, had devised a system of surprising complexity, involving the use of an imaginary island which serves as a nexus of directional information. They had achieved navigational accuracy, which could only be based on a deep knowledge of navigational rules and relationships. Within this system, complex relationships of wind, current, and direction became integrated and yielded pragmatic performances of great accuracy. Yet, it is fully conceivable that the highly skilled Puluwat navigator would be unable to perform in a reasonable way on some standard test of intelligence or deductive reasoning.

An important source of input for a contextualized theory of cognition would be to use those systems of human behavior that appear to be common to human groups wherever they are found. LaBarre (1954) has indicated several important areas to look at such as language, cosmology (mythological or scientific formulations of the nature of the world), and technology (tool use).

While cosmology and tool-use have been little looked at within the psychological tradition (but see Horton 1967a, b; Levi-Strauss 1963, and Wilson 1970, for important treatments of these issues within the anthropological and sociological traditions), studies of language and language acquisition have assumed increasing importance in framing psychological theories of mental functioning.

The basic importance of the study of language acquisition for considerations of cognition in a cross-cultural context is based upon several considerations. First, all human groups have language. Second, the fact that we share the capacity for language implies at least that those cognitive capacities related to language use are shared. Third, it seems, at present, that the capacities involved in language use are of a high conceptual order.

The issue has been most strongly put by Chomsky (1968):

The native speaker has acquired a grammar on the basis of very restricted and degenerate evidence; the grammar has empirical consequences that extend far beyond the evidence. At one level, the phenomena with which the grammar deals are explained by the rules of the grammar itself and the interaction of these rules. At a deeper level, these same phenomena are explained by the principles that determine the selection of the grammar on the basis of the restricted and degenerate evidence available to the person who has acquired knowledge of the language, who has constructed for himself this particular grammar. The principles that determine the form of the grammar and that select a grammar of the appropriate form on the basis of certain data constitute a subject that might, following traditional usage, be termed "universal grammar." The study of universal grammar, so understood, is a study of the nature of human intellectual processes. It tries to formulate the necessary and sufficient conditions that a system must meet to qualify as a potential human language, conditions that are not accidentally true of existing human languages, but that are rather rooted in the human "language capacity," and thus constitutes the innate organization that determines what counts as linguistic experience. Universal grammar, then, constitutes an explanatory theory of a much deeper sort than particular grammar (pp. 23–24).

The comparative study of language acquisition has been the focus of the Berkeley cross-cultural project. The reader is referred to Slobin (1971) for an impressive review of evidence finding similar forms of syntax in early language acquisition for groups as diverse as Finnish speakers and speakers of African languages such as Luo. Studies of early referential functions of language (semantics) suggests a universality of early forms of reference as well (Slobin 1971, pp. 44–45).

The important empirical work is as yet at an early stage, but there are clear indications at this point that this work will be of fundamental importance in conditioning our views of human cognitive functioning. Most students of the area agree that one must presuppose a great degree of selectivity and a rather impressive amount of abstractive ability in order to account for the facts of language acquisition.

Whether these abilities are specific to language acquisition processes or are general cognitive abilities is in doubt at this point (Chomsky 1965; McNeill 1966, 1970; Sinclair-de-Zwart 1969, 1971; Greenfield, Nelson, and Saltzman 1972; Bever 1970). What is clear is that an impressive array of cognitive capacities is involved in language use, no matter what the language is.

All of this evidence suggests that the behaviors that people do perform and live through in the course of everyday life are highly structured behaviors involving sophisticated and complex laws of structuring (Goodnow and Levine 1973; Greenfield and Childs 1971). This seems to be the very stuff of cognitive capacity.

Summary

1. It is apparent that cross-cultural studies on conceptual development have given few definitive answers to questions about the etiological factors in development. While there have been claims for the important influences of schooling and language on cognitive functioning, the cross-culture literature is contradictory or weak with respect to these specific influences.

Similarly, arguments for biological or interactional determinants have as yet but tentative support in the source literature.

2. Facts often conflict. Sometimes a look beneath the surface reveals similarities between diverse peoples where none appeared to exist and differences where none were suspected. If there is an overriding order to the array of literature reviewed, it is that we have much to learn before fundamental etiological questions can be answered.

3. Two related considerations must be applied to questions of etiology. The first is that etiological questions are most properly asked after there has been considerable descriptive work tying down the processes involved in the behaviors for which we seek causes. Stated more simply, one must know what it is that is being caused before one can talk about its causes. In all of these areas the question of cause can only be raised after some notion of process has been achieved. *One cannot proceed etiologically without corresponding descriptive analysis.*

4. A second consideration bears on the problem of inferring cognitive abilities or lack of them from performance on any specific behavioral test. *We do not know the relationship between cognitive capacities and the conditions of their application.* In the review of literature on conceptual development we have encountered instances where conceptual behavior varies considerably with the manner in which it is elicited. Sometimes behavior differs as a function of the type of material used, and sometimes it differs as a function of the way in which a task is presented. Inferences about the conceptual abilities of the group in question would vary accordingly.

CODA

These considerations and the literature reviewed in this chapter suggest the outlines of an approach to psychological experimentation as applied to understanding cognitive development in a cross-cultural perspective. The elements blended in this approach are: an interest in the cognitive capacities revealed in normal, everyday functioning, or what might be called "mundane cognition" (Glick and Slobin 1972); and a recognition of the need for discovery procedures which will allow us to better proceed with the analysis of the performance determinants that govern the application of cognitive capacities embedded in everyday life to other situations.

The approach taken by Cole et al. (Cole 1972; Cole et al. 1971; Glick 1968, 1969) has been to transform the experimental approach into one that is compatible with ethnographic analyses and other analyses which are pointed toward analyses of spontaneous and organized activities.

Accordingly, everyday activities, such as speaking, doing ordinary tasks, and, in general, being a competent human being—whether in hunting, gathering, working a computer, or telling and understanding a myth—are regarded as important data inputs about the human cognizer's abilities. The cognitive structural description of these activities becomes then a "theory" of cognitive abilities that might be manifested in specifically designed experimental tasks.

In this approach, what is sought is experimental confirmation of an hypothesis derived from ethnographic description. If a particular experimental test fails to confirm that "theory," a new test is tried. This approach provides an inquiry device which looks to the parameters of experimental situations as being important features of the analysis of cognitive function. Some situations will yield expected results, others will not. An attempt can be made to analyze the *dimensions of these different classes of situations*. This approach, then, becomes both activity-centered and context-centered—with the cognitive analysis of everyday activities being coupled with an analysis of the contexts within which behavior occurs. In this way, a theory of cultural variation might be built which escapes many of the methodological limitations of approaches which are measure- rather than process-centered. This approach provides a promising alternative to the more traditional approaches to cross-cultural study of development.

References

Armstrong, R. E., Rubin, E. V., Stewart, M., & Kuntner, L. Susceptibility to the Muller-Lyer, Sander parallelogram and Ames distorted room illusions as a function of age, sex and retinal pigmentation in urban Midwestern children. Duplicated research report, 1970, Dept. of Psychology, Northwestern University.

Berlin, B. & Kay, P. *Basic Color Terms: Their Universality and Evolution.* Berkeley: University of California Press, 1969.

Berry, J. W. Temne and Eskimo perceptual skills. *International Journal of Psychology*, 1966, *1*, 207–229.

————. Ecology, perceptual development and the Muller-Lyer illusion. *British Journal of Psychology*, 1968, *59*, 205–210.

————. Muller-Lyer susceptibility: culture, ecology or race? *International Journal of Psychology*, 1971, *6*, 193–197.

Bever, T. G. The cognitive basis for linguistic structures. In J. R. Hayes, ed., *Cognition and the Development of Language.* New York: John Wiley, 1970.

Biesheuval, S. Psychological tests and their application to non-European peoples. In G. B. Jeffrey, ed., *The Yearbook of Education, Exams,* 1949, 90–104. Reprinted in D. Price-Williams, ed., *Cross-Cultural Studies.* Baltimore: Penguin Books, 1970.

Brian, C. & Goodenough, F. The relative potency of color and form perception at various ages. *Journal of Experimental Psychology*, 1929, *12*, 197–213.

Brislin, R. W. Back translation for cross-cultural research. *Journal of Cross-Cultural Psychology*, 1970, *1*, 185–216.

Brown, R. & Lenneberg, E. A study in language and cognition. *Journal of Abnormal and Social Psychology*, 1954, *49*, 454–462.

Bruner, J. S., Goodnow, J. J., & Austin, G. A. *A Study of Thinking*. New York: John Wiley, 1956.

Brunswick, E. *Perception and the Representative Design of Psychological Experiments*. Berkeley: University of California Press, 1956.

Cassirer, E. *The Philosophy of Symbolic Forms*. Vol. 1: *Language*. New Haven: Yale University Press, 1953.

Carroll, J. B. & Cassagrande, J. B. The function of language classification. In E. E. Maccoby et al., eds., *Readings in Social Psychology*. 3d ed. New York: Holt, Rinehart, & Winston, 1958.

Chomsky, N. *Aspects of the Theory of Syntax*. Cambridge: MIT Press, 1965.

———. *Cartesian Linguistics*. New York: Harper & Row, 1966.

———. *Language and Mind*. New York: Harcourt Brace Jovanovich, 1968.

Ciborowski, T. & Cole, M. Cultural differences in learning conceptual rules. *International Journal of Psychology*, 1971, *6*, 25–37.

Cole, M. Toward an experimental anthropology of thinking. Paper presented at the Joint Meeting of the American Ethnological Society and Council on Anthropology and Education, Montreal, April, 1972.

Cole, M. & Bruner, J. Cultural differences and inferences about psychological processes. *American Psychologist*, 1971, *26*, 867–876.

Cole, M., Gay, J., & Glick, J. Some studies in Kpelle quantitative behavior. *Psychonomic Monographs*, 1968, *2*, 173–190.

———. The development of communication skills among Liberian tribal people. Paper presented at the Society for Research in Child Development meetings, Santa Monica, California, 1969.

Cole, M., Gay, J., Glick, J., & Sharp, D. Linguistic structure and transposition. *Science*, 1969, *164*, 90–91.

———. *The Cultural Context of Learning and Thinking*. New York: Basic Books, 1971.

Conklin, H. C. Hunanoo color categories. *Southwestern Journal of Anthropology*, 1955, *11*, 335–344.

Corah, N. L. Color and form preferences in children's perceptual behavior. *Perceptual and Motor Skills*, 1964, *18*, 313–316.

Coren, S. & Girgus, J. S. Density of human lens pigmentation: in vivo measures over an extended age range. *Vision Research*, 1972, *12*, 343–346.

Dasen, P. R. Cross-cultural Piagetian research: a summary. *Journal of Cross-Cultural Psychology*, 1972a, *3*, 23–40.

———. Preliminary study of cognitive development among Ivorian children (Baoule and Ebrie): sensori-motor intelligence and concrete operations, Manuscript, University of Geneva, 1972b.

———. The development of conservation in aboriginal children: a replication study. *International Journal of Psychology*, 1972c, *7*, 75–85.

Dawson, J. L. M. Cultural and physiological influences upon spatial-perceptual processes in West Africa, Part I. *International Journal of Psychology*, 1967a, *2*, 115–125.

———. Cultural and physiological influences upon spatial-perceptual processes in West Africa, Part II. *International Journal of Psychology*, 1967b, *2*, 171–185.

DeLacey, P. R. A cross-cultural study of classificatory ability in Australia. *Journal of Cross-Cultural Psychology*, 1970, *1*, 293–304.

DeLemos, M. M. The development of conservation in aboriginal children. *International Journal of Psychology*, 1969, *4*, 255–269.

Deregowski, J. B. Difficulties in pictorial perception in Africa. *British Journal of Psychology*, 1968, *59*, 195–204.

———. Orientation and perception of pictorial depth. *International Journal of Psychology*, 1971, *6* (2), 111–114.

Deregowski, J. B. & Byth, W. Hudson's pictures in Pandora's box. *Journal of Cross-Cultural Psychology*, 1970, *1*, 315–323.

Deregowski, J. B. & Serpell, R. Performance on a sorting task: a cross-cultural experiment. *International Journal of Psychology,* 1971, *6,* 273–281.

Fingeston, P. Symbolism and reality. *Journal of Psycholinguistic Research,* 1971, *1,* 95–112.

Flavell, J. H. Developmental studies of mediated memory. In L. Lipsitt & H. Reese, eds., *Advances in Child Development and Behavior.* Vol. 5. New York: Academic Press, 1970.

———. *The Developmental Psychology of Jean Piaget.* Princeton, N. J.: Van Nostrand, 1963.

Frake, C. D. The ethnographic study of cognitive systems. In T. Gladwin & W. C. Sturtevant, eds., *Anthropology and Human Behavior.* Washington, D.C.: Anthropological Society of Washington, 1962.

Furth, H. G. *Piaget and Knowledge.* Englewood Cliffs, N. J.: Prentice-Hall, 1969.

Garfinkel, H. *Studies in Ethnomethodology.* Englewood Cliffs, N. J.: Prentice-Hall, 1967.

Gay, J. H. & Cole, M. *The New Mathematics and an Old Culture: A Study of Learning Among the Kpelle.* New York: Holt, Rinehart & Winston, 1967.

Gibson, E. J. *Principles of Perceptual Learning and Development.* New York: Appleton-Century-Crofts, 1969.

Gibson, E. J., Gibson, J. J., Pick, A. D., & Osser, H. A developmental study of the discrimination of letter-like forms. *Journal of Comparative and Physiological Psychology,* 1962, *55,* 897–906.

Gladwin, T. *East is a Big Bird: Navigation and Logic on Pulawat Atoll.* Cambridge: Harvard University Press, 1970.

Glick, J. Cognitive style among the Kpelle of Liberia. Paper presented at American Educational Research Association meeting, Chicago, 1968.

———. Culture and cognition: some theoretical and methodological concerns. Paper presented at the American Anthropological Association meeting, New Orleans, La., 1969.

Glick, J. & Slobin, D. Mundane cognition: Proposal for a conference, submitted to the Social Science Research Council Committee on Cognition, 1972.

Goffman, E. *Strategic Interaction.* New York: Basic Books, 1971.

Golden, M. & Birns, B. Social class and cognitive development in infancy. *Merrill Palmer Quarterly,* 1968, *14,* 139–149.

Goodnow, J. J. Problems in research in culture and thought. In D. Elkind & J. Flavell, eds., *Studies in Cognitive Development.* New York: Oxford University Press, 1969.

———. Cultural variations in cognitive skills. In D. R. Price-Williams, ed., *Cross-Cultural Studies.* New York: Penguin, 1970.

———. Rules and repertoires, rituals and tricks of the trade: social and informational aspects to cognitive and representational development. In S. Farnham-Diggory, ed., *Information Processing in Children.* New York: Academic Press, 1972.

Goodnow, J. J. & Levine, R. The grammar of action: sequences and syntax in children's copying. *Cognitive Psychology,* 1973, in press.

Goody, J. & Watt, I. The consequences of literacy. *Comparative Studies in Sociology and History,* 1962, *5,* 304–345.

Greenberg, J. H. Language universals. In T. Sebeck, ed., *Current Trends in Linguistics.* Vol. 3. The Hague: Mouton, 1966.

Greenfield, P. M. Comparing dimensional categorization in natural and artificial contexts: a developmental study among the Zinacantecos of Mexico. Manuscript, Harvard University, 1972.

———. On culture and conservation. In J. S. Bruner, R. R. Olver, P. M. Greenfield et al., eds., *Studies in Cognitive Growth.* New York: John Wiley, 1966.

Greenfield, P. M. & Bruner, J. S. Culture and cognitive growth. In D. A. Goslin, ed., *Handbook of Socialization Research*. New York: Rand-McNally, 1969.

Greenfield, P. M. & Bruner, J. S. Culture and cognitive growth. *International Journal of Psychology*, 1966, *1*, 89–107.

Greenfield, P. M. & Childs, C. Weaving skill, color, terms and pattern representation among the Zinacantecos of Southern Mexico: a developmental study. Manuscript, Harvard University, 1971.

Greenfield, P. M., Nelson, K., & Saltzman, E. The development of rulebound strategies for manipulating seriated cups: a parallel between action and grammar. *Cognitive Psychology*, 1972, *3*, 291–310.

Greenfield, P. M., Reich, L. C., & Olver, R. R. On culture and equivalence II. In J. S. Bruner, R. R. Olver, P. M. Greenfield et al., eds., *Studies in Cognitive Growth*. New York: John Wiley, 1966.

Gregor, A. J. & McPherson, D. A. A study of susceptibility to geometrical illusions among cultural subgroups of Australian aborigines. *Psychologia Africana*, 1965, *11*, 1–13.

Hagan, M. How children see pictures: the development of the perception of surface layout, as pictured in art. Unpublished special area paper, University of Minnesota, 1972*a*.

———. Picture perception: infants, chimpanzees and primitives. Unpublished paper, University of Minnesota, 1972*b*.

Halle, M. On the basis of phonology. In J. A. Fodor & J. J. Katz, eds., *The Structure of Language*. Englewood Cliffs, N. J.: Prentice-Hall, 1967.

Hallowell, A. I. Cultural factors in the structuralization of perception. In J. H. Rohrer & M. Sherif, eds., *Social Psychology at the Crossroads*. New York: Harper & Row, 1951.

Heider, E. R. On the internal structure of perceptual and semantic categories. In T. M. Moore, ed., *Cognitive Development and the Acquisition of Language*. New York: Academic Press, 1972*a*, in press.

———. Universals in color naming and memory. *Journal of Experimental Psychology*, 1972*b*, in press.

Heider, E. R. & Olivier, D. C. The structure of the color space in naming and memory for two languages. *Cognitive Psychology*, 1972, *3*, 337–354.

Horton, R. African traditional thought and Western science. Part I: From tradition to science. *Africa*, 1967*a*, *37*, 50–71.

———. African traditional thought and Western science. Part II: The closed and open predicaments. *Africa*, 1967*b*, *37*, 155–187.

Hudson, W. Pictorial depth perception in sub-cultural groups in Africa. *Journal of Social Psychology*, 1960, *52*, 183–208.

———. The study of pictorial perception among unacculturated groups. *International Journal of Psychology*, 1967, *2*, 90–107.

Inhelder, B. & Piaget, J. *The Growth of Logic in the Child*. New York: Harper & Row, 1964.

Irwin, A. M. & McLaughlin, D. H. Ability and preference in category sorting by Mano school children and adults. *Journal of Social Psychology*, 1970, *82*, 15–24.

Jahoda, G. Geometric illusions and environment: a study in Ghana. *British Journal of Psychology*, 1966, *57*, 193–199.

———. Retinal pigmentation, illusion susceptibility and space perception. *International Journal of Psychology*, 1971, *6*, 199–208.

Jahoda, G. & Stacy, B. Susceptibility to geometrical illusions according to culture and professional training. *Perception and Psychophysics*, 1970, *7*, 179–184.

Jung, C. G. *Two Essays on Analytical Psychology*. New York: Meridian Books, 1956.

Kellaghan, T. Abstraction and categorization in African children. *International Journal of Psychology*, 1968, *3*, 115–120.

Kubany, E. S., Gallimore, R., & Buell, J. The effects of intrinsic factors on achievement-oriented behavior: a non-Western case. *Journal of Transcultural Psychology,* 1970, *1,* 77–84

LaBarre, W. *The Human Animal.* Chicago: University of Chicago Press, 1954.

Labov, W. The logic of non-standard English. In F. Williams, ed., *Language and Poverty.* Chicago: Markham, 1970.

Lantz, D. L. & Stefflre, V. Language and cognition revisited. *Journal of Abnormal and Social Psychology,* 1964, *69,* 472–481.

Leibowitz, H. & Pick, H. A. Cross-cultural and educational aspects of the Ponzo illusion. Paper presented at the Eastern Psychological Association meetings, April 1, 1971.

Lenneberg, E. *Biological Foundation of Language.* New York: John Wiley, 1967.

————. Color naming, color recognition, color discrimination: a reappraisal. *Perceptual and Motor Skills,* 1961, *12,* 375–382.

LeVine, R. Cross-cultural study in child psychology. In P. Mussen, ed., *Carmichael's Manual of Child Psychology.* Vol. 2. New York: John Wiley, 1970.

Levi-Strauss, C. *Structural Anthropology.* New York: Basic Books, 1963.

————. *The Savage Mind.* Chicago: University of Chicago Press, 1966.

Lloyd, B. B. The intellectual development of Yoruba children: a re-examination. *Journal of Cross-Cultural Psychology,* 1971, *2* (1), 29–38.

Luria, A. R. Towards the problem of the historical nature of psychological processes. *International Journal of Psychology,* 1971, *6,* 259–272.

Luria, A. R. & Yudovitch, F. I. *Speech and the Development of Mental Processes in the Child.* Trans. Joan Simon. London: Staples, 1959.

MacArthur, R. Sex differences in field dependence for the Eskimo: replication of Berry's findings. *International Journal of Psychology,* 1967, *2,* 139–140.

Maccoby, M. & Modiano, N. On culture and equivalence, I. In J. S. Bruner, R. R. Olver, P. M. Greenfield, et al., eds., *Studies in Cognitive Growth.* New York: John Wiley, 1966.

Madsen, M. C. Developmental and cross-cultural differences in the cooperative and competitive behavior of young children. *Journal of Cross-Cultural Psychology,* 1971, *2,* 365–371.

Mandler, G. From associations to structure. *Psychological Review,* 1962, *69,* 415–426.

Maranda, P. & Maranda, E. K. *Structural Analysis of Oral Tradition.* Philadelphia: University of Pennsylvania Press, 1971.

McNeill, D. Anthropological psycholinguistics. Unpublished paper, Harvard University, 1965.

————. Developmental psycholinguistics. In F. Smith & G. A. Miller, eds., *The Genesis of Language: A Psycholinguistic Approach.* Cambridge: MIT Press, 1966.

————. The development of language. In P. Mussen, ed., *Carmichael's Manual of Child Psychology.* New York: John Wiley, 1970.

Mehler, J. & Bever, T. G. The study of competence in cognitive psychology. *International Journal of Psychology,* 1968, *3,* 273–280.

Mermelstein, E., & Shulman, L. S. Lack of formal schooling and the acquisition of conservation. *Child Development,* 1967, *38,* 39–51.

Miller, G. A., Galanter, E., & Pribram, K. *Plans and the Structure of Behavior.* New York: Holt, Rinehart, & Winston, 1960.

Mundy-Castle, A. C. Pictorial depth perception in Ghanaian children. *International Journal of Psychology,* 1966, *1,* 290–300.

Okonji, D. M. A cross-cultural study of the effects of familiarity on classificatory behavior. *Journal of Cross-Cultural Psychology,* 1971, *2,* 39–40.

Piaget, J. Nécessité et signification des recherches comparatives en psychologie génétique. *International Journal of Psychology,* 1966, *1,* 3–13.

————. Piaget's theory. In P. Mussen, ed., *Carmichael's Handbook of Child Psychology.* New York: John Wiley, 1970.

————. *The Origins of Intelligence in Children.* New York: International Universities Press, 1952.

Pike, W. L. *Language in Relation to a Unified Theory of the Structure of Human Behavior.* Part 1. (Preliminary edition.) Glendale: Summer Institute of Linguistics, 1954.

Pollack, R. The carpentered world: or biology stay away from my door. Paper delivered at City University Graduate School and University Center, New York, N. Y., December, 1972.

Pollack, R. H. & Silvar, S. D. Magnitude of the Muller-Lyer illusion in children as a function of pigmentation of the Fundus oculi. *Psychonomic Science,* 1967, *8,* 83–84.

Price-Williams, D. R. A study concerning concepts of conservation of quantities among primitive children. *Acta Psychologica,* 1961, *18,* 293–305.

————. Abstract and concrete modes of classification in a primitive society. *British Journal of Educational Psychology,* 1962, *32,* 50–61.

Price-Williams, D. R., ed., *Cross-Cultural Studies.* New York: Penguin, 1970.

Romney, A. K. & D'Andrade, R. G. Transcultural studies in cognition. *American Anthropologist,* 1964, Part II, *66.*

Sapir, E. *Language: An Introduction to the Study of Speech.* New York: Harcourt Brace, 1921.

Schmidt, W. H. O. & Nzimande, A. Cultural preferences in color/form preference and in classificatory behavior. *Human Development,* 1970, *13,* 140–148.

Sechrest, L. Fay, T. L., & Zaidi, S. M. H. Problems of translation in cross-cultural research. *Journal of Cross-Cultural Psychology,* 1972, *3,* 41–56.

Segall, M. H., Campbell, D. T., & Herskovitz, M. J. *The Influence of Culture on Visual Perception.* Indianapolis: Bobbs-Merrill, 1966.

Serpell, R. Cultural differences in attentional preference for color over form. *International Journal of Psychology,* 1969, *4,* 183–194.

Serpell, R. Preference for specific orientation of abstract shapes among Zambian children. *Journal of Cross-Cultural Psychology,* 1971, *2,* 225–239.

Silvar, S. D. & Pollack, R. H. Racial differences in pigmentation of the Fundus oculi, *Psychonomic Science,* 1967, *7,* 159–160.

Sinclair-de-Zwart, H. Developmental psycholinguistics. In D. Elkind & J. Flavell, eds., *Studies in Cognitive Development.* New York: Oxford University Press, 1969.

————. Sensorimotor action patterns as a condition for the acquisition of syntax. In R. Huxley & E. Ingram, eds., *Language Acquisition: Models and Methods.* New York: Academic Press, 1971.

Slobin, D. J. *Psycholinguistics.* Glenview, Ill.: Scott-Foresman, 1971.

Stefflre, V., Castillo-Vales, N., & Morley, L. Language and cognition in Yucatan: a cross-cultural replication. *Journal of Personality and Social Psychology,* 1966, *4,* 112–115.

Strodtbeck, F. Considerations of metamethod in cross-cultural studies. *American Anthropologist,* 1964, *66,* 223–229. Reprinted in D. R. Price-Williams, eds., *Cross-Cultural Studies.* New York: Penguin, 1970.

Suchman, R. G. Cultural differences in children's color and form preferences. *Journal of Social Psychology,* 1966, *70,* 3–10.

Tyler, S. A. *Cognitive Anthropology.* New York: Holt, Rinehart & Winston, 1969.

Vygotskii, L. S. *Thought and Language.* Cambridge: MIT Press, 1962.

Wason, P. C. The contexts of plausible denial. *Journal of Verbal Learning and Verbal Behavior,* 1965, *4,* 7–11.

Werner, H. *The Comparative Psychology of Mental Development.* New York: International Universities Press, 1957.

Werner, H. & Kaplan, B. The developmental approach to cognition. *American Anthropologist,* 1956, *50,* 866–881.

————. *Symbol Formation.* New York: John Wiley, 1963.

Glick

Werner, O. & Campbell, D. T. Translating, working through interpreters, and the problem of decentering. In A. Narral & R. Cohen, eds., *A Handbook of Method in Cultural Anthropology*. Garden City, N. Y.: The Natural History Press, 1970.

Whorf, B. L. *Four Articles on Metalinguistics*. Washington: Foreign Service Institute, 1952.

————. *Language, Thought, and Reality: Selected Writings*. Cambridge: Technology Press, 1956.

Wilson, B. R., ed. *Rationality*. New York: Harper & Row, 1970.

Witkin, H. A. A cognitive style approach to cross-cultural research. *International Journal of Psychology*, 1967, *2*, 233–250.

Witkin, H. A., Dyk, R. B., Faterson, H. F., Goodenough, D. E., et al. *Psychological Differentiation*. New York: John Wiley, 1962.

Wober, M. Adapting Witkin's field dependence theory to accommodate new information from Africa. *British Journal of Psychology*, 1967, *58*, 29–38.

————. Distinguishing centri-cultural from cross-cultural tests and research. *Perceptual and Motor Skills*, 1969, *28*, 488.

Zigler, C. & Butterfield, E. C. Motivational aspects of changes in IQ test performance of culturally deprived nursery school children. *Child Development*, 1968, *39*, 1–14.

Author Index

655

Index of Subjects